Inflation Rate
(GNP Deflator)

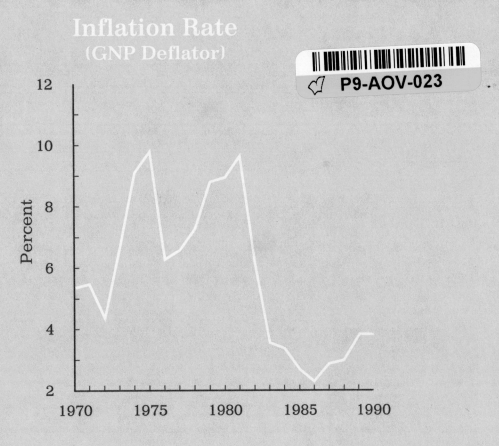

Nominal Interest Rate
(Three-month Treasury bills)

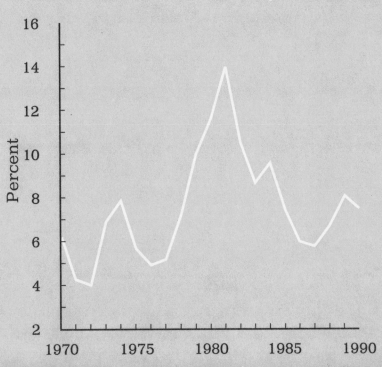

Macroeconomics

Macroeconomics

N. Gregory Mankiw

Harvard University

Worth Publishers

Development editors: Paul Shensa and Lisa Pinto

Design: Malcolm Grear Designers

Art director: George Touloumes

Production editor: Toni Scaramuzzo

Production supervisor: Stacey B. Alexander

Layout: Pat Lawson

Composition: Ruttle, Shaw & Wetherill, Inc.

Printing and binding: R. R. Donnelley & Sons Company

Photo Credit: p. vii © Linda Haas, Cambridge, MA.

Worth Publishers

33 Irving Place

New York, New York 10003

About the Author

N. Gregory Mankiw is Professor of Economics at Harvard University, where he has been teaching both undergraduate and graduate courses since 1985. He began his study of economics as an undergraduate at Princeton University and received his Ph.D. in economics from MIT in 1984.

Professor Mankiw has worked at the Council of Economic Advisers in Washington, D.C., and he is now a research associate at the National Bureau of Economic Research, a nonprofit think tank in Cambridge, Massachusetts. His research ranges across the entire field of macroeconomics and includes work on consumer behavior, price rigidity, financial markets, monetary and fiscal policy, housing, and economic growth.

Professor Mankiw is a regular contributor to scholarly journals, having published over 50 articles in the past 10 years. He is currently on the editorial boards of the *Review of Economics and Statistics* and the *Journal of Economic Perspectives*. He is also a frequent lecturer in both the United States and Europe. In 1991, Harvard economics students awarded him the Galbraith Prize for Teaching.

Professor Mankiw lives in Wellesley, Massachusetts, with his wife, Deborah, who also works at the National Bureau of Economic Research. In his free time, he plays with his border terrier, Keynes.

To Deborah

Those branches of politics, or of the laws of social life, in which there exists a collection of facts sufficiently sifted and methodized to form the beginning of a science should be taught *ex professo*. Among the chief of these is Political Economy, the sources and conditions of wealth and material prosperity for aggregate bodies of human beings. . . .

The same persons who cry down Logic will generally warn you against Political Economy. It is unfeeling, they will tell you. It recognises unpleasant facts. For my part, the most unfeeling thing I know of is the law of gravitation: it breaks the neck of the best and most amiable person without scruple, if he forgets for a single moment to give heed to it. The winds and waves too are very unfeeling. Would you advise those who go to sea to deny the winds and waves—or to make use of them, and find the means of guarding against their dangers? My advice to you is to study the great writers on Political Economy, and hold firmly by whatever in them you find true; and depend upon it that if you are not selfish or hard-hearted already, Political Economy will not make you so.

John Stuart Mill
1867

Brief Table of Contents

Preface   xxvii

Part One

Introduction   1
1   The Science of Macroeconomics   3
2   The Data of Macroeconomics   15

Part Two

The Economy in the Long Run   41
3   National Income: Its Production, Distribution, and Allocation   42
4   Economic Growth   77
5   Unemployment   118
6   Inflation   140
7   The Open Economy   176

Part Three

The Economy in the Short Run   213
8   Introduction to Economic Fluctuations   214
9   Aggregate Demand I   235
10   Aggregate Demand II   263
11   Aggregate Supply   287
12   The Macroeconomic Policy Debate   322
13   The Open Economy in the Short Run   345
14   The Theory of Real Business Cycles   374

Part Four

More on the Microeconomics Behind Macroeconomics   391
15   Consumption   392
16   Two Views of Government Debt   423
17   Investment   440
18   Money Supply and Money Demand   463
    Epilogue: What We Know, What We Don't   482
    Glossary   489
    Index   499

Table of Contents

Preface xxvii

Part One

Introduction   1

Chapter 1
The Science of Macroeconomics   3

1-1 Why Study Macroeconomics? 3

    CASE STUDY 1-1 Presidential Elections and the Economy 5

1-2 How Economists Think 6

    The Use of Economic Models 6
        FYI Using Functions to Express Relationships Among Variables 9
    The Role of Microeconomics in Macroeconomics 10
    Eclectic Macroeconomics 11
    Prices: Flexible versus Sticky 11

1-3 How This Book Proceeds 12

Chapter 2
The Data of Macroeconomics   15

2-1 Measuring the Value of Economic Activity: Gross National Product 16

    Income, Expenditure, and the Circular Flow 16
        FYI Stocks and Flows 18
    Some Rules for Computing GNP 19
        The Treatment of Inventories 19
        Adding Apples and Oranges 19
        Intermediate Goods and Value-Added 20
        Housing Services and Other Imputations 20
    Real GNP versus Nominal GNP 21
        CASE STUDY 2-1 Real GNP in the United States 22
    The GNP Deflator 23
    Other Statistics in the National Income Accounts 24
        The Components of Expenditure 24
        CASE STUDY 2-2 GNP and Its Components 25
        Alternative Measures of Income 26
        CASE STUDY 2-3 The Seasonal Cycle and Seasonal Adjustment 28

2-2 Measuring the Cost of Living: The Consumer Price Index 29

    The Price of a Basket of Goods 29

The CPI versus the GNP Deflator   30
  CASE STUDY 2-4   The Inflation of 1978–1981   32

2-3 Measuring Joblessness: The Unemployment Rate   33
  CASE STUDY 2-5   Unemployment, GNP, and Okun's Law   35

2-4 Conclusion: From Economic Statistics to Economic Models   37

Part Two

The Economy in the Long Run   41

Chapter 3
National Income: Its Production, Distribution, and Allocation   42

3-1 The Production of Goods and Services   44

The Factors of Production   44
The Production Function   45
The Fixed Supply of Goods and Services   45

3-2 Distributing National Income to the Factors of Production   46

Factor Prices   46
The Problem Facing the Competitive Firm   47
The Firm's Demand for Factors   48
  The Marginal Product of Labor   48
  From the Marginal Product of Labor to Labor Demand   49
  The Marginal Product of Capital and Capital Demand   51
The Division of National Income   51
  CASE STUDY 3-1   The Black Death and Factor Prices   53
  CASE STUDY 3-2   The Senator, the Mathematician, and the
  Constancy of Factor Shares   53

3-3 The Demand for Goods and Services   56

Consumption   56
  CASE STUDY 3-3   The Consumption Function in U.S. Data   58
Investment   58
  FYI   What Is Investment?   61
Government Purchases   61

3-4 Equilibrium and the Interest Rate   62

Equilibrium in the Market for Goods and Services: The Supply and
Demand for the Economy's Output   63
Equilibrium in the Financial Markets: The Supply and Demand for
Loanable Funds   64
Changes in Saving: The Effects of Fiscal Policy   65
  An Increase in Government Purchases   66
  CASE STUDY 3-4   Wars and Interest Rates in the
  United Kingdom, 1730–1920   67
  A Decrease in Taxes   68
  CASE STUDY 3-5   Fiscal Policy in the 1980s   69
Changes in Investment Demand   69
  FYI   The Identification Problem   72

3-5 Conclusion   74

Chapter 4
Economic Growth   77

4-1 The Accumulation of Capital   79

The Supply and Demand for Goods   79
    The Supply of Goods and the Production Function   79
    The Demand for Goods and the Consumption Function   80
The Steady-State Level of Capital   81
Approaching the Steady State   84
Approaching the Steady State: A Numerical Example   84
    CASE STUDY 4-1 Japanese and German Postwar Economic Growth   86
Changes in the Saving Rate   87
    CASE STUDY 4-2 Saving in Rich and Poor Countries   88

4-2 The Golden Rule Level of Capital   89

Comparing Steady States   89
Comparing Steady States: A Numerical Example   91
The Transition to the Golden Rule Steady State   93
    Starting With More Capital Than in the Golden Rule   93
    Starting With Less Capital Than in the Golden Rule   94

4-3 Population Growth   96

The Steady State With Population Growth   96
The Effects of Population Growth   98
    CASE STUDY 4-3 Population Growth in Rich and Poor Countries   99

4-4 Technological Progress   100

The Efficiency of Labor   100
The Steady State With Technological Progress   100
The Effects of Technological Progress   101
    CASE STUDY 4-4 Steady-State Growth in the United States   102

4-5 Saving, Growth, and Economic Policy   103

Evaluating the Rate of Saving   103
Changing the Rate of Saving   104
    CASE STUDY 4-5 Social Security and Saving   105
Encouraging Technological Progress   105
    CASE STUDY 4-6 The Worldwide Slowdown in Economic Growth   106

4-6 Conclusion: Beyond the Solow Model   107

Appendix: Accounting for the Sources of Economic Growth   112

Increases in the Factors of Production   112
    Increases in Capital   112
    Increases in Labor   113
    Increases in Capital and Labor   113
Technological Progress   114
The Sources of Growth in the United States   116

Chapter 5
Unemployment   118

5-1 Job Loss, Job Finding, and the Natural Rate of Unemployment   119

5-2 Job Search and Frictional Unemployment   121

Public Policy and Frictional Unemployment   122

CASE STUDY 5-1 Interwar British Unemployment 123
CASE STUDY 5-2 Unemployment Insurance and the Rate of Job Finding 124

5-3 Real-Wage Rigidity and Wait Unemployment 126

Minimum-Wage Laws 127
CASE STUDY 5-3 The Minimum Wage and the Working Poor 128
Unions and Collective Bargaining 128
CASE STUDY 5-4 Unionization and Unemployment in the
United States and Canada 129
Efficiency Wages 130
CASE STUDY 5-5 Henry Ford's $5 Workday 131

5-4 Patterns of Unemployment 132

The Duration of Unemployment 132
Variation in the Unemployment Rate Across Demographic Groups 133
The Upward Trend in Unemployment 134
Transitions Into and Out of the Labor Force 136

5-5 Conclusion 137

Chapter 6
Inflation   **140**

6-1 What Is Money? 141

The Functions of Money 141
The Types of Money 142
CASE STUDY 6-1 Money in a POW Camp 143
How Fiat Money Evolves 144
CASE STUDY 6-2 Money on the Island of Yap 144
How the Quantity of Money Is Controlled 145
How the Quantity of Money Is Measured 146

6-2 The Quantity Theory of Money 147

Transactions and the Quantity Equation 147
From Transactions to Income 148
The Money Demand Function and the Quantity Equation 149
The Assumption of Constant Velocity 150
Money, Prices, and Inflation 150
FYI Products and Percentage Changes 151
CASE STUDY 6-3 A Century of Money Growth and Inflation 152

6-3 Seigniorage: The Revenue From Printing Money 152

CASE STUDY 6-4 Paying for the American Revolution 154

6-4 Inflation and Interest Rates 154

Two Interest Rates: Real and Nominal 155
The Fisher Effect 155
CASE STUDY 6-5 Inflation and Nominal Interest Rates 156
Two Real Interest Rates: *Ex Ante* and *Ex Post* 157
CASE STUDY 6-6 Nominal Interest Rates in the Nineteenth Century 157

6-5 The Nominal Interest Rate and the Demand for Money 158

The Cost of Holding Money 158
Future Money and Current Prices 159
How to Stop a Hyperinflation 160
CASE STUDY 6-7 Hyperinflation in Interwar Germany 162

6-6 The Social Costs of Inflation   164

Expected Inflation   164
    C A S E S T U D Y 6 - 8   Life During the Bolivian Hyperinflation   166
Unexpected Inflation   166
    C A S E S T U D Y 6 - 9   The Free Silver Movement, the Election of 1896,
and the Wizard of Oz   168
The Level and Variability of Inflation   169

6-7 Conclusion: The Classical Dichotomy   169

Appendix: The Impact of Current and Future Money on the Price Level   173

Chapter 7
The Open Economy   176

7-1 National Income Accounting in an Open Economy   178

The Role of Net Exports   178
GNP versus GDP   180
The Capital Account and the Current Account   181

7-2 The International Flows of Capital and Goods   183

A Model of the Small Open Economy   183
How Policies Influence the Capital Account and the Current Account   185
    Fiscal Policy at Home   185
    C A S E S T U D Y 7 - 1   The Twin Deficits of the 1980s   186
    Fiscal Policy Abroad   188
    Shifts in Investment Demand   188
Evaluating Economic Policy   189

7-3 Exchange Rates   190

Nominal and Real Exchange Rates   190
    The Nominal Exchange Rate   190
    F Y I   How Newspapers Report the Exchange Rate   191
    The Real Exchange Rate   192
The Real Exchange Rate and Net Exports   193
    C A S E S T U D Y 7 - 2   How Business Firms Respond to the Exchange Rate   194
The Determinants of the Real Exchange Rate   194
How Policies Influence the Real Exchange Rate   196
    Fiscal Policy at Home   196
    Fiscal Policy Abroad   196
    Shifts in Investment Demand   197
The Effects of Trade Policies   198
The Determinants of the Nominal Exchange Rate   199
    C A S E S T U D Y 7 - 3   Inflation and Nominal Exchange Rates   200
The Special Case of Purchasing-Power Parity   201
    C A S E S T U D Y 7 - 4   The Big Mac Around the World   203

7-4 Conclusion: The United States as a Large Open Economy   204

Appendix: A Model of the Large Open Economy   208

The Flow of Capital From Abroad   208
The Elements of the Model   209
The Effects of Economic Policies   211

Part Three
The Economy in the Short Run   213

Chapter 8
Introduction to Economic Fluctuations   214

8-1 How the Short Run and Long Run Differ   215
> CASE STUDY 8-1   The Puzzle of Sticky Magazine Prices   217

8-2 Aggregate Demand   217

The Quantity Equation as Aggregate Demand   218
Why the Aggregate Demand Curve Slopes Downward   218
Shifts in the Aggregate Demand Curve   219

8-3 Aggregate Supply   220

The Long Run: The Vertical Aggregate Supply Curve   221
The Short Run: The Horizontal Aggregate Supply Curve   222
From the Short Run to the Long Run   224
> CASE STUDY 8-2   Gold, Greenbacks, and the Contraction of the 1870s   226

8-4 Stabilization Policy   226

Shocks to Aggregate Demand   227
> CASE STUDY 8-3   Velocity and the 1982 Recession   228
Shocks to Aggregate Supply   229
> CASE STUDY 8-4   How OPEC Helped Cause Stagflation in the 1970s and
> Euphoria in the 1980s   231

8-5 Conclusion   233

Chapter 9
Aggregate Demand I   235

9-1 The Goods Market and the *IS* Curve   237

The Keynesian Cross   237
> Planned Expenditure   237
> The Economy in Equilibrium   238
> Fiscal Policy and the Multiplier: Government Purchases   240
> Fiscal Policy and the Multiplier: Taxes   243
> CASE STUDY 9-1   Kennedy, Keynes, and the 1964 Tax Cut   244
The Interest Rate, Investment, and the *IS* Curve   244
How Fiscal Policy Shifts the *IS* Curve   246
A Loanable-Funds Interpretation of the *IS* Curve   247
The Simple Algebra of the *IS* Curve   248

9-2 The Money Market and the *LM* Curve   250

The Theory of Liquidity Preference   250
> CASE STUDY 9-2   Paul Volcker, Tight Money, and Rising Interest Rates   254
Income, Money Demand, and the *LM* Curve   254
How Monetary Policy Shifts the *LM* Curve   255
A Quantity-Equation Interpretation of the *LM* Curve   257
The Simple Algebra of the *LM* Curve   258

9-3 Conclusion: The Short-Run Equilibrium   259

Chapter 10
Aggregate Demand II   263

10-1 Explaining Fluctuations With the *IS-LM* Model   264

Changes in Fiscal Policy   264
Changes in Monetary Policy   265
The Interaction Between Monetary and Fiscal Policy   266
     C A S E S T U D Y 10 - 1   Policy Analysis With Macroeconometric Models   268
Shocks in the *IS-LM* Model   269

10-2 *IS-LM* as a Theory of Aggregate Demand   270

From the *IS-LM* Model to the Aggregate Demand Curve   270
The Simple Algebra of the Aggregate Demand Curve   273
     C A S E S T U D Y 10 - 2   The Effectiveness of Monetary and Fiscal Policy   274
The *IS-LM* Model in the Short Run and Long Run   275

10-3 The Great Depression   277

The Spending Hypothesis: Shocks to the *IS* Curve   278
The Money Hypothesis: A Shock to the *LM* Curve   280
The Money Hypothesis Again: The Effects of Falling Prices   280
     The Stabilizing Influences of Deflation   281
     The Destabilizing Influences of Deflation   281
Could the Depression Happen Again?   283

10-4 Conclusion   283

Chapter 11
Aggregate Supply   287

11-1 Four Models of Aggregate Supply   288

The Sticky-Wage Model   288
The Worker-Misperception Model   291
     C A S E S T U D Y 11 - 1   The Cyclical Behavior of the Real Wage   294
The Imperfect-Information Model   295
The Sticky-Price Model   296
     C A S E S T U D Y 11 - 2   International Differences in the Aggregate
     Supply Curve   299
Summary and Implications   300

11-2 Inflation, Unemployment, and the Phillips Curve   302

From Aggregate Supply to Phillips Curve   303
     F Y I   The History of the Phillips Curve   304
Expectations and Inflation Inertia   305
The Two Causes of Rising and Falling Inflation   305
     C A S E S T U D Y 11 - 3   Inflation and Unemployment in the United States   306
The Short-Run Tradeoff Between Inflation and Unemployment   307
Disinflation and the Sacrifice Ratio   308
Rational Expectations and Painless Disinflation   309
     C A S E S T U D Y 11 - 4   The Cost of Paul Volcker's Disinflation   311

11-3 Recent Developments: New Keynesian Economics   312

Small Menu Costs and Aggregate Demand Externalities   313
The Staggering of Wages and Prices   314
Recessions as Coordination Failure   315
     C A S E S T U D Y 11 - 5   Experimental Evidence on Coordination Games   316

Hysteresis and the Challenge to the Natural-Rate Hypothesis   317
    C A S E   S T U D Y   11 - 6   Unemployment in the United Kingdom in the 1980s   318

11-4 Conclusion   319

Chapter 12
The Macroeconomic Policy Debate   322

12-1 Should Policy Be Active or Passive?   323

Lags in the Implementation and Effects of Policies   324
    C A S E   S T U D Y   12 - 1   Profit Sharing as an Automatic Stabilizer   325
The Difficult Job of Economic Forecasting   326
    C A S E   S T U D Y   12 - 2   Two Episodes in Economic Forecasting   326
Ignorance, Expectations, and the Lucas Critique   328
The Historical Record   329
    C A S E   S T U D Y   12 - 3   Is the Stabilization of the Economy a Figment
of the Data?   329

12-2 Should Policy Be Conducted by Rule or by Discretion?   330

Distrust of Policymakers and the Political Process   331
    C A S E   S T U D Y   12 - 4   The Economy Under Republican and Democratic
Presidents   332
The Time Inconsistency of Discretionary Policy   333
    C A S E   S T U D Y   12 - 5   Alexander Hamilton versus Time Inconsistency   335
Rules for Monetary Policy   336
Rules for Fiscal Policy   337
    C A S E   S T U D Y   12 - 6   The Debt-GNP Ratio Over Two Hundred Years   338

12-3 Conclusion: Making Policy in an Uncertain World   339

Appendix: Time Inconsistency and the Tradeoff Between Inflation and
Unemployment   342

Chapter 13
The Open Economy in the Short Run   345

13-1 The Mundell-Fleming Model   346

Components of the Model   346
The Model on a *Y-r* Graph   347
The Model on a *Y-e* Graph   349

13-2 The Small Open Economy Under Floating Exchange Rates   352

Fiscal Policy   352
Monetary Policy   353
    C A S E   S T U D Y   13 - 1   The Rise in the Dollar, 1979–1982   354
Trade Policy   354

13-3 The Small Open Economy Under Fixed Exchange Rates   356

How a Fixed Exchange-Rate System Works   356
    C A S E   S T U D Y   13 - 2   The International Gold Standard   358
Fiscal Policy   359
Monetary Policy   359
Trade Policy   361
Summary of the Mundell-Fleming Model   362

13-4 Should Exchange Rates Be Floating or Fixed?   362

    C A S E   S T U D Y 13 - 3   The European Monetary System   364

13-5 A Concluding Reminder   364

   Appendix: A Short-Run Model of the Large Open Economy   368

   Fiscal Policy   370
   Monetary Policy   370
   A Rule of Thumb   373

Chapter 14
The Theory of Real Business Cycles

                                                                 374

14-1 A Review of the Economy Under Flexible Prices   375

14-2 A Real-Business-Cycle Model   377

   Intertemporal Substitution and Labor Supply   377
   Real Aggregate Supply and Real Aggregate Demand   378
   Changes in Fiscal Policy   379
   Shocks to Technology   380

14-3 The Debate Over Real-Business-Cycle Theory   382

   The Importance of Technology Shocks   382
      C A S E   S T U D Y 14 - 1   The Solow Residual and the Business Cycle   383
   The Interpretation of Unemployment   384
      C A S E   S T U D Y 14 - 2   Looking for Intertemporal Substitution   385
   The Neutrality of Money   386
   The Flexibility of Wages and Prices   386
      F Y I   What Is New Classical Economics?   387

14-4 Conclusion   388

Part Four

More on the Microeconomics Behind Macroeconomics

                                                 391

Chapter 15
Consumption

                                               392

15-1 John Maynard Keynes and the Consumption Function   393

   Keynes's Conjectures   393
   The Early Empirical Successes   395
   Secular Stagnation, Simon Kuznets, and the Consumption Puzzle   395

15-2 Irving Fisher and Intertemporal Choice   397

   The Intertemporal Budget Constraint   397
   Consumer Preferences   400
   Optimization   401
   How Changes in Income Affect Consumption   402
   How Changes in the Real Interest Rate Affect Consumption   403
      C A S E   S T U D Y 15 - 1   Consumption and the Real Interest Rate   404
   Constraints on Borrowing   405
      C A S E   S T U D Y 15 - 2   The High Japanese Saving Rate   408

15-3 Franco Modigliani and the Life-Cycle Hypothesis   409

   The Hypothesis   409

Implications 410
    CASE STUDY 15-3 The Consumption and Saving of the Elderly 412
    CASE STUDY 15-4 Saving and the Fear of Nuclear War 412

15-4 Milton Friedman and the Permanent-Income Hypothesis 414

The Hypothesis 414
Implications 415
    CASE STUDY 15-5 The 1964 Tax Cut and the 1968 Tax Surcharge 416
Rational Expectations and Consumption 417
    CASE STUDY 15-6 Do Consumers Anticipate Future Income? 418

15-5 Conclusion 419

Chapter 16
Two Views of Government Debt 423

16-1 The Traditional View of Government Debt 424

16-2 The Ricardian View of Government Debt 426

The Basic Logic of Ricardian Equivalence 426
The Government Budget Constraint 427

16-3 Consumers and Future Taxes 429

Myopia 430
Borrowing Constraints 430
Future Generations 432
    CASE STUDY 16-1 Why Do Parents Leave Bequests? 433

16-4 Conclusion: Making a Choice 433

Appendix: Is the Government Budget Deficit Correctly Measured? 436

Measurement Problem No. 1: Inflation 436
Measurement Problem No. 2: Capital Assets 432
Measurement Problem No. 3: Uncounted Liabilities 438
Whither the Budget Deficit? 439

Chapter 17
Investment 440

17-1 Business Fixed Investment 441

The Rental Price of Capital 442
The Cost of Capital 443
The Determinants of Investment 445
Taxes and Investment 448
    CASE STUDY 17-1 The Swedish Investment Funds System 449
The Stock Market and Tobin's *q* 450
Financing Constraints 451

17-2 Residential Investment 452

The Stock Equilibrium and the Flow Supply 452
Changes in Housing Demand 453
    FYI What Price House Can You Afford? 454
    CASE STUDY 17-2 Taxes, Babies, and the Housing Boom
    of the 1970s 455

17-3 Inventory Investment 456

Reasons for Holding Inventories 456
   CASE STUDY 17-3 Seasonal Fluctuations and Production
   Smoothing 457
The Accelerator Model of Inventories 458
   CASE STUDY 17-4 The Evidence for the Accelerator Model 458
Inventories and the Real Interest Rate 459

17-4 Conclusion 460

Chapter 18
Money Supply and Money Demand   463

18-1 Money Supply 463

100-Percent-Reserve Banking 464
Fractional-Reserve Banking 465
A Model of the Money Supply 467
The Three Instruments of Monetary Policy 469
   CASE STUDY 18-1 Bank Failures and the Money Supply in the
   1930s 470

18-2 Money Demand 472

Portfolio Theories of Money Demand 472
   CASE STUDY 18-2 Currency and the Underground Economy 474
Transactions Theories of Money Demand 474
The Baumol-Tobin Model of Cash Management 474
   CASE STUDY 18-3 Empirical Studies of Money Demand 478

18-3 Conclusion: Microeconomic Models for Macroeconomics 479

Epilogue
What We Know, What We Don't   482

The Four Most Important Lessons of Macroeconomics 482
   Lesson No. 1: In the long run, a country's capacity to produce goods and
   services determines the standard of living of its citizens 483
   Lesson No. 2: In the short run, aggregate demand influences the amount of
   goods and services that a country produces 483
   Lesson No. 3: In the long run, the rate of money growth determines the rate of
   inflation, but it does not affect the rate of unemployment 483
   Lesson No. 4: In the short run, policymakers who control monetary and fiscal
   policy face a tradeoff between inflation and unemployment 484

The Four Most Important Unresolved Questions of Macroeconomics 485
   Question No. 1: How should policymakers try to raise the economy's natural
   rate of output? 485
   Question No. 2: Should policymakers try to stabilize the economy? 486
   Question No. 3: How costly is inflation, and how costly is reducing
   inflation? 486
   Question No. 4: What are the consequences of government budget deficits? 487

Glossary 489

Index 499

List of Case Studies

1-1 Presidential Elections and the Economy   5

2-1 Real GNP in the United States   22
2-2 GNP and Its Components   25
2-3 The Seasonal Cycle and Seasonal Adjustment   28
2-4 The Inflation of 1978–1981   32
2-5 Unemployment, GNP, and Okun's Law   35

3-1 The Black Death and Factor Prices   53
3-2 The Senator, the Mathematician, and the Constancy of Factor Shares   53
3-3 The Consumption Function in U.S. Data   58
3-4 Wars and Interest Rates in the United Kingdom, 1730–1920   67
3-5 Fiscal Policy in the 1980s   69

4-1 Japanese and German Postwar Economic Growth   86
4-2 Saving in Rich and Poor Countries   88
4-3 Population Growth in Rich and Poor Countries   99
4-4 Steady-State Growth in the United States   102
4-5 Social Security and Saving   105
4-6 The Worldwide Slowdown in Economic Growth   106

5-1 Interwar British Unemployment   123
5-2 Unemployment Insurance and the Rate of Job Finding   124
5-3 The Minimum Wage and the Working Poor   128
5-4 Unionization and Unemployment in the United States and Canada   129
5-5 Henry Ford's $5 Workday   131

6-1 Money in a POW Camp   143
6-2 Money on the Island of Yap   144
6-3 A Century of Money Growth and Inflation   152
6-4 Paying for the American Revolution   154
6-5 Inflation and Nominal Interest Rates   156
6-6 Nominal Interest Rates in the Nineteenth Century   157
6-7 Hyperinflation in Interwar Germany   162
6-8 Life During the Bolivian Hyperinflation   166
6-9 The Free Silver Movement, the Election of 1896, and the Wizard
     of Oz   168

7-1 The Twin Deficits of the 1980s   186
7-2 How Business Firms Respond to the Exchange Rate   194

7-3 Inflation and Nominal Exchange Rates 200

7-4 The Big Mac Around the World 203

8-1 The Puzzle of Sticky Magazine Prices 217

8-2 Gold, Greenbacks, and the Contraction of the 1870s 226

8-3 Velocity and the 1982 Recession 228

8-4 How OPEC Helped Cause Stagflation in the 1970s and Euphoria in the 1980s 231

9-1 Kennedy, Keynes, and the 1964 Tax Cut 244

9-2 Paul Volcker, Tight Money, and Rising Interest Rates 254

10-1 Policy Analysis With Macroeconometric Models 268

10-2 The Effectiveness of Monetary and Fiscal Policy 274

11-1 The Cyclical Behavior of the Real Wage 294

11-2 International Differences in the Aggregate Supply Curve 299

11-3 Inflation and Unemployment in the United States 306

11-4 The Cost of Paul Volcker's Disinflation 311

11-5 Experimental Evidence on Coordination Games 316

11-6 Unemployment in the United Kingdom in the 1980s 318

12-1 Profit Sharing as an Automatic Stabilizer 325

12-2 Two Episodes in Economic Forecasting 326

12-3 Is the Stabilization of the Economy a Figment of the Data? 329

12-4 The Economy Under Republican and Democratic Presidents 332

12-5 Alexander Hamilton versus Time Inconsistency 335

12-6 The Debt-GNP Ratio Over Two Hundred Years 338

13-1 The Rise in the Dollar, 1979–1982 354

13-2 The International Gold Standard 358

13-3 The European Monetary System 364

14-1 The Solow Residual and the Business Cycle 383

14-2 Looking for Intertemporal Substitution 385

15-1 Consumption and the Real Interest Rate 404

15-2 The High Japanese Saving Rate 408

15-3 The Consumption and Saving of the Elderly 412

15-4 Saving and the Fear of Nuclear War 412

15-5 The 1964 Tax Cut and the 1968 Tax Surcharge 416

15-6 Do Consumers Anticipate Future Income? 418

16-1 Why Do Parents Leave Bequests? 433

17-1 The Swedish Investment Funds System 449

17-2 Taxes, Babies, and the Housing Boom of the 1970s 455

17-3 Seasonal Fluctuations and Production Smoothing 457

17-4 The Evidence for the Accelerator Model 458

18-1 Bank Failures and the Money Supply in the 1930s 470

18-2 Currency and the Underground Economy 474

18-3 Empirical Studies of Money Demand 478

Preface

Why write a textbook?

I was asked this question many times during the three years I worked on this book. Sometimes, sorting through the piles of suggestions from reviewers and editors, I asked it myself. My answer was always the same: although several good textbooks for intermediate courses in macroeconomics were already available, I envisioned a book that was very different and, I believed, much better.

Having invested so much time in this book, I am not objective enough to judge whether it is in fact better. That is a task for others. But I can say without hesitation that it is different. Although in some ways the approach I take in this book is traditional, in other ways it tries to redefine—or at least reorient—the teaching of macroeconomics.

First, I attempt to achieve a balance between short-run and long-run macroeconomics. Courses in macroeconomics will always present the theory of short-run economic fluctuations, for it provides the basis for understanding most discussions of monetary and fiscal policy. Yet if students are to understand fully the implications of public policies, courses must give ample attention to long-run topics as well, including economic growth, the natural rate of unemployment, persistent inflation, and government debt. As if we needed reminding, the past decade has highlighted the importance of understanding the effects of policies at all time horizons: any intelligent discussion of continuing budget deficits requires balancing short-run and long-run concerns.

Second, I integrate the insights of both Keynesian and classical economics. The prominent role of the Keynesian approach to economic fluctuations in this and most other textbooks is testament to the influence and importance of Keynes's *General Theory*. Yet, in the aftermath of the Keynesian revolution, too many economists forgot that classical economics provides the right answers to many fundamental questions. In this book I incorporate many of the contributions of the classical economists before Keynes and the new classical economists of the past two decades. Substantial coverage is given, for example, to the loanable-funds theory of the interest rate, the quantity theory of money, and the problem of time inconsistency. At the same time, however, I recognize that many of the ideas of Keynes and the new Keynesians are necessary to understand economic fluctuations. Substantial coverage is given also to the *IS-LM* model of aggregate demand, the short-run tradeoff between inflation and unemployment, and modern theories of wage and price rigidity.

Third, I present macroeconomics using a variety of simple models. Instead of pretending that there is one model that is complete enough to explain all facets of the economy, I encourage students to learn how to use and compare a set of prominent models. This approach has the pedagogical value that each model can be kept relatively simple and can be presented within one or two chapters. More important, this approach asks students to think like economists, who always keep a variety of models in mind when analyzing economic events or public policies.

Fourth, I emphasize that macroeconomics is an empirical discipline, motivated and guided by a wide variety of historical experience. This book contains many case studies that use macroeconomic theory to shed light on real-world data or events. I have chosen the case studies to highlight the broad applicability of the basic theory. The reader learns how to analyze the policies of John Kennedy, Henry Ford, and Alexander Hamilton, and how to apply economic principles to issues from fourteenth-century Europe, the island of Yap, and the land of Oz.

In these four ways, this book differs markedly from those I used as a student. I have found that these changes work well with the current generation of students. During the years I was writing this book, students at Berkeley, Brown, Harvard, Illinois, Michigan, Michigan State, Rochester, Smith, Vanderbilt, and Yale used early drafts of the manuscript in their courses. The response was heartening. The feedback I received individually and from questionnaires kept me going during the long process of writing and rewriting.

The Arrangement of Topics

My basic strategy when teaching this course is first to examine the long run when prices are flexible, and then to examine the short run when prices are sticky. That is, I begin with classical models of the economy and explain fully the long-run equilibrium before discussing deviations from that equilibrium. This strategy has several advantages:

- Students learn first the material that is less controversial among macroeconomists.

- Beginning with market-clearing models makes clearer the link between macroeconomics and microeconomics.

- When I turn to short-run fluctuations, students understand fully the long-run equilibrium around which the economy is fluctuating.

- Because the classical dichotomy permits the separation of real and monetary issues, the long-run material is easier for students to understand.

The book follows this organizational strategy. It is made up of four parts (including 18 chapters) and an epilogue. Here is a whirlwind tour:

Part One: Introduction

I have kept the introductory material as brief as possible in order to get to the core topics quickly. Chapter 1 discusses the broad questions that macroeconomists address and the economist's approach of building models to explain the world. Chapter 2 introduces the key data of macroeconomics, emphasizing gross national product, the consumer price index, and the unemployment rate.

Part Two: The Economy in the Long Run

Part Two examines the long run over which prices are flexible. Chapter 3 presents the basic classical model of national income. In this model, the factors of production and the production technology determine the level of income, and the marginal products of the factors determine its distribution to households. In addition, the model shows how fiscal policy influences the allocation of the economy's resources among consumption, investment, and government purchases, and it highlights how the real interest rate equilibrates the supply and demand for goods and services.

Chapter 4 makes the classical analysis of the economy dynamic. It uses the Solow growth model to examine the evolution of the economy over time. The Solow model provides the basis for discussing why the standard of living varies so widely across countries and how public policies influence the level and growth of the standard of living.

Chapter 5 relaxes the assumption of full employment by discussing the dynamics of the labor market and the natural rate of unemployment. It examines various causes of unemployment, including job search, minimum-wage laws, union power, and efficiency wages. It also presents some important facts about patterns of unemployment.

Money and the price level are introduced in Chapter 6. Because prices are assumed to be fully flexible, the chapter presents the prominent ideas of classical monetary theory. It discusses the quantity theory of money, the inflation tax, the Fisher effect, the causes of hyperinflation, and the social costs of inflation.

The study of open-economy macroeconomics begins in Chapter 7. Maintaining the assumption of full employment, this chapter presents models to explain the current account, the capital account, and the real and nominal exchange rates. It addresses various issues of economic policy: the relation between the budget deficit and the current-account deficit, the macroeconomic impact of protectionist trade policies, and the effect of monetary policy on the value of a currency in the market for foreign exchange.

Part Three: The Economy in the Short Run

Part Three examines the short run when prices are sticky. It begins in Chapter 8 by introducing the model of aggregate supply and aggregate demand as well as the role of stabilization policy. Subsequent chapters refine the ideas introduced here.

Chapters 9 and 10 look more closely at aggregate demand. Chapter 9 presents the Keynesian cross and the theory of liquidity preference, and it uses these models as building blocks for the *IS-LM* model. Chapter 10 uses the *IS-LM* model to explain economic fluctuations and the aggregate demand curve. It concludes with an extended case study of the Great Depression.

Chapter 11 looks more closely at aggregate supply. It examines the various approaches to explaining the short-run aggregate supply curve, and it discusses the short-run tradeoff between inflation and unemployment. It also discusses some recent new Keynesian developments in the theory of aggregate supply.

After the model of aggregate supply and aggregate demand has been fully developed, Chapter 12 turns to the hotly contested issue of how this model should be applied to economic policy. It emphasizes two broad questions. Should monetary and fiscal policy be active or passive? Should policy be conducted by rule or by discretion? The chapter presents arguments on both sides of the debate.

The study of open-economy macroeconomics continues in Chapter 13, which discusses short-run fluctuations in an open economy. This chapter presents the Mundell-Fleming model and shows how monetary and fiscal policy affect the economy under floating and fixed exchange-rate systems. It also discusses the debate over whether exchange rates should be floating or fixed.

Finally, Chapter 14 presents the theory of real business cycles as an alternative way to view economic fluctuations. It discusses the basic elements of this new classical approach and the arguments advanced by both its advocates and critics.

Part Four: More on the Microeconomics Behind Macroeconomics

After developing the long-run and short-run models, the book discusses several topics that refine our understanding of the economy by analyzing more fully the microeconomics behind macroeconomics. Chapter 15 presents the various theories of consumer behavior, including the Keynesian consumption function, Fisher's model of intertemporal choice, Modigliani's life-cycle hypothesis, and Friedman's permanent-income hypothesis. Chapter 16 discusses the debate between the traditional and Ricardian views of government debt, emphasizing that the argument is ultimately over how consumers behave. Chapter 17 presents the theory behind the investment function. Chapter 18 provides additional material on the money market, including the role of the banking system in determining the money supply and the Baumol-Tobin model of money demand.

Epilogue

The book ends with a brief epilogue, which reviews the broad lessons about which most macroeconomists would agree and some of the most important unresolved questions. Here and throughout the book, I emphasize that despite the disagreements among macroeconomists, there is much we know about how the economy works.

Alternative Syllabus

Economics professors differ in the importance they place on various topics and the sequence in which they prefer to cover these topics. In writing this book, I have tried to make it as flexible as possible. Many of the chapters are self-contained. Instructors can change the emphases of their courses by rearranging the chapters or by omitting some chapters entirely.

One possible alternative syllabus is presented here as an example. This syllabus maintains the strategy of first examining output and prices in the long run when prices are flexible, but it introduces sticky prices and short-run fluctuations earlier in the course. It defers all open-economy macroeconomics until after the study of fluctuations, and it defers the study of economic growth and the natural rate of unemployment until the end of the course.

Introduction
1. The Science of Macroeconomics
2. The Data of Macroeconomics

Income and Prices
3. National Income: Its Production, Distribution, and Allocation
6. Inflation
8. Introduction to Economic Fluctuations
9. Aggregate Demand I
10. Aggregate Demand II
11. Aggregate Supply
12. Macroeconomic Policy
14. The Theory of Real Business Cycles

Open-Economy Macroeconomics
7. The Open Economy
13. The Open Economy in the Short Run

More on the Microeconomics Behind Macroeconomics
15. Consumption
16. Two Views of Government Debt
17. Investment
18. Money Supply and Money Demand
5. Unemployment
4. Economic Growth

Learning Tools

I have made every effort to keep this text user-friendly. Students are continually asked to use and review what they have learned.

Case Studies

Economics comes to life when it is applied to understand the world. Therefore, the 74 case studies in this text are its most important learning tool. The frequency with which they occur ensures that a student does not need to grapple with an overdose of theory before seeing the theory applied. Students report that the case studies are their favorite part of the book.

FYI Boxes

These boxes present ancillary material "for your information." I use these boxes to clarify difficult concepts, to provide additional information about the tools of economics, and to show how economics relates to our daily lives.

Mathematical Notes

I use occasional mathematical footnotes to keep more difficult material out of the body of the text. These notes make an argument more rigorous or present a proof of a mathematical result. They are designed for students who know basic calculus and can easily be skipped by those who don't.

Chapter Summaries

Every chapter ends with a brief, nontechnical summary of its major lessons. Students can use the summaries to place the material in perspective and to review for exams.

Key Concepts

Every chapter includes a number of key concepts. Within the chapter, each key concept is **boldfaced** when it is introduced. At the end of the chapter, the key concepts are listed for review.

Questions for Review

After finishing a chapter, students can immediately test their understanding of its basic lessons by answering the Questions for Review.

Problems and Applications

Each chapter includes a number of Problems and Applications designed for homework assignments. Some of these are numerical applications of the theory in the chapter. Others encourage the student to go beyond the material in the chapter by addressing new issues that are closely related to the chapter topics.

Chapter Appendices

Six chapters include appendices presenting additional material, sometimes at a higher level of mathematical sophistication. These are designed so that professors can cover certain topics in greater depth if they wish. The appendices can be skipped altogether without any loss of continuity.

Glossary

Like all fields, macroeconomics has its own language. To help students become familiar with this new language, a glossary of more than 250 terms is provided at the end of the book.

Supplements

Worth Publishers and I have put together a talented team of economics professors to develop the supplements that accompany this book.

Student Guide and Workbook

Roger Kaufman of Smith College has written a superb study guide for students. It provides an abundance of ways for students to learn the material in the text and assess their understanding.

- *Fill-In Questions* give students the opportunity to review and check their knowledge of the key terms and concepts in the chapter.
- *Multiple-Choice Questions* allow students to test themselves on the chapter material.
- *Exercises* guide students step by step through the various models using graphs and numerical examples.
- *Problems* ask students to apply the models on their own.
- *Questions to Think About* require critical thinking as well as economic analysis.
- *Data Questions* ask students to obtain and learn about readily available economic data.

Student Software

David Weil of Brown University has developed an innovative software package that students can use throughout the course. *MacroBytes* provides a range of activities to aid and motivate the student:

- *Self-Tests.* Students can test their knowledge of the material in the book by taking multiple-choice tests on any chapter or combination of chapters. After the student responds, the program explains the answer and directs the student to specific sections in the book for additional study.

- *Data Plotter.* Students can explore macroeconomic data with time-series graphs and scatterplots.

- *Macro Models.* These modules provide simulations of the models presented in the book. Students can change the exogenous variables and see the outcomes in terms of shifting curves and recalculated numerical values of the endogenous variables. Each module contains exercises that instructors can assign as homework. These exercises help ensure mastery of the models in the book.

- *2001: A Game for Macroeconomists.* The game allows students to become President of the United States in the year 2001 and to make macroeconomic policy decisions based on news events, economic statistics, and approval ratings. It gives students a sense of the complex interconnections that influence the economy.

The *Instructor's Resource Manual* gives suggestions on various ways to integrate the software into the course. *MacroBytes* is available for the IBM PC.

Instructor's Resource Manual

Andrew John of Michigan State University has developed an extensive resource manual which instructors will find invaluable. Each chapter contains notes to the instructor, a detailed lecture outline, a series of "briefs," an annotated reading list, and suggestions on ways to incorporate the *MacroBytes* software into the course. The notes to the instructor provide a clear and concise discussion of the approach and goals of each chapter. These notes complement the detailed lecture outlines, which cover all of the topics in each text chapter.

A special feature of the *Instructor's Resource Manual* is the series of briefs for each chapter. These lively supplemental discussions address current economic events and emerging research, give additional case studies, and take in-depth looks at selected topics in the text. Instructors can use these briefs to enrich their lectures, or they can reproduce the briefs as handouts for students.

Test Bank and Computerized Test-Generation System

Charles Bischoff of the State University of New York at Binghamton has written a test bank of over 500 multiple-choice questions to accompany the text. Several numerical problems are also provided for each chapter. Professors can obtain either a printed and bound copy of the test bank, a disk, or both. The disk includes a test-generation program and is available for both the IBM PC and Macintosh computers.

Transparency Masters

Worth Publishers will provide enlarged master copies of all the figures in the text. Instructors can use these to prepare overhead transparencies for use in lecture.

Solutions Manual

Harvard graduate students John Fernald and Paula DeMasi have prepared a *Solutions Manual* for instructors' use. The manual contains answers to all the end-of-chapter questions, including both the Questions for Review and the Problems and Applications. It also contains answers for selected problems from the *Student Guide* and for all the questions in the *MacroBytes* software. Instructors can use the *Solutions Manual* to prepare answer sheets for their students.

Acknowledgments

When writing this book, I benefited from the input of many editors, reviewers, and colleagues. In addition, over 1,000 students at nearly a dozen universities read the manuscript at various stages of revision. Their comments and suggestions have made this a better book.

I would like to thank individually those who read and commented on large portions of the manuscript. They include:

Francis Ahking, *University of Connecticut*

Steven Allen, *North Carolina State University*

Robert Barry, *College of William and Mary*

Susanto Basu, *Harvard University*

Charles Bischoff, *State University of New York at Binghamton*

John Campbell, *Princeton University*

Charles DeLorme Jr., *University of Georgia*

Paula DeMasi, *Harvard University*

William Dickens, *University of California at Berkeley*

Donald Dutkowsky, *Syracuse University*

Karen Dynan, *Harvard University*

Douglas Elmendorf, *Harvard University*

Gerald Epstein, *University of Massachusetts*

Antonio Fatas, *Harvard University*

John Fernald, *Harvard University*

Chris Hanes, *University of Pennsylvania*

Daniel Himarios, *University of Texas at Arlington*

Steven Holland, *University of Kentucky*

Dennis Jansen, *Texas A&M University*

Nancy Jianakoplos, *Colorado State University*

Klaus Dieter John, *Johannes Gutenberg University*

John Laitner, *University of Michigan*

John Lapp, *North Carolina State University*

Deborah Mankiw, *NBER*

W. Douglas McMillin, *Louisiana State University*

Starr McMullen, *Oregon State University*

David Meinster, *Temple University*

Andrew Metrick, *Harvard University*

Jeffrey Miron, *Boston University*

Neil Niman, *University of New Hampshire*

Stefan Oppers, *Harvard University*

Joseph Ritter, *University of Texas at Austin*

Bennett Rushkoff

Amy Salsbury, *Harvard University*

Boris Simkovich, *Harvard University*

David Spencer, *Brigham Young University*

Lowell Taylor, *Carnegie-Mellon University*

Ping Wang, *Pennsylvania State University*

I am especially grateful to those instructors who not only gave me their own comments but also class-tested the manuscript with their students. They include:

Robert Barsky, *University of Michigan*

Andrew John, *Michigan State University*

David Johnson, *Harvard University*

Roger Kaufman, *Smith College*

Bill Maloney, *University of Illinois at Urbana-Champaign*

David Parsley, *Vanderbilt University*

Changyong Rhee, *University of Rochester*

David Romer, *University of California at Berkeley*

Matthew Shapiro, *University of Michigan*

David Weil, *Brown University*

The people at Worth Publishers were consistently gracious and helpful, as were the free-lance editors who worked on the manuscript. I am grateful to Marjorie Anderson, Lisa Pinto, Toni Scaramuzzo, Wendy Schechter, Jonathan Shapiro, Paul Shensa, and Bob Worth.

I am also grateful to Jeanette DeHaan, my secretary at Harvard. As always, her work went beyond the call of duty.

Finally, I would like to encourage those who use this book to send me their reactions—both positive and negative. Regular revision is necessary to keep a textbook up-to-date. Suggestions from teachers and students were invaluable in writing this first edition, and I am sure they will be again when I start writing the second.

N. Gregory Mankiw

Cambridge, Massachusetts
May 1991

Part One

Introduction

Chapter 1

The Science of Macroeconomics

*The whole of science is nothing more than the
refinement of everyday thinking.*

Albert Einstein

1-1 Why Study Macroeconomics?

Why are incomes higher today than they were in 1950, and why were
they higher in 1950 than in 1900? Why do some countries have high rates
of inflation while others have stable prices? What causes recessions and
depressions—the recurrent periods of falling incomes and rising unemployment—and how can public policy be used to avoid them? **Macroeconomics**, the study of the economy as a whole, attempts to answer
these and many related questions.

To appreciate the importance of macroeconomics, you need only to
read the newspaper or listen to the news. The media report macroeconomic developments daily. Headlines such as DISPOSABLE INCOME RISES
FIVE PERCENT, FEDERAL RESERVE MOVES TO COMBAT INFLATION, or STOCK MARKET
FALLS AMID FEARS OF RECESSION are routine.

Macroeconomic events touch the lives of all of us. Business executives forecasting the demand for their products must guess how fast
consumers' incomes will grow. Senior citizens living on fixed incomes
wonder how fast prices will rise. Unemployed workers looking for jobs
hope that the economy will boom and that firms will be hiring. All are
affected by the state of the economy.

It is no surprise that macroeconomic issues play a central role in
political debate. In the 1970s, Presidents Richard Nixon, Gerald Ford,
and Jimmy Carter all wrestled unsuccessfully with a rising rate of inflation. In the 1980s, Presidents Ronald Reagan and George Bush con-
tended with a large federal budget deficit. The popularity of the incumbent president rises during booms and falls during recessions. Voters
are keenly aware of macroeconomic events, and politicians are equally
aware of the importance of macroeconomic policy.

Macroeconomic issues also play a pivotal role in international relations. In the 1950s and 1960s, most major industrial countries maintained a constant rate of exchange between their currency and that of other countries. In the early 1970s, this system of fixed exchange rates broke down, and a new era of flexible and highly volatile exchange rates began. In the 1980s, the United States imported many more goods than it exported, and it financed these imports by borrowing heavily in world financial markets. International economic developments like these are often a source of tension, even among close allies.

Macroeconomists are the scientists who try to explain the working of the economy as a whole. They collect data on incomes, prices, unemployment, and many other economic variables from different periods of time and from different countries. They then attempt to formulate general theories that help to explain these data.

Figure 1-1 shows three types of macroeconomic data for the U.S. economy: growth in real GNP, the inflation rate, and the unemployment rate. Each of these variables measures some aspect of economic performance. GNP measures the total income of everyone in the economy; the inflation rate measures how quickly prices are rising; and the unemployment rate measures the fraction of the labor force that is unemployed. Macroeconomists study how these variables are determined, why they change over time, and how they interact with each other.

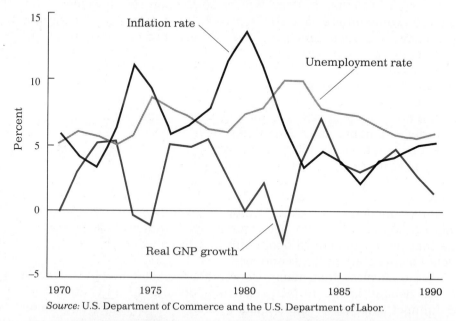

Source: U.S. Department of Commerce and the U.S. Department of Labor.

Figure 1-1   **Three Key Macroeconomic Variables.** This figure shows the growth in real GNP, the inflation rate (according to the consumer price index), and the unemployment rate for the U.S. economy since 1970.

Subsequent chapters discuss how these variables are measured and the theories that macroeconomists have developed to explain them.

Like astronomers studying the evolution of stars or biologists study-ing the evolution of species, macroeconomists cannot conduct controlled experiments—experimenting with the economy would be too costly. In-stead, they must rely on natural experiments. Macroeconomists observe that economies differ from one another and that economies change over time. These observations provide both the motivation for developing macroeconomic theories and the data for testing them.

To be sure, macroeconomics is a young and imperfect science. The macroeconomist's ability to predict the future course of economic events is no better than the meteorologist's ability to predict next month's weather. But, as you will see, we do know quite a lot about how the economy works.

Our goal in studying macroeconomics, however, is not just to explain economic events but also to improve economic policy. The monetary and fiscal tools of government can influence the economy in powerful ways—both for good and for ill—and macroeconomics helps policymakers eval-uate alternative policies. Macroeconomists are asked to explain the eco-nomic world as it is and to consider what it could be.

CASE STUDY 1-1

Presidential Elections and the Economy

The influence of economic events on politics is most apparent during presidential elections. Economic policy provides a primary topic of de-bate for the candidates, and the state of the economy has a powerful influence on the outcome of the election. In fact, according to economist Ray Fair, one can forecast the outcome of a presidential election with remarkable accuracy by looking at how well the economy is doing. His-tory shows that the incumbent party is helped by growing incomes and is hurt by rising prices.

Fair has used the historical evidence to produce an equation that forecasts the election outcome using the following information:

- which party is currently in power,
- whether an incumbent is running for reelection,
- the growth in total income in the six months before the election, and
- the rate at which prices are rising in the two years before the elec-tion.

Fair's equation would have correctly predicted the outcomes of 13 of the 16 presidential elections from 1916 to 1976. The three elections it would have missed were all close: Kennedy-Nixon in 1960, Humphrey-Nixon in 1968, and Carter-Ford in 1976.

Since Fair first came up with his forecasting method in 1978, three presidential elections have taken place: Carter-Reagan in 1980, Mon-dale-Reagan in 1984, and Dukakis-Bush in 1988. Fair predicted each outcome correctly. In fact, he predicted a narrow Bush victory in 1988, at a time when Bush was far behind in the political polls.[1]

1-2 How Economists Think

Economics as a subject is distinguished not only by the questions it addresses but also by the tools it uses—the terminology, the data, and the way of thinking. Like any science, economics can seem foreign and arcane to the uninitiated. The best way to become familiar with the tools of economics, of course, is to practice using them. This book will afford you ample opportunity to do so. To make these tools less forbidding, however, let's discuss some of them here.

The Use of Economic Models

Economists try to understand the economy by using simplified theories called **models**. Models summarize, often in mathematical terms, the relationships among economic variables. Models are useful because they help us to dispense with irrelevant details and to focus on important economic connections more clearly.

Models have two kinds of variables: **exogenous variables** and **endogenous variables**. Exogenous variables come from outside the model—they are the inputs into the model. Endogenous variables come from inside the model—they are the model's output. In other words, exogenous variables are fixed at the moment they enter the model, whereas endogenous variables are determined within the model. As Figure 1-2 illustrates, the purpose of a model is to show how the exogenous variables affect the endogenous variables.

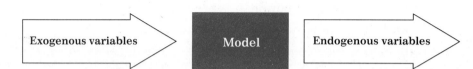

Figure 1-2 **How Models Work.**   Models are simplified theories that show the key relationships among economic variables. The exogenous variables are those that come from outside the model. The endogenous variables are those that the model explains. The model shows how a change in one of the exogenous variables affects all the endogenous variables.

[1] Ray C. Fair, "The Effect of Economic Events on Votes for President," *The Review of Economics and Statistics* 60 (May 1978):159–173; Ray C. Fair, "The Effect of Economic Events on Votes for President: 1984 Update," *Political Behavior* 10, no. 2 (1988):168–179.

For example, consider how an economist might develop a model of the market for bread. The economist supposes that the quantity of bread demanded by consumers, Q^d, depends on the price of bread, P_b, and on aggregate income, Y. This relationship is expressed in the equation

$$Q^d = D(P_b, Y).$$

Similarly, the economist supposes that the quantity of bread supplied by bakers, Q^s, depends on the price of bread, P_b, and on the price of flour, P_f, since flour is used to make bread:

$$Q^s = S(P_b, P_f).$$

Finally, the economist assumes that the price of bread adjusts to equilibrate supply and demand:

$$Q^s = Q^d.$$

These three equations compose a model of the market for bread.

The economist illustrates the model with the supply-and-demand diagram, as in Figure 1-3. The demand curve shows the relationship between the quantity of bread demanded and the price of bread, while holding aggregate income constant. The demand curve slopes downward because the greater the price of bread, the more consumers switch to other foods and the less bread they buy. The supply curve shows the relationship between the quantity of bread supplied and the price of bread, while holding the price of flour constant. The supply curve slopes upward because the greater the price of bread, the more bread bakers produce. The equilibrium for the market is the price and quantity at which the supply and demand curves intersect.

This model of the bread market has two exogenous variables and two endogenous variables. The exogenous variables are aggregate in-

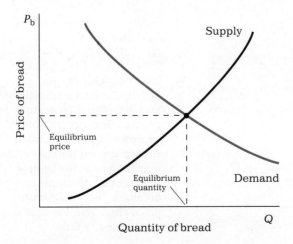

Figure 1-3 **Supply and Demand Curves.** The most famous economic model is that of supply and demand for a good or service—in this case, bread. The demand curve is a downward-sloping curve relating the price of bread to the quantity of bread that consumers demand. The supply curve is an upward-sloping curve relating the price of bread to the quantity of bread that bakeries supply. The price of bread adjusts until supply equals demand. The point where the two curves cross is the market equilibrium, which shows the equilibrium price of bread and the equilibrium quantity of bread.

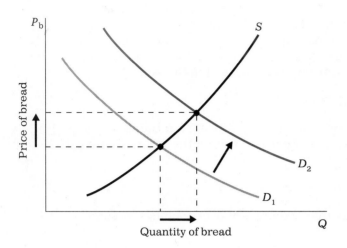

Figure 1-4 **An Increase in Demand.** An increase in aggregate income increases the demand for bread—at any given price, consumers now want to buy more bread. This is represented by an outward shift in the demand curve. The price of bread rises until the supply again equals demand. The equilibrium price and the equilibrium quantity of bread rise.

come and the price of flour. The model does not attempt to explain them but takes them as already determined (perhaps to be explained by another model). The endogenous variables are the price of bread and the quantity of bread exchanged. These are the variables that the model attempts to explain.

The model shows how a change in one of the exogenous variables affects both endogenous variables. For example, if aggregate income increases, then the demand for bread increases, as illustrated in Figure 1-4. The model shows that both the equilibrium price and the equilibrium quantity of bread rise. Similarly, if the price of flour increases, then the supply of bread decreases, as illustrated in Figure 1-5. The model shows that in this case the equilibrium price of bread rises and the equilibrium quantity of bread falls. Thus, the model shows in a simple way how changes in aggregate income or in the price of flour affect the market for bread.

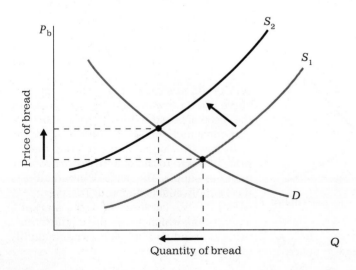

Figure 1-5 **A Decrease in Supply.** If the price of flour rises, the supply of bread falls—at any given price, bakeries find that the sale of bread is less profitable and therefore choose to produce less bread. This is represented by an inward shift in the supply curve. The market moves to the new intersection of supply and demand. The equilibrium price rises, and the equilibrium quantity falls.

Like all models, this model of the bread market makes many simplifying assumptions. The model does not take into account, for example, that every bakery is in a different location. For each customer, one bakery is more convenient than the others, and thus bakeries have some ability to set their own prices. Although the model assumes that there is a single price for bread, in fact there could be a different price at every bakery.

How should we react to the model's lack of realism? Should we discard the simple model of bread supply and bread demand? Should we attempt to build a more complex model that allows for diverse bread prices? The answers to these questions depend on our purpose. On the one hand, if our goal is to explain how the price of flour affects the average price of bread and the amount of bread sold, then the diversity of bread prices is probably not important. The simple model of the bread market does a good job of answering that question. On the other hand, if our goal is to explain why towns with three bakeries have lower bread prices than towns with one bakery, the simple model is less useful.

The art in economics is in judging when an assumption is clarifying and when it is misleading. Any model constructed to be completely realistic would be too complicated for anyone to understand. Simplification is a necessary part of building a useful model. Yet models lead to incorrect conclusions when they ignore crucial features of the economy. Judging what is crucial is sometimes difficult because an assumption that is reasonable for some questions may be misleading for others. Economic modeling therefore requires the use of care and common sense.

///

F Y I **Using Functions to Express Relationships Among Variables**

All economic models express relationships among economic variables. Often, these relationships are expressed as functions. A *function* is a mathematical concept that shows the dependence of one set of variables on another. For example, in the model of the bread market, we said that the quantity of bread demanded depends on the price of bread and on aggregate income. To express this, we wrote

$$Q^{d} = D(P_{b}, Y).$$

This equation says that the quantity of bread demanded Q^{d} is a function of the price of bread P_{b} and aggregate income Y. In functional notation, the variable preceding the parentheses denotes the function. Thus, in this case, $D(\ )$ is a function of the variables in parentheses.

In the model for bread, the notation $Q^d = D(P_b, Y)$ expresses the determinants of bread demand. If we knew more about the demand for bread, we might be able to write

$$Q^d = 60 - 10P_b + 2Y.$$

In this case, the demand function is

$$D(P_b, Y) = 60 - 10P_b + 2Y.$$

For any price of bread and aggregate income, this function gives the corresponding quantity of bread demanded. For example, if aggregate income is 10, and the price of bread is 2, then the quantity of bread demanded is 60; if the price of bread rises to 3, the quantity of bread demanded falls to 50.

Functional notation allows us to express a relationship among variables even when the precise numerical relationship among the variables is unknown. For example, we might know that the quantity of bread demanded falls when the price rises from 2 to 3, but we might not know by how much it falls. In this situation, functional notation is useful: as long as we know that a relationship among the variables exists, we can express it using functional notation.

The Role of Microeconomics in Macroeconomics

Microeconomics, the study of the economy in the small, examines the activities of individual units in the economy. Microeconomists study how households and firms make decisions, and how these decisionmakers interact in the marketplace. The central principle of microeconomics is that households and firms "optimize"—they do the best they can given their objectives and the constraints they face. In microeconomic models, households choose their purchases to maximize utility, and firms make production decisions to maximize profit.

Because the economy-wide events studied by macroeconomists arise from the interaction of many households and many firms, macroeconomics and microeconomics are inextricably linked. When we study the economy as a whole, we must consider the decisions of individual economic actors. For example, to understand the determinants of aggregate consumption, we must think about a family deciding how much to spend today and how much to save for the future. To understand the determinants of aggregate investment, we must think about a firm deciding whether to build a new factory. Because aggregate variables are simply the sum of the variables describing many individual decisions, macroeconomics is inevitably founded in microeconomics.

Although microeconomic decisions always underlie economic models, in many models the optimizing behavior of households and firms is implicit rather than explicit. The model of the bread market we discussed earlier is an example. Households' decisions about how much bread to buy underlie the demand for bread, and bakeries' decisions about how much bread to produce underlie the supply of bread. Presumably, households make their decisions to maximize utility, and bakeries make their decisions to maximize profit. Yet the model did not focus on these microeconomic decisions; it left them in the background. Similarly, in much of macroeconomics, the optimizing behavior of households and firms is left implicit.

Eclectic Macroeconomics

Macroeconomists address many different questions. For example, they examine the influence of fiscal policy on national saving, the impact of unemployment insurance on the unemployment rate, and the role of monetary policy in maintaining stable prices. Macroeconomics is as diverse as the economy.

Because no single model can answer all questions, macroeconomists use many different models. One of the most important and difficult tasks for the student of macroeconomics is to keep in mind that there is no single "correct" model. Instead, there are many models—each of which is useful for a different purpose.

This book therefore presents many different models that address different questions and make different assumptions. Remember that a model is only as good as its assumptions, and that an assumption that is useful for some purposes may be misleading for others. When using a model to address a question, the macroeconomist must keep in mind the underlying assumptions and judge whether these assumptions are reasonable for the matter at hand.

Prices: Flexible versus Sticky

One of the most crucial assumptions of macroeconomic models concerns the adjustment of wages and prices. Some of the major disagreements among macroeconomists are over this issue.

Economists normally presume that the price of a good or a service adjusts to equilibrate supply and demand. In other words, they assume that, at the going price, demanders have bought all they want and suppliers have sold all they want. This assumption is called **market clearing** and is central to the model of the bread market discussed earlier. For answering most questions, economists use market-clearing models.

But the assumption of continuous market clearing is not entirely realistic. For markets to clear continuously, prices must adjust instantly to changes in supply and demand. In fact, however, many wages and prices adjust slowly. Labor contracts often set wages for up to three years. Many firms leave their product prices unchanged for long periods of time—for example, magazine publishers change their newsstand prices only every three or four years. Although market-clearing models assume that all wages and prices are **flexible**, in the real world it appears that some wages and prices are **sticky**.

The apparent stickiness of prices does not necessarily make market-clearing models useless. After all, prices are not stuck forever; eventually, they do adjust to changes in supply and demand. Market-clearing models might not describe the economy at every instant, but they do describe the equilibrium to which the economy slowly gravitates. Therefore, most macroeconomists believe that price flexibility is a reasonable assumption for studying long-run issues, such as the economic growth we observe from decade to decade.

Yet, for studying short-run issues, such as year-to-year economic fluctuations, the assumption of price flexibility is less plausible. Over short periods, many prices are fixed at their predetermined levels. Therefore, most macroeconomists believe that price stickiness is a better assumption for studying the behavior of the economy in the short run.

1-3 How This Book Proceeds

This book has four parts. This chapter and the one following form the "Introduction." Chapter 2 discusses how economists measure economic variables, such as aggregate income, the inflation rate, and the unemployment rate.

Part Two, "The Economy in the Long Run," presents the classical model of the economy. The distinguishing feature of the classical model is that, with only a few exceptions, it assumes that prices adjust to equilibrate markets; that is, it assumes market clearing. For the reasons we have cited, the classical model is best viewed as describing the economy in the long run.

Part Three, "The Economy in the Short Run," examines the time horizon over which prices are sticky. It describes a non-market-clearing model of the economy and shows that many of the conclusions of the classical model need to be modified when the stickiness of prices is taken into account. This model with sticky prices is designed to analyze short-run issues, such as the reasons for economic fluctuations and the role of monetary and fiscal policy in stabilizing the economy.

The last chapter of Part Three presents an alternative view of economic fluctuations. It examines a "new classical" theory that attempts to explain the economy in the short run without invoking the assumption that prices are sticky. This approach stands in stark contrast to the one advocated by most economists, which posits that the failure of prices to equilibrate supply and demand is crucial for explaining short-run economic fluctuations.

Part Four, "More on the Microeconomics Behind Macroeconomics," examines some of the microeconomic models that are useful for analyzing macroeconomic issues. For example, it examines the household's decisions regarding how much to consume and how much money to hold and the firm's decision regarding how much to invest. These individual decisions together form the larger macroeconomic picture. The goal of studying these microeconomic decisions in detail is to refine our understanding of the economy.

Summary

1. Macroeconomics is the study of the economy as a whole—including the growth in incomes, the stability of prices, and the rate of unemployment. Macroeconomists attempt both to explain economic events and to devise policies to improve economic performance.

2. Economists use models—simplified theories that show how exogenous variables influence endogenous variables—to understand the economy. The art in economics is in judging whether a model usefully captures the important economic relationships.

3. Microeconomics is the study of how firms and individuals make decisions and how these decisionmakers interact. Since macroeconomic events arise from many microeconomic interactions, macroeconomists use many of the tools of microeconomics.

4. No single model can answer all questions. Macroeconomists therefore use different models for different purposes.

5. Whether prices are flexible or sticky is a crucial assumption for a macroeconomic model. Most macroeconomists believe that market-clearing models describe the economy in the long run, but that prices are sticky in the short run.

KEY CONCEPTS

Macroeconomics

Models

Exogenous variables

Endogenous variables

Microeconomics

Market clearing

Flexible and sticky prices

QUESTIONS FOR REVIEW

1. Explain the difference between macroeconomics and microeconomics. How are these two fields related?

2. Why do economists build models?

3. What is a market-clearing model? When is the assumption of market clearing appropriate?

PROBLEMS AND APPLICATIONS

1. What macroeconomic issues have been in the news lately?

2. What do you think are the defining characteristics of a science? Does the study of the economy have these characteristics? Do you think macroeconomics should be called a science? Why or why not?

3. How often does the price you pay for a haircut change? What does your answer imply about the usefulness of market-clearing models for analyzing the market for haircuts?

Chapter 2

The Data of Macroeconomics

*It is a capital mistake to theorize before one has
data. Insensibly one begins to twist facts to suit
theories, instead of theories to fit facts.*

Sherlock Holmes

Like all sciences, macroeconomics relies on an interplay between theory
and observation. Since our goal in studying macroeconomics is to understand how the economy works, observing the economy provides the
basis for our theories. Once we have developed these theories, we turn
again to observation to test them.

Casual observation provides one source of information about the
economy. When you go shopping, you see how fast prices are rising.
When you look for a job, you learn whether firms are hiring. Because we
are all participants in the economy, we all gain some sense of economic
conditions as we go about our lives.

Economic statistics provide a more systematic and objective source
of information. The government regularly surveys individuals and firms
to learn about their economic activity—how much they are earning, what
they are buying, what prices they are charging, and so on. From these
surveys, various statistics are computed that summarize the state of the
economy. These statistics are the data with which macroeconomists
study the economy, and they help policymakers monitor economic developments and formulate appropriate policies.

This chapter focuses on the three economic statistics that are used
most frequently to study the economy and to evaluate economic policy.
Gross national product, or **GNP**, tells us the nation's total income and
the total expenditure on its output of goods and services. The **consumer
price index** measures the level of prices. The **unemployment rate** tells
us the fraction of workers who are unemployed. We see how these statistics are computed and what they tell us about the economy.

2-1 Measuring the Value of Economic Activity: Gross National Product

GNP is often considered the best measure of how well the economy is performing. This statistic, which the U.S. Department of Commerce computes every three months, attempts to summarize in a single number the dollar value of economic activity. More precisely, GNP equals

- the total income of everyone in the economy, and
- the total expenditure on the economy's output of goods and services.

GNP is a measure of economic performance because people would rather have more income than less. Similarly, an economy with a large output of goods and services can better satisfy the demands of individuals, firms, and the government.

GNP can measure both the economy's income and the expenditure on its output because these two functions are really the same: for an economy as a whole, income must equal expenditure. To see why this is so, we must discuss **national income accounting**, the accounting system that measures GNP and many related statistics.

Income, Expenditure, and the Circular Flow

Imagine an economy that produces a single good, bread, from a single input, labor. Figure 2-1 illustrates all the economic transactions that occur between households and firms in this economy.

The inner loop in Figure 2-1 represents the flow of bread and labor. The households sell their labor to the firms. The firms use the labor of their workers to produce bread, which the firms in turn sell to the households. Hence, labor flows from households to firms, and bread flows from firms to households.

The outer loop in Figure 2-1 represents the corresponding flow of dollars. The households buy bread from the firms. The firms use some of the revenue from these sales to pay the wages of their workers, and the remainder is the profit belonging to the owners of the firms (who themselves are part of the household sector). Hence, expenditure on bread flows from households to firms, and income in the form of wages and profit flows from firms to households.

GNP measures the flow of dollars in this economy. We can compute it in two ways. GNP is the total income from the production of bread, which equals the sum of wages and profit—the top half of the circular flow of dollars. GNP is also the total expenditure on purchases of bread—the bottom half of the circular flow of dollars. Thus, we can look at the flow of dollars from firms to households or at the flow of dollars from households to firms.

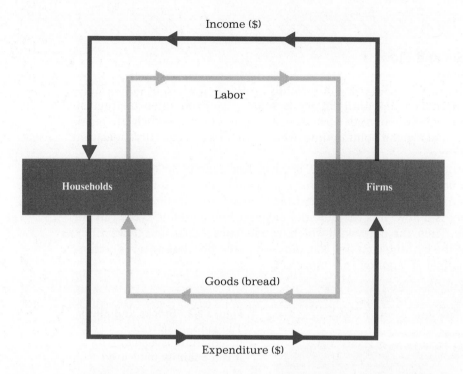

Figure 2-1 **The Circular Flow.** This figure illustrates the flows between firms and households in an economy that produces one good, bread, from one input, labor. The inner loop represents the flows of labor and bread: households sell their labor to firms, and the firms sell the bread they produce to households. The outer loop represents the corresponding flows of dollars: households pay the firms for the bread, and the firms pay wages and profit to the households. In this economy, GNP is both the total expenditure on bread and the total income from the production of bread.

The equality of income and expenditure arises from an accounting rule: all expenditure on purchases of products is necessarily income to the producers of the products. According to this rule, every transaction that affects expenditure must affect income, and every transaction that affects income must affect expenditure. For example, suppose that a firm produces and sells one more loaf of bread to a household. Clearly this transaction increases total expenditure on bread, but it also has an equal effect on total income. If the firm produces the extra loaf by hiring more labor, then wages are increased. If the firm produces the extra loaf without hiring any more labor (such as by making the production process more efficient), then profit is increased. In both cases, expenditure and income are increased equally.

F Y I **Stocks and Flows**

Many of the variables that economists study involve a quantity of something—a quantity of money, a quantity of goods, and so on. Economists distinguish between two types of quantity variables: stocks and flows. A **stock** is a quantity measured at a given point in time, whereas a **flow** is a quantity measured per unit of time.

The bathtub, shown in Figure 2-2, is the classic example used to illustrate stocks and flows. The amount of water in the tub is a stock: it is the quantity of water in the tub at a given point in time. The amount of water coming out of the faucet is a flow: it is the quantity of water being added to the tub per unit of time. Thus, the units with which we measure stocks and flows differ. We say that the bathtub contains 50 *gallons* of water, but that water is coming out of the faucet at 5 *gallons per minute*.

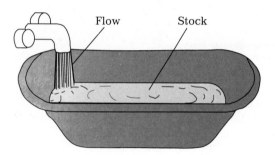

Flow   Stock

Figure 2-2 **Stocks and Flows.** The amount of water in a bathtub is a stock: it is a quantity measured at a given moment in time. The amount of water coming out of the faucet is a flow: it is a quantity measured per unit of time.

When we build theories to explain variables, there are often relationships linking stocks and flows. These relationships are clear in the case of the bathtub. The stock of water in the tub represents the accumulation of the flow out of the faucet. Equivalently, the flow of water represents the change in the stock. When studying economic variables, it is often useful to think about whether the variables are stocks or flows and whether any relationships link them.

The following are some examples of related stocks and flows that we study in future chapters:

- A consumer's wealth is a stock; his income and expenditure are flows.

- The number of unemployed people is a stock; the number of people losing their jobs is a flow.

- The amount of capital in the economy is a stock; the amount of investment is a flow.

- The government debt is a stock; the government budget deficit is a flow.

Some Rules for Computing GNP

In the hypothetical economy that produces only bread, we can compute GNP merely by adding up total expenditure on bread. By contrast, computing U.S. GNP is a more ambitious task. Because the economy is so large and complex, adding up the expenditure on all goods and services is less straightforward. Although we do not learn in this book all the details of how GNP is computed, to interpret GNP correctly we must understand some of the rules that govern its construction.

The Treatment of Inventories Suppose that a firm in our one-good economy hires workers to produce more bread, pays their wages, and then fails to sell the additional bread. How does this transaction affect GNP?

The answer depends on what happens to the unsold bread. On the one hand, if the bread spoils, then profit is reduced by the amount that wages are increased—the firm has paid the workers more wages but has not received any benefit from doing so. Because the transaction affects neither expenditure nor income, it leaves GNP unaltered (although more is distributed as wages and less as profit). On the other hand, if the bread is put into inventory to be sold at a later date, the rules of national income accounting treat the transaction differently. In this case, profit is not reduced, and the owners of the firm are assumed to have "purchased" the bread for the firm's inventory. GNP therefore rises: income rises because of the higher wages, and expenditure rises because of the inventory accumulation.

The general rule is that when a firm increases its inventory of goods, this investment in inventory is counted both as part of expenditure and as part of income. Thus, production for inventory increases GNP just as production for final sale does.

Adding Apples and Oranges We have been discussing GNP as if bread were the only item produced. Our economy, however, produces many different goods and services—bread, hamburgers, automobiles, haircuts, and so on. GNP combines the value of these different goods and services into one summary measure. The diversity of products in the economy complicates the calculation of GNP, because different products have different values.

Suppose, for example, that the economy produces four apples and three oranges. How do we find GNP? We could simply add apples and oranges and conclude that GNP equals seven pieces of fruit. But this makes sense only if apples and oranges have equal value, which is generally not true. (This would be even clearer if the economy had produced four watermelons and three grapes.)

To compute the total value of different goods and services, we use the market price as the measure of value. The market price is used because it reflects how much people are willing to pay for a particular good or service. Thus, if apples cost $0.50 each and oranges cost $1.00 each, GNP would be

$$
\begin{aligned}
\text{GNP} &= (\text{Price of Apples} \times \text{Quantity of Apples}) + \\
&\quad\ (\text{Price of Oranges} \times \text{Quantity of Oranges}) \\
&= (\$0.50 \times 4) + (\$1.00 \times 3) \\
&= \$5.00.
\end{aligned}
$$

GNP equals $5.00—the value of all the apples, $2.00, plus the value of all the oranges, $3.00.

Intermediate Goods and Value-Added   Many goods are produced in stages: raw materials are processed into intermediate goods by one firm and then sold to another firm for final processing. How should we treat such products when computing GNP? For example, suppose a cattle rancher sells one-quarter pound of meat to McDonald's for $0.50, and then McDonald's sells you a hamburger for $1.50. Should GNP include both the meat and the hamburger (a total of $2.00), or just the hamburger ($1.50)?

The answer is that GNP includes only the value of final goods. Thus, the hamburger is included in GNP but the meat is not: GNP increases by $1.50, not by $2.00. The reason is that the value of intermediate goods is already included as part of the price of the final goods. To add the intermediate goods to the final goods would be double-counting—that is, the meat would be counted twice. Hence, GNP is the total value of final goods and services produced.

One way to compute the value of all final goods and services is to sum the value-added at each stage of production. The **value-added** of a firm equals the value of the firm's output less the value of the intermediate goods that the firm purchases. In the case of the hamburger, the value-added of the rancher is $0.50 (assuming the rancher bought no intermediate goods), and the value-added of McDonald's is $1.50 − $0.50, which is $1.00. Total value-added is $0.50 + $1.00, or $1.50. For the economy as a whole, the sum of all value-added must equal the market value of all final goods and services. Hence, GNP is also the total value-added of all firms in the economy.

Housing Services and Other Imputations   Although most goods and services are valued at their market prices when computing GNP, some goods and services are not sold in the marketplace and therefore do not have market prices. If GNP is to include the value of these goods and services, we must use an estimate of their value. Such an estimate is called an **imputed value**.

One area in which imputations are important is housing. A person who rents a house is buying housing services and is providing income for the landlord; the rent is part of GNP, both as expenditure of the renter and as income of the landlord. Many people, however, live in their own homes. Although they do not pay rent to a landlord, they are enjoying housing services similar to those of renters. Therefore, to take account of the housing services enjoyed by homeowners, GNP includes the "rent" that these homeowners "pay" to themselves. Of course, homeowners do not in fact pay themselves this rent. The Department of Commerce estimates what the market rent for a house would be if it were rented and includes that imputed rent as part of GNP. This imputed rent is included both in the homeowner's expenditure and in the homeowner's income.

Another area in which imputations arise is in valuing the services provided by the government. For example, police officers, fire fighters, and senators provide services to the public. Measuring the value of these services is difficult, because they are not sold in a marketplace and therefore do not have a market price. GNP includes these services by valuing them at their cost. Thus, the wages of these public servants are used as a measure of the value of their output.

In many circumstances, an imputation is called for in principle but is not made in practice. Since GNP includes the imputed rent on owner-occupied houses, one might expect it also to include the imputed rent on cars, lawn mowers, jewelry, and other durable goods owned by households; yet the value of these services is left out of GNP. In addition, some of the output of the economy is produced and consumed at home and never enters the marketplace. For example, meals cooked at home are not very different from meals cooked at a restaurant, yet the value-added in meals at home is left out of GNP. Finally, GNP excludes the value of goods produced and sold in illegal activities such as the drug trade.

Since the imputations necessary for computing GNP are imperfect, and since the value of many goods and services is left out altogether, GNP is an imperfect measure of economic activity. Yet these imperfections need not reduce the usefulness of GNP. As long as the imperfections in GNP do not change much over time, GNP is useful for comparing economic activity from year to year or from decade to decade.

Real GNP versus Nominal GNP

Now that we have examined some of the rules used in constructing GNP, let us return to the question of whether GNP is a good measure of economic well-being. Consider once again the economy that produces only apples and oranges. In this economy GNP is the sum of the value of all the apples produced and the value of all the oranges produced. That is,

$$\text{GNP} = (\text{Price of Apples} \times \text{Quantity of Apples}) + (\text{Price of Oranges} \times \text{Quantity of Oranges}).$$

GNP can increase either because of increases in the prices or because of increases in the quantities.

GNP computed this way is not a good measure of economic well-being. That is, it does not accurately reflect how well the economy can satisfy the demands of consumers, firms, and the government. If all prices doubled without any change in quantities, GNP would double. Yet it would be misleading to say that the economy's ability to satisfy demands doubled, because the quantity of every good produced remained the same. Economists call the value of goods and services measured at current prices **nominal GNP**.

A better measure of economic well-being would measure the economy's output of goods and services and would not be influenced by changes in prices. For this purpose, economists use **real GNP**, which is the value of goods and services measured at constant prices. To compute real GNP, a base year is chosen—say, 1982. Goods and services are then added up using 1982 prices to value the different goods. In our apple-and-orange economy, real GNP for 1990 would be

Real GNP = (1982 Price of Apples × 1990 Quantity of Apples) +
(1982 Price of Oranges × 1990 Quantity of Oranges).

Similarly, real GNP in 1991 would be

Real GNP = (1982 Price of Apples × 1991 Quantity of Apples) +
(1982 Price of Oranges × 1991 Quantity of Oranges).

Because the prices are being held constant, real GNP varies from year to year only if the quantities vary. Thus, real GNP summarizes the output of the economy, measured in base-year (in this case, 1982) dollars. Because a society's ability to provide economic satisfaction for its members ultimately depends on the quantities of goods and services produced, real GNP provides a better measure of economic well-being than nominal GNP.

CASE STUDY 2-1

Real GNP in the United States

What does an examination of real GNP tell us about the performance of the economy? Figure 2-3 shows real GNP in the United States since 1960. Two aspects of this figure are noteworthy. First, real GNP grows over time. The output of the economy today is more than twice its output in 1960. Second, the growth in real GNP is not steady. There are repeated periods during which real GNP is falling, such as in 1975 and 1982. Such periods are called **recessions**. In the chapters that follow, we build models to explain both the long-run growth and the short-run fluctuations in real GNP.

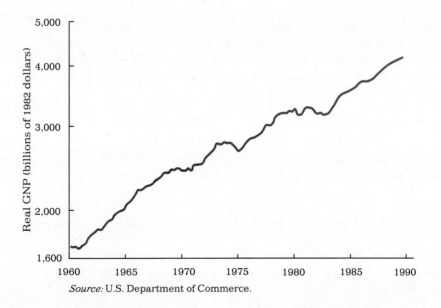

Figure 2-3 **Real GNP in the United States.** This plot of real GNP in the United States shows that output rises over time but that this growth is frequently interrupted by periods of falling output, called recessions.

Note: Real GNP is plotted here on a logarithmic scale. On such a scale, equal distances on the vertical axis represent equal *percentage* changes. Thus, the distance between $1,600 billion and $2,000 billion is the same as the distance between $4,000 billion and $5,000 billion.

The GNP Deflator

From nominal GNP and real GNP we can compute a third important statistic: the GNP deflator. The **GNP deflator**, also called the implicit price deflator for GNP, is defined as

$$\text{GNP Deflator} = \frac{\text{Nominal GNP}}{\text{Real GNP}}.$$

Thus, the GNP deflator is the ratio of nominal GNP to real GNP.

To understand clearly nominal GNP, real GNP, and the GNP deflator, consider again an economy with only one good, bread. In any year, nominal GNP is the total number of dollars spent on bread in that year. Real GNP is the number of loaves of bread produced in that year times the price of bread in some base year. The GNP deflator is the price of bread in that year relative to the price of bread in the base year.

Actual economies, however, produce many goods. Nominal GNP, real GNP, and the GNP deflator aggregate the many different prices and quantities. Consider an economy with apples and oranges. Letting P denote the price of a good, Q the quantity, and a superscript "82" the base year 1982, the GNP deflator would be

$$\text{GNP Deflator} = \frac{(P_{\text{apples}} \times Q_{\text{apples}}) + (P_{\text{oranges}} \times Q_{\text{oranges}})}{(P^{82}_{\text{Apples}} \times Q_{\text{apples}}) + (P^{82}_{\text{oranges}} \times Q_{\text{oranges}})}.$$

The numerator of this expression is nominal GNP; the denominator is real GNP. Both nominal GNP and real GNP can be viewed as the price of a basket of goods: in this case, the basket consists of the quantities of apples and oranges currently produced. The GNP deflator compares the current price of this basket to the price of the same basket in the base year.

The definition of the GNP deflator allows us to separate nominal GNP into two parts: one part measures quantities and the other measures prices. That is,

$$\text{Nominal GNP} = \text{Real GNP} \times \text{GNP Deflator.}$$

Nominal GNP measures the dollar value of the output of the economy. Real GNP measures the amount of output—that is, output valued at constant (base-year) prices. The GNP deflator measures the price of the typical unit of output relative to its price in the base year.

Other Statistics in the National Income Accounts

We have seen that GNP measures both total expenditure and total income in the economy—the two halves of the circular flow of dollars. Most of the other statistics in the national income accounts provide more detailed information on these flows. We can group these statistics into one of two categories: the components of expenditure and alternative measures of income.

The Components of Expenditure   Economists and policymakers care not only about the economy's total output of goods and services but also about the allocation of this output among alternative uses. The national income accounts divide the expenditures included in GNP into four broad categories:

- Consumption (*C*)
- Investment (*I*)
- Government purchases (*G*)
- Net exports (*NX*).

Thus, letting *Y* stand for GNP,

$$Y = C + I + G + NX.$$

GNP is the sum of consumption, investment, government purchases, and net exports. Every expenditure in GNP is included in one of these categories. This equation is an identity—an equation that holds by the definition of the variables. It is called the **national income accounts identity**.

Consumption consists of the goods and services bought by households. It is divided into three subcategories: nondurable goods, durable goods, and services. Nondurable goods are goods that last only a short period of time, such as food and clothing. Durable goods are goods that last a long period of time, such as automobiles and washing machines. Services are the purchase of the personal services of individuals, such as haircuts and visits to doctors.

Investment consists of the goods purchased for use in the future. Investment is also divided into three subcategories: nonresidential fixed investment, residential fixed investment, and inventory investment. Nonresidential fixed investment is the purchase of new plants and equipment by firms. Residential investment is the purchase of new housing by households and landlords. Inventory investment is the increase in firms' inventory of goods (if the inventory is falling, inventory investment is negative).

Government purchases are the goods and services bought by federal, state, and local governments. This category includes military equipment, highways, and the services that government workers provide. It does *not* include transfer payments to individuals, such as Social Security and welfare. Because these payments are not made in exchange for goods and services, they are not part of GNP.

The last category, net exports, takes into account trade with other countries. Net exports are the value of goods and services exported to other countries minus the value of goods and services that foreigners provide us. If trade were always in balance, the value of exports would equal the value of imports, and net exports would always be zero; in this case, GNP would be the sum of domestic expenditure, $C + I + G$. If, however, we export more than we import, then we are net sellers in world markets, so GNP exceeds domestic expenditure. Similarly, if we import more than we export—as the United States did throughout the 1980s—then we are net buyers in world markets, net exports are negative, and our expenditure exceeds our production.

CASE STUDY 2-2

GNP and Its Components

In 1989 the GNP of the United States totaled $5.2 trillion. This number is so large that it is almost impossible to comprehend. We can make it easier to understand by dividing it by the 1989 U.S. population of 248 million. In this way, we obtain GNP per person—the amount of expenditure for the average American—which equaled $21,036 in 1989.

How did we use this GNP? Table 2-1 shows that about two-thirds of it, or $13,949 per person, was spent on consumption. Investment was $3,123 per person. Government purchases were $4,167 per person, $1,217 of which was spent by the federal government on national defense.

Table 2-1   GNP and the Components of Expenditure: 1989

	Total (billions of 1989 dollars)	Per Person (1989 dollars)
Gross National Product	**$5,233.2**	**$21,036**
Consumption	**$3,470.3**	**$13,949**
Nondurable goods	1,122.6	4,512
Durable goods	473.6	1,904
Services	1,874.1	7,533
Investment	**777.1**	**3,123**
Nonresidential fixed investment	512.5	2,060
Residential fixed investment	235.2	945
Inventory investment	29.4	118
Government Purchases	**1,036.7**	**4,167**
Federal	404.1	1,624
Defense	302.8	1,217
Nondefense	101.3	407
State and local	632.5	2,542
Net Exports	**−50.9**	**−205**
Exports	624.4	2,510
Imports	675.2	2,714

Note: Numbers do not add up to totals shown due to rounding.
Source: U.S. Department of Commerce.

The average person purchased $2,714 of goods imported from abroad and produced $2,510 of goods that were exported to other countries. Thus, net exports were negative. Since foreigners earned more from selling to us than they spent on our goods, they must have used some of the proceeds from their sales to give us loans (or, equivalently, to buy our assets). Thus, the average American borrowed $205 from abroad in 1989.

Alternative Measures of Income   Although GNP is the most common measure of the total income of everyone in the economy, the national income accounts include other measures of income that differ slightly in definition from GNP. The distinctions among the different measures of income are often not important in practice, since the measures move closely together. We should, however, be aware of the various measures, because economists and the press often refer to them.

We can see most clearly how the alternative measures of income relate to each other by starting with GNP and subtracting various quantities. To obtain net national product (NNP), we subtract the depreciation of capital—the amount of the economy's stock of plants, equipment, and residential structures that wears out during the year:

$$NNP = GNP - Depreciation.$$

In the national income accounts, depreciation is called the capital consumption allowance. It equals about 10 percent of GNP. Since the depreciation of capital is a cost of producing the output of the economy, subtracting depreciation from GNP shows the net result of economic activity. For this reason, some economists believe that NNP is a better measure of economic well-being than GNP.

The next adjustment in the national income accounts is for indirect business taxes, such as sales taxes. These kinds of taxes, which make up about 10 percent of NNP, place a wedge between the price that consumers pay for a good and the price that firms receive. Because firms never receive this tax wedge, it is not really part of their income. Once we subtract indirect business taxes from NNP, we obtain a measure called national income:

$$National\ Income = NNP - Indirect\ Business\ Taxes.$$

National income is a measure of how much everyone in the economy has earned.

The national income accounts divide national income into five components, depending on the way the income is earned. The five categories, and the approximate percentage of national income that each comprises, are:

- Compensation of employees (73%): the wages and fringe benefits earned by workers.

- Proprietors' income (7%): the income of noncorporate businesses, such as small farms, mom-and-pop stores, and law partnerships.

- Rental income (2%): the profit that individuals earn as landlords, including the profit from imputed rent they "pay" to themselves.

- Corporate profits (11%): the income of corporations after the payments to their workers and creditors.

- Net interest (7%): the interest domestic businesses pay minus the interest they receive, plus interest earned from foreigners.

A series of adjustments takes us from national income to personal income, the amount of income that households and noncorporate businesses receive. Three of these adjustments are most important. First, we reduce national income by the amount corporations earn but do not pay out, either because the corporations are retaining earnings or because they are paying taxes to the government; this adjustment is made by subtracting corporate profits and adding dividends. Second, we increase national income by the amount the government pays out in transfer payments on net; this adjustment equals government transfers to individuals minus social insurance contributions paid to the government. Third, we adjust national income to include the interest that households earn rather than the interest that businesses pay; this adjustment is made by adding personal interest income and subtracting net interest. (The difference between personal interest and net interest arises in part from the interest on the government debt.) Thus, personal income is

Personal Income = National Income
  − Corporate Profits
  − Social Insurance Contributions
  − Net Interest
  + Dividends
  + Government Transfers to Individuals
  + Personal Interest Income.

Next, if we subtract personal tax payments and certain nontax payments to the government (such as traffic tickets), we obtain disposable personal income:

Disposable Personal Income = Personal Income
  − Personal Tax and Nontax Payments.

Disposable personal income is the amount households and noncorporate businesses have available to spend after satisfying their tax obligations to the government.

CASE STUDY 2-3

The Seasonal Cycle and Seasonal Adjustment

If we look at what happens to real GNP and other measures of income over the year, we find a regular seasonal pattern. The output of the economy rises over the course of the year, reaching a peak in the fourth quarter (October, November, and December), and then falling in the first quarter (January, February, and March). These regular seasonal changes are substantial. From the fourth quarter to the first quarter, real GNP falls on average about 8 percent.[1]

[1] Robert B. Barsky and Jeffrey A. Miron, "The Seasonal Cycle and the Business Cycle," *Journal of Political Economy* 97 (June 1989): 503–534.

It is not surprising that real GNP follows a seasonal cycle. Some of these seasonal changes are attributable to changes in our ability to produce: for example, it is more difficult to construct housing in the cold weather of the winter. In addition, people have seasonal tastes: they have preferred times for such activities as vacations and Christmas shopping.

When economists study fluctuations in real GNP and other economic variables, they often want to eliminate the portion of fluctuations that is attributable to these seasonal movements. You will find that most of the economic statistics reported in the newspaper are seasonally adjusted—that is, statisticians have adjusted the data to remove the regular seasonal fluctuations. Therefore, when you observe a change in real GNP or any other data series, you must look beyond the seasonal cycle to explain the change.

2-2 Measuring the Cost of Living: The Consumer Price Index

A dollar today doesn't buy as much as it did ten years ago. The cost of almost everything has gone up. This increase in the overall level of prices is called **inflation**, and it is one of the primary concerns of economists and policymakers. In later chapters we examine in detail the causes and effects of inflation. Here we discuss how economists measure changes in the cost of living.

The Price of a Basket of Goods

The most commonly used measure of the level of prices is the **consumer price index (CPI)**. The Bureau of Labor Statistics, which is part of the U.S. Department of Labor, has the job of computing the CPI. It begins by collecting the prices of thousands of goods and services. Just as GNP turns the quantities of many goods and services into a single number measuring the value of production, the CPI turns the prices of many goods and services into a single index measuring the overall level of prices.

How should economists aggregate the many prices in the economy into a single index that reliably measures the price level? They could simply compute the average of all prices. But this approach would treat all goods and services equally. Since people consume more chicken than caviar, the price of chicken should have a greater weight in the CPI than the price of caviar does. The Bureau of Labor Statistics weights different items by computing the price of a basket of goods and services purchased by a typical consumer. The CPI is the price of this basket of goods and services relative to the price of the same basket in some base year.

For example, suppose that the typical consumer buys 5 apples and 2 oranges every month. That is, the basket of goods consists of 5 apples and 2 oranges. The CPI is

$$CPI = \frac{(5 \times \text{Current Price of Apples}) + (2 \times \text{Current Price of Oranges})}{(5 \times 1982\,\text{Price of Apples}) + (2 \times 1982\,\text{Price of Oranges})}.$$

In this CPI, 1982 is the base year. The index tells us how much it costs now to buy 5 apples and 2 oranges relative to how much it cost to buy the same basket of fruit in 1982.

The consumer price index is the most closely watched index of prices, but it is not the only such index. Another is the producer price index, which measures the price of a typical basket of goods bought by firms rather than by consumers. In addition to these overall price indices, the Bureau of Labor Statistics computes indices for specific types of goods, such as food, housing, and energy.

The CPI versus the GNP Deflator

Earlier in this chapter we discussed another measure of prices—the implicit price deflator for GNP, which is the ratio of nominal GNP to real GNP. The GNP deflator and the CPI give somewhat different information about the overall level of prices in the economy. There are three key differences between the two measures.

The first difference is that the GNP deflator measures the prices of all goods and services produced, whereas the CPI measures the prices of only the goods and services bought by consumers. Thus, an increase in the price of goods bought by firms or the government will show up in the GNP deflator but not in the CPI.

The second difference is that the GNP deflator includes only those goods produced by U.S. citizens. Goods imported from abroad are not part of GNP and do not show up in the GNP deflator. Hence, an increase in the price of a Toyota produced in Japan and sold in this country affects the CPI, because the Toyota is bought by consumers, but it does not affect the GNP deflator.

The third and most subtle difference concerns how the two measures aggregate the many prices in the economy. The CPI assigns fixed weights to the prices of different goods, whereas the GNP deflator assigns changing weights. In other words, the CPI is computed using a fixed basket of goods, whereas the GNP deflator allows the basket of goods to change over time as the composition of GNP changes. To see how this works, consider an economy that produces and consumes two goods—apples and oranges. The GNP deflator is

$$\text{GNP Deflator} = \frac{\text{Nominal GNP}}{\text{Real GNP}}$$

$$= \frac{(P_{\text{apples}} \times Q_{\text{apples}}) + (P_{\text{oranges}} \times Q_{\text{oranges}})}{(P^{82}_{\text{apples}} \times Q_{\text{apples}}) + (P^{82}_{\text{oranges}} \times Q_{\text{oranges}})}.$$

The CPI is

$$\text{CPI} = \frac{(P_{\text{apples}} \times Q^{82}_{\text{apples}}) + (P_{\text{oranges}} \times Q^{82}_{\text{oranges}})}{(P^{82}_{\text{apples}} \times Q^{82}_{\text{apples}}) + (P^{82}_{\text{oranges}} \times Q^{82}_{\text{oranges}})}.$$

These equations show that both the CPI and the GNP deflator compare the cost of a basket of goods today with the cost of that same basket in the base year. The difference between the two measures is whether the basket changes over time. The CPI uses a fixed basket (base-year quantities), whereas the GNP deflator uses a changing basket (current quantities).

To see the effects of these different approaches to aggregating prices, consider the following example. Suppose that a major frost in Florida destroys the orange crop: the quantity of oranges produced falls to zero, and the price of the few oranges that remain on grocers' shelves is driven sky-high. Because oranges are no longer part of GNP, the increase in the price of oranges does not show up in the GNP deflator. But because the CPI is computed with a fixed basket of goods that includes oranges, the increase in the price of oranges causes a substantial rise in the CPI.

Economists call a price index with a fixed basket of goods a **Laspeyres index** and a price index with a changing basket a **Paasche index**. Economic theorists have studied the properties of these different types of price indices to determine which is better. The answer, it turns out, is that neither is clearly superior.

The purpose of any price index is to measure the cost of living—that is, how much it costs to maintain a given standard of living. When prices of different goods are changing by different amounts, a Laspeyres index tends to overstate the increase in the cost of living, whereas a Paasche index tends to understate it. A Laspeyres index uses a fixed basket and thus does not take into account that consumers have the opportunity to substitute less expensive goods for more expensive ones. By contrast, a Paasche index accounts for the substitution of alternative goods, but it does not reflect the reduction in consumers' satisfaction that may result from such substitutions.

The example of the Florida frost illustrates the problems with Laspeyres and Paasche price indices. Because the CPI is a Laspeyres index, it overstates the impact of the increase in orange prices on consumers: by using a fixed basket of goods, it ignores consumers' ability to substitute apples for oranges. By contrast, because the GNP deflator is a Paasche index, it understates the impact on consumers: the GNP deflator shows no rise in prices, yet surely the high price of oranges makes consumers worse off.

Luckily, however, the difference between the GNP deflator and the CPI is usually not large in practice. That is, the CPI moves closely with the GNP deflator. Figure 2-4 shows the percentage change in the GNP deflator and the percentage change in the CPI yearly since 1948. Both measures usually tell the same story about how quickly prices are rising.

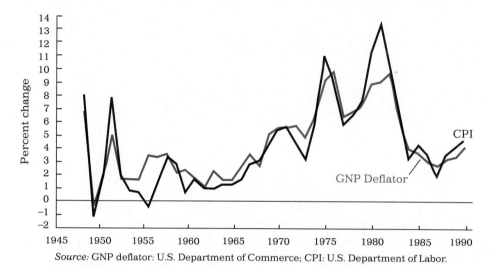

Source: GNP deflator: U.S. Department of Commerce; CPI: U.S. Department of Labor.

Figure 2-4 **The GNP Deflator and the CPI.** This figure shows the percentage change in the GNP deflator and in the CPI for every year since 1948. Although sometimes these two measures of prices diverge, usually they tell the same story about how quickly prices are rising. Both the CPI and the GNP deflator show that prices rose slowly in most of the 1950s and 1960s, that they rose much more quickly in the 1970s, and that they rose slowly again in the 1980s.

CASE STUDY 2-4

The Inflation of 1978-1981

From 1978 to 1981 prices in the United States rose faster than at any time in recent history. But exactly how fast did they rise? This question was asked by public policymakers who had to judge the seriousness of the inflation problem. It was also asked by private decisionmakers: many private contracts, such as wage agreements and pensions, are indexed to correct for the effects of rising prices.

The magnitude of the price rise depends on which measure of prices one uses. According to the GNP deflator, prices rose an average of 9.1 percent per year during these three years. According to the CPI, prices rose 11.2 percent per year. Over the three-year period, the accumulated difference is over 6 percent.

This discrepancy is partly attributable to the large increase in the price of energy products, which was caused by the sharp rise in the price of oil charged by the Organization of Petroleum Exporting Countries (OPEC), the international oil cartel. The increase in energy prices helps to account for the discrepancy in two ways. First, the GNP deflator reflects efforts to conserve energy and the substitution of other sources of energy for oil. (A fixed-weight price index for the goods and services in GNP, which like the CPI uses a fixed basket of goods, shows that prices rose 9.7 percent per year—0.6 of a percentage point higher than the GNP deflator.) Second, the United States imports much of the oil it consumes. Since imports are not part of GNP, oil prices have a greater impact on the CPI than on the GNP deflator.

When price indices differ, as they did from 1978 to 1981, it is usually possible to identify the sources of the differences. Yet accounting for the differences is easier than deciding which index provides the better measure. Furthermore, which index one should use in practice is not merely a question of measurement; it also depends on one's purpose.

2-3 Measuring Joblessness: The Unemployment Rate

One aspect of economic performance is how well an economy uses its resources. Since an economy's workers are its chief resource, keeping workers employed is a paramount concern of economic policymakers. The unemployment rate is the statistic that measures the percentage of those people who would like to work who do not have jobs.

Every month the U.S. Bureau of Labor Statistics computes the unemployment rate and many other statistics with which economists and policymakers monitor developments in the labor market. These statistics come from a survey of about 60,000 households. Based on survey questions, each person in each household is placed into one of three categories: employed, unemployed, or not in the labor force. A person is employed if he or she spent most of the previous week working at a job, as opposed to keeping house, going to school, or doing something else. A person is unemployed if he or she is not employed and is waiting for the start date of a new job, is on temporary layoff, or has been looking for a job. A person who fits neither of the first two categories (such as a student or a homemaker) is not in the labor force; such a person does not have a job and is not waiting or looking for a job.

The **labor force** is defined as the sum of the employed and the unemployed, and the **unemployment rate** is defined as the percentage of the labor force that is unemployed. That is,

Labor Force = Number of Employed + Number of Unemployed,

and

$$\text{Unemployment Rate} = \frac{\text{Number of Unemployed}}{\text{Labor Force}} \times 100.$$

Another statistic the Bureau of Labor Statistics computes is the **labor-force participation rate**, the percentage of the adult population that is in the labor force:

$$\text{Labor-Force Participation Rate} = \frac{\text{Labor Force}}{\text{Adult Population}} \times 100.$$

These statistics are computed for the overall population and for groups within the population: men and women, whites and blacks, teenagers and prime-age workers.

Figure 2-5 shows the breakdown of the population into the three categories for 1989. In this year, the labor force was

Labor Force = 119.0 + 6.5 = 125.5 million,

the unemployment rate was

Unemployment Rate = (6.5/125.5) × 100 = 5.2%,

and the labor-force participation rate was

Labor-Force Participation Rate = (125.5/188.1) × 100 = 66.7%.

Hence, about two-thirds of the adult population was in the labor force, and about 5 percent of those in the labor force did not have a job.

Drawing M. Stevens; © 1980
The New Yorker Magazine, Inc.

"Well, so long Eddie, the recession's over."

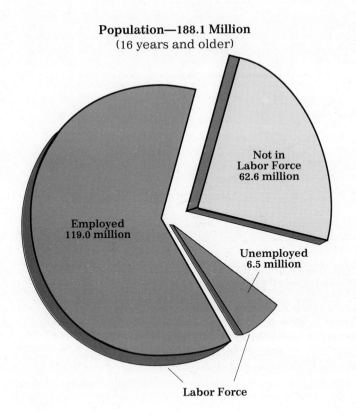

Population—188.1 Million
(16 years and older)

Not in
Labor Force
62.6 million

Employed
119.0 million

Unemployed
6.5 million

Labor Force

Figure 2-5 **The Three Groups of the Population.** When the Bureau of Labor Statistics surveys the population, it places everyone in one of three categories: employed, unemployed, or not in the labor force. This figure shows the number of people in each category in 1989.
Source: U.S. Department of Labor.

CASE STUDY 2-5

Unemployment, GNP, and Okun's Law

What relationship would you expect to find between unemployment and real GNP? Since employed workers help to produce goods and services and unemployed workers do not, one would expect increases in the unemployment rate to be associated with decreases in real GNP. This negative relationship between unemployment and GNP is called **Okun's law**, after Arthur Okun, the economist who first studied it.[2]

Figure 2-6 uses annual data for the United States to illustrate Okun's law. This figure is a scatterplot—a scatter of points where each point represents one observation (in this case, the data for a particular year). The horizontal axis represents the change in the unemployment rate from the previous year, and the vertical axis represents the percentage change in GNP. This figure shows clearly that year-to-year changes in the unemployment rate are closely associated with year-to-year changes in real GNP.

---

[2] Arthur M. Okun, "Potential GNP: Its Measurement and Significance," in *Proceedings of the Business and Economics Statistics Section, American Statistical Association* (Washington, D.C.: American Statistical Association, 1962), 98–103; reprinted in Arthur M. Okun, *Economics for Policymaking* (Cambridge, Mass.: MIT Press, 1983), 145–158.

Source: U.S. Department of Commerce and U.S. Department of Labor.

Figure 2-6 **Okun's Law.** This figure is a scatterplot of the change in the unemployment rate on the horizontal axis and the percentage change in real GNP on the vertical axis. Each point represents one year. The negative correlation between these variables shows that increases in unemployment tend to be associated with decreases in real GNP.

We can be more precise about the magnitude of the Okun's law relationship. The line drawn through the scatter of points tells us that

$$\text{Percent Change in Real GNP} = 3\% - 2 \times \text{Change in the Unemployment Rate.}$$

If the unemployment rate remains the same, real GNP grows by about 3 percent; this normal growth is due to population growth, capital accumulation, and technological progress. In addition, for every percentage point the unemployment rate rises, real GNP growth typically falls by 2 percent. Hence, if the unemployment rate rises from 6 to 8 percent, then real GNP growth would be

$$\text{Percent Change in Real GNP} = 3 - 2 \times (8 - 6)$$
$$= -1\%.$$

In this case, Okun's law says that GNP would fall by 1 percent, indicating that the economy was in a recession.

2-4 Conclusion: From Economic Statistics to Economic Models

The three statistics discussed in this chapter—gross national product, the consumer price index, and the unemployment rate—provide a way to quantify the performance of the economy. Public and private decisionmakers use these statistics to monitor changes in the economy and to formulate appropriate policies. Economists use these statistics to develop and test theories about how the economy works.

In the chapters that follow, we examine some of these theories. Chapters 3 and 4 study GNP, Chapter 5 studies unemployment, and Chapter 6 studies inflation. We build models to help us understand how these variables are determined and how economic policy affects them. Having learned how to measure economic performance, we now learn how to explain it.

Summary

1. Gross national product (GNP) measures both the income of everyone in the economy and the total expenditure on the economy's output of goods and services.

2. Nominal GNP values goods and services at current prices, and real GNP values goods and services at constant prices. Thus, real GNP rises only when the amount of goods and services has increased, whereas nominal GNP can rise either because output has increased or because prices have increased.

3. GNP is the sum of four categories of expenditure: consumption, investment, government purchases, and net exports.

4. The consumer price index (CPI) measures the price of a basket of goods and services purchased by a typical consumer. Like the GNP deflator, which is the ratio of nominal GNP to real GNP, the CPI measures the overall level of prices.

5. The unemployment rate shows what fraction of those who would like to work do not have a job. Increases in the unemployment rate are typically associated with decreases in real GNP.

KEY CONCEPTS

Gross national product (GNP)

National income accounting

Stocks and flows

Value-added

Imputed value

Nominal versus real GNP

Recessions

GNP deflator

National income accounts identity

Inflation

Consumer price index (CPI)

Laspeyres versus Paasche index

Labor force

Unemployment rate

Labor-force participation rate

Okun's law

QUESTIONS FOR REVIEW

1. List the two things GNP measures. How can GNP measure two things at once?

2. What does the consumer price index measure?

3. List the three categories used by the Bureau of Labor Statistics to classify everyone in the economy. How does the Bureau compute the unemployment rate?

4. Explain Okun's law.

PROBLEMS AND APPLICATIONS

1. Look at the newspapers for the past few days. What new economic statistics have been released? How do you interpret these statistics?

2. A farmer grows wheat and sells it to a miller for $1.00; the miller turns the wheat into flour and then sells the flour to a baker for $3.00; the baker uses the flour to make bread and sells the bread to an engineer for $6.00; the engineer eats the bread. What is the value added by each person? What is GNP?

3. Suppose that a woman marries her butler. After they are married, her husband continues to wait on her as before, and she continues to support him as before (but as a husband rather than as a wage earner). How do you think the marriage affects GNP? How should it affect GNP?

4. Find data on GNP and its components, and compute the percentage of GNP of the following components for 1950, 1970, and 1990.

   a. Personal consumption expenditures

   b. Gross private domestic investment

   c. Government purchases

   d. Net exports

   e. National defense purchases

   f. State and local purchases

   g. Imports

Do you see any stable relationships in the data? Do you see any trends? (*Hint:* A good place to look for data is the statistical appendices of the *Economic Report of the President*, which is written each year by the Council of Economic Advisers.)

	Year 2000	Year 2010
Price of an automobile	$50,000	$60,000
Price of a loaf of bread	$10	$20
Number of automobiles produced	100	120
Number of loaves of bread produced	500,000	400,000

5. Consider an economy that produces and consumes bread and automobiles. In the table above are data for two different years.

   a. Using the year 2000 as the base year, compute for each year nominal GNP, real GNP, the implicit price deflator for GNP, and a fixed-weight price index such as the CPI.

   b. How much have prices risen between year 2000 and year 2010? Compare the answers given by the Laspeyres and Paasche price indices. Explain the difference.

   c. Suppose you were a senator writing a bill on indexing Social Security and federal pensions—that is, on adjusting these benefits for changes in the cost of living. Would you use the GNP deflator or the CPI? Why?

6. When Senator Robert Kennedy was running for president in 1968, he said in a speech:

   The gross national product does not allow for the health of our children, the quality of their education, or the joy of their play. It does not include the beauty of our poetry or the strength of our marriages, the intelligence of our public debate or the integrity of our public officials. It measures neither our courage, nor our wisdom, nor our devotion to our country. It measures everything, in short, except that which makes life worthwhile, and it can tell us everything about America except why we are proud that we are Americans.

Was Robert Kennedy right? If so, why do we care about GNP?

Part Two

The Economy in the
Long Run

National Income: Its Production, Distribution, and Allocation

*A large income is the best recipe for happiness
I ever heard of.*

Jane Austen

The macroeconomic variables introduced in Chapter 2 allow economists and policymakers to measure and compare various aspects of economic performance from year to year and from country to country. Our goal, however, is not merely to measure economic performance but also to explain it. That is, we want to build economic models that help us to understand the behavior of the economy, the relationships among different economic variables, and the effects of economic policy.

Perhaps the most important economic variable is Gross National Product (GNP), which is both the economy's output of goods and services and its income. This chapter addresses four groups of questions about the sources and uses of GNP:

- How much do the firms in the economy produce? What determines a nation's total income?

- Who gets the income from production? How much goes to compensate workers, and how much goes to compensate owners of capital?

- Who buys the output of the economy? How much do households purchase for consumption, how much do households and firms purchase for investment, and how much does the government buy for public purposes?

- What equilibrates the demand for goods and services and the supply? What ensures that the sum of consumption, investment, and government purchases equals the level of production?

To answer these questions, we must examine how the parts of the economy interact.

A good place to start is the circular flow diagram. In Chapter 2, we discussed the circular flow of dollars in a hypothetical economy that produced one product, bread, from labor services. Figure 3-1 more accurately reflects how real economies function. It shows the linkages among the economic actors—households, firms, and the government, each represented by a gray box in the figure—and how dollars flow among them through the various markets in the economy.

Let's look at the flows of dollars from the points of view of these economic actors. Households receive income and use it to pay taxes to the government, to save through the financial markets, and to consume goods and services. Firms receive revenue from the sale of goods and services and use it to pay for the factors of production. The government receives revenue from taxes, uses it to pay for government purchases, and, if it spends more than it receives, borrows the deficit in the financial markets.

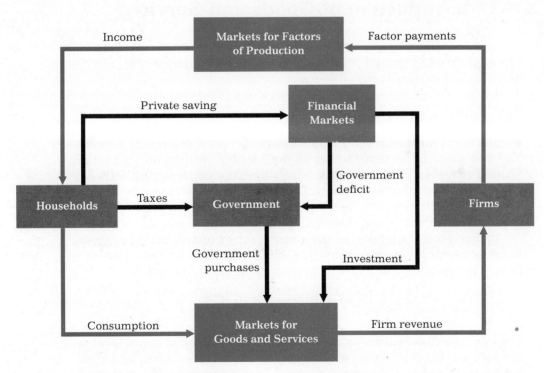

Figure 3-1 **The Circular Flow of Dollars Through the Economy.** This figure is a more elaborate and realistic version of the circular flow diagram found in Chapter 2. Each gray box represents an economic actor —households, firms, and the government.

Each blue box represents a type of market—the markets for goods and services, the markets for the factors of production, and financial markets. The arrows show the flow of dollars among the economic actors through these three types of markets.

In this chapter we examine the economic interactions depicted in this diagram. We begin with firms, where we look at what determines their level of production, which, in turn, equals the level of national income. Then we examine how this income is distributed to households through the markets for the factors of production. Next, we consider how much of this income households consume and how much they save. In addition to our discussion of the demand for goods and services arising from the consumption of households, we also discuss the demand arising from investment and government purchases. Finally, we come full circle and examine how the demand for goods and services (the sum of consumption, investment, and government purchases) and the supply of goods and services (the level of production) are brought into balance.

3-1   The Production of Goods and Services

The economy's output of goods and services—its GNP—depends on two elements: the factors of production and the production function. We discuss each in turn.

The Factors of Production

Factors of production are the inputs used to produce goods and services. The two most important factors of production are capital and labor. *Capital* is the set of tools that workers use: the construction worker's crane, the accountant's calculator, and this author's personal computer. *Labor* is the time people spend working. We use the symbol K to denote the amount of capital and the symbol L to denote the amount of labor.

In this chapter we take the economy's factors of production as given. In other words, to keep our analysis simple, we assume that there is a fixed amount of capital and a fixed amount of labor. We write

$$K = \overline{K}.$$
$$L = \overline{L}.$$

The bar over these variables means that they are fixed at some level. In the real world, the factors of production change over time, as we examine in Chapter 4. For now, however, we assume fixed amounts of capital and labor.

We also assume here that the factors of production are fully utilized— that is, that no resources are wasted. Again, in the real world, part of the labor force is unemployed, and some capital lies idle. In Chapter 5 we examine the reasons for unemployment, but for now we assume that capital and labor are fully employed.

The Production Function

The available production technology determines how much output is produced from given amounts of capital and labor. Economists express the available technology mathematically using a **production function**, which shows how the factors of production determine the amount of output produced. Letting Y denote the amount of output, we write the production function as

$$Y = F(K, L).$$

This equation states that output is a function of the amount of capital and the amount of labor.

The production function reflects the available technology. That is, the available technology is implicit in the way this function turns capital and labor into output. If someone invents a better way to produce a good, the result is more output from the same amounts of capital and labor. Thus, technological change alters the production function.

Many production functions have a feature called **constant returns to scale**. A production function has constant returns to scale if an increase of an equal percentage in all factors of production causes an increase in output of the same percentage. Thus, if the production function has constant returns to scale, we get 10 percent more output if we increase capital and labor each by 10 percent. Mathematically, a production function has constant returns to scale if

$$zY = F(zK, zL)$$

for any positive number z. This equation says that if we multiply both the amount of capital and the amount of labor by some amount z, the amount of output is also multiplied by z. We see in the next section that the assumption of constant returns to scale has an important implication for how the income from production is distributed.

As an example of a production function, consider production at a bakery. The kitchen and its equipment are the bakery's capital, the workers hired to make the bread are its labor, and the loaves of bread are its output. The bakery's production function shows that the number of loaves produced depends on the amount of equipment and the number of workers. The property of constant returns to scale states that if we double the amount of equipment and double the number of workers, we also double the amount of bread produced.

The Fixed Supply of Goods and Services

We can now see that the factors of production and the production function together determine the supply of goods and services, which equals the economy's output. To express this mathematically, we write

$$Y = F(\overline{K}, \overline{L})$$
$$= \overline{Y}.$$

At any particular point in time, the output of the economy is fixed because the supplies of capital and labor and the technology for turning capital and labor into goods and services are fixed. Over time, however, output changes when factor supplies change or when technology changes. The greater the amount of capital or the amount of labor, the greater the output. The better the available technology as summarized in the production function, the greater the output.

3-2 Distributing National Income to the Factors of Production

As we discussed in Chapter 2, the total output of an economy equals its total income. Because the factors of production and the production function together determine the total output of goods and services, they also determine national income. The circular flow diagram in Figure 3-1 shows that this national income flows from firms to households through the markets for the factors of production.

In this section we discuss how these factor markets work. Economists have long studied factor markets in order to understand the distribution of income. (For example, Karl Marx, the noted nineteenth-century economist, spent much time trying to explain the incomes of capital and labor. The political philosophy of communism was in part based on Marx's now-discredited theory.) Here we examine the modern theory of how national income is divided between the factors of production. This theory, called the *neoclassical theory of distribution*, is accepted by most economists today.

Factor Prices

The distribution of national income is determined by factor prices. **Factor prices** are the amounts paid to the factors of production—the wage workers earn and the rent the owners of capital collect. As Figure 3-2 illustrates, the price each factor of production receives for its services is in turn determined by the supply and demand for that factor. Because we have assumed that the economy's factors of production are fixed, the factor supply curve in Figure 3-2 is vertical. The intersection of the downward-sloping factor demand curve and the vertical supply curve determines the equilibrium factor price.

To understand factor prices and the distribution of income, we must examine the demand for the factors of production. Factor demand arises from the thousands of firms that use the factors of production. We now look at the decisions faced by a typical firm.

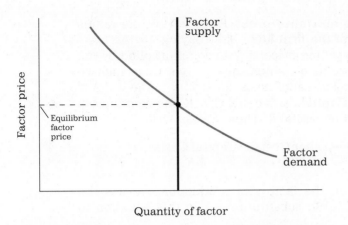

Figure 3-2 **How a Factor of Production Is Compensated.** The price paid to any factor of production depends on the supply and demand for that factor's services. Because we have assumed that supply is fixed, the supply curve is vertical. The equilibrium factor price is where the downward-sloping demand curve crosses the vertical supply curve.

The Problem Facing the Competitive Firm

The simplest assumption to make about a typical firm is that it is **competitive**. A competitive firm is one that is small relative to the markets in which it trades, so it has little influence on market prices. For example, our firm produces a good and sells it at the market price. Because it is one of many firms producing the good, the firm can increase its sales as much as it wants without causing the price of the good to fall, or it can stop selling altogether without causing the price of the good to rise. Nor can the firm have much effect on the wages of the workers it hires, because many other local firms are also hiring workers. The firm has no reason to pay above the market wage and, if it tried to pay less, its workers would go elsewhere. Therefore, the competitive firm takes prices—both of its output and of its inputs—as given.

To manufacture its product, the firm requires two factors of production, capital and labor. As we did for the aggregate economy, we represent the firm's production technology by the production function

$$Y = F(K, L),$$

where Y is the number of units produced (the firm's output), K the number of machines used (its capital), and L the number of hours worked by the firm's employees (its labor). The firm produces more output if it has more machines or if its employees work more hours.

The firm sells its output at a price P, hires workers at a wage W, and rents capital at a rate R. Notice that, when we speak of firms renting capital, we are assuming that households own the economy's stock of capital. In this analysis, households rent out their capital, just as they sell their labor. The firm obtains both factors of production from the households who own them.[1]

---

[1] More realistically, the ownership of capital is indirect, because firms own capital and households own the firms. In the real world, firms have two functions: owning capital and producing output. To help us understand how the factors of production are compensated, however, we assume that households own capital directly, thus separating the ownership of capital from the production of output.

The goal of the firm is to maximize profit. *Profit* is revenue minus costs—it is what the owners of the firm keep after paying for the costs of production. *Revenue* is the selling price of the good multiplied by the amount of the good the firm produces, which equals $P \times Y$. *Costs* include both labor costs and capital costs. Labor costs equal $W \times L$, the wage W times the amount of labor L. Capital costs equal $R \times K$, the rental price of capital R times the amount of capital K. Thus, we can write

$$\text{Profit} = \text{Revenue} - \text{Labor Costs} - \text{Capital Costs}$$
$$= \quad PY \quad - \quad WL \quad - \quad RK.$$

To see how profit depends on the factors of production, we use the production function $Y = F(K, L)$ to substitute for Y in this equation to obtain

$$\text{Profit} = PF(K, L) - WL - RK.$$

The equation states that profit depends on the product price P, the factor prices W and R, and the factor quantities L and K. The competitive firm takes the product price and the factor prices as given and chooses the amounts of labor and capital that maximize its profit.

The Firm's Demand for Factors

We can now see how this firm decides how much labor to hire and how much capital to rent.

The Marginal Product of Labor   The more labor the firm employs, the more output it produces. The **marginal product of labor (*MPL*)** is the extra amount of output the firm gets from one extra unit of labor. In other words, if the firm hires an additional hour of labor, its production increases by *MPL* units. We can express this algebraically using the production function:

$$MPL = F(K, L + 1) - F(K, L).$$

The first term is the amount of output produced with K units of capital and $L + 1$ units of labor; the second term is the amount of output produced with K units of capital and L units of labor. This equation states that the marginal product of labor is the difference between the amount of output produced with $L + 1$ units of labor and the amount produced with only L units of labor.

Most production functions have the property of **diminishing marginal product**: holding the amount of capital fixed, the greater the amount of labor, the smaller the marginal product of an extra unit of labor. For example, consider again the production of bread at a bakery. As a bakery hires more labor, it produces more bread. The *MPL* is the amount of extra bread produced when an extra unit of labor is hired. With each additional unit of labor, however, the *MPL* is smaller. Fewer additional loaves are produced, because workers are less productive when the kitchen is more crowded. In other words, holding the size of the kitchen fixed, each additional unit of labor adds fewer loaves of bread to the bakery's output.

Figure 3-3 graphs the production function. It illustrates what happens to the amount of output when we hold the amount of capital constant and vary the amount of labor. This figure shows that the marginal product of labor is the slope of the production function. As the amount of labor increases, the production function becomes flatter, indicating diminishing marginal product.

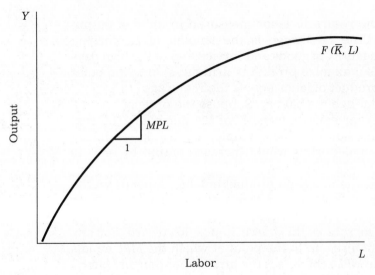

Figure 3-3 **The Production Function.** This curve shows how output depends on labor input, holding the amount of capital constant. The marginal product of labor (*MPL*) is the change in output when the labor input is increased by one unit. That is, $MPL = F(K, L + 1) - F(K, L)$. As the amount of labor increases, the production function becomes flatter, indicating diminishing marginal product.

From the Marginal Product of Labor to Labor Demand When the competitive, profit-maximizing firm is deciding whether to hire an additional unit of labor, it considers how that decision affects profits. It therefore compares the extra revenue from the increased production that results from the added labor to the extra cost of a higher wage bill. The increase in revenue from an additional unit of labor depends on both the marginal product of labor and the price of the output. Because an extra unit of labor produces *MPL* units of output, and each unit of output sells for *P* dollars, the extra revenue is $P \times MPL$. The extra cost from hiring one more unit of labor is the wage *W*. Thus, the change in profit from hiring an additional unit of labor is:

$$\Delta\text{Profit} = \Delta\text{Revenue} - \Delta\text{Cost}$$
$$= (P \times MPL) - W.$$

The symbol Δ (called *delta*) denotes a change in a variable.

We can now answer the question we asked at the beginning of this section: How much labor does the firm hire? The firm's manager knows that as long as the extra revenue $P \times MPL$ exceeds the wage W, an extra unit of labor increases profit. Therefore, the manager continues to hire labor until the next unit would no longer be profitable—that is, until the MPL falls to the point where the extra revenue equals the wage. The firm's demand for labor is determined by

$$P \times MPL = W.$$

We can write this as

$$MPL = W/P.$$

W/P is the **real wage**, the return to labor measured in units of output rather than in dollars. The real wage is the amount of purchasing power—measured as a quantity of goods and services—that the firm pays for each unit of labor. To maximize profit, the firm hires up to the point at which the marginal product of labor equals the real wage.

For example, consider again a bakery. Suppose the price of bread P is $2 per loaf, and a worker earns a wage W of $20 per hour. The real wage W/P is 10 loaves per hour. In this example, the firm keeps hiring workers until an additional worker would increase output by only 10 loaves per hour.

Figure 3-4 shows how the marginal product of labor depends on the amount of labor employed (holding the firm's capital stock constant). That is, this figure graphs the MPL schedule. Because the MPL diminishes as the amount of labor increases, this curve slopes downward. For any given real wage, the firm hires up to the point at which the MPL equals the real wage. Hence, the MPL schedule is the firm's labor demand curve.

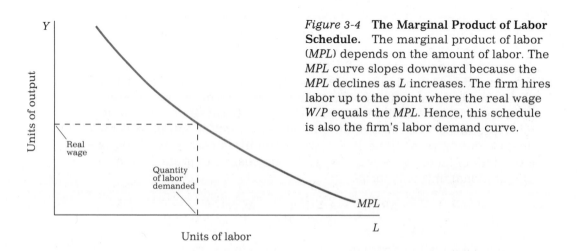

Figure 3-4 **The Marginal Product of Labor Schedule.** The marginal product of labor (MPL) depends on the amount of labor. The MPL curve slopes downward because the MPL declines as L increases. The firm hires labor up to the point where the real wage W/P equals the MPL. Hence, this schedule is also the firm's labor demand curve.

The Marginal Product of Capital and Capital Demand   The firm decides how much capital to rent in the same way it decides how much labor to hire. The **marginal product of capital** *(MPK)* is the amount of extra output the firm gets from an extra unit of capital,

$$MPK = F(K + 1, L) - F(K, L).$$

Thus, the marginal product of capital is the difference between the amount of output produced with $K + 1$ units of capital and that produced with only K units of capital. Like labor, capital is subject to diminishing marginal product.

The increase in profit from renting an additional machine is the extra revenue from selling the output of that machine minus the machine's rental price:

$$\Delta\text{Profit} = \Delta\text{Revenue} - \Delta\text{Cost}$$
$$= (P \times MPK) - R.$$

To maximize profit, the firm continues to rent more capital until the *MPK* falls to equal the real rental price:

$$MPK = R/P.$$

The **real rental price** is the rental price measured in units of goods rather than in dollars.

To sum up, the competitive, profit-maximizing firm follows a simple rule about how much labor to hire and how much capital to rent. *The firm demands each factor of production until that factor's marginal product falls to equal its real factor price.*

The Division of National Income

Having analyzed the factor demand for the individual firm, we can now explain how the income of the overall economy is divided. If all firms in the economy are competitive and profit-maximizing, then each factor of production is paid its marginal contribution to the production process. In other words, the real wage paid to each worker equals the *MPL*, and the real rental price paid to each owner of capital equals the *MPK*. The total real wage bill is therefore $MPL \times L$, and the total real return to capital owners is $MPK \times K$.

The income that remains after the firms have paid the factors of production is the **economic profit** of the owners of the firms. Real economic profit is

$$\text{Economic Profit} = Y - (MPL \times L) - (MPK \times K).$$

Since we want to examine the distribution of national income, we rearrange the terms as follows:

$$Y = (MPL \times L) + (MPK \times K) + \text{Economic Profit.}$$

Total income is thus divided among the return to labor, the return to capital, and economic profit.

If we assume that the production function has the property of constant returns to scale, however, economic profit must be zero. That is, nothing is left after the factors of production are paid. This surprising conclusion follows from a famous mathematical result called *Euler's theorem*, which states that if the production function has constant returns to scale, then[2]

$$F(K, L) = (MPK \times K) + (MPL \times L).$$

If each factor of production is paid its marginal product, then the sum of these factor payments equals total output. In other words, constant returns to scale, profit maximization, and competition together imply that economic profit is zero.

If economic profit is zero, however, how can we explain the existence of "profit" in the economy? The answer is that the term "profit" as normally used is different from economic profit. We have been assuming that there are three types of agents: laborers, owners of capital, and owners of firms. Total income is therefore divided among wages, return to capital, and economic profit. In the real world, however, most firms own rather than rent the capital they use. Hence, the owners of firms also own the capital. The term "profit" usually includes both economic profit and the return to capital. If we call this alternative definition **accounting profit**, we can say that

$$\text{Accounting Profit} = \text{Economic Profit} + (MPK \times K).$$

Under our assumptions—constant returns to scale, profit-maximization, and competition—economic profit is zero. If these assumptions approximately describe the world, then the "profit" in the national income accounts must be mostly the return to capital.

We can now answer the question posed at the beginning of this chapter about how the income of the economy is distributed from firms to households. Each factor of production is paid its marginal product, and these factor payments exhaust total output. *Therefore, total output is divided between the payments to capital and the payments to labor, depending on their marginal productivities.*

---

[2] *Mathematical Note*: To prove Euler's theorem, begin with the definition of constant returns to scale

$$zY = F(zK, zL).$$

Now differentiate with respect to z and evaluate at $z = 1$.

CASE STUDY 3-1

The Black Death and Factor Prices

According to our analysis of the distribution of the economy's income, factor prices equal the marginal products of the factors of production. Because the marginal products depend on the quantities of the factors, a change in the quantity of any one factor alters the marginal products of all the factors. Therefore, a change in the supply of a factor alters equilibrium factor prices.

Fourteenth-century Europe provides a vivid example of how factor quantities affect factor prices. The outbreak of the bubonic plague—the Black Death—in 1348 reduced the population of Europe by about one-third within a few years. Because the marginal product of labor increases as the amount of labor falls, this massive reduction in the labor force raised the marginal product of labor. (The economy moved to the left along the curves in Figure 3-3 and Figure 3-4.) Therefore, real wages increased substantially—doubling, by some estimates. The peasants who were fortunate enough to survive the plague enjoyed economic prosperity.

The reduction in the labor force caused by the plague also affected the return to land, the other major factor of production in medieval Europe. With fewer workers available to farm the land, an additional unit of land produced less additional output. This fall in the marginal product of land led to a decline in real rents of 50 percent or more. While the peasant classes prospered, the landed classes suffered reduced incomes.[3]

CASE STUDY 3-2

The Senator, the Mathematician, and the Constancy of Factor Shares

In 1927 Paul Douglas, an economist who later served as U.S. senator from Illinois from 1949 to 1966, noted that the division of national income between capital and labor had been roughly constant over a long period. In other words, as the output of the economy grew, workers and the owners of capital shared equally in the greater prosperity. This observation caused Douglas to wonder what conditions lead to constant factor shares.

Douglas asked Charles Cobb, a mathematician, what production function, if any, would produce constant factor shares if factors always earned their marginal products. The production function would need to

---

[3] Carlo M. Cipolla, *Before the Industrial Revolution: European Society and Economy, 1000–1700*, 2d ed. (New York: Norton, 1980), 200–202.

have the property that

$$\text{Capital Income} = MPK \times K = \alpha Y, \text{ and}$$
$$\text{Labor Income} = MPL \times L = (1 - \alpha) Y,$$

where α is a constant between zero and one that measures capital's share of income—that is, α determines what share of income goes to capital and what share goes to labor. Cobb showed that the function with this property is

$$Y = F(K, L) = AK^{\alpha}L^{1 - \alpha},$$

where A is a parameter greater than zero that measures the productivity of the available technology. This became known as the *Cobb-Douglas production function*.

Many economists have found that the Cobb-Douglas production function accurately describes how the economy turns capital and labor into output. Let's therefore take a closer look at some of its properties.

First, the Cobb-Douglas production function has constant returns to scale. That is, if capital and labor are increased by the same proportion, then output increases by that proportion as well.[4]

Next, we look at the marginal products for the Cobb-Douglas production function. The marginal product of labor is[5]

$$MPL = (1 - \alpha) AK^{\alpha}L^{-\alpha},$$

and the marginal product of capital is

$$MPK = \alpha AK^{\alpha - 1}L^{1 - \alpha}.$$

From these equations, recalling that α is between zero and one, we can see what causes the marginal products of the two factors to change. An increase in the amount of capital raises the *MPL* and reduces the *MPK*. Similarly, an increase in the amount of labor reduces the *MPL* and raises the *MPK*. A technological advance that increases the parameter A raises the marginal product of both factors proportionately.

---

[4] *Mathematical Note*: To prove that the Cobb-Douglas production function has constant returns to scale, examine what happens when we multiply capital and labor by a constant z:
$$F(zK, zL) = A(zK)^{\alpha}(zL)^{1 - \alpha}.$$
Expanding terms on the right,
$$F(zK, zL) = Az^{\alpha}K^{\alpha}z^{1 - \alpha}L^{1 - \alpha}.$$
Rearranging to bring like terms together, we get
$$F(zK, zL) = z^{\alpha}z^{1 - \alpha}AK^{\alpha}L^{1 - \alpha}.$$
Since $z^{\alpha}z^{1 - \alpha} = z$, our function becomes
$$F(zK, zL) = zAK^{\alpha}L^{1 - \alpha}.$$
But $AK^{\alpha}L^{1 - \alpha} = F(K, L)$. Thus,
$$F(zK, zL) = zF(K, L) = zY.$$
Hence, the amount of output Y increases by the same factor z, which implies that this production function has constant returns to scale.

[5] *Mathematical Note*: Obtaining the formulas for the marginal products from the production function requires a bit of calculus. To find the *MPL*, differentiate the production function with respect to L. This is done by multiplying by the exponent $(1 - \alpha)$, and then subtracting one from the old exponent to obtain the new exponent, $-\alpha$. Similarly, to obtain the *MPK*, differentiate the production function with respect to K.

The marginal products for the Cobb-Douglas production function can also be written as[6]

$$MPL = (1 - \alpha)Y/L,$$
$$MPK = \alpha Y/K.$$

The *MPL* is proportional to output per worker, and the *MPK* is proportional to output per unit of capital. *Y/L* is called *average labor productivity*, and *Y/K* is called *average capital productivity*. If the production function is Cobb-Douglas, then the marginal productivity of a factor is proportional to its average productivity.

We can now verify that, if factors earn their marginal products, then the parameter α indeed tells us how much income goes to labor and how much goes to capital. The total wage bill, which we have seen is *MPL* × *L*, is simply $(1 - \alpha)Y$. Therefore, $(1 - \alpha)$ is labor's share of output. Similarly, the total return to capital, *MPK* × *K*, is αY, and α is capital's share of output. The ratio of labor income to capital income is a constant, $(1 - \alpha)/\alpha$, just as Douglas observed. The factor shares depend only on the parameter α, not on the amounts of capital or labor or on the state of technology as measured by the parameter *A*.

More recent data are also consistent with the Cobb-Douglas production function. Figure 3-5 shows the ratio of labor income to capital income in the United States from 1948 to 1989. Despite the many changes in the economy over the past four decades, this ratio has remained between 2 and 3. This division of income is easily explained by a Cobb-Douglas production function in which the capital share α is about 0.3.

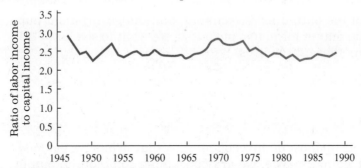

Figure 3-5   **The Ratio of Labor Income to Capital Income.**   Labor income has been between two and three times capital income in the United States. This approximate constancy of factor shares is evidence for the Cobb-Douglas production function. (This figure is produced from national income accounts data. Labor income is compensation of employees. Capital income is the sum of corporate profits, net interest, rental income, and depreciation. Proprietors' income is excluded from these calculations, because it is a combination of labor income and capital income.) *Source:* U.S. Department of Commerce.

---

[6] *Mathematical Note:* To check these expressions for the marginal products, substitute in the production function for *Y* to show that these expressions are equivalent to the earlier formulas for the marginal products.

3-3 The Demand for Goods and Services

We have seen what determines the level of production and how the income from production is divided between workers and owners of capital. We now continue our tour of the circular flow diagram, Figure 3-1, and examine how the output from production is used.

In Chapter 2, we discussed the four components of GNP:

- Consumption (*C*)
- Investment (*I*)
- Government purchases (*G*)
- Net exports (*NX*).

Only the first three components are found in the circular flow diagram. For now, to simplify the analysis, we assume a closed economy—a country that does not trade with other countries. Therefore, its net exports are always zero. In Chapter 7 we examine the macroeconomics of open economies.

A closed economy has three uses for the goods and services it produces. These three components of GNP are expressed in the national income accounts identity:

$$Y = C + I + G.$$

Households consume some of the economy's output; firms and households use some of the output for investment; and the government purchases some of the output for public purposes. We want to see how GNP is allocated among these three uses.

Consumption

Consumption takes up most of the economy's output. When we eat food, wear clothing, or go to a movie, we are consuming some of the output of the economy. Together all forms of consumption compose two-thirds of GNP, which makes the consumption decision one of the most important issues in economics. In Chapter 15 we examine this decision in detail. Here we consider the simplest story of consumer behavior.

Households receive income from their labor and their ownership of capital, pay taxes to the government, and then decide how much of their after-tax income to consume and how much to save. As we discussed in Section 3-2, the income that households receive equals the output of the economy *Y*. The government then taxes households an amount *T*. Although the government imposes many kinds of taxes, such as personal and corporate income taxes and sales taxes, for simplicity we lump all these taxes together. We define income after the payment of all taxes, $Y - T$, as **disposable income**. People divide their disposable income between consumption and saving.

We assume that consumption depends directly on the level of disposable income. The higher disposable income is, the greater consumption is. Thus,

$$C = C(Y - T).$$

This equation states that consumption is a function of disposable income. The relationship between consumption and disposable income is called the **consumption function**.

The **marginal propensity to consume (*MPC*)** is the amount consumption changes when disposable income increases by one dollar. We normally expect the *MPC* to be between zero and one: an extra dollar of income increases consumption, but by less than one dollar. Thus, if households obtain an extra dollar of income, they save a portion of it. For example, if the *MPC* is 0.7, then households spend 70 cents of each additional dollar of disposable income on consumer goods and services and save 30 cents.

Figure 3-6 illustrates the consumption function. The slope of the consumption function tells us how much consumption increases when disposable income increases by one dollar. That is, the slope of the consumption function is the *MPC*.

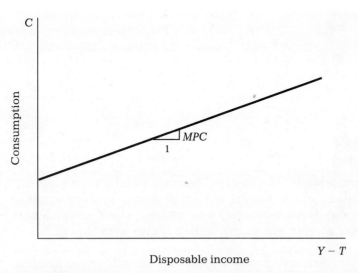

Figure 3-6 **The Consumption Function.** The consumption function relates consumption C to disposable income $Y - T$. The marginal propensity to consume *MPC* is the amount that consumption increases when income increases by one dollar.

CASE STUDY 3-3

The Consumption Function in U.S. Data

It is easy to find the consumption function in U.S. data. Figures 3-7A and 3-7B use annual data from the national income accounts on consumption per person and disposable income per person to illustrate the consumption function in two different ways. Figure 3-7A, a scatterplot of the level of income and the level of consumption, emphasizes the long-run relationship between these two variables. As income has risen over time, so has consumption. Figure 3-7B, a scatterplot of the year-to-year changes

Figure 3-7 **The Consumption Function in U.S. Data.** These two scatterplots show the relationship between consumption C and disposable income $Y - T$ using annual data from 1950 to 1989. (Both variables are measured in 1982 dollars.)

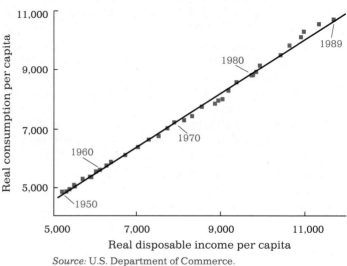

Source: U.S. Department of Commerce.

(A)

Investment

Both firms and households purchase investment goods. Firms buy investment goods to add to their stock of capital and to replace existing capital as it wears out. Households buy new houses, which are also part of investment. Total investment in the United States averages about 15 percent of GNP.

The quantity of investment goods demanded depends on the interest rate. For an investment project to be profitable, its return must exceed its cost. Because the interest rate measures the cost of funds to finance investment, an increase in the interest rate results in fewer investment projects being profitable and, therefore, a decrease in the demand for investment goods.

in disposable income and the year-to-year changes in consumption, emphasizes the short-run relationship. In those years when income rises by a large amount, consumption also rises by a large amount; in those years when income stays the same or falls, consumption also stays the same or falls. However we look at the data, we see a close relationship between consumption and income—a relationship summarized by the consumption function.

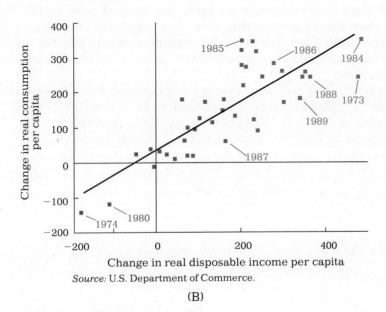

Source: U.S. Department of Commerce.

(B)

For example, suppose that a firm is considering whether it should build a $1 million factory that would yield a return of $80,000 per year, or 8 percent. The firm compares this return to the cost of borrowing the $1 million. If the interest rate is below 8 percent, the firm borrows money in financial markets and makes the investment. If the interest rate is above 8 percent, the firm forgoes the opportunity and does not build the factory.

A person wanting to buy a new house faces a similar decision. The higher the interest rate, the greater is the cost of carrying a mortgage. A $100,000 mortgage costs $8,000 per year if the interest rate is 8 percent and $10,000 per year if the interest rate is 10 percent. As the interest rate rises, the cost of owning a home rises, and the demand for new homes falls.

Economists distinguish between the **nominal interest rate** and the **real interest rate**. This distinction arises during periods of inflation or deflation—that is, when prices are not stable. The nominal interest rate is the interest rate as the term is normally used: it is the rate of interest that investors pay to borrow money. The real interest rate is the nominal interest rate corrected for the effects of inflation.

To see how nominal and real interest rates differ, consider a firm that decides to build a new factory and borrows the money from a bank at an interest rate of 8 percent. The nominal interest rate is therefore 8 percent—that is, the amount the firm owes to the bank grows by 8 percent per year. But if prices are rising, say by 5 percent per year, the dollars with which the firm will repay the bank are losing 5 percent of their value per year. Each year the firm owes 8 percent more dollars, but the dollars are worth 5 percent less. The real interest rate is therefore only 3 percent, the difference between the nominal interest rate and the rate of inflation.

In Chapter 6 we discuss the relation between nominal and real interest rates in more detail. Here it is sufficient to note that the real interest rate measures the true cost of borrowing. We therefore expect investment to depend on the real rather than the nominal interest rate.

The link between the real interest rate r and investment I can be expressed as

$$I = I(r).$$

This equation states that investment depends on the interest rate. Figure 3-8 shows this investment function. It slopes downward, because as the interest rate rises, the quantity of investment demanded falls.

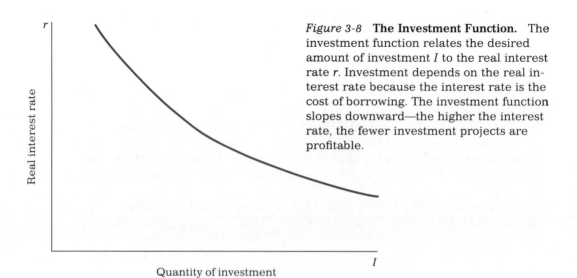

Figure 3-8 **The Investment Function.** The investment function relates the desired amount of investment I to the real interest rate r. Investment depends on the real interest rate because the interest rate is the cost of borrowing. The investment function slopes downward—the higher the interest rate, the fewer investment projects are profitable.

//

F Y I **What Is Investment?**

The term "investment" sometimes creates confusion for newcomers to macroeconomics. The confusion arises because what looks like investment for an individual may not be investment for the economy as a whole.

Suppose we observe these two events:

• Smith buys for himself a 100-year-old Victorian house.

• Jones builds for herself a brand-new contemporary house.

What is total investment here? One house, two houses, or none?

A macroeconomist seeing these two transactions counts only the Jones house as investment. Smith's transaction has not created new housing for the economy; it has merely reallocated existing housing. Smith's purchase is investment for Smith, but it is disinvestment for the person selling the house. Jones, in contrast, has added new housing to the economy; hence, her new house is counted as investment.

The general rule is that purchases that reallocate existing assets among different individuals are not investment for the economy. Investment, as macroeconomists use the term, entails the creation of new capital.

//

Government Purchases

Government purchases are the third component of the demand for goods and services. The federal government buys guns, missiles, and the services of government employees. Local governments buy library books, build schools, and hire teachers. Governments at all levels build roads and other public works. All these transactions make up government purchases of goods and services, which account for about 20 percent of GNP in the United States.

These purchases are only one type of government spending. The other type involves transfer payments to households, such as welfare for the poor and Social Security payments for the elderly. Unlike government purchases, however, transfer payments do not directly use the economy's output of goods and services. Therefore, they are not included in the variable *G*.

Transfer payments, however, do affect the demand for goods and services indirectly. Transfer payments are the opposite of taxes: they increase households' disposable income, just as taxes reduce disposable income. Therefore, an increase in transfer payments financed by an increase in taxes leaves aggregate disposable income unchanged. We can now revise our definition of T as taxes minus transfer payments. Disposable income, $Y - T$, includes both the negative impact of taxes and the positive impact of transfer payments.

If government purchases equal taxes minus transfers, then $G = T$, and the government has a *balanced budget*. If G exceeds T, the government runs a *budget deficit*, which it funds by issuing government debt—that is, by borrowing in the financial markets. If G is less than T, the government runs a *budget surplus*, which it can use to repay some of its outstanding loans and reduce its debt.

We do not try to explain the political process that leads to a particular fiscal policy—that is, to the level of government purchases and taxes. Instead, we take government purchases and taxes as exogenous variables. To denote that these variables are fixed outside of the model, we write

$$G = \overline{G}.$$
$$T = \overline{T}.$$

We do want to examine, however, the impact of fiscal decisions on the variables determined within the model, the endogenous variables. The endogenous variables here are consumption, investment, and the interest rate.

To see how the exogenous variables affect the endogenous variables, we must first solve our model. This is the subject of the next section.

3-4   Equilibrium and the Interest Rate

We have now come full circle in the circular flow diagram, Figure 3-1. We began by examining the supply of goods and services, and we have just discussed the demand for them.

How can we be certain that all these flows balance? In other words, what ensures that the sum of consumption, investment, and government purchases equals the amount of output produced? We will see that the interest rate has the crucial role of equilibrating supply and demand.

Equilibrium in the Market for Goods and Services: The Supply and Demand for the Economy's Output

The following equations summarize the discussion in Section 3-3 of the demand for goods and services:

$$Y = C + I + G$$
$$C = C(Y - T)$$
$$I = I(r)$$
$$G = \overline{G}$$
$$T = \overline{T}.$$

The demand for the economy's output comes from consumption, investment, and government purchases. Consumption depends on disposable income; investment depends on the real interest rate; and government purchases and taxes are the exogenous fiscal policy variables.

In addition to the demand for goods and services, we now consider the supply. As we discussed in Section 3-1, the factors of production and the production function determine the amount of output:

$$Y = F(\overline{K}, \overline{L})$$
$$= \overline{Y}.$$

Now let's combine these equations describing the supply and demand for output. If we substitute the consumption function and the investment function in the national income accounts identity, we obtain

$$Y = C(Y - T) + I(r) + G.$$

Since the variables G and T are fixed by policy, and the level of output Y is fixed by the factors of production and the production function, we can write:

$$\overline{Y} = C(\overline{Y} - \overline{T}) + I(r) + \overline{G}.$$

This equation states that the supply of output equals its demand, which is the sum of consumption, investment, and government purchases.

Now you can see why the interest rate r plays a key role: it must adjust to ensure that the demand for goods equals the supply. The greater the interest rate, the lower the level of investment, and thus the lower the demand for goods and services, $C + I + G$. If the interest rate is too high, investment is too low, and the demand for output falls short of the supply. If the interest rate is too low, investment is too high, and the demand exceeds the supply. *At the equilibrium interest rate, the demand for goods and services equals the supply.*

Equilibrium in the Financial Markets: The Supply and Demand for Loanable Funds

Because the interest rate is the cost of borrowing and the return to lending in financial markets, we can better understand the role of the interest rate by thinking about the financial markets. To do this, rewrite the national income accounts identity as

$$Y - C - G = I.$$

The term $Y - C - G$ is the output that remains after the demands of consumers and the government have been satisfied; it is called **national saving** or simply **saving** (S). In this form, the national income accounts identity states that saving equals investment.

   We can split national saving into two parts to separate the saving of households from that of the government:

$$(Y - T - C) + (T - G) = I.$$

The term $Y - T - C$ is disposable income minus consumption, which is **private saving**. The term $T - G$ is government revenue minus government spending, which is **public saving**. (If government spending exceeds government revenue, the government runs a budget deficit, and public saving is negative.) National saving is the sum of private and public saving. The circular flow diagram in Figure 3-1 reveals an interpretation of this equation: this equation states that the flows into and out of the financial markets must balance.

   To see the role of the interest rate in equilibrating financial markets, substitute the consumption function and the investment function into the national income accounts identity:

$$Y - C(Y - T) - G = I(r).$$

Next, make G and T fixed by policy and Y fixed by the factors of production and the production function:

$$\overline{Y} - C(\overline{Y} - \overline{T}) - \overline{G} = I(r)$$
$$\overline{S} = I(r).$$

The left-hand side of this equation shows that national saving depends on income, Y, and the fiscal policy variables, G and T. For fixed values of Y, G, and T, national saving S is also fixed. The right-hand side of the equation shows that investment depends on the interest rate.

   Figure 3-9 is a graph of both saving and investment as a function of the interest rate. The saving function is a vertical line, because in this model saving does not depend on the interest rate (although we relax this assumption later). The investment function slopes downward: the higher the interest rate, the fewer investment projects are profitable.

   From a quick glance at Figure 3-9, one might think it was a supply

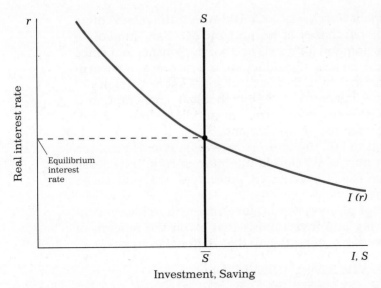

Figure 3-9 **Saving, Investment, and the Interest Rate.** The interest rate adjusts to ensure that saving equals desired investment. The vertical line represents saving—the supply of loans. The downward-sloping line represents desired investment—the demand for loans. These two curves intersect at the equilibrium interest rate.

and demand diagram for a particular good. In fact, saving and investment can be interpreted in terms of supply and demand. In this case, the "good" is loanable funds, and its "price" is the interest rate. Saving is the supply of loans—individuals lend their saving to investors or they deposit their saving in a bank that makes the loans for them. Investment is the demand for loans—investors borrow from the public directly by selling bonds or indirectly by borrowing from banks. Since investment depends on the interest rate, the demand for these loans also depends on the interest rate.

The interest rate adjusts until investment equals saving. If the interest rate is too low, investors want more of the economy's output than individuals want to save. Equivalently, the demand for loans exceeds the supply. When this happens, the interest rate rises. Conversely, if the interest rate is too high, saving exceeds investment; because the supply of loans is greater than the demand, the interest rate falls. The equilibrium interest rate is found where the two curves cross. *At the equilibrium interest rate, saving equals investment, and the supply of loans equals the demand.*

Changes in Saving: The Effects of Fiscal Policy

Fiscal policy affects the demand for the economy's output of goods and services. It also affects national saving and, thereby, investment and the equilibrium interest rate. The model we have developed helps us evaluate the impact of changes in government purchases and taxes on the rest of the economy.

An Increase in Government Purchases   Consider first the effects of an increase in government purchases of an amount ΔG. The immediate impact is to increase the demand for goods and services by ΔG. But since total output is fixed by the factors of production, the increase in government purchases must be met by a decrease in some other category of demand. Since disposable income $Y - T$ is unchanged, consumption C is also unchanged. The increase in government purchases must therefore be met by an equal decrease in investment.

To induce investment to fall, the interest rate must rise. Hence, the increase in government purchases causes the interest rate to increase and investment to decrease. Government purchases are said to be **crowding out** investment.

To grasp the effects of an increase in government purchases, consider the impact on saving and investment—that is, on the amount of loanable funds available to investors. Recall that national saving is

$$\overline{S} = \text{Private Saving} + \text{Public Saving}$$
$$= (\overline{Y} - \overline{T} - C(\overline{Y} - \overline{T})) + (\overline{T} - \overline{G})$$
$$= \overline{Y} - C(\overline{Y} - \overline{T}) - \overline{G}.$$

Since the increase in G is not accompanied by an increase in T, the government finances the additional spending by borrowing—that is, by reducing public saving. This government borrowing in turn reduces national saving. As Figure 3-10 shows, a reduction in national saving is represented by a leftward shift in the supply of loanable funds available for investment. At the initial interest rate, the demand for loans exceeds the supply. The equilibrium interest rate rises to the point where the investment schedule crosses the new saving schedule. Thus, an increase in government purchases raises the interest rate.

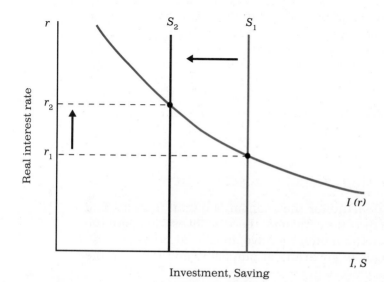

Figure 3-10 **A Reduction in Saving.** Any reduction in saving, possibly the result of a change in fiscal policy, shifts the vertical line to the left. In other words, a reduction in saving is a reduction in the supply of loans. The new equilibrium is where the new saving line crosses the investment schedule. A reduction in saving lowers the amount of investment and raises the interest rate. Fiscal policy actions that reduce saving are said to crowd out investment.

CASE STUDY 3-4

Wars and Interest Rates in the United Kingdom, 1730–1920

Wars are traumatic—both for those who fight them and for a nation's economy. Because the economic changes accompanying them are often large, wars provide a natural experiment with which economists can test their theories. We can learn about the economy by seeing how in wartime the endogenous variables respond to the major changes in the exogenous variables.

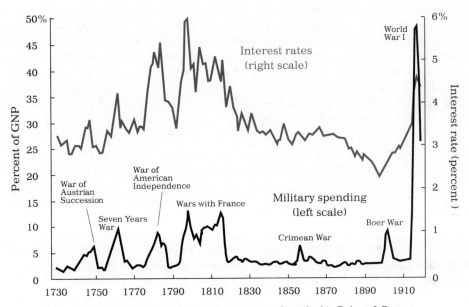

Source: Series constructed from various sources described in Robert J. Barro, "Government Spending, Interest Rates, Prices, and Budget Deficits in the United Kingdom, 1701–1918," *Journal of Monetary Economics* 20 (Sept. 1987): 221–248.

Figure 3-11 **Military Spending and the Interest Rate in the United Kingdom.** This figure shows military spending as a percentage of GNP in the United Kingdom from 1730 to 1919. Not surprisingly, military spending rose substantially during each of the eight wars of this period. This figure also shows that the interest rate (here the rate on a government bond called a *consol*) tended to rise when military spending rose.

The level of government purchases is one exogenous variable that changes substantially in wartime. Figure 3-11 shows military spending as a percent of GNP for the United Kingdom from 1730 to 1919, when the United Kingdom was a leading world power. This figure shows, as one would expect, that government purchases rose suddenly and dramatically during the eight wars of this period.

Our model of the economy predicts that this wartime increase in government purchases should have increased the demand for goods and services and thus raised the interest rate. In other words, the increase in government borrowing to finance the wars should have reduced the supply of loanable funds and thus raised the interest rate.

To test this prediction, Figure 3-11 also shows the interest rate on long-term government bonds, called *consols* in the United Kingdom. A positive association between military purchases and interest rates is apparent in this figure. Thus, these data support the model's prediction: interest rates do tend to rise when government purchases increase.[7]

One of the problems with using wars to test theories is that many things may be happening to the economy at the same time. For example, in World War II, while government purchases increased dramatically, rationing also restricted consumption of many goods. In addition, the risk of losing the war and of the government defaulting on its debt presumably increases the interest rate the government must pay. Economic models predict what happens when one exogenous variable changes and all the other exogenous variables remain constant. In the real world, however, many different exogenous variables may change at once. Unlike controlled laboratory experiments, the natural experiments on which economists must rely are not always easy to interpret.

A Decrease in Taxes   Now consider a reduction in taxes of ΔT. The immediate impact of this reduction is to increase disposable income and thus also to increase consumption. Disposable income increases by ΔT, and consumption increases by ΔT times the marginal propensity to consume. The higher the *MPC*, the greater is the impact of the tax cut on consumption.

Since total output is fixed by the factors of production and the level of government purchases is fixed by the government, the increase in consumption must be met by a decrease in investment. For investment to fall, the interest rate must rise. Hence, a reduction in taxes, like an increase in government purchases, crowds out investment and raises the interest rate.

We can also analyze the effect of a tax cut by looking at saving and investment. Since the tax cut raises disposable income by ΔT, consumption goes up by the $MPC \times \Delta T$. Since saving is $Y - C - G$, it falls by the same amount as consumption rises. As in Figure 3-10, the reduction in saving shifts the supply of loanable funds to the left, which increases the equilibrium interest rate and crowds out investment.

---

[7] Daniel K. Benjamin and Levis A. Kochin, "War, Prices, and Interest Rates: A Martial Solution to Gibson's Paradox," in M. D. Bordo and A. J. Schwartz, eds., *A Retrospective on the Classical Gold Standard, 1821–1931* (Chicago: University of Chicago Press, 1984), 587–612; Robert J. Barro, "Government Spending, Interest Rates, Prices, and Budget Deficits in the United Kingdom, 1701–1918," *Journal of Monetary Economics* 20 (September 1987): 221–248.

CASE STUDY 3-5

Fiscal Policy in the 1980s

One of the most dramatic macroeconomic events in recent history was the large change in U.S. fiscal policy in 1981. In 1980 Ronald Reagan was elected President on a platform to increase military spending and reduce taxes. The result of this combination of policies was, not surprisingly, a substantial budget deficit. In the 1970s, the federal budget was roughly balanced on average—that is, revenue approximately equaled spending. In the 1980s, the budget deficit averaged almost 4 percent of GNP, and the federal government borrowed at a rate unprecedented in peacetime.[8]

As our model of the economy predicts, this change in fiscal policy led to higher interest rates and lower national saving. The real interest rate (measured as the difference between the yield on government bonds and the inflation rate) rose from 0.4 percent in the 1970s to 5.7 percent in the 1980s. Gross national saving as a percent of GNP fell from 16.7 percent in the 1970s to 14.1 percent in the 1980s. The change in fiscal policy in the 1980s had the effects that our simple model of the economy predicted it would have.

Changes in Investment Demand

Thus far, we have discussed how fiscal policy can change national saving. We can also use the model to examine the other side of the market—the demand for investment. In this section we look at why the demand for investment changes and the effects of such changes.

One reason that investment demand might increase is technological innovation. Suppose, for example, that someone invents a new technology, such as the railroad or the computer. Before a firm or household can use the innovation, it must buy investment goods. The invention of the railroad had no value until railroad cars were produced and tracks were laid. The idea of the computer was not productive until computers were manufactured. Thus, technological innovation leads to an increase in investment demand.

Investment demand may also change because the government encourages or discourages investment through the tax laws. For example, suppose that the government increases personal income taxes and uses the extra revenue to provide tax cuts for those who invest in new capital. (This situation occurs when the government offers an investment tax

---

[8] These figures for the government budget deficit differ from government figures by correcting for the effects of inflation. In government accounting practices, the nominal interest paid on the government debt is counted as expenditure. In these figures, and in the deficit figures used in the rest of this book, only the real interest on the government debt is counted as expenditure. See the appendix to Chapter 16 for a discussion of this correction.

credit, which we discuss in Chapter 17.) Such a change in the tax laws makes more investment projects profitable and, like a technological innovation, increases the demand for investment goods.

Figure 3-12 shows the effects of an increase in investment demand. At any given interest rate, the demand for investment goods (and also for loans) is higher—this is represented by a shift in the investment schedule to the right. The economy moves from the old equilibrium, point E_1, to the new equilibrium, point E_2.

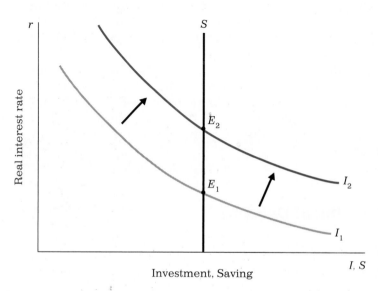

Investment, Saving

Figure 3-12 **An Increase in Desired Investment.**   An increase in the demand for investment goods, perhaps because of technological innovation or tax incentives for investment, shifts the investment schedule outward. At any given interest rate, the desired amount of investment is greater. The new equilibrium is the point where the new investment schedule crosses the vertical line representing saving. Because the amount of saving is fixed, the increase in investment demand raises the interest rate while leaving the equilibrium amount of investment unchanged.

The surprising implication of Figure 3-12 is that in equilibrium the amount of investment is unchanged. Under our assumptions, the fixed level of saving determines the equilibrium amount of investment; in other words, there is a fixed supply of loans. An increase in investment demand merely increases the equilibrium interest rate.

We would reach a different conclusion, however, if we modified our simple consumption function and allowed consumption to depend on the interest rate. Since the interest rate is the return to saving (as well

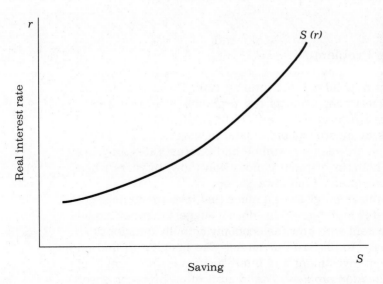

Figure 3-13 **Saving as a Function of the Interest Rate.** Here saving is positively related to the interest rate. A positive relation occurs if a higher interest rate induces people to consume less and save more.

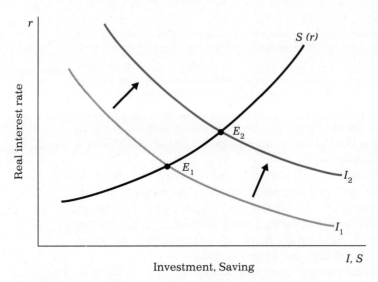

Figure 3-14 **An Increase in Desired Investment When Saving Depends on the Interest Rate.** If saving depends on the interest rate, then a shift outward in the investment schedule increases the interest rate and the amount of investment. The higher interest rate induces people to increase saving, which in turn allows investment to increase.

as the cost of borrowing), a higher interest rate might reduce consumption and increase saving. If so, the saving schedule would be upward-sloping, as it is in Figure 3-13, rather than vertical.

With an upward-sloping saving schedule, an increase in investment demand would increase both the equilibrium interest rate and the equilibrium quantity of investment. Figure 3-14 illustrates such a change. The increase in the interest rate causes households to consume less and save more. The decrease in consumption frees resources for investment.

//

F Y I **The Identification Problem**

In our model, investment depends on the interest rate. The higher the interest rate, the fewer investment projects are profitable. The investment schedule therefore slopes downward.

Economists who look at macroeconomic data, however, usually fail to find an obvious association between investment and interest rates. In years when interest rates are high, investment is not always low. In years when interest rates are low, investment is not always high.

How do we interpret this finding? Does it mean that investment does not depend on the interest rate? More generally, does it suggest that our model of the economy is inconsistent with how the economy actually functions?

Luckily, we do not have to discard our model. The inability to find an empirical relation between investment and interest rates is an example of what is called *the identification problem*. The identification problem arises when variables are related in more than one way. When we look at data, therefore, we are observing a combination of these different relationships, and it is difficult to "identify" any one of them.

To understand this problem more concretely, consider the relationships among saving, investment, and the interest rate. Suppose, on the one hand, that all changes in the interest rate resulted from changes in saving—that is, from shifts in the saving schedule. Then, as shown in the left-hand side of panel A in Figure 3-15, all changes would represent movement *along* the investment schedule. We would therefore observe a negative relationship between investment and interest rates. As the right-hand side of panel A shows, the data would trace out the investment schedule; that is, we would "identify" the investment schedule.

Suppose, on the other hand, that all changes in the interest rate resulted from technological innovations—that is, from shifts in the investment schedule. Then, as shown in panel B, all changes would represent movements *in* the investment schedule. We would observe a positive relationship between investment and interest rates. As the right-hand side of panel B shows, when we plot the data, we would "identify" the saving schedule.

More realistically, interest rates change sometimes because of shifts in the saving schedule and sometimes because of shifts in the investment schedule. In this mixed case, as shown in panel C, a plot of the data would reveal no recognizable relation between interest rates and the quantity of investment, just as economists observe in actual data. The moral of the story is simple and is applicable to many other situations: the empirical relationship we expect to observe depends crucially on which exogenous variables we think are changing.

//

A. Shifting Saving Schedules

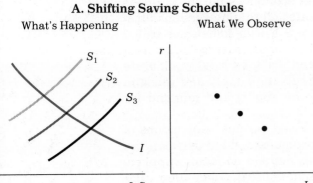

What's Happening   What We Observe

B. Shifting Investment Schedules

What's Happening   What We Observe

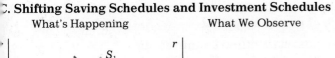

C. Shifting Saving Schedules and Investment Schedules

What's Happening   What We Observe

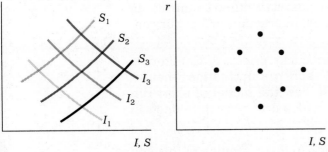

Figure 3-15 **Identifying the Investment Function.** When we look at data on interest rates r and investment I, what we find depends on which exogenous variables are changing. In panel A, the saving schedule is shifting, perhaps because of changes in fiscal policy; we would observe a negative association between r and I. In panel B, the investment schedule is shifting, perhaps because of technological innovations; we would observe a positive association between r and I. In the more realistic situation shown in panel C, both schedules are shifting. In the data, we would observe no association between r and I, which is in fact what researchers typically find.

3-5 Conclusion

In this chapter we have developed a model that explains the production, distribution, and allocation of the economy's output of goods and services. Because the model incorporates all the interactions illustrated in the circular flow diagram, Figure 3-1, it is sometimes called a *general equilibrium model*. The model emphasizes the adjustment of prices to equilibrate supply and demand. Factor prices equilibrate factor markets. The interest rate equilibrates the supply and demand for goods and services (or, equivalently, the supply and demand for loanable funds).

Throughout the chapter, we have discussed various applications of the model. The model can explain how income is divided between the factors of production and how factor prices depend on factor supplies. We have also used the model to discuss how fiscal policy alters the allocation of output among its alternative uses—consumption, investment, and government purchases—and how it affects the equilibrium interest rate.

At this point it is useful to review some of the simplifying assumptions we have made in this chapter. In the following chapters we relax some of these assumptions in order to address a greater range of questions.

- We have assumed that the capital stock, the labor force, and the technology are fixed. In Chapter 4 we see how changes over time in each of these lead to growth in the economy's output of goods and services.

- We have assumed that the labor force is fully employed. In Chapter 5 we examine the reasons for unemployment, and we see how public policy influences the level of unemployment.

- We have ignored the role of money, the asset with which goods and services are bought and sold. In Chapter 6 we discuss how money affects the economy and the influence of monetary policy.

- We have assumed that there is no trade with other countries. In Chapter 7 we consider how international interactions affect our conclusions.

- We have ignored the role of short-run sticky prices. In Chapters 8, 9, 10, and 11, we develop a model of short-run fluctuations that includes sticky prices. We then discuss how the model of short-run fluctuations relates to the model of national income developed in this chapter.

Before going on to these chapters, go back to the beginning of this one and make sure you can answer the four groups of questions about national income that begin the chapter.

Summary

1. The factors of production and the production technology determine the economy's output of goods and services. An increase in one of the factors of production or a technological advance raises output.

2. Competitive, profit-maximizing firms hire labor until the marginal product of labor (*MPL*) equals the real wage. Similarly, these firms hire capital until the marginal product of capital (*MPK*) equals the real rental price. Therefore, each factor of production is paid its marginal product. If the production function has constant returns to scale, all output is used to compensate the inputs.

3. The economy's output is used for consumption, investment, and government purchases. Consumption depends positively on disposable income. Investment depends negatively on the real interest rate. Government purchases and taxes are the exogenous variables of fiscal policy.

4. The real interest rate adjusts to equilibrate the supply and demand for the economy's output—or, equivalently, to equilibrate the supply of loanable funds (saving) and the demand for loanable funds (investment). A decrease in national saving, perhaps because of an increase in government purchases or a decrease in taxes, reduces the equilibrium amount of investment and raises the interest rate. An increase in investment demand, perhaps because of a technological innovation or a tax incentive for investment, also raises the interest rate. An increase in investment demand increases the quantity of investment only if higher interest rates stimulate additional saving.

KEY CONCEPTS

Factors of production	Accounting profit
Production function	Disposable income
Constant returns to scale	Consumption function
Factor prices	Marginal propensity to consume (*MPC*)
Competition	Nominal interest rate
Marginal product of labor (*MPL*)	Real interest rate
Diminishing marginal product	National saving (saving)
Real wage	Private saving
Marginal product of capital (*MPK*)	Public saving
Real rental price of capital	Crowding out
Economic profit	

QUESTIONS FOR REVIEW

1. What determines the amount of output an economy produces?

2. Explain how a competitive, profit-maximizing firm decides how much of each factor of production to demand.

3. What is the role of constant returns to scale in the distribution of income?

4. What determines consumption and investment?

5. Explain the difference between government purchases and transfer payments. Give two examples of each.

6. What makes the demand for the economy's output of goods and services equal the supply?

7. Explain what happens to consumption, investment, and the interest rate when the government increases taxes.

PROBLEMS AND APPLICATIONS

1. If a 10 percent increase in both capital and labor causes output to increase by less than 10 percent, the production function is said to exhibit *decreasing returns to scale*. If it causes output to increase by more than 10 percent, the production function is said to exhibit *increasing returns to scale*. Why might a production function exhibit decreasing or increasing returns to scale?

2. Suppose that the production function is Cobb-Douglas with parameter $\alpha = 0.3$.

   a. What fractions of income do capital and labor receive?

   b. Suppose that the labor force increases by 10 percent (for example, because of immigration). What happens to total output (in percent)? The rental price of capital? The real wage?

3. The government raises taxes by $100 billion. If the marginal propensity to consume is 0.6, what happens to

   a. Public saving?

   b. Private saving?

   c. National saving?

   d. Investment?

4. Suppose that an increase in consumer confidence raises consumers' expectations of future income and thus the amount they want to consume today. This might be interpreted as an upward shift in the consumption function. How does this shift affect investment and the interest rate?

5. Suppose that the government increases taxes and government purchases by equal amounts. What happens to the interest rate and investment in response to this balanced budget change? Does your answer depend on the marginal propensity to consume?

6. If consumption depended on the interest rate, how would that affect the conclusions reached in this chapter about the effects of fiscal policy?

Chapter **4**

Economic Growth

*The primary economic goal of my administration
is to achieve the highest possible rate of sustainable
economic growth. . . . Growth is the key to raising
living standards, to leaving a legacy of prosperity
for our children, to uplifting those most in need, and
to maintaining America's leadership in the world.*

George Bush

Over the course of U.S. economic history, we can observe substantial increases in national income. Each generation of Americans has enjoyed higher incomes than their parents, and these higher incomes have allowed them to consume greater quantities of goods and services. Higher levels of consumption have led to a higher standard of living.

To measure this economic growth, economists use data on gross national product, which measures the total income of everyone in the economy. The real GNP of the United States today is more than three times its 1950 level, and real GNP per person is more than twice its 1950 level. These differences in national income over time are large, and as the quotation at the beginning of this chapter suggests, they affect many facets of American society.

In any given year, we can also observe large differences in the standard of living among countries. Table 4-1 shows income per person in 1985 of the 12 most populous countries in the world. The United States tops the list with an income of $16,217 per person. Nigeria has an income per person of only $752—less than 5 percent of the figure for the United States.

Our goal in this chapter is to understand these differences in income over time and across countries. In Chapter 3 we identified the factors of production—capital and labor—and the production technology as the sources of the economy's output and, thus, of its income. Differences in income, therefore, must come from differences in capital, labor, and technology.

Our primary task is to develop a model of economic growth, called the **Solow growth model**. Our analysis in Chapter 3 enabled us to de-

Table 4-1   International Differences in the Standard of Living: 1985

Country	Income Per Person (in 1985 U.S. dollars)
United States	$16,217
West Germany	13,857
Japan	12,225
Soviet Union	8,109
Mexico	5,161
Brazil	4,247
China	3,163
Indonesia	1,624
Pakistan	1,492
India	971
Bangladesh	837
Nigeria	752

Source: Robert Summers and Alan Heston, "A New Set of International Comparisons of Real Product and Price Levels: Estimates for 130 Countries," *The Review of Income and Wealth* (March 1988): 1–25.
Note: Many analysts believe that faulty reporting of data in the Soviet Union and China render the statistics from those countries highly unreliable, and that income per person is actually much lower than reported.

scribe the production, distribution, and allocation of the economy's output at a given point in time. This analysis was static—a snapshot of the economy. To explain rising living standards, we must refine our analysis so that it describes changes in the economy over time. We want to make our analysis dynamic, so that it is more like a motion picture than a photograph. The Solow growth model shows how saving, population growth, and technological progress affect the growth of output over time. The model also identifies some of the reasons that countries vary so widely in their standards of living.[1]

Our second task is to examine how economic policy can influence the level and growth of the standard of living. Our model provides a framework with which we can address one of the most important questions in economics: How much of the economy's output should be consumed today, and how much should be saved for the future? Since an economy's saving equals its investment, saving determines the amount of capital an economy will have for future production. National saving is influenced directly and indirectly by government policies. Evaluating these policies requires an understanding of the costs and benefits to society of alternative rates of saving.

---

[1] The Solow growth model is named after economist Robert Solow and was developed in the 1950s and 1960s. In 1987 Solow won the Nobel Prize in Economics for his work in economic growth. The model was introduced in Robert M. Solow, "A Contribution to the Theory of Economic Growth," *Quarterly Journal of Economics* (February 1956): 65–94.

4-1 The Accumulation of Capital

We want to develop the Solow growth model in order to find out how growth in the capital stock, growth in the labor force, and advances in technology interact, and how they affect output. As our first step in building the model, we examine how the supply and demand for goods determine the accumulation of capital over time. To do this, we hold the labor force and the technology fixed. As the discussion proceeds, we relax these assumptions and make the analysis more realistic by first introducing changes in the labor force and then introducing changes in technology.

The Supply and Demand for Goods

The supply and demand for goods, which were crucial elements of our static model of the economy in Chapter 3, are also crucial elements of the Solow model. As in Chapter 3, the supply of goods determines how much output is produced at any given point in time, and the demand determines how this output is allocated to alternative uses.

The Supply of Goods and the Production Function   The supply of goods in the Solow model is based on the now familiar production function:

$$Y = F(K, L).$$

Output depends on the capital stock and the labor input. The Solow growth model assumes that the production function has constant returns to scale. Recall that a production function has constant returns to scale if

$$zY = F(zK, zL)$$

for any positive number z. That is, if we multiply both capital and labor by z, we also multiply the amount of output by z.

To keep the analysis simple, we express all quantities relative to the size of the labor force. Production functions with constant returns to scale are convenient for this purpose because output per worker depends only on the amount of capital per worker. To see that this is true, set $z = 1/L$ in the above definition of constant returns to scale to obtain

$$Y/L = F(K/L, 1).$$

This equation states that output per worker Y/L is a function of capital per worker K/L.

We use lowercase letters to denote quantities per worker. That is, $y = Y/L$ is output per worker, and $k = K/L$ is capital per worker. Then we can write the production function as

$$y = f(k),$$

where $f(k) = F(k,1)$. It is more convenient to analyze the economy using this production function relating capital per worker to output per worker. Figure 4-1 illustrates this production function.

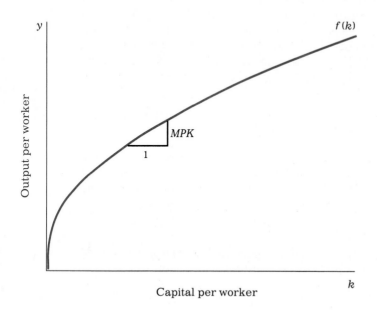

y | Output per worker

$f(k)$

MPK

1

Capital per worker

k

Figure 4-1 **The Production Function.** The production function shows how the amount of capital per worker k determines the amount of output per worker $y = f(k)$. The slope of the production function is the marginal product of capital: if k increases by 1 unit, y increases by *MPK* units. The production function becomes flatter as k increases, indicating diminishing marginal product.

The slope of this production function tells us how much extra output per worker we get from an extra unit of capital per worker. This amount is the marginal product of capital *MPK*. Mathematically, we say that

$$MPK = f(k + 1) - f(k).$$

Note that in Figure 4-1, as the amount of capital increases, the production function becomes flatter—that is, the slope decreases. The production function exhibits diminishing marginal product of capital: each incremental unit of capital produces less output than did the preceding unit. When there is only a little capital, an extra unit of capital is very useful and produces much additional output. When there is a lot of capital, an extra unit is less useful and produces less additional output.

The Demand for Goods and the Consumption Function The demand for goods in the Solow model comes from consumption and investment. In other words, output per worker y is divided between consumption per worker c and investment per worker i:

$$y = c + i.$$

This equation is the national income accounts identity for the economy. It differs slightly from the identity in Chapter 3 because it omits government purchases (which for present purposes we can ignore) and because it expresses y, c, and i as quantities per worker.

The Solow model assumes that the consumption function takes the simple form

$$c = (1 - s)y,$$

where s, the saving rate, is a number between zero and one. This consumption function states that consumption is proportional to income. Each year a fraction $(1 - s)$ of income is consumed, and a fraction s is saved.

To see what this consumption function implies, substitute $(1 - s)y$ for c in the national income accounts identity:

$$y = (1 - s)y + i.$$

Rearrange the terms to obtain

$$i = sy.$$

This equation states that investment, like consumption, is proportional to income. Since investment equals saving, the rate of saving s is also the fraction of output devoted to investment.

The Steady-State Level of Capital

Having introduced the two main ingredients of the Solow model—the production function and the consumption function—we can now examine how increases in the capital stock over time result in economic growth. The capital stock changes for two reasons:

- Investment adds to the stock of capital.

- Some of the old capital wears out—that is, it depreciates—lowering the stock of capital.

To understand how the capital stock changes, we must understand the determinants of investment and depreciation.

We noted previously that investment per worker is a fraction of output per worker, sy. By substituting the production function for y, we can express investment per worker as a function of the capital stock per worker:

$$i = sf(k).$$

The higher the level of capital k, the greater the levels of output $f(k)$ and investment i. This equation, which incorporates both the production and consumption functions, relates the existing stock of capital k to the

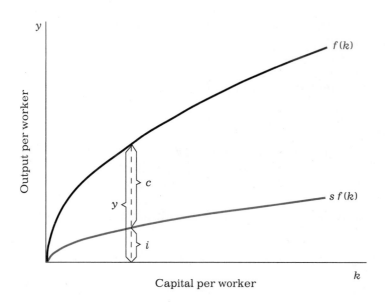

Figure 4-2 **Output, Consumption, and Investment.** The saving rate *s* determines the split of output between consumption and investment. At any level of capital *k*, output is $f(k)$, investment is $sf(k)$, and consumption is $f(k) - sf(k)$.

accumulation of new capital *i*. Figure 4-2 shows how the saving rate determines the split of output between consumption and investment for every value of *k*.

To incorporate depreciation into the model, we assume that a certain fraction δ of the capital stock wears out each year. We call δ the *depreciation rate*. For example, if capital lasts an average of 25 years, then the depreciation rate is 4 percent per year (δ = 0.04). Thus, the amount of capital that depreciates each year is δ*k*. Figure 4-3 shows how depreciation depends on the capital stock.

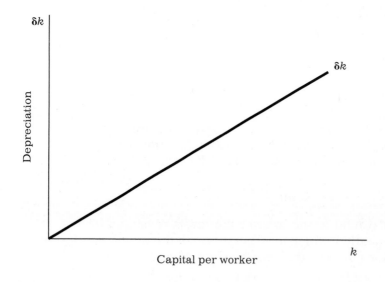

Figure 4-3 **Depreciation.** A constant fraction δ of the capital stock wears out every year. Depreciation is therefore proportional to the capital stock.

We can express the impact of investment and depreciation on the capital stock with this adjustment equation:

$$\text{Change in Capital Stock} = \text{Investment} - \text{Depreciation}$$
$$\Delta k = i - \delta k,$$

where Δk is the change in the capital stock between one year and the next. Because investment equals saving, we can write the change in the capital stock as

$$\Delta k = sf(k) - \delta k.$$

This equation states that the change in the capital stock equals investment $sf(k)$ minus the depreciation of existing capital δk.

Figure 4-4 graphs investment and depreciation for different levels of the capital stock k. The higher the capital stock, the greater the amounts of output and investment. Yet the higher the capital stock, the greater also the amount of depreciation.

Figure 4-4 shows that there is a single capital stock at which the amount of investment equals the amount of depreciation. If the economy has this capital stock, the capital stock will not change over time because the two forces acting to change it—investment and depreciation—just balance. That is, at this level of the capital stock, $\Delta k = 0$. We call this the **steady-state** level of capital and designate it as k^*.

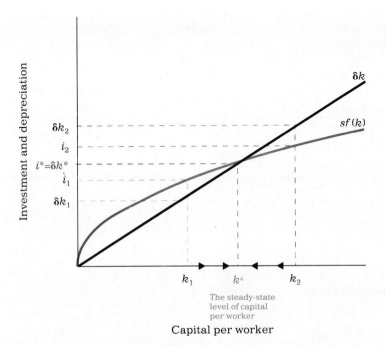

Figure 4-4 **Investment, Depreciation, and the Steady State.** Since the saving rate s is constant and saving equals investment, the amount of investment is $sf(k)$. Since capital depreciates at a constant rate δ, the amount of depreciation is δk. The steady-state level of capital k^* is the level at which investment equals depreciation; at k^* the two curves cross. Below k^* investment exceeds depreciation, so the capital stock grows. Above k^* investment is less than depreciation, so the capital stock shrinks.

Approaching the Steady State

The steady state represents the long-run equilibrium of the economy. Regardless of the level of capital with which the economy begins, it eventually ends up in the steady state.

Suppose that the capital stock starts below the steady-state level, such as at level k_1 in Figure 4-4. In this case, the level of investment exceeds the amount of depreciation. Thus, over time, the capital stock will rise and will continue to grow—along with output—until it approaches the steady state k^*.

Similarly, suppose that the capital stock starts above the steady-state level, such as at level k_2. In this case, investment is less than depreciation: capital is wearing out faster than it is being replaced. Thus, the capital stock will fall, again approaching the steady-state level. Once the capital stock reaches the steady-state level, investment equals depreciation, and the capital stock neither increases nor decreases.

Approaching the Steady State: A Numerical Example

Let's use a numerical example to see how the Solow model works and how the economy approaches the steady state. For this example, we assume that the production function takes the form

$$Y = K^{1/2}L^{1/2}.$$

This production function is Cobb-Douglas with the parameter α equal to 1/2.

The per-worker production function $f(k)$ is derived as follows. Begin with the definition of y:

$$y = \frac{Y}{L}.$$

Substitute the production function for Y:

$$y = \frac{K^{1/2}L^{1/2}}{L}.$$

Rearrange to obtain

$$y = \left(\frac{K}{L}\right)^{1/2}$$

Since $k = K/L$, this becomes

$$y = k^{1/2}.$$

This equation can also be written as

$$y = \sqrt{k}.$$

Output per worker is the square root of capital per worker.

To complete this example, we assume that 30 percent of output is saved ($s = 0.3$), that 10 percent of the capital stock depreciates every year ($\delta = 0.1$), and that the economy starts off with 4 units of capital stock per worker ($k = 4$). We can now examine what happens to this economy over time.

We begin by looking at the production and allocation of output in the first year. According to the production function, the 4 units of capital per worker produce 2 units of output per worker. Since 70 percent of output is consumed and 30 percent is saved and invested, $c = 1.4$ and $i = 0.6$. Also, since 10 percent of the capital stock depreciates, $\delta k = 0.4$. With investment of 0.6 and depreciation of 0.4, the change in the capital stock is $\Delta k = 0.2$. Therefore, the second year begins with 4.2 units of capital per worker.

Table 4-2 shows how this economy progresses year by year. Every year, new capital is added and output grows. Over many years, the economy reaches a steady state with 9 units of capital per worker. In this steady state, investment of 0.9 exactly offsets depreciation of 0.9, so that the capital stock and output are no longer growing.

Table 4-2   **Approaching the Steady State: A Numerical Example**

Assumptions: $y = \sqrt{k}$	$s = 0.3$		$\delta = 0.1$		Initial $k = 4.0$	
Year	k	y	c	i	δk	Δk
1	4.000	2.000	1.400	0.600	0.400	0.200
2	4.200	2.049	1.435	0.615	0.420	0.195
3	4.395	2.096	1.467	0.629	0.440	0.189
4	4.584	2.141	1.499	0.642	0.458	0.184
5	4.768	2.184	1.529	0.655	0.477	0.178
.						
.						
.						
10	5.602	2.367	1.657	0.710	0.560	0.150
.						
.						
.						
25	7.321	2.706	1.894	0.812	0.732	0.080
.						
.						
.						
100	8.962	2.994	2.096	0.898	0.896	0.002
.						
.						
.						
∞	9.000	3.000	2.100	0.900	0.900	0.000

Following the progress of the economy for many years is one way to find the steady-state capital stock, but another way requires fewer calculations. Recall that

$$\Delta k = sf(k) - \delta k.$$

This equation shows how k evolves over time. Since $\Delta k = 0$ in the steady state, we know that

$$0 = sf(k^*) - \delta k^*,$$

or, equivalently,

$$\frac{k^*}{f(k^*)} = \frac{s}{\delta}.$$

This equation for the capital-output ratio provides a way of finding the steady-state level of capital per worker, k^*. Substituting in our example, we obtain

$$\frac{k^*}{\sqrt{k^*}} = \frac{0.3}{0.1}.$$

We can solve for k^* by squaring both sides of this equation. We find that the steady-state capital stock is 9 units per worker, confirming the calculation of the steady state in Table 4-2.

CASE STUDY 4-1

Japanese and German Postwar Economic Growth

Japan and Germany are two success stories of economic growth. Today they are economic superpowers, but in 1945 at the end of World War II the economies of both countries were in shambles. The war had destroyed much of their capital stocks. In the decades after the war, however, these two countries experienced some of the most rapid growth rates on record. Between 1948 and 1972, output per person grew at 8.2 percent per year in Japan and 5.7 percent per year in Germany, compared to only 2.2 percent per year in the United States.

Are the postwar experiences of Japan and Germany so surprising from the standpoint of the Solow growth model? Consider an economy in steady state. Now suppose that a war destroys some of its capital stock. (In Figure 4-4, the capital stock falls from k^* to k_1.) Not surprisingly, the level of output is immediately reduced. But as long as the saving rate—the fraction of output devoted to saving and investment—is unchanged, the economy will eventually return to its old steady state. To do this requires a period of high growth. This high growth occurs because, at the lower capital stock, investment exceeds depreciation—that is, output increases because more capital is added by investment than is removed by depreciation. Hence, although destroying part of the capital stock immediately reduces output, it is followed by higher than normal growth. The "miracle" of rapid growth in Japan and Germany, as it is often described in the business press, is in many ways what the Solow model predicts for countries in which war has greatly reduced the capital stock.

The explanation of Japanese and German economic growth is not this simple, however. Both countries also have higher saving rates than the United States, and thus are approaching a different steady state. To understand more fully the differences among countries, we must consider the effects of different saving rates.

Changes in the Saving Rate

Consider what happens to an economy when the saving rate increases. Figure 4-5 illustrates such a change. We assume that the economy begins in a steady state with saving rate s_1 and capital stock k_1^*. The saving rate then increases from s_1 to s_2, causing an upward shift in the $sf(k)$ curve. At the initial saving rate s_1 and the initial capital stock k_1^*, the amount of investment just offset the amount of depreciation. The moment after the saving rate rises, investment is higher, but the capital stock and thus depreciation are unchanged. Therefore, investment exceeds depreciation. The capital stock will gradually rise until the economy reaches the new steady state, k_2^*, which has a higher capital stock and a higher level of output than the old steady state.

The Solow model shows that the saving rate is a key determinant of the steady-state capital stock. If the saving rate is high, the economy will have a large capital stock and a high level of output. If the saving rate is low, the economy will have a small capital stock and a low level of output.

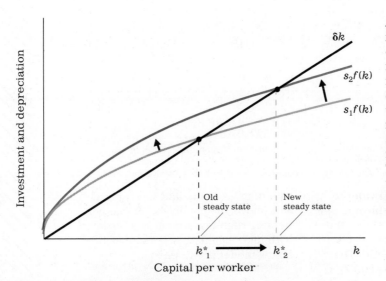

Investment and depreciation

δk

$s_2 f(k)$

$s_1 f(k)$

Old steady state

New steady state

k_1^* ⟶ k_2^* k

Capital per worker

Figure 4-5 **An Increase in the Saving Rate.** An increase in the saving rate s implies that the amount of investment at any given capital stock is higher. It therefore shifts the saving function upward. At the old steady state, investment now exceeds depreciation. The capital stock rises until the economy reaches a new steady state with more capital and output.

What is the relationship between saving and economic growth? Higher saving leads to faster growth, but only in the short run. An increase in the rate of saving raises growth until the economy reaches the new steady state. If the economy maintains a high saving rate, it will also maintain a large capital stock and a high level of output, but it will not maintain a high rate of growth forever.

CASE STUDY 4-2

Saving in Rich and Poor Countries

According to the Solow model, a nation that devotes a high fraction of its income to saving will have a high steady-state capital stock and thus also a high level of income. This is not just a theoretical conclusion, however—it is also supported by considerable evidence.

Figure 4-6 is a scatterplot of data from 112 countries. The figure includes most of the world's economies. (It excludes major oil-producing countries and countries that were communist during the period 1960–

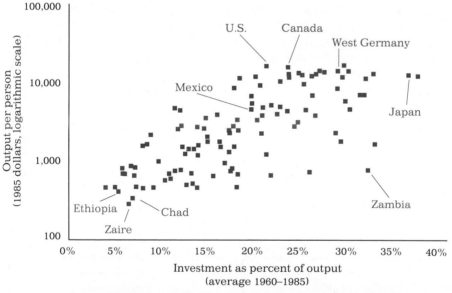

Source: Adapted from Robert Summers and Alan Heston, "A New Set of International Comparisons of Real Product and Price Levels: Estimates for 130 Countries," *The Review of Income and Wealth* (March 1988): 1–25.

Figure 4-6 **International Evidence on Investment Rates and Income per Person.** This scatterplot shows the experience of 112 countries, each represented by a single point. The horizontal axis shows the country's rate of investment, and the vertical axis shows the country's income per person. High investment is associated with high income per person, as the Solow model predicts.

1985.) The data show a positive relationship between the fraction of output devoted to investment and the level of income per person. That is, countries with high rates of investment, such as the United States, Canada, and Japan, usually have high incomes, whereas countries with low rates of investment, such as Ethiopia, Zaire, and Chad, have low incomes. The international evidence is therefore consistent with the Solow model's prediction that the rate of saving is an important determinant of whether a country is rich or poor.

The figure also shows, however, that the fit between saving and income is far from perfect. There must be other determinants of income per person. We return to the international differences later in the chapter to see what other variables enter the picture.

4-2 The Golden Rule Level of Capital

Now that we have examined the link between the rate of saving and the steady-state levels of capital and income, we can discuss what amount of capital accumulation is optimal. Later, in Section 4-5, we describe how government policies alter the saving rate and thus influence the economy's levels of capital and output. But first, in this section, we present the theory behind these policy decisions. To keep our analysis as simple as possible, we assume that a policymaker can simply choose the rate of saving and thus the steady state. We consider what steady state the policymaker should choose.

Comparing Steady States

When choosing a steady state, the policymaker's goal is to maximize the economic well-being of the individual members of society. Individuals themselves do not care about the amount of capital in the economy, or even the amount of output. They care about the amount of goods and services they can consume. Thus, a policymaker interested in economic well-being would want to choose the steady state with the highest level of consumption. The steady state with the highest consumption is called the **Golden Rule level of capital accumulation** and is denoted k^{**}.[2]

How can we tell whether an economy is at the Golden Rule level? To answer this question, we must first determine steady-state consumption per worker. Then we can see which steady state provides the greatest consumption.

---

[2] Edmund Phelps, "The Golden Rule of Accumulation: A Fable for Growthmen," *American Economic Review* 51 (September 1961): 638–643.

To find steady-state consumption per worker, we begin with the national income accounts identity

$$y = c + i,$$

and rearrange it as

$$c = y - i.$$

That is, consumption is simply output minus investment. Since we want to find steady-state consumption, we substitute steady-state values for output and investment. Steady-state output per worker is $f(k^*)$, where k^* is the steady-state capital stock per worker. Furthermore, in the steady state, the capital stock is not changing; therefore, investment is equal to depreciation, δk^*. Substituting $f(k^*)$ for y and δk^* for i, we can write steady-state consumption per worker as

$$c^* = f(k^*) - \delta k^*.$$

This equation states that steady-state consumption is the difference between steady-state output and steady-state depreciation. It shows that increased capital has two effects on steady-state consumption: it causes greater output, but more output must be used to replace depreciating capital.

Figure 4-7 graphs steady-state output and steady-state depreciation as a function of the steady-state capital stock. Steady-state consumption is the gap between output and depreciation. This figure shows that there

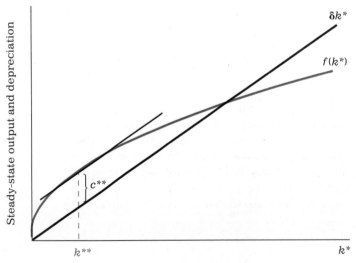

Figure 4-7 Steady-State Consumption. The economy's output is used for consumption or investment. In the steady state, investment equals depreciation. Therefore, steady-state consumption is the difference between output $f(k^*)$ and depreciation δk^*. The steady state that maximizes steady-state consumption is called the Golden Rule. The Golden Rule capital stock is denoted k^{**}, and the Golden Rule consumption is denoted c^{**}.

is one level of the capital stock—the Golden Rule level k^{**}—that maximizes consumption.

When we compare steady states, we must take into account the effects of higher capital on both output and depreciation. On the one hand, if the capital stock is below the Golden Rule level, an increase in the capital stock increases output more than depreciation, so that consumption rises. In this case, the production function is steeper than the δk^* line, so the gap between these two curves—which equals consumption—grows as k^* rises. On the other hand, if the capital stock is above the Golden Rule level, an increase in the capital stock reduces consumption, since the increase in output is smaller than the increase in depreciation. In this case, the production function is flatter than the δk^* line, so the gap between the curves—consumption—shrinks as k^* rises. At the Golden Rule level of capital, the production function and the δk^* line have the same slope, and consumption is at its greatest level.

To make the point somewhat differently, suppose that the economy starts at some capital stock k^* and that the policymaker is considering increasing the capital stock to $k^* + 1$. The amount of extra output would then be $f(k^* + 1) - f(k^*)$, which is the marginal product of capital *MPK*. The amount of extra depreciation from having one more unit of capital is the depreciation rate δ. The net effect of this extra unit of capital on consumption is then $MPK - \delta$, which is the marginal product of capital less the depreciation rate. If the steady-state capital stock is below the Golden Rule level, increases in capital increase consumption because the marginal product of capital is greater than the depreciation rate. If the steady-state capital stock exceeds the Golden Rule level, increases in capital reduce consumption because the marginal product of capital is less than the depreciation rate. Therefore, the following condition describes the Golden Rule:

$$MPK = \delta.$$

At the Golden Rule level of capital, the marginal product of capital equals the rate of depreciation. In other words, at the Golden Rule, the marginal product net of depreciation, $MPK - \delta$, equals zero.

Comparing Steady States: A Numerical Example

Consider the decision of a policymaker choosing a steady state in the following economy. The production function is the same as in our earlier example

$$y = \sqrt{k}.$$

Output per worker is the square root of capital per worker. Depreciation is again 10 percent of capital. This time, the policymaker chooses the saving rate s and thus the economy's steady state.

To see the outcomes available to the policymaker, recall that the steady-state capital-output ratio is

$$\frac{k^*}{f(k^*)} = \frac{s}{\delta}.$$

In this economy, this equation becomes

$$\frac{k^*}{\sqrt{k^*}} = \frac{s}{0.1}.$$

Squaring both sides of this equation yields a solution for the steady-state capital stock. We find

$$k^* = 100s^2.$$

Using this result, we can compute the steady-state capital stock for any saving rate.

Table 4-3 presents calculations showing the steady states that result from various saving rates. We see that higher saving leads to higher capital, which in turn leads to higher output and higher depreciation. Steady-state consumption, the difference between output and depreciation, first rises with higher saving rates and then declines. Consumption is highest when the saving rate is 0.5; this saving rate produces the Golden Rule steady state.

Table 4-3   Comparing Steady States: A Numerical Example

Assumptions:
$y = \sqrt{k}$
$\delta = 0.1$

s	k^*	y^*	δk^*	c^*	MPK	MPK $-\ \delta$
0.0	0.0	0.0	0.0	0.0	∞	∞
0.1	1.0	1.0	0.1	0.9	0.500	0.400
0.2	4.0	2.0	0.4	1.6	0.250	0.150
0.3	9.0	3.0	0.9	2.1	0.167	0.067
0.4	16.0	4.0	1.6	2.4	0.125	0.025
0.5	25.0	5.0	2.5	2.5	0.100	0.000
0.6	36.0	6.0	3.6	2.4	0.083	-0.017
0.7	49.0	7.0	4.9	2.1	0.071	-0.029
0.8	64.0	8.0	6.4	1.6	0.062	-0.038
0.9	81.0	9.0	8.1	0.9	0.056	-0.044
1.0	100.0	10.0	10.0	0.0	0.050	-0.050

Another way to identify the Golden Rule steady state is from the marginal product of capital. Recall from Chapter 3 that, for the Cobb-

Douglas production function, $MPK = \alpha y/k$. Using this formula, and the fact that $\alpha = 1/2$ in our example, the last two columns of Table 4-3 present the value of $MPK - \delta$ in the different steady states. Note, again, that in the Golden Rule steady state, the marginal product of capital net of depreciation equals zero.

The Transition to the Golden Rule Steady State

Let's now make our policymaker's problem more realistic. So far, we have been assuming that the policymaker can simply choose the economy's steady state. In this case, the policymaker would choose the steady state with highest consumption—the Golden Rule steady state. But now suppose that the economy has reached a steady state other than the Golden Rule. What happens to consumption, investment, and capital when the economy makes the transition between steady states? Might the impact of the transition deter the policymaker from trying to achieve the Golden Rule?

We must consider two cases: the economy might begin with more capital than in the Golden Rule steady state, or with less. The second case—too little capital—presents far greater difficulties; it forces the policymaker to evaluate the benefits of current consumption relative to future consumption. As we see in Section 4-5, this is the situation of actual economies, including that of the United States.

Starting With More Capital Than in the Golden Rule   We first consider the case in which the economy begins with more capital than it would have in the Golden Rule steady state. In this case, the policymaker should pursue policies aimed at reducing the rate of saving in order to reduce the steady-state capital stock. Suppose that these policies succeed and that, at some point in time—call it t_0—the saving rate falls to the level that will eventually lead to the Golden Rule steady state.

Figure 4-8 shows what happens to output, consumption, and investment when the saving rate is reduced. The reduction in the saving rate causes an immediate increase in the level of consumption and a decrease in the level of investment. Investment is now lower than depreciation, so the economy is no longer in a steady state. Gradually, as the capital stock falls, output, consumption, and investment also fall to the new steady state. Because the new steady state is the Golden Rule steady state, we know that the level of consumption is now higher than it was before the change in the saving rate, even though output and investment are lower.

Note that, compared to the old steady state, consumption is higher not just in the new steady state but also along the entire path to it. When the capital stock exceeds the Golden Rule level, reducing saving is clearly a good policy, for it increases consumption at every point in time.

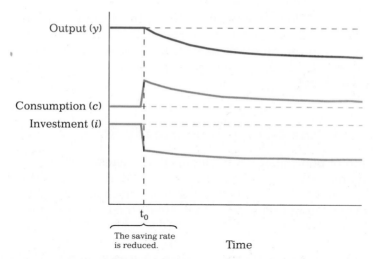

Output (y)

Consumption (c)
Investment (i)

t_0

The saving rate
is reduced.   Time

Figure 4-8 **Reducing Saving When Starting
With More Capital Than in the Golden Rule
Steady State.**   This figure shows what happens over time to output, consumption, and
investment when the economy begins with
more capital than the Golden Rule and the
saving rate is reduced. The reduction in the
saving rate (at time t_0) causes an immediate
increase in consumption and an equal decrease in investment. Over time, as the capital stock falls, output, consumption, and investment fall together. Since the economy
began with too much capital, the new
steady state has a higher level of consumption than the initial steady state.

Starting With Less Capital Than in the Golden Rule   When the economy
begins with less capital than in the Golden Rule steady state, the policymaker must increase the rate of saving to reach the Golden Rule.
Figure 4-9 shows what happens. The increase in the rate of saving at
time t_0 causes an immediate fall in consumption and a rise in investment.
Over time, higher investment causes the capital stock to rise. As capital
accumulates, output, consumption, and investment gradually increase,
eventually approaching the new steady-state levels. Because the initial
steady state was below the Golden Rule, the increase in saving eventually leads to a higher level of consumption than that which prevailed
initially.

Does the increase in saving leading to the Golden Rule steady state
raise economic welfare? Eventually, it does, because the steady-state
level of consumption is higher. But achieving that new steady state requires an initial period of reduced consumption. Note the contrast to
the case in which the economy begins above the Golden Rule. *When the
economy begins above the Golden Rule, reaching the Golden Rule produces higher consumption at all points in time. When the economy begins
below the Golden Rule, reaching the Golden Rule requires reducing consumption today to increase consumption in the future.*

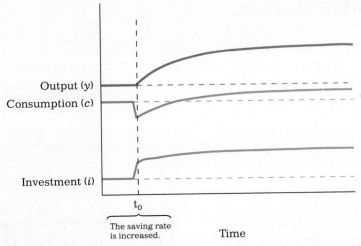

Output (*y*)

Consumption (*c*)

Investment (*i*)

t_0

The saving rate
is increased.

Time

Figure 4-9 **Increasing Saving When Starting With Less Capital Than in the Golden
Rule Steady State.** This figure shows what
happens over time to output, consumption,
and investment when the economy begins
with less capital than the Golden Rule, and
the saving rate is increased. The increase in
the saving rate (at time t_0) causes an immediate drop in consumption and an equal
jump in investment. Over time, as the capital stock grows, output, consumption, and
investment increase together. Since the
economy began with less capital than the
Golden Rule, the new steady state has a
higher level of consumption than the
initial steady state.

Deciding whether to try to reach the Golden Rule steady state is
especially difficult because the population of consumers changes over
time. Reaching the Golden Rule achieves the highest steady-state level
of consumption and thus benefits future generations. But, when the economy is below the Golden Rule, reaching the Golden Rule requires raising
investment and thus lowering the consumption of current generations.

When choosing whether to increase capital accumulation, the policymaker must compare the welfare of different generations. A policymaker who cares more about current generations than about future
generations may decide not to pursue policies to reach the Golden Rule
steady state. By contrast, a policymaker who cares about all generations
equally will choose to reach the Golden Rule. Even though current generations will consume less, an infinite number of future generations will
benefit by moving to the Golden Rule.

Thus, optimal capital accumulation depends crucially on how we
weigh the interests of current and future generations. The biblical
Golden Rule tells us to "do unto others as you would have them do unto
you." If we heed this advice, we give all generations equal weight. In this
case, it is optimal to reach the Golden Rule level of capital—which is
why it is called the "Golden Rule."

4-3 Population Growth

The basic Solow model shows that capital accumulation, by itself, cannot explain persistent economic growth. High rates of saving lead to high growth temporarily, but the economy eventually approaches a steady state in which capital and output are constant. To explain the persistent economic growth that we observe in most parts of the world, we must expand the Solow model to incorporate the other two sources of economic growth: population growth and technological progress. In this section we add population growth to the model.

Instead of assuming that the population is fixed, as we did in Sections 4-1 and 4-2, we now suppose that the population and the labor force grow at a constant rate n. For example, in the United States, the population grows about 1 percent per year, so $n = 0.01$. This means that if 150 million people are working one year, then 151.5 million (1.01×150) are working the next year, and 153.015 million (1.01×151.5) the year after that, and so on.

The Steady State With Population Growth

How does population growth affect the steady state? To answer this question, we must discuss how population growth, along with investment and depreciation, influences the accumulation of capital per worker. As we noted before, investment raises the capital stock, and depreciation reduces it. But now there is a third force acting to change the amount of capital per worker: the growth in the number of workers causes capital per worker to fall.

We continue to let lowercase letters stand for quantities per worker. Thus, $k = K/L$ is capital per worker, and $y = Y/L$ is output per worker. Keep in mind, however, that the number of workers is growing over time.

The change in the capital stock per worker is

$$\Delta k = i - \delta k - nk.$$

The three terms on the right-hand side of this equation show the effects of new investment, depreciation, and population growth on the per-worker capital stock. New investment increases k, whereas depreciation and population growth decrease k. We have seen this equation before in the special case in which $n = 0$.

To make use of this equation, substitute $sf(k)$ for i and rearrange terms. The equation can then be written as

$$\Delta k = sf(k) - (\delta + n)k.$$

We have added together the effects of depreciation and population growth. The equation shows that population growth reduces the accumulation of capital per worker much the way depreciation does. Depreciation reduces *k* by making the capital stock wear out, whereas population growth reduces *k* by spreading the capital stock more thinly among a larger population of workers.

You can think of the term $(\delta + n)k$ as *break-even investment*: the amount of investment necessary to keep the capital stock per worker constant. Break-even investment includes the depreciation of existing capital, which equals δk. It also includes the amount of investment necessary to provide new workers with capital. The amount of investment necessary for this purpose is nk, because there are *n* new workers for each old worker, and because *k* is the amount of capital for each worker.

To see what determines the steady-state level of capital per worker, we use Figure 4-10, which extends the analysis of Figure 4-4 to include the effects of population growth. An economy is in a steady state if capital per worker *k* is unchanging. We designate the steady-state value of *k* as *k**. If *k* is less than *k**, investment is greater than break-even investment, so *k* rises. If *k* is greater than *k**, investment is less than break-even investment, so *k* falls.

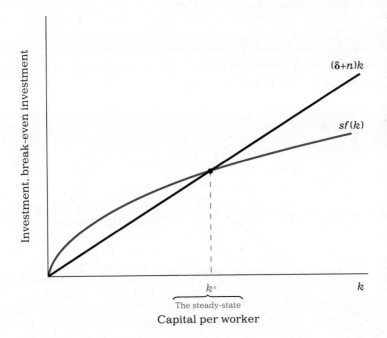

Figure 4-10 Population Growth in the Solow Model. Like depreciation, population growth is one reason the capital stock per worker shrinks. If *n* is the rate of population growth and δ is the rate of depreciation, then $(\delta + n)k$ is the amount of investment necessary to keep constant the capital stock per worker *k*. For the economy to be in a steady state, investment $sf(k)$ must offset the effects of depreciation and population growth $(\delta + n)k$—this is represented by the crossing of the two curves.

In the steady state, the positive effect of investment on the capital stock per worker just balances the negative effects of depreciation and population growth. That is, at *k**, $\Delta k = 0$ and $i^* = \delta k^* + nk^*$. Once the economy is in the steady state, investment has two purposes. Some of it (δk^*) replaces the depreciated capital, and the rest (nk^*) provides the new workers with the steady-state amount of capital.

The Effects of Population Growth

Population growth alters the basic Solow model in three ways. First, it brings us closer to explaining persistent economic growth. In the steady state with population growth, capital per worker and output per worker are unchanging. Because the number of workers is growing at rate n, total capital and total output are also growing at the rate n. Hence, population growth cannot explain persistent growth in standards of living, because output per worker is constant in the steady state. But population growth can explain persistent growth in total output.

Second, population growth gives us another explanation of why some countries are rich and others are poor. Consider the effects of an increase in population growth. Figure 4-11 shows that an increase in the rate of population growth from n_1 to n_2 reduces the steady-state level of capital per worker from k_1^* to k_2^*. Since k^* is lower, and since $y^* = f(k^*)$, the level of output per worker y^* is also lower. Thus, the Solow model predicts that countries with higher population growth will have lower levels of GNP per person.

Finally, population growth affects the Golden Rule level of capital accumulation. Remember that consumption per worker is

$$c = y - i.$$

Since the steady-state output is $f(k^*)$ and steady-state investment is $(\delta + n)k^*$, we can write steady-state consumption as

$$c^* = f(k^*) - (\delta + n)k^*.$$

The level of k^* that maximizes consumption is the one at which

$$MPK = \delta + n,$$

or equivalently,

$$MPK - \delta = n.$$

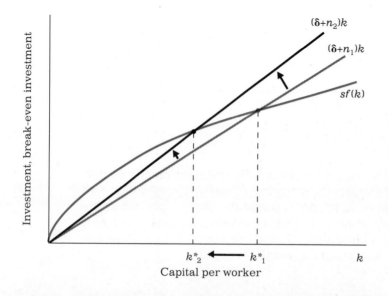

Figure 4-11 **The Impact of Population Growth.** An increase in the rate of population growth n shifts the line representing population growth and depreciation upward. The new steady state has a lower level of capital per worker. Thus, the Solow model predicts that economies with higher rates of population growth will have lower levels of capital per worker and therefore lower incomes.

At the Golden Rule steady state, the marginal product of capital net of depreciation equals the rate of population growth.

CASE STUDY 4-3

Population Growth in Rich and Poor Countries

According to the Solow model, a nation with a high rate of population growth will have a low steady-state capital stock per worker and thus also a low level of income per worker. In other words, high population growth tends to impoverish a country, because it is hard to maintain a high level of capital per worker when the number of workers is growing quickly. To see whether the evidence supports this conclusion, we again turn to international data.

Figure 4-12 is a scatterplot of data for the same 112 countries examined in Case Study 4-2. The figure shows that countries with high rates of population growth tend to have low levels of income per person. Thus, the evidence is consistent with the Solow model's prediction that the rate of population growth is one of the determinants of a country's standard of living.

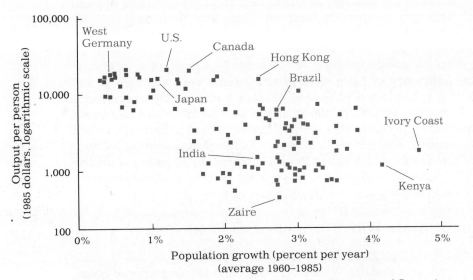

Source: Adapted from Robert Summers, "A New Set of International Comparisons of Real Product and Price Levels: Estimates for 130 Countries," *The Review of Income and Wealth* (March 1988): 1–25.

Figure 4-12 **International Evidence on Population Growth and Income per Person.** This figure is a scatterplot of 112 countries showing that countries with high rates of population growth tend to have low levels of income per person, as the Solow model predicts.

4-4 Technological Progress

We now incorporate technological progress, the third source of economic growth, into the Solow model. So far, we have been assuming an
unchanging relationship between the inputs of capital and labor and the
output of goods and services. The model can be modified, however, to
allow for exogenous increases in society's ability to produce.

The Efficiency of Labor

To incorporate technological progress, we must return to the production
function that relates total capital K and total labor L to total output Y.
Thus far, the production function has been

$$Y = F(K, L).$$

We now write the production function as

$$Y = F(K, L \times E),$$

where E is a new variable called the **efficiency of labor**. The efficiency
of labor depends on the health, education, skill, and knowledge of the
labor force.
     The term $L \times E$ is the labor force measured in **efficiency units**. It
takes into account the number of workers L and the efficiency of each
worker E. This new production function states that total output Y depends on the number of units of capital K and on the number of efficiency
units of labor, $L \times E$.
     The simplest assumption about technological progress is that it
causes the efficiency of labor E to grow at some constant rate g. For
example, if $g = 0.02$, then each unit of labor becomes 2 percent more
efficient each year: output increases as if the labor force had increased
by an additional 2 percent. This form of technological progress is called
labor-augmenting, and g is called the rate of labor-augmenting technological progress. Since the labor force L is growing at rate n, and the
efficiency of each unit of labor E is growing at rate g, the number of
efficiency units of labor $L \times E$ is growing at rate $n + g$.

The Steady State With Technological Progress

Expressing technological progress as labor-augmenting makes it analogous to population growth. We analyze the economy in terms of quantities per efficiency unit of labor. That is, let $k = K/(L \times E)$ stand for
capital per efficiency unit, and $y = Y/(L \times E)$ stand for output per efficiency unit. With these definitions, we can again write $y = f(k)$.
     Our analysis of the economy proceeds just as it did with population
growth. The equation showing the evolution of k over time now changes
to

$$\Delta k = sf(k) - (\delta + n + g)k.$$

The new term involving g, the rate of technological progress, arises because k is the amount of capital per efficiency unit of labor. If g is high, then the number of efficiency units is growing quickly, and the amount of capital per efficiency unit tends to fall.

As shown in Figure 4-13, the inclusion of technological progress does not substantially alter our analysis of the steady state. There is one level of k, denoted k^*, at which capital per efficiency unit and output per efficiency unit are constant. This steady state represents the long-run equilibrium of the economy.

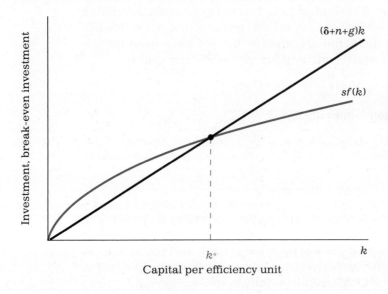

Figure 4-13 Introducing Technological Progress. Including labor-augmenting technological progress at rate g affects our analysis in much the same way as did population growth. Now that k is defined as the amount of capital per efficiency unit of labor, increases in the number of efficiency units because of technological progress tend to decrease k. In the steady state, investment $sf(k)$ offsets the reductions in k due to depreciation, population growth, and technological progress.

The Effects of Technological Progress

Table 4-4 shows how some variables behave in the steady state with technological progress. As we have just seen, capital per efficiency unit k is constant in the steady state. Since $y = f(k)$, output per efficiency unit is also constant. Remember, though, that the number of efficiency units per worker is growing at rate g. Hence, output per worker ($Y/L = y \times E$) also grows at rate g. Total output [$Y = y \times (E \times L)$] grows at rate $n + g$.

Table 4-4   Steady-State Growth Rates in the Solow Model With Technological Progress

Variable	Symbol	Growth Rate
Capital per efficiency unit	$k = K/(E \times L)$	0
Output per efficiency unit	$y = Y/(E \times L) = f(k)$	0
Output per worker	$Y/L = y \times E$	g
Total output	$Y = y \times (E \times L)$	$n + g$

Thus, with the addition of technological progress, our model can finally explain the persistent increases in standards of living that we observe. That is, we have shown that technological progress can lead to sustained growth in output per worker. By contrast, a high rate of saving leads to a high rate of growth only until the steady state is reached. Once the economy is in steady state, the rate of growth of output per worker depends only on the rate of technological progress. *The Solow model shows that only technological progress can explain persistently rising living standards.*

The introduction of technological progress also modifies the condition for the Golden Rule. The Golden Rule level of capital accumulation is defined as the steady state that maximizes consumption per efficiency unit of labor. Following the same arguments that we have used before, we can show that steady-state consumption per efficiency unit is

$$c^* = f(k^*) - (\delta + n + g)k^*.$$

Steady-state consumption is maximized if

$$MPK = \delta + n + g,$$

or

$$MPK - \delta = n + g.$$

That is, at the Golden Rule level of capital, the net marginal product of capital, $MPK - \delta$, equals the rate of growth of total output, $n + g$. Because actual economies experience both population growth and technological progress, we must use this condition to evaluate whether they have more or less capital than at the Golden Rule steady state.

CASE STUDY 4-4

Steady-State Growth in the United States

Now that we have introduced technological progress into the Solow model and explained persistent growth in standards of living, we should ask how well our theory fits the facts. The Solow model predicts that technological progress causes many variables to grow together. In the steady state, output per worker and the capital stock per worker both grow at the rate of technological progress. Data for the United States over the past 40 years show that output per worker-hour and the capital stock per worker-hour have in fact grown at approximately the same rate—about 2 percent per year.

Technological progress also affects factor prices. Problem 8(d) at the end of the chapter asks you to show that, in the steady state, the real wage grows at the rate of technological progress. The real rental price of capital, however, is constant over time. Again, these predictions hold true for the United States. Over the past 40 years, the real wage has increased about 2 percent per year; it thus increased about the same amount as real GNP per worker-hour. Yet the real rental price of capital (measured as real capital income divided by the capital stock) has remained about the same.

The Solow model's prediction about factor prices—and the success of this prediction—is especially noteworthy when contrasted with Karl Marx's theory of the development of capitalist economies. Marx predicted that the return to capital would decline over time and that this would lead to economic and political crisis. Economic history has not supported Marx's prediction, which partly explains why we now study Solow's theory of growth rather than Marx's.

4-5 Saving, Growth, and Economic Policy

Having used the Solow model to uncover the relationships among the different sources of economic growth, we can now use the theory to help guide our thinking about economic policy. Here we address three policy questions. First, should our society save more or save less? Second, how can economic policy influence the rate of saving? Third, how can economic policy influence the rate of technological progress?

Evaluating the Rate of Saving

The Solow growth model shows how the saving rate determines the steady-state levels of capital and output. One particular saving rate produces the Golden Rule steady state, which maximizes consumption per worker and thus economic well-being. These results help us address the first question for economic policy: Is the rate of saving in the economy too low, too high, or about right?

If the marginal product of capital net of depreciation is greater than the growth rate, the economy is operating with less capital than in the Golden Rule steady state. In this case, increasing the rate of saving will eventually lead to a steady state with higher consumption. On the other hand, if the net marginal product of capital is below the growth rate, the economy is operating with too much capital, and the rate of saving should be reduced. To evaluate a nation's rate of capital accumulation, one needs to compare the growth rate and the net return to capital.

This comparison requires an estimate of the growth rate $(n + g)$ and an estimate of the net marginal product of capital $(MPK - \delta)$. Real GNP in the United States grows an average of 3 percent per year, so $n + g = 0.03$. We can estimate the net marginal product of capital from the following three facts:

1. The capital stock is about 2.5 times one year's GNP.

2. Depreciation of capital is about 10 percent of GNP.

3. Capital's share in output is about 30 percent.

Fact 1 states that $k = 2.5y$, and fact 2 states that $\delta k = 0.1y$. Therefore,

$$\begin{aligned} \delta &= (\delta k)/k \\ &= (0.1y)/(2.5y) \\ &= 0.04. \end{aligned}$$

That is, about 4 percent of the capital stock depreciates each year. To obtain the marginal product of capital from facts 1 and 3, recall our conclusion in Chapter 3 that capital is paid its marginal product. Therefore,

$$\begin{aligned} \text{Capital's Share} &= (MPK \times K)/Y \\ &= MPK \times (K/Y). \end{aligned}$$

Now substitute the numbers from facts 1 and 3 into this equation,

$$0.30 = MPK \times 2.5.$$

This implies that

$$MPK = 0.30/2.5 = 0.12.$$

Thus, the marginal product of capital is about 12 percent per year. The net marginal product of capital ($MPK - \delta$) is about 8 percent per year, well in excess of the average growth rate of 3 percent per year.

The high return to capital implies that the capital stock in the U.S. economy is well below the Golden Rule level. This finding suggests that policymakers should want to increase the rate of saving and investment. In fact, for many years they have. Increasing capital formation has long been a high priority of economic policy.

Changing the Rate of Saving

Public policy can raise national saving in two ways: directly by increasing public saving, and indirectly by providing incentives to stimulate private saving.

Public saving is the difference between government revenue and government spending. If spending exceeds revenue, the government runs a budget deficit, which is negative saving. The government funds the deficit by issuing government bonds—in other words, by borrowing. As we saw in Chapter 3, the government budget deficit crowds out investment. The reduced capital stock is part of the burden of the national debt on future generations. On the other hand, if revenue exceeds spending, the government runs a budget surplus. It can then retire some of the national debt and stimulate investment.

Private saving can be affected by various sorts of government policies. Although not included in the Solow model, the saving decisions of households may depend on the rate of return; the greater the return to saving, the more attractive saving becomes. Tax incentives, such as tax-exempt retirement accounts for individuals and the investment tax credit for corporations, increase the rate of return and thus encourage private saving.

CASE STUDY 4-5

Social Security and Saving

One government program that is often thought to affect private saving is the Social Security system. Social Security is a transfer system that is designed to maintain individuals' income in their old age. A payroll tax on the working-age population pays for these transfers to the elderly. This system reduces the need for individuals to save for their own retirement and, therefore, may also reduce capital formation.

To counteract the reduction in national saving attributed to Social Security, many economists have proposed that the Social Security system be reformed. The system is now *pay as you go*—most of the current tax receipts are paid out to the current elderly population. One suggestion is that Social Security should be *fully funded*. Under this plan, the government would put aside in a trust fund the payments a generation makes when it is young and working; the government would then pay out the principal and accumulated interest to this same generation when it has reached old age and retired. Under a fully funded Social Security system, an increase in public saving would offset the reduction in private saving.

Because the impact of Social Security on national saving is potentially so important, many economists have attempted to estimate the magnitude of this effect. The evidence, however, is mixed. Therefore, economists do not agree about whether Social Security reduces national saving or, if it does, by how much.[3]

Encouraging Technological Progress

The Solow model shows that prolonged growth in income per worker must come from technological progress. The Solow model, however, takes technological progress as exogenous; it does not explain it. Unfortunately, the determinants of technological progress are not well understood.

---

[3] To get the flavor of the debate, see Martin S. Feldstein, "Social Security, Induced Retirement, and Aggregate Capital Accumulation," *Journal of Political Economy* 82 (September/October 1974): 905–926; Dean R. Leimer and Selig D. Lesnoy, "Social Security and Private Saving: New Time Series Evidence," *Journal of Political Economy* 90 (June 1982): 606–629; and Martin S. Feldstein, "Social Security and Private Saving: Reply," *Journal of Political Economy* 90 (June 1982): 630–642.

Despite this limited understanding, many public policies are designed to stimulate technological progress by encouraging research. For example, the patent system gives a temporary monopoly to inventors of new products. The tax code offers tax breaks for research and development. Government agencies, such as the National Science Foundation, subsidize basic research. All of these public policies encourage individuals to devote resources to technological innovation.

CASE STUDY 4-6

The Worldwide Slowdown in Economic Growth

One of the most perplexing problems that policymakers have faced over the past 20 years is the worldwide slowdown in economic growth that began in the early 1970s. Table 4-5 presents data on the growth in real GNP per person for the seven major world economies. Growth in the United States fell from 2.2 percent to 1.7 percent. Other countries experienced similar or more severe declines.

Table 4-5	The Slowdown in Growth Around the World	
	Growth in Output Per Person (percent per year)	
Country	1948–72	1972–88
Canada	2.9	2.6
France	4.3	2.1
West Germany	5.7	2.2
Italy	4.9	2.8
Japan	8.2	3.3
United Kingdom	2.4	2.1
United States	2.2	1.7

Source: Angus Maddison, *Phases of Capitalist Development* (Oxford: Oxford University Press, 1982); International Financial Statistics.

Studies have shown that the slowdown in growth is attributable to a slowdown in the rate at which the production function is improving over time. The appendix to this chapter explains how economists measure the improvement in the production function using a variable called *total factor productivity*; this variable is closely related to the efficiency of labor in the Solow model. The growth in total factor productivity has slowed by about 1 percent per year starting around 1970. Accumulated over many years, even such a small change substantially affects economic welfare: because of this 1 percent decline in productivity growth, real income in the United States is about 20 percent lower today than it would have been.

Many economists have attempted to explain this adverse change. Here are some of their explanations:

- The composition of the labor force has been changing. The entrance of the younger baby-boom generation into the labor force beginning in the 1970s lowered the average level of experience and, therefore, the productivity of labor.

- An increase in government regulations, such as those to protect the environment, requires firms to use less productive production methods. The regulations reduce growth in productivity and incomes (even if they are socially desirable).

- Large changes in oil prices in the 1970s caused by OPEC, the oil cartel, made some of the capital stock prematurely obsolete. Firms may have retired some of their machinery that was heavily dependent on fuel.

- The world has started to run out of new ideas about how to produce. We have entered an age of slower technological progress.

Which of these suspects is the culprit? All of them have some plausibility, but it is difficult to prove beyond a reasonable doubt that any one of them is guilty. The worldwide slowdown in economic growth largely remains a mystery.[4]

4-6 Conclusion: Beyond the Solow Model

Although the Solow model provides the best framework with which to start studying economic growth, it is only a beginning. The model simplifies many aspects of the world, and it omits many others altogether. Economists who study economic growth try to build more sophisticated models that allow them to address a broader range of questions.

These advanced models usually turn one of the exogenous variables in the Solow model into an endogenous variable. For example, the Solow model takes the rate of saving as exogenous. As we see in Chapter 15, consumption arises from the decisions of households about how much to consume today and how much to save for the future. More sophisticated growth models replace the consumption function of the Solow

---

[4] For various views on the growth slowdown, see "Symposium: The Slowdown in Productivity Growth," *The Journal of Economic Perspectives* 2 (Fall 1988): 3–98. This symposium is a collection of papers written by Zvi Griliches, Dale W. Jorgenson, Mancur Olson, and Michael J. Boskin, and includes a summary by Stanley Fischer.

model with an explicit theory of household behavior.[5] As another example, the Solow model takes the rate of population growth as exogenous. Some more sophisticated models explicitly incorporate fertility decisions to see how the choice regarding family size interacts with other aspects of economic growth.[6]

Perhaps most important, economists have tried to build models to explain the level of and growth in the efficiency of labor. Some economists have emphasized the acquisition of knowledge and skills through education—that is, the accumulation of *human capital*.[7] Others have suggested that technological progress occurs as a beneficial by-product of certain economic activities; such a by-product is called an *externality*. For example, new and improved production processes may be devised during the process of accumulating capital. If this speculation is correct, then the benefits of capital accumulation to society may be much greater than the Solow model suggests.[8]

The Solow model shows that sustained growth in standards of living can arise only from technological progress. Therefore, our understanding of economic growth will not be complete until we understand how private decisions and public policy affect technological progress. That is a topic on which much more research is needed.

Summary

1. The Solow growth model shows that an economy's rate of saving determines the size of its capital stock and thus its level of production. The higher the rate of saving, the higher the stock of capital and the higher the level of output.

2. An increase in the rate of saving causes a period of high growth until the new steady state is reached. In the long run, the saving rate does not affect the growth rate. Sustained growth of output per worker depends on technological progress.

3. The level of capital that maximizes consumption is called the Golden Rule level. At this level, the net marginal product of capital equals the growth rate of output. Estimates for actual economies, such as the United

---

[5] The integration of the household's consumption decision and the model of capital accumulation can take several forms. To appreciate the different approaches, see Chapters 2 and 3 of the graduate-level textbook by Olivier Jean Blanchard and Stanley Fischer, *Lectures on Macroeconomics* (Cambridge, Mass.: MIT Press, 1989).

[6] Robert J. Barro and Gary S. Becker, "Fertility Choice in a Model of Economic Growth," *Econometrica* (March 1989): 481–502.

[7] Robert E. Lucas, Jr., "On the Mechanics of Economic Development," *Journal of Monetary Economics* 22 (1988): 3–42; N. Gregory Mankiw, David Romer, and David N. Weil, "A Contribution to the Empirics of Economic Growth," *Quarterly Journal of Economics*, forthcoming.

[8] Paul Romer, "Crazy Explanations for the Productivity Slowdown," *NBER Macroeconomics Annual* 2 (1987): 163–201.

States, suggest that the capital stock is well below the Golden Rule level. To reach the Golden Rule requires increased investment and thus lower consumption for current generations.

4. Economic policymakers often claim that the rate of capital accumulation should be increased. Increased public saving and tax incentives for private saving are two ways to encourage capital accumulation.

5. The Solow model shows that an economy's rate of population growth is another determinant of the standard of living. The higher the rate of population growth, the lower the level of output per worker.

6. In the early 1970s, the rate of growth fell substantially in most industrialized countries. The cause of this slowdown is not well understood.

KEY CONCEPTS

Solow growth model

Steady state

Golden Rule level of capital
 accumulation

Efficiency of labor

Efficiency units of labor

Labor-augmenting technological progress

QUESTIONS FOR REVIEW

1. In the Solow model, how does the saving rate affect the steady-state level of income? How does it affect the steady-state rate of growth?

2. Why might an economic policymaker choose the Golden Rule level of capital?

3. Might a policymaker choose a steady state with more capital than in the Golden Rule steady state? With less capital than in the Golden Rule steady state?

4. In the Solow model, how does the rate of population growth affect the steady-state level of income? How does it affect the steady-state rate of growth?

5. What determines the steady-state rate of growth of income per worker?

6. How can economic policy influence the saving rate?

7. What has happened to the rate of growth over the past 40 years?

PROBLEMS AND APPLICATIONS

1. Country A and country B both have the production function

$$Y = F(K, L) = K^{1/2}L^{1/2}.$$

a. Does this production function have constant returns to scale? Explain.

b. What is the per-worker production function, $y = f(k)$?

c. Assume that neither country has population growth or technological progress and that 5 percent of capital depreciates each year. Assume further that country A saves 10 percent of output each year and country B saves 20 percent of output each year. Use your answer from part b and the steady-state condition that investment equals depreciation to find the steady-state level of capital per worker for each country. Then find the steady-state levels of income per worker and consumption per worker.

d. Suppose that both countries start off with a capital stock per worker of 2. What are the levels of income per worker and consumption per worker? Remembering that the change in the capital stock is investment less depreciation, use a calculator to show how the capital stock per worker will evolve over time in both countries. For each year, calculate income per worker and consumption per worker. How many years will it be before the consumption in country B is higher than the consumption in country A?

2. In the discussion of German and Japanese postwar growth, the text describes what happens when part of the capital stock is destroyed in a war. By contrast, suppose that a war does not directly affect the capital stock, but that casualties reduce the labor force.

a. What is the immediate impact on total output and on output per person?

b. Assuming that the saving rate is unchanged and that the economy was in a steady state before the war, what happens subsequently to output per worker in the postwar economy? Is the growth rate of output per worker after the war smaller or greater than normal?

3. The 1983 *Economic Report of the President* contained the following statement: "Devoting a larger share of national output to investment would help restore rapid productivity growth and rising living standards." Do you agree with this claim? Explain.

4. Suppose the production function is

$$y = \sqrt{k}.$$

a. Solve for the steady-state value of y as a function of s, n, g, and δ.

b. A developed country has a saving rate of 28 percent and a population growth rate of 1 percent per year. A less-developed country has a saving rate of 10 percent and a population growth rate of 4 percent per year. In both countries, $g = 0.02$ and $\delta = 0.04$. Find the steady-state value of y for each country.

c. What policies might the less-developed country pursue to raise its level of income?

5. In the United States, gross capital income is about 30 percent of GNP; the average growth in output is about 3 percent per year; the depreciation rate is about 4 percent per year; and the capital-output ratio is about 2.5. Suppose that the production function is Cobb-Douglas, so that the capital share in output is constant, and that the United States has been in a steady state.

a. What must the saving rate be in the initial steady state? (*Hint:* Use the steady-state relationship, $sy = (\delta + n + g)k$.)

b. What is the marginal product of capital in the initial steady state?

c. Suppose that public policy raises the saving rate so that the economy reaches the Golden Rule level of capital. What will the marginal product of capital be at the Golden Rule steady state? Compare the marginal product at the Golden Rule steady state to the marginal product in the initial steady state. Explain.

d. What will the capital-output ratio be at the Golden Rule steady state? (*Hint:* For the Cobb-Douglas production function, the capital-output ratio is simply related to the marginal product of capital. See the discussion of the Cobb-Douglas function in Chapter 3.)

e. What must the saving rate be to reach the Golden Rule steady state?

6. One view of the consumption function, sometimes advocated by Marxist economists, is that workers have high propen-

sities to consume and capitalists have low propensities to consume. To explore the implications of this view, suppose an economy consumes all wage income and saves all capital income. Show that if the factors of production earn their marginal product, this economy reaches the Golden Rule level of capital accumulation.

(*Hint:* Begin with the identity that saving equals investment. Then use the steady-state condition that investment is just enough to keep up with depreciation, population growth, and technological progress, and the fact that saving equals capital income in this economy.)

7. Many demographers predict that the United States will have zero population growth in the twenty-first century, in contrast to average population growth of about 1 percent per year in the twentieth century. Use the Solow model to forecast the effect of this slowdown in population growth on the growth of total output and the growth of output per person. Consider the effects both in the steady state and in the transition between steady states.

8. Prove each of the following statements about the steady state with population growth and technological progress.

a. The capital-output ratio is constant.

b. The capital and labor shares of income are constant. (*Hint:* Recall the definition $MPK = f(k + 1) - f(k)$.)

c. Total capital income and total labor income both grow at the rate of population growth plus the rate of technological progress $(n + g)$.

d. The real rental price of capital is constant, and the real wage grows at the rate of technological progress g. (*Hint:* The real rental price of capital equals total capital income divided by the capital stock, and the real wage equals total labor income divided by the labor force.)

9. The amount of education the typical person receives varies substantially among countries. Suppose you were to compare a country with a highly educated labor force and a country with a less educated labor force. Assume that the countries have the same saving rate, the same population growth rate, and the same rate of technological progress. Using the Solow model, what would you predict for the following variables?

a. The rate of growth of total income.

b. The level of income per worker.

c. The real rental price of capital.

d. The real wage.

10. In the Solow model, population growth leads to growth in total output, but not in output per worker. Do you think this would still be true if the production function exhibited increasing or decreasing returns to scale? Explain. (For the definitions of increasing and decreasing returns to scale, see Chapter 3, Problems and Applications, No. 1.)

11. Suppose that the production function does not exhibit diminishing marginal product of capital and that, instead, the production function is

$$y = Ak,$$

where A is a positive constant.

a. Show that this production function implies that the marginal product of capital is constant.

b. Show that, in this case, a higher saving rate leads to a permanently higher growth rate. (Remember that growth in a variable X is defined to be $\Delta X/X$.)

c. Why does this conclusion differ from that in the Solow model?

d. Do you think this production function is reasonable? Explain.

Accounting for the Sources of Economic Growth

Real GNP in the United States has grown an average of 3 percent per year over the past 40 years. What accounts for this growth? In Chapter 3 we linked the output of the economy to the factors of production—capital and labor—and to the production technology. Here we divide the growth in output into three different sources: increases in capital, increases in labor, and advances in technology. This breakdown provides us with a measure of the rate of technological change.

Increases in the Factors of Production

We first examine how increases in the factors of production contribute to increases in output. We assume there is no technological change. Therefore, the production function relating output Y to capital K and labor L does not change over time:

$$Y = F(K, L).$$

In this case, the amount of output changes only because the amount of capital or labor changes.

Increases in Capital   First, consider changes in capital. If the amount of capital increases by ΔK units, how much does the amount of output increase? To answer this question, we need to recall the definition of the marginal product of capital MPK:

$$MPK = F(K + 1, L) - F(K, L).$$

The marginal product of capital tells us how much output increases when capital increases by one unit. Therefore, when capital increases by ΔK units, output increases by approximately $MPK \times \Delta K$.[9]

---

[9] Note the word "approximately" here. This answer is only an approximation because the marginal product of capital varies: it falls as the amount of capital increases. An exact answer would take into account that each unit of capital has a different marginal product. If the change in K is not too large, however, the approximation of a constant marginal product is very accurate.

For example, suppose that the marginal product of capital is 1/5; that is, an additional unit of capital increases the amount of output produced by one-fifth of a unit. If we increase the amount of capital by 10 units, we can compute the amount of additional output as follows:

$$\Delta Y = \quad MPK \quad \times \quad \Delta K$$
$$= 1/5 \, \frac{\text{output}}{\text{capital}} \times 10 \text{ capital}$$
$$= 2 \text{ output.}$$

By increasing capital by 10 units, we obtain 2 more units of output per year. Thus, we use the marginal product of capital to convert changes in capital into changes in output.

Increases in Labor   Next, consider changes in labor. If the amount of labor increases by ΔL units, how much does output increase? We answer this question the same way we answered the question about capital. The marginal product of labor *MPL* tells us how much output changes when labor increases by one unit—that is,

$$MPL = F(K, L + 1) - F(K, L).$$

Therefore, when the amount of labor increases by ΔL units, output increases by approximately $MPL \times \Delta L$.

For example, suppose that the marginal product of labor is 2; that is, an additional unit of labor increases the amount of output produced by 2 units. If we increase the amount of labor by 10 units, we can compute the amount of additional output as follows:

$$\Delta Y = \quad MPL \quad \times \quad \Delta L$$
$$= 2 \, \frac{\text{output}}{\text{labor}} \times 10 \text{ labor}$$
$$= 20 \text{ output.}$$

By increasing labor by 10 units, we obtain 20 more units of output per year. We thus use the marginal product of labor to convert changes in labor into changes in output.

Increases in Capital and Labor   Finally, let's consider the more realistic case in which both factors of production change. Suppose that the amount of capital increases by ΔK and the amount of labor increases by ΔL. The increase in output then comes from two sources: more capital and more labor. We can divide this increase into the two sources using the marginal products of the two inputs:

$$\Delta Y = (MPK \times \Delta K) + (MPL \times \Delta L).$$

The first term in parentheses is the increase in output resulting from the increase in capital, and the second term in parentheses is the increase in output resulting from the increase in labor. This equation shows us how to attribute growth to each factor of production.

We now want to convert this last equation into a form that is easier to interpret and apply to the available data. First, with some algebraic rearrangement, the equation becomes[10]

$$\frac{\Delta Y}{Y} = \left(\frac{MPK \times K}{Y}\right)\frac{\Delta K}{K} + \left(\frac{MPL \times L}{Y}\right)\frac{\Delta L}{L}.$$

This form of the equation relates the growth rate of output, $\Delta Y/Y$, to the growth rate of capital, $\Delta K/K$, and the growth rate of labor, $\Delta L/L$.

Next, we need to find some way to measure the terms in parentheses in the last equation. In Chapter 3 we showed that the marginal product of capital equals its real rental price. Therefore, $MPK \times K$ is the total return to capital, and $(MPK \times K)/Y$ is capital's share of output. Similarly, the marginal product of labor equals the real wage. Therefore, $MPL \times L$ is the total compensation that labor receives, and $(MPL \times L)/Y$ is labor's share of output. Under the assumption that the production function has constant returns to scale, Euler's theorem tells us that these two shares sum to one. In this case, we can write

$$\frac{\Delta Y}{Y} = \alpha\frac{\Delta K}{K} + (1 - \alpha)\frac{\Delta L}{L}.$$

where α is capital's share and $(1 - \alpha)$ is labor's share.

This last equation gives us a simple formula for showing how changes in inputs lead to changes in output. In particular, we must weight the growth rates of the inputs by the factor shares. As we discussed in Chapter 3, capital's share in the United States is about 30 percent—that is, $\alpha = 0.30$. Therefore, a 10 percent increase in the amount of capital $(\Delta K/K = 0.10)$ leads to a 3 percent increase in the amount of output $(\Delta Y/Y = 0.03)$. Similarly, a 10 percent increase in the amount of labor $(\Delta L/L = 0.10)$ leads to a 7 percent increase in the amount of output $(\Delta Y/Y = 0.07)$.

Technological Progress

Thus far in our analysis of the sources of growth, we have assumed that the production function does not change over time. In practice, however, technological progress improves the production function. For the same amount of inputs, we get more output today than we did in the past. We now extend our analysis to allow for technological progress.

---

[10] *Mathematical Note:* To see that this is equivalent to the previous equation, note that we can multiply both sides by Y and thereby cancel Y from three places in which it appears. We can cancel the K in the top and bottom of the first term on the right-hand side and the L from the top and bottom of the second term on the right-hand side. These algebraic manipulations turn this equation into the previous one.

We include the effects of the changing technology by writing the production function as

$$Y = AF(K, L),$$

where A is a measure of the current level of technology called *total factor productivity*. Output now increases not only because of increases in capital and labor but also because of increases in total factor productivity. If total factor productivity increases by 1 percent and if the inputs are unchanged, then output increases by 1 percent.

Allowing for a changing technology adds an additional term to our equation accounting for economic growth:

$$\frac{\Delta Y}{Y} = \alpha\frac{\Delta K}{K} + (1 - \alpha)\frac{\Delta L}{L} + \frac{\Delta A}{A}$$

$$\begin{array}{ccccc} \text{Growth in} & = & \text{Contribution} & + & \text{Contribution} & + & \text{Growth in Total} \\ \text{Output} & & \text{of Capital} & & \text{of Labor} & & \text{Factor Productivity.} \end{array}$$

This is the key equation of growth accounting. It identifies and allows us to measure the three sources of growth: changes in the amount of capital, in the amount of labor, and in total factor productivity.

Because total factor productivity is not observable directly, it is measured indirectly. We have data on the growth in output, capital, and labor; we also have data on capital's share of output. From these data and the growth accounting equation, we can compute the growth in total factor productivity to make sure that everything adds up:

$$\frac{\Delta A}{A} = \frac{\Delta Y}{Y} - \alpha\frac{\Delta K}{K} - (1 - \alpha)\frac{\Delta L}{L}.$$

$\Delta A/A$ is the change in output that cannot be explained by changes in inputs. Thus, the growth in total factor productivity is computed as a residual—that is, as the amount of output growth that remains after we have accounted for the determinants of growth that we can measure. Indeed, $\Delta A/A$ is sometimes called the *Solow residual*, after Robert Solow, who first showed how to compute it.[11]

Total factor productivity can change for many reasons. Changes most often arise because of increased knowledge about production methods. The Solow residual is therefore often viewed as a measure of technological progress. Yet other factors, such as education and government regulation, can affect total factor productivity as well. For example, if higher public spending raises the quality of education, then workers may become more productive and output may rise, which implies higher total

---

[11] Robert M. Solow, "Technical Change and the Aggregate Production Function," *Review of Economics and Statistics* 39 (1957): 312–320. One might ask how growth in labor efficiency E relates to growth in total factor productivity. One can show that $\Delta A/A = (1 - \alpha)\Delta E/E$, where α is capital's share.

factor productivity. As another example, if government regulations require firms to purchase capital to reduce pollution or increase worker safety, then the capital stock may rise without any increase in measured output, which implies lower total factor productivity. *Thus, total factor productivity captures anything that changes the relation between measured inputs and measured output.*

The Sources of Growth in the United States

Having learned how to measure the sources of economic growth, we now look at the data. Table 4-1A uses U.S. data to measure the contributions of the three sources of growth between 1950 and 1985.

Table 4-1A   Accounting for Economic Growth in the United States

Years	Output Growth	Source of Growth		
		Capital	Labor	Total Factor Productivity
	$\dfrac{\Delta Y}{Y}$ =	$\alpha \dfrac{\Delta K}{K}$ +	$(1-\alpha)\dfrac{\Delta L}{L}$ +	$\dfrac{\Delta A}{A}$
	(average percent increase per year)			
1950–1960	3.3	1.2	0.5	1.6
1960–1970	3.8	1.2	1.0	1.6
1970–1980	2.8	0.8	1.3	0.7
1980–1985	2.5	1.1	0.9	0.5
1950–1985	3.2	1.1	0.9	1.2

Note: Y is real GNP, K is the nonresidential capital stock, and L is total employment times average weekly hours. These calculations assume $\alpha = 0.3$.
Source: U.S. Department of Commerce, U.S. Department of Labor, and the author's calculations.

This table shows that real GNP has grown an average of 3.2 percent per year since 1950. Of this 3.2 percent, 1.1 percent is attributable to increases in the capital stock, 0.9 percent to increases in total hours worked, and 1.2 percent to increases in total factor productivity. These data show that increases in capital, labor, and productivity have contributed almost equally to economic growth in the United States.

Table 4-1A also shows that the growth in total factor productivity slowed substantially around 1970. In Case Study 4-6 we discussed some hypotheses to explain this productivity slowdown.

MORE PROBLEMS AND APPLICATIONS

1. In the economy of Solovia, the owners of capital get two-thirds of national income, and the workers receive one-third.

   a. The men of Solovia stay at home performing household chores, while the women work in factories. If some of the men decided to start working outside of the home, so that the labor force increased by 5 percent, what would happen to the measured output of the economy? Does labor productivity—defined as output per worker—increase, decrease, or stay the same? Does total factor productivity increase, decrease, or stay the same?

   b. In year 1, the capital stock was 6, the labor input was 3, and output was 12. In year 2, the capital stock was 7, the labor input was 4, and output was 14. What happened to total factor productivity between the two years?

2. Labor productivity is defined as Y/L, the amount of output divided by the amount of labor input. Start with the growth accounting equation and show that the growth in labor productivity depends on growth in total factor productivity and growth in the capital-labor ratio. In particular, show that

$$\frac{\Delta(Y/L)}{Y/L} = \frac{\Delta A}{A} + \alpha\frac{\Delta(K/L)}{K/L}.$$

Hint: You many find the following mathematical trick helpful. If $z = wx$, then the growth rate of z is approximately the growth rate of w plus the growth rate of x. That is,

$$\Delta z/z = \Delta w/w + \Delta x/x.$$

3. Suppose an economy described by the Solow model is in a steady state with population growth n of 1.0 percent per year and technological progress g of 2.0 percent per year. Total output and total capital are thus growing at 3.0 percent per year. Suppose further that the capital share of output is 0.3. If you used the growth accounting equation to divide output growth into three sources—capital, labor, and total factor productivity—how much would you attribute to each source? Compare your results to the figures we found for the United States in Table 4-1.

Chapter 5

Unemployment

Unemployment is the macroeconomic problem that affects individuals most directly and severely. For most people, the loss of a job means a reduced living standard and psychological distress. It is therefore no surprise that unemployment is a frequent topic of political debate. Many politicians have used the "misery index"—the sum of the inflation and unemployment rates—to measure the health of the economy and the success or failure of economic policies.

Economists study unemployment to identify its causes and to help improve the public policies that affect the unemployed. Some of these policies, such as job training programs, assist people in regaining employment. Others, such as unemployment insurance, alleviate some of the economic hardships that the unemployed face. Still others affect the prevalence of unemployment inadvertently. For example, most economists believe that laws prescribing a high minimum wage lead to greater unemployment. By pointing out a policy's unintended side effects, economists can help policymakers to evaluate alternative options.

When discussing the labor market in previous chapters, we ignored unemployment. In our study of national income in Chapter 3 and of economic growth in Chapter 4, we simply assumed that the economy reaches full employment. In reality, of course, not everyone in the labor force has a job all the time: all free-market economies experience some unemployment.

Figure 5-1 presents the rate of unemployment—the percentage of the labor force unemployed—in the United States since 1948. The figure shows that there is always some unemployment, although the amount fluctuates from year to year. In this chapter we begin our study of unemployment by discussing why there is unemployment and what determines its level. We do not study the year-to-year fluctuations in the rate of unemployment until Part Three of this book, which examines short-run economic fluctuations. Here we examine the determinants of the **natural rate of unemployment**—the average rate of unemployment around which the economy fluctuates.

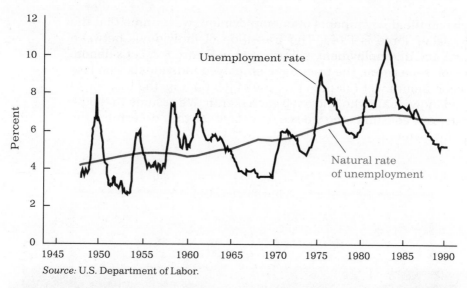

Source: U.S. Department of Labor.

Figure 5-1 **The Unemployment Rate and the Natural Rate of Unemployment in the United States.** There is always some unemployment. The natural rate of unemployment is the average level around which the unemployment rate fluctuates. (The natural rate of unemployment for any particular year is estimated here by averaging all the unemployment rates from ten years earlier to ten years later.)

5-1 Job Loss, Job Finding, and the Natural Rate of Unemployment

Every day some workers lose or quit their jobs, and some unemployed workers are hired. This perpetual ebb and flow determines the fraction of the labor force that is unemployed. In this section we develop a model of labor-force dynamics which shows what determines the natural rate of unemployment.[1]

Let L denote the labor force, E the number of employed workers, and U the number of unemployed workers. Because every worker is either employed or unemployed,

$$L = E + U.$$

Thus, the labor force is the sum of the employed and unemployed. The rate of unemployment is U/L.

[1] Robert E. Hall, "A Theory of the Natural Rate of Unemployment and the Duration of Unemployment," *Journal of Monetary Economics* 5 (April 1979): 153–169.

To focus on the determinants of unemployment, we assume that the size of the labor force is fixed. The transition of individuals between employment and unemployment is illustrated in Figure 5-2. Let *s* denote the rate of job separation, the fraction of employed individuals who lose their job each month. Let *f* denote the rate of job finding, the fraction of unemployed individuals who find a job each month. We assume that both of these rates are constant, and we see how together they determine the rate of unemployment.

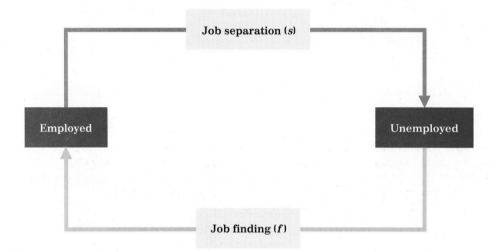

Figure 5-2 **The Transitions Between Employment and Unemployment.** In every period, a fraction *s* of the employed lose their jobs, and a fraction *f* of the unemployed find jobs. The rates of job separation and job finding determine the rate of unemployment.

If the rate of unemployment is neither rising nor falling—that is, if the labor market is in a steady state—then the number of people finding jobs must equal the number of people losing jobs. Because fU is the number of people finding jobs and sE the number of people losing jobs, these two values must be equal:

$$fU = sE.$$

We can rearrange this equation to find the steady-state unemployment rate. Note that $E = L - U$, that is, the number of employed equals the labor force minus the number of unemployed. This implies that

$$fU = s(L - U).$$

Divide both sides of this equation by L to obtain

$$f\frac{U}{L} = s(1 - \frac{U}{L}).$$

Then solve for U/L to find

$$\frac{U}{L} = \frac{s}{s + f}.$$

This equation states that the rate of unemployment U/L depends on the rates of job separation s and job finding f. The higher the rate of job separation, the higher the unemployment rate. The higher the rate of job finding, the lower the unemployment rate.

Here's a numerical example. Suppose that 1 percent of the employed lose their jobs each month ($s = 0.01$), which implies that the average job lasts 100 months, or about 8 years. Suppose further that about 20 percent of the unemployed find a job each month ($f = 0.20$), which implies that the average spell of unemployment lasts 5 months. In this case, the steady-state rate of unemployment is:

$$\frac{U}{L} = \frac{0.01}{0.01 + 0.20}$$
$$= 0.0476.$$

Thus, the rate of unemployment in this example is about 5 percent.

This model of the natural rate of unemployment has an obvious but important implication for public policy. *Any policy aimed at lowering the natural rate of unemployment must either reduce the rate of job separation or increase the rate of job finding. Similarly, any policy that affects the rate of job separation or job finding also changes the natural rate of unemployment.*

Although this model is useful in relating the unemployment rate to job separation and job finding, it does not answer a central question: Why is there unemployment in the first place? If a person could always find a job quickly, then the rate of job finding would be very high, and the rate of unemployment would be near zero. This model of the unemployment rate assumes that job finding is not instantaneous, but it fails to explain why. In the next two sections, we examine two underlying reasons for unemployment: job search and wage rigidity.

5-2 Job Search and Frictional Unemployment

One reason for unemployment is that it takes time to match workers and jobs. The equilibrium model of the aggregate labor market discussed in Chapter 3 assumes that all workers and all jobs are identical, and therefore that all workers are equally well suited for all jobs. If this were really true and the labor market were in equilibrium, then a job loss would not cause unemployment: a laid-off worker would immediately find a new job at the market wage.

In fact, however, workers have different preferences and abilities, and jobs have different attributes. Furthermore, the flow of information about job candidates and job vacancies is imperfect, and the geographic mobility of workers is not instantaneous. Searching for an appropriate job takes time and effort. Indeed, because different jobs require different skills and pay different wages, unemployed workers may not accept the first job offer they receive. The unemployment caused by the time it takes to match workers and jobs is called **frictional unemployment**.

Some frictional unemployment is inevitable in a changing economy. The demand for different goods always fluctuates, which in turn causes fluctuations in the demand for the labor that produces those goods. The invention of the personal computer, for example, reduced the demand for typewriters and, as a result, for labor by typewriter manufacturers. At the same time, it increased the demand for labor in the electronics industry. Similarly, because different regions produce different goods, the demand for labor may be rising in one part of the country while it is falling in another. An increase in the price of oil, for example, may cause the demand for labor to rise in oil-producing states such as Texas and fall in auto-producing states such as Michigan. Economists call such a change in the composition of demand among industries or regions a **sectoral shift**. Because sectoral shifts are always occurring, and because it takes time for workers to change sectors, there is always frictional unemployment.

Sectoral shifts are not the only cause of job separation and frictional unemployment. In addition, workers find themselves unexpectedly out of work when their firm fails, when their job performance is deemed unacceptable, or when their particular skills are no longer needed. Workers also may quit their jobs to change careers or to move to different parts of the country. As long as the supply and demand for labor among firms is changing, frictional unemployment is unavoidable.

Public Policy and Frictional Unemployment

Many public policies seek to decrease the natural rate of unemployment by reducing frictional unemployment. Government employment agencies disseminate information about job vacancies in order to match jobs and workers more efficiently. Public retraining programs are designed to ease the transition of workers from declining to growing industries. To the extent that these programs increase the rate of job finding, they decrease the natural rate of unemployment.

Unemployment insurance, however, is a government program that increases the amount of frictional unemployment. Under this program, unemployed workers can collect a fraction of their wages for a certain period after losing their jobs. Although the precise terms of the program differ from year to year and state to state, a typical worker covered by unemployment insurance in the United States receives 50 percent of his or her former wages for 26 weeks.

By softening the economic hardship of unemployment, unemployment insurance increases the amount of frictional unemployment and raises the natural rate. The unemployed who receive unemployment insurance benefits are less pressed to search for new employment, and they are more likely to turn down unattractive job offers. This reduces the rate of job finding. In addition, unemployment insurance may make employers less reluctant to lay off workers and may thus increase the rate of job separation.

That unemployment insurance raises the natural rate of unemployment does not necessarily imply that the policy is undesirable. The program has the benefit of reducing workers' uncertainty about their income. Moreover, inducing workers to reject unattractive job offers may lead to a better matching between workers and jobs. Evaluating the costs and benefits of different systems of unemployment insurance is a difficult task that continues to be a topic of much research.

Economists who study unemployment insurance often propose ways to reform the system in order to reduce the amount of unemployment. One common proposal is to require a firm that lays off a worker to pay for that worker's unemployment benefits in full. Such a system is called *100 percent experience rated*, because the rate that each firm pays for unemployment insurance fully reflects the unemployment experience of its own workers. Most current programs are *partially experience rated*. Under this system, when a firm lays off a worker, it is charged only part of the worker's benefits; the remainder comes from the program's general revenue. Because a firm pays only a fraction of the cost of the unemployment it causes, it has an incentive to lay off workers when its demand for labor is temporarily low. By reducing that incentive, the proposed reform may reduce the prevalence of temporary layoffs.

CASE STUDY 5-1

Interwar British Unemployment

Between World War I and World War II, Britain experienced persistently high unemployment. From 1920 to 1938 the unemployment rate in Britain averaged 14 percent and never fell below 9 percent.

Economists Daniel Benjamin and Levis Kochin have suggested that Britain's generous unemployment insurance can largely explain this high rate of unemployment. They cite three pieces of evidence to support their view. First, they found that increases in British unemployment benefits from 1920 to 1938 were associated with increases in the economy's unemployment rate. Second, they noted that teenagers, who received few or no unemployment benefits, had much lower unemployment rates than adults. Third, they showed that when the benefits for married women were reduced in 1932, their unemployment rate dropped significantly relative to that for men. All three pieces of evidence suggest a connection between unemployment benefits and unemployment rates.

This explanation of interwar British unemployment is controversial among economists who study this period. One difficulty in interpreting this evidence is that the data on unemployment benefits and unemployment rates may reflect two different relationships—one economic and one political. On the one hand, the higher the level of benefits, the more likely it is that an unemployed person will turn down an unattractive job offer, and thus the higher the level of frictional unemployment. On the other hand, the higher the rate of unemployment, the more pressing unemployment becomes as a political issue, and thus the higher the level of benefits the government chooses to offer. Hence, high unemployment rates may have caused high unemployment benefits, rather than the other way around. When we observe an empirical relationship between unemployment rates and unemployment benefits, we cannot tell whether we have identified an economic connection, a political connection, or some combination of the two.[2]

CASE STUDY 5-2

Unemployment Insurance and the Rate of Job Finding

Another way to demonstrate the effect of unemployment insurance on job search is to examine how the economic incentives facing unemployed workers influence their rate of job finding. To do this, one needs to examine data on unemployed individuals, rather than data on economy-wide rates of unemployment. Individual data sometimes provide evidence that is less open to alternative interpretations.

One of the findings from these data is that when unemployed workers become ineligible for unemployment insurance, the probability of their finding a new job rises markedly. Figure 5-3 shows how the rate of job finding depends on the number of weeks of eligibility remaining. The spike at zero shows that the probability of finding a new job approximately doubles when unemployment insurance benefits run out, which suggests that an absence of benefits greatly increases the search effort of unemployed workers.[3]

---

[2] Daniel Benjamin and Levis Kochin, "Searching for an Explanation of Unemployment in Interwar Britain," *Journal of Political Economy* 87 (June 1979): 441–478. For critical comments on this article and a reply by the authors, see *Journal of Political Economy* 90 (April 1982): 369–436.

[3] Lawrence F. Katz and Bruce D. Meyer, "Unemployment Insurance, Recall Expectations, and Unemployment Outcomes," *Quarterly Journal of Economics* 105 (November 1990): 973–1002.

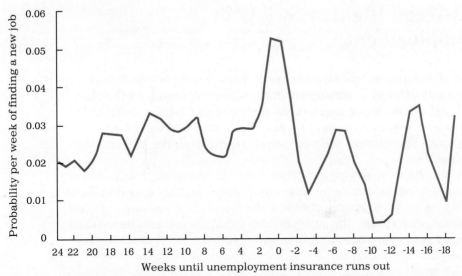

Source: Adapted from Lawrence F. Katz and Bruce D. Meyer, "Unemployment Insurance, Recall Expectations, and Unemployment Outcomes." *Quarterly Journal of Economics* 105 (November 1990): 973–1002.

Figure 5-3 **The Rate of Job Finding.** This figure shows how the probability of finding a new job changes as eligibility for unemployment insurance runs out. The spike at zero shows a substantial increase in the rate of job finding in the week when eligibility expires.

Note: The large week-to-week variation in the rate of job finding in the later weeks is a statistical artifact. Because individuals leave the sample when they find work, the rate of job finding is estimated less precisely as time passes.

Additional evidence on how economic incentives affect job search comes from an experiment that the state of Illinois ran in 1985. Randomly selected new claimants for unemployment insurance were each offered a $500 bonus if they found employment within 11 weeks. The subsequent experience of this group was compared to that of a control group not offered this incentive. The average duration of unemployment for the group offered the $500 incentive was 17.0 weeks, compared to 18.3 weeks for the control group. This experiment offers clear evidence that the economic incentives provided by the unemployment insurance system do influence the rate of job finding.[4]

---

[4] Stephen A. Woodbury and Robert G. Spiegelman, "Bonuses to Workers and Employers to Reduce Unemployment: Randomized Trials in Illinois," *American Economic Review* 77 (September 1987): 513–530.

5-3   Real-Wage Rigidity and Wait Unemployment

A second reason for unemployment is **wage rigidity**—the failure of the wage to adjust until labor supply equals labor demand. In the equilibrium model of the labor market, as outlined in Chapter 3, the real wage adjusts to equilibrate supply and demand. Yet wages are not always flexible. Sometimes the real wage is stuck above the market-clearing level.

Figure 5-4 shows why wage rigidity leads to unemployment. When the real wage is above the level that equilibrates supply and demand, the quantity of labor supplied exceeds the quantity demanded. Firms must in some way ration the scarce jobs among workers. Real-wage rigidity reduces the rate of job finding and raises the level of unemployment.

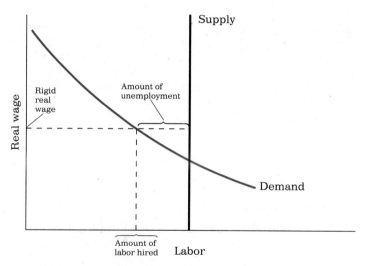

Figure 5-4 **Real-Wage Rigidity Leads to Job Rationing.** If the real wage is stuck above the equilibrium level, then the supply of labor exceeds the demand. The result is unemployment.

The unemployment resulting from wage rigidity and job rationing is called **wait unemployment**. Workers are unemployed not because they are actively searching for the jobs that best suit their individual skills but because, at the going wage, the supply of labor exceeds the demand. These workers are simply waiting for jobs to become available.

To understand wage rigidity and wait unemployment, we must examine why the labor market does not clear. When the real wage exceeds the equilibrium level and the supply of workers exceeds the demand, we might expect firms to lower the wages they pay. Wait unemployment arises because firms fail to reduce wages despite an excess supply of labor. We now turn to three causes of this wage rigidity: minimum-wage laws, the monopoly power of unions, and efficiency wages.

Minimum-Wage Laws

The government causes wage rigidity when it prevents wages from falling to equilibrium levels. Minimum-wage laws set a legal minimum on the wages that firms pay their employees. Since the passage of the Fair Labor Standards Act of 1938, the federal government in the United States has enforced a minimum wage that usually has been between 30 and 50 percent of the average wage in manufacturing. For most workers, this minimum wage is not binding, because they earn well above the minimum. Yet for some workers, especially the unskilled and inexperienced, the minimum wage raises their wage above its equilibrium level. It therefore reduces the quantity of their labor that firms demand.

The minimum wage is often thought to have its greatest impact on teenage unemployment, because the equilibrium wages of teenagers tend to be low. There are two reasons for this. First, because teenagers are among the least skilled and least experienced members of the labor force, they tend to have low marginal products. Second, teenagers often take some of their "compensation" in the form of on-the-job training rather than as direct pay. An apprenticeship is a classic example of this. For both of these reasons, the wage at which the supply of teenage workers equals the demand is low. The minimum wage is therefore more often binding for teenagers than for others in the labor force.

Many economists have studied the impact of the minimum wage on teenage employment. These researchers compare the variation in the minimum wage over time with the variation in the number of teenagers with jobs. These studies find that a 10 percent increase in the minimum wage reduces teenage employment by between 1 and 3 percent.[5]

To mitigate the effects on teenage unemployment, some economists and policymakers have long advocated exempting young workers from the regular minimum wage. This would permit a lower wage for teenagers, thereby reducing their unemployment and enabling them to get training and job experience. A limited exemption of this kind went into effect in 1990. Opponents of this exemption argue that it gives firms an incentive to substitute teenagers for unskilled adults, thereby raising unemployment among that group.

---

[5] Charles Brown, "Minimum Wage Laws: Are They Overrated?" *Journal of Economic Perspectives* 2 (Summer 1988): 133–146.

CASE STUDY 5-3

The Minimum Wage and the Working Poor

The minimum wage is a perennial source of political debate. Advocates of a higher minimum wage view it as a means of raising the income of the working poor. Certainly, the minimum wage provides only a meager standard of living. In 1988, when the minimum wage was $3.35 per hour, a person would have to work 52 hours every week to exceed the $9,044 official poverty level for a family of three.

Opponents of a higher minimum wage argue that it is not the best way to help the working poor. They contend not only that the increased labor costs would raise unemployment, but also that the minimum wage is poorly targeted. Many minimum-wage earners are teenagers from middle-class homes working for discretionary spending money. Of the approximately 5 million workers who earn the minimum wage, heads of households represent less than 25 percent, whereas teenagers make up 37 percent.

Many economists and policymakers believe that tax credits provide a better way to help the working poor. The *earned income tax credit* is an amount that poor working families are allowed to subtract from the taxes they owe. The lower their income, the higher is their credit. Compared to the minimum wage, the earned income tax credit has the advantage of not raising labor costs to firms and, therefore, not reducing the quantity of labor firms demand. It has the disadvantage, however, of reducing the government's tax revenue.

Unions and Collective Bargaining

A second cause of wage rigidity is the monopoly power of unions. About one-fifth of the U.S. labor force is unionized. The wages of these workers are determined not by the equilibrium of supply and demand but by collective bargaining between union leaders and firm management. Often, the final agreement raises the wage above the equilibrium level and allows the firm to decide how many workers to employ. In this case, the result is a reduction in the number of workers hired and an increase in wait unemployment.

Some evidence on the effects of unionization comes from comparing unemployment in different states. As one might expect, states with a more highly unionized labor force tend to have higher rates of unemployment. According to a study of data for 1985, an increase of 10 percentage points in the proportion of the labor force that is unionized increases the unemployment rate by 1.2 percentage points.[6]

---

[6] Lawrence H. Summers, "Why Is the Unemployment Rate So Very High Near Full Employment?" *Brookings Papers on Economic Activity* no. 2 (1986): 339–383.

Unions can also influence the wages paid by firms whose work forces are not unionized, because the threat of unionization can keep wages above the equilibrium level. Most firms dislike unions. Unions not only raise wages but they also increase the bargaining power of labor on many other issues, such as hours of employment and working conditions. A firm may choose to pay its workers high wages to keep them happy and thus to discourage them from forming a union.

The unemployment caused by unions and by the threat of unionization is an instance of conflict between different groups of workers—**insiders** and **outsiders**. Those workers already employed by a firm, the insiders, typically try to keep their firm's wages high. The unemployed workers who might otherwise have been hired, the outsiders, bear part of the cost of higher wages. Tension between the interests of these two groups is inevitable. The effect of any bargaining process on wages and employment depends crucially on the relative influence of each group.

The conflict between insiders and outsiders is resolved differently in different countries. In some countries, such as the United States, wage bargaining takes place at the level of the firm or plant. In other countries, such as Sweden, wage bargaining takes place at the national level—with the government often playing a key role. Despite a highly unionized labor force, unemployment in Sweden is low. One possible explanation is that the centralization of wage bargaining and the role of the government in the bargaining process may give more influence to the outsiders and may thus keep wages closer to the equilibrium level.[7]

CASE STUDY 5-4

Unionization and Unemployment in the United States and Canada

Throughout the 1960s the United States and Canada had similar labor markets. The rates of unemployment in the two countries were about the same on average, and the rates fluctuated together. In the mid-1970s, their experiences began to diverge. In 1985, when the unemployment rate in the United States was 7.2 percent, the unemployment rate in Canada was 10.5 percent.

The changing roles of unions in the two countries is one possible explanation for this divergence. In the 1960s, about 30 percent of the labor force was unionized in each country. But Canadian labor laws did more to foster unionization than U.S. laws did. By 1985, unionization had risen to about 40 percent in Canada and had declined to about 20 percent in the United States.

As one might have predicted, changes in real wages accompanied the change in unionization. The real wage in Canada increased by about 30 percent relative to the real wage in the United States. This evidence

[7] Michael Bruno and Jeffrey Sachs, *Economics of Worldwide Stagflation* (Cambridge, Mass.: Harvard University Press, 1985).

suggests that unions in Canada pushed the real wage further above the equilibrium level, leading to more wait unemployment.

The divergence in the two unemployment rates may also be attributable to the increase in the availability of unemployment insurance benefits in Canada. Not only does unemployment insurance raise search times and the amount of frictional unemployment but it also interacts in two ways with the effects of unionization. First, unemployment insurance makes unemployed workers more willing to wait for a high-wage job in a unionized firm, rather than take a lower-wage job in a nonunion firm. Second, unemployment insurance makes unions more willing to press for high wages at the expense of lower employment.[8]

Efficiency Wages

Besides minimum-wage laws and unionization, a third cause of wage rigidity is suggested by **efficiency-wage** theories, which hold that high wages make workers more productive. The influence of wages on worker efficiency may explain the failure of firms to cut wages despite an excess supply of labor. Even though a wage reduction would lower a firm's wage bill, it would also—if the theories are correct—lower worker productivity and the firm's profits.

There are various theories about how wages affect worker productivity. One efficiency-wage theory, which is applied mostly to less-developed countries, holds that wages influence nutrition. Better-paid workers can afford a more nutritious diet, and healthier workers are more productive. A firm in a less-developed country may decide to pay a wage above the equilibrium level to maintain a healthy work force. Obviously, this consideration is not important for employers in developed countries such as the United States, where the equilibrium wage is well above the level necessary to maintain good health.

A second efficiency-wage theory, which is more relevant for developed countries, holds that high wages reduce labor turnover. Workers quit jobs for many reasons—to accept better positions at other firms, to change careers, or to move to other parts of the country. The more a firm pays its workers, the greater their incentive to stay with the firm. By paying a high wage, a firm reduces the frequency of quits, thereby decreasing the time spent hiring and training new workers.

A third efficiency-wage theory holds that the average quality of a firm's work force depends on the wage it pays its employees. If a firm reduces its wage, the best employees may take jobs elsewhere, leaving the firm with inferior employees who have fewer alternative opportuni-

---

[8] Herbert G. Grubel, "Drifting Apart: Canadian and U.S. Labor Markets," *Contemporary Policy Issues* 6 (January 1988): 39–55, also in *Journal of Economic and Monetary Affairs* 2 (Winter 1988): 59–75.

ties. Economists call this unfavorable sorting *adverse selection*. By paying a wage above the equilibrium level, the firm may avoid adverse selection, improve the average quality of its work force, and thereby increase productivity.

A fourth efficiency-wage theory holds that a high wage improves worker effort. This theory posits that firms cannot perfectly monitor their employees' work effort, and that employees must themselves decide how hard to work. Workers can choose to work hard, or they can choose to shirk and risk getting caught and fired. Economists call this possibility of dishonest behavior *moral hazard*. The firm can reduce the problem of moral hazard by paying a high wage. The higher the wage, the greater the cost to the worker of getting fired. By paying a higher wage, a firm induces more of its employees not to shirk and thus increases their productivity.

All of these efficiency-wage theories share the theme that the firm operates more efficiently if it pays its workers a high wage. These theories therefore imply that it is sometimes in the firm's interest to keep wages above the equilibrium level. The result of this wage rigidity is wait unemployment.[9]

CASE STUDY 5-5

Henry Ford's $5 Workday

In 1914 the Ford Motor Company instituted the $5 workday. Since the prevailing wage at the time was between $2 and $3 a day, Ford's wage was well above the equilibrium level. Not surprisingly, long lines of job-seekers waited outside the Ford plant gates hoping for a chance to earn $5 a day.

What was Ford's motive? Henry Ford later wrote, "We wanted to pay these wages so that the business would be on a lasting foundation. We were building for the future. A low wage business is always insecure. . . . The payment of five dollars a day for an eight hour day was one of the finest cost cutting moves we ever made."

Ford was apparently using the wage to increase worker efficiency. Evidence suggests that paying such a high wage did indeed benefit the company. According to an engineering report written at the time, "The Ford high wage does away with all the inertia and living force resistance. . . . The workingmen are absolutely docile, and it is safe to say that since the last day of 1913, every single day has seen major reductions in Ford shops' labor costs." Absenteeism, for example, fell by 75 percent, sug-

---

[9] For more extended discussions of efficiency wages, see Janet Yellen, "Efficiency Wage Models of Unemployment," *American Economic Review Papers and Proceedings* (May 1984): 200–205; and Lawrence Katz, "Efficiency Wages: A Partial Evaluation," *NBER Macroeconomics Annual* (1986): 235–276.

gesting a substantial increase in worker effort. Alan Nevins, an historian who studied the early Ford Motor Company, wrote, "Ford and his associates freely declared on many occasions that the high wage policy had turned out to be good business. By this they meant that it had improved the discipline of the workers, given them a more loyal interest in the institution, and raised their personal efficiency."[10]

5-4 Patterns of Unemployment

We now turn to some additional facts about unemployment, which will help us to evaluate our theories of unemployment and assess public policies aimed at reducing it.

The Duration of Unemployment

When people become unemployed, are they likely to face a short or a long spell of unemployment? The answer is important because it indicates the reasons for the unemployment and what policy response is appropriate. On the one hand, if unemployment is short-term, one might argue that it is frictional and, perhaps, unavoidable. Individuals may require a short spell of unemployment to search for the job that is best suited to their skills and tastes. On the other hand, long-term unemployment cannot easily be attributed to the time it takes to match jobs and workers: we would not expect this matching process to take many months. Long-term unemployment is more likely to be wait unemployment. Thus, data on the duration of unemployment can affect our view about the reasons for unemployment.

The answer to our question turns out to be subtle. The data show that most spells of unemployment are short, but that most weeks of unemployment are attributable to the long-term unemployed. In 1974, for example, when the unemployment rate was 5.6 percent, 60 percent of the spells of unemployment ended within one month. In that same year, 69 percent of the weeks of unemployment occurred in spells that lasted two or more months.[11]

---

[10] Jeremy I. Bulow and Lawrence H. Summers, "A Theory of Dual Labor Markets With Application to Industrial Policy, Discrimination, and Keynesian Unemployment," *Journal of Labor Economics* 4 (July 1986): 376–414; Daniel M. G. Raff and Lawrence H. Summers, "Did Henry Ford Pay Efficiency Wages?" *Journal of Labor Economics* 5 (October 1987, Part 2): S57–S86.

[11] Kim B. Clark and Lawrence H. Summers, "Labor Market Dynamics and Unemployment: A Reconsideration," *Brookings Papers on Economic Activity* no. 1 (1979): 13–72.

To see how both these facts can be true, consider the following example. Suppose that 14 people are unemployed for part of a given year. Of these 14 people, 12 are unemployed for one month, and 2 are unemployed for 12 months, totaling 36 months of unemployment. In this example, most spells of unemployment are short: 12 of the 14 unemployment spells, or 86 percent, end in one month. Yet most months of unemployment are attributable to the long-term unemployed: 24 of the 36 months of unemployment, or 67 percent, are experienced by the two workers who are unemployed for 12 months. Depending on whether one looks at spells of unemployment or months of unemployment, most unemployment can appear to be short-term or long-term.

This evidence on the duration of unemployment has an important implication for public policy. If the goal is to lower substantially the rate of unemployment, policies must aim at the long-term unemployed, because these individuals account for a large amount of unemployment. Yet policies must be carefully targeted, because the long-term unemployed also constitute a small minority of those who become unemployed. Most people who become unemployed find work within a short time.

Variation in the Unemployment Rate Across Demographic Groups

The rate of unemployment varies substantially across different groups within the population. Table 5-1 presents the U.S. unemployment rates for different demographic groups for 1985, when the overall rate was 7.2 percent.

Table 5-1   Unemployment Rate by Demographic Groups: 1985

Age	White Male	White Female	Black Male	Black Female
16–17	19.2%	17.2%	42.9%	44.3%
18–19	14.7	13.1	40.0	36.4
20–24	9.7	8.5	23.5	25.6
25–54	4.9	5.4	11.6	11.5
55+	3.8	3.9	8.1	5.9

Source: U.S. Department of Labor.

This table shows that younger workers have much higher unemployment rates than older ones. To explain this difference, recall our model of the natural rate of unemployment. The model isolates two possible causes for a high rate of unemployment: a low rate of job finding, or a high rate of job separation. When economists study data on the transition of individuals between employment and unemployment, they find that those groups with high unemployment tend to have high rates of job separation. They find less variation across groups in the rate of job finding. For example, an employed white male is four times more likely to become unemployed if he is a teenager than if he is middle-aged; once unemployed, his rate of job finding is not closely related to his age.

These findings suggest that the higher unemployment rates for younger workers may be desirable. Younger workers have only recently entered the labor market, and they are often uncertain about their career plans. It may be optimal for them to try different types of jobs before making a long-term commitment to a specific occupation. If so, we should expect a higher rate of job separation and a higher rate of frictional unemployment for this group.

Another fact that stands out from Table 5-1 is that unemployment rates are much higher for blacks than for whites. This phenomenon is not well understood. Data on transitions between employment and unemployment show that the higher unemployment rates for blacks, and especially for black teenagers, arise because of both higher rates of job separation and lower rates of job finding. Possible reasons for the lower rates of job finding include reduced access to informal job-finding networks and discrimination by employers.

The Upward Trend in Unemployment

Over the past 40 years, the rate of unemployment in the United States has drifted upward. As Figure 5-5 shows, unemployment averaged 4.4 percent in the 1950s, 4.7 percent in the 1960s, 6.1 percent in the 1970s,

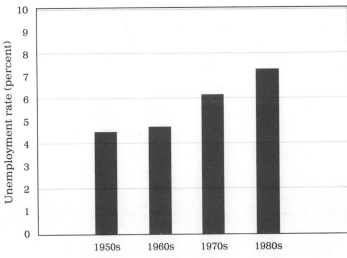

Figure 5-5 **The Upward Drift in the Unemployment Rate.** The rate of unemployment in the United States has gradually drifted upward: the average in each decade since 1950 has exceeded that in the previous decade.

Source: U.S. Department of Labor.

and 7.3 percent in the 1980s. Although economists do not have a conclusive explanation for this trend, they have proposed various hypotheses.

One explanation stresses the changing composition of the U.S. labor force. After World War II, birth rates rose dramatically, producing a baby-boom generation that began entering the labor force around 1970. Because younger workers have higher unemployment rates, this influx of baby-boomers into the labor force increased the average level of unemployment. At roughly the same time, the participation of women in the labor force was also increasing significantly. In 1960 women made up 33 percent of the labor force; by 1980 this proportion had risen to 43 percent. Since historically women have had higher unemployment rates than men (a difference that has disappeared in recent years), the increasing proportion of women in the labor force may have raised the average unemployment rate.

These two demographic changes, however, cannot fully explain the upward trend in unemployment, because the trend was also apparent for men between the ages of 25 and 54. This group's average unemployment rate was 3.4 percent in the 1950s, 3.0 percent in the 1960s, 3.7 percent in the 1970s, and 6.1 percent in the 1980s. Hence, the increase in unemployment is not merely the result of a change in the composition of the labor force.

A second explanation is that the increase in female labor-force participation, by increasing the number of two-income households, also increased the unemployment rate for men. The reasoning here is that unemployed men with working wives are more likely to turn down unattractive job offers than are men who are the sole breadwinners. If so, the resulting decrease in the rate of job finding by men would increase their unemployment rate.

Though plausible, this explanation is hard to reconcile with the evidence. Contrary to what one might expect, men with working wives have lower unemployment rates than men whose wives do not work.[12] Moreover, the unemployment rate for single men has also drifted upward, indicating that the two-income household cannot explain the upward drift in overall unemployment.

A third possible explanation for the upward trend in unemployment is that sectoral shifts have become more prevalent. The greater the amount of sectoral reallocation, the greater the rate of job separation and the higher the level of frictional unemployment.[13] One source of sectoral shifts has been the large changes in oil prices caused by the international oil cartel, OPEC. As shown in Figure 5-6, the relative price

---

[12] Kevin M. Murphy and Robert H. Topel, "The Evolution of Unemployment in the United States: 1968–1985," *NBER Macroeconomics Annual* (1987): 11–68.

[13] David M. Lilien, "Sectoral Shifts and Cyclical Unemployment," *Journal of Political Economy* 90 (August 1982): 777–793.

of oil was stable until the early 1970s. The large changes in oil prices since 1972 may have required reallocating labor between more-energy-intensive and less-energy-intensive sectors. If so, this oil-price volatility may have increased the rate of unemployment. This explanation, however, has proven hard to evaluate.

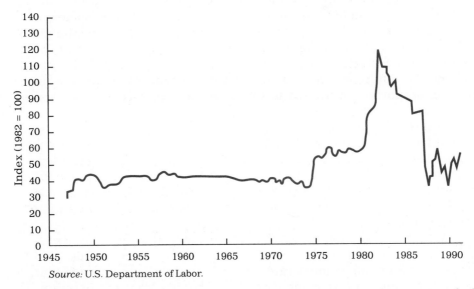

Source: U.S. Department of Labor.

Figure 5-6 **The Relative Price of Oil: A Source of Sectoral Shifts.** This figure shows the relative price of oil, as measured by the producer price index for crude petroleum divided by the producer price index for all commodities. It shows that, since the early 1970s, the relative price of oil has been highly volatile. Changes in this relative price are a possible source of sectoral shifts and, therefore, may help to explain the increase in the unemployment rate over time.

In the end, the upward drift in the unemployment rate remains a mystery. Some of the proposed explanations are plausible, but none seems conclusive. Perhaps there is no single answer—the upward drift in the unemployment rate may be the result of several unrelated developments.

Transitions Into and Out of the Labor Force

So far we have been ignoring an important aspect of labor market dynamics: the movement of individuals into and out of the labor force. Our model of the natural rate of unemployment assumes that the labor force is fixed. In this case, the sole reason for unemployment is job separation, and the sole reason for leaving unemployment is job finding.

In fact, changes in the labor force are important. About one-third of the unemployed have only recently entered the labor force. Some of these entrants are young workers still looking for their first jobs; the others have worked before but had temporarily left the labor force. In addition, not all unemployment ends with job finding: almost half of all spells of unemployment end in the unemployed person's withdrawal from the labor market.

These individuals entering and leaving the labor force make unemployment statistics more difficult to interpret. On the one hand, some individuals calling themselves unemployed may not be seriously looking for a job and perhaps should best be viewed as out of the labor force. Their "unemployment" may not represent a social problem. On the other hand, some individuals may want a job but, after an unsuccessful search, have given up looking. These **discouraged workers** are counted as being out of the labor force and therefore do not show up in unemployment statistics. Even though their joblessness is unmeasured, it may nonetheless be a social problem.

5-5 Conclusion

Unemployment represents wasted resources. Unemployed workers have the potential to contribute to national income but are not doing so. Those searching for jobs to suit their skills are happy when the search is over, and those waiting for jobs in firms that pay above-equilibrium wages are happy when positions open up. Clearly, the unemployed would rather be employed.

Unfortunately, there is no simple way to reduce unemployment. The government cannot make job search an instantaneous process, nor can it easily bring wages closer to equilibrium levels. Zero unemployment is beyond reach in an economy such as ours.

Yet public policy is not completely powerless in the fight to reduce unemployment. Job-training programs, the unemployment insurance system, the minimum wage, and the laws governing collective bargaining are frequently the topics of political debate. The policies we choose are likely to have important effects on the prevalence of unemployment.

Summary

1. The natural rate of unemployment is the steady-state rate of unemployment. It depends on the rate of job separation and the rate of job finding.

2. Because it takes time for workers to search for the job that best suits their individual skills and tastes, some frictional unemployment is inevitable. Various government policies, such as unemployment insurance, alter the amount of frictional unemployment.

3. Wait unemployment results when the real wage remains above the level that equilibrates labor supply and labor demand. Minimum-wage legislation is one cause of wage rigidity. Another cause is unions and the threat of unionization. Finally, efficiency-wage theories suggest that, for various reasons, a firm may find it profitable to keep its wage high despite an excess supply of labor.

4. Whether one concludes that most unemployment is short-term or long-term depends on how one looks at the data. Most spells of unemployment are fairly short. Yet most weeks of unemployment are attributable to the small number of long-term unemployed.

5. The unemployment rates among demographic groups differ substantially. In particular, the unemployment rates for younger workers are much greater than for older workers. This difference results from a difference in the rate of job separation rather than from a difference in the rate of job finding.

6. The unemployment rate has gradually drifted upward over the past 40 years. Various explanations have been proposed, including the changing demographic composition of the labor force, the increase in the number of two-earner households, and an increase in sectoral shifts.

7. Individuals who have recently entered the labor force, including both new entrants and reentrants, make up about one-third of the unemployed. The transitions into and out of the labor force make unemployment statistics more difficult to interpret.

KEY CONCEPTS

Natural rate of unemployment

Frictional unemployment

Sectoral shift

Unemployment insurance

Wage rigidity

Wait unemployment

Insiders versus outsiders

Efficiency wages

Discouraged workers

QUESTIONS FOR REVIEW

1. What determines the natural rate of unemployment?

2. Describe the difference between frictional unemployment and wait unemployment.

3. Give three explanations for why the real wage may remain above the level that equilibrates labor supply and labor demand.

4. Is most unemployment long-term or short-term? Explain your answer.

5. How do economists explain the upward drift in the rate of unemployment over the past 40 years?

PROBLEMS AND APPLICATIONS

1. Answer the following questions about your own experience in the labor force:

   a. When you or one of your friends is looking for a part-time job, how many weeks does it typically take? After you find a job, how many weeks does it typically last?

   b. From your estimates, calculate (in a rate per week) your rate of job finding f and your rate of job separation s. (*Hint:* If f is the rate of job finding, then the average spell of unemployment is $1/f$.)

   c. What is the natural rate of unemployment for the population you represent?

2. In this chapter we saw that the steady-state rate of unemployment is $U/L = s/(s + f)$. Suppose that the unemployment rate does not begin at this level. Show that unemployment will evolve over time and reach this steady state. (*Hint:* Express ΔU, the change in the number of unemployed, as a function of s, f, and U. Then show that if unemployment is above the natural rate, unemployment falls, and if unemployment is below the natural rate, unemployment rises.)

3. Some economists who have studied differences across countries in labor markets have suggested that the relationship between unemployment and unionization resembles an inverted letter "U." That is, they find that the natural rate of unemployment is low if unionization is very low or very high, and that intermediate levels of unionization lead to the highest rates of unemployment. Why might this be true?

4. Suppose that a country experiences a reduction in productivity—that is, an adverse shock to the production function.

   a. What happens to the labor demand curve?

   b. How would this change affect the labor market—that is, employment, unemployment, and real wages—if the labor market were always in equilibrium?

   c. How would this change affect the labor market if unions constrained real wages to remain unaltered?

5. In any city at any time, some of the stock of usable office space is vacant. This vacant office space is unemployed capital. How would you explain this phenomenon? Is it a social problem?

Chapter 6

Inflation

*Lenin is said to have declared that the best way to
destroy the Capitalist System was to debauch the
currency. . . . Lenin was certainly right. There is no
subtler, no surer means of overturning the existing
basis of society than to debauch the currency. The
process engages all the hidden forces of economic
law on the side of destruction, and does it in a
manner which not one man in a million is able to
diagnose.*

John Maynard Keynes

In 1970 the *New York Times* cost 15 cents, the median price of a single-family home was $23,000, and the average wage in manufacturing was $3.35 per hour. In 1990 the *Times* cost 40 cents, the price of a home was $96,000, and the average wage was $10.83 per hour. This overall increase in prices is called **inflation**, and it is the subject of this chapter.

The rate of inflation—the percentage change in the overall level of prices—varies substantially over time and across countries. In the United States, prices rose an average of 2.7 percent per year in the 1960s, 7.1 percent per year in the 1970s, and 4.9 percent per year in the 1980s. By international standards, the experience of the United States has been moderate: other countries have often experienced much higher rates of inflation. In Israel in the early 1980s, prices increased over 100 percent every year. In Germany between December 1922 and December 1923, prices rose an average of 500 percent per month. Such an episode of extraordinarily high inflation is called a **hyperinflation**.

Many people consider inflation to be a major social problem. Certainly economic policymakers monitor inflation closely. In the 1970s President Gerald Ford declared inflation to be "public enemy number one," and in the 1980s President Ronald Reagan called inflation "the cruelest tax." Opinion polls show that the general public also views inflation as pernicious.

In this chapter we examine the causes, effects, and social costs of inflation. Because inflation is the increase in the price level, we begin our study by examining how prices are determined. A price is the rate at which money is exchanged for a good or a service. To understand prices, we must understand money—what it is, what affects its supply and demand, and what influence it has on the economy. This chapter is therefore an introduction to a branch of economics called *monetary economics.*

The "hidden forces of economic law" that lead to inflation are not as mysterious as suggested in the quotation that opened this chapter. Section 6-1 begins our analysis of inflation by discussing the economist's concept of "money" and how, in our economy, the government controls the number of dollars in the hands of the public. Section 6-2 shows that the quantity of money determines the price level, and that the rate of growth in the quantity of money determines the rate of inflation.

Inflation in turn has numerous effects of its own on the economy. Section 6-3 discusses the revenue that the government raises by printing money, sometimes called the *inflation tax.* Section 6-4 examines how inflation affects the nominal interest rate. Section 6-5 discusses how the nominal interest rate in turn affects the quantity of money people wish to hold and, thereby, the price level. All of these issues come into play when a government faces the formidable task of ending a hyperinflation.

After completing our analysis of the causes and effects of inflation, in Section 6-6 we address what is perhaps the most important question about inflation: is it a major social problem? Does inflation really amount to "overturning the existing basis of society"?

6-1 What Is Money?

Economists use a particular and specialized definition of the term **money**. To an economist, *money is the stock of assets used for transactions.* Roughly speaking, the dollars in the hands of the public make up the nation's stock of money.

The Functions of Money

Money has three purposes. It is a **store of value**, a **unit of account**, and a **medium of exchange**.

As a store of value, money is a way to transfer purchasing power from the present to the future. If I work today and earn $100, I can hold onto the money and spend it tomorrow, next week, or next month. Of course, money is an imperfect store of value: if prices are rising, the real value of money is falling. Even so, people hold money because they can trade the money for goods and services at some time in the future.

As a unit of account, money provides the terms in which prices are quoted and debts are recorded. Microeconomics teaches us that resources are allocated according to relative prices—the prices of goods relative to other goods—yet stores post their prices in dollars and cents. A car dealer tells you that a car costs $12,000, not 400 shirts (even though it may amount to the same thing). Similarly, most debts require the debtor to deliver a specified number of dollars in the future, not a specified amount of some commodity. Money is the yardstick with which we measure economic transactions.

As a medium of exchange, money is what we use to buy goods and services. "This note is legal tender for all debts, public and private" is printed on the U.S. dollar. When we walk into stores, we are confident that the shopkeepers will accept money in exchange for the items they are selling.

To better understand the functions of money, try to imagine an economy without it: a barter economy. In such a world, trade requires the **double coincidence of wants**—the unlikely happenstance of two people each having a good that the other wants. A barter economy permits only simple economic transactions.

Money makes more indirect transactions possible. A professor uses her salary to buy books; the book publisher uses its revenue from the sale of books to buy paper; the paper company uses its revenue from the sale of paper to pay the lumberjack; the lumberjack uses his income to send his child to college; and the college uses its tuition receipts to pay the salary of the professor. In a complex, modern economy, trade is usually indirect and requires the use of money.

The Types of Money

Money takes many forms. In the U.S. economy we make transactions with an item whose sole function is to act as money: dollar bills. These pieces of green paper with George Washington's picture would have little value if they were not widely accepted as money. Money that has no intrinsic value is called **fiat money,** since it is established as money by government decree.

Although fiat money is the norm in most economies today, historically most societies have used for money a commodity with some intrinsic value. Money of this sort is called **commodity money**.

Gold is the most widespread example of commodity money. An economy in which gold serves as money is said to be on a **gold standard**. Gold is a form of commodity money because it can be used for various purposes—jewelry, dental fillings, etc.—as well as for transactions. The United States and most other countries were on some form of a gold standard throughout most of the nineteenth century.

CASE STUDY 6-1

Money in a POW Camp

An unusual form of commodity money developed in the Nazi prisoner of war (POW) camps during World War II. The Red Cross supplied the prisoners with various goods—food, clothing, cigarettes, and so on. Yet these rations were allocated without close attention to personal preferences, so naturally the allocation was not always efficient. One prisoner may have preferred chocolate, while another may have preferred cheese, and a third may have wanted a new shirt. The differing tastes and endowments of the prisoners led to trade among them.

Barter proved to be an inconvenient way to allocate these resources, however, because it required the double coincidence of wants. In other words, a barter system was not the easiest way to ensure that each prisoner received the goods he valued most. Even the limited economy of the POW camp needed some form of money to facilitate transactions.

Eventually, cigarettes became the established "currency" in which prices were quoted and with which trades were made. A shirt, for example, cost about 80 cigarettes. Wages were also quoted in cigarettes: some prisoners offered to do other prisoners' laundry for 2 cigarettes per garment. Even non-smokers were happy to accept cigarettes in exchange, knowing they could trade the cigarettes in the future for some good they did enjoy. Within the POW camp the cigarette became the store of value, the unit of account, and the medium of exchange.[1]

Drawing by Bernard Schoenbaum; © 1979
The New Yorker Magazine, Inc.

"And how would you like your funny money?"

---

[1] R.A. Radford, "The Economic Organisation of a P.O.W. Camp," *Economica* (November 1945): 189–201. The use of cigarettes as money is not limited to this example. In the Soviet Union in the late 1980s, packs of Marlboros were preferred to the ruble in the large underground economy.

How Fiat Money Evolves

It is not surprising that some form of commodity money arises to facilitate exchange: people are willing to accept a commodity currency such as gold because it has intrinsic value. The development of fiat money, however, is more perplexing. What would make people begin to value something that has no intrinsic worth?

To understand how the evolution from commodity money to fiat money takes place, imagine an economy in which individuals carry around bags of gold. When a purchase is made, the buyer must measure out the appropriate amount of gold. If the seller is convinced that the weight and purity of the gold are right, the buyer and seller make the exchange.

The government first intervenes to save on transaction costs. Using raw gold as money is costly because it takes time to verify the purity of the gold and to measure the correct quantity. To help save on these costs, the government mints gold coins of known purity and weight. The coins are easier to use than gold bullion because their values are widely recognized.

The next step is for the government to issue gold certificates—pieces of paper that can be redeemed for a certain quantity of gold. If people believe the government's promise to pay, these bills are just as valuable as the gold itself. In addition, because the bills are lighter than the gold, they are easier to use in transactions. Eventually, no one carries around gold at all, and these gold-backed government bills become the monetary standard.

Finally, the necessity of the gold backing becomes irrelevant. If no one ever bothers to redeem the bills for gold, no one cares if redemption is abandoned. As long as everyone continues to accept the paper certificates in exchange, they will have value and serve as money. Thus, the system of commodity money gradually turns into a system of fiat money.

CASE STUDY 6-2

Money on the Island of Yap

The economy of Yap, a small island in the Pacific, once had a type of money that was something between commodity and fiat money. The traditional medium of exchange in the Yap economy was *fei*, stone wheels up to 12 feet in diameter. These stones had holes in the center, so that they could be carried on poles and used for exchange.

Large stone wheels are obviously not a convenient form of money. The stones were heavy; it took substantial effort for a new owner to take his *fei* home after completing a bargain. Although the monetary system facilitated exchange, it did so at great cost.

As one might expect, it became common practice for the new owner of the *fei* not to bother to take physical possession of the stone. Instead, the new owner merely accepted a claim to the *fei* without moving it. In future bargains, he traded this claim for goods that he wanted. Having physical possession of the stone became less important than having legal claim to it.

This practice was put to a test when an extremely valuable stone was lost at sea during a storm. Because the owner lost his money by accident rather than through negligence, it was universally agreed that his claim to the *fei* remained valid. Even generations later, when no one alive had ever seen this stone, the claim to this *fei* was still valued in exchange.[2]

How the Quantity of Money Is Controlled

The quantity of money available is called the **money supply**. In an economy that uses commodity money, the money supply is the quantity of that commodity. In an economy that uses fiat money, such as the U.S. economy today, the government controls the supply of money: legal restrictions give the government a monopoly on the printing of dollar bills. Just as the level of taxation and the level of government purchases are policy instruments of the government, so is the supply of money.

In the United States and many other countries, the control of the money supply is delegated to a partially independent institution called the **central bank**. The central bank of the United States is the **Federal Reserve**—often called the Fed. If you look at a U.S. dollar bill, you will see it is called a Federal Reserve Note. The members of the Federal Reserve Board, who are appointed by the President and confirmed by Congress, together decide on the money supply. The control of the money supply is called **monetary policy**.

The primary way in which the Fed controls the supply of money is through **open-market operations**—the purchase and sale of government bonds. To increase the supply of money, the Fed uses dollars to buy government bonds from the public. This purchase increases the quantity of dollars in circulation. To decrease the supply of money, the Fed sells some of its government bonds. This open-market sale of bonds takes some dollars out of the hands of the public.

In Chapter 18 we discuss in detail how the Fed controls the supply of money. For our current discussion of money, however, these details are not crucial. It is sufficient to assume that the Fed has direct control over the supply of money.

---

[2] Norman Angell, *The Story of Money* (New York: Frederick A. Stokes Company, 1929), 88–89.

How the Quantity of Money Is Measured

One of the goals of this chapter is to determine how the money supply affects the economy; we turn to that problem in the next section. As a background for that analysis, let's first discuss how economists measure the quantity of money.

Because money is the stock of assets used for transactions, the quantity of money is simply the quantity of those assets. In simple economies, this quantity is easily measured. In the POW camp, for example, the quantity of money was the quantity of cigarettes in the camp. But how can we measure the quantity of money in more complex economies such as ours? The answer is not obvious, because no single asset is used for all transactions. People can use various assets to make transactions, although some assets are more convenient than others. This ambiguity leads to numerous measures of the quantity of money.

The most obvious asset that has claim to being included in the quantity of money is **currency**, the sum of outstanding paper money and coins. Most day-to-day transactions use currency as the medium of exchange.

A second type of asset used for transactions is **demand deposits**, the funds people hold in their checking accounts. If most sellers accept personal checks, assets in a checking account are almost as convenient as currency. In both cases, the assets are in a form ready to facilitate a transaction. Demand deposits are therefore usually added to currency when measuring the quantity of money.

Once we admit the logic of including demand deposits in the measured money stock, many other assets become candidates for inclusion. Funds in savings accounts, for example, are readily transferred into checking accounts; these assets are almost as convenient for transactions. Money market mutual funds allow investors to write checks against their accounts, although often restrictions apply with regard to the size of the check or the number of checks written. Because all of these assets can be easily used for transactions, they should arguably be included in the quantity of money.

Since it is unclear exactly which assets should be included in the money stock, various measures are available. Table 6-1 presents the five measures of the money stock that the Federal Reserve calculates for the U.S. economy. Listed from the smallest to the largest, they are designated C, $M1$, $M2$, $M3$, and L. The most commonly used measures for studying the effects of money on the economy are $M1$ and $M2$. There is no consensus, however, about which measure of the money stock is best. Disagreements about monetary policy sometimes arise because different measures of money are moving in different directions. Luckily, the different measures normally move together and so tell the same story about whether the quantity of money is growing quickly or slowly.

Table 6-1   The Measures of Money

Symbol	Assets Included	Amount in 1990 (billions of dollars)
C	Currency	$ 228
M1	Sum of currency, demand deposits, traveler's checks, and other checkable deposits	805
M2	Sum of M1 and overnight repurchase agreements, Eurodollars, money market deposit accounts, money market mutual fund shares, and savings and small time deposits	3,266
M3	Sum of M2 and large time deposits and term repurchase agreements	4,064
L	Sum of M3 and savings bonds, short-term Treasury securities, and other liquid assets	4,895

Source: Federal Reserve.

6-2 The Quantity Theory of Money

Having defined what money is and described how it is controlled and measured, we can now examine how the quantity of money affects the economy. To do this, we must see how the quantity of money is related to other economic variables.

Transactions and the Quantity Equation

People hold money to engage in transactions. The more money they need for transactions, the more money they hold. Thus, the quantity of money in the economy is closely related to the number of dollars exchanged in transactions.

The link between transactions and money is expressed in the following equation, called the **quantity equation,**

$$\text{Money} \times \text{Velocity} = \text{Price} \times \text{Transactions}.$$
$$M \times V = P \times T.$$

We now examine each of the four variables in this equation.

The right-hand side of the quantity equation tells us about transactions. T represents the total number of transactions during some period of time, say, a year. In other words, T is the number of times in a year that any two individuals exchange goods or services for money. P is the price of a typical transaction—the number of dollars exchanged. The product of the price of a transaction and the number of transactions, PT, equals the number of dollars exchanged in a year.

The left-hand side of the quantity equation tells us about the money used to make the transactions. M is the quantity of money. V is called the **transactions velocity of money** and measures the rate at which money circulates in the economy. In other words, velocity tells us the number of times a dollar bill changes hands in a given period of time.

For example, suppose that 60 loaves of bread are sold in a given year at $0.50 per loaf. Then T equals 60 loaves per year and P equals $0.50 per loaf. The total number of dollars exchanged is

$$PT = \$0.50/\text{loaf} \times 60 \text{ loaves/year} = \$30.00/\text{year}.$$

The right-hand side of the quantity equation equals 30 dollars per year, which is the dollar value of all transactions.

Suppose further that the quantity of money in the economy is $10. Then we can compute velocity as

$$\begin{aligned} V &= PT/M \\ &= (\$30/\text{year})/(\$10) \\ &= 3 \text{ times per year.} \end{aligned}$$

That is, for $30 of transactions per year to take place with $10 of money, each dollar must change hands 3 times per year.

The quantity equation is merely an *identity:* the definitions of the four variables make it true. The equation is useful, however, because it tells us that if one of the variables changes, one or more of the others must also change to maintain the equality. For example, if the quantity of money increases and the velocity of money stays unchanged, then either the price or the number of transactions must increase.

From Transactions to Income

Economists usually use a slightly different version of the quantity equation than the one just introduced. The problem with the first equation is that the number of transactions is difficult to measure. To solve this problem, the number of transactions T is replaced by the total output of the economy Y.

Transactions and output are closely related, because the more the economy produces, the more goods are bought and sold. They are not the same, however. When one person sells a used car to another person, for example, they perform a transaction using money, even though the used car is not part of current output. Nonetheless, the dollar value of transactions is roughly proportional to the dollar value of output.

If Y denotes the amount of output and P denotes the price of one unit of output, then the dollar value of output is PY. We encountered measures for these variables when we discussed the national income accounts introduced in Chapter 2: Y is real GNP, P the GNP deflator, and

PY nominal GNP. The quantity equation now becomes

$$\text{Money} \times \text{Velocity} = \text{Price} \times \text{Output.}$$
$$M \quad \times \quad V \quad = \quad P \quad \times \quad Y.$$

Because *Y* is also total income, *V* in this version of the quantity equation is called the **income velocity of money**. The income velocity of money tells us the number of times a dollar bill enters someone's income in a given period of time. This version of the quantity equation is the most common, and it is the one we use from now on.

The Money Demand Function and the Quantity Equation

When analyzing the effects of money on the economy, it is often convenient to express the quantity of money in terms of the quantity of goods and services it can buy. This amount is *M/P* and is called **real money balances**.

A **money demand function** is an equation that shows what determines the quantity of real money balances people wish to hold. A simple money demand function is

$$(M/P)^{\text{d}} = kY,$$

where *k* is a constant. This equation states that the quantity of real balances demanded is proportional to income.

The money demand function is like the demand function for a particular good. Here the "good" is the convenience of holding real money balances. Just as owning an automobile makes it easier for an individual to travel, holding money makes it easier to engage in transactions. Therefore, just as higher national income leads to a greater demand for automobiles, higher national income also leads to a greater demand for real money balances.

From this money demand function, we can derive the quantity equation. To do so we add the condition that the demand for real balances $(M/P)^{\text{d}}$ must equal the supply *M/P*. Therefore,

$$M/P = kY.$$

A simple rearrangement of terms changes this equation into

$$M(1/k) = PY,$$

which can be written as

$$MV = PY,$$

where $V = 1/k$. Hence, when we use the quantity equation, we are assuming that the supply of real money balances equals the demand, and that the demand is proportional to income.

The Assumption of Constant Velocity

One can view the quantity equation as merely defining velocity as the ratio of nominal GNP to the quantity of money. Yet we can turn the equation into a useful theory—called the **quantity theory of money**—by making the additional assumption that velocity is constant.

Like many of the assumptions in economics, we can justify the assumption of constant velocity only as an approximation. Velocity does change if the money demand function changes. For example, the introduction of the automatic teller machine allows people to reduce their average money holdings, which reduces the money demand parameter k; the machines raise the rate at which money circulates in the economy, which implies greater velocity V. Yet economists have found that the assumption of constant velocity provides a good approximation in many situations. Let's therefore assume that velocity is constant and determine what this assumption implies about the effects of the money supply on the economy.

Once we assume that velocity is constant, the quantity equation can be seen as a theory of nominal GNP. The quantity equation says

$$M\overline{V} = PY,$$

where the bar over V means that velocity is fixed. Therefore, a change in the quantity of money (M) must cause a proportionate change in nominal GNP (PY). That is, the quantity of money determines the dollar value of the economy's output.

Money, Prices, and Inflation

We now have the elements of a theory that can help us to explain what determines the overall level of prices in the economy:

1. The factors of production and the production function determine the level of output Y. We borrow this conclusion from Chapter 3.

2. The money supply determines the nominal value of output PY. This conclusion follows from the quantity equation and the assumption that the velocity of money is fixed.

3. The price level P is then the ratio of the nominal value of output PY to the level of output Y.

In other words, the productive capability of the economy determines real GNP, the quantity of money determines nominal GNP, and the GNP deflator is the ratio of nominal GNP to real GNP.

This theory explains what happens when the Fed changes the supply of money. Because velocity is fixed, any change in the supply of money leads to a proportionate change in nominal GNP. Because the factors of production and the production function have already determined real GNP, the change in nominal GNP must represent a change in the price level. Hence, the quantity theory implies that the price level is proportional to the money supply.

Because the inflation rate is the percentage change in the price level, this theory of the price level is also a theory of the inflation rate. The quantity equation, written in percentage-change form, is

% Change in M + % Change in V = % Change in P + % Change in Y.

Consider each of these four terms. First, the percentage change in the quantity of money is under the control of the central bank. Second, the percentage change in velocity reflects shifts in money demand; we have assumed velocity is constant, so the percentage change in velocity is zero. Third, the percentage change in the price level is the rate of inflation; this is the variable in the equation that we would like to explain. Fourth, the percentage change in output depends on growth in the factors of production and on technological progress; we can take the growth of output to be a constant. This analysis tells us that (except for a constant that depends on exogenous growth in output) the growth in the money supply determines the rate of inflation.

Thus, the quantity theory of money states that the central bank, which controls the money supply, has the ultimate control over the rate of inflation. If the central bank keeps the money supply stable, the price level will be stable. If the central bank increases the money supply quickly, the price level will rise quickly.

//

F Y I **Products and Percentage Changes**

When manipulating the quantity equation and many other relationships in economics, there is an arithmetic trick that is useful to remember: *the percentage change of a product of two variables is approximately the sum of the percentage changes in each of the variables.* We used this trick when we wrote the quantity equation in percentage changes.

To see how this trick works, let's apply it to the GNP deflator (P), real GNP (Y), and nominal GNP ($P \times Y$). The trick states that

% Change in $(P \times Y) \approx$ (% Change in P) + (% Change in Y).

For example, suppose that in one year, real GNP is 100 and the GNP deflator is 2; the next year real GNP is 103 and the GNP deflator is 2.1. We can calculate that real GNP rose by 3 percent, and the GNP deflator rose by 5 percent. Nominal GNP rose from 200 the first year to 216.3 the second year, an increase of 8.15 percent. Notice that the growth in nominal GNP (8.15 percent) is approximately the sum of the growth in the GNP deflator (5 percent) and the growth in real GNP (3 percent).

//

CASE STUDY 6-3

A Century of Money Growth and Inflation

Milton Friedman, who for many years was a professor at the University of Chicago and who won the Nobel Prize for economics in 1976, once said, "Inflation is always and everywhere a monetary phenomenon." The quantity theory of money indeed leads us to agree that the growth in the quantity of money is the primary determinant of the inflation rate. Yet Friedman's claim is empirical, not theoretical. To evaluate his claim, and to judge the usefulness of our theory, we need to look at data on money and prices.

Friedman, together with fellow economist Anna Schwartz, wrote two treatises on monetary history that documented the sources and effects of changes in the quantity of money over the past century.[3] Figure 6-1 uses some of their data and plots the average rate of money growth and the average rate of inflation in the United States over each decade since the 1870s. The data verify the link between growth in the quantity of money and inflation. Decades with high money growth tend to have high inflation, and decades with low money growth tend to have low inflation.

If we looked at month-to-month changes in money growth and inflation, rather than decade-to-decade changes, we would not see as close a connection between these two variables. Our theory of inflation works best in the long run, not in the short run. We examine the short-run impact of changes in the quantity of money when we turn to economic fluctuations beginning in Chapter 8.

---

[3] Milton Friedman and Anna J. Schwartz, *A Monetary History of the United States, 1867–1960* (Princeton, N.J.: Princeton University Press, 1963); Milton Friedman and Anna J. Schwartz, *Monetary Trends in the United States and the United Kingdom: Their Relation to Income, Prices, and Interest Rates, 1867–1975* (Chicago: University of Chicago Press, 1982).

6-3 Seigniorage: The Revenue From Printing Money

The government can finance its spending in three ways. First, it can raise revenue through taxes, such as personal and corporate income taxes. Second, it can borrow from the public. Third, it can simply print money.

The revenue raised through the printing of money is called **seigniorage**. The term comes from *seigneur*, the French word for feudal lord. In

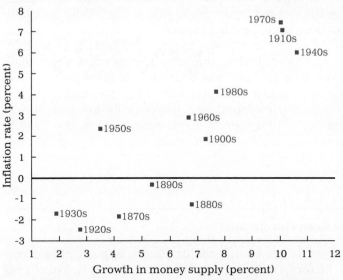

Source: For data through the 1960s: Milton Friedman and Anna J. Schwartz, *Monetary Trends in the United States and the United Kingdom: Their Relaton to Income, Prices, and Interest Rates 1867–1975*. (Chicago: University of Chicago Press, 1982). For recent data: U.S. Department of Commerce, Federal Reserve Board.

Figure 6-1   **Money Growth and Inflation in the Decades Since 1870.**   In this scatterplot of money growth and inflation, each point represents a decade. The horizontal axis shows the average growth in the money supply (as measured by *M*2) over the decade, and the vertical axis shows the average rate of inflation (as measured by the GNP deflator). The positive association between money growth and inflation is evidence for the quantity theory's prediction that high money growth leads to high inflation.

the Middle Ages, the lord had the exclusive right on his manor to coin money. Today that right belongs to the government, and it is one source of revenue.

When the government prints money to finance expenditure, it increases the money supply. For the reasons we have already discussed, the increase in the money supply leads to inflation. Therefore, printing money to raise revenue is like imposing an *inflation tax.*

At first it may not be obvious that inflation can be viewed as a tax. After all, no one receives a bill for this tax—the government merely prints the money it needs. Who then pays the inflation tax? The answer is: the holders of money. As prices rise, the real value of the dollars you are holding in your wallet falls. When the government prints new money for its use, it makes the old money in the hands of the public less valuable. Thus, inflation is a tax on holding money.

The amount raised by printing money varies substantially from country to country. In the United States, the amount has been very small: seigniorage has accounted for less than 3 percent of government revenue. In Italy and Greece, seigniorage has been over 10 percent of government revenue.[4] In countries experiencing hyperinflation, seigniorage is often the government's chief source of revenue—indeed, the need to print money to finance expenditure is a primary cause of hyperinflation.

CASE STUDY 6-4

Paying for the American Revolution

Although seigniorage has not been a major source of government revenue in recent U.S. history, the situation was very different two centuries ago. Beginning in 1775 the Continental Congress needed to find a way to finance the Revolution, but it had limited ability to raise revenue through taxation. It therefore relied heavily on the printing of fiat money to help pay for the war.

The Continental Congress's reliance on seigniorage increased over time. In 1775 new issues of continental currency were approximately $6 million. This amount increased to $19 million in 1776, $13 million in 1777, $63.4 million in 1778, and $124.8 million in 1779.

Not surprisingly, this rapid growth in the money supply led to massive inflation. By the end of the war, the price of gold measured in continental dollars had increased to more than 100 times its level of only a few years earlier. The large quantity of the continental currency made the continental dollar nearly worthless. Even today we use the expression "not worth a continental" to mean that something has little real value.

6-4 Inflation and Interest Rates

So far we have examined the link between money growth and inflation. We now examine the link between inflation and interest rates.

---

[4] Stanley Fischer, "Seigniorage and the Case for a National Money," *Journal of Political Economy* 90 (April 1982): 295–313.

Two Interest Rates: Real and Nominal

Suppose you deposit your savings in a bank account that pays 8 percent interest annually. Next year, you withdraw your savings and the accumulated interest. Are you 8 percent richer than you were when you made the deposit a year earlier?

The answer depends on what "richer" means. Certainly, you have 8 percent more dollars than you had before. But if prices have risen, so that each dollar buys less, then your purchasing power has not risen by 8 percent. If the inflation rate was 5 percent, then the amount of goods you can buy has increased by only 3 percent. And if the inflation rate was 10 percent, then your purchasing power actually fell by 2 percent.

Economists call the interest rate that the bank pays the **nominal interest rate** and the increase in your purchasing power the **real interest rate**. If i denotes the nominal interest rate, r the real interest rate, and π the rate of inflation, then the relationship between these three variables can be written as

$$r = i - \pi.$$

The real interest rate is the difference between the nominal interest rate and the rate of inflation.

The Fisher Effect

Rearranging terms in our equation for the real interest rate, we can show that the nominal interest rate is the sum of the real interest rate and the inflation rate:

$$i = r + \pi.$$

The equation written in this way is called the **Fisher equation**, after economist Irving Fisher (1867–1947). It shows that the nominal interest rate can change for two reasons: because the real interest rate changes or because the inflation rate changes.

Once we separate the nominal interest rate into these two parts, we can use this equation to develop a theory of the nominal interest rate. Chapter 3 showed that the real interest rate adjusts to equilibrate saving and investment. This chapter shows that the rate of money growth determines the rate of inflation. The Fisher equation then tells us to add the real interest rate and the inflation rate together to determine the nominal interest rate.

The quantity theory and the Fisher equation together tell us the effect of money growth on the nominal interest rate. *According to the quantity theory, an increase in the rate of money growth of 1 percent causes a 1 percent increase in the rate of inflation. According to the Fisher equation, a 1 percent increase in the rate of inflation in turn causes a 1 percent increase in the nominal interest rate.* This one-for-one relation between the inflation rate and the nominal interest rate is called the **Fisher effect**.

Inflation and Nominal Interest Rates

Figure 6-2 shows the nominal interest rate and the inflation rate in the United States since 1952. It is apparent that years of high inflation tend to be years of high nominal interest rates. The link between inflation and interest rates is well known to Wall Street investment firms; many of them hire *Fed watchers* to monitor monetary policy and news about inflation in order to anticipate changes in interest rates.

Figure 6-2 also shows that inflation is not the only determinant of the nominal interest rate—the real interest rate changes as well. Because the real interest rate is the difference between the nominal interest rate and the inflation rate, the real interest rate is shown in this figure as the distance between the two lines. We can see, for example, that the real interest rate was low (and sometimes negative) in the 1970s and high in the 1980s. As we discussed in Chapter 3, the high real interest rates in the 1980s are often attributed to the large federal budget deficits that reduced national saving.

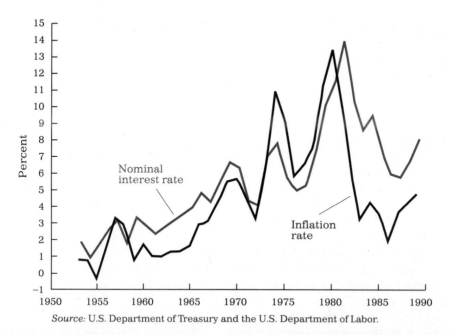

Source: U.S. Department of Treasury and the U.S. Department of Labor.

Figure 6-2 **Inflation and Nominal Interest Rates.** This figure plots the nominal interest rate (the yield on three-month Treasury bills) and the inflation rate (the percentage change in the CPI). It shows the Fisher effect: higher inflation leads to a higher nominal interest rate.

Two Real Interest Rates: *Ex Ante* and *Ex Post*

When a borrower and a lender agree on a nominal interest rate, they do not know what the inflation rate over the term of the loan will be. Therefore, we must distinguish between two concepts of the real interest rate: the real interest rate the borrower and lender expect when the loan is made, called the **ex ante real interest rate**, and the real interest rate actually realized, called the **ex post real interest rate**.

Although borrowers and lenders cannot predict future inflation with certainty, they do have some expectation of the inflation rate. Let π denote actual future inflation and π^e the expectation of future inflation. The *ex ante* real interest rate is then $i - \pi^e$, and the *ex post* real interest rate is $i - \pi$. The two real interest rates differ when actual inflation π differs from expected inflation π^e.

How does this distinction between actual and expected inflation modify the Fisher effect? Obviously, the nominal interest rate cannot adjust to actual inflation, because actual inflation is not known when the nominal interest rate is set. The nominal interest rate can adjust only to expected inflation. The Fisher effect is therefore more precisely written as

$$i = r + \pi^e.$$

The *ex ante* real interest rate r is determined by equilibrium in the market for goods and services, as described by the model in Chapter 3. The nominal interest rate i moves one-for-one with changes in expected inflation π^e.

CASE STUDY 6-6

Nominal Interest Rates in the Nineteenth Century

Although recent data show a positive relationship between nominal interest rates and inflation rates, this finding is not universal. In data from the late nineteenth and early twentieth centuries, high nominal interest rates did not accompany high inflation. The apparent absence of any Fisher effect during this time puzzled even Irving Fisher. He suggested that inflation "caught merchants napping."

How should we interpret the absence of an apparent Fisher effect in nineteenth-century data? Does this period of history provide evidence against the adjustment of nominal interest rates to inflation? Recent research suggests that this period has little to tell us about the validity of the Fisher effect. The reason is that the Fisher effect relates the nominal interest rate to expected inflation and, according to this research, inflation at this time was largely unexpected.

Although expectations cannot be directly observed, we can draw inferences about them by examining the persistence of inflation. In recent experience, inflation has been highly persistent: when it is high one year, it tends to be high the next year as well. Therefore, when people have observed high inflation, it has been rational for them to expect high inflation in the future. During the nineteenth century, however, when the gold standard was in effect, inflation had little persistence. High inflation in one year was just as likely to be followed the next year by low inflation as by high inflation. Therefore, high inflation did not imply high expected inflation and did not lead to high nominal interest rates. So, in a sense, Fisher was right to say that inflation "caught merchants napping."[5]

6-5 The Nominal Interest Rate and the Demand for Money

The quantity theory is based on a simple money demand function: it assumes that the demand for real balances is proportional to income. Although the quantity theory is a good place to start when analyzing the role of money, it is not the whole story. Here we introduce another determinant of the quantity of money demanded—the nominal interest rate.

The Cost of Holding Money

The dollars you hold in your wallet do not earn interest. If instead of holding those dollars you used them to buy government bonds or deposited them in a savings account, you would earn the nominal interest rate. The nominal interest rate is what you give up by holding money rather than bonds: it is the opportunity cost of holding money.

We can see that the cost of holding money equals the nominal interest rate by looking at the real returns on alternative assets. Assets other than money, such as government bonds, earn the real return r. Money, however, is expected to decline in real value at the rate of inflation; its expected real return is $-\pi^e$. When you hold money, you give up the difference between these two returns. Thus, the cost of holding money is $r - (-\pi^e)$, which the Fisher equation tells us is the nominal interest rate i.

Just as the quantity of bread demanded depends on the price of bread, the quantity of money demanded depends on the price of holding money. Hence, the demand for real balances depends both on the level

[5] Robert B. Barsky, "The Fisher Effect and the Forecastability and Persistence of Inflation," *Journal of Monetary Economics* 19 (January 1987): 3–24.

of income and on the nominal interest rate. We write the general money demand function as

$$(M/P)^d = L(i, Y).$$

The letter L is used to denote money demand, because money is the *liquid* asset—the asset most easily used to make transactions. This equation states that the demand for the liquidity of real money balances is a function of income and the nominal interest rate. The higher the income Y, the greater the demand for real balances. The higher the nominal interest rate i, the lower the demand for real balances.

Future Money and Current Prices

Consider how this general money demand function changes our theory of the price level. First, equate the supply of real balances M/P to the demand $L(i, Y)$:

$$M/P = L(i, Y).$$

Next, use the Fisher equation to write the nominal interest rate as the sum of the real interest rate and the expected inflation rate:

$$M/P = L(r + \pi^e, Y).$$

This equation states that the level of real balances depends on the expected rate of inflation.

The general money demand equation tells a more sophisticated story than the quantity theory about what determines the price level. The quantity theory of money says that today's money supply determines today's price level. This conclusion remains partly true: if the nominal interest rate and the level of output are held constant, the price level moves proportionately with the money supply. Yet the nominal interest rate is not constant; it depends on expected inflation, which in turn depends on money growth. The presence of the nominal interest rate in the money demand function yields an additional channel through which money supply affects the price level.

This general money demand equation implies that the price level depends not just on today's money supply but also on the money supply expected in the future. To see why, suppose the Fed announces that it will raise the money supply in the future but does not change the money supply today. If people believe the Fed's announcement, they will expect higher money growth and higher inflation. Through the Fisher effect, this increase in expected inflation will increase the nominal interest rate. The higher nominal interest rate immediately reduces the demand for real money balances. Because nominal balances have not been changed, the reduced demand for real balances leads to a higher price level. Hence, higher expected money growth in the future leads to a higher price level today.

The effect of money on prices is fairly complex. The appendix to this chapter works out the mathematics relating the price level to current and future money. The conclusion of that analysis is that the price level depends on a weighted average of the current money supply and the money supply expected to prevail in the future.

How to Stop a Hyperinflation

The sensitivity of real money balances to the nominal interest rate complicates the problem of stopping a hyperinflation. If the quantity theory were completely true and the nominal interest rate did not affect money demand, then stopping a hyperinflation would be easy: the central bank would merely need to stop printing money. As soon as the quantity of money stabilized, the price level would stabilize.

But if money demand depends on the nominal interest rate, ending a hyperinflation is more complicated. The fall in inflation will lead to a fall in the cost of holding money and, therefore, an increase in real money balances. If the central bank merely stops printing money (that is, keeps M constant), the increase in real balances (M/P) necessitates a fall in prices. Hence, the apparently simple task of ending a hyperinflation will, if the central bank is not careful, lead to falling prices. In this case, the central bank will not have achieved its goal of price stability.

What monetary policy should the central bank pursue to achieve stable prices? That is, what path should the money supply follow to end the inflation without causing deflation? To answer this question, we work backwards. We begin with the goal of price stabilization and find the path of the money supply that is consistent with that objective. Figure 6-3 shows the five steps to determining the path of the money supply.

1. The desired path of the price level is at the top of this figure. The price level is rising during the hyperinflation. Then the new monetary policy goes into effect and prices stabilize.

2. Next is the rate of inflation π, which is the growth in the price level. It is high until the period of price stability, when it drops to zero.

3. The nominal interest rate i adjusts one-for-one with the rate of inflation. This is required by the Fisher effect. Therefore, the nominal interest rate also is high until prices stabilize and then falls to a lower level.

4. This fall in the nominal interest rate leads to a jump up in real balances, because the cost of holding money has declined.

5. Since we now know the path of the price level P and the path of real balances M/P, we can infer the required path of money M. At the moment the hyperinflation ends, the money supply must jump up to accommodate the increase in real balances. After the jump, the money supply stays constant to ensure price stability.

One issue that this analysis does not address is the central bank's credibility. For the expected inflation and the nominal interest rate to fall, people must expect that the central bank will stop printing so much

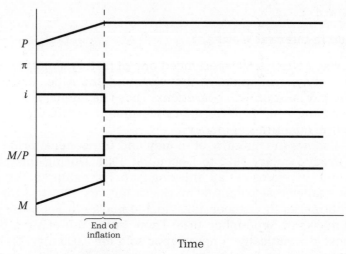

Note: Each variable is drawn on its own scale.

Figure 6-3 **How to Stop Inflation When Real Balances Depend on the Nominal Interest Rate.** By examining the paths we expect the key monetary variables to follow, we can derive the path that the money supply must follow to end an inflation. (1) At top is the desired path of the price level P. (2) Next is the rate of inflation π, which is high until the period of price stability, when it drops to zero. (3) The nominal interest rate i adjusts one-for-one with the rate in inflation. (4) The fall in the nominal interest rate leads to a jump up in real balances M/P. (5) The path of the money supply M then depends on the path of the price level P and the path of real balances M/P.

money. This expectation is hard to create in the midst of a hyperinflation. Indeed, if the central bank follows our advice and makes the money supply jump up, it may have trouble convincing the public that the hyperinflation is over. Yet if the central bank does not achieve credibility, expected inflation and the nominal interest rate will not fall, real balances will not rise, and the jump in the money supply will lead to more inflation.

In practice, the central bank usually achieves credibility by removing the underlying cause of the hyperinflation: the need for seigniorage. Most hyperinflations begin when the government needs to print money to pay for expenditures. As long as the need for seigniorage exists, the public is not likely to believe the central bank's announcements about price stability. For this reason, the ends of hyperinflations usually coincide with fiscal reforms—reductions in government spending and increases in taxes—that reduce the need for seigniorage. Hence, even if inflation is always and everywhere a monetary phenomenon, the end of hyperinflation is often a fiscal phenomenon as well.[6]

[6] Thomas J. Sargent, "The End of Four Big Inflations," in Robert Hall, ed., *Inflation* (Chicago: University of Chicago Press, 1983), 41–98; Rudiger Dornbusch and Stanley Fischer, "Stopping Hyperinflations: Past and Present," *Weltwirtschaftliches Archiv* 122 (April 1986):1–47.

Hyperinflation in Interwar Germany

After World War I Germany experienced one of history's most spectacular examples of hyperinflation. At the war's end, the Allies demanded that Germany pay substantial reparations. These payments led to fiscal deficits in Germany, which the German government eventually financed by printing large quantities of money.

Figure 6-4 shows the quantity of money and the general price level in Germany from January 1922 to December 1924. During this period both money and prices rose at an amazing rate. For example, the price of a daily newspaper rose from 0.30 marks in January 1921 to 1 mark in May 1922, to 8 marks in October 1922, to 100 marks in February 1923, and to 1,000 marks in September 1923. Then, in the fall of 1923, prices rose even more dramatically: a newspaper sold for 2,000 marks on October 1, 20,000 marks on October 15, 1 million marks on October 29, 15 million marks on November 9, and 70 million marks on November 17. In December 1923 the money supply and prices abruptly stabilized.[7]

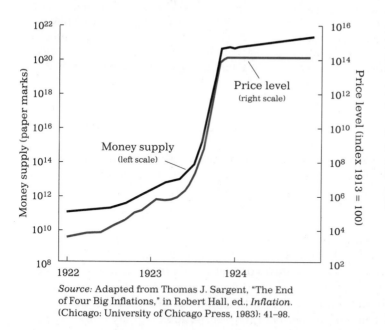

Figure 6-4 **Money and Prices in Interwar Germany.** This figure shows the money supply and the price level in Germany from January 1922 to December 1924. The immense increases in the money supply and the price level provide one of the most dramatic illustrations of the effects of printing large amounts of money.

Source: Adapted from Thomas J. Sargent, "The End of Four Big Inflations," in Robert Hall, ed., *Inflation.* (Chicago: University of Chicago Press, 1983): 41–98.

---

[7] The data on newspaper prices are from Michael Mussa, "Sticky Individual Prices and the Dynamics of the General Price Level," *Carnegie-Rochester Conference on Public Policy* 15 (Autumn 1981): 261–296.

Just as fiscal problems caused the German hyperinflation, a fiscal reform ended it. At the end of 1923, the number of government employees was cut by one-third, and the reparations payments were temporarily suspended and eventually reduced. At the same time, a new central bank, the Rentenbank, replaced the old central bank, the Reichsbank. The Rentenbank was committed to not financing the government by printing money.

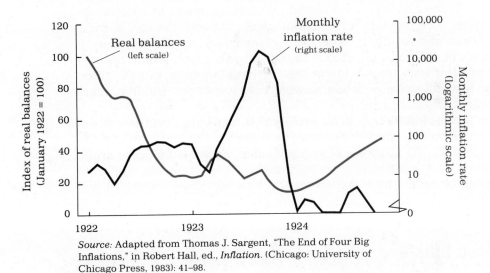

Source: Adapted from Thomas J. Sargent, "The End of Four Big Inflations," in Robert Hall, ed., *Inflation.* (Chicago: University of Chicago Press, 1983): 41–98.

Figure 6-5 **Inflation and Real Balances in Interwar Germany.** This figure shows inflation and real balances in Germany from January 1922 to December 1924. As inflation rose, real balances fell. When the inflation ended, real balances rose.

According to our theoretical analysis, an end to a hyperinflation should lead to an increase in real money balances. Figure 6-5 shows that real balances in Germany did fall as inflation increased, and then increased again as inflation fell. Yet in contrast to our theoretical analysis, the increase in real balances was not instantaneous. Perhaps the adjustment of real balances to the cost of holding money is a gradual process. Or perhaps it took time for people in Germany to believe that the inflation had really ended, so that the expected rate of inflation fell more gradually than actual inflation.

6-6 The Social Costs of Inflation

Our discussion of the causes and effects of inflation does not tell us much about the social problems that result from inflation. We turn to those problems now.

If you ask the average person why inflation is a social problem, he will probably say that inflation makes him poorer. "Each year my boss gives me a raise, but prices go up and that takes some of my raise away from me." The implicit assumption in this statement is that if there were no inflation, he would get the same raise and be able to buy more goods.

This complaint about inflation is a common fallacy. From Chapters 3 and 4, we know that increases in the purchasing power of labor come from capital accumulation and technological progress; the real wage is independent of how much money the government chooses to print. If the government slowed the rate of money growth, prices would not rise as quickly. But workers would not see their real wage increasing more rapidly. Instead, when inflation slowed, they would get smaller raises each year.

Why then is inflation a social problem? It turns out that the costs of inflation are subtle. Indeed, economists disagree about the size of the social costs. To the surprise of many laymen, some economists argue that the costs of inflation are not very great—at least for the moderate rates of inflation we have experienced in recent years in the United States.[8]

Expected Inflation

Consider first the case of expected inflation. Suppose that every month the price level rose by 1 percent. What would be the social costs of such a steady and predictable 12 percent annual inflation?

One cost is the distortion of the inflation tax on holding money. As we have already discussed, a higher inflation rate leads to a higher nominal interest rate, which in turn leads to lower real money balances. If people are to hold lower money balances on average, they must make more frequent trips to the bank to withdraw money—for example, they might withdraw $50 twice a week rather than $100 once a week. The inconvenience of reducing money holding is metaphorically called the **shoeleather cost** of inflation, because walking to the bank more often causes one's shoes to wear out more quickly.

---

[8] See, for example, Chapter 2 of Alan Blinder, *Hard Heads, Soft Hearts: Tough-Minded Economics for a Just Society* (Reading, Mass.: Addison Wesley, 1987).

A second cost of inflation arises because high inflation induces firms to change their posted prices more often. Changing prices is sometimes costly: for example, it may require printing and distributing a new catalog. These costs are called **menu costs**, because the higher the rate of inflation, the more often restaurants have to print new menus.

A third cost of inflation arises because firms facing menu costs change prices infrequently; therefore, the higher the rate of inflation, the greater the variability in relative prices. For example, suppose a firm issues a new catalog every January. If there is no inflation, then the firm's prices relative to those of other goods are constant over the year. Yet if inflation is 1 percent per month, then from the beginning to the end of the year the firm's relative prices fall by 12 percent. Thus, inflation induces variability in relative prices. Since free-market economies rely on relative prices to allocate resources efficiently, inflation leads to microeconomic inefficiencies.

A fourth cost of inflation is attributable to the way the tax laws are written. Many provisions of the tax code do not take into account the effects of inflation. Thus, inflation can alter individuals' tax liability, often in ways that lawmakers did not intend.

One example of the failure of the tax code to deal with inflation is the income tax's treatment of nominal capital gains. Suppose you buy some stock today and sell it a year from now at the same real price. It would seem reasonable for the government not to levy a tax, since you have earned no real income from this investment. Indeed, if there is no inflation, a zero tax liability would be the outcome. But suppose the rate of inflation is 10 percent and you initially paid $100 per share for the stock; for the real price to be the same a year later, you must sell the stock for $110 per share. In this case the tax code, which ignores the effects of inflation, says that you have earned $10 per share in income, and the government taxes you on this capital gain. The problem, of course, is that the tax code measures income as the nominal rather than the real capital gain. In this example, and in many others, inflation distorts how taxes are levied.

A fifth cost of inflation is the inconvenience of living in a world with a changing price level. Money is the yardstick with which we measure economic transactions. When there is inflation, that yardstick is changing in length. Suppose, for example, that Congress passed a law specifying that a yard would equal 36 inches in 1990, 35 inches in 1991, 34 inches in 1992, and so on. Although the law would result in no ambiguity, it would be highly inconvenient. When someone measured a distance in yards, it would be necessary to specify whether the measurement was in 1990 yards or 1991 yards; to compare distances measured in different years, one would need to make an "inflation" correction. Similarly, the dollar is a less useful measure when its value is always changing.

CASE STUDY 6-8

Life During the Bolivian Hyperinflation

The costs of inflation become most apparent when inflation reaches extreme levels. The following article from the *Wall Street Journal* shows what life was like during the hyperinflation in Bolivia in 1985. Note the costs of inflation that the article emphasizes. Does the Bolivian experience conform to the assessment of Lenin and Keynes in the quotation that began this chapter?

Precarious Peso - Amid Wild Inflation, Bolivians Concentrate on Swapping Currency

LA PAZ, Bolivia - When Edgar Miranda gets his monthly teacher's pay of 25 million pesos, he hasn't a moment to lose. Every hour, pesos drop in value. So, while his wife rushes to market to lay in a month's supply of rice and noodles, he is off with the rest of the pesos to change them into black-market dollars.

Mr. Miranda is practicing the First Rule of Survival amid the most out-of-control inflation in the world today. Bolivia is a case study of how runaway inflation undermines a society.

Price increases are so huge that the figures build up almost beyond comprehension. In one six-month period, for example, prices soared at an annual rate of 38,000%. By official count, however, last year's inflation reached 2,000%, and this year's is expected to hit 8,000%—though other estimates range many times higher. In any event, Bolivia's rate dwarfs Israel's 370% and Argentina's 1,100%—two other cases of severe inflation.

It is easier to comprehend what happens to the 38-year-old Mr. Miranda's pay if he doesn't quickly change it into dollars. The day he was paid 25 million pesos, a dollar costs 500,000 pesos. So he received $50. Just days later, with the rate at 900,000 pesos, he would have received $27.

Unexpected Inflation

Unexpected inflation has an effect that is perhaps more pernicious than any of the costs of steady, anticipated inflation: it arbitrarily redistributes wealth among individuals. You can see how this works by examining long-term loans. Loan agreements typically specify a nominal interest rate, which is based on the expected rate of inflation. If inflation turns out differently from what was expected, the *ex post* real return that the debtor pays to the creditor differs from what both parties anticipated. On the one hand, if inflation turns out to be higher than expected, the debtor wins and the creditor loses because the debtor repays the loan with less valuable dollars. On the other hand, if inflation turns out to be lower than expected, the creditor wins and the debtor loses because the repayment is worth more than the two parties anticipated.

Consider, for example, a person taking out a mortgage in 1960. At the time, a 30-year mortgage had an interest rate of about 6 percent per

"We think only about today and converting every peso into dollars," says Ronald MacLean, the manager of a gold-mining firm. "We have become myopic."

And intent on survival. Civil servants won't hand out a form without a bribe. Lawyers, accountants, hairdressers, even prostitutes have almost given up working to become money-changers in the streets. Workers stage repeated strikes and steal from their bosses. The bosses smuggle production abroad, take out phony loans, duck taxes—anything to get dollars for speculation.

The production at the state mines, for example, dropped to 12,000 tons last year from 18,000. The miners pad their wages by smuggling out the richest ore in their lunch pails, and the ore goes by a contraband network into neighboring Peru. Without a major tin mine, Peru now exports some 4,000 metric tons of tin a year.

"We don't produce anything. We are all currency speculators," a heavy-equipment dealer in La Paz says. "People don't know what's good and bad anymore. We have become an amoral society. . . ."

It is an open secret that practically all of the black-market dollars come from the illegal cocaine trade with the U.S. Cocaine traffickers earn an estimated $1 billion a year. . . .

But meanwhile the country is suffering from inflation largely because the government's revenues cover a mere 15% of its expenditures and its deficit has widened to nearly 25% of the country's total annual output. The revenues are hurt by a lag in tax payments, and taxes aren't being collected largely because of widespread theft and bribery.

Source: Reprinted by permission of the *Wall Street Journal,* © August 13, 1985, page 1, Dow Jones & Company, Inc. All Rights Reserved Worldwide.

year. This rate was based on a low rate of expected inflation—inflation over the previous decade had averaged only 2½ percent. The creditor probably expected to receive a real return of about 3½ percent, and the debtor expected to pay this real return. In fact, however, over the life of the mortgage, the inflation rate averaged 5 percent, so the *ex post* real return was only 1 percent. This unanticipated inflation benefited the debtor at the expense of the creditor.

Unanticipated inflation also hurts individuals on fixed pensions. Workers and firms often agree on a fixed nominal pension when the worker retires (or even earlier). Since the pension is deferred earnings, the worker is essentially providing the firm a loan: the worker provides labor services to the firm while young, but does not get fully paid until old age. Like any creditor, the worker is hurt when inflation is higher than anticipated. Like any debtor, the firm is hurt when inflation is lower than anticipated.

These situations provide a clear argument against highly variable inflation. The more variable the rate of inflation, the greater the uncertainty that both debtors and creditors face. Since most people are *risk averse*—they dislike uncertainty—the unpredictability caused by highly variable inflation hurts almost everyone.

Given these effects of inflation uncertainty, it is puzzling that nominal contracts are so prevalent. One might expect debtors and creditors to protect themselves from this uncertainty by writing contracts in real terms—that is, by indexing to some measure of the price level. In economies with extremely high and variable inflation, indexation is often widespread; sometimes this indexation takes the form of writing contracts using a more stable foreign currency. In economies with moderate inflation, such as the United States, indexation is less common. Yet even in the United States, some long-term obligations are indexed: for example, Social Security benefits for the elderly are adjusted automatically in response to changes in the consumer price index.

CASE STUDY 6-9

The Free Silver Movement, the Election of 1896, and the Wizard of Oz

The redistributions of wealth caused by unexpected changes in the price level are often a source of political turmoil, as evidenced by the Free Silver movement in the late nineteenth century. From 1880 to 1896 the price level in the United States fell 23 percent. This deflation was good for creditors, the bankers of the Northeast, but it was bad for debtors, the farmers of the South and West. One proposed solution to this problem was to replace the gold standard with a bimetallic standard, under which both gold and silver could be minted into coin. The move to a bimetallic standard would increase the money supply and stop the deflation.

The silver issue dominated the presidential election of 1896. William McKinley, the Republican nominee, campaigned on a platform of preserving the gold standard. William Jennings Bryan, the Democratic nominee, supported the bimetallic standard. In a famous speech, Bryan proclaimed, "You shall not press down upon the brow of labor this crown of thorns, you shall not crucify mankind upon a cross of gold." Not surprisingly, McKinley was the candidate of the conservative eastern establishment, while Bryan was the candidate of the southern and western populists.

This debate over silver found its most memorable expression in a children's book, *The Wizard of Oz*. Written by a midwestern journalist, Frank Baum, just after the 1896 election, it tells the story of Dorothy, a girl lost in a strange land far from her home in Kansas. Dorothy (representing traditional American values) makes three friends: a scarecrow (the farmer), a tin woodman (the industrial worker), and a lion whose roar exceeds his might (William Jennings Bryan). Together, the four of them make their way along a perilous yellow brick road (the gold standard), hoping to find the Wizard who will help Dorothy return home. Eventually they arrive in Emerald City (Washington), where everyone sees the world through green glasses (money). The Wizard (William McKinley) tries to be all things to all people but turns out to be a fraud. Dorothy's problem is solved only when she learns about the magical power of her silver slippers.[9]

Although the Republicans won the election of 1896 and the United States stayed on a gold standard, the Free Silver advocates got what they ultimately wanted: inflation. Around the time of the election, gold was discovered in Alaska, Australia, and South Africa. In addition, gold refiners devised the cyanide process, which facilitated the extraction of gold from ore. These developments led to increases in the money supply and in prices. From 1896 to 1910 the price level rose 35 percent.

The Level and Variability of Inflation

No discussion of inflation would be complete without mentioning an important but little understood fact: high inflation is variable inflation. That is, when economists study the experiences of different countries, they find that countries with high average inflation also have inflation rates that change greatly from year to year. The implication is that if a country decides to pursue a high-inflation monetary policy, it will likely have to accept highly variable inflation as well. For the reasons discussed previously, highly variable inflation increases uncertainty for both creditors and debtors by subjecting them to arbitrary and potentially large wealth redistributions. The social cost of this uncertainty is hard to evaluate, but it is most likely substantial.

6-7 Conclusion: The Classical Dichotomy

We have finished our discussion of money and inflation. Let's now step back and examine an important assumption that has been implicit in our discussion.

In Chapters 3, 4, and 5, we explained numerous macroeconomic variables, such as real GNP, the capital stock, the real wage, and the real interest rate. These variables fall into two categories. The first category is *quantities*. For example, real GNP is the quantity of goods produced in a given year; the capital stock is the amount of capital

---

[9] The movie made 40 years later hid much of the allegory by changing Dorothy's slippers from silver to ruby. For more on this topic, see Henry M. Littlefield, "The Wizard of Oz: Parable on Populism," *American Quarterly* 16 (Spring 1964): 47–58; and Hugh Rockoff, "The Wizard of Oz as a Monetary Allegory," *Journal of Political Economy* 98 (August 1990): 739–760.

available at a given time. The second category is *relative prices*. For example, the real wage is the relative price of consumption and leisure; the real interest rate is the price of output today relative to output tomorrow. Together these two categories—quantities and relative prices—are called **real variables**.

In this chapter we examined **nominal variables**. Nominal variables are expressed in terms of money. There are many nominal variables: the price level, the inflation rate, the wage a person earns (the number of dollars he receives for working).

In previous chapters we were able to explain many important real variables without introducing nominal variables or the existence of money. We studied the level and allocation of the economy's output without mentioning the rate of inflation. Our theory of the labor market explained the real wage without explaining the nominal wage.

The **classical dichotomy** is the term macroeconomists give to this theoretical separation of real and nominal variables. It is the hallmark of classical macroeconomic theory. It allows us to examine real variables, as we have done, while ignoring nominal variables. The classical dichotomy arises because, in the models we have developed, changes in the money supply do not influence real variables. This irrelevance of money for real variables is called **monetary neutrality**. For many purposes—in particular for studying long-run issues—monetary neutrality is approximately correct.

Yet monetary neutrality does not fully describe the world in which we live. Beginning in Chapter 8, we discuss departures from the classical model and monetary neutrality. These departures are crucial for understanding many macroeconomic phenomena, such as short-run economic fluctuations.

Summary

1. Money is the stock of assets used for transactions. It serves as a store of value, a unit of account, and a medium of exchange. Different sorts of assets are used as money: commodity money systems use an asset with intrinsic value, whereas fiat money systems use an asset whose sole function is to serve as money. In modern economies, a central bank such as the Federal Reserve has the responsibility for controlling the supply of money.

2. The quantity theory of money states that nominal GNP is proportional to the stock of money or, equivalently, that the demand for real balances is proportional to real GNP. Because the factors of production and the production function determine real GNP, the quantity theory implies that the price level is proportional to the quantity of money. Therefore, the rate of growth in the quantity of money determines the inflation rate.

3. Seigniorage is the revenue that the government raises by printing money. It is a tax on money holding. Although seigniorage is quantitatively small in most economies, it is often a major source of government revenue in economies experiencing hyperinflation.

4. The nominal interest rate is the sum of the real interest rate and the inflation rate. The Fisher effect says that the nominal interest rate moves one-for-one with expected inflation.

5. The nominal interest rate is the cost of holding money. One might therefore expect the demand for real balances to depend on the nominal interest rate. If real balances depend on the nominal interest rate, stopping inflation is a tricky task because real balances will rise when inflation stops.

6. The costs of expected inflation include shoeleather costs, menu costs, the cost of relative price variability, tax distortions, and the inconvenience of making inflation corrections. The cost of unexpected inflation is the arbitrary redistribution of wealth between debtors and creditors.

7. The classical model of the economy assumes that the money supply does not affect real variables. This classical dichotomy allows us to study first how real variables are determined. The equilibrium in the money market then determines the price level and, as a result, all other nominal variables.

KEY CONCEPTS

Inflation	Demand deposits
Hyperinflation	Quantity equation
Money	Transactions velocity of money
Store of value	Income velocity of money
Unit of account	Real money balances
Medium of exchange	Money demand function
Double coincidence of wants	Quantity theory of money
Fiat money	Seigniorage
Commodity money	Nominal and real interest rates
Gold standard	Fisher equation and Fisher effect
Money supply	*Ex ante* and *ex post* real interest rates
Central bank	Shoeleather costs
Federal Reserve	Menu costs
Monetary policy	Real and nominal variables
Open-market operations	Classical dichotomy
Currency	Monetary neutrality

QUESTIONS FOR REVIEW

1. List the functions of money.

2. What is fiat money? What is commodity money?

3. Who controls the money supply and how?

4. Write down the quantity equation and explain it.

5. What does the assumption of constant velocity imply?

6. Who pays the inflation tax?

7. If inflation rises from 6 to 8 percent, what happens to real and nominal interest rates according to the Fisher effect?

8. Explain what happens to real balances at the end of hyperinflations.

9. List all the costs of inflation you can think of, and rank them according to how important you think they are.

PROBLEMS AND APPLICATIONS

1. What are the three functions of money? Which of the functions do the following items satisfy? Which do they not satisfy?

   a. a credit card

   b. a Rembrandt painting

   c. a subway token

2. Suppose you are advising a small country (such as Bermuda) on whether to print its own money or to use the money of its larger neighbor (such as the United States). What are the costs and benefits of a national money? Does the relative political stability of the two countries have any role in this decision?

3. During World War II, both Germany and England had plans for a paper weapon: they each printed the other's currency with the intention of dropping large quantities by airplane. Why might this have been an effective weapon?

4. Calvin Coolidge once said that "inflation is repudiation." What might he have meant by this? Do you agree? Why or why not? Does it matter whether the inflation is expected or unexpected?

5. Some economic historians have noted that during the period of the gold standard, gold discoveries were most likely to occur after a long deflation. (The discoveries of 1896 are an example.) Why might this be true?

6. Suppose that consumption depends on the level of real balances (on the grounds that real balances are part of wealth). Show that if real balances depend on the nominal interest rate, then an increase in the rate of money growth now affects consumption, investment, and the real interest rate. Does the nominal interest rate adjust more than one-for-one or less than one-for-one to expected inflation?

   This deviation from the classical dichotomy and the Fisher effect is called the *Mundell-Tobin effect.* How might you decide whether the Mundell-Tobin effect is important in practice?

The Impact of Current and Future Money on the Price Level

In this chapter we showed that if the quantity of real balances demanded depends on the cost of holding money, the price level depends both on the current money supply and on the future money supply. We now examine more explicitly how this works.

To keep the math as simple as possible, we posit a money demand function that is linear in the logarithms of all the variables. The money demand function is

$$m_t - p_t = -\gamma(p_{t+1} - p_t), \tag{A1}$$

where m_t is the log of the quantity of money at time t, p_t is the log of the price level at time t, and γ is a parameter which governs the sensitivity of money demand to the rate of inflation. By the property of logarithms, $m_t - p_t$ is the log of real balances, and $p_{t+1} - p_t$ is the inflation rate between period t and period $t + 1$. This equation states that if inflation goes up by one percentage point, real balances fall by γ percent.

We have made a number of assumptions in writing the money demand function in this way. First, by excluding the level of output as a determinant of money demand, we are implicitly assuming that it is constant. Second, by including the rate of inflation rather than the nominal interest rate, we are assuming that the real interest rate is constant. Third, by including actual inflation rather than expected inflation, we are assuming perfect foresight. All of these assumptions are for simplification.

We want to solve Equation A1 to express the price level as a function of current and future money. To do this, note that Equation A1 can be written as

$$p_t = \left(\frac{1}{1+\gamma}\right) m_t + \left(\frac{\gamma}{1+\gamma}\right) p_{t+1}. \tag{A2}$$

This equation states that the current price level is a weighted average of the current money supply and next period's price level. Next period's price level will be determined the same way as this period's price level:

$$p_{t+1} = \left(\frac{1}{1+\gamma}\right) m_{t+1} + \left(\frac{\gamma}{1+\gamma}\right) p_{t+2}. \tag{A3}$$

Use this equation to substitute for p_{t+1} in Equation A2 to obtain

$$p_t = \frac{1}{1+\gamma} m_t + \frac{\gamma}{(1+\gamma)^2} m_{t+1} + \frac{\gamma^2}{(1+\gamma)^2} p_{t+2}. \tag{A4}$$

This equation states that the current price level is a weighted average of the current money supply, next period's money supply, and the following period's price level. Once again, the price level in $t + 2$ is determined as in Equation A2:

$$p_{t+2} = \left(\frac{1}{1+\gamma}\right) m_{t+2} + \left(\frac{\gamma}{1+\gamma}\right) p_{t+3}. \tag{A5}$$

Now use Equation A5 to substitute into Equation A4 to obtain

$$p_t = \frac{1}{1+\gamma} m_t + \frac{\gamma}{(1+\gamma)^2} m_{t+1} + \frac{\gamma^2}{(1+\gamma)^3} m_{t+2} + \frac{\gamma^3}{(1+\gamma)^3} p_{t+3}. \tag{A6}$$

By now you see the pattern. We can continue to use Equation A2 to substitute for the future price level. If we do this an infinite number of times, we find

$$p_t = \left(\frac{1}{1+\gamma}\right) \left[m_t + \left(\frac{\gamma}{1+\gamma}\right) m_{t+1} + \left(\frac{\gamma}{1+\gamma}\right)^2 m_{t+2} + \left(\frac{\gamma}{1+\gamma}\right)^3 m_{t+3} + \dots \right], \tag{A7}$$

where "..." indicates an infinite number of terms. According to Equation A7, the current price level is a weighted average of the current and all future money supplies.

Note the importance of γ, the parameter governing the sensitivity of real balances to inflation. The weights on the future money supplies decline geometrically at rate $\gamma/(1+\gamma)$. If γ is small, then $\gamma/(1+\gamma)$ is small, and the weights decline quickly. In this case, the current money supply is the primary determinant of the price level. If γ is large, then $\gamma/(1+\gamma)$ is close to 1, and the weights decline slowly. In this case, the future money supplies play a key role in determining today's price level.

Finally, let's relax the assumption of perfect foresight. If the future is not known with certainty, then we should write the money demand function as

$$m_t - p_t = -\gamma(Ep_{t+1} - p_t), \tag{A8}$$

where Ep_{t+1} is the expected price level. Equation A8 states that real balances depend on expected inflation. By following the same sort of reasoning as above, we can show that

$$p_t = \left(\frac{1}{1+\gamma}\right)\left[m_t + \left(\frac{\gamma}{1+\gamma}\right)Em_{t+1} + \left(\frac{\gamma}{1+\gamma}\right)^2 Em_{t+2} + \left(\frac{\gamma}{1+\gamma}\right)^3 Em_{t+3} + \dots\right]. \quad \text{(A9)}$$

Equation A9 states that the price level depends on current and future expected money.

Equation A9 is relevant to the discussion in the text on stopping hyperinflations. When a hyperinflation ends, individuals revise downward their expectations of future money; this tends to reduce the current price level. To offset this downward effect of future money on current prices, the current money supply can rise even as prices stabilize.

Chapter 7

The Open Economy

No nation was ever ruined by trade.

Benjamin Franklin

Many of the goods and services we enjoy are produced abroad. We eat Norwegian salmon as well as Texan beef, drive cars made in Japan as well as Michigan, and vacation in Mexico as well as Florida. The freedom to import and export benefits the citizens of all countries. Trade allows each country to specialize in what it produces best, and it provides everyone with a greater variety of goods and services.

Over the past four decades the volume of international trade has been increasing, making the economies of the world more interdependent. Figure 7-1 displays imports and exports as a percentage of GNP for the United States. It shows clearly the upward trend in international trade. In the 1950s imports were less than 5 percent of GNP; today they are approaching 15 percent.

While international trade is important for the United States, it plays an even more vital role in most other countries. Figure 7-2 shows imports and exports as a percentage of output for seven major industrial countries. In Canada and the United Kingdom, for example, imports are over 25 percent of domestic output. In these countries, international trade is central to analyzing economic developments and formulating economic policies.

Because the world's economies are so interdependent, international economic issues have a central role in world politics. When world leaders meet, economic matters are often high on their agenda. Economic policymakers must pay close attention to the international implications of their own country's policies and also to those of other nations.

In previous chapters we simplified our analysis by assuming that the economy does not trade internationally. That is, we assumed that the economy is closed. As we have just seen, however, actual economies export goods and services abroad, and they import goods and services from abroad. In this chapter we begin our study of open-economy macroeconomics.

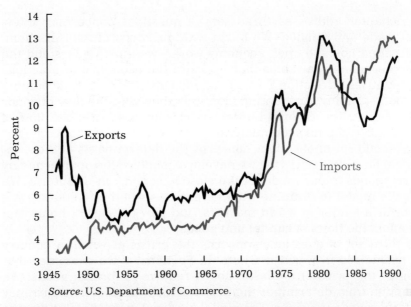

Source: U.S. Department of Commerce.

Figure 7-1 **U.S. Imports and Exports as a Percentage of Output.** International trade has become an increasingly important feature of the U.S. economy.

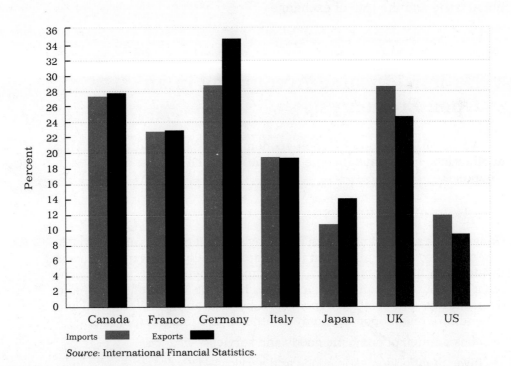

Source: International Financial Statistics.

Figure 7-2 **Imports and Exports as a Percentage of Output: 1988.** While international trade is important for the United States, it is even more vital for smaller countries.

This chapter addresses three sets of questions concerning international trade and finance. We begin with questions of measurement. To understand how the open economy works, we must understand the key macroeconomic variables that measure the economic interactions among countries. In Section 7-1 we examine national income accounting for an open economy. Accounting identities show that the flow of goods and services across national borders is closely related to the flow of funds to finance capital accumulation.

The second set of questions concerns the determinants of these international flows. In Section 7-2 we develop a model of the open economy that corresponds to our model of the closed economy in Chapter 3. We can use the model to examine what determines whether a country is a borrower or a lender in world markets, and how policies at home and abroad affect the flows of capital and goods.

The third set of questions concerns the prices at which a country makes exchanges in world markets. In Section 7-3 we examine what determines the price of domestic goods relative to foreign goods. We also examine what determines the rate at which the domestic currency trades for foreign currencies. The model we develop will help us discuss how protectionist trade policies—policies designed to protect domestic industries from foreign competition—influence the amount of international trade and the rate of exchange.

7-1 National Income Accounting in an Open Economy

We begin our study of open-economy macroeconomics by taking another look at national income accounting, which we first discussed in Chapter 2.

The Role of Net Exports

Consider the expenditure on an economy's output of goods and services. In a closed economy, all output is sold domestically, and expenditure is divided into three components: consumption, investment, and government purchases. In an open economy, however, some output is sold domestically, and some is exported to be sold abroad. We can divide expenditure on an open economy's output Y into four components:

- consumption of domestic goods and services—C^d,
- investment of domestic goods and services—I^d,
- government purchases of domestic goods and services—G^d, and
- exports of domestic goods and services—EX.

The division of expenditure into these four components is expressed in the identity

$$Y = C^d + I^d + G^d + EX.$$

The sum of the first three components, $C^d + I^d + G^d$, is domestic spending on domestic goods and services. The fourth component, EX, is foreign spending on domestic goods and services.

We now want to turn this identity into a more useful form. To do this, note that domestic spending on *all* goods and services is the sum of domestic spending on domestic goods and services *and* on foreign goods and services. Hence, total consumption C equals consumption of domestic goods and services C^d plus consumption of foreign goods and services C^f; total investment I equals investment of domestic goods and services I^d plus investment of foreign goods and services I^f; and total government purchases G equals government purchases of domestic goods and services G^d plus government purchases of foreign goods and services G^f. We write this as:

$$C = C^d + C^f.$$
$$I = I^d + I^f.$$
$$G = G^d + G^f.$$

We substitute these three equations into the identity above:

$$Y = (C - C^f) + (I - I^f) + (G - G^f) + EX.$$

We can rearrange to obtain

$$Y = C + I + G + EX - (C^f + I^f + G^f).$$

The sum of domestic spending on foreign goods and services ($C^f + I^f + G^f$) is expenditure on imports (IM). We can thus write the national income accounts identity as

$$Y = C + I + G + EX - IM.$$

Because spending on imports is included in domestic spending ($C + I + G$), and because goods and services imported from abroad are not part of a country's output, this equation subtracts spending on imports. Defining **net exports** to be exports minus imports ($NX = EX - IM$), the identity becomes

$$Y = C + I + G + NX.$$

This equation states that expenditure on domestic output is the sum of consumption, investment, government purchases, and net exports. This form of the national income accounts identity is the most common; it should be familiar from Chapter 2.

The national income accounts identity shows how expenditures on domestic output, domestic spending, and net exports are related. In particular,

$$NX \quad = \quad Y \quad - \quad (C + I + G)$$

Net Exports = Output − Domestic Spending.

If output exceeds domestic spending, we export the difference: net exports are positive. If output falls short of domestic spending, we import the difference: net exports are negative.

GNP versus GDP

National income accounting—in both closed and open economies—tells us that the total expenditure on an economy's output of goods and services equals the economy's total income. In an open economy, there are two measures of total income:

- **Gross National Product (GNP)** is the income earned by nationals (that is, by citizens of a nation). It includes the income that nationals earn abroad, but it does *not* include the income of the factors of production within a country that are owned by foreigners.

- **Gross Domestic Product (GDP)** is the income earned domestically. It includes income earned domestically by foreigners, but does *not* include income earned by nationals on foreign ground.

These two measures of income differ because factors of production are not always owned by the citizens of the country in which they are used.

To understand the difference between GNP and GDP, let's consider several examples. Suppose a Mexican citizen comes temporarily to the United States to work. The income he earns in the United States is part of U.S. GDP, because it is earned domestically. But the income is not part of U.S. GNP, because the worker is not a U.S. national. Similarly, if a U.S. citizen works in Mexico, her income is part of U.S. GNP, but it is not part of U.S. GDP.

As another example, suppose a Japanese citizen owns an apartment building in New York. The rent he earns is part of U.S. GDP, because this income is earned domestically. But the rent is not part of U.S. GNP, because the landlord is not a U.S. national. Similarly, if a U.S. citizen owns a factory in Haiti, the profit she makes is part of U.S. GNP, but it is not part of U.S. GDP.

Now look again at the national income accounts identity:

$$Y = C + I + G + NX.$$

Is Y in this identity equal to GNP or GDP? The answer depends on the interpretation of NX. As long as our treatment of NX is consistent with our treatment of Y, Y can be either GNP or GDP.

Consider, for example, what happens when a U.S. citizen earns income working abroad. Two related questions arise about our handling of this transaction:

- Should we include this income as part of *Y*?
- Should we treat the labor services the U.S. citizen is providing abroad as an export and thus part of *NX*?

It doesn't matter how we answer these questions as long as we answer both of them the same way. On the one hand, if we choose *Y* to be GDP, then the income earned abroad is not part of *Y*, and the labor services should not be part of *NX*. On the other hand, if we choose *Y* to be GNP, then the income earned abroad is included in *Y*, and the labor services are included in *NX*.

In this book, *Y* denotes GNP. This choice means that *NX* includes the services from factors of production—capital and labor—owned domestically and used abroad.

The Capital Account and the Current Account

In an open economy, as in the closed economy we discussed in Chapter 3, financial markets and goods markets are closely related. To see the relationship, we must rewrite the national income accounts identity in terms of saving and investment. Begin with the identity

$$Y = C + I + G + NX.$$

Subtract *C* and *G* from both sides to obtain

$$Y - C - G = I + NX.$$

Recall from Chapter 3 that $Y - C - G$ is national saving (*S*), the sum of private saving $(Y - T - C)$ and public saving $(T - G)$. Therefore,

$$S = I + NX.$$

Bringing all the terms to the same side of the equation, we can write the national income accounts identity as

$$(I - S) + NX = 0.$$

This form of the national income accounts identity shows the relationship between the international flow of funds for capital accumulation $(I - S)$ and the international flow of goods and services (*NX*).

Each part of this identity has its own name. $I - S$ is called the **capital account**. The capital account is the excess of domestic investment over domestic saving. Investment can exceed saving because investors can finance investment projects by borrowing in world financial markets. Therefore, the capital account equals the amount of domestic capital accumulation that is being financed by loans from abroad. *NX* is called the **current account**. The current account is the net amount we are currently receiving from abroad in exchange for our net export of goods and services (including the net amount received for the use of our factors of production).

The national income accounts identity says that the capital account and the current account balance. That is,

$$\text{Capital Account} + \text{Current Account} = 0$$
$$(I - S) \qquad + \qquad NX \qquad = 0.$$

If $I - S$ is positive and *NX* is negative, we have a capital-account surplus and a current-account deficit. In this case, we are borrowing in world financial markets, and we are importing more goods than we are exporting. If $I - S$ is negative and *NX* is positive, we have a capital-account deficit and a current-account surplus. In this case, we are lending in world financial markets, and we are exporting more goods than we are importing.[1]

The balance of the capital account and the current account shows that the international flow of funds to finance capital accumulation, and the international flow of goods and services, are two sides of the same coin. On the one hand, if our saving exceeds our investment, the saving that does not get invested domestically is used to make loans to foreigners. They require these loans because we are providing them with more goods and services than they are providing us—that is, *NX* is positive. On the other hand, if our investment exceeds our saving, the extra investment must be financed from abroad. Foreigners must be lending to us. These foreign loans enable us to import more goods and services than we export—that is, *NX* is negative.

Note that the international flow of capital can take many forms. It is easiest to assume—as we have done so far—that when we run a capital-account surplus, foreigners make loans to us. This happens, for example, when the Japanese buy the debt issued by U.S. corporations or by the U.S. government. But, equivalently, the flow of capital can take the form of foreigners buying domestic assets. For example, when Japanese investors bought Rockefeller Center, that transaction was part of the capital-account surplus. In both the case of foreigners buying domestically-issued debt and the case of foreigners buying domestically owned assets, foreigners are obtaining a claim to the future returns to domestic capital. In other words, in both cases, foreigners end up owning some of the domestic capital stock.

---

[1] This analysis leaves out another accounting category, called *Official Reserve Transactions*, which keeps the capital account from precisely equalling $I - S$ and keeps the capital account from precisely balancing the current account. This category arises because certain forms of public saving and dissaving, such as the purchase and sale of foreign currency by the central bank, are not included in the capital account. For our purposes, we can assume that this third category equals zero.

7-2 The International Flows of Capital and Goods

So far, our discussion of the international flows has merely involved accounting identities. That is, we have defined some of the variables that measure transactions in an open economy, and we have shown the links among these variables that follow from their definitions. Our next step is to develop a model that explains economic behavior in an open economy. We then use the model to answer questions such as how the capital account and the current account respond to changes in economic policy.

A Model of the Small Open Economy

Here we present a model of the international flows of capital and goods. Since the capital account is investment minus saving, our model explains the capital account by explaining investment and saving. The model also explains the current account, because the current account must balance the capital account.

To develop this model, we use some of the elements of the model of national income in Chapter 3. In contrast to the model in Chapter 3, however, we now do not assume that the real interest rate equilibrates saving and investment. Instead, we allow the economy to run a capital-account surplus and borrow from abroad, or to run a capital-account deficit and lend to abroad.

If the real interest rate does not equilibrate saving and investment in this model, what does determine the real interest rate? The simplest assumption is that the economy we are examining is a **small open economy** with access to world financial markets. By "small" we mean that this economy is a small part of the world market and thus, by itself, can have only a negligible effect on the world interest rate. By "access to world financial markets" we mean that the government of this country does not impede international borrowing and lending. Thus, the interest rate in a small open economy equals the **world interest rate** r^*, the real interest rate prevailing in world financial markets. We write

$$r = r^*.$$

The small open economy takes the world real interest rate as given.

Let us discuss for a moment what determines the world real interest rate. In a closed economy, the equilibrium of saving and investment determines the interest rate. Surely, the world economy—barring interplanetary trade—is a closed economy. Therefore, the equilibrium of world saving and world investment determines the world interest rate. Our small open economy has a negligible effect on the world real interest rate because, being a small part of the world, it has a negligible effect on world saving and world investment.

To build the model of the small open economy, we take three assumptions from Chapter 3:

- The output of the economy Y is fixed by the factors of production and the production function. We write this as

$$Y = \overline{Y} = F(\overline{K}, \overline{L}).$$

- The greater the disposable income $Y - T$, the greater is consumption. We write the consumption function as

$$C = C(Y - T).$$

- The higher the real interest rate r, the lower is investment. We write the investment function as

$$I = I(r).$$

These are the three key elements of our model. If you do not understand any of them, review Chapter 3 before proceeding with the following analysis.

We can now return to the accounting identity and write it as

$$\text{Current Account} = - \text{Capital Account}$$
$$NX = S - I$$
$$NX = (Y - C - G) - I.$$

Substituting our three assumptions from Chapter 3, and the condition that the interest rate equals the world interest rate, we obtain

$$NX = [\overline{Y} - C(\overline{Y} - T) - G] - I(r^*)$$
$$= \qquad \overline{S} \qquad - I(r^*).$$

This equation shows what determines saving and investment—and thus the capital account $(I - S)$ and the current account (NX). Remember that saving depends on fiscal policy (G and T): lower government purchases or higher taxes raise national saving. Investment depends on the world real interest rate (r^*): high interest rates make some investment projects unprofitable. Therefore, the capital account and the current account depend on these variables as well. We can use this equation to examine how the capital account and the current account respond to changes in the economy, such as changes in fiscal policy.

In Chapter 3 we graphed saving and investment as in Figure 7-3. In the closed economy of that chapter, the real interest rate adjusts to equilibrate saving and investment—that is, the real interest rate is found where the saving and investment curves cross. In the small open economy, however, the real interest rate equals the world real interest rate. *The capital account and the current account are determined by the difference between saving and investment at the world interest rate.*

At this point, one might wonder about the mechanism that causes the current account to balance the capital account. The determinants of

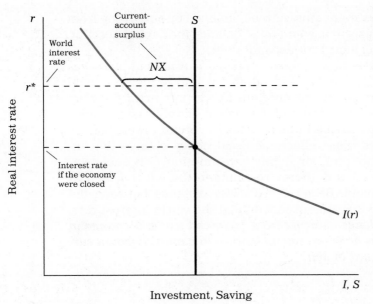

Figure 7-3 **Saving and Investment as a Function of the Real Interest Rate.**
In a closed economy, the real interest rate adjusts to equilibrate saving and investment. In a small open economy, the interest rate is determined in the world financial markets. The difference between saving and investment determines the capital account and thus the current account. Here there is a current-account surplus, because at the world interest rate, saving exceeds investment.

the capital account are easy to understand. When domestic saving falls short of domestic investment, investors borrow from abroad; when saving exceeds investment, the excess is lent to other countries. But what causes those who import and export to behave in a way that ensures that the international flow of goods exactly balances this international flow of capital? For now we leave this question unanswered, but we return to it later in the chapter when we discuss what determines exchange rates.

How Policies Influence the Capital Account and the Current Account

Suppose that the economy begins in a position of balanced trade—that is, its exports exactly balance its imports. In other words, at first, both the current account *NX* and the capital account *I* − *S* are at zero. Let's use our model to predict the effects of government policies at home and abroad.

Fiscal Policy at Home   Consider first what happens to the small open economy if the government expands domestic spending by increasing government purchases. The increase in *G* reduces national saving, because *S* = *Y* − *C* − *G*. With an unchanged world real interest rate, investment remains the same. Therefore, the excess of investment over saving, *I* − *S*, rises. The reduced saving leads to a capital-account surplus, because some investment must now be financed by borrowing from abroad. Of course, the current account must balance the capital account, so *NX* must fall, implying a current-account deficit.

The same logic applies to a decrease in taxes *T*. A tax cut increases disposable income *Y − T*, stimulates consumption, and reduces national saving. (Even though some of the tax cut finds its way into private saving, public saving falls by the full amount of the tax cut; in total, saving falls.) The reduction in national saving in turn raises *I − S* and lowers *NX*.

Figure 7-4 illustrates these effects. A fiscal policy change that increases private consumption *C* or public consumption *G* reduces national saving (*Y − C − G*) and, therefore, shifts to the left the vertical line that represents saving. Because *NX* is the distance between the saving schedule and the investment schedule at the world interest rate, this shift reduces *NX*. *Hence, starting from balanced trade, a change in fiscal policy that reduces national saving leads to a capital-account surplus and a current-account deficit.*

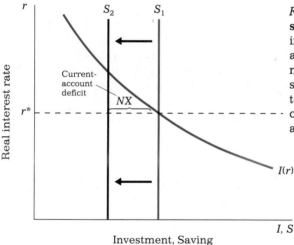

Figure 7-4 **A Fiscal Expansion at Home.** An increase in government purchases or a reduction in taxes reduces national saving and thus shifts the saving schedule to the left. This leads to a capital-account surplus and a current-account deficit.

CASE STUDY 7-1

The Twin Deficits of the 1980s

The United States experienced an unusual episode of expansionary fiscal policy in the 1980s. With the support of President Ronald Reagan, the Congress passed legislation in 1981 that substantially cut personal income taxes over the next three years. Because of these tax cuts, the federal budget deficit—the excess of government spending over tax revenue—was almost 4 percent of GNP for much of the decade. Our model says that such a tax cut should cause a reduction in national saving and a current-account deficit.

Figure 7-5 shows the federal budget deficit and the current-account deficit as a percent of GNP since 1960. Before 1980, the federal budget was, on average, roughly in balance. In fact, the budget averaged a small surplus, as the World War II debt was gradually being paid off. During this time, the current account was in surplus of about 1 percent of GNP. Americans were saving more than they were investing at home, and the difference was invested abroad.

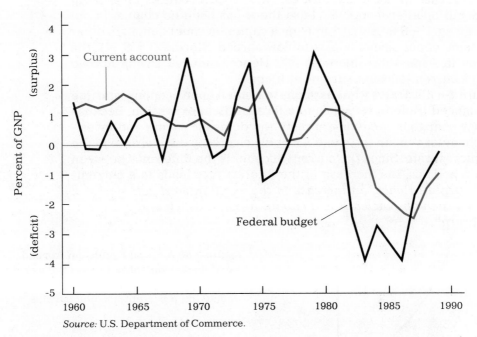

Source: U.S. Department of Commerce.

Figure 7-5 **The Current Account and the Federal Budget in the United States.** This figure shows the federal budget deficit and the current-account deficit as a percentage of GNP since 1960. Positive numbers represent a surplus, and negative numbers represent a deficit. In the 1980s, the federal government began running large budget deficits, which reduced national saving and led to large current-account deficits. (The numbers for the budget deficit are corrected for the effects of inflation: only the real interest on the debt is counted as expenditure. For a discussion of this correction, see the appendix to Chapter 16. The numbers for the current account are net exports in current dollars from the national income accounts.)

In the 1980s, however, the federal government ran a budget deficit unprecedented in peacetime. The government, borrowing to cover the deficit, reduced national saving, leading to a current-account deficit and a capital-account surplus. That is, other countries started lending to the United States. The United States went from being the world's largest creditor to being the world's largest debtor.

Fiscal Policy Abroad   Consider now what happens to our small open economy when foreign governments increase their government purchases. If these foreign countries are a small part of the world economy, then their fiscal change has a negligible impact on other countries. But if these foreign countries are a large part of the world economy, their increase in purchases reduces world saving and thus raises the world interest rate.

The increase in the world interest rate in turn reduces investment in our small open economy. Because there has been no change in domestic saving, $I - S$ must fall, implying a capital-account deficit. In other words, some of our saving begins to flow abroad. Since $NX = S - I$, the reduction in I must also increase NX. Hence, reduced saving abroad leads to a current-account surplus at home.

Figure 7-6 illustrates what happens to a small open economy starting from balanced trade in response to a foreign fiscal expansion. Because the policy change is occurring abroad, the domestic saving and investment schedules remain the same. The only change is the increase in the world interest rate. Since the current account is the difference between the two schedules, the increase in the interest rate leads to a current-account surplus. *Hence, an increase in the world interest rate due to a fiscal expansion abroad leads to a capital-account deficit and a current-account surplus.*

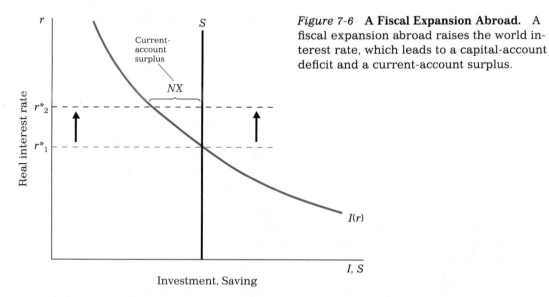

Figure 7-6 **A Fiscal Expansion Abroad.**   A fiscal expansion abroad raises the world interest rate, which leads to a capital-account deficit and a current-account surplus.

Shifts in Investment Demand   Consider what happens to our small open economy if its investment schedule shifts outward. This shift would occur if, for example, the government changes the tax laws in a way that encourages domestic investment, such as by providing an investment tax credit. Figure 7-7 illustrates the impact of a shift in the investment schedule. At a given world interest rate, investment is now higher. Because saving is unchanged, this investment must be financed by borrowing from abroad. The capital account $(I - S)$ rises, and the current account $(NX = S - I)$ falls. *Hence, an outward shift in the investment schedule causes a capital-account surplus and a current-account deficit.*

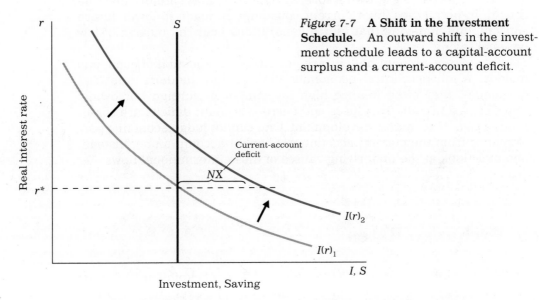

Figure 7-7 **A Shift in the Investment Schedule.** An outward shift in the investment schedule leads to a capital-account surplus and a current-account deficit.

Evaluating Economic Policy

The central message of our model of the open economy is that the flow of goods and services measured by the current account is inextricably connected to the flow of funds for capital accumulation measured by the capital account. Because the capital account is investment minus saving, the impact of economic policies on these international flows can always be found by examining their impact on investment and saving. Policies that increase investment push the capital account toward surplus and the current account toward deficit. Policies that increase saving push the capital account toward deficit and the current account toward surplus.

Our analysis of the open economy has been positive, not normative. That is, our analysis of how economic policies influence the international flows of capital and goods does not tell us whether these policies are desirable. Evaluating economic policies and their impact on the open economy is a frequent topic of debate among economists and policy-makers.

In the United States in the 1980s, policymakers confronted the question of whether the current-account deficit represented a national problem. Many economists viewed the current-account deficit as a symptom, but not as a problem in itself. The current-account deficit of the 1980s reflected a low saving rate. A low saving rate means that we are putting away less for the future. In a closed economy, low saving leads to low investment and thus a smaller future capital stock. In an open economy, low saving leads to a growing foreign debt, which eventually must be repaid. In both cases, high current consumption leads to lower future consumption, implying that future generations bear the burden of low national saving.

Yet current-account deficits are not always a reflection of economic malady. When poor rural economies develop into modern industrial economies, they often finance high investment by foreign borrowing. Thus, capital-account surpluses and current-account deficits are sometimes a sign of economic development. One cannot judge economic performance from the current account and capital account alone. Instead, one must look at the underlying causes of these international flows.

7-3　Exchange Rates

Having built a model of the international flows of capital and of goods and services in the small open economy, we now examine the prices that apply to these transactions. The *exchange rate* between two countries is the price at which exchanges between them take place. In this section we first examine precisely what the exchange rate measures, and then discuss how exchange rates are determined.

Nominal and Real Exchange Rates

Economists distinguish between two exchange rates: the nominal exchange rate and the real exchange rate. Let's discuss each in turn and see how they are related.

The Nominal Exchange Rate　The **nominal exchange rate** is the relative price of the currency of two countries. If, for example, the exchange rate between the U.S. dollar and the Japanese yen is 120 yen per dollar, then you can exchange one dollar for 120 yen in world markets for foreign currency. A Japanese wanting to obtain dollars would thus pay 120 yen for each dollar he bought. An American wanting to obtain yen would obtain 120 yen for each dollar he paid. When people refer to "the exchange rate" between two countries, they usually mean the nominal exchange rate.

FYI How Newspapers Report the Exchange Rate

You can find exchange rates reported daily in many newspapers. Here's how they are reported in the *Wall Street Journal*:

EXCHANGE RATES
Tuesday, February 5, 1991

The New York foreign exchange selling rates below apply to trading among banks in amounts of $1 million and more, as quoted at 3 p.m. Eastern time by Bankers Trust Co. Retail transactions provide fewer units of foreign currency per dollar.

Country	U.S. $ equiv. Tues.	U.S. $ equiv. Mon.	Currency per U.S. $ Tues.	Currency per U.S. $ Mon.
Argentina (Austral) ...	.0001121	.0001059	8918.00	9440.00
Australia (Dollar)	.7775	.7825	1.2862	1.2780
Austria (Schilling)	.09749	.09713	10.26	10.30
Bahrain (Dinar)	2.6525	2.6525	.3770	.3770
Belgium (Franc)				
Commercial rate ...	.03332	.03319	30.01	30.13
Brazil (Cruzeiro)	.00448	.00437	223.10	229.00
Britain (Pound)	1.9925	1.9815	.5019	.5047
30-Day Forward	1.9815	1.9706	.5047	.5075
90-Day Forward	1.9600	1.9485	.5102	.5132
180-Day Forward	1.9325	1.9213	.5175	.5205
Canada (Dollar)	.8636	.8626	1.1580	1.1593
30-Day Forward	.8607	.8597	1.1619	1.1632
90-Day Forward	.8556	.8547	1.1688	1.1700
180-Day Forward	.8507	.8496	1.1755	1.1770
Chile (Official rate) ...	.003055	.002967	327.29	337.00
China (Renminbi)	.191205	.191205	5.2300	5.2300
Colombia (Peso)	.001769	.001727	565.40	579.00
Denmark (Krone)	.1781	.1772	5.6150	5.6425
Ecuador (Sucre)				
Floating rate	.001072	.001072	932.50	932.50
Finland (Markka)	.28209	.28102	3.5450	3.5585
France (Franc)	.20151	.20074	4.9625	4.9815
30-Day Forward	.20094	.20020	4.9765	4.9951
90-Day Forward	.19980	.19903	5.0050	5.0243
180-Day Forward	.19808	.19732	5.0485	5.0680
Germany (Mark)	.6863	.6833	1.4570	1.4635
30-Day Forward	.6851	.6820	1.4597	1.4663
90-Day Forward	.6822	.6792	1.4658	1.4724
180-Day Forward	.6781	.6748	1.4748	1.4820
Greece (Drachma)	.006380	.006414	156.75	155.90
Hong Kong (Dollar) ...	.12827	.12827	7.7960	7.7960
India (Rupee)	.05382	.05382	18.58	18.58
Indonesia (Rupiah)	.0005305	.0005305	1885.01	1885.01
Ireland (Punt)	1.8190	1.8160	.5498	.5507
Israel (Shekel)	.5071	.4998	1.9720	2.0008
Italy (Lira)	.0009124	.0009083	1096.00	1101.00

Country	U.S. $ equiv. Tues.	U.S. $ equiv. Mon.	Currency per U.S. $ Tues.	Currency per U.S. $ Mon.
Japan (Yen)	.007722	.007660	129.50	130.55
30-Day Forward	.007714	.007652	129.64	130.69
90-Day Forward	.007696	.007634	129.94	131.00
180-Day Forward	.007678	.007614	130.25	131.33
Jordan (Dinar)	1.4995	1.4995	.6669	.6669
Malta (Lira)	3.4014	3.4014	.2940	.2940
Mexico (Peso)				
Floating rate	.0003375	.0003375	2963.00	2963.00
Netherland (Guilder) .	.6088	.6062	1.6425	1.6495
New Zealand (Dollar)	.6005	.6007	1.6653	1.6647
Norway (Krone)	.1753	.1745	5.7061	5.7296
Pakistan (Rupee)	.0454	.0454	22.02	22.02
Peru (New Sol)	1.9153	1.9608	.52	.51
Philippines (Peso)	.03676	.03676	27.20	27.20
Portugal (Escudo)	.007749	.007749	129.05	129.05
Saudi Arabia (Riyal) ..	.26667	.26667	3.7500	3.7500
Singapore (Dollar)	.5831	.5821	1.7150	1.7180
South Africa (Rand)				
Commercial rate	.3956	.3958	2.5278	2.5268
Financial rate	.3185	.3106	3.1400	3.2200
South Korea (Won)	.0013947	.0013947	717.00	717.00
Spain (Peseta)	.010917	.010864	91.60	92.05
Sweden (Krona)	.1828	.1823	5.4690	5.4845
Switzerland (Franc) ..	.8039	.7997	1.2440	1.2505
30-Day Forward	.8028	.7986	1.2456	1.2522
90-Day Forward	.8010	.7964	1.2485	1.2556
180-Day Forward	.7986	.7938	1.2522	1.2598
SDR	1.44774	1.44525	.69073	.69192
ECU	1.39933	1.40198	.....	.....

Special Drawing Rights (SDR) are based on exchange rates for the U.S., German, British, French and Japanese currencies. Source: International Monetary Fund.

European Currency Unit (ECU) is based on a basket of community currencies. Source: European Community Commission.

Source: Reprinted by permission of the *Wall Street Journal*, © 1991 Dow Jones & Company, Inc. All Rights Reserved Worldwide.

Notice that each exchange rate is reported in two ways. On this Tuesday, a dollar bought 129.50 yen, and a yen bought 0.007722 dollars. We can say the exchange rate is 129.50 yen per dollar, or we can say the exchange rate is 0.007722 dollars per yen. Since 0.007722 equals 1/129.50, these two ways of expressing the exchange rate are equivalent. This book always expresses the exchange rate in units of foreign currency per dollar.

The exchange rate on this Tuesday of 129.50 yen per dollar was down from 130.55 yen per dollar on Monday. Such a fall in the exchange rate is called a *depreciation* of the dollar; a rise in the exchange rate is called an *appreciation*.

The Real Exchange Rate   The **real exchange rate** is the relative price of the goods of two countries. That is, the real exchange rate tells us the rate at which we can trade the goods of one country for the goods of another. The real exchange rate is sometimes called the *terms of trade*.

To see the relation between the real and nominal exchange rates, consider a single good produced in many countries: cars. Suppose an American car costs $10,000 and a similar Japanese car costs 2,400,000 yen. To compare the prices of the two cars, we must convert them into a common currency. If a dollar is worth 120 yen, then the American car costs 1,200,000 yen. Thus, comparing the price of the American car (1,200,000 yen) and the price of the Japanese car (2,400,000 yen), we conclude that the American car costs one-half of what the Japanese car costs. In other words, at current prices, we can exchange 2 American cars for 1 Japanese car.

The car example shows that the real exchange rate—the relative price of goods in two countries—depends on the nominal exchange rate and the prices of the goods measured in the domestic currencies. We can summarize our calculation above as follows:

$$\frac{\text{Real Exchange}}{\text{Rate}} = \frac{(120 \text{ yen/dollar}) \times (10{,}000 \text{ dollars/American Car})}{(2{,}400{,}000 \text{ yen/Japanese Car})}$$

$$= 0.5 \frac{\text{Japanese Car}}{\text{American Car}}.$$

At these prices and this exchange rate, we obtain one-half of a Japanese car per American car. More generally, we can write this calculation as

$$\frac{\text{Real Exchange}}{\text{Rate}} = \frac{\text{Nominal Exchange Rate} \times \text{Price of Domestic Good}}{\text{Price of Foreign Good}}.$$

The rate at which we exchange foreign and domestic goods depends on the prices of the goods in the local currencies and on the rate at which the currencies are exchanged.

This calculation for the real exchange rate for a single good suggests how we should define the real exchange rate for a broader basket of goods. Let e be the nominal exchange rate (the number of yen per dollar), P be the price level in the United States (measured in dollars), and P^* be the price level in Japan (measured in yen). Then the real exchange rate ϵ is

$$\begin{array}{ccc} \text{Real} & \text{Nominal} & \text{Ratio of} \\ \text{Exchange} = \text{Exchange} \times & \text{Price} \\ \text{Rate} & \text{Rate} & \text{Levels} \\ \epsilon \quad = \quad e & \times \quad (P/P^*) \end{array}.$$

The real exchange rate between two countries is computed from the nominal exchange rate and the price levels in the two countries. *If the real exchange rate is high, foreign goods are relatively cheap, and do-*

mestic goods are relatively expensive. If the real exchange rate is low, foreign goods are relatively expensive, and domestic goods are relatively cheap.

The Real Exchange Rate and Net Exports

Just as the price of bread affects the demand for bread, the relative price of domestic and foreign goods affects the demand for these goods. If the real exchange rate is low so that domestic goods are relatively cheap, domestic residents will purchase few imported goods: they will buy Fords rather than Toyotas, drink Coors rather than Heineken, and vacation in California rather than Europe. For the same reason, foreigners will buy many of our goods. Therefore, our net exports will be high.

The opposite occurs if the real exchange rate is high and, therefore, domestic goods are expensive relative to foreign goods. Domestic residents will buy many imported goods, and foreigners will buy few of our goods. Therefore, our net exports will be low.

"How about Nebraska? The dollar's still strong in Nebraska."

We write this relationship between the real exchange rate and net exports as

$$NX = NX(\epsilon).$$

This equation states that net exports are a function of the real exchange rate. Figure 7-8 illustrates this negative relationship. Remember that *NX* is also the current account, so Figure 7-8 provides a relationship between the current account and the real exchange rate.

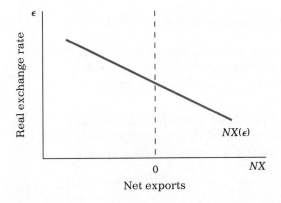

Figure 7-8 **Net Exports and the Real Exchange Rate.** The figure shows the relationship between the real exchange rate and net exports: the lower the real exchange rate, the less expensive are domestic goods relative to foreign goods, and thus the greater are our net exports. Note that a portion of the horizontal axis measures negative values of *NX*: because imports can exceed exports, net exports can be less than zero.

CASE STUDY 7-2

How Business Firms Respond to the Exchange Rate

Businesses engaged in international trade are heavily dependent on the exchange rate. This lesson was made clear in the 1980s, a decade of highly volatile exchange rates. The following article from the *New York Times* shows how one American industry responded in 1988 to a fall in the real exchange rate. What do you think foreign companies were doing at this time?

Steel Exports Rise as Dollar Slides

Several American steelmakers, anticipating continued weakness in the dollar and a tightening supply of steel, are taking steps to increase their exports to the highest level in years.

The USX corporation, for example, the nation's largest steel producer, recently reopened its long-dormant export subsidiary, United States Steel International, Inc. The company also said it planned to increase exports to 10 percent of its shipments within two years. The company now ships less than 1 percent of its steel overseas.

Similarly, Armco Inc., a steel producer based in Parsippany, N.J., said it planned to double its exports, which are currently 5 percent of its total shipments, within two years. . . .

Steel company executives say their renewed interest in exports stems from their belief that the dollar will remain relatively weak for some time and foreign customers will increasingly see American steel as competitively priced. A weak dollar helps American exports by reducing the prices of those goods in other currencies. . . .

"Since the dollar weakened, we've expanded the number of people in our international sales operation by 20 percent," said Charles A. Stitt, vice president of Armco's advanced materials subsidiary. "We believe that the weaker dollar will allow us to increase our exports significantly."

From the *New York Times*, June 13, 1988.

The Determinants of the Real Exchange Rate

To construct a model of the real exchange rate, we combine the relationship between net exports and the real exchange rate with our model of the current account. We find that two forces determine the real exchange rate:

- The real exchange rate is related to the current account. The higher is the real exchange rate, the more expensive are domestic goods relative to foreign goods, the lower is the net demand for exports, and the smaller is the current account.

- The current account must balance the capital account, which implies that the current account equals the difference between saving and investment. Saving is fixed by the consumption function and fiscal policy; investment is fixed by the investment function and the world interest rate.

Figure 7-9 illustrates these two conditions. The line showing the relationship between the current account and the real exchange rate slopes downward because a high real exchange rate leads to low net exports. The line representing the excess of saving over investment, $S - I$, is vertical, since neither saving nor investment depend on the real exchange rate. The crossing of these two lines determines the equilibrium exchange rate.

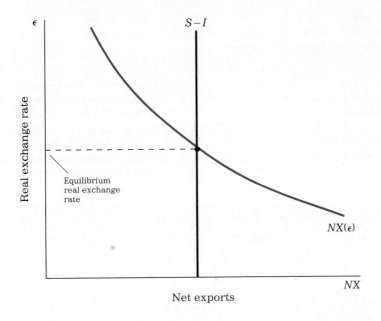

Figure 7-9 **How the Real Exchange Rate Is Determined.** The real exchange rate is determined by the crossing of the vertical line representing saving minus investment and the downward-sloping net-exports schedule. At this intersection, the quantity of dollars supplied for capital-account transactions equals the quantity of dollars demanded for current-account transactions.

Figure 7-9 looks like an ordinary supply-and-demand diagram. In fact, you can think of this diagram as representing the supply and demand for foreign currency exchange. The vertical line, $S - I$, represents the excess of our saving over our investment, and thus the supply of dollars to be exchanged into foreign currency and invested abroad. The downward-sloping line, NX, represents the net demand for dollars coming from foreigners who want dollars to buy our goods. *At the equilibrium real exchange rate, the supply of dollars available for foreign lending balances the demand for dollars by foreigners buying our net exports. In other words, at the equilibrium real exchange rate, the supply of dollars for capital-account transactions balances the demand for dollars for current-account transactions.*

How Policies Influence the Real Exchange Rate

We can use this model to show how the changes in economic policy we discussed earlier affect the real exchange rate.

Fiscal Policy at Home   What happens to the real exchange rate if the government reduces national saving by increasing government purchases or cutting taxes? As we discussed earlier, this reduction in saving lowers $S - I$ and thus NX. That is, the reduction in saving pushes the current account toward deficit.

Figure 7-10 shows how the equilibrium real exchange rate adjusts to ensure that NX falls. The policy change shifts the vertical $S - I$ line to the left, lowering the supply of dollars to be invested abroad. The lower supply causes the equilibrium real exchange rate to rise—that is, the dollar becomes more valuable. Because of the rise in the value of the dollar, domestic goods become more expensive relative to foreign goods, which causes exports to fall and imports to rise.

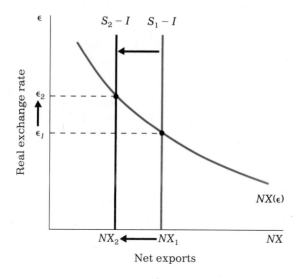

Figure 7-10 **The Impact of Expansionary Fiscal Policy at Home on the Real Exchange Rate.** Expansionary fiscal policy at home reduces national saving, which reduces the supply of dollars and raises the equilibrium real exchange rate.

Fiscal Policy Abroad   What happens to the real exchange rate if foreign governments increase government purchases or cut taxes? This change in fiscal policy reduces world saving and therefore raises the world interest rate. The increase in the world interest rate reduces domestic investment I, which raises $S - I$ and thus NX. That is, the increase in the world interest rate pushes the current account toward surplus.

Figure 7-11 shows that this policy change shifts the vertical $S - I$ line to the right, raising the supply of dollars to be invested abroad. The equilibrium real exchange rate falls. That is, the dollar becomes less valuable, and domestic goods become less expensive relative to foreign goods.

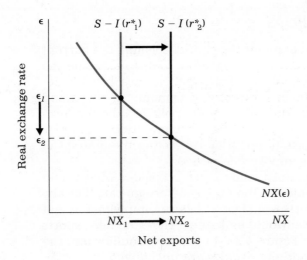

Figure 7-11 **The Impact of Expansionary Fiscal Policy Abroad on the Real Exchange Rate.** Expansionary fiscal policy abroad reduces world saving, raises the world interest rate, and therefore reduces investment at home. The reduction in investment raises the supply of dollars and lowers the equilibrium real exchange rate.

Shifts in Investment Demand What happens to the real exchange rate if investment demand at home increases, perhaps because Congress passes an investment tax credit? At the given world interest rate, the increase in investment demand leads to higher investment. A higher value of I means lower values of $S - I$ and NX. That is, the increase in investment demand pushes the current account toward deficit.

Figure 7-12 shows that the increase in investment demand shifts the vertical $S - I$ line to the left, reducing the supply of dollars to be invested abroad. The equilibrium real exchange rate rises. Hence, when the investment tax credit makes investing in the United States more attractive, it also makes the U.S. dollar more valuable, so that domestic goods become more expensive relative to foreign goods.

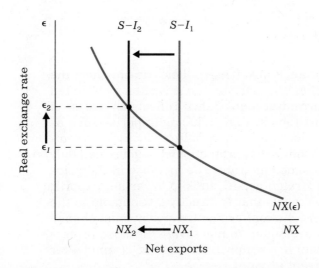

Figure 7-12 **The Impact of an Outward Shift of Investment Demand on the Real Exchange Rate.** An increase in investment demand raises the quantity of domestic investment. It therefore reduces $S - I$, which reduces the supply of dollars and raises the equilibrium real exchange rate.

The Effects of Trade Policies

Now that we have a model that explains the capital account, the current account, and the real exchange rate, we have the tools to examine the macroeconomic effects of trade policies. Trade policies are, broadly defined, policies designed to influence directly the amount of goods and services exported or imported. Most often, trade policies take the form of protecting domestic industries from foreign competition—either by placing a tax on foreign imports (a tariff) or restricting the amount of goods and services that can be imported (a quota).

As an example of a protectionist trade policy, consider what would happen if the government prohibited the import of foreign cars. For any given real exchange rate, imports would now be lower, implying that net exports (exports minus imports) would be higher. Thus, the net exports schedule shifts outward, as in Figure 7-13. In the new equilibrium, the real exchange rate is higher, and net exports are unchanged.

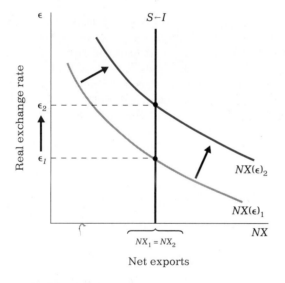

Figure 7-13 **The Impact of Protectionist Trade Policies on the Real Exchange Rate.** A protectionist trade policy, such as a ban on imported cars, raises the demand for net exports and thus raises the real exchange rate.

This analysis shows that protectionist trade policies do not affect the current account. This conclusion is important, but it is often overlooked in popular debate. Since a current-account deficit reflects an excess of imports over exports, one might guess that reducing imports—such as by prohibiting the import of foreign cars—would reduce a current-account deficit. Yet our model shows that protectionist policies lead only to an appreciation of the real exchange rate. The increase in the price of domestic goods relative to foreign goods tends to lower net exports, offsetting the increase in net exports that is directly attributable to the trade restriction. To change the current account, a policy must change the capital account, which is investment minus saving. Because protectionist policies do not alter either investment or saving, they cannot alter the capital account or the current account.

Protectionist policies do affect the amount of trade, however. As we have seen, because the real exchange rate appreciates, the goods and services we produce become more expensive relative to foreign goods and services. We therefore export less in the new equilibrium. Since net exports are unchanged, we must import less as well. Thus, protectionist policies reduce both the quantity of imports and the quantity of exports.

This reduction in the total amount of trade is the reason economists almost always oppose protectionist policies. International trade benefits all countries by allowing each country to specialize in what it produces best and by providing each country with a greater variety of goods and services. Protectionist policies diminish these gains from trade. Although these policies benefit certain groups within society—for example, a ban on imported cars helps domestic car producers—society on average is worse off when policies reduce the amount of international trade.

The Determinants of the Nominal Exchange Rate

We now turn our attention from the real exchange rate to the nominal exchange rate—the rate at which the currency of two countries trades. Recall the relation between the real and the nominal exchange rate:

$$\begin{array}{ccc} \text{Real} & \text{Nominal} & \text{Ratio of} \\ \text{Exchange} = \text{Exchange} \times & \text{Price} \\ \text{Rate} & \text{Rate} & \text{Levels} \\ \epsilon & = & e \times (P/P^*) \end{array}$$

We can write the nominal exchange rate as

$$e = \epsilon \times (P^*/P).$$

This equation shows what determines the nominal exchange rate: it depends on the real exchange rate and the price levels in the two countries. If the domestic price P rises, then the nominal exchange rate e will fall: because a dollar is worth less, a dollar will buy fewer yen. On the other hand, if the Japanese price level P^* rises, then the nominal exchange rate will increase: because the yen is worth less, a dollar will buy more yen.

It is instructive to consider changes in exchange rates over time. The exchange rate equation can be written

% Change in e = % Change in ϵ + % Change in P^* − % Change in P.

The percentage change in ϵ is the change in the real exchange rate. The percentage change in P is our inflation rate, π, and the percentage change in P^* is the foreign country's inflation rate, π^*. Thus, the percentage change in the nominal exchange rate is

% Change in e =   % Change in ϵ + $(\pi^* - \pi)$

$$\frac{\text{Percent Change in}}{\text{Nominal Exchange Rate}} = \frac{\text{Percent Change in}}{\text{Real Exchange Rate}} + \frac{\text{Difference in}}{\text{Inflation Rates.}}$$

This equation states that the change in the nominal exchange rate between the currency of two countries equals the change in the real exchange rate plus the difference in their inflation rates. *If a country has a high rate of inflation relative to the United States, a dollar will buy an increasing amount of the foreign currency over time. If a country has a low rate of inflation relative to the United States, a dollar will buy a decreasing amount of the foreign currency over time.*

This analysis shows the influence of monetary policy on the nominal exchange rate. We know from Chapter 6 that high growth in the money supply leads to high inflation. One consequence of high inflation is a depreciating currency: high π implies falling e. In other words, just as growth in the amount of money raises the price of goods measured in terms of money, it also tends to raise the price of foreign currencies measured in terms of the domestic currency.

CASE STUDY 7-3

Inflation and Nominal Exchange Rates

If we look at data on exchange rates and price levels of different countries, we quickly see the importance of inflation for explaining changes in the nominal exchange rate. The most dramatic examples come from periods of hyperinflation. For example, the price level in Mexico rose by 2,300 percent from 1983 to 1988. Because of this inflation, the number of pesos a person could buy with a U.S. dollar rose from 144 in 1983 to 2,281 in 1988.

The same relationship holds true for countries with more moderate inflation. Figure 7-14 is a scatterplot showing the relationship between inflation and the exchange rate for six prominent countries. On the horizontal axis is the difference between each country's average inflation rate and the average inflation rate of the United States. On the vertical axis is the average percent change in the exchange rate between each country's currency and the U.S. dollar. The positive relationship between these two variables is clear in this figure. Countries with relatively high inflation tend to have depreciating currencies, and countries with relatively low inflation tend to have appreciating currencies.

As an example, consider the exchange rate between German marks and U.S. dollars. Both Germany and the United States have experienced inflation over the past twenty years, so both the mark and the dollar buy fewer goods than they once did. But, as Figure 7-14 shows, inflation in Germany has been lower than inflation in the United States. This means that the value of the mark has fallen less than the value of the dollar. Therefore, the number of German marks one can buy with a U.S. dollar has been falling over time.

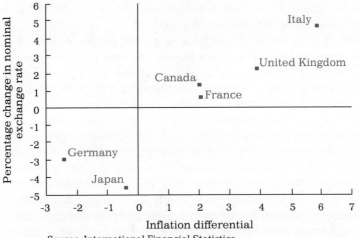

Source: International Financial Statistics.

Figure 7-14 **Inflation Differentials and the Exchange Rate.** This scatterplot shows the relationship between inflation and the nominal exchange rate. The horizontal axis shows the country's average inflation rate minus the U.S. average inflation rate over the period 1970–1988. The vertical axis is the average percentage change in the country's exchange rate (per U.S. dollar) over that period. This figure shows that countries with relatively high inflation tend to have depreciating currencies, and that countries with relatively low inflation tend to have appreciating currencies.

The Special Case of Purchasing-Power Parity

A basic tenet in economics, called the *law of one price*, says that the same good cannot sell for different prices in different locations at the same time. If a bushel of wheat sold for less in New York than in Chicago, it would be profitable to buy wheat in New York and then sell it in Chicago. Always ready to take advantage of such opportunities, astute arbitragers would increase the demand for wheat in New York and increase the supply in Chicago. This would drive the price up in New York and down in Chicago—thereby ensuring that prices are equalized in the two markets.

The law of one price applied to the international marketplace is called **purchasing-power parity**. It states that if international arbitrage is possible, then a dollar (or any other currency) must have the same purchasing power in every country. The argument goes as follows. If a dollar could buy more wheat domestically than abroad, there would then be opportunities to profit by buying wheat domestically and selling it abroad. Profit-seeking arbitragers would thus drive up the domestic price of wheat relative to the foreign price. Similarly, if a dollar could buy more wheat abroad than domestically, the arbitragers would buy wheat abroad and sell it domestically, driving down the domestic price

relative to the foreign price. Thus, profit-seeking by international arbitragers drives international wheat prices to equality.

We can interpret the doctrine of purchasing-power parity using our
model of the real exchange rate. The quick action of these international
arbitragers implies that net exports are highly sensitive to small movements in the real exchange rate. A small decrease in the price of domestic goods relative to foreign goods—that is, a small decrease in the
real exchange rate—causes arbitragers to buy goods domestically and
sell them abroad. Similarly, a small increase in the relative price of
domestic goods causes arbitragers to import goods from abroad. Therefore, as in Figure 7-15, the net-exports schedule is very flat at the real
exchange rate that equalizes purchasing power among countries: any
small movement in the real exchange rate leads to a large change in
net exports. This extreme sensitivity of net exports guarantees that the
equilibrium real exchange rate is always close to the level ensuring
purchasing-power parity.

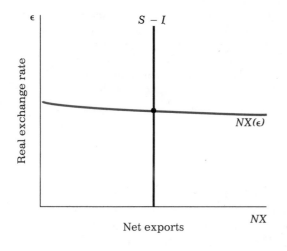

Figure 7-15 **Purchasing-Power Parity.** The
law of one price applied to the international
marketplace suggests that net exports are
highly sensitive to small movements in the
real exchange rate.

Purchasing-power parity has two important implications. First, since
the net-exports schedule is flat, changes in saving or investment do not
substantially influence the real or nominal exchange rate. Second, since
the real exchange rate is fixed, all changes in the nominal exchange
rate result from changes in price levels.

Is this doctrine of purchasing-power parity realistic? Most economists believe that, despite its appealing logic, purchasing-power parity
does not provide a completely accurate description of the world. First,
many goods are not easily traded. For example, a haircut can be more
expensive in Tokyo than in New York, yet there is no room for international arbitrage since it is impossible to transport haircuts. Second, even
goods that are traded are not always perfect substitutes. For example,
some consumers prefer Toyotas, and others prefer Fords. Thus, the relative price of Toyotas and Fords can vary to some extent without leaving

any profit opportunities. For these reasons, real exchange rates do in fact vary over time.

Although the doctrine of purchasing-power parity is not perfectly descriptive of the world, it does provide a reason to expect limited movement in the real exchange rate. There is much validity to its underlying logic: the farther the real exchange rate drifts from the level predicted by purchasing-power parity, the greater the incentive for individuals to engage in international arbitrage in goods. Hence, although we cannot rely on purchasing-power parity to eliminate all movements in the real exchange rate, this doctrine does provide a reason to expect that movements in the real exchange rate will typically be small or temporary.

CASE STUDY 7-4

The Big Mac Around the World

The doctrine of purchasing-power parity says that, after adjusting for exchange rates, goods should sell for the same price everywhere. Conversely, it says that the exchange rate between two currencies should depend on the price levels in the two countries.

To see how well this doctrine works, *The Economist*, an international news magazine, collected data on the price of a good sold in many countries: the McDonald's Big Mac hamburger. According to purchasing-power parity, the price of a Big Mac should have been closely related to the country's nominal exchange rate. The higher the price of a Big Mac in the local currency, the higher the exchange rate (measured per U.S. dollar) should have been.

Table 7-1 presents the international prices in 1990, when a Big Mac sold for $2.20 in the United States. With these data one can use the doctrine of purchasing-power parity to predict nominal exchange rates. For example, since a Big Mac costs 370 yen in Japan, one would predict that the exchange rate between the dollar and the yen was 370/2.20, or 168, yen per dollar. At this exchange rate, a Big Mac would have cost the same in Japan and in the United States.

Table 7-1 shows the predicted and actual exchange rates for 18 countries. You can see that the evidence on purchasing-power parity is mixed. In some cases, the predicted and actual exchange rates differed substantially.[2] Yet, for almost all countries, the predicted and actual exchange rates were in the same ballpark; in some cases, they were very close. For example, the predicted exchange rate of 168 yen per dollar was not far from the actual rate of 159 yen per dollar. Although not exact, purchasing-power parity does provide a rough guide to the level of exchange rates.

---

[2] The largest error was for the ruble. According to the doctrine of purchasing-power parity, the ruble's value was much less than the actual (government-mandated) exchange rate indicated. The black market for currency exchange in the Soviet Union agreed with purchasing-power parity: one could buy many more rubles for a dollar in the underground economy.

Table 7-1   Big Mac Prices and the Exchange Rate: An Application of Purchasing-Power Parity

Country	Currency	Price of a Big Mac	Exchange Rate (per U.S.$) Predicted	Exchange Rate (per U.S.$) Actual
Australia	Dollar	2.30	1.05	1.32
Belgium	Franc	97.00	44.00	34.65
Britain	Pound	1.40	0.64	0.61
Canada	Dollar	2.19	1.00	1.16
Denmark	Crown	25.50	11.60	6.39
France	Franc	17.70	8.05	5.63
Germany	Mark	4.30	1.95	1.68
Hong Kong	Dollar	8.60	3.90	7.79
Ireland	Punt	1.30	0.59	0.63
Italy	Lira	3900.00	1773.00	1230.00
Japan	Yen	370.00	168.00	159.00
Netherlands	Guilder	5.25	2.39	1.88
Singapore	Dollar	2.60	1.18	1.88
South Korea	Won	2100.00	955.00	707.00
Spain	Peseta	295.00	134.00	106.00
Sweden	Crown	24.00	10.90	6.10
U.S.S.R.	Ruble	3.75	1.70	0.60
Yugoslavia	Dinar	16.00	7.27	11.72
United States	Dollar	2.20	1.00	1.00

NOTE: The predicted exchange rate is the exchange rate that would make the price of a Big Mac in that country equal to its price in the United States.
Source: The Economist, May 5, 1990, page 92. © 1990 The Economist Newspaper Limited. Reprinted with permission.

7-4 Conclusion: The United States as a Large Open Economy

In this chapter we have seen how a small open economy works. We have examined the determinants of the international flow of funds for capital accumulation and the international flow of goods and services. We have also examined the determinants of a country's real and nominal exchange rates. Our analysis shows how various economic policies—monetary policies, fiscal policies, and trade policies—affect these flows of capital and goods and the exchange rate.

The economy we have studied is "small" in the sense that its interest rate is fixed by world financial markets. That is, we have assumed that this economy's actions and policies do not affect the world interest rate, and that the economy can borrow and lend at the world interest rate in unlimited amounts. This assumption stands in stark contrast to the assumption made in Chapter 3. In the closed economy of that chapter, the domestic interest rate adjusts to equilibrate domestic saving and domestic investment, implying that policies that influence saving or investment alter the equilibrium interest rate.

Which of these analyses should one apply to an economy like the United States? The answer is a little of both. On the one hand, the United States is not so large or so isolated that it is immune to developments occurring abroad. The large capital-account surpluses of the 1980s show the importance of international financial markets for funding U.S. investment. Hence, the analysis of a closed economy in Chapter 3 cannot by itself fully explain the impact of policies on the U.S. economy.

On the other hand, the U.S. economy is not so small and so open that the analysis of this chapter applies perfectly either. First, the United States is large enough that its actions can have a significant impact on world financial markets. Indeed, U.S. fiscal policy was blamed for the high real interest rates that prevailed throughout the world in the 1980s. Second, capital may not be perfectly mobile among countries. If individuals prefer holding their wealth in domestic rather than foreign assets, funds for capital accumulation will not flow freely to equate interest rates in all countries. For these two reasons, we cannot directly apply our model of the small open economy to the United States.

When analyzing policy for a country like the United States, we need to apply both the closed-economy logic developed in Chapter 3 and the open-economy logic developed in this chapter. The appendix to this chapter builds a model of an economy between these two extremes. In this intermediate case, there is international borrowing and lending, but the interest rate is not fixed by the world economy. Instead, the more the economy borrows from abroad, the higher the interest rate it must offer to foreign investors. The results, not surprisingly, are a mixture of the two polar cases we have already examined.

Consider, for example, a reduction in national saving due to a fiscal expansion. As in the closed economy, this policy change raises the interest rate and crowds out investment. As in the small open economy with perfect capital mobility, it also causes a capital-account surplus, a current-account deficit, and an appreciation of the real exchange rate. Hence, although the model of the small open economy examined here does not precisely describe an economy like the United States, it does provide approximately the right answer to how policies affect the current account, the capital account, and the exchange rate.

Summary

1. Net exports are the difference between exports and imports. They are equal to the difference between what we produce and what we demand for consumption, investment, and government purchases.

2. There are two measures of income for an open economy. Gross National Product is the income earned by domestic citizens both here and abroad. Gross Domestic Product is the income earned domestically both by domestic citizens and by foreigners.

3. The capital account is the excess of investment over saving; it shows the amount of investment being financed by borrowing from abroad. The capital account must always balance the current account, which is the amount we receive from abroad for our net export of goods and services.

4. Anything that alters saving or investment—such as changes in fiscal policy or changes in the world interest rate—alters the capital account and thus the current account.

5. The nominal exchange rate is the rate at which one can exchange the currency of one country for the currency of another country. The real exchange rate is the rate at which one can exchange the goods produced by the two countries. The real exchange rate equals the nominal exchange rate multiplied by the ratio of the price levels in the two countries.

6. The higher our real exchange rate, the lower the demand for our net exports. At the equilibrium real exchange rate, the demand for net exports equals saving minus investment. Equivalently, at the equilibrium real exchange rate, the net demand for dollars for current-account transactions equals the net supply of dollars for capital-account transactions.

7. The nominal exchange rate is determined by the real exchange rate and the price levels in the two countries. Other factors being equal, a high rate of inflation leads to a depreciating currency.

KEY CONCEPTS

Net exports

Gross National Product versus Gross Domestic Product

Capital account and current account

Small open economy

World interest rate

Nominal exchange rate

Real exchange rate

Purchasing-power parity

QUESTIONS FOR REVIEW

1. Define the two notions of income in the open economy. When an American works in Canada, are his earnings part of U.S. GNP? U.S. GDP? Canadian GNP? Canadian GDP?

2. What are the current account and the capital account? Explain how they are related.

3. Define the nominal exchange rate and the real exchange rate.

4. If the United States cuts defense spending, what happens to the current account, the capital account, and the exchange rate?

5. If the United States bans the import of Japanese VCRs, what happens to the current account, the capital account, and the exchange rate?

6. If Germany has low inflation and Italy has high inflation, what will happen to the exchange rate between the German mark and the Italian lira?

PROBLEMS AND APPLICATIONS

1. Use the model of this chapter to predict what would happen to the capital account, the current account, the real exchange rate, and the nominal exchange rate in response to each of the following events.

   a. A fall in consumer confidence about the future induces consumers to spend less and save more.

   b. The introduction of a stylish line of Toyotas makes some consumers prefer foreign cars over domestic cars.

   c. The introduction of automatic teller machines reduces the demand for money.

2. What will happen to the current account and the real exchange rate when government purchases increase, such as during a war? Does your answer depend on whether this is a local war or a world war?

3. Suppose that some foreign countries begin to subsidize investment by instituting an investment tax credit.

   a. What happens to world investment demand as a function of the world interest rate?

   b. What happens to the world interest rate?

   c. What happens to investment in our country?

   d. What happens to our current account and our capital account?

   e. What happens to our real exchange rate?

4. "Traveling in Italy is much cheaper now than it was ten years ago," says a friend. "Ten years ago, one dollar bought 1,000 lire; this year, one dollar buys 1,500 lire."

   Is your friend right or wrong? Given that total inflation over this period was 25 percent in the United States and 100 percent in Italy, has it become more or less expensive to travel in Italy? Write your answer using a concrete example—like a cup of American coffee versus a cup of Italian espresso—that will convince your friend.

5. The newspaper reports that the nominal interest rate is 12 percent per year in Canada and 8 percent per year in the United States. Suppose that the real interest rates are equalized in the two countries and that purchasing-power parity holds.

   a. Using the Fisher equation, which was discussed in Chapter 6, what can you infer about expected inflation in Canada and in the United States?

   b. What can you infer about the expected change in the exchange rate between the Canadian dollar and the U.S. dollar?

   c. A friend proposes a get-rich-quick scheme: borrow from a U.S. bank at 8 percent, deposit the money in a Canadian bank at 12 percent, and make a 4 percent profit. What's wrong with this scheme?

Appendix

A Model of the Large Open Economy

In this appendix we develop a model of a large open economy. This model combines some of the features of the small open economy with some of the features of the closed economy.

The Flow of Capital From Abroad

Although the small open economy we examined in this chapter takes its interest rate as determined by world financial markets, actual open economies are somewhat more complex. In practice, the interest rate of an open economy—especially a large one such as the United States—is not fixed by world markets. Instead, its interest rate is determined in part by the policies it pursues. Foreigners are not willing to borrow and lend funds at a fixed world interest rate in unlimited amounts: the more a country wishes to borrow from abroad, the higher the interest rate it must pay.

Consider how the capital flow *CF* into a country depends on the domestic interest rate *r*. Three cases are illustrated in Figure 7-16. The first case is the closed economy we discussed in Chapter 3. In the closed economy, there is no international borrowing or lending, so *CF* = 0 regardless of the interest rate. The second case is the small open economy with perfect capital mobility. In this case, which was discussed in

Figure 7-16 **How the Capital Flow From Abroad Depends on the Interest Rate.** In Case A, the closed economy, the capital flow is zero for all interest rates. In Case B, the small open economy with perfect capital mobility, the capital flow is perfectly elastic at the world interest rate *r**. In Case C, the large open economy, higher capital flows from abroad require a higher interest rate.

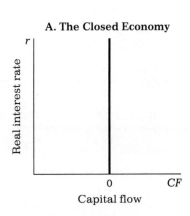

A. The Closed Economy

r

Real interest rate

0   *CF*

Capital flow

this chapter, capital flows freely into and out of the country at the world interest rate, so *CF* is perfectly elastic at $r = r^*$. That is, the country can borrow or lend as much as it wants at the world interest rate r^*.

The third case is the intermediate case, which applies best to an economy like the United States. Here, the capital flow is positively related to the domestic interest rate: the greater the interest rate, the more attractive our assets become to foreign investors, and the more funds for capital accumulation flow in from abroad. We write this as

$$CF = CF(r).$$

This equation states that the capital flow—that is, the capital account—is a function of the domestic interest rate.

The Elements of the Model

The model of the large open economy proceeds as earlier in this chapter, except for the assumption about the flow of capital. The model is summarized in the following equations:

1. $Y = \overline{Y} = F(\overline{K}, \overline{L})$.
2. $Y = C + I + G + NX$.
3. $C = C(Y - T)$.
4. $I = I(r)$.

5. $NX = NX(\epsilon)$.
6. $CF = CF(r)$.
7. $NX + CF = 0$.

These equations tell us the following:

1. Output depends on the fixed amounts of capital and labor and on the production function.

2. Output is the sum of consumption, investment, government purchases, and net exports.

3. Consumption depends on disposable income.

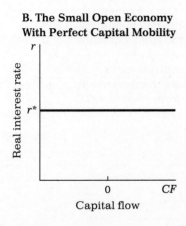

B. The Small Open Economy With Perfect Capital Mobility

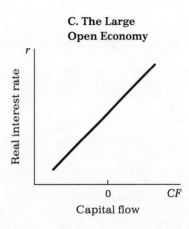

C. The Large Open Economy

4. Investment depends on the real interest rate.

5. The current account depends on the real exchange rate.

6. The capital account depends on the domestic interest rate.

7. The current account and the capital account must balance.

The implications of this model of the economy are most easily derived by analyzing the market for loans. As before, national saving S is defined as $Y - C - G$. The national income accounts identity tells us that

$$S = I + NX.$$

Since $NX = -CF$, we can write this equation as

$$S + CF = I.$$

This equation states that the supply of loans (domestic saving plus the capital flow from abroad) equals the demand for loans (domestic investment).

Now substitute the determinants of saving, capital flow, and investment into this last equation to obtain

$$[\overline{Y} - C(\overline{Y} - T) - G] + CF(r) = I(r)$$
$$\underbrace{\phantom{[\overline{Y} - C(\overline{Y} - T) - G]}}_{\overline{S}} + CF(r) = I(r).$$

This equation is illustrated in Figure 7-17. The supply curve for loans, $S + CF$, slopes upward because a higher interest rate induces capital to flow in from abroad. The demand curve for loans, I, slopes downward because a higher interest rate reduces investment. The equilibrium interest rate is found where the supply and demand curves cross.

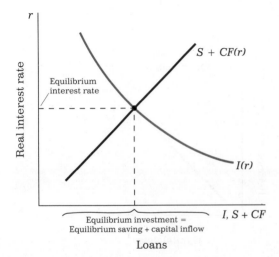

Figure 7-17 **The Equilibrium Interest Rate in the Large Open Economy.**   At the equilibrium interest rate, the supply of loans from saving and international borrowing $(S + CF)$ balances the demand for loans from investment (I).

The Effects of Economic Policies

We can now use this model to examine the impact of economic policies on the variables that are endogenous to the model, such as the interest rate, the exchange rate, and the current account. Consider the impact of expansionary fiscal policy: an increase in government purchases or a decrease in taxes. Such a policy reduces national saving S and thereby reduces the supply of loans, as in Figure 7-18. The equilibrium interest rate rises. The higher interest rate leads to a reduction in investment and an increase in the capital flow into the country—that is, I falls and CF rises. Since the current account and the capital account always balance, a fall in NX must accompany the rise in CF. Since NX is negatively associated with the real exchange rate, the real exchange rate ϵ must rise.

Note that the impact of fiscal policy in this model is a combination of its impact in the closed economy of Chapter 3 and its impact in the small open economy of this chapter. As in the closed economy, a fiscal expansion in a large open economy raises the interest rate and crowds out investment. As in the small open economy with perfect capital mobility, a fiscal expansion causes a capital inflow, a current-account deficit, and an appreciation in the real exchange rate.

To understand this model more fully, try using it to examine the impact of other policies. Consider the following changes:

- An investment tax credit shifts investment demand outward.

- An import quota shifts the demand for net exports outward.

- Political instability abroad shifts the capital flow into the United States outward.

In each case, what happens to the interest rate, investment, the capital account, the current account, and the exchange rate?

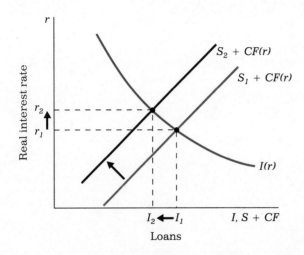

Loans

Figure 7-18 **A Reduction in National Saving in the Large Open Economy.** A reduction in national saving lowers the supply of loans. The equilibrium interest rate rises, which crowds out investment and increases the capital flow from abroad.

Part Three

The Economy in the Short Run

Chapter 8

Introduction to Economic Fluctuations

The modern world regards business cycles much as the ancient Egyptians regarded the overflowing of the Nile. The phenomenon recurs at intervals, it is of great importance to everyone, and natural causes of it are not in sight.

John Bates Clark, 1898

Economic fluctuations present a recurring problem for economists and policymakers. As you can see in Figure 8-1, real GNP does not grow smoothly. Recessions—periods of falling incomes and rising unemployment—are frequent. In the severe U.S. recession of 1982, real GNP fell 2.5 percent, and the unemployment rate rose to over 10 percent. Recessions are also associated with shorter workweeks: more workers have part-time jobs, and fewer workers work overtime.

Economists sometimes call these fluctuations in output and employment *the business cycle*. Although this term suggests that fluctuations in the economy are regular and predictable, neither is the case. Recessions are as irregular as they are common. Sometimes they are close together, such as the recessions in 1980 and 1982. Sometimes they are far apart: after 1982, the United States experienced a long period of uninterrupted growth.

In Part Two of this book, we developed models to identify the determinants of national income, unemployment, inflation, and other economic variables. Yet we did not examine why these variables fluctuate so much from year to year. Here in Part Three we develop a model to explain these short-run fluctuations. Because real GNP is the best single measure of economic well-being, it is the focus of our model.

Just as Egypt has attempted to stem the flooding of the Nile Valley with the Aswan Dam, modern society tries to control the business cycle

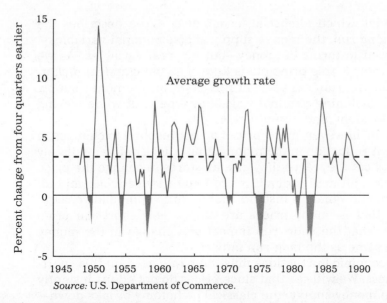

Source: U.S. Department of Commerce.

Figure 8-1 **Real GNP Growth in the United States.** The growth in real GNP averages about 3 percent per year, as indicated by the dashed line, but there is wide variation around this average. Recessions are periods during which real GNP falls—that is, during which real GNP growth is negative.

with appropriate economic policies. The model we develop over the next several chapters shows how monetary and fiscal policies influence the business cycle. It shows that these policies can either stabilize or exacerbate economic fluctuations.

8-1 How the Short Run and Long Run Differ

To build a model of short-run fluctuations, we must first decide how that model will differ from the long-run classical model that we developed in Chapters 3 through 7. Most macroeconomists believe that the crucial difference between the short run and the long run is the behavior of prices. *In the long run, prices are flexible and therefore can respond to changes in supply or demand. In the short run, however, many prices are "stuck" at some predetermined level.* Because prices behave differently in the short run than in the long run, economic policies have different effects over different time horizons.

To see how the short run and the long run differ, consider the effects of a change in monetary policy. Suppose, for example, that the Federal Reserve suddenly reduced the money supply by 5 percent. According to the classical model, which almost all economists agree describes the economy in the long run, the money supply affects nominal variables—variables measured in terms of money—but not real variables. As we discussed in Chapter 6, this principle is known as the *classical dichotomy*. Thus, in the long run, a 5 percent reduction in the money supply lowers all prices (including nominal wages) by 5 percent while leaving real wages, employment, and output unaltered.

In the short run, however, many prices do not respond to changes in monetary policy. A reduction in the money supply does not immediately induce all firms to cut the wages they pay, all stores to change the price tags on their goods, all mail-order firms to issue new catalogs, and all restaurants to print new menus. Instead, there is little immediate change in many prices; that is, many prices are sticky. This short-run price stickiness implies that the short-run impact of a change in the money supply is not the same as the long-run impact.

A model of economic fluctuations must take into account this short-run price stickiness. We will see that since prices do not adjust instantly to changes in the money supply, the classical dichotomy breaks down—monetary policy does have a potent effect on output and employment. The failure of prices to adjust to changes in the money supply implies that, in the short run, output and employment must do some of the adjusting instead.

The general principle is that if prices are sticky, the amount of output produced can deviate from the level implied by the classical model. In the classical model, the amount of output depends on the supplies of capital and labor and on the available technology. We will see that flexible prices play a key role here: in the classical model, prices adjust to ensure that the quantity of output demanded equals the quantity supplied. When prices are sticky, however, output also depends on the demand for goods. Demand in turn is influenced by monetary policy, fiscal policy, and a variety of other factors. Thus, price stickiness provides a rationale for the usefulness of monetary and fiscal policy in stabilizing the economy.

In the remainder of this chapter we introduce a model that can explain short-run economic fluctuations. The model of supply and demand, which we used to discuss the market for bread in Chapter 1, provides perhaps the most fundamental insight of all of economics. This model shows how the supply and demand for any good jointly determine the good's price and the quantity sold, and how changes in exogenous variables affect the price and quantity. Here we present what is sometimes called the "economy-size" version of this model—*the model of aggregate supply and aggregate demand*. This macroeconomic model allows us to study how the aggregate price level and the quantity of aggregate output are determined. It also provides a way to compare how the economy behaves in the long run and how it behaves in the short run.

CASE STUDY 8-1

The Puzzle of Sticky Magazine Prices

How sticky are prices? The answer to this question depends on what price we consider. Some commodities, such as wheat, soybeans, and pork bellies, are traded on organized exchanges, and their prices change every minute. No one would call these prices sticky. Yet the prices of most goods and services change much less frequently. One survey found that 37.7 percent of firms change their prices once a year, and another 17.4 percent change their prices less than once a year.[1]

The reasons for price stickiness are not always apparent. Consider, for example, the market for magazines. A study has documented that magazines change their newsstand prices very infrequently. The typical magazine allows inflation to erode its real price by about 25 percent before it raises its nominal price. Hence, if inflation is 4 percent per year, the typical magazine changes its price about every six years.[2]

Why do magazines change their prices so infrequently? Economists do not have a definitive answer. The question is puzzling because it would seem that, for magazines, the cost of a price change is small: to change prices, a mail-order firm must issue a new catalog and a restaurant must print a new menu, but a magazine publisher can simply print a new price on the cover of the next issue. Perhaps the cost to the publisher of charging the wrong price is also not very great. Or maybe customers would find it inconvenient if the price of their favorite magazine changed every month.

Thus, it is often not easy to explain sticky prices at the microeconomic level. The cause of price stickiness is, therefore, an active area of research. In Chapter 11 we discuss some recent theories about why prices are sticky.

Although not yet fully explained, price stickiness is widely believed to be crucial for understanding economic fluctuations. In this chapter we begin to develop the link between sticky prices and economic fluctuations.

8-2 Aggregate Demand

Aggregate demand is the relation between the quantity of output demanded and the aggregate price level. In other words, the aggregate demand curve tells us the quantity of goods and services people will buy for any given level of prices.

[1] Alan S. Blinder, "Why Are Prices Sticky? Preliminary Results from an Interview Study," *American Economic Review Papers and Proceedings,* 81 (May 1991): 89–96.

[2] Stephen G. Cecchetti, "The Frequency of Price Adjustment: A Study of the Newsstand Prices of Magazines," *Journal of Econometrics* 31 (1986): 255–274.

The Quantity Equation as Aggregate Demand

We can derive a simple theory of aggregate demand from the quantity theory of money. Recall from Chapter 6 that the quantity theory tells us that

$$MV = PY,$$

where M is the money supply, V is the velocity of money (which for now we assume is constant), P is the price level, and Y is the amount of output. This equation states that the money supply determines the nominal value of output, which in turn is the product of the price level and the amount of output.

You might recall from Chapter 6 that the quantity equation can be rewritten in terms of the supply and demand for real money balances:

$$M/P = (M/P)^d = kY,$$

where $k = 1/V$. In this form, the quantity equation states that the supply of real money balances M/P equals the demand $(M/P)^d$, and that the demand is proportional to the amount of output Y.

For any fixed money supply, the quantity equation yields a negative relationship between the price level P and output Y. Figure 8-2 graphs the combinations of P and Y that satisfy the quantity equation holding the money supply constant. This is called the aggregate demand curve.

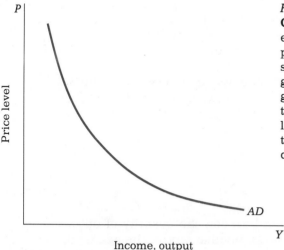

Figure 8-2 **The Aggregate Demand Curve.** The aggregate demand curve AD expresses the relationship between the price level P and the quantity of goods and services demanded Y. It is drawn for a given value of the money supply M. The aggregate demand curve slopes downward: the higher the price level P, the lower the level of real balances M/P, and therefore the lower the quantity of goods and services demanded Y.

Why the Aggregate Demand Curve Slopes Downward

The aggregate demand curve slopes downward. For any fixed money supply, the quantity equation fixes the nominal value of output PY. Therefore, if the price level P goes up, output Y must go down.

One way to understand the negative relationship between P and Y is to consider the link between money and transactions. Because we have assumed that the velocity of money is fixed, the money supply determines the dollar value of all transactions in the economy. If the price level rises, so that each transaction requires more dollars, the quantity of transactions and thus the quantity of goods and services purchased must fall.

Equivalently, we could look at the supply and demand for real money balances. If output is higher, people engage in more transactions and therefore need higher real balances M/P. For a fixed money supply M, higher real balances imply a lower price level. Conversely, if the price level is lower, real money balances are higher; the higher level of real balances allows a greater volume of transactions and thus a higher level of output.

Shifts in the Aggregate Demand Curve

The aggregate demand curve is drawn for a fixed value of the money supply. In other words, it tells us the possible combinations of P and Y for a given value of M. If the money supply changes, then the possible combinations of P and Y change—that is, the aggregate demand curve shifts. Let's examine some situations in which a shift may occur.

First, consider what happens if the Federal Reserve reduces the money supply. The quantity equation, $MV = PY$, tells us that the reduction in the money supply leads to a proportionate reduction in the nominal value of output, PY. Therefore, for any given price level, the amount of output is lower; and for any given amount of output, the price level is lower. As in Figure 8-3, the aggregate demand curve relating P and Y shifts inward.

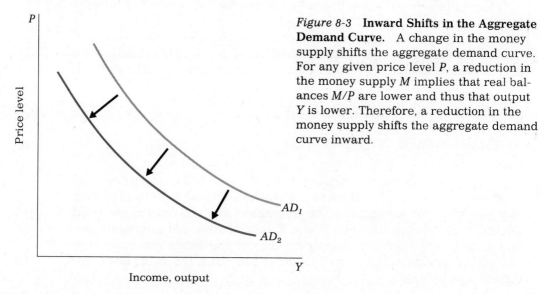

Figure 8-3 **Inward Shifts in the Aggregate Demand Curve.** A change in the money supply shifts the aggregate demand curve. For any given price level P, a reduction in the money supply M implies that real balances M/P are lower and thus that output Y is lower. Therefore, a reduction in the money supply shifts the aggregate demand curve inward.

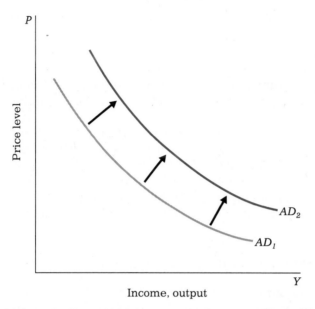

Income, output

Figure 8-4 Outward Shifts in the Aggregate Demand Curve. For any given price level P, an increase in the money supply M implies that real balances M/P are higher and thus that output Y is higher. Therefore, an increase in the money supply shifts the aggregate demand curve outward.

Next, consider what happens if the Fed increases the money supply. The quantity equation tells us that there is an increase in PY. Therefore, for any given price level, the amount of output is higher; and for any given amount of output, the price level is higher. As shown in Figure 8-4, the aggregate demand curve shifts outward.

Fluctuations in the money supply are not the only source of fluctuations in aggregate demand. Even if the money supply is held constant, the aggregate demand curve shifts because of changes in the velocity of money. We study the aggregate demand curve more fully in Chapters 9 and 10, where we consider many possible reasons that it might shift.

8-3 Aggregate Supply

By itself, the aggregate demand curve does not tell us the price level or the amount of output; it merely gives a relationship between these two variables. To accompany the aggregate demand curve, we need another relationship between P and Y that crosses the aggregate demand curve—an aggregate supply curve. The aggregate demand curve and the aggregate supply curve together pin down the price level and the amount of output.

Aggregate supply is the relationship between the quantity of goods and services supplied and the price level. This relationship depends crucially on the time horizon under consideration. We therefore need to discuss two different aggregate supply curves: the long-run aggregate supply curve and the short-run aggregate supply curve. We also need to discuss the transition from the short run to the long run.

The Long Run: The Vertical Aggregate Supply Curve

Since the classical model describes how the economy behaves in the long run, we derive the long-run aggregate supply curve from the classical model. Recall from Chapter 3 that the amount of output produced depends on the fixed amounts of capital and labor and on the available technology. To show this, we write

$$Y = F(\overline{K}, \overline{L})$$
$$= \overline{Y}.$$

Thus, according to the classical model, output does not depend on the price level. Therefore, the aggregate supply curve is vertical, as shown in Figure 8-5. The intersection of the aggregate demand curve with this vertical aggregate supply curve determines the price level.

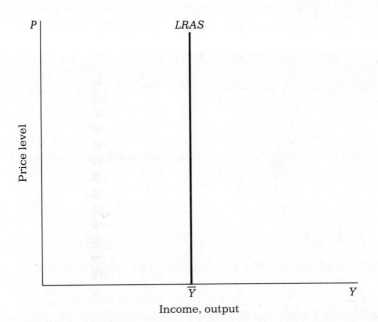

Figure 8-5 **The Long-Run Aggregate Supply Curve.** In the long run, the level of output is determined by the amounts of capital and labor and by the available technology. Thus, it does not depend on the price level. The long-run aggregate supply curve, LRAS, is vertical.

If the aggregate supply curve is vertical, then changes in aggregate demand affect prices but not output. For example, if the money supply falls, the aggregate demand curve shifts downward, as in Figure 8-6. The economy moves from the old intersection of aggregate supply and aggregate demand, point E_1, to the new intersection, point E_2. Since the aggregate supply curve is vertical, the shift in aggregate demand affects only prices.

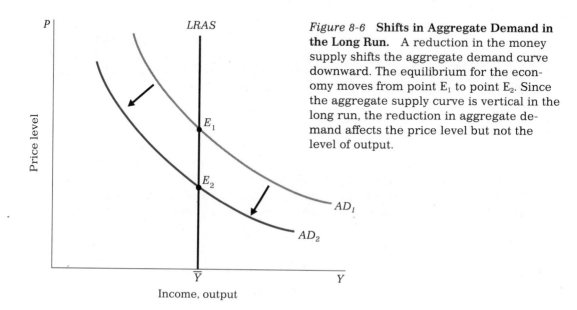

Figure 8-6 **Shifts in Aggregate Demand in the Long Run.**   A reduction in the money supply shifts the aggregate demand curve downward. The equilibrium for the economy moves from point E_1 to point E_2. Since the aggregate supply curve is vertical in the long run, the reduction in aggregate demand affects the price level but not the level of output.

The vertical aggregate supply curve satisfies the classical dichotomy, since it implies that the level of output is independent of aggregate demand and thus independent of the money supply. This long-run level of output, $\overline{Y}$, is called the *full-employment* or *natural-rate* level of output: it is the level of output at which the economy's resources are fully employed or, more realistically, at which unemployment is at its natural rate.

The Short Run: The Horizontal Aggregate Supply Curve

The classical model and the vertical aggregate supply curve apply only in the long run. In the short run, some prices are sticky and, therefore, do not adjust to changes in demand. This price stickiness implies that the short-run aggregate supply curve is not vertical.

As an extreme example, suppose that all firms have issued price catalogs and that it is costly for them to issue new ones. Therefore, all prices are stuck at predetermined levels. At these prices, firms are willing to sell as much as their customers are willing to buy. They hire

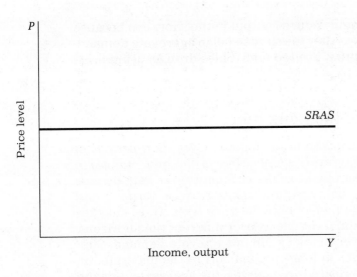

Figure 8-7 **The Short-Run Aggregate Supply Curve.** In this extreme example, all prices are fixed in the short run. Therefore, the short-run aggregate supply curve, SRAS, is horizontal.

just enough labor to produce the amount demanded. Since the price level is fixed, we represent this situation in Figure 8-7 by a horizontal aggregate supply curve.

The short-run equilibrium of the economy is the intersection of the aggregate demand curve and this horizontal short-run aggregate supply curve. In this case, changes in aggregate demand do affect the level of output. For example, if the Fed suddenly reduces the money supply, the aggregate demand curve shifts inward, as in Figure 8-8. The economy moves from the old intersection of aggregate demand and aggregate supply, point E_1, to the new intersection, point E_2. Since the price level is fixed, the shift in aggregate demand causes output to fall.

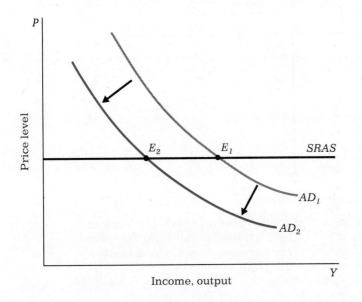

Figure 8-8 **Shifts in Aggregate Demand in the Short Run.** A reduction in the money supply shifts the aggregate demand curve downward. The equilibrium for the economy moves from point E_1 to point E_2. Since the aggregate supply curve is horizontal in the short run, the reduction in aggregate demand reduces the level of output.

A fall in aggregate demand reduces output in the short run because prices do not adjust instantly. After the sudden fall in aggregate demand, firms are stuck with prices that are too high. Sales drop, causing firms to reduce employment and production.

From the Short Run to the Long Run

We can summarize our analysis so far as follows: *Over short periods of time, prices are sticky, the aggregate supply curve is flat, and changes in aggregate demand affect the output of the economy. Over long periods of time, prices are flexible, the aggregate supply curve is vertical, and changes in aggregate demand affect only the price level.* Thus, changes in aggregate demand have different effects over different time horizons.

Let's trace the effects over time of a fall in aggregate demand. Suppose that the economy begins in long-run equilibrium, as illustrated in Figure 8-9. In this figure, there are three curves: the aggregate demand

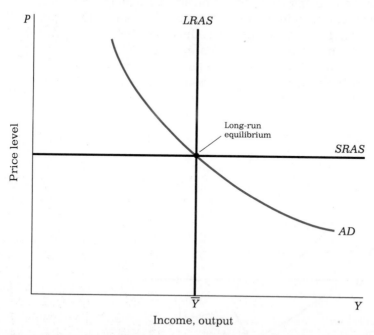

Figure 8-9 **Long-Run Equilibrium.** In the long run, the economy finds itself at the intersection of the long-run aggregate supply curve and the ag-gregate demand curve. Since prices have adjusted to this level, the short-run aggregate supply curve crosses this point as well.

curve, the long-run aggregate supply curve, and the short-run aggregate supply curve. The long-run equilibrium is the point at which aggregate demand crosses the long-run aggregate supply curve. Prices have adjusted to reach this equilibrium. Therefore, when the economy is in its long-run equilibrium, the short-run aggregate supply curve must cross this point as well.

Now suppose that the Fed reduces the money supply and the aggregate demand curve shifts downward, as in Figure 8-10. In the short run, prices are sticky, so the economy moves from point A to point B. Output and employment fall below their natural-rate levels, which means the economy is in a recession. Over time, in response to the low demand, wages and prices fall. The gradual reduction in the price level moves the economy downward along the aggregate demand curve to point C, which is the new long-run equilibrium. In the new long-run equilibrium (point C), output and employment are back to their natural-rate levels, but prices are lower than in the old long-run equilibrium (point A).

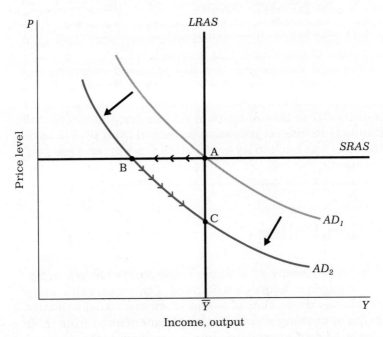

Figure 8-10 **A Reduction in Aggregate Demand.** The economy begins in long-run equilibrium, point A. A reduction in aggregate demand, perhaps caused by a decrease in the money supply, moves the economy from point A to point B, where output is below its natural-rate level. As prices fall, the economy gradually recovers from the recession, moving from point B to point C.

CASE STUDY 8-2

Gold, Greenbacks, and the Contraction of the 1870s

The experience of the United States in the 1870s illustrates the effects of contractionary monetary policy. The story begins in the 1860s with the monetary changes caused by the Civil War. Before the war, the United States had been on a gold standard. The Treasury stood ready to convert paper dollars into gold. Therefore, the quantity of gold determined the money supply and the price level.

In 1862, after the Civil War began, the Treasury announced that it would no longer exchange gold for dollars. In essence, this act placed the United States on a fiat money system. Over the next few years, the government printed large quantities of paper currency—called *greenbacks* for their color—and used the seigniorage to finance wartime expenditure. Because of this increase in the money supply, the price level approximately doubled during the war.

When the war was over, much political debate centered on the question of whether to return to the gold standard. The Greenback Party was formed with the primary goal of maintaining the system of fiat money. Eventually, however, policymakers decided to retire the greenbacks gradually in order to reinstate the gold standard at the rate of exchange between dollars and gold that had prevailed before the war. Their goal was to return the value of the dollar to its former level.

Returning to the gold standard in this way required reversing the wartime rise in prices, which meant a fall in aggregate demand. (Or, to be more precise, the growth in aggregate demand needed to fall short of the growth in the natural rate of output.) As the price level fell, the economy experienced the longest recession on record from 1873 to 1879. By 1879, the price level was back to its level before the war, and the gold standard was resumed.

8-4 Stabilization Policy

Fluctuations in the economy as a whole come from changes in aggregate supply or changes in aggregate demand. Economists call exogenous changes in these curves **shocks** to the economy. Shocks disrupt economic well-being by pushing output and employment away from their natural rates. The model of aggregate supply and aggregate demand shows how shocks cause economic fluctuations.

The model is also useful for evaluating how macroeconomic policy can respond to shocks in order to dampen fluctuations. **Stabilization policy** is public policy that is aimed at keeping output and employment at their natural rates. Because the money supply has a potent impact on aggregate demand, monetary policy is an important component of stabilization policy.

Shocks to Aggregate Demand

Consider an example of a shock to aggregate demand: the invention of automatic teller machines. These machines make cash easier to obtain and, therefore, reduce the demand for money. For example, suppose that before the introduction of teller machines, everyone goes to the bank once a week, withdraws $100, and then spends the money gradually over the week; in this case, average money holdings equal $50. After the introduction of teller machines, everyone goes to the bank twice a week and withdraws $50; now, average money holdings equal $25. Hence, in this example, money demand falls by half.

This reduction in money demand is equivalent to an increase in the velocity of money. To see this, remember that

$$M/P = kY,$$

where $k = 1/V$. A decrease in real money balances for any given amount of output implies a decrease in k and an increase in V. Because the introduction of automatic teller machines allows people to hold fewer dollars in their wallets, the dollars circulate more quickly. That is, because people obtain money more frequently, there is less time between when a dollar is received and when it is spent. Hence, velocity increases.

If the money supply is held constant, the increase in velocity causes the aggregate demand curve to shift outward, as in Figure 8-11. In the short run, the increase in aggregate demand raises the output of the economy—it causes an economic boom. At the old prices, firms sell more output. Therefore, they hire more workers, ask their existing workers to work longer hours, and make greater use of their factories and equipment.

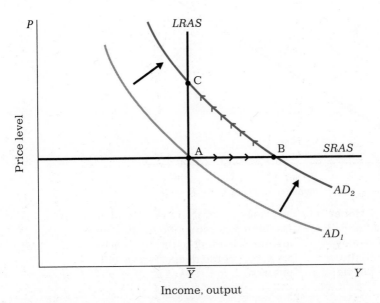

Figure 8-11 **An Increase in Aggregate Demand.** The economy begins in long-run equilibrium, point A. An increase in aggregate demand, due to an increase in the velocity of money, moves the economy from point A to point B, where output is above its natural-rate level. As prices rise, output gradually returns to its natural rate, and the economy moves from point B to point C.

Over time, the high level of aggregate demand pulls up wages and prices. As the price level rises, the quantity of output demanded declines, and the economy gradually approaches the natural rate of production. But during the transition to the higher price level, the economy's output is higher than the natural rate.

What can the Fed do to dampen this boom and keep output closer to the natural rate? The Fed might reduce the money supply to offset the increase in velocity. Offsetting the change in velocity would stabilize aggregate demand. The Fed has the potential to reduce or even eliminate the impact of demand shocks on output and employment by skillfully controlling the money supply.

CASE STUDY 8-3

Velocity and the 1982 Recession

Is the velocity of money steady, or is it highly volatile? The answer to this question influences how the Fed should conduct monetary policy. On the one hand, if velocity is steady, then it is easy to stabilize aggregate demand: the Fed only needs to keep the money supply constant, or growing at a steady rate. On the other hand, if velocity is highly volatile, then stabilizing aggregate demand requires adjusting the money supply frequently to offset the changes in velocity.

The deep recession that the United States experienced in 1982 is partly attributable to a large, unexpected, and still mostly unexplained decline in velocity. Figure 8-12 graphs velocity (measured here as nom-

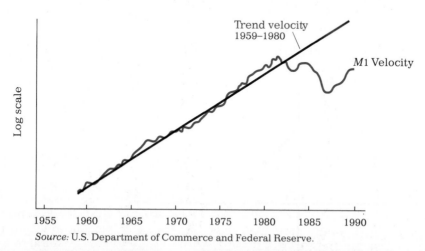

Source: U.S. Department of Commerce and Federal Reserve.

Figure 8-12 **The Velocity of Money.** For reasons that are still not fully understood, the velocity of money (measured here as *M*1) fell in the early 1980s substantially below its previous upward trend. This fall contributed to a reduction in aggregate demand, leading to the 1982 recession, one of the deepest in recent history.

inal GNP divided by *M*1) since 1959. The figure shows that velocity rose steadily in the 1960s and 1970s but then fell markedly after 1981. The experience of the early 1980s shows that the Fed cannot rely on the velocity of money remaining stable.

In 1982 the Fed could have offset the decrease in velocity by increasing the money supply. Containing inflation was the Fed's primary concern in the early 1980s, however, so it reduced the rate of money growth instead, further depressing aggregate demand. The combination of these two forces—falling velocity and anti-inflationary monetary policy—led to the deepest recession since the Great Depression of the 1930s.

How should we evaluate the Fed's actions? It attained its goal of lower inflation (even more quickly than it expected), but the cost was a substantial fall in output and employment. The 1982 recession highlights the conflicting goals of the Fed: maintaining full employment and keeping inflation under control. Stabilization policy often involves a tradeoff between these two objectives.[3]

Shocks to Aggregate Supply

Shocks to aggregate demand are not the only source of economic fluctuations; the other is shocks to aggregate supply. A supply shock is a shock to the economy that alters the cost of producing goods and services and, as a result, the prices that firms charge. Because supply shocks have a direct impact on the price level, they are sometimes called price shocks. Examples are:

- A drought that destroys crops—the reduction in food supply pushes up food prices.

- A new environmental protection law requiring firms to reduce their emissions of pollutants—firms pass on the added costs to customers in higher prices.

- An increase in union aggressiveness—this pushes up wages and the prices of the goods produced by union workers.

- The organization of an international oil cartel—by curtailing competition, the major oil producers can raise the world price of oil.

All these events are adverse supply shocks: they push up costs and prices. A favorable supply shock, such as the breakup of an international oil cartel, reduces costs and prices.

---

[3] For two views of what we learned about monetary policy from the experience of the 1980s, see Benjamin M. Friedman, "Lessons on Monetary Policy from the 1980s," *Journal of Economic Perspectives* 2 (Summer 1988): 51–72; and William Poole, "Monetary Policy Lessons of Recent Inflation and Disinflation," *Journal of Economic Perspectives* 2 (Summer 1988): 73–100.

Figure 8-13 shows the effect of an adverse supply shock. The short-run aggregate supply curve shifts upward. (The supply shock may also lower the natural-rate level of output, and thus shift the long-run aggregate supply curve to the left, but we ignore that effect here.) If aggregate demand is held constant, the economy moves from point A to point B: the price level rises and the amount of output falls below the natural rate. An experience like this is called **stagflation**, because it combines stagnation (falling output) with inflation (rising prices).

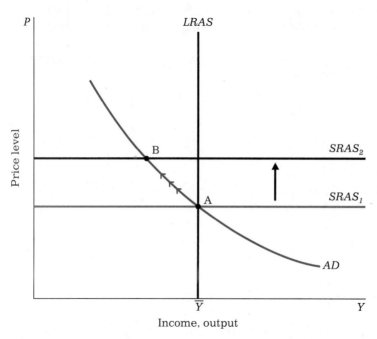

Figure 8-13   An Adverse Supply Shock.   An adverse supply shock pushes up costs and thus prices. If aggregate demand is held constant, the economy moves from point A to point B, leading to a combination of increasing prices and falling output. Eventually, as prices fall, the economy returns to the natural rate, point A.

Faced with an adverse supply shock, a policymaker controlling aggregate demand, such as the Fed, has a difficult choice between two options. The first option, implicit in Figure 8-13, is to hold aggregate demand constant. In this case, output and employment are lower than the natural rate. Eventually, prices will fall to restore full employment at the old price level (point A). But the cost of this process is a painful recession.

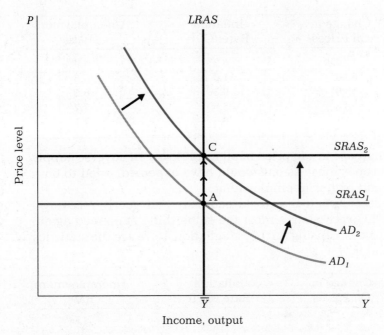

Figure 8-14 **Accommodating an Adverse Supply Shock.** In response to an adverse supply shock, the Fed can increase aggregate demand to prevent a reduction of output. The economy moves from point A to point C. The cost of this policy, however, is a permanently higher level of prices.

The second option, illustrated in Figure 8-14, is to expand aggregate demand to bring the economy toward the natural rate more quickly. If the increase in aggregate demand coincides with the shock to aggregate supply, the economy goes from point A to point C. In this case, the Fed is said to *accommodate* the supply shock. The drawback of this option, of course, is that the price level is permanently higher. There is no way to adjust aggregate demand both to maintain full employment and to keep the price level stable.

CASE STUDY 8-4

How OPEC Helped Cause Stagflation in the 1970s and Euphoria in the 1980s

The most disruptive supply shocks of the past forty years are attributable to OPEC, the Organization of Petroleum Exporting Countries. In the early 1970s, OPEC's coordinated reduction in the supply of oil nearly doubled the world price. This increase in oil prices caused stagflation in most industrial countries. These statistics show what happened in the United States:

Year	Change in Oil Prices	Inflation Rate (CPI)	Unemployment Rate
1973	11.0%	6.2%	4.9%
1974	68.0	11.0	5.6
1975	16.0	9.1	8.5
1976	3.3	5.8	7.7
1977	8.1	6.5	7.1

The 68 percent increase in the price of oil in 1974 was an adverse supply shock of major proportions. As one would have expected, it led to both higher inflation and higher unemployment.

A few years later, when the world economy had nearly recovered from the first OPEC recession, almost the same thing happened again. OPEC raised oil prices, causing further stagflation. Here are the statistics for the United States:

Year	Change in Oil Prices	Inflation Rate (CPI)	Unemployment Rate
1978	9.4%	7.7%	6.1%
1979	25.4	11.3	5.8
1980	47.8	13.5	7.0
1981	44.4	10.3	7.5
1982	−8.7	6.1	9.5

The increases in oil prices in 1979, 1980, and 1981 again led to double-digit inflation and higher unemployment.

In the mid-1980s, political turmoil among the Arab countries weakened OPEC's ability to restrain supplies of oil. Oil prices fell, reversing the stagflation of the 1970s and the early 1980s. Here's what happened:

Year	Change in Oil Prices	Inflation Rate (CPI)	Unemployment Rate
1983	−7.1%	3.2%	9.5%
1984	−1.7	4.3	7.4
1985	−7.5	3.6	7.1
1986	−44.5	1.9	6.9
1987	18.3	3.6	6.1

In 1986 oil prices fell by nearly half. This favorable supply shock led to one of the lowest inflation rates experienced in recent U.S. history and to falling unemployment.[4]

---

[4] Some economists have suggested that changes in oil prices played a major role in economic fluctuations even before the 1970s. See James D. Hamilton, "Oil and the Macroeconomy Since World War II," *Journal of Political Economy* 91 (April 1983): 228–248.

8-5 Conclusion

In this chapter we have introduced a framework to study economic fluctuations. Our model of aggregate supply and aggregate demand is built on the assumption that prices are sticky in the short run and flexible in the long run. The model shows how shocks to the economy cause output to deviate temporarily from the level implied by the classical model.

The model also highlights the role of monetary policy. Poor monetary policy can be a source of shocks to the economy. A well-run monetary policy, however, can respond to shocks and stabilize the economy.

Although the model of aggregate supply and aggregate demand resembles the model of supply and demand for a single good, we have to be careful: the analogy is imprecise. When we study supply and demand for a single good, we are analyzing only a single market. Macroeconomists need to model the whole economy at once. The model of aggregate supply and aggregate demand is really quite a sophisticated model that incorporates the interactions among many markets.

In the chapters that follow, we refine this model and our analysis of stabilization policy. Chapters 9 and 10 go beyond the quantity equation to refine our theory of aggregate demand. This refinement shows that aggregate demand depends on fiscal policy as well as monetary policy. Chapter 11 examines aggregate supply in more detail, and discusses why wages and prices are sticky. Chapter 12 examines the debate over the virtues and limits of stabilization policy.

Summary

1. The crucial difference between the long run and the short run is that prices are flexible in the long run but sticky in the short run. The model of aggregate supply and aggregate demand provides a framework to analyze economic fluctuations and to see how the impact of policies varies over different time horizons.

2. The aggregate demand curve tells us that the lower the price level, the greater the aggregate demand for goods and services.

3. In the long run, the aggregate supply curve is vertical: output is determined by the amounts of capital and labor and by the available technology. Therefore, shifts in aggregate demand affect the price level but not output or employment.

4. In the short run, the aggregate supply curve is horizontal, since wages and prices are predetermined. Therefore, shifts in aggregate demand affect output and employment.

5. Shocks to aggregate demand and aggregate supply cause economic

fluctuations. Since the Fed can shift the aggregate demand curve, it can attempt to offset these shocks to maintain output and employment at the natural rate.

KEY CONCEPTS

Aggregate demand

Aggregate supply

Shocks

Stabilization policy

Stagflation

QUESTIONS FOR REVIEW

1. Give an example of a price that is sticky in the short run and flexible in the long run.

2. Why does the aggregate demand curve slope downward?

3. Explain the impact of an increase in the money supply in the short run and in the long run.

4. Why is it easier for the Fed to deal with demand shocks than with supply shocks?

PROBLEMS AND APPLICATIONS

1. Suppose that a change in government regulations allows banks to start paying interest on checking accounts. Recall that the money stock is the sum of currency and demand deposits, including checking accounts, so this regulatory change makes holding money more attractive.

 a. How does this change affect the demand for money?

 b. What happens to the velocity of money?

 c. If the Fed keeps the money supply the same, what will happen to output and prices in the short run and long run?

 d. Should the Fed keep the money supply the same in response to this regulatory change? Why or why not?

2. The Fed reduces the money supply by 5 percent.

 a. What happens to the aggregate demand curve?

 b. What happens to the level of output and the price level in the short run and in the long run?

 c. According to Okun's law, what happens to unemployment in the short run and in the long run? (*Hint:* Okun's law is the relationship between output and unemployment discussed in Chapter 2.)

 d. What happens to the real interest rate in the short run and in the long run? (*Hint:* Use the model of the real interest rate in Chapter 3 to see what happens when output changes.)

3. Let's examine how the goals of the Fed influence its response to shocks. Suppose Fed A cares only about keeping the price level stable, and Fed B cares only about keeping output and employment at their natural rates. Explain how each Fed would respond to

 a. an exogenous decrease in the velocity of money.

 b. an exogenous increase in the price of oil.

Chapter 9

Aggregate Demand I

*I shall argue that the postulates of the classical theory
are applicable to a special case only and not to the
general case. . . . Moreover, the characteristics of the
special case assumed by the classical theory happen not
to be those of the economic society in which we actually
live, with the result that its teaching is misleading and
disastrous if we attempt to apply it to the facts of
experience.*

John Maynard Keynes
The General Theory

The most disruptive economic fluctuation in U.S. history was the Great
Depression. In the 1930s the United States experienced massive unemployment and greatly reduced incomes. In the worst year, 1933, one-
fourth of the U.S. labor force was unemployed, and real GNP was 30
percent below its 1929 level.

This devastating episode caused many economists to question the
validity of classical economic theory—the theory we examined in Chapters 3 through 7. The theory seemed incapable of explaining the Depression. Classical theory states that national income depends on factor
supplies and the available technology, but none of these changed substantially from 1929 to 1933. After the onset of the Depression, many
economists believed that a new model was needed not only to explain
such a large and sudden economic downturn but also to suggest government policies that might reduce the economic hardship so many people
faced.

In 1936 the British economist John Maynard Keynes revolutionized
economics with his book, *The General Theory of Employment, Interest,
and Money*. Keynes proposed a new way to analyze the economy, which
he presented as an alternative to classical theory. Keynes's theory
quickly became a center of controversy. From his vision of how the
economy works, a new understanding of economic fluctuations gradually
developed.

Keynes proposed that low aggregate demand is responsible for the low income and high unemployment that characterize economic downturns. He criticized classical theory for assuming that aggregate supply alone—capital, labor, and technology—determines national income. Economists today reconcile these two views with the model of aggregate demand and aggregate supply introduced in Chapter 8. In the long run, prices are flexible, and aggregate supply determines income. But in the short run, prices are sticky, so changes in aggregate demand influence income.

In this chapter and the next one, we continue our study of economic fluctuations by looking more closely at aggregate demand. Our goal is to identify the variables that shift the aggregate demand curve, causing fluctuations in national income. We also examine more fully the tools policymakers can use to influence aggregate demand. In Chapter 8 we derived the aggregate demand curve from the quantity theory of money, and we showed that monetary policy can shift the aggregate demand curve. In this chapter we see that government can influence aggregate demand with both monetary and fiscal policy.

The model of aggregate demand developed in this chapter, called the **IS-LM model**, is the leading interpretation of Keynes's theory. The *IS-LM* model takes the price level as exogenous and then shows what determines national income. There are two ways to view the *IS-LM* model. One can view it as showing what causes income to change in the short run when the price level is fixed. Alternatively, one can view the *IS-LM* model as showing what causes the aggregate demand curve to shift. These two ways of viewing the model are equivalent because, as Figure 9-1 illustrates, changes in income for a fixed price level are the

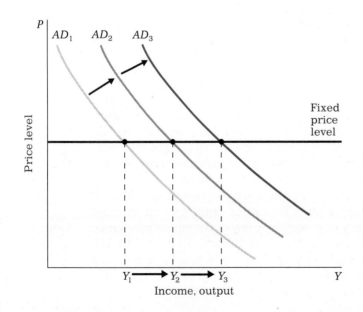

Figure 9-1 **Shifts in Aggregate Demand.** For a given price level, aggregate output and income fluctuate because of shifts in the aggregate demand curve. The *IS-LM* model takes the price level as given and shows what causes income to change. The model therefore shows what causes aggregate demand to shift.

same as shifts in the aggregate demand curve. That is, in the short run when the price level is fixed, shifts in the aggregate demand curve determine changes in income.

The two parts of the *IS-LM* model are, not surprisingly, the **IS curve** and the **LM curve**. *IS* stands for "investment" and "saving." The *IS* curve represents the market for goods and services we discussed in Chapter 3. *LM* stands for "liquidity" and "money." The *LM* curve represents the supply and demand for money we discussed in Chapter 6. Because the interest rate influences both investment and money demand, it is the variable that links the two halves of the *IS-LM* model. The model shows how interactions between these markets determine aggregate demand.[1]

9-1 The Goods Market and the *IS* Curve

The *IS* curve plots the relationship between the interest rate and the level of income that arises in the market for goods and services. To understand this relationship, we begin with a simple theory of the demand for goods and services, called the **Keynesian cross**.

The Keynesian Cross

The Keynesian cross is the simplest interpretation of Keynes's theory of national income. It provides a useful building block for the more complex and realistic *IS-LM* model. Many of the elements of the Keynesian cross should be familiar from our discussion of the market for goods and services in Chapter 3.

Planned Expenditure   To derive the Keynesian cross, we begin by looking at the determinants of planned expenditure. Planned expenditure is the amount households, firms, and government plan to spend on goods and services. Actual expenditure differs from planned expenditure when firms are forced to make unplanned inventory investment—that is, when firms unexpectedly raise or lower their stock of inventories in response to unexpectedly low or high sales.

Assuming that the economy is closed, so that net exports are zero, we write planned expenditure *E* as the sum of consumption *C*, planned investment *I*, and government purchases *G*:

$$E = C + I + G.$$

To this equation, we add the consumption function

$$C = C(Y - T).$$

---

[1] The *IS-LM* model was introduced in a classic article by the Nobel-prize-winning economist John R. Hicks, "Mr. Keynes and the Classics: A Suggested Interpretation," *Econometrica* 5 (1937): 147–159.

The consumption function states that consumption depends on disposable income $(Y - T)$. Disposable income is total income Y minus taxes T. In addition, we assume that planned investment is fixed

$$I = \bar{I},$$

and that fiscal policy—the levels of government purchases and taxes—is fixed:

$$G = \bar{G}.$$
$$T = \bar{T}.$$

Combining these equations, we obtain

$$E = C(Y - \bar{T}) + \bar{I} + \bar{G}.$$

This equation states that planned expenditure is a function of income Y, the exogenous level of planned investment $\bar{I}$, and the exogenous fiscal policy variables $\bar{G}$ and $\bar{T}$.

Figure 9-2 graphs planned expenditure as a function of the level of income. This line slopes upward because higher income leads to higher consumption and thus higher planned expenditure. The slope of this line is the marginal propensity to consume, the *MPC*: it shows how much planned expenditure increases when income rises by one dollar.

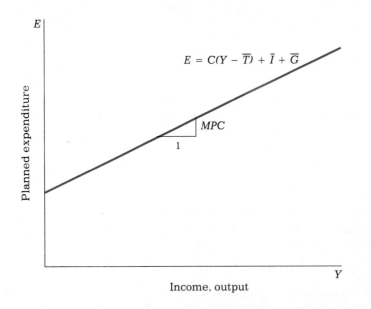

Figure 9-2 **Planned Expenditure as a Function of Income.** Planned expenditure depends on income because higher income leads to higher consumption. The slope of this line is the marginal propensity to consume (*MPC*).

The Economy in Equilibrium   We now assume that the economy is in equilibrium when actual expenditure equals planned expenditure. Recall that GNP has two meanings: the economy's income and the economy's expenditure. Therefore, Y equals not only total income but also actual expenditure on goods and services. We write the equilibrium condition as

$$\text{Actual Expenditure} = \text{Planned Expenditure}$$
$$Y = E.$$

The 45-degree line in Figure 9-3 plots the points where this condition holds. With the addition of the planned-expenditure function, this diagram becomes the Keynesian cross. The equilibrium of this economy is at point A, where the planned-expenditure function crosses the 45-degree line.

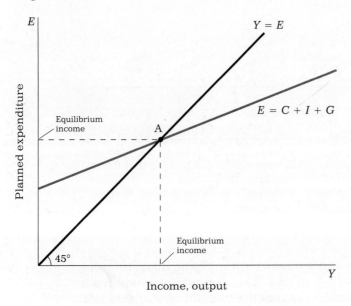

Figure 9-3 **The Keynesian Cross.** The equilibrium in the Keynesian cross is at point A, where income equals planned expenditure.

How does the economy get to the equilibrium? For many firms, inventories play an important role in the adjustment process. If firms produce more goods than people want to buy, the firms add the additional goods to their inventories. Conversely, if firms produce less than people want to buy, the firms use up some of their inventories. These unplanned changes in inventories then induce firms to change production levels.

For example, suppose GNP is at a level greater than the equilibrium level, such as the level Y_1 in Figure 9-4. In this case, planned expenditure is E_1, which is less than Y_1. Because planned expenditure is less than production, firms are selling less than they produce. Therefore, inventories increase: this inventory accumulation is unplanned investment by the owners of firms. The increase in inventories induces firms to lay off workers and reduce production, which reduces GNP. This process of unintended inventory accumulation and falling income continues until income falls to the equilibrium level. At the equilibrium, income equals planned expenditure.

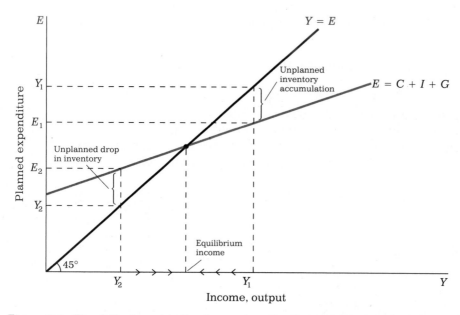

Figure 9-4 **The Adjustment to Equilibrium in the Keynesian Cross.** If firms are producing at level Y_1, then planned expenditure E_1 falls short of production, so that firms accumulate inventories. This inventory accumulation induces firms to reduce production. Similarly, if firms are producing at level Y_2, then planned expenditure E_2 exceeds production, so that firms run down their inventories. This fall in inventories induces firms to raise production.

Similarly, suppose GNP is at a level lower than the equilibrium level, such as the level Y_2 in Figure 9-4. In this case, planned expenditure is E_2, which is more than Y_2. Because planned expenditure exceeds production, firms are selling more than they are producing. Inventories fall, so firms hire more workers and increase production, raising GNP. This process continues until income equals planned expenditure.

In summary, the Keynesian cross shows how income Y is determined for given levels of planned investment I and fiscal policy G and T. We can use this model to show how income changes when one of these exogenous variables changes.

Fiscal Policy and the Multiplier: Government Purchases We first use the Keynesian cross to consider the impact of a change in government purchases. Because government purchases are one component of expenditure, an increase in government purchases means that, for any given level of income, planned expenditure increases. If government purchases increase by ΔG, then the planned-expenditure schedule shifts upward by ΔG, as Figure 9-5 illustrates. The equilibrium of the economy moves from point A to point B.

This graph shows that an increase in government purchases leads

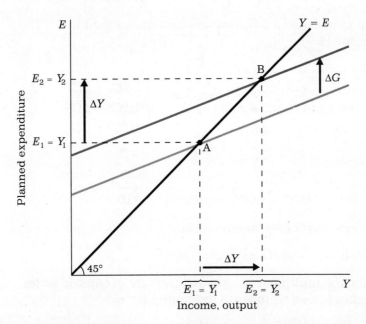

Figure 9-5 **An Increase in Government Purchases in the Keynesian Cross.** An increase in government purchases of ΔG raises planned expenditure by that amount for any given level of income. The equilibrium moves from point A to point B, and income rises from Y_1 to Y_2. Note that the increase in income (ΔY) exceeds the increase in government purchases (ΔG). Thus, fiscal policy has a multiplied effect on income.

to an even greater increase in income. That is, ΔY is larger than ΔG. The ratio $\Delta Y/\Delta G$ is called the **government-purchases multiplier**; it tells us how much income rises in response to a one-dollar increase in government purchases. An implication of the Keynesian cross is that the government-purchases multiplier is larger than one.

Why does fiscal policy have a multiplied effect on income? The reason is that, according to the consumption function, higher income causes higher consumption. Because an increase in government purchases raises income, it also raises consumption, which further raises income, which further raises consumption, and so on. Therefore, in this model, an increase in government purchases causes a greater increase in income.

How big is the multiplier? To answer this question, we trace through each step of the change in income. The process begins when expenditure rises by ΔG, which implies that income rises by ΔG as well. This increase in income in turn raises consumption by $MPC \times \Delta G$, where MPC is the marginal propensity to consume. This increase in consumption raises expenditure and income once again. This second increase in income of $MPC \times \Delta G$ again raises consumption, this time by $MPC \times (MPC \times \Delta G)$, which again raises expenditure and income, and so on. This feedback from consumption to income to consumption continues indefinitely. The total effect on income is:

Initial Change in Government Purchases = $\quad\quad \Delta G$

First Change in Consumption $\quad\quad = MPC \times \Delta G$

Second Change in Consumption $\quad\quad = MPC^2 \times \Delta G$

Third Change in Consumption $\quad\quad = MPC^3 \times \Delta G$

.
.
.

$$\Delta Y = (1 + MPC + MPC^2 + MPC^3 + \ldots)\Delta G.$$

Thus, the government-purchases multiplier is

$$\Delta Y/\Delta G = 1 + MPC + MPC^2 + MPC^3 + \ldots.$$

This expression for the multiplier is called an *infinite geometric series*. A result from algebra allows us to write the multiplier as[2]

$$\Delta Y/\Delta G = 1/(1 - MPC).$$

For example, if the marginal propensity to consume is 0.6, the multiplier is

$$\Delta Y/\Delta G = 1 + 0.6 + 0.6^2 + 0.6^3 + \ldots$$
$$= 1/(1 - 0.6)$$
$$= 2.5.$$

In this case, a $1.00 increase in government purchases raises equilibrium income by $2.50.[3]

---

[2] *Mathematical Note:* We prove this algebraic result as follows. Let
$$z = 1 + x + x^2 + \ldots.$$
Multiply both sides of this equation by x:
$$xz = x + x^2 + x^3 + \ldots.$$
Subtract the second equation from the first:
$$z - xz = 1.$$
Rearrange this last equation to obtain:
$$z(1 - x) = 1,$$
which implies
$$z = 1/(1 - x).$$
This completes the proof.

[3] *Mathematical Note:* The government-purchases multiplier is most easily derived using a little calculus. Begin with the equation
$$Y = C(Y - T) + I + G.$$
Differentiate to obtain
$$dY = C'dY + dG,$$
and then rearrange to find
$$dY/dG = 1/(1 - C').$$
This is the same as the equation in the text.

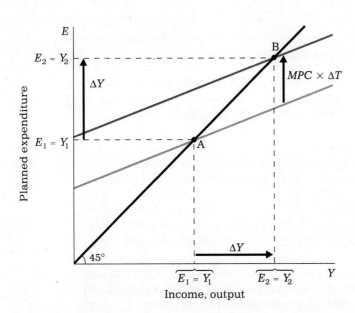

Figure 9-6 **A Decrease in Taxes in the Keynesian Cross.** A decrease in taxes of ΔT raises planned expenditure by $MPC \times \Delta T$ for any given level of income. The equilibrium moves from point A to point B, and income rises from Y_1 to Y_2. Again, fiscal policy has a multiplied effect on income.

Fiscal Policy and the Multiplier: Taxes We now consider the impact of a change in taxes on equilibrium income. A decrease in taxes of ΔT immediately raises disposable income $Y - T$ by ΔT and, therefore, consumption by $MPC \times \Delta T$. For any given level of income Y, planned expenditure is now higher. Thus, as in Figure 9-6, the planned-expenditure schedule shifts upward by $MPC \times \Delta T$. The equilibrium of the economy moves from point A to point B.

Just as the increase in government purchases has a multiplied effect on income, so does a decrease in taxes. As before, the initial change in expenditure is multiplied by $1/(1 - MPC)$. The overall effect on income of the change in taxes is

$$\Delta Y / \Delta T = -MPC/(1 - MPC).$$

This expression is the **tax multiplier:** the amount income changes in response to a one-dollar change in taxes. For example, if the marginal propensity to consume is 0.6, then the tax multiplier is

$$\Delta Y / \Delta T = -0.6/(1 - 0.6) = -1.5.$$

In this example, a $1.00 cut in taxes raises equilibrium income by $1.50.[4]

---

[4] *Mathematical Note:* As before, the multiplier is most easily derived using a little calculus. Begin with the equation

$$Y = C(Y - T) + I + G.$$

Differentiate to obtain

$$dY = C'(dY - dT),$$

and then rearrange to find

$$dY/dT = -C'/(1 - C').$$

This is the same as the equation in the text.

Kennedy, Keynes, and the 1964 Tax Cut

When John F. Kennedy became president in 1961, he brought to Washington some of the bright young economists of the day to work on the Council of Economic Advisers. These economists, who had been schooled in the economics of Keynes, brought Keynesian ideas to discussions of economic policy at the highest level.

One of the Council's first proposals was to expand national income by reducing taxes. This eventually led to a substantial cut in personal and corporate income taxes in 1964. This tax cut was intended to stimulate expenditure on consumption and investment, leading to higher levels of income and employment. When a reporter asked Kennedy why he advocated a tax cut, Kennedy replied, "To stimulate the economy. Don't you remember your Economics 101?"

As these economic advisers predicted, the passage of the tax cut was followed by an economic boom. Growth in real GNP was 5.3 percent in 1964 and 6.0 percent in 1965. The unemployment rate fell from 5.7 percent in 1963, to 5.2 percent in 1964, and then to 4.5 percent in 1965.

Economists continue to debate the source of this rapid growth in the early 1960s. A group called *supply-siders* argues that the economic boom resulted from the incentive effects of the cut in income tax rates. According to supply-siders, when workers are allowed to keep a higher fraction of their earnings, they supply substantially more labor and expand the aggregate supply of goods and services. Keynesians, however, emphasize the impact of tax cuts on aggregate demand. They view the 1964 tax cut as a successful experiment with expansionary fiscal policy and as a confirmation of Keynesian economics.[5]

The Interest Rate, Investment, and the *IS* Curve

The Keynesian cross is only a stepping-stone on our road to developing the *IS-LM* model. The Keynesian cross is useful because it shows what determines the economy's income for any given level of planned investment. Yet it is simplistic because it assumes that the level of planned investment is fixed. Chapter 3 explains that planned investment in fact depends on the interest rate.

To add this relationship between the interest rate and investment to our model, we write the level of planned investment as

$$I = I(r).$$

[5] For an analysis of the 1964 tax cut by one of Kennedy's economists, see Arthur Okun, "Measuring the Impact of the 1964 Tax Reduction," in W. W. Heller, ed., *Perspectives on Economic Growth* (New York: Random House, 1968); reprinted in Arthur M. Okun, *Economics for Policymaking* (Cambridge, Mass.: MIT Press, 1983), 405–423.

This investment function is graphed in Figure 9-7A. Because the interest rate is the cost of borrowing to finance investment projects, an increase in the interest rate reduces planned investment.

Figure 9-7 **Deriving the *IS* Curve.** Panel A shows the investment function: an increase in the interest rate from r_1 to r_2 reduces planned investment from $I(r_1)$ to $I(r_2)$. Panel B shows the Keynesian cross: a decrease in planned investment from $I(r_1)$ to $I(r_2)$ reduces income from Y_1 to Y_2. Panel C shows the *IS* curve summarizing this relationship between the interest rate and income: the higher the interest rate, the lower the level of income.

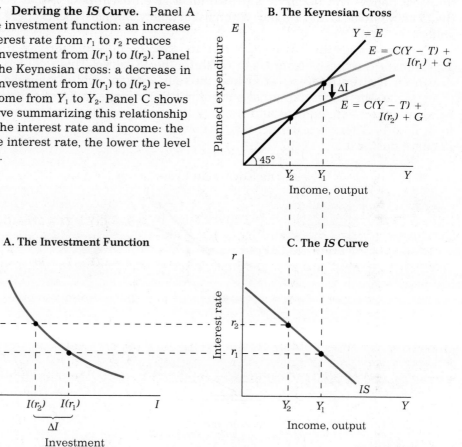

We can use the investment function and the Keynesian-cross diagram to determine how income changes when the interest rate increases. Because investment is inversely related to the interest rate, an increase in the interest rate from r_1 to r_2 reduces the quantity of investment from $I(r_1)$ to $I(r_2)$. The reduction in planned investment, in turn, shifts the expenditure function downward, as in Figure 9-7B. The shift in the expenditure function leads to a lower level of income. Hence, an increase in the interest rate lowers income.

The *IS* curve summarizes this relationship between the interest rate and the level of income that results from the investment function and the Keynesian cross. The higher the interest rate, the lower the level of planned investment, and thus the lower the level of income. For this reason, the *IS* curve slopes downward, as in Figure 9-7C.

How Fiscal Policy Shifts the *IS* Curve

The *IS* curve shows us the level of income for any given interest rate. As we learned from the Keynesian cross, the level of income also depends on fiscal policy. The *IS* curve is drawn for a given fiscal policy; that is, the *IS* curve holds G and T fixed. When fiscal policy changes, the *IS* curve shifts.

Figure 9-8 uses the Keynesian cross to examine how an increase in government purchases from G_1 to G_2 shifts the *IS* curve. This figure is drawn for a given interest rate $\bar{r}$ and thus for a given level of planned investment. The Keynesian cross shows that this change in fiscal policy raises planned expenditure and thereby increases equilibrium income from Y_1 to Y_2. Therefore, an increase in government purchases shifts the *IS* curve outward.

A. The Keynesian Cross

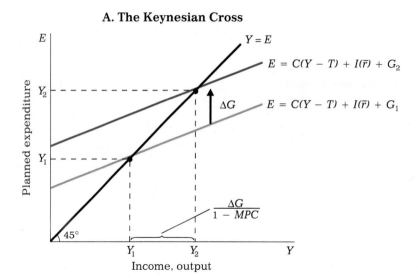

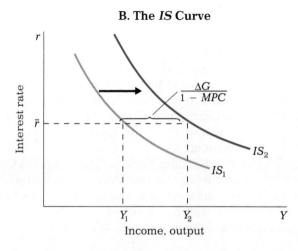

B. The *IS* Curve

Figure 9-8 **An Increase in Government Purchases Shifts the *IS* Curve Outward.** Panel A shows that an increase in government purchases raises planned expenditure. For any given interest rate, the upward shift in planned expenditure of ΔG leads to an increase in income of $\Delta G/(1 - MPC)$. Therefore, in panel B, the *IS* curve shifts to the right by this amount.

We can use the Keynesian cross to see how other changes in fiscal policy shift the *IS* curve. Because a decrease in taxes also expands expenditure and income, it too shifts the *IS* curve outward. A decrease in government purchases or an increase in taxes reduces income; therefore, such a change in fiscal policy shifts the *IS* curve inward.

In summary, the IS *curve shows the relationship between the interest rate and the level of income that arises from the market for goods and services. The* IS *curve is drawn for a given fiscal policy. Changes in fiscal policy that raise the demand for goods and services shift the* IS *curve to the right. Changes in fiscal policy that reduce the demand for goods and services shift the* IS *curve to the left.*

A Loanable-Funds Interpretation of the *IS* Curve

When we first studied the market for goods and services in Chapter 3, we noted an equivalence between the supply and demand for goods and services and the supply and demand for loanable funds. This equivalence provides another way to interpret the *IS* curve.

Recall that the national income accounts identity can be written as

$$Y - C - G = I$$
$$S = I.$$

The left-hand side of this equation is national saving S, the sum of private saving $Y - T - C$ and public saving $T - G$, and the right-hand side is investment I. National saving represents the supply of loanable funds, and investment represents the demand for these funds.

To see how the market for loanable funds produces the *IS* curve, substitute the consumption function for C and the investment function for I:

$$Y - C(Y - T) - G = I(r).$$

The left-hand side of this equation states that the supply of loanable funds depends on income and fiscal policy. The right-hand side states that the demand for loanable funds depends on the interest rate. The interest rate adjusts to equilibrate the supply and demand for loans.

As Figure 9-9 illustrates, we can interpret the *IS* curve as showing the interest rate that equilibrates the market for loanable funds for any given level of income. When income rises from Y_1 to Y_2, national saving, which equals $Y - C - G$, increases. (Consumption rises by less than income, because the marginal propensity to consume is less than one.) The increased supply of loanable funds drives down the interest rate from r_1 to r_2. The *IS* curve summarizes this relationship: higher income implies higher saving, which in turn implies a lower equilibrium interest rate. For this reason, the *IS* curve slopes downward.

A. The Market for
Loanable Funds

B. The *IS* Curve

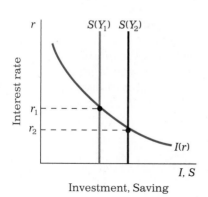

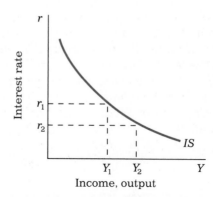

Figure 9-9 **A Loanable-Funds Interpretation of the *IS* Curve.** Panel A
shows that an increase in income
from Y_1 to Y_2 raises saving and thus
lowers the interest rate that equilibrates the supply and demand for
loanable funds. The *IS* curve in panel
B expresses this negative relationship
between income and the interest rate.

This alternative interpretation of the *IS* curve also explains why a
change in fiscal policy shifts the *IS* curve. An increase in government
purchases or a decrease in taxes reduces national saving for any given
level of income. The reduced supply of loanable funds raises the interest
rate that equilibrates the market. Because the interest rate is now higher
for any given level of income, the *IS* curve shifts upward in response to
the expansionary change in fiscal policy.

The Simple Algebra of the *IS* Curve

One way to think about the *IS* curve is that it describes the combinations
of income Y and the interest rate r that satisfy an equation we first saw
in Chapter 3:

$$Y = C(Y - T) + I(r) + G.$$

This equation combines the national income accounts identity, the consumption function, and the investment function. It states that the quantity of goods produced, Y, must equal the quantity of goods demanded,
$C + I + G$.

We can learn more about the *IS* curve by considering the special
case in which the consumption function and investment function are
linear. We begin with the national income accounts identity

$$Y = C + I + G.$$

Now suppose that the consumption function is

$$C = a + b(Y - T),$$

where a and b are numbers greater than zero, and the investment function is

$$I = c - dr,$$

where c and d also are numbers greater than zero. The parameter b is the marginal propensity to consume, so we expect b to be between zero and one. The parameter d determines how much investment responds to the interest rate; because investment rises when the interest rate falls, there is a minus sign in front of d.

From these three equations, we can derive an algebraic expression for the *IS* curve and see what influences the *IS* curve's position and slope. If we substitute the consumption and investment functions into the national income accounts identity, we obtain

$$Y = [a + b(Y - T)] + (c - dr) + G.$$

Note that Y shows up on both sides of this equation. We can simplify this equation by bringing all the Y terms to the left-hand side and rearranging the terms on the right-hand side:

$$Y - bY = (a + c) + (G - bT) - dr.$$

We solve for Y to get

$$Y = \frac{a + c}{1 - b} + \frac{1}{1 - b}G + \frac{-b}{1 - b}T + \frac{-d}{1 - b}r.$$

This equation expresses the *IS* curve algebraically. It tells us the level of income Y for any given interest rate r and fiscal policy G and T. Holding fiscal policy fixed, it gives us a relationship between the interest rate and the level of income: the higher the interest rate, the lower the level of income. The *IS* curve graphs this equation for different values of Y and r and for fixed values of G and T.

Using this last equation, we can verify our previous conclusions about the *IS* curve. First, because the coefficient of the interest rate is negative, the *IS* curve slopes downward: higher interest rates lead to lower income. Second, because the coefficient of government purchases is positive, an increase in government purchases shifts the *IS* curve outward. Third, because the coefficient of taxes is negative, an increase in taxes shifts the *IS* curve inward.

The coefficient of the interest rate, $-d/(1 - b)$, tells us what determines whether the *IS* curve is steep or flat. If investment is highly sensitive to the interest rate, then d is large, and income is highly sensitive to the interest rate as well. In this case, small changes in the interest rate lead to large changes in income: the *IS* curve is relatively flat.

Conversely, if investment is not very sensitive to the interest rate, then d is small, and income is also not very sensitive to the interest rate. In this case, large changes in interest rates lead to small changes in income: the *IS* curve is relatively steep.

Similarly, the slope of the *IS* curve depends on the marginal propensity to consume, b. The larger the marginal propensity to consume, the larger the change in income resulting from a given change in the interest rate. The reason is that a large marginal propensity to consume leads to a large multiplier for changes in investment. The larger the multiplier, the larger the impact of a change in investment on income, and the flatter the *IS* curve.

The marginal propensity to consume, b, also determines how much changes in fiscal policy shift the *IS* curve. The coefficient of G, $1/(1 - b)$, is the government-purchases multiplier in the Keynesian cross. Similarly, the coefficient of T, $-b/(1 - b)$, is the tax multiplier in the Keynesian cross. The larger the marginal propensity to consume, the greater the multiplier, and thus the greater the shift in the *IS* curve that arises from a change in fiscal policy.

Finally, remember that the *IS* curve does not determine either income Y or the interest rate r. Instead, the *IS* curve only provides a relationship between Y and r arising in the market for goods and services. To determine the equilibrium of the economy, we need another relationship between these two variables, to which we now turn our attention.

9-2 The Money Market and the *LM* Curve

The *LM* curve is the relationship between the interest rate and the level of income that arises in the market for money balances. To understand this relationship, we begin by looking at a simple theory of the interest rate, called the **theory of liquidity preference**.

The Theory of Liquidity Preference

The theory of liquidity preference is the simplest interpretation of Keynes's theory of the interest rate. Just as the Keynesian cross provides a building block for the *IS* curve, the theory of liquidity preference provides a building block for the *LM* curve. The theory explains how the supply and demand for real money balances, which we studied in Chapter 6, determine the interest rate.

We begin with the supply of real money balances. If M stands for the supply of money and P stands for the price level, then M/P is the supply of real money balances. The theory of liquidity preference assumes there is a fixed supply of real balances. That is,

$$(M/P)^s = \overline{M}/\overline{P}.$$

M is the level of the money supply chosen by the Federal Reserve; thus, it is an exogenous policy variable. The price level P is also an exogenous variable in this model. (We take the price level as given because the *IS-LM* model—our ultimate goal in this chapter—considers the short run when the price level is fixed.) These assumptions imply that the supply of real balances is fixed and, therefore, that it does not depend on the interest rate. Hence, when we plot the supply of real money balances against the interest rate in Figure 9-10, we obtain a vertical supply curve.

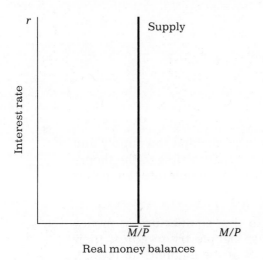

Figure 9-10 **The Supply of Real Money Balances.** The supply curve of real balances is vertical because the supply does not depend on the interest rate.

Next, we turn to the demand for real money balances. People hold money because it is a "liquid" asset—that is, because it is easily used to make transactions. The theory of liquidity preference postulates that the quantity of real money balances demanded depends on the interest rate. The interest rate is the opportunity cost of holding money: it is what you forgo by holding money, which does not bear interest, instead of interest-bearing bank deposits or bonds. Just as the price of bread affects the quantity of bread demanded, the price of holding money affects the quantity of real balances demanded. Therefore, when the interest rate rises, people want to hold less of their wealth in the form of money.

We write the demand for real money balances as

$$(M/P)^d = L(r),$$

where the function $L(\ )$ denotes the demand for the liquid asset—money.

This equation states that the quantity of real balances demanded is a function of the interest rate. Figure 9-11 shows the relationship between the interest rate and the quantity of real balances demanded. This demand curve slopes downward because higher interest rates reduce the quantity of real balances demanded.[6]

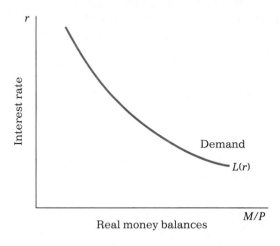

Figure 9-11   **The Demand for Real Money Balances.** Because the interest rate is the cost of holding money, a higher interest rate lowers the quantity of real balances demanded.

To obtain a theory of the interest rate, we combine the supply and demand for real money balances in Figure 9-12. According to the theory of liquidity preference, the interest rate adjusts to equilibrate the money market. At the equilibrium interest rate, the quantity of real balances demanded equals the quantity supplied.

The adjustment of the interest rate to this equilibrium of money supply and money demand occurs because people try to adjust their portfolios of assets if the interest rate is not at the equilibrium level. If the interest rate is too high, the quantity of real balances supplied exceeds the quantity demanded. Individuals holding the excess supply of money try to convert some of their non-interest-bearing money into interest-bearing bank deposits or bonds. Banks and bond issuers, who prefer to pay lower interest rates, respond to this excess supply of money by lowering the interest rates they offer. Conversely, if the interest rate is too low, so that the quantity of money demanded exceeds the quantity supplied, individuals try to obtain money by selling bonds or making bank withdrawals, which drives the interest rate upward. At the equilibrium interest rate people are content with their portfolio of monetary and non-monetary assets.

---

[6] Note that r is being used to denote the interest rate here, as it was in our discussion of the *IS* curve. More accurately, it is the nominal interest rate that determines money demand and the real interest rate that determines investment. To keep things simple, we are ignoring expected inflation, which creates the difference between the real and the nominal interest rate. The role of expected inflation in the *IS-LM* model is explored in Chapter 10.

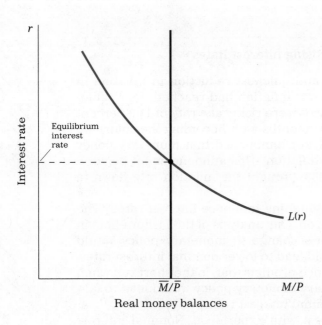

Figure 9-12 **The Theory of Liquidity Preference.** The interest rate adjusts until the quantity of real balances demanded equals the supply.

The theory of liquidity preference implies that decreases in the money supply raise the interest rate and that increases in the money supply lower the interest rate. To see why, suppose that the Fed reduces the money supply. A reduction in M reduces M/P, since P is fixed in the model. Therefore, the supply of real balances shifts to the left, as in Figure 9-13. The equilibrium interest rate rises from r_1 to r_2. The higher interest rate induces people to hold a smaller quantity of real money balances.

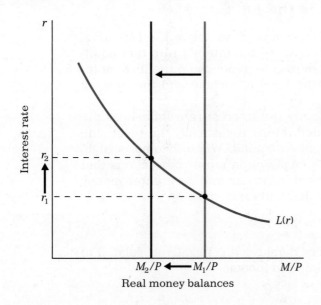

Figure 9-13 **A Reduction in the Money Supply in the Theory of Liquidity Preference.** A reduction in the money supply from M_1 to M_2 reduces the supply of real balances, since the price level is fixed. The equilibrium interest rate therefore rises from r_1 to r_2.

CASE STUDY 9-2

Paul Volcker, Tight Money, and Rising Interest Rates

The early 1980s saw the largest and quickest reduction in inflation in recent U.S. history. By the late 1970s inflation had reached the double-digit range; in 1979, consumer prices were rising at a rate of 11.3 percent per year. In October 1979, only two months after becoming the chairman of the Federal Reserve, Paul Volcker announced that monetary policy would aim to reduce the rate of inflation. This announcement began a period of tight money that, by 1983, brought the inflation rate down to about 3 percent.

How does such a monetary tightening influence interest rates? The answer depends on the time horizon. Our analysis of the Fisher effect in Chapter 6 suggests that Volcker's change in monetary policy would lower inflation, which in turn would lead to lower nominal interest rates. Yet the theory of liquidity preference predicts that, in the short run when prices are sluggish, anti-inflationary monetary policy would lead to falling real balances and higher nominal interest rates.

Both conclusions are consistent with experience. Nominal interest rates did fall in the 1980s as inflation fell. But comparing the year before the October 1979 announcement and the year after, we find that real balances ($M1$ divided by the CPI) fell 8.3 percent and the nominal interest rate (on commercial paper) rose from 10.1 percent to 11.9 percent. Hence, although a monetary tightening leads to lower interest rates in the long run, it leads to higher interest rates in the short run.

Income, Money Demand, and the *LM* Curve

We now use the theory of liquidity preference to derive the *LM* curve. We see that the equilibrium interest rate—the interest rate that equilibrates money supply and money demand—depends on the level of income. This relationship between the level of income and the interest rate is expressed in the *LM* curve.

So far we have assumed that only the interest rate influences the quantity of real balances demanded. More realistically, however, the level of income Y also affects money demand. When income is high, expenditure is high, so people are engaging in more transactions that require the use of money. Thus, greater income implies greater money demand. We now write the money demand function as

$$(M/P)^d = L(r, Y).$$

The quantity of real money balances demanded is negatively related to the interest rate and positively related to income.

Using the theory of liquidity preference, we can see what happens to the interest rate when the level of income changes. For example, consider what happens when income increases from Y_1 to Y_2. As Figure 9-14A illustrates, this increase in income shifts the money demand curve outward. To equilibrate the market for real money balances, the interest rate must rise from r_1 to r_2. Therefore, higher income leads to a higher interest rate.

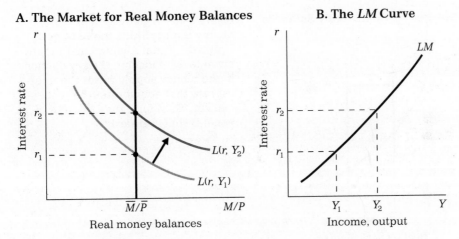

A. The Market for Real Money Balances   **B. The *LM* Curve**

Figure 9-14 **Deriving the *LM* Curve.** Panel A shows the market for real balances: an increase in income from Y_1 to Y_2 raises the demand for money and thus the interest rate from r_1 to

r_2. Panel B shows the *LM* curve summarizing this relationship between the interest rate and income: the higher the level of income, the higher the interest rate.

The *LM* curve plots this relationship between the level of income and the interest rate. The higher the level of income, the higher the demand for real money balances, and thus the higher the equilibrium interest rate. For this reason, the *LM* curve slopes upward, as in Figure 9-14B.

How Monetary Policy Shifts the *LM* Curve

The *LM* curve tells us the interest rate that equilibrates the money market for any given level of income. The theory of liquidity preference shows that the equilibrium interest rate depends also on the supply of real balances. The *LM* curve is drawn for a given supply of real money balances. If real balances change—for example, if the Fed changes the money supply—the *LM* curve shifts.

We can use the theory of liquidity preference to understand how monetary policy shifts the *LM* curve. Suppose that the Fed decreases the money supply from M_1 to M_2, which causes the supply of real balances to fall from M_1/P to M_2/P. Figure 9-15 shows what happens. Holding constant the amount of income and thus the demand curve for real balances, a reduction in the supply of real balances raises the interest rate that equilibrates the money market. Hence, a decrease in real balances shifts the *LM* curve upward.

A. The Market for Real Money Balances

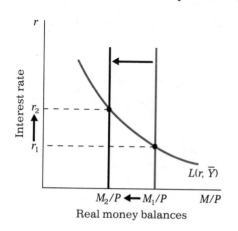

Figure 9-15   **A Reduction in the Money Supply Shifts the *LM* Curve Upward.**   Panel A shows that for any given level of income ($\overline{Y}$), a reduction in the money supply raises the interest rate that equilibrates the money market. Therefore, the *LM* curve in panel B shifts upward.

B. The *LM* Curve

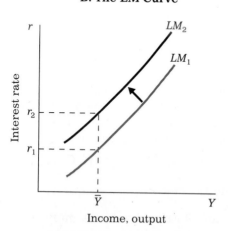

In summary, the LM *curve shows the relationship between the interest rate and the level of income that arises in the market for real money balances. The* LM *curve is drawn for a given supply of real money*

balances. Decreases in the supply of real money balances shift the LM *curve upward. Increases in the supply of real money balances shift the* LM *curve downward.*

A Quantity-Equation Interpretation of the *LM* Curve

When we first discussed aggregate demand and the short-run determination of income in Chapter 8, we derived the aggregate demand curve from the quantity theory of money. We wrote the quantity equation,

$$MV = PY,$$

and assumed that velocity V is constant. This assumption implies that, for any given price level, the supply of money alone determines the level of income. Because this level of income does not depend on the interest rate, the quantity theory is equivalent to a vertical *LM* curve.

We can derive the more realistic upward-sloping *LM* curve from the quantity equation by relaxing the assumption that velocity is constant. The assumption of constant velocity is equivalent to the assumption that the demand for real money balances depends only on the level of income. In reality, the demand for real money balances also depends on the interest rate: a higher interest rate raises the cost of holding money and reduces money demand. As people respond to a higher interest rate by reducing the amount of money they hold, each dollar in the economy circulates from person to person more quickly—that is, the velocity of money increases. We can write this as

$$MV(r) = PY.$$

The velocity function $V(r)$ indicates that velocity is positively related to the interest rate.

This form of the quantity equation yields an *LM* curve that slopes upward. Because an increase in the interest rate raises the velocity of money, it raises the level of income for any given money supply and price level. The *LM* curve expresses this positive relationship between the interest rate and income.

This equation also shows why changes in the money supply shift the *LM* curve. For any given interest rate and price level, an increase in the money supply raises the level of income. Thus, increases in the money supply shift the *LM* curve to the right, and decreases in the money supply shift the *LM* curve to the left.

Finally, keep in mind that the quantity equation merely provides another way to express the theory behind the *LM* curve. This interpretation of the *LM* curve is substantively the same as that provided by the theory of liquidity preference. In both cases, the *LM* curve represents a positive relationship between income and the interest rate that arises from the money market.

The Simple Algebra of the *LM* Curve

One way to think about the *LM* curve is that it describes the combinations of income *Y* and the interest rate *r* that satisfy the money-market equilibrium condition

$$M/P = L(r, Y).$$

This equation simply equates money supply and money demand.

We can learn more about the *LM* curve by considering the case in which the money demand function is linear—that is,

$$L(r, Y) = eY - fr,$$

where *e* and *f* are numbers greater than zero. The value of *e* determines how much the demand for money rises when income rises. The value of *f* determines how much the demand for money falls when the interest rate rises. There is a minus sign in front of the interest rate term because money demand is inversely related to the interest rate.

The equilibrium in the money market is now described by

$$M/P = eY - fr.$$

To see what this equation implies, rearrange the terms so that *r* is on the left-hand side. We obtain

$$r = (e/f)Y - (1/f)M/P.$$

This equation gives us the interest rate that equilibrates the money market for any values of income and real money balances. The *LM* curve graphs this equation for different values of *Y* and *r* and for a fixed value of *M/P*.

From this last equation, we can verify some of our conclusions about the *LM* curve. First, because the coefficient of income is positive, the *LM* curve slopes upward: higher income requires a higher interest rate to equilibrate the money market. Second, because the coefficient of real money balances is negative, decreases in real balances shift the *LM* curve upward, and increases in real balances shift the *LM* curve downward.

From the coefficient of income, *e/f*, we can see what determines whether the *LM* curve is steep or flat. If money demand is not very sensitive to the level of income, then *e* is small. In this case, only a small change in the interest rate is necessary to offset the small increase in money demand caused by a change in income: the *LM* curve is relatively flat. Similarly, if the quantity of money demanded is not very sensitive to the interest rate, then *f* is small. In this case, a shift in money demand due to a change in income leads to a large change in the equilibrium interest rate: the *LM* curve is relatively steep.

Finally, note that the *LM* curve by itself does not determine either income *Y* or the interest rate *r*. Like the *IS* curve, it is only a relationship between these two endogenous variables. The equilibrium in the economy is determined by the *IS* and *LM* curves together.

9-3 Conclusion: The Short-Run Equilibrium

We now have all the components of the *IS-LM* model. The two equations of this model are

$$Y = C(Y - T) + I(r) + G \qquad IS$$
$$M/P = L(r, Y). \qquad LM$$

The model takes fiscal policy, *G* and *T*, monetary policy *M*, and the price level *P* as exogenous. Given these exogenous variables, the *IS* curve provides the combinations of *r* and *Y* that satisfy the equation representing the goods market, and the *LM* curve provides the combinations of *r* and *Y* that satisfy the equation representing the money market. These two curves are shown together in Figure 9-16.

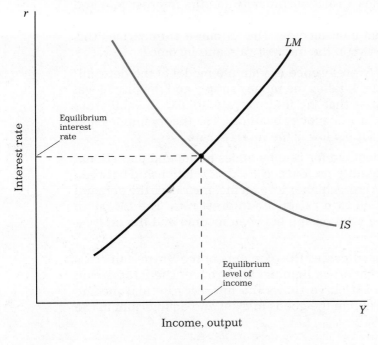

Figure 9-16 **Equilibrium in the *IS-LM* Model.** The intersection of *IS* and *LM* represents simultaneous equilibrium in the market for goods and services and in the market for real money balances.

The equilibrium of the economy is the point at which the *IS* curve and the *LM* curve cross. This point gives the interest rate r and the level of income Y that satisfy both the goods-market equilibrium condition and the money-market equilibrium condition. In other words, at this intersection, actual expenditure equals planned expenditure, and the demand for real money balances equals the supply.

Economists use the *IS-LM* model to analyze the short-run effects of policy changes and other events on national income. We apply it to that purpose in the next chapter, where we also examine how the *IS-LM* model explains the position and slope of the aggregate demand curve.

Summary

1. The Keynesian cross is a simple model of income determination. It takes fiscal policy and planned investment as exogenous and then shows that there is one level of national income at which actual expenditure equals planned expenditure. It shows that changes in fiscal policy have a multiplied impact on income.

2. Once we allow planned investment to depend on the interest rate, the Keynesian cross yields a relationship between the interest rate and national income. A higher interest rate lowers planned investment, which in turn lowers national income. The *IS* curve summarizes this negative relationship between the interest rate and income.

3. The theory of liquidity preference is a simple model of the determination of the interest rate. It takes the money supply and the price level as exogenous and assumes that the interest rate adjusts to equilibrate the supply and demand for real money balances. The theory implies that increases in the money supply lower the interest rate.

4. Once we allow the demand for real balances to depend on national income, the theory of liquidity preference yields a relationship between income and the interest rate. A higher level of income raises the demand for real balances, which in turn raises the interest rate. The *LM* curve summarizes this positive relationship between income and the interest rate.

5. The *IS-LM* model encompasses the elements of the Keynesian cross and the elements of the theory of liquidity preference. The intersection of the *IS* curve and the *LM* curve shows the interest rate and income that satisfy both equilibrium in the goods market and equilibrium in the money market.

KEY CONCEPTS

IS-LM model

IS curve

LM curve

Keynesian cross

Government-purchases multiplier

Tax multiplier

Theory of liquidity preference

QUESTIONS FOR REVIEW

1. Use the Keynesian cross to explain why fiscal policy has a multiplied effect on national income.

2. Use the theory of liquidity preference to explain why an increase in the money supply lowers the interest rate. What does this explanation assume about the price level?

3. Why does the *IS* curve slope downward?

4. Why does the *LM* curve slope upward?

PROBLEMS AND APPLICATIONS

1. Use the Keynesian cross to examine the impact of:

   a. an increase in government purchases.

   b. an increase in taxes.

   c. an equal increase in government purchases and taxes.

2. In the Keynesian cross, assume that the consumption function is given by

$$C = 200 + 0.75 \ (Y - T).$$

Planned investment is 100; government purchases and taxes are both 100.

   a. Graph planned expenditure as a function of income.

   b. What is the equilibrium level of income?

   c. If government purchases increase to 125, what is the new equilibrium income?

   d. What level of government purchases is needed to achieve an income of 1,600?

3. Although our development of the Keynesian cross in this chapter assumes that taxes are a fixed amount, in many countries taxes depend on income. Let's represent the tax system by writing tax revenue as

$$T = \overline{T} + tY,$$

where $\overline{T}$ and t are parameters of the tax code. The parameter t is the marginal tax rate: if income rises by \$1.00, taxes rise by $t \times \$1.00$.

   a. How does this tax system change the way consumption responds to changes in GNP?

b. How does this tax system alter the response of the economy to a change in government purchases?

c. In the *IS-LM* model, how does this tax system alter the slope of the *IS* curve?

4. Consider the impact of an increase in thriftiness in the Keynesian cross. Suppose the consumption function is

$$C = \overline{C} + c(Y - T),$$

where $\overline{C}$ is a parameter called *autonomous consumption* and c is the marginal propensity to consume.

a. What happens to equilibrium income when the society becomes more thrifty, as represented by a decline in $\overline{C}$?

b. What happens to equilibrium saving?

c. Why do you suppose this result is called the *paradox of thrift*?

d. Does this paradox arise in the classical model of Chapter 3? Why or why not?

5. Suppose that the money demand function is

$$(M/P)^d = 1000 - 100r,$$

where r is the interest rate in percent. The money supply M is 1,000 and the price level P is 2.

a. Graph the supply and demand for real money balances.

b. What is the equilibrium interest rate?

c. Assuming the price level is fixed, what happens to the equilibrium interest rate if the supply of money is raised from 1,000 to 1,200?

d. If the Fed wishes to raise the interest rate to 7 percent, what money supply should it set?

Chapter 10

Aggregate Demand II

Science is a parasite: the greater the patient population the better the advance in physiology and pathology; and out of pathology arises therapy. The year 1932 was the trough of the great depression, and from its rotten soil was belatedly begot a new subject that today we call macroeconomics.

Paul Samuelson

In Chapter 9 we assembled the pieces of the *IS-LM* model. We saw that the *IS* curve represents the equilibrium in the market for goods and services, that the *LM* curve represents the equilibrium in the market for real money balances, and that the *IS* and *LM* curves together determine national income in the short run when the price level is fixed. Now we turn our attention to applying the model. This chapter uses the *IS-LM* model to analyze three issues.

First, we examine the potential causes of fluctuations in national income. To be more precise, we use the *IS-LM* model to see how changes in the exogenous variables influence the endogenous variables. Because monetary and fiscal policy are among the exogenous variables, the *IS-LM* model shows how these policies influence the economy in the short run. The model also shows how various shocks to the money and goods markets influence the economy.

Second, we discuss how the *IS-LM* model fits into the model of aggregate supply and aggregate demand we developed in Chapter 8. In particular, we examine how the *IS-LM* model provides a theory of the aggregate demand curve. Here we relax the assumption that the price level is fixed, and we show that the *IS-LM* model implies a negative relationship between the price level and national income.

Third, we study the Great Depression, the episode that motivated Keynes to emphasize aggregate demand as a key determinant of national income. As the quotation at the beginning of this chapter indicates, the Great Depression is the event that gave birth to short-run macroeconomic theory. We can use the *IS-LM* model to discuss the various explanations of this traumatic economic downturn.

10-1 Explaining Fluctuations With the *IS-LM* Model

The intersection of the *IS* curve and the *LM* curve determines the level of national income. National income fluctuates when one of these curves shifts, changing the short-run equilibrium of the economy. In this section we examine how changes in policy and exogenous shocks to the economy can cause these curves to shift.

Changes in Fiscal Policy

We first examine the impact of changes in fiscal policy on the economy. Recall that changes in fiscal policy shift the *IS* curve. The *IS-LM* model shows how these shifts in the *IS* curve affect income and the interest rate.

Consider the effect of an increase in government purchases of ΔG. The government-purchases multiplier in the Keynesian cross tells us that, at any given interest rate, this change in fiscal policy raises the level of income by $\Delta G/(1 - MPC)$. Therefore, as Figure 10-1 illustrates, the *IS* curve shifts outward by this amount. The equilibrium of the economy moves from point A to point B. The increase in government purchases raises both income and the interest rate.

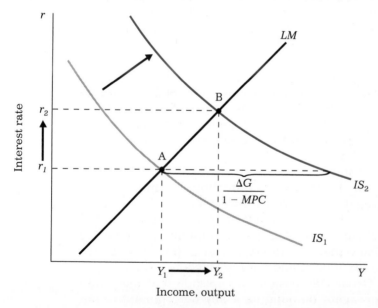

Figure 10-1 **An Increase in Government Purchases in the *IS-LM* Model.** An increase in government purchases shifts the *IS* curve to the right. The equilibrium moves from point A to point B. Income rises from Y_1 to Y_2, and the interest rate rises from r_1 to r_2.

Similarly, consider the effect of a decrease in taxes of ΔT. The tax multiplier in the Keynesian cross tells us that, at any given interest rate, this change in policy raises the level of income by $\Delta T \times MPC/(1 - MPC)$.

Therefore, as Figure 10-2 illustrates, the *IS* curve shifts outward by this amount. The equilibrium of the economy moves from point A to point B. The tax cut raises both income and the interest rate.

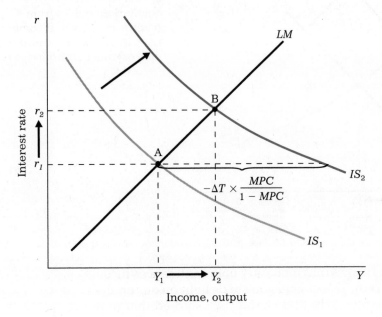

Figure 10-2 **A Decrease in Taxes in the *IS-LM* Model.** A decrease in taxes shifts the *IS* curve to the right. The equilibrium moves from point A to point B. Income rises from Y_1 to Y_2, and the interest rate rises from r_1 to r_2.

Note that the increase in income in response to a fiscal expansion is smaller in the *IS-LM* model than in the Keynesian cross. You can see this in Figures 10-1 and 10-2: the increase in equilibrium income is smaller than the horizontal shift in the *IS* curve. The difference arises because the Keynesian cross assumes that investment is fixed, whereas the *IS-LM* model takes into account that investment falls when the interest rate rises. In the *IS-LM* model, a fiscal expansion raises the interest rate and crowds out investment.

Changes in Monetary Policy

We now examine the impact of a change in monetary policy. Recall that a change in monetary policy shifts the *LM* curve. The *IS-LM* model shows how a shift in the *LM* curve affects income and the interest rate.

Consider the impact of an increase in the money supply. An increase in *M* leads to an increase in *M/P*, since *P* is fixed. The theory of liquidity preference shows that, for any given level of income, an increase in real money balances leads to a lower interest rate. Therefore, the *LM* curve shifts downward, as in Figure 10-3. The equilibrium moves from point A to point B. The increase in the money supply lowers the interest rate and raises the level of income.

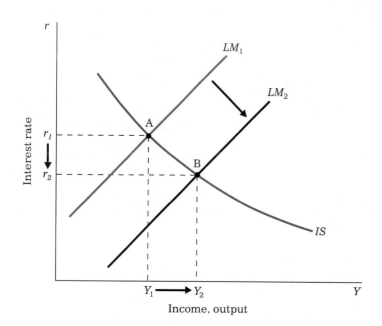

Figure 10-3   **An Increase in the Money Supply in the *IS-LM* Model.**   An increase in the money supply shifts the *LM* curve downward. The equilibrium moves from point A to point B. Income rises from Y_1 to Y_2, and the interest rate falls from r_1 to r_2.

Thus, the *IS-LM* model shows that monetary policy influences income by changing the interest rate. This conclusion sheds light on our analysis of monetary policy in Chapter 8. In that chapter we showed that in the short run, when prices are sticky, an expansion in the money supply raises income. But we did not discuss how an increase in the money supply induces greater spending on goods and services—a process that is called the **monetary transmission mechanism**. The *IS-LM* model shows that an increase in the money supply lowers the interest rate, which stimulates investment and thereby expands the demand for goods and services.

The Interaction Between Monetary and Fiscal Policy

When analyzing any change in monetary or fiscal policy, it is important to keep in mind that these policies may not be independent of each other. A change in one may influence the other. This interdependence may alter the impact of a policy change.

For example, suppose that Congress, concerned about a budget deficit, raises taxes to balance the budget. What effect would that policy change have on the economy? The answer depends on how the Federal Reserve responds to the tax increase.

Figure 10-4 shows three of the many possible outcomes. In Figure 10-4A, the Fed holds the money supply constant. The tax increase shifts the *IS* curve inward, which reduces income and the interest rate. In Figure 10-4B, the Fed wants to hold the interest rate constant. In this case, when the tax increase shifts the *IS* curve inward, the Fed must decrease the money supply to keep the interest rate at its original level. This shifts the *LM* curve upward. The interest rate does not fall, but income falls by a larger amount than if the Fed had held the money supply constant. In Figure 10-4C, the Fed wants to prevent the tax increase from lowering income; therefore, it must increase the money supply. In this case, the tax increase does not cause a recession, but it does cause a large fall in the interest rate.

A. Fed Holds Money Supply Constant

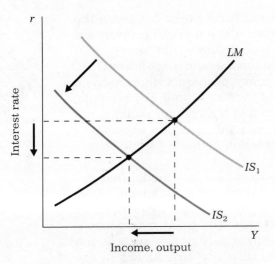

B. Fed Holds Interest Rate Constant

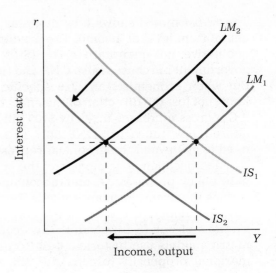

Figure 10-4 **The Response of the Economy to a Tax Increase.** How the economy responds to a tax increase depends on how monetary policy responds. In panel A the Fed holds the money supply constant. In panel B the Fed holds the interest rate constant by reducing the money supply. In panel C the Fed holds the level of income constant by raising the money supply.

C. Fed Holds Income Constant

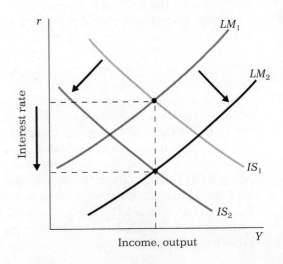

From this example we can see that the impact of the change in fiscal policy depends on the policy the Fed pursues—that is, on whether it holds the money supply, the interest rate, or the level of income constant. More generally, whenever analyzing a change in one policy, one must make an assumption about its effects on the other policy. What assumption is most appropriate depends on the case at hand and the many political considerations that lie behind economic policymaking.

CASE STUDY 10-1
_____

Policy Analysis With Macroeconometric Models

The *IS-LM* model shows how monetary and fiscal policy influence the equilibrium level of income. The predictions of the model, however, are qualitative, not quantitative. The *IS-LM* model shows that increases in government purchases raise GNP and that increases in taxes lower GNP. But when economists analyze specific policy proposals, they need to know not just the direction of the effect but the size as well. For example, if Congress increases taxes by $100 billion and if monetary policy is not altered, how much will GNP fall? To answer this question economists need to go beyond the graphical representation of the *IS-LM* model.

Macroeconometric models of the economy provide one way to evaluate policy proposals. A **macroeconometric model** is a model that describes the economy quantitatively, rather than just qualitatively. Many of these models are essentially more complicated and more realistic versions of our *IS-LM* model. The economists who build macroeconometric models use historical data to estimate parameters such as the marginal propensity to consume, the sensitivity of investment to the interest rate, and the sensitivity of money demand to the interest rate. Once a model is built, economists can simulate the effects of alternative policies with the help of a computer.

Table 10-1 shows the fiscal-policy multipliers implied by one widely used macroeconometric model, the Data Resources Incorporated (DRI) model, named for the economic forecasting firm that developed it. The multipliers are given for two assumptions about how the Fed might respond to the change in fiscal policy.

One assumption about monetary policy is that the Fed keeps the nominal interest rate constant. That is, when fiscal policy shifts the *IS* curve to the right or to the left, the Fed adjusts the money supply to shift the *LM* curve in the same direction. Because there is no crowding out of investment due to a changing interest rate, the fiscal-policy multipliers are similar to those from the Keynesian cross. The DRI model indicates that, in this case, the government-purchases multiplier is 1.93, and the tax multiplier is −1.19. That is, a $100 billion increase in government purchases raises GNP by $193 billion, and a $100 increase in taxes lowers GNP by $119 billion.

The second assumption about monetary policy is that the Fed keeps the money supply constant so that the *LM* curve does not shift. In this case, there is substantial crowding out. The government-purchases multiplier is 0.60, and the tax multiplier is −0.26. That is, a $100 increase in government purchases raises GNP by $60 billion, and a $100 increase in taxes lowers GNP by $26 billion.

Table 10-1 shows that the fiscal-policy multipliers are very different under the two assumptions about monetary policy. The impact of any change in fiscal policy depends crucially on how the Fed responds to that change.

Table 10-1	The Fiscal-Policy Multipliers in the DRI Model		
Assumption About Monetary Policy		$\Delta Y/\Delta G$	$\Delta Y/\Delta T$
Nominal Interest Rate Held Constant		1.93	−1.19
Money Supply Held Constant		0.60	−0.26

NOTE: This table gives the fiscal-policy multipliers for a sustained change in government purchases or in personal income taxes. These multipliers are for the fourth quarter after the policy change is made.
Source: Otto Eckstein, *The DRI Model of the U.S. Economy* (New York: McGraw-Hill, 1983), 169.

Shocks in the *IS-LM* Model

Because the *IS-LM* model shows how national income is determined in the short run, we can use the model to examine how various economic disturbances affect income. So far we have seen how changes in fiscal policy shift the *IS* curve and how changes in monetary policy shift the *LM* curve. Similarly, we can group other disturbances into two categories: shocks to the *IS* curve and shocks to the *LM* curve.

Shocks to the *IS* curve are exogenous changes in the demand for goods and services. Some economists, including Keynes, have emphasized that changes in demand can arise from investors' *animal spirits*— exogenous and perhaps self-fulfilling waves of optimism and pessimism. For example, suppose that firms become pessimistic about the future of the economy and that this pessimism causes them to build fewer new factories. This reduction in the demand for investment goods causes a contractionary shift in the investment function: at every interest rate, firms want to invest less. The fall in investment shifts the *IS* curve inward, which reduces income and employment. This fall in equilibrium income in part validates the firms' initial pessimism.

Shocks to the *IS* curve may also arise from changes in the demand for consumer goods. Suppose that a reduction in consumer confidence in the economy induces consumers to save more for the future and consume less today. We can interpret this change as a downward shift in the consumption function. This shift in the consumption function causes the *IS* curve to shift inward, lowering income.

Shocks to the *LM* curve arise from exogenous changes in the demand for money. Suppose that the demand for money increases substantially, as it did in the early 1980s. An increase in money demand implies that, for any given level of income, the interest rate necessary to equilibrate the money market is higher. Hence, an increase in money demand shifts the *LM* curve upward, which tends to raise the interest rate and depress income.

In summary, several kinds of events can cause economic fluctuations by shifting the *IS* curve or the *LM* curve. Remember, however, that such fluctuations are not inevitable. Monetary and fiscal policy can respond to exogenous shocks. If changes in policy are well timed, shocks to the *IS* or *LM* curves will not lead to fluctuations in income or employment.

10-2 *IS-LM* as a Theory of Aggregate Demand

We have been using the *IS-LM* model to explain national income in the short run when the price level is fixed. To see how the *IS-LM* model fits into the model of aggregate supply and aggregate demand developed in Chapter 8, we now examine what happens in the *IS-LM* model as the price level changes. As was promised when we began our study of this model, the *IS-LM* model provides a theory of the aggregate demand curve.

From the *IS-LM* Model to the Aggregate Demand Curve

Recall from Chapter 8 that the aggregate demand curve is a relationship between the price level and the level of national income. In Chapter 8 this relationship was derived from the quantity theory of money. For a given money supply, a higher price level implies a lower level of income. Increases in the money supply shift the aggregate demand curve outward, and decreases in the money supply shift the aggregate demand curve inward.

We now use the *IS-LM* model, rather than the quantity theory, to derive the aggregate demand curve. First, we use the *IS-LM* model to show that national income falls as the price level rises; the downward-sloping aggregate demand curve expresses this relationship. Second, we examine what causes the aggregate demand curve to shift.

Why does the aggregate demand curve slope downward? To answer this question, we examine what happens in the *IS-LM* model when the price level changes. Figure 10-5 illustrates the impact of a changing price level. For any given money supply M, a higher price level P causes a lower supply of real money balances M/P. A lower supply of real money balances shifts the LM curve upward and lowers the equilibrium level of income, as in Figure 10-5A. Here we see that when the price level increases from P_1 to P_2, national income falls from Y_1 to Y_2. By shifting the LM curve, changes in the price level lead to different levels of income. The aggregate demand curve in Figure 10-5B plots the negative relationship between national income and the price level that arises from the IS-LM model.

A. The *IS-LM* Model

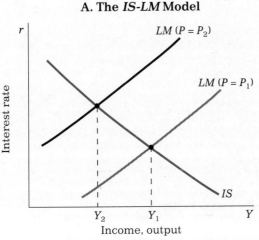

Income, output

Figure 10-5 **Deriving the Aggregate Demand Curve With the *IS-LM* Model.** Panel A shows the *IS-LM* model: an increase in the price level from P_1 to P_2 lowers real money balances and thus shifts the LM curve upward. The shift in the LM curve lowers income from Y_1 to Y_2. Panel B shows the aggregate demand curve summarizing this relationship between the price level and income: the higher the price level, the lower the level of income.

B. The Aggregate Demand Curve

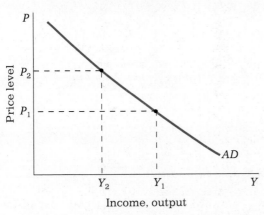

Income, output

What causes the aggregate demand curve to shift? Because the aggregate demand curve summarizes the results of the IS-LM model, shocks that shift the IS curve or the LM curve cause the aggregate demand curve to shift. Expansionary monetary or fiscal policy raises income in the *IS-LM* model and thus shifts the aggregate demand curve outward, as in Figure 10-6. Similarly, contractionary monetary or fiscal policy lowers income in the *IS-LM* model and thus shifts the aggregate demand curve inward.

A. Expansionary Monetary Policy

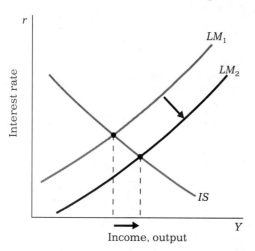
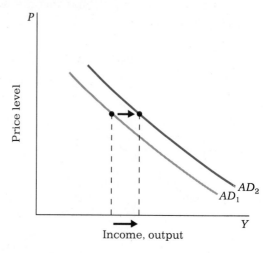

B. Expansionary Fiscal Policy

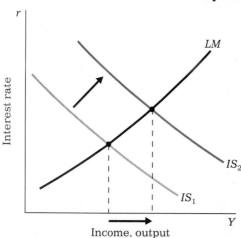
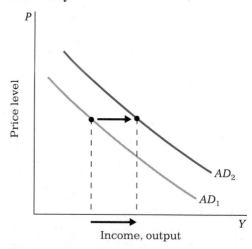

Figure 10-6   **How Monetary and Fiscal Policy Shift the Aggregate Demand Curve.**
Panel A shows a monetary expansion. For any given price level, an increase in the money supply raises real money balances, shifts the *LM* curve downward, and raises income. Hence, an increase in the money supply shifts the aggregate demand curve outward. Panel B shows a fiscal expansion, such as an increase in government purchases or a decrease in taxes. The fiscal expansion shifts the *IS* curve outward and, for any given price level, raises income. Hence, a fiscal expansion shifts the aggregate demand curve outward.

We can summarize these results as follows. A change in income in the IS-LM *model resulting from a change in the price level represents a movement along the aggregate demand curve. A change in income in the* IS-LM *model for a fixed price level represents a shift in the aggregate demand curve.*

The Simple Algebra of the Aggregate Demand Curve

We can learn more about the aggregate demand curve by deriving the curve algebraically. In Chapter 9 we examined the *IS* and *LM* curves for the case in which the consumption function, the investment function, and the money demand function are linear. That is,

$$C = a + b(Y - T).$$
$$I = c - dr.$$
$$L(r, Y) = eY - fr.$$

We concluded that the *IS* curve is

$$Y = \frac{a + c}{1 - b} + \frac{1}{1 - b}G + \frac{-b}{1 - b}T + \frac{-d}{1 - b}r,$$

and that the *LM* curve is

$$r = (e/f)Y - (1/f)M/P,$$

where *a*, *b*, *c*, *d*, *e*, and *f* are parameters greater than zero. From these two equations, we can solve for the equation of the aggregate demand curve.

To find the aggregate demand equation, we must find the level of income that satisfies both the *IS* equation and the *LM* equation. To do this, substitute the *LM* equation for the interest rate *r* into the *IS* equation to obtain

$$Y = \frac{a + c}{1 - b} + \frac{1}{1 - b}G + \frac{-b}{1 - b}T + \frac{-d}{1 - b}[(e/f)Y - (1/f)M/P].$$

With some algebraic manipulation, we can solve for *Y*. The final equation for *Y* is

$$Y = \frac{z(a + c)}{1 - b} + \frac{z}{1 - b}G + \frac{-zb}{1 - b}T + \frac{d}{(1 - b)[f + de/(1 - b)]}M/P,$$

where $z = f/[f + de/(1 - b)]$ is a composite of some of the parameters and is between zero and one.

This last equation expresses the aggregate demand curve algebraically. It says that income depends on fiscal policy, *G* and *T*, monetary policy *M*, and the price level *P*. The aggregate demand curve graphs this equation for different values of *Y* and *P* and for fixed values of *G*, *T*, and *M*.

The Effectiveness of Monetary and Fiscal Policy

Economists have long debated whether monetary or fiscal policy exerts a more powerful influence on aggregate demand. According to the *IS-LM* model, the answer to this question depends on the parameters of the *IS* and *LM* curves. Therefore, economists have spent much energy arguing about the size of these parameters. The most hotly contested parameters are those that describe the influence of the interest rate on economic decisions.

Those economists who believe that fiscal policy is more potent than monetary policy argue that the responsiveness of investment to the interest rate—measured by the parameter *d*—is small. If you look at the algebraic equation for aggregate demand, you will see that a small value of *d* implies a small effect of the money supply on income. The reason is that when *d* is small, the *IS* curve is nearly vertical, so that shifts in the *LM* curve do not cause much of a change in income. In addition, a small

We can verify several features of the aggregate demand curve from this equation. First, the aggregate demand curve slopes downward, since an increase in *P* lowers *M/P* and therefore lowers *Y*. Second, increases in the money supply raise income and therefore shift the aggregate demand curve outward. Third, increases in government purchases or decreases in taxes also raise income and thus shift the aggregate demand curve outward. Note that, because *z* is less than one, the multipliers for fiscal policy are smaller in the *IS-LM* model than in the Keynesian cross. Hence, the parameter *z* reflects the crowding out of investment discussed earlier.

Finally, this equation shows the relationship between the aggregate demand curve derived in this chapter from the *IS-LM* model and the aggregate demand curve derived in Chapter 8 from the quantity theory of money. The quantity theory assumes that the interest rate does not influence the quantity of real money balances demanded. Put differently, the quantity theory assumes that the parameter *f* equals zero. If *f* equals zero, then the composite parameter *z* also equals zero, so that fiscal policy does not influence aggregate demand. Thus, the aggregate demand curve derived in Chapter 8 is a special case of the aggregate demand curve derived here.

value of d implies a large value of z, which in turn implies that fiscal policy has a large effect on income. The reason for this large effect is that when investment is not very responsive to the interest rate, there is little crowding out.

Those economists who believe that monetary policy is more potent than fiscal policy argue that the responsiveness of money demand to the interest rate—measured by the parameter f—is small. When f is small, z is small, so that fiscal policy has a small effect on income; in this case, the *LM* curve is nearly vertical. In addition, when f is small, changes in the money supply have a large effect on income.

Most economists today do not endorse either of these extreme views. The evidence indicates that the interest rate affects both investment and money demand. This finding implies that both monetary and fiscal policy are important determinants of aggregate demand.

The *IS-LM* Model in the Short Run and Long Run

The *IS-LM* model is designed to explain the economy in the short run when the price level is fixed. Yet, now that we have seen how a change in the price level influences the equilibrium, we can use the *IS-LM* model also to describe the economy in the long run when the price level adjusts to ensure that the economy produces at its natural rate. By using the *IS-LM* model to describe the long run, we can show clearly how the Keynesian model of national income differs from the classical model of Chapter 3.

Figure 10-7A shows the three curves that are necessary for understanding the short-run and long-run equilibria: the *IS* curve, the *LM* curve, and the vertical line representing the natural rate of output $\bar{Y}$. The *LM* curve is, as always, drawn for a fixed price level, P_1. The short-run equilibrium of the economy is point K, where the *IS* curve crosses the *LM* curve.

Figure 10-7B shows the same situation in the diagram of aggregate supply and aggregate demand. At the price level P_1, the quantity of output demanded is below the natural rate. In other words, at the existing price level, there is insufficient demand for goods and services to keep the economy at its natural rate.

A. The *IS-LM* Model

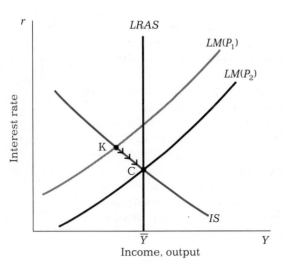

B. The Model of Aggregate Supply and Aggregate Demand

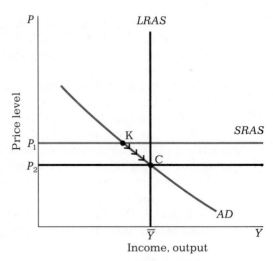

Figure 10-7 **The Short-Run and Long-Run Equilibria.** We can compare the short-run and long-run equilibria using either the *IS-LM* diagram in panel A or the aggregate supply-aggregate demand diagram in panel B. In the short run, the price level is stuck at P_1. The short-run equilibrium of the economy is therefore point K. In the long run, the price level adjusts so that the economy is at the natural rate. The long-run equilibrium is therefore point C.

In these two diagrams we can examine the short-run equilibrium at which the economy finds itself and the long-run equilibrium to which the economy evolves. Point K describes the short-run equilibrium, because it assumes that the price level is stuck at P_1. Eventually, the low demand for goods and services causes prices to fall, which helps restore the economy to its natural rate. When the price level reaches P_2, the economy is at point C, which is the long-run equilibrium. The diagram of aggregate supply and aggregate demand shows that, at point C, the quantity of goods and services demanded equals the natural rate of output. This long-run equilibrium is achieved in the *IS-LM* diagram by a shift in the *LM* curve: the fall in the price level raises real money balances and therefore shifts the *LM* curve to the right.

In these diagrams we can see the key difference between Keynesian and classical approaches to the determination of national income. The Keynesian assumption (represented by point K) is that the price level is stuck. Depending on monetary policy, fiscal policy, and the other determinants of aggregate demand, output may deviate from the natural rate. The classical assumption (represented by point C) is that the price level is flexible. The price level adjusts to ensure that national income is always at the natural rate.

To make the same point somewhat differently, we can think of the economy as being described by three equations. The first two are the *IS* and *LM* equations:

$$Y = C(Y - T) + I(r) + G \qquad\qquad IS$$
$$M/P = L(r, Y). \qquad\qquad\qquad LM$$

These two equations contain three variables of interest: Y, P, and r. The Keynesian approach is to complete the model with the assumption of fixed prices, so the third equation is

$$P = P_1.$$

This assumption implies that r and Y must adjust to satisfy the *IS* and *LM* equations. The classical approach is to complete the model with the assumption that output reaches the natural rate, so the third equation is

$$Y = \overline{Y}.$$

This assumption implies that r and P must adjust to satisfy the *IS* and *LM* equations.

Which assumption is most appropriate? The answer depends on the time horizon. The classical assumption best describes the long run. Hence, our long-run analysis of national income in Chapter 3 and prices in Chapter 6 assumes that output equals the natural rate. The Keynesian assumption best describes the short run. Therefore, our analysis of economic fluctuations relies on the assumption of a fixed price level.

10-3 The Great Depression

Now that we have developed the model of aggregate demand, let's use it to address the question that originally motivated Keynes: what caused the Great Depression? Even today, more than half a century after the event, economists continue to debate the cause of this major economic downturn. The Great Depression provides an extended case study to show how economists use the *IS-LM* model to analyze economic fluctuations.[1]

Before turning to the explanations economists have proposed, look at Table 10-2, which presents some statistics regarding the Depression. These statistics are the battlefield on which debate about the Depression takes place. What do you think happened? An *IS* shift? An *LM* shift? Or something else?

---

[1] For a flavor of the debate, see Milton Friedman and Anna J. Schwartz, *A Monetary History of the United States, 1867–1960* (Princeton, N.J.: Princeton University Press, 1963); Peter Temin, *Did Monetary Forces Cause the Great Depression?* (New York: W. W. Norton, 1976); and the essays in Karl Brunner, ed., *The Great Depression Revisited* (Boston: Martinus Nijhoff Publishing, 1981).

Table 10-2   What Happened During the Great Depression?

Year	Unemployment Rate	Real GNP	Consumption	Investment	Government Purchases
1929	3.2	203.6	139.6	40.4	22.0
1930	8.9	183.5	130.4	27.4	24.3
1931	16.3	169.5	126.1	16.8	25.4
1932	24.1	144.2	114.8	4.7	24.2
1933	25.2	141.5	112.8	5.3	23.3
1934	22.0	154.3	118.1	9.4	26.6
1935	20.3	169.5	125.5	18.0	27.0
1936	17.0	193.2	138.4	24.0	31.8
1937	14.3	203.2	143.1	29.9	30.8
1938	19.1	192.9	140.2	17.0	33.9
1939	17.2	209.4	148.2	24.7	35.2
1940	14.6	227.2	155.7	33.0	36.4

Source: Historical Statistics of the United States, Colonial Times to 1970, Parts I and II, U.S. Department of Commerce, Bureau of Census, 1975, Washington, D.C. The unemployment rate is series D9. Real GNP, consumption, investment, and government purchases are series: F3, F48, F52, and F66, and are measured in billions of 1958 dollars. The interest rate is the prime Com-

The Spending Hypothesis: Shocks to the *IS* Curve

Since the decline in income in the early 1930s coincided with falling interest rates, some economists have suggested that the cause of the decline was a contractionary shift in the *IS* curve. This view is sometimes called the *spending hypothesis,* because it places primary blame for the Depression on an exogenous fall in spending on goods and services. Economists have attempted to explain this decline in spending in several ways.

Some argue that a downward shift in the consumption function caused the contractionary shift in the *IS* curve. The stock market crash of 1929 may have been partly responsible for this decline in consumption. By reducing wealth and increasing uncertainty, the crash may have induced consumers to save more of their income.

Others explain the decline in spending by pointing to the large drop in investment in housing. Some economists believe that the residential investment boom of the 1920s was excessive, and that once this "over-building" became apparent, the demand for residential investment declined drastically. Another possible explanation for the fall in residential investment is the reduction in immigration in the 1930s: a more slowly growing population leads to a smaller demand for new housing.

Once the Depression began, several events occurred that could have reduced spending further. First, the widespread bank failures may have reduced investment. Banks play the crucial role of getting the funds available for investment to those investors who can best use them. The

Year	Nominal Interest Rate	Money Supply	Price Level	Inflation	Real Money Balances
1929	5.9	26.6	50.6	—	52.6
1930	3.6	25.8	49.3	−2.6	52.3
1931	2.6	24.1	44.8	−10.1	54.5
1932	2.7	21.1	40.2	−9.3	52.5
1933	1.7	19.9	39.3	−2.2	50.7
1934	1.0	21.9	42.2	7.4	51.8
1935	0.8	25.9	42.6	0.9	60.8
1936	0.8	29.6	42.7	0.2	62.9
1937	0.9	30.9	44.5	4.2	69.5
1938	0.8	30.5	43.9	−1.3	69.5
1939	0.6	34.2	43.2	−1.6	79.1
1940	0.6	39.7	43.9	1.6	90.3

mercial Paper rate, 4–6 months, series x445. The money supply is series x414, currency plus demand deposits, measured in billions of dollars. The price level is the GNP deflator (1958 = 100), series E1. The inflation rate is the percent change in the price level series. Real money balances, calculated by dividing the money supply by the price level and multiplying by 100, are in billions of 1958 dollars.

closing of many banks in the early 1930s may have prevented some investors from getting the funds they needed and thus may have led to a further contractionary shift in the investment function.[2]

In addition, the fiscal policy of the 1930s caused a contractionary shift in the *IS* curve. Politicians at that time were more concerned with balancing the budget than with using fiscal policy to stimulate the economy. The Revenue Act of 1932 increased various taxes, especially those falling on lower- and middle-income consumers.[3] The Democratic platform of that year expressed concern about the budget deficit and advocated an "immediate and drastic reduction of governmental expenditures." In the midst of historically high unemployment, policymakers searched for ways to raise taxes and reduce government spending.

There are, therefore, several ways to explain a contractionary shift in the *IS* curve. Keep in mind that these different views are not inconsistent with each other. There may be no single explanation for the decline in spending. It is possible that all of these changes coincided, and together they led to a major reduction in spending.

---

[2] Ben Bernanke, "Non-Monetary Effects of the Financial Crisis in the Propagation of the Great Depression," *American Economic Review* 73 (June 1983): 257–276.

[3] E. Cary Brown, "Fiscal Policy in the 'Thirties: A Reappraisal," *American Economic Review* 46 (December 1956): 857–879.

The Money Hypothesis: A Shock to the *LM* Curve

We can see in Table 10-2 that the money supply fell 25 percent from 1929 to 1933, during which time the unemployment rate rose from 3.2 percent to 25.2 percent. This fact provides the motivation and support for what is called the *money hypothesis*, which places primary blame for the Depression on the Federal Reserve for allowing the money supply to fall by such a large amount.[4] The best known advocates of this interpretation are Milton Friedman and Anna Schwartz, who defend it in their treatise on monetary history. Friedman and Schwartz argue that contractions in the money supply have caused most economic downturns and that the Great Depression is a particularly vivid example.

Using the *IS-LM* model, we might interpret the money hypothesis as explaining the Depression by a contractionary shift in the *LM* curve. Seen in this way, however, the money hypothesis runs into two problems.

The first problem is the behavior of real money balances. Monetary policy leads to a contractionary shift in the *LM* curve only if real money balances fall. Yet from 1929 to 1931 real money balances rose slightly, since the fall in the money supply was accompanied by an even greater fall in the price level. Although the monetary contraction may be responsible for the rise in unemployment from 1931 to 1933, when real money balances did fall, it probably should not be blamed for the initial downturn from 1929 to 1931.

The second problem for the money hypothesis is the behavior of interest rates. If a contractionary shift in the *LM* curve triggered the Depression, we should have observed higher interest rates. Yet interest rates fell continuously from 1929 to 1933.

These two reasons appear sufficient to reject the view that the Depression was instigated by a contractionary shift in the *LM* curve. But was the fall in the money stock irrelevant? Below we turn to another mechanism through which monetary policy might have been responsible for the severity of the Depression—the deflation of the 1930s.

The Money Hypothesis Again: The Effects of Falling Prices

From 1929 to 1933 the price level fell 25 percent. Many economists blame this deflation for the severity of the Great Depression. They argue that the deflation may have turned what in 1931 was a typical economic downturn into an unprecedented period of high unemployment and depressed income. If correct, this argument gives new life to the money hypothesis. Since the falling money supply was, plausibly, responsible

---

[4] We discuss the reason for this large decrease in the money supply in Chapter 18 (Case Study 18-1), where we examine the money supply process in more detail.

for the falling price level, it could be responsible for the severity of the Depression. To evaluate this argument, we must discuss how changes in the price level affect income in the *IS-LM* model.

The Stabilizing Influences of Deflation   In the *IS-LM* model we have developed so far, falling prices increase income. For any given supply of money M, a lower price level implies higher real money balances M/P. An increase in real money balances causes an expansionary shift in the *LM* curve, which leads to higher income.

Another channel through which falling prices expand income is called the **Pigou effect**. Arthur Pigou, a prominent classical economist in the 1930s, pointed out that real money balances are part of households' wealth. As prices fall and real money balances rise, consumers should feel wealthier and therefore spend more. This increase in consumer spending should cause an expansionary shift in the *IS* curve, also leading to higher income.

These two reasons led some economists in the 1930s to believe that falling prices would help the economy restore itself to full employment. Yet other economists were less confident in the economy's ability to correct itself; they pointed to other effects of falling prices, to which we now turn.

The Destabilizing Influences of Deflation   Economists have proposed two theories to explain how falling prices could depress income rather than raise it. The first, called **debt-deflation**, concerns the effects of unexpected falls in the price level. The second concerns the effects of expected deflation.

The debt-deflation theory begins with an observation that should be familiar from Chapter 6: unanticipated changes in the price level redistribute wealth between debtors and creditors. If a debtor owes a creditor $100, then the real amount of this debt is $100/P$, where P is the price level. A fall in the price level raises the real amount of this debt—the amount of purchasing power the debtor owes. Therefore, an unexpected deflation enriches creditors and impoverishes debtors.

The debt-deflation theory then posits that this redistribution of wealth alters spending on goods and services. In response to this redistribution from debtors to creditors, debtors spend less and creditors spend more. If these two groups have equal spending propensities, there is no aggregate impact. But it seems reasonable to assume that debtors have higher propensities to spend than creditors—perhaps that is why the debtors are in debt in the first place. In this case, debtors reduce their spending by more than creditors increase theirs. The net effect is a reduction in spending, a contractionary shift in the *IS* curve, and thus lower national income.

To understand how *expected* changes in prices can affect income, we need to add a new variable to the *IS-LM* model. Our discussion of the model has so far not distinguished between the nominal interest rate and the real interest rate. Yet we know from previous chapters that investment depends on the real interest rate and that money demand depends on the nominal interest rate. If i is the nominal interest rate and π^e is expected inflation, then the *ex ante* real interest rate is $i - \pi^e$. We can therefore write the *IS-LM* model as

$$Y = C(Y - T) + I(i - \pi^e) + G \qquad\qquad IS$$
$$M/P = L(i, Y). \qquad\qquad LM$$

Expected inflation enters as a variable in the *IS* curve. Thus, changes in expected inflation shift the *IS* curve.

Let's use this extended *IS-LM* model to examine how changes in expected inflation influence the level of income. We begin by assuming that everyone expects the price level to remain the same. In this case, there is no expected inflation ($\pi^e = 0$), and these two equations produce the familiar *IS-LM* model. Now suppose that everyone suddenly expects that the price level will fall in the future, so that π^e becomes negative. Figure 10-8 shows what happens. At any given nominal interest rate, the real interest rate is higher, which depresses investment spending. This decrease in planned investment causes a contractionary shift in the *IS* curve. An expected deflation thus leads to a reduction in national income from Y_1 to Y_2. The nominal interest rate falls from i_1 to i_2, while the real interest rate rises from r_1 to r_2.

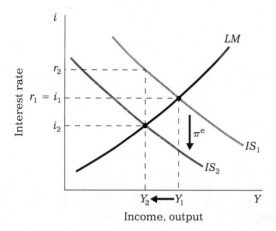

Figure 10-8 **Expected Deflation in the *IS-LM* Model.** An expected deflation raises the real interest rate for any given nominal interest rate, which reduces desired investment. This reduction in investment shifts the *IS* curve downward. The level of income falls from Y_1 to Y_2. The nominal interest rate falls from i_1 to i_2, and the real interest rate rises from r_1 to r_2.

Note that there is a common thread in these two stories of destabilizing deflation. In both, falling prices depress national income by causing a contractionary shift in the *IS* curve. Since a deflation of the size observed from 1929 to 1933 is unlikely except in the presence of a major contraction in the money supply, these two explanations give some of the responsibility for the Depression—especially its severity—to the Fed. In other words, if falling prices are destabilizing, then a contraction in the money supply can lead to a fall in income, even without a decrease in real money balances or a rise in nominal interest rates.

Could the Depression Happen Again?

Economists study the Depression both because of its intrinsic interest as a major economic event and to provide guidance to policymakers so that it will not happen again. To state with confidence whether this event could recur one would need to know why it happened. Since there is not yet agreement on the causes of the Great Depression, it is impossible to rule out with certainty another depression of this magnitude.

Yet most economists believe that the mistakes that led to the Great Depression are unlikely to be repeated. The Fed seems unlikely to allow the money supply to fall by one fourth. Many economists believe that the deflation of the early 1930s was responsible for the depth and length of the Depression. And it seems likely that such a prolonged deflation was possible only in the presence of a falling money supply.

Fiscal policy is another area in which mistakes are unlikely to be repeated. Fiscal policy in the 1930s not only failed to help but actually further depressed aggregate demand. Few economists today would advocate such a rigid adherence to a balanced budget in the face of massive unemployment.

In addition, there are many institutions today that would help to prevent the events of the 1930s from recurring. The system of Federal Deposit Insurance makes widespread bank failures less likely. The income tax causes an automatic reduction in taxes when income falls, which stabilizes the economy. Finally, economists know more about how the economy works today than they did in the 1930s. Our knowledge of how the economy works, limited as it still is, should help policymakers formulate better policies to combat such widespread unemployment.

10-4 Conclusion

The purpose of this chapter and the previous one has been to deepen our understanding of aggregate demand. We now have the tools to analyze monetary and fiscal policy in the long run and in the short run. In the long run, prices are flexible, and we use the classical analysis of Part Two of this book. In the short run, prices are sticky, and we use the *IS-LM* model to examine how changes in policy influence the economy.

Although the model presented in this chapter provides the basic framework for analyzing aggregate demand, it is not the whole story. In later chapters, we examine in more detail the elements of this model and thereby refine our understanding of aggregate demand. In Chapter 15, for example, we study theories of consumption. Since the consumption function is a crucial element of the *IS-LM* model, a change in our analysis of consumption may modify our view of the impact of monetary and fiscal policy on the economy. The simple *IS-LM* model presented in Chapters 9 and 10 provides the benchmark for this further analysis.

Summary

1. The *IS-LM* model provides a general theory of aggregate demand. The exogenous variables in the model are fiscal policy, monetary policy, and the price level. The model explains two endogenous variables: the interest rate and the level of national income.

2. The *IS* curve represents the negative relationship between the interest rate and the level of income that arises from equilibrium in the market for goods and services. The *LM* curve represents a positive relationship between the interest rate and the level of income that arises from equilibrium in the market for real money balances. Equilibrium in the *IS-LM* model—the intersection of the *IS* and *LM* curves—represents simultaneous equilibrium in the market for goods and services and in the market for real money balances.

3. Expansionary fiscal policy—an increase in government purchases or a decrease in taxes—shifts the *IS* curve outward. This shift in the *IS* curve increases the interest rate and income. The increase in income represents an outward shift in the aggregate demand curve. Similarly, contractionary fiscal policy shifts the *IS* curve inward, lowers the interest rate and income, and shifts the aggregate demand curve inward.

4. Expansionary monetary policy shifts the *LM* curve downward. This shift in the *LM* curve lowers the interest rate and raises income. The increase in income represents an outward shift of the aggregate demand curve. Similarly, contractionary monetary policy shifts the *LM* curve upward, raises the interest rate and lowers income, and shifts the aggregate demand curve inward.

KEY CONCEPTS

Monetary transmission mechanism	Pigou effect
Macroeconometric model	Debt-deflation theory

QUESTIONS FOR REVIEW

1. Explain why the aggregate demand curve slopes downward.

2. What is the impact of an increase in taxes on the interest rate, income, consumption, and investment?

3. What is the impact of a decrease in the money supply on the interest rate, income, consumption, and investment?

4. Describe the possible effects of falling prices on equilibrium income.

PROBLEMS AND APPLICATIONS

1. According to the *IS-LM* model, what happens to the interest rate, income, consumption, and investment when

   a. the central bank increases the money supply?

   b. the government increases government purchases?

   c. the government increases taxes?

   d. the government increases government purchases and taxes by equal amounts?

2. Consider the economy of Hicksonia.

   a. The consumption function is given by

   $$C = 200 + 0.75(Y - T).$$

   The investment function is

   $$I = 200 - 25r.$$

   Government purchases and taxes are both 100. For this economy, graph the *IS* curve for *r* ranging from 0 to 8.

   b. The money demand function in Hicksonia is

   $$(M/P)^d = Y - 100r.$$

   The money supply *M* is 1,000 and the price level *P* is 2. For this economy, graph the *LM* curve for *r* ranging from 0 to 8.

   c. Find the equilibrium interest rate *r* and level of income *Y*.

   d. Suppose that government purchases

are raised from 100 to 150. How much does the *IS* curve shift? What is the new equilibrium interest rate and level of income?

   e. Suppose instead that the money supply is raised from 1,000 to 1,200. How much does the *LM* curve shift? What is the new equilibrium interest rate and level of income?

   f. With the initial values for monetary and fiscal policy, suppose that the price level rises from 2 to 4. What happens? What is the new equilibrium interest rate and level of income?

   g. Derive and graph an equation for the aggregate demand curve. What happens to this aggregate demand curve if fiscal or monetary policy changes, as in parts d and e?

3. Explain why each of the following statements is true. Discuss the impact of monetary and fiscal policy in each of these special cases.

   a. If investment does not depend on the interest rate, the *IS* curve is vertical.

   b. If money demand does not depend on the interest rate, the *LM* curve is vertical.

   c. If money demand does not depend on income, the *LM* curve is horizontal.

   d. If money demand is extremely sensitive to the interest rate, the *LM* curve is horizontal.

4. Suppose that the government wants to raise investment but keep output constant. In the *IS-LM* model, what mix of monetary and fiscal policy will achieve this goal? In the early 1980s, the U.S. government cut taxes and ran a budget deficit while the Fed pursued tight monetary policy. What effect should this policy mix have?

5. Use the *IS-LM* diagram to describe the short-run and long-run impact on national income, the price level, and the interest rate of

   a. an increase in the money supply.

   b. an increase in government purchases.

   c. an increase in taxes.

6. The Fed is considering two alternative monetary policies:

   • holding the money supply constant,

   • adjusting the money supply to hold the interest rate constant.

In the *IS-LM* model, which policy will better stabilize output if

   a. all shocks to the economy arise from exogenous changes in the demand for goods and services?

   b. all shocks to the economy arise from exogenous changes in the demand for money?

7. Suppose that the demand for real money balances depends on consumption rather than on total expenditure. That is, the money demand function is

$$M/P = L(r, C).$$

Using the *IS-LM* model, discuss whether this change in the money demand function alters

   a. the analysis of changes in government purchases,

   b. the analysis of changes in taxes.

(*Hint:* Substitute the consumption function, $C = C(Y - T)$, into the money demand function.)

Chapter 11

Aggregate Supply

There is always a temporary tradeoff between inflation and unemployment; there is no permanent tradeoff. The temporary tradeoff comes not from inflation per se, but from unanticipated inflation, which generally means, from a rising rate of inflation.

Milton Friedman

We now turn our attention to aggregate supply. In Chapters 9 and 10, we used the *IS-LM* model to show how changes in monetary and fiscal policy and exogenous shocks to the money and goods markets shift the aggregate demand curve. When we add the aggregate supply curve to our analysis, we can see how these shifts in aggregate demand affect the quantity of output and the level of prices. To understand fluctuations in output and in the price level, we must understand what determines the position and slope of the aggregate supply curve. That is our goal in this chapter.

When we introduced the aggregate supply curve in Chapter 8, we established that aggregate supply behaves very differently in the short run than in the long run. In the long run, prices are flexible, and the aggregate supply curve is vertical. A vertical aggregate supply curve means that shifts in the aggregate demand curve affect the price level but do not affect aggregate output. In the short run, however, prices are sticky, and the aggregate supply curve is not vertical. In this case, shifts in aggregate demand do lead to fluctuations in aggregate output. In Chapter 8 we took a simplified view of this price stickiness by drawing the short-run aggregate supply curve as a horizontal line, representing the extreme situation in which all prices are fixed.

To refine our understanding of aggregate supply, we begin by looking more closely at explanations for the slope of the short-run aggregate supply curve. Because no consensus exists among economists about how to explain aggregate supply, we examine four prominent models. Although different in some important details, these models share a common theme about what makes the short-run and long-run aggregate supply curves differ and a common conclusion that the short-run aggregate supply curve is upward-sloping.

After examining the models, we see that the short-run aggregate supply curve implies a tradeoff between two measures of economic performance: inflation and unemployment. This tradeoff states that to reduce the rate of inflation policymakers must temporarily raise unemployment, and to reduce unemployment they must accept higher inflation. As the quotation at the beginning of the chapter suggests, the tradeoff between inflation and unemployment holds only in the short run.

Finally, because aggregate supply is an active area of research, we examine some recent developments in the theory of aggregate supply. It is not yet clear which of these developments will prove most useful, but they show how macroeconomists are attempting to gain new insights into aggregate supply.

11-1   Four Models of Aggregate Supply

Here we present four prominent models of aggregate supply, roughly in the order of their development. In all of these models, the short-run aggregate supply curve is not vertical because of some market imperfection. As a result, shifts in the aggregate demand curve cause the level of output to deviate temporarily from the natural rate.

All four models imply an aggregate supply equation of the form

$$Y = \overline{Y} + \alpha(P - P^e) \qquad \alpha > 0,$$

where Y is output, $\overline{Y}$ is the natural rate of output, P is the price level, and P^e is the expected price level. This equation states that output deviates from its natural rate when the price level deviates from the expected price level. The parameter α indicates how responsive output is to unexpected changes in the price level; $1/\alpha$ is the slope of the aggregate supply curve.

Each of the four models tells a different story about what lies behind this equation. In other words, each highlights a particular reason that unexpected price movements are associated with fluctuations in aggregate output.

The Sticky-Wage Model

To explain why the short-run aggregate supply curve is not vertical, many economists stress the sluggish behavior of nominal wages. In many industries, especially those that are unionized, nominal wages are set by contracts, so they cannot adjust quickly when economic conditions change. Even in industries not covered by formal contracts, implicit agreements between workers and firms may limit wage changes. Wages may also depend on social norms and notions of fairness that evolve slowly. For these reasons, many economists believe that nominal wages are sluggish, or "sticky," in the short run.

The **sticky-wage model** shows what a sticky nominal wage implies for aggregate supply. To preview the model, consider what happens to the amount of output produced when the price level rises.

1. When the nominal wage is stuck, a rise in the price level lowers the real wage, making labor cheaper.

2. The lower real wage induces firms to hire more labor.

3. The greater quantity of labor hired raises output.

This positive relationship between the price level and the amount of output means that the aggregate supply curve slopes upward during the time when the nominal wage cannot adjust.

To develop this story of aggregate supply more formally, assume that workers and firms bargain over and agree on the nominal wage before they know what the price level will be when their agreement takes effect. The bargaining parties—the workers and the firms—have in mind a target real wage. This target may be the real wage at which labor supply equals labor demand. More likely, however, it also depends on the various factors that keep the real wage above the equilibrium level—union power, efficiency-wage considerations, and so on—that we discussed in Chapter 5.

The two parties set the nominal wage W based on this target real wage ω and on their expectation of the price level P^e. The nominal wage they set is

$$W \quad = \quad \omega \quad \times \quad P^e$$

$$\frac{\text{Nominal}}{\text{Wage}} = \frac{\text{Target}}{\text{Real}} \times \frac{\text{Expected}}{\text{Price}}$$
$$\qquad\qquad \text{Wage} \qquad \text{Level}$$

After the nominal wage has been set and before labor has been hired, firms learn the actual price level P. The real wage turns out to be

$$W/P \quad = \quad \omega \quad \times \quad (P^e/P)$$

$$\frac{\text{Real}}{\text{Wage}} = \frac{\text{Target}}{\text{Real}} \times \frac{\text{Expected Price Level}}{\text{Actual Price Level}}.$$
$$\qquad\qquad \text{Wage}$$

This equation shows that the real wage deviates from the target wage if the actual price level differs from the expected price level. When the actual price level is greater than expected, the real wage is less than its target; when the actual price level is less than expected, the real wage is greater than its target.

The final assumption of the model is that the quantity of labor demanded determines employment. In other words, the bargain between the workers and the firms does not determine the level of employment in advance; instead, the workers agree to provide as much labor as the firms wish to buy at the predetermined wage. We describe the firms' hiring decisions by the labor demand function,

$$L = L^d(W/P),$$

which states that the lower the real wage, the more labor is hired, as shown in panel A of Figure 11-1. Output is determined by the production function

$$Y = F(L),$$

which states that the more labor is hired, the more output is produced, as shown in panel B of Figure 11-1. Panel C of Figure 11-1 shows the resulting aggregate supply curve.

A. Labor Demand

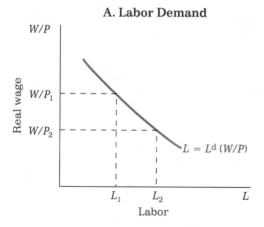

B. Production Function

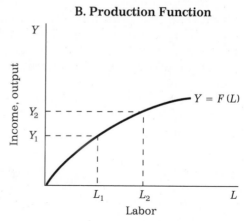

C. Aggregate Supply

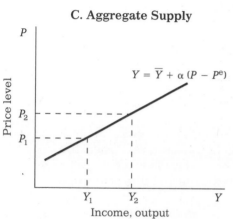

Figure 11-1 **The Sticky-Wage Model.** Panel A shows the labor demand curve. Since the nominal wage W is stuck, an increase in the price level from P_1 to P_2 reduces the real wage from W/P_1 to W/P_2. The lower real wage raises the quantity of labor demanded from L_1 to L_2. Panel B shows the production function. An increase in the quantity of labor from L_1 to L_2 raises the quantity of output produced from Y_1 to Y_2. Panel C shows the aggregate supply curve summarizing this relationship between the price level and output. An increase in the price level from P_1 to P_2 raises the quantity of output from Y_1 to Y_2.

Hence, according to the sticky-wage model, unexpected price changes move the real wage away from the target real wage. The change in the real wage in turn influences the amounts of labor hired and output produced. The aggregate supply curve can be written as

$$Y = \overline{Y} + \alpha(P - P^e).$$

Output deviates from its natural-rate level if the price level deviates from the expected price level.[1]

The Worker-Misperception Model

The next model of the short-run aggregate supply curve also focuses on the labor market. Unlike the sticky-wage model, however, the **worker-misperception model** assumes that wages are free to equilibrate supply and demand. Its key assumption is that workers temporarily confuse real and nominal wages.

The two components of the worker-misperception model are labor supply and labor demand. As before, the quantity of labor demanded depends on the real wage:

$$L^d = L^d(W/P).$$

The labor supply curve is new:

$$L^s = L^s(W/P^e).$$

This equation states that the quantity of labor supplied depends on the real wage that workers expect. Workers know their nominal wage W, but they do not know the overall price level P. When deciding how much to work, they consider the expected real wage, which equals the nominal wage W divided by their expectation of the price level P^e. We can write the expected real wage as

$$\frac{W}{P^e} = \frac{W}{P} \times \frac{P}{P^e}.$$

The expected real wage is the product of the actual real wage, W/P, and workers' misperception of the level of prices, P/P^e. To see what determines labor supply, we can substitute this expression for W/P^e and write

$$L^s = L^s(W/P \times P/P^e).$$

The quantity of labor supplied depends on the real wage and on workers' misperceptions.

---

[1] For more on the sticky-wage model, see JoAnna Gray, "Wage Indexation: A Macroeconomic Approach," *Journal of Monetary Economics* 2 (April 1976): 221–235; and Stanley Fischer, "Long-term Contracts, Rational Expectations, and the Optimal Money Supply Rule," *Journal of Political Economy* 85 (February 1977): 191–205.

To see the implications of this model for aggregate supply, consider the equilibrium in the labor market, shown in Figure 11-2. As is usual, the labor demand curve slopes downward, the labor supply curve slopes upward, and the wage adjusts to equilibrate supply and demand. Note that the position of the labor supply curve and thus the equilibrium in the labor market depend on worker misperception P/P^e.

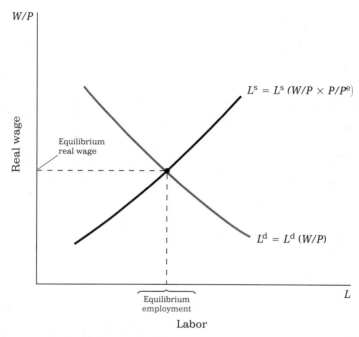

Figure 11-2 **The Worker-Misperception Model: Equilibrium in the Labor Market.** In the worker-misperception model, the labor market clears, so the intersection of the labor supply and labor demand curves determines the quantity of labor hired. Remember that the position of the labor supply curve depends on workers' misperceptions of the price level.

Consider two possibilities for what happens when the price level changes. First, suppose that the price level P goes up and that workers had correctly expected this. In this case, P^e rises proportionately with P, so neither labor supply nor labor demand changes. The real wage and the level of employment remain the same. The nominal wage rises by the same amount as prices.

Second, suppose that the price level rises without workers having expected it to and without their being aware of it. In this case, P^e remains the same. Then, at every real wage, workers are willing to supply more labor because they believe that their real wage is higher than it actually is. The increase in P/P^e shifts the labor supply curve outward, as in Figure 11-3. The outward shift in labor supply lowers the real wage and raises the level of employment. In essence, the increase in the nominal wage caused by the rise in the price level leads workers to think that their real wage is higher, which induces them to supply more labor. In ac-

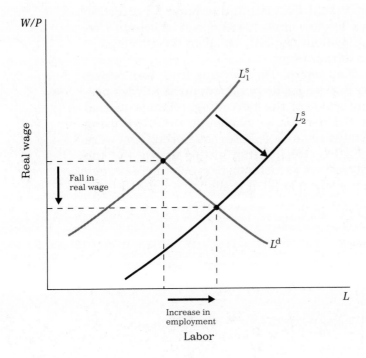

Figure 11-3 **The Worker-Misperception Model: An Unexpected Increase in the Price Level.** If the price level rises unexpectedly, workers are willing to supply more labor at any given real wage, since they believe the real wage is higher than it actually is. The equilibrium level of employment therefore rises.

tuality, the nominal wage rises by less than the price level. Firms are assumed to be better informed than workers and to recognize the fall in the real wage, so they hire more labor and produce more output.

To sum up, the worker-misperception model says that deviations of prices from expected prices induce workers to alter their supply of labor. The model implies an aggregate supply curve of the same form as the sticky-wage model:

$$Y = \overline{Y} + \alpha(P - P^e).$$

Output deviates from the natural rate when the price level deviates from the expected price level.[2]

---

[2] The worker-misperception model as presented here comes from the classic article by Milton Friedman, "The Role of Monetary Policy," *American Economic Review* 68 (March 1968): 1–17.

CASE STUDY 11-1

The Cyclical Behavior of the Real Wage

In any model with an unchanging labor demand curve, such as the two we just discussed, employment rises when the real wage falls. In the sticky-wage and worker-misperception models, an unexpected rise in the price level lowers the real wage and thereby raises the quantity of labor hired and the amount of output produced. Hence, the real wage should be *countercyclical:* it should fluctuate in the opposite direction from employment and output. Keynes himself wrote in *The General Theory* that "an increase in employment can only occur to the accompaniment of a decline in the rate of real wages."

The earliest attacks on *The General Theory* came from economists who presented data showing that wages do not fluctuate as Keynes predicted. Figure 11-4 is a scatterplot of the percentage change in real compensation per hour and the percentage change in real GNP using annual data for the United States since 1953. If Keynes's prediction were correct, we should see a negative relationship in this figure. Yet the figure shows that there is only a weak association between the real wage and output. If the real wage is cyclical at all, it is slightly *procyclical:* the real wage tends to rise when output rises.

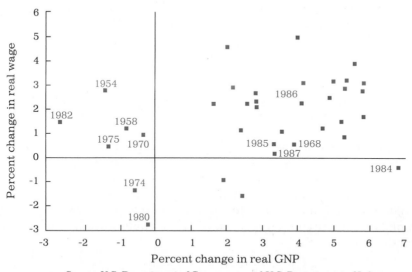

Source: U.S. Department of Commerce and U.S. Department of Labor.

Figure 11-4 **The Cyclical Behavior of the Real Wage.** This figure is a scatterplot of the percent change in real GNP and the percent change in the real wage (real compensation per hour). It shows that as output fluctuates, the real wage typically moves in the same direction. That is, the real wage is somewhat procyclical. This observation is inconsistent with the sticky-wage and worker-misperception models.

This figure suggests that abnormally high labor costs cannot explain the low employment and output observed in recessions. This evidence leads many economists to believe that the sticky-wage and worker-misperception models cannot by themselves provide a complete explanation of aggregate supply.

The evidence is not decisive, however. Some economists believe that measures of the real wage are misleading, because these measures are averages over many workers with very different wages. The composition of employment may change during the business cycle in ways that distort the average wage. For example, if high-wage workers get laid off disproportionately in recessions, then the average real wage can be falling, even when individuals' real wages are rising. It remains possible that the real wages of some workers are countercyclical, as the sticky-wage and worker-misperception models predict.[3]

The Imperfect-Information Model

The third model of aggregate supply, the **imperfect-information model**, also assumes that markets clear and that the short-run and long-run aggregate supply curves differ because of short-run misperceptions about prices. But unlike the worker-misperception model, it does not assume that firms are better informed than their workers. In its simplest form, the model does not distinguish between workers and firms at all.

The imperfect-information model assumes that each supplier in the economy produces a single good and consumes many goods. Because the number of goods is so large, suppliers cannot observe all prices at all times. They monitor closely the prices of what they produce but less closely the prices of all the goods that they consume. Because of imperfect information, they sometimes confuse changes in the overall level of prices with changes in relative prices. This confusion influences decisions about how much to supply, and it leads to a short-run relationship between the price level and output.

Consider the decision facing a single supplier, say, a corn farmer. Because the farmer earns income from selling corn and uses this income to buy goods and services, the amount of corn she chooses to produce depends on the price of corn relative to the prices of other goods and services in the economy. If the relative price of corn is high, the farmer is motivated to work hard and produce more corn, because the reward is great. If the relative price of corn is low, she would prefer to enjoy more leisure and produce less corn.

---

[3] For some of the recent work on this topic, see Patrick T. Geary and John Kennan, "The Employment-Real Wage Relationship: An International Study," *Journal of Political Economy* 90 (August 1982): 854–871; Mark J. Bils, "Real Wages over the Business Cycle: Evidence from Panel Data," *Journal of Political Economy* 93 (1985): 666–689; and Scott Sumner and Stephen Silver, "Real Wages, Employment, and the Phillips Curve," *Journal of Political Economy* 97 (June 1989): 706–720.

When the corn farmer makes her production decision, however, she does not know the relative price of corn. Being a corn producer, she monitors the price of corn closely and therefore knows its nominal price. But she does not know the prices of all the other goods in the economy. She must, therefore, estimate the relative price of corn using the nominal price of corn and her expectation of the overall price level.

Consider how the farmer responds if all prices in the economy, including the price of corn, increase. One possibility is that she expected this change in prices. So when she observes an increase in the price of corn, her estimate of its relative price is unchanged. She does not work any harder.

The other possibility is that the farmer did not expect the price level to increase (or to increase by this much). When she observes the increase in the price of corn, she is not sure whether other prices have risen (in which case corn's relative price is unchanged) or if only the price of corn has risen (in which case its relative price is higher). The rational inference is that some of each has happened. In other words, the farmer infers from the increase in the nominal price of corn that its relative price has risen somewhat. So she works harder and produces more.

Our corn farmer is not unique. When the price level rises unexpectedly, all suppliers in the economy observe increases in the prices of the goods they produce. They all infer, rationally but mistakenly, that the relative prices of the goods they produce have risen. They work harder and produce more.

To sum up, the imperfect-information model says that when prices exceed expected prices, suppliers infer that the relative prices of the goods they produce have risen, which induces them to raise their output. The model implies an aggregate supply curve that is now familiar:

$$Y = \overline{Y} + \alpha(P - P^e).$$

Output deviates from the natural rate when the price level deviates from the expected price level.[4]

The Sticky-Price Model

Our fourth and final model of aggregate supply, the **sticky-price model**, emphasizes that firms do not instantly adjust the prices they charge in response to changes in demand. Sometimes prices are set by long-term contracts between firms and customers. Even without formal agreements, firms may hold prices steady to prevent annoying their regular

---

[4] To read more on the imperfect-information model, see Robert E. Lucas, Jr., "Understanding Business Cycles," *Stabilization of the Domestic and International Economy*, vol. 5 of Carnegie-Rochester Conference on Public Policy (Amsterdam: North-Holland Publishing Company, 1977); reprinted in Robert E. Lucas, Jr., *Studies in Business Cycle Theory* (Cambridge, Mass.: MIT Press, 1981).

customers with frequent price changes. Some prices are sticky because of the way markets are structured: once a firm has printed and distributed its catalog or price list, it is costly to alter prices.

To see what sticky prices imply for aggregate supply, we must first consider the pricing decisions of individual firms. We can then add together the decisions of many firms to obtain the aggregate supply curve.

Consider the decision facing a single firm that has some monopoly control over the price it charges. The firm's desired price p depends on two macroeconomic variables:

- The overall level of prices P. A higher price level implies that the firm's costs are higher. Hence, the higher the overall price level, the more the firm would like to charge for its product.

- The level of aggregate income Y. A higher level of income raises the demand for the firm's product. Because marginal cost increases at higher levels of production, the higher the demand, the higher the firm's desired price.

We therefore write the firm's desired price as

$$p = P + a(Y - \overline{Y}),$$

where a is a parameter greater than zero. This equation says that the desired price p depends on the overall level of prices P and on the level of aggregate output relative to the natural rate $Y - \overline{Y}$.[5]

Now assume that there are two types of firms. Some have flexible prices: they always set their prices according to this equation. Others have sticky prices: they announce their prices in advance based on what they expect economic conditions to be. These firms set prices according to

$$p = P^e + a(Y^e - \overline{Y}^e),$$

where, as before, a superscript "e" represents an expectation of the variable. For simplicity, assume that these firms expect output to be at its natural rate, so that the last term, $a(Y^e - \overline{Y}^e)$, is zero. Then these firms set the price

$$p = P^e.$$

That is, they set their prices based on what they expect other firms to charge.

We can use the pricing rules of the two groups of firms to derive the aggregate supply equation. To do this, we find the overall price level in the economy, which is the weighted average of the prices set by the two groups. If s is the fraction of firms with sticky prices and $1 - s$ the fraction

---

[5] *Mathematical Note:* If you interpret p and P as the logarithm of the firm's price and the price level, then this equation states that the desired relative price depends on the deviation of output from the natural rate.

with flexible prices, then the overall price level is

$$P = sP^e + (1 - s)[P + a(Y - \overline{Y})].$$

The first term is the price of the sticky-price firms weighted by their fraction in the economy, and the second term is the price of the flexible-price firms weighted by their fraction. Now subtract $(1 - s)P$ from both sides of this equation to obtain

$$sP = sP^e + (1 - s)[a(Y - \overline{Y})].$$

Divide both sides by s to solve for the overall price level:

$$P = P^e + [(1 - s)a/s](Y - \overline{Y}).$$

The two terms in this equation are explained as follows:

- When firms expect a high price level, they expect high costs. Those firms that fix prices in advance set their prices high. These high prices cause the other firms to set high prices also. Hence, a high expected price level leads to a high actual price level.

- When output is high, the demand for goods is high. Those firms with flexible prices set their prices high, which leads to a high price level. The effect of output on the price level depends on the proportion of firms with flexible prices.

Hence, the overall price level depends on the expected price level and on the level of output.

Algebraic rearrangement puts this aggregate pricing equation in a more familiar form:

$$Y = \overline{Y} + \alpha(P - P^e),$$

where $\alpha = s/[(1 - s)a]$. Like the other models, the sticky-price model says that the deviation of output from the natural rate is associated with the deviation of the price level from the expected price level.

Although the sticky-price model emphasizes the goods market, consider briefly what is happening in the labor market. If a firm's price is stuck in the short run, then a reduction in aggregate demand reduces the amount that the firm is able to sell. The firm responds to the drop in sales by reducing its production and its demand for labor. Hence, in the sticky-price model, fluctuations in output are associated with shifts in the labor demand curve, rather than movements along a fixed labor demand curve. In this model, therefore, the real wage can be procyclical.[6]

---

[6] For a more advanced development of the sticky-price model, see Julio Rotemberg, "Monopolistic Price Adjustment and Aggregate Output," *Review of Economic Studies* 49 (1982): 517–531; or Laurence Ball, N. Gregory Mankiw, and David Romer, "The New Keynesian Economics and the Output-Inflation Tradeoff," *Brookings Papers on Economic Activity* no. 1 (1988): 1–65.

CASE STUDY 11-2

International Differences in the Aggregate Supply Curve

Economists often use the models of aggregate supply to predict differences in the short-run aggregate supply curve across countries. They then examine data to test these predictions. The purpose of this work is to try to evaluate the alternative models and to use the models to help understand international differences in economic fluctuations.

When economist Robert Lucas proposed the imperfect-information model in the early 1970s, he pointed out a simple prediction about how the aggregate supply curve should differ across countries. Lucas noted that the slope of the aggregate supply curve should depend on the variability of aggregate demand. In countries where aggregate demand fluctuates widely, the aggregate price level fluctuates widely as well. Because most movements in prices in these countries do not represent movements in relative prices, suppliers should have learned not to respond much to unexpected changes in the price level. Therefore, the aggregate supply curve should be relatively steep (that is, α will be small.) Conversely, in countries where aggregate demand is relatively stable, suppliers should have learned that most price changes are relative price changes. Accordingly, in these countries, suppliers should be more responsive to unexpected price changes, making the aggregate supply curve relatively flat (that is, α will be large).

Lucas tested this prediction by examining international data on output and prices. He found that changes in aggregate demand have the biggest effect on output in those countries where aggregate demand and prices are most stable. Lucas concluded that the evidence supports the imperfect-information model.[7]

The sticky-price model also makes predictions about the slope of the short-run aggregate supply curve. If infrequent price adjustment is the key reason that the short-run aggregate supply curve is not vertical, then the average rate of inflation should influence the curve's slope. The higher the average rate of inflation, the more frequently firms adjust individual prices to keep up with the rising overall price level. More frequent price adjustment in turn causes prices to respond more quickly to shocks to aggregate demand. Hence, a high rate of inflation should make the short-run aggregate supply curve steeper.

Comparisons of different countries support this prediction of the sticky-price model. In countries with low average inflation, the short-run aggregate supply curve is relatively flat: fluctuations in aggregate demand have large effects on output and are slowly reflected in prices.

---

[7] Robert E. Lucas, Jr., "Some International Evidence on Output-Inflation Tradeoffs," *American Economic Review* 63 (June 1973): 326–334; reprinted in Robert E. Lucas, Jr., *Studies in Business Cycle Theory* (Cambridge, Mass.: MIT Press, 1981).

High-inflation countries have steep short-run aggregate supply curves. Fluctuations in their aggregate demand have small effects on output because prices respond quickly. In other words, high inflation appears to erode the frictions that cause prices to be sticky.[8]

Note that the sticky-price model provides another interpretation of Lucas's finding that countries with variable aggregate demand have steep aggregate supply curves. If the price level is highly variable, few firms will commit to prices in advance (s will be small). Hence, the aggregate supply curve will be steep (α will be small).

Summary and Implications

Figure 11-5 lists the four models of aggregate supply and the market imperfection that each uses to explain why the short-run aggregate supply curve is not vertical. The figure divides the models according to two characteristics by which they differ. The first is whether the model assumes that markets clear—that is, whether wages and prices are free to equilibrate supply and demand. The second is whether the model emphasizes the labor or the goods market as the location of the market imperfection.

Market With Imperfection

	Labor	Goods
Yes	**Worker-Misperception Model:** Workers confuse nominal wage changes with real wage changes.	**Imperfect-Information Model:** Suppliers confuse changes in the price level with changes in relative prices.
Markets Clear?		
No	**Sticky-Wage Model:** Nominal wages adjust slowly.	**Sticky-Price Model:** The prices of goods and services adjust slowly.

Figure 11-5 **Comparison of Models of Aggregate Supply.** The four models of aggregate supply differ by two characteristics: whether they assume that markets clear and whether the key market imperfection lies in the goods market or in the labor market.

---

[8] Laurence Ball, N. Gregory Mankiw, and David Romer, "The New Keynesian Economics and the Output-Inflation Tradeoff," *Brookings Papers on Economic Activity* no. 1 (1988): 1–65.

Keep in mind that these models of aggregate supply are not necessarily incompatible with each other. We need not accept one model and
reject the others. The world may contain all four of these market imperfections, and all may contribute to the behavior of short-run aggregate supply.

Although the four models of aggregate supply differ in their assumptions and emphases, their implications for the economy are similar. All
can be summarized in the equation

$$Y = \overline{Y} + \alpha(P - P^e).$$

This equation, illustrated in Figure 11-6, relates deviations of output from
the natural rate to deviations of the price level from the expected price
level. *If the price level is greater than the expected price level, output
exceeds its natural rate. If the price level is less than the expected price
level, output falls short of its natural rate.*

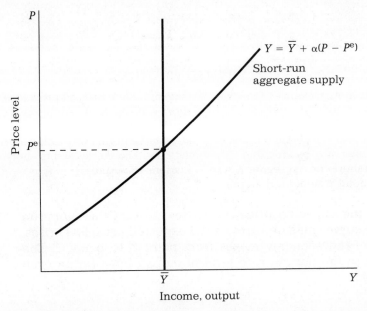

Figure 11-6 **The Short-Run Aggregate**   the natural rate if the price level devi-
Supply Curve. Output deviates from   ates from the expected price level.

Figure 11-7 uses this aggregate supply equation to show what happens in response to an unexpected increase in aggregate demand. In
the short run, the equilibrium of the economy moves from point A to
point B. The increase in aggregate demand raises the price level above
the expected price level and, therefore, output above the natural rate.

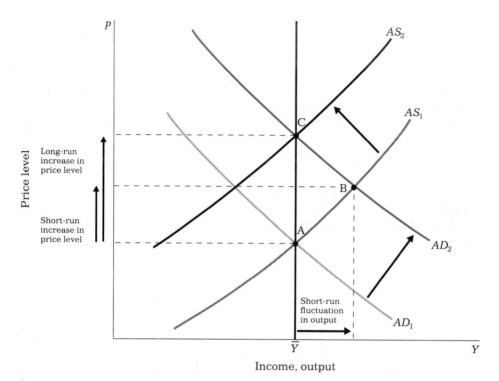

Figure 11-7 **A Shift in Aggregate Demand.** When aggregate demand increases unexpectedly, the price level rises above the expected price level and output rises above the natural rate, moving the economy along the short-run aggregate supply curve from point A to point B. In the long run, the expected price level rises, the short-run aggregate supply curve shifts upward, and output returns to the natural rate at point C. In this way, shifts in the aggregate demand curve lead to short-run fluctuations in output.

In the long run, the expected price level rises, so that the short-run aggregate supply curve shifts upward. As the expected price level rises, the equilibrium of the economy moves from point B to point C. The economy returns to the natural-rate level of output, but with an even higher price level.

11-2 Inflation, Unemployment, and the Phillips Curve

Two goals of economic policymakers are low inflation and low unemployment. Here we examine a relationship between inflation and unemployment called the **Phillips curve**. The Phillips curve is an alternative way to express aggregate supply; thus, we can view the models of aggregate supply we have just examined as providing the theory behind the Phillips curve. The Phillips curve is useful to policymakers who influence aggregate demand because it provides a simple way to analyze the tradeoff between inflation and unemployment implied by the short-run aggregate supply curve.

The Phillips curve posits that the inflation rate—the percentage change in the price level—depends on three forces:

- expected inflation,

- the deviation of unemployment from the natural rate, called *cyclical unemployment*, and

- supply shocks.

These three forces are expressed in the following equation:

$$\pi \quad = \quad \pi^e \quad - \quad \beta(u - u^n) \quad + \quad \epsilon$$

$$\text{Inflation} = \frac{\text{Expected}}{\text{Inflation}} - \left(\beta \times \frac{\text{Cyclical}}{\text{Unemployment}} \right) + \frac{\text{Supply,}}{\text{Shock}}$$

where β is a parameter greater than zero. Notice that there is a minus sign before the cyclical unemployment term: high unemployment tends to reduce inflation.

From Aggregate Supply to the Phillips Curve

To see that the Phillips curve and the aggregate supply curve express essentially the same relationship, write the aggregate supply equation as

$$P = P^e + (1/\alpha)(Y - \overline{Y}).$$

With one subtraction, one substitution, and one addition, we can derive the Phillips curve.

First, subtract last year's price level P_{-1} from both sides of this equation to obtain

$$(P - P_{-1}) = (P^e - P_{-1}) + (1/\alpha)(Y - \overline{Y}).$$

The term on the left-hand side, $P - P_{-1}$, is the difference between the current price level and last year's price level, which is inflation π.[9] The term on the right-hand side, $P^e - P_{-1}$, is the difference between the expected price level and last year's price level, which is expected inflation π^e. Therefore, we can replace $P - P_{-1}$ with π and $P^e - P_{-1}$ with π^e:

$$\pi = \pi^e + (1/\alpha)(Y - \overline{Y}).$$

Next, recall from Chapter 2 that Okun's law gives a relationship between output and unemployment. One version of Okun's law states that the deviation of output from its natural rate is inversely related to the de-

---

[9] *Mathematical Note:* This statement is not precise, because inflation is really the percentage change in the price level. To make the statement more precise, let p be the price level and P be the logarithm of the price level. Then the change in P is roughly the inflation rate, because $dP = d(\log p) = dp/p$.

viation of unemployment from its natural rate; that is, when output is higher than the natural rate of output, unemployment is lower than the natural rate of unemployment. Using this relationship, we can substitute $-\beta(u - u^n)$ for $(1/\alpha)(Y - \overline{Y})$. The equation becomes

$$\pi = \pi^e - \beta(u - u^n).$$

Finally, add a supply shock to represent exogenous influences on prices, such as a change in oil prices, a change in the minimum wage, or the imposition of government controls on prices:

$$\pi = \pi^e - \beta(u - u^n) + \epsilon.$$

Thus, we obtain the Phillips curve from the aggregate supply equation.

Now step back from this algebra. Notice that the Phillips curve retains the key feature of the short-run aggregate supply curve: a link between real and nominal variables that causes the classical dichotomy to fail. More precisely, the Phillips curve demonstrates the connection between real economic activity and unexpected changes in the price level. *The Phillips curve is merely a convenient way to express and analyze aggregate supply.*

///

F Y I **The History of the Phillips Curve**

The Phillips curve is named after British economist A. W. Phillips. In 1958 Phillips observed a negative relationship between the unemployment rate and the rate of wage inflation.[10] The Phillips curve that economists use today differs from the relationship Phillips examined in three ways.

First, the modern Phillips curve substitutes price inflation for wage inflation. This difference is not crucial, because price inflation and wage inflation are closely related. In periods when wages are rising quickly, prices are rising quickly as well.

Second, the modern Phillips curve includes expected inflation. This addition is due to Milton Friedman and Edmund Phelps. In developing the worker-misperception model in the late 1960s, these two economists emphasized the importance of expectations for aggregate supply.

Third, the modern Phillips curve includes supply shocks. This addition is due to OPEC, the Organization of Petroleum Exporting Countries. In the 1970s OPEC caused large increases in the world price of oil, which made economists more aware of the importance of shocks to aggregate supply.

///

[10] A. W. Phillips, "The Relationship between Unemployment and the Rate of Change of Money Wages in the United Kingdom, 1861–1957," *Economica* 25 (November 1958): 283–299.

Expectations and Inflation Inertia

To make the Phillips curve useful for analyzing the choices facing policymakers, we need to say what determines expected inflation. A simple and often plausible assumption is that people form their expectations of inflation based on recently observed inflation. For example, suppose that people expect prices will rise this year at the same rate they did last year. Then

$$\pi^e = \pi_{-1}.$$

In this case, we can write the Phillips curve as

$$\pi = \pi_{-1} - \beta(u - u^n) + \epsilon,$$

which states that inflation depends on past inflation, cyclical unemployment, and a supply shock.

The first term in this form of the Phillips curve, π_{-1}, implies that inflation is inertial. That is, if unemployment is at its natural rate and if there are no supply shocks, prices will continue to rise at the prevailing rate of inflation. This inertia arises because past inflation influences expectations of future inflation and because these expectations influence the wages and prices that people set. Robert Solow captured the concept of inflation inertia well when, during the high inflation of the 1970s, he wrote, "Why is our money ever less valuable? Perhaps it is simply that we have inflation because we expect inflation, and we expect inflation because we've had it."

In the model of aggregate supply and aggregate demand, inflation inertia is interpreted as follows. If prices have been rising quickly, people will expect them to continue to rise quickly. Because the position of the short-run aggregate supply curve depends on the expected price level, the short-run aggregate supply curve will be shifting upward over time. It will continue to shift upward until some event, such as a recession or a supply shock, changes inflation and thereby changes expectations of inflation.

The Two Causes of Rising and Falling Inflation

Although inflation is inertial, it does rise and fall. The second and third terms in the Phillips curve show the two forces that can change the rate of inflation.

The second term, $\beta(u - u^n)$, shows that cyclical unemployment—the deviation of unemployment from its natural rate—exerts upward or downward pressure on inflation. Low unemployment pulls the inflation rate up. This is called **demand-pull inflation** because high aggregate demand is responsible for this type of inflation. High unemployment pulls the inflation rate down. The parameter β measures how responsive inflation is to cyclical unemployment.

The third term, ϵ, shows that inflation also rises and falls because of supply shocks. An adverse supply shock, such as the rise in world oil prices in the 1970s, implies a positive value of ϵ and causes inflation to rise. This is called **cost-push inflation** because adverse supply shocks are typically events that push up the costs of production. A beneficial supply shock, such as the oil glut that led to a fall in oil prices in the 1980s, implies a negative value of ϵ and causes inflation to fall.

CASE STUDY 11-3

Inflation and Unemployment in the United States

Because inflation and unemployment are such important measures of economic performance, macroeconomic developments are often viewed through the lens of the Phillips curve. Figure 11-8 displays the history of inflation and unemployment in the United States since 1961. In it we can trace the rises and falls in inflation over the past three decades.

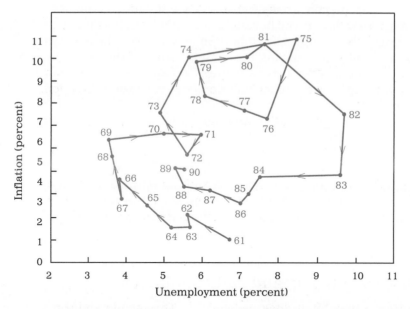

Figure 11-8 **Inflation and Unemployment in the United States Since 1961.** This figure uses annual data on the unemployment rate and the inflation rate (percent change in the GNP deflator) to illustrate macroeconomic developments over the past three decades.

In the 1960s, expansionary policy lowered unemployment and raised inflation. The tax cut in 1964, together with expansionary monetary policy, pushed the unemployment rate to below 5 percent. The continuing expansion of the economy in the late 1960s was a by-product of government spending for the Vietnam War. Unemployment fell lower and inflation rose higher than policymakers intended.

The 1970s were a period of economic turmoil. The decade began with policymakers trying to lower the inflation inherited from the 1960s. Temporary controls on wages and prices and a demand-induced recession reduced the inflation rate only slightly. The effects of wage and price controls ended when the controls were lifted, and the recession was too small to counteract the inflationary impact of the boom that had preceded it. By 1972 the unemployment rate was the same as a decade earlier, while inflation was three percentage points higher.

Beginning in 1973 policymakers had to cope with the large supply shocks caused by the Organization of Petroleum Exporting Countries (OPEC). OPEC first raised oil prices in the mid-1970s, pushing up the inflation rate to about 10 percent. A recession in 1975 reduced inflation somewhat, but further OPEC price hikes pushed inflation up again in the late 1970s.

The 1980s began with high inflation and high expectations of inflation. Under the leadership of Chairman Paul Volcker, the Federal Reserve doggedly pursued monetary policies aimed at reducing inflation. In 1982 and 1983 the unemployment rate reached its highest level in 40 years. High unemployment, aided by a fall in oil prices in 1986, pulled the inflation rate down from about 10 percent to about 3 percent. By 1987 the unemployment rate of about 6 percent was close to most estimates of the natural rate. At the end of the 1980s, unemployment fell somewhat below the natural rate, beginning a new round of demand-pull inflation.

Thus, recent macroeconomic history exhibits the many causes of inflation. The 1960s and the 1980s show the two sides of demand-pull inflation: in the 1960s low unemployment pulled inflation up, and in the 1980s high unemployment pulled inflation down. The 1970s show the effects of cost-push inflation.

The Short-Run Tradeoff Between Inflation and Unemployment

Consider the options the Phillips curve gives to a policymaker who can influence aggregate demand. At any given time, expected inflation and the supply shock are beyond the policymaker's immediate control. Yet, through monetary and fiscal policy, the policymaker can alter output and unemployment. The policymaker can expand aggregate demand to lower unemployment and raise inflation. Or the policymaker can depress aggregate demand to raise unemployment and lower inflation.

Figure 11-9 shows the short-run tradeoff between inflation and unemployment implied by the Phillips curve equation. The policymaker can manipulate aggregate demand to choose a combination of inflation and unemployment on this curve, called the *short-run Phillips curve.*

Notice that the short-run Phillips curve depends on expected inflation. If expected inflation rises, the curve shifts upward, and the tradeoff the policymaker faces becomes worse: inflation is higher for any level of unemployment. Figure 11-10 shows how the tradeoff depends on expected inflation.

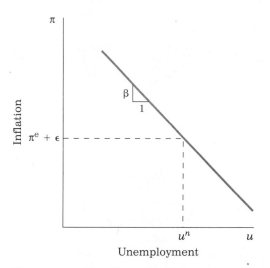

Figure 11-9 **The Short-Run Tradeoff Between Inflation and Unemployment.** In the short run, there is a negative relationship between inflation and unemployment. At any point in time, a policymaker who controls aggregate demand can choose a combination of inflation and unemployment on this short-run Phillips curve.

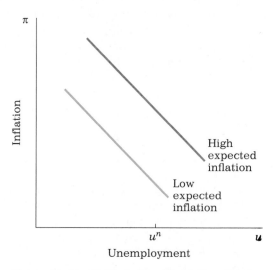

Figure 11-10 **Shifts in the Short-Run Tradeoff.** The short-run tradeoff between inflation and unemployment depends on expected inflation. The higher expected inflation is, the higher this curve is.

Because people adjust their expectations of inflation over time, this tradeoff between inflation and unemployment holds only in the short run. The policymaker cannot keep inflation above expected inflation forever: expectations eventually adapt to whatever inflation rate the policymaker chooses. In the long run, the classical dichotomy holds, unemployment returns to its natural rate, and there is no tradeoff between inflation and unemployment.

Disinflation and the Sacrifice Ratio

What would happen to unemployment and output if the Fed pursued a policy to reduce inflation from 6 percent to 2 percent?

The Phillips curve shows that, in the absence of a beneficial supply shock, lowering inflation requires a period of high unemployment and reduced output. But by how much and for how long would unemployment need to rise above the natural rate? Before deciding whether to reduce inflation, policymakers must know how much output would be lost during the transition to lower inflation. This cost can then be compared with the benefits of lower inflation.

Much research has used the available data to examine the Phillips curve quantitatively. The results of these studies are often summarized in a number called the **sacrifice ratio**, the percentage of a year's real GNP that must be forgone to reduce inflation by one percentage point. Although estimates of the sacrifice ratio vary substantially, a typical estimate is about five: for every percentage point that inflation is to fall, five percent of one year's GNP must be sacrificed.[11]

We can also express the sacrifice ratio in terms of unemployment. Okun's law says that a change of one percentage point in the unemployment rate translates into a change of two percentage points in GNP. Therefore, reducing inflation by one percentage point requires about two and one-half percentage point-years of cyclical unemployment.

We can use the sacrifice ratio to estimate by how much and for how long unemployment must rise to reduce inflation. Since reducing inflation by one percentage point requires a sacrifice of 5 percent of a year's GNP, reducing inflation by four percentage points requires a sacrifice of 20 percent of a year's GNP. Equivalently, this reduction in inflation requires a sacrifice of 10 percentage point-years of unemployment.

This disinflation could take a variety of forms, each totaling the same sacrifice of 20 percent of a year's GNP. For example, a rapid disinflation would lower output by 10 percent for two years: this is sometimes called the *cold turkey* solution to inflation. A moderate disinflation would lower output by 5 percent for four years. An even more gradual disinflation would depress output by 2 percent for a decade.

Rational Expectations and Painless Disinflation

Because the expectation of inflation influences the short-run tradeoff between inflation and unemployment, a crucial question is how people form expectations. So far, we have been assuming that expected inflation depends on recently observed inflation. Although this assumption about expectations is plausible, it is probably too simple to be applicable in all circumstances.

An approach called **rational expectations** assumes that people optimally use all the available information, including information about current policies, to forecast the future. Because monetary and fiscal policies

---

[11] Arthur M. Okun, "Efficient Disinflationary Policies," *American Economic Review* 68 (May 1978): 348–352; Robert J. Gordon and Stephen R. King, "The Output Cost of Disinflation in Traditional and Vector Autoregressive Models," *Brookings Papers on Economic Activity* no. 1 (1982): 205–245.

influence inflation, expected inflation should also depend on the monetary and fiscal policies in effect. According to the theory of rational expectations, a change in monetary or fiscal policy will change expectations, and an evaluation of any policy change must incorporate this effect on expectations. This approach implies that inflation is less inertial than it first appears.

Here is how Thomas Sargent, a prominent advocate of rational expectations, describes the implications for the Phillips curve:

> An alternative "rational expectations" view denies that there is any inherent momentum to the present process of inflation. This view maintains that firms and workers have now come to expect high rates of inflation in the future and that they strike inflationary bargains in light of these expectations. However, it is held that people expect high rates of inflation in the future precisely because the government's current and prospective monetary and fiscal policies warrant those expectations. . . . Thus inflation only seems to have a momentum of its own; it is actually the long-term government policy of persistently running large deficits and creating money at high rates which imparts the momentum to the inflation rate. An implication of this view is that inflation can be stopped much more quickly than advocates of the "momentum" view have indicated and that their estimates of the length of time and the costs of stopping inflation in terms of foregone output are erroneous. . . . [Stopping inflation] would require a change in the policy regime: there must be an abrupt change in the continuing government policy, or strategy, for setting deficits now and in the future that is sufficiently binding as to be widely believed. . . . How costly such a move would be in terms of foregone output and how long it would be in taking effect would depend partly on how resolute and evident the government's commitment was.[12]

Thus, advocates of rational expectations argue that the short-run Phillips curve does not accurately represent the options available. They believe that if policymakers are credibly committed to reducing inflation, rational people will understand the commitment and quickly lower their expectations of inflation. According to the theory of rational expectations, traditional estimates of the sacrifice ratio are not useful for evaluating the impact of alternative policies. Under a credible policy, the costs of reducing inflation may be much lower than estimates of the sacrifice ratio suggest.

In the most extreme case, one can imagine reducing the rate of inflation without causing any recession at all. A painless disinflation has

---

[12] Thomas J. Sargent, "The Ends of Four Big Inflations," in Robert E. Hall, ed., *Inflation: Causes and Effects* (Chicago: University of Chicago Press, 1982).

two requirements. First, the plan to reduce inflation must be announced before the crucial expectations are formed. Second, those setting wages and prices must believe the announcement; otherwise, they will not reduce their expectations of inflation. If both requirements are met, the announcement will immediately shift the short-run tradeoff between inflation and unemployment downward, permitting a lower rate of inflation without higher unemployment.

Although the rational-expectations approach remains controversial, almost all economists agree that expectations of inflation influence the short-run tradeoff between inflation and unemployment. The credibility of a policy to reduce inflation is therefore one determinant of how costly the policy will be. Unfortunately, it is often difficult to predict whether the public will view the announcement of a new policy as credible. The central role of expectations makes forecasting the results of alternative policies far more difficult.

CASE STUDY 11-4

The Cost of Paul Volcker's Disinflation

The 1980s began with some of the highest rates of inflation in U.S. history. Yet because of the tight monetary policies that the Fed pursued under Chairman Paul Volcker, the rate of inflation fell substantially in the first few years of the decade. This episode provides a natural experiment with which to estimate how much output is lost in the process of disinflation.

The first question is, how much did inflation fall? As measured by the GNP deflator, inflation reached a peak of 9.7 percent in 1981. It is natural to end the episode in 1985 because oil prices plunged in 1986—a large, beneficial supply shock unrelated to Fed policy. In 1985, inflation was 3.0 percent, so the Fed engineered a reduction in inflation of 6.7 percentage points over four years.

The second question is, how much output was lost during this period? Table 11-1 shows the unemployment rate from 1982 to 1985. Assuming

Table 11-1	Unemployment During the Volcker Disinflation		
Year	Unemployment Rate	Natural Rate	Cyclical Unemployment
1982	9.5%	6.0%	3.5%
1983	9.5	6.0	3.5
1984	7.4	6.0	1.4
1985	7.1	6.0	1.1
		Total	9.5%

that the natural rate of unemployment was 6 percent, we can compute the amount of cyclical unemployment in each year. In total over this period, there were 9.5 point-years of cyclical unemployment. Okun's law says that one percentage point of unemployment implies two percentage points of GNP. Therefore, 19.0 percent of a year's GNP were lost during the disinflation.

Now we can compute the sacrifice ratio for this episode. We know that 19.0 point-years of GNP were lost, and that inflation fell by 6.7 percentage points. Hence, 19.0/6.7, or 2.8, point-years of GNP were lost for each percentage-point reduction in inflation. The estimate of the sacrifice ratio from the Volcker disinflation is 2.8.

This estimate of the sacrifice ratio is smaller than the estimates made before Volcker was appointed Fed chairman. In other words, Volcker reduced inflation at a smaller cost than many economists had predicted. One explanation is that Volcker's tough stand was credible enough to influence directly expectations of inflation. Yet the change in expectations was not large enough to make the disinflation painless: in 1982 unemployment reached its highest level since the Great Depression.

11-3   Recent Developments: New Keynesian Economics

Economists do not agree on the best way to explain economic fluctuations and, in particular, the short-run aggregate supply curve. There are two predominate schools of thought: new classical and new Keynesian economics.

New classical economists advocate models in which wages and prices adjust quickly to clear markets. The market-clearing models we examined earlier—the worker-misperception and imperfect-information models—were popular among new classical economists in the 1970s. Today, however, many new classical economists have turned their attention to *real-business-cycle theory*, which applies the tenets of the classical model—price flexibility and monetary neutrality—to explain economic fluctuations. We discuss this theory in Chapter 14.

New Keynesian economists believe that market-clearing models cannot explain short-run economic fluctuations, and so they advocate models with sticky wages and prices. In *The General Theory* Keynes urged economists to abandon the classical presumption that wages and prices always adjust to equilibrate markets. He emphasized that aggregate demand is a primary determinant of national income in the short run. This result requires that the short-run aggregate supply curve not be vertical, as it is in the classical model. New Keynesian economists accept these basic conclusions.

In their research, new Keynesian economists try to explain why the classical model does not adequately describe the economy; in the process, they put the Keynesian approach to economic fluctuations on a firmer theoretical foundation. Much of this new Keynesian research is aimed at explaining why wages and prices are not flexible in the short run. This work tries to identify more precisely the market imperfections that make wages and prices sticky and that cause the economy to return only slowly to the natural rate. In addition, some new Keynesian research challenges an underlying premise of our model of economic fluctuations. In this section we discuss these recent developments.

Small Menu Costs and Aggregate-Demand Externalities

One reason that prices do not adjust immediately in the short run is that there are costs involved in adjusting prices. To change its prices, a firm may need to send out a new catalog to customers, distribute new price lists to its sales staff, or, in the case of a restaurant, print new menus. These costs of price adjustment, called **menu costs**, cause firms to adjust prices intermittently rather than continuously.

Economists disagree about whether menu costs explain the short-run stickiness of prices. Skeptics point out that menu costs are usually very small. How can small menu costs help to explain recessions, which are very costly for society? Proponents reply that small does not mean inconsequential: even though menu costs are small for the individual firm, they can have large effects on the economy as a whole.

Proponents of the menu-cost hypothesis describe the situation as follows. To understand why prices adjust slowly, one must acknowledge that there are externalities to price adjustment: a price reduction by one firm benefits other firms in the economy. When a firm lowers the price it charges, it lowers slightly the average price level and thereby raises real money balances. The increase in real money balances expands aggregate income (by shifting the *LM* curve outward). The economic expansion in turn raises the demand for the products of all firms. This macroeconomic impact of one firm's price adjustment on the demand for all other firms' products is called an **aggregate-demand externality**.

In the presence of this aggregate-demand externality, small menu costs can make prices sticky, and this stickiness can have a large cost to society. Suppose that a firm originally sets its price too high and later must decide whether to cut its price. Because of the aggregate-demand externality, the benefit to society of the price cut would exceed the benefit to the firm. Because the firm ignores this externality when making its decision, it sometimes fails to pay the menu cost and cut its price even though the price cut is socially desirable. *Hence, sticky prices may be optimal for those setting prices, even though they are undesirable for the economy as a whole.*[13]

The Staggering of Wages and Prices

Not everyone in the economy sets new wages and prices at the same time. Instead, the adjustment of wages and prices throughout the economy is staggered. *Staggering makes the overall level of wages and prices adjust slowly, even when individual wages and prices change frequently.*

Consider the following example. Suppose first that price setting is synchronized: every firm adjusts its price on the first day of every month. If the money supply and aggregate demand rise on May 10, output will be higher from May 10 to June 1 because prices are fixed during this interval. But on June 1 all firms will raise their prices in response to the higher demand, ending the boom.

Now suppose that price setting is staggered: half the firms set prices on the first of each month and half on the fifteenth. If the money supply rises on May 10, then half the firms can raise their prices on May 15. But these firms will probably not raise their prices very much. Because half of the firms will not be changing their prices on the fifteenth, a price increase by any firm will raise that firm's *relative* price, which will cause it to lose customers. (In contrast, if all firms are synchronized, all firms can raise prices together, leaving relative prices unaffected.) If the May 15 price-setters make little adjustment in their prices, then the other firms will make little adjustment when their turn comes on June 1, because they also want to avoid relative price changes. And so on. The price level rises slowly as the result of small price increases on the first and the fifteenth of each month. Hence, staggering makes the price level sluggish, because no firm wishes to be the first to post a substantial price increase.

Staggering also affects wage determination. Consider, for example, how a fall in the money supply works its way through the economy. A smaller money supply implies reduced aggregate demand, which in turn requires a proportionate fall in nominal wages to maintain full employment. Each worker might be willing to take a cut in his nominal wage if all other wages were to fall proportionately. But each worker is reluctant to be the first to take a pay cut, knowing that this means, at least temporarily, a fall in his relative wage. Since the setting of wages is stag-

---

[13] For more on this topic, see N. Gregory Mankiw, "Small Menu Costs and Large Business Cycles: A Macroeconomic Model of Monopoly," *Quarterly Journal of Economics* 100 (May 1985): 529–537; George A. Akerlof and Janet L. Yellen, "A Near Rational Model of the Business Cycle, with Wage and Price Inertia," *Quarterly Journal of Economics* 100 (Supplement 1985): 823–838; and Olivier Jean Blanchard and Nobuhiro Kiyotaki, "Monopolistic Competition and the Effects of Aggregate Demand," *American Economic Review* 77 (September 1987): 647–666. These three articles are reprinted in N. Gregory Mankiw and David Romer, eds., *New Keynesian Economics* (Cambridge, Mass.: MIT Press, 1991).

gered, the reluctance of each worker to reduce his wage first makes the overall level of wages slow to respond to changes in aggregate demand. In other words, the staggered setting of individual wages makes the overall level of wages sticky.[14]

Recessions as Coordination Failure

Some economists suggest that recessions result from a failure of coordination. In recessions, output is low, workers are unemployed, and factories sit idle. It is possible to imagine allocations of resources in which everyone is better off—for example, the high output and employment of the 1920s is clearly preferable to the low output and employment of the 1930s. If society fails to reach an outcome that is feasible and that everyone prefers, then the members of society have failed to coordinate in some way.

Coordination problems can arise in the setting of wages and prices because those who set them must anticipate the actions of other wage and price setters. Union leaders negotiating wages are concerned about the concessions other unions will win. Firms setting prices are mindful of the prices other firms will charge.

To see how a recession could arise as a failure of coordination, consider the following parable. The economy is made up of two firms. After a fall in the money supply, each firm must decide whether to cut its price. Each firm wants to maximize its profit, but its profit depends not only on its pricing decision, but also the decision made by the other firm.

The choices facing each firm are listed in Figure 11-11, which shows how the profits of the two firms depend on their actions. If neither firm cuts its price, real money balances are low, a recession ensues, and each

Firm 2

		Cut Price	Keep High Price
Firm 1	Cut Price	Firm 1 makes $30 Firm 2 makes $30	Firm 1 makes $ 5 Firm 2 makes $15
	Keep High Price	Firm 1 makes $15 Firm 2 makes $ 5	Firm 1 makes $15 Firm 2 makes $15

Figure 11-11 **Price Setting and Coordination Failure.** This figure shows a hypothetical "game" between two firms, each of which is deciding whether to cut prices after a fall in the money supply. Each firm must choose a strategy without knowing the strategy the other firm will choose. What outcome would you expect?

[14] For more on the effects of staggering, see John Taylor, "Staggered Price Setting in a Macro Model," *American Economic Review* 69 (May 1979): 108–113; and Olivier J. Blanchard, "Price Asynchronization and Price Level Inertia," in R. Dornbusch and Mario Henrique Simonsen, eds., *Inflation, Debt, and Indexation* (Cambridge, Mass.: MIT Press, 1983), 3–24. Both are reprinted in N. Gregory Mankiw and David Romer, eds., *New Keynesian Economics* (Cambridge, Mass.: MIT Press, 1991).

firm makes a profit of only $15. If both firms cut their prices, real money balances are high, a recession is avoided, and each firm makes a profit of $30. Although both firms prefer to avoid a recession, neither can do so by its own actions. If one firm cuts its price while the other does not, a recession follows. The firm making the price cut makes only $5, while the other firm makes $15.

The essence of this parable is that each firm's decision influences the set of outcomes available to the other firm. When one firm cuts its price, it improves the position of the other firm, because the other firm can then avoid the recession. This positive impact of one firm's price cut on the other firm's profit opportunities might arise because of an aggregate-demand externality.

What outcome should we expect in this economy? On the one hand, if each firm expects the other to cut its price, both will cut prices, resulting in the preferred outcome in which each makes $30. On the other hand, if each firm expects the other to maintain its price, both will maintain their prices, resulting in the inferior solution in which each makes $15. Hence, either of these outcomes is possible: economists say that there are *multiple equilibria*.

The inferior outcome, in which each firm makes $15, is an example of a **coordination failure**. If the two firms could coordinate, they would both cut their price and reach the preferred outcome. In the real world, unlike in our parable, coordination is often difficult because the number of firms setting prices is large. *The moral of the story is that prices can be sticky simply because people expect them to be sticky, even though stickiness is in no one's interest.*[15]

CASE STUDY 11-5

Experimental Evidence on Coordination Games

What happens when economic actors, such as the firms in our parable, face a problem of coordination? Do they somehow manage to choose the preferred outcome, knowing that this outcome makes them both better off? Or do they fail to coordinate?

One way to answer this question is by experimentation. In two recent studies, student volunteers were asked to play coordination games, such as the "game" in Figure 11-11. To maintain anonymity, the students played each other through computer terminals. To ensure earnest play, the students were rewarded with small amounts of money depending on how many points they won in the game.

---

[15] For more on coordination failure, see Russell Cooper and Andrew John, "Coordinating Coordination Failures in Keynesian Models," *Quarterly Journal of Economics* 103 (1988): 441–463; reprinted in N. Gregory Mankiw and David Romer, eds., *New Keynesian Economics* (Cambridge, Mass.: MIT Press, 1991); and Laurence Ball and David Romer, "Sticky Prices as Coordination Failure," *American Economic Review*, 81 (June 1991): 539–552.

Consider what strategy you would choose if you were playing the game in Figure 11-11. Remember that you don't know the strategy of the other player: you only know that the other player is facing the same decision you are. Would you cut your price or keep it high? Would your strategy change if the payoffs in the upper left corner were $100 instead of $30? Or if they were only $16?

The experimental evidence shows that economic actors do not always coordinate by choosing the preferred outcome. Whether coordination occurs depends on the payoffs and therefore varies from game to game. But, in some games, coordination failure is the most common outcome.[16]

Hysteresis and the Challenge to the Natural-Rate Hypothesis

Our discussion of economic fluctuations has been based on an assumption called the **natural-rate hypothesis**, summarized in the following statement.

> *Fluctuations in aggregate demand affect output and employment only in the short run. In the long run, the economy returns to the levels of output, employment, and unemployment described by the classical model.*

The natural-rate hypothesis allows macroeconomists to study separately short-run and long-run developments in the economy.

Recently, some economists have challenged the natural-rate hypothesis by suggesting that aggregate demand may affect output and employment even in the long run. They have pointed out a number of mechanisms through which recessions might leave permanent scars on the economy by altering the natural rate of unemployment. **Hysteresis** is the term used to describe the long-lasting influence of history on the natural rate.

A recession can have permanent effects if it changes the people who become unemployed. For instance, workers might lose valuable job skills when unemployed, lowering their ability to find a job even after the recession ends. Alternatively, a long period of unemployment may change an individual's attitude toward work and reduce the desire to

---

[16]Russell Cooper, Douglas V. DeJong, Robert Forsythe, and Thomas W. Ross, "Selection Criteria in Coordination Games: Some Experimental Results," *American Economic Review* 80 (March 1990): 218–233; John B. Van Huyck, Raymond C. Battalio, and Richard O. Beil, "Tacit Coordination Games, Strategic Uncertainty, and Coordination Failure," *American Economic Review* 80 (March 1990): 234–248.

find employment. In either case, the recession permanently inhibits the process of job search and raises the amount of frictional unemployment.

Another way in which a recession can permanently affect the economy is by changing the process that determines wages. Those who become unemployed may lose their influence on the wage-setting process. Unemployed workers may lose their status as union members, for example. More generally, some of the *insiders* in the wage-setting process become *outsiders*. If the smaller group of insiders cares more about high real wages and less about high employment, then the recession may permanently push real wages higher above the equilibrium level and raise the amount of wait unemployment.

Hysteresis remains a controversial topic. It is still not clear whether this phenomenon is significant, or why it might be more pronounced in some countries than in others. Yet the topic is important, because hysteresis implies that recessions are much more costly than the natural-rate hypothesis would suggest. Put another way, hysteresis raises the sacrifice ratio.

CASE STUDY 11-6

Unemployment in the United Kingdom in the 1980s

Doubts about the natural-rate hypothesis and interest in hysteresis arose largely in response to the experience in the 1980s of several European countries, especially the United Kingdom. In the 1970s U.K. unemployment averaged 3.4 percent, whereas in the 1980s it averaged 9.4 percent. This rise in unemployment presented a problem for policymakers and a puzzle for economists.

The rise in unemployment was caused in large part by the policies designed by the Thatcher government to reduce inflation. Soon after the Conservative party won control and Margaret Thatcher became prime minister in 1979, inflation was running as high as 18 percent per year. Contractionary monetary and fiscal policies caused the rate of unemployment to rise from 4.3 percent in 1979 to 11.1 percent in 1984. As the Phillips curve predicts, the rise in unemployment lowered inflation to less than 5 percent in 1984.

The puzzle is that unemployment remained high even after inflation had stabilized. Since this high unemployment did not lower inflation further, it appeared that the natural rate of unemployment had risen. Theories of hysteresis provide reasons that the recession might have raised the natural rate of unemployment.[17]

---

[17] Olivier J. Blanchard and Lawrence H. Summers, "Beyond the Natural Rate Hypothesis," *American Economic Review* 78 (May 1988): 182–187.

11-4 Conclusion

In this chapter we have discussed four models of aggregate supply, the implied tradeoff between inflation and unemployment, and some recent theoretical developments. We saw that the four prominent models of aggregate supply are similar in their implications for the aggregate economy. We also saw that the Phillips curve, according to which inflation depends on expected inflation, cyclical unemployment, and supply shocks, provides a convenient way to express and analyze aggregate supply.

Although this chapter summarizes economists' present understanding of aggregate supply, keep in mind that not all economists agree with the models presented here. In the last section, we discussed briefly some recent developments in the theory of aggregate supply. Some of these developments, such as the theories of hysteresis, challenge traditional views about aggregate supply. If you find it difficult to fit all the pieces together, you are not alone. The study of aggregate supply remains one of the most unsettled—and therefore one of the most exciting—research areas in macroeconomics.

Summary

1. The four theories of aggregate supply—the sticky-wage, worker-misperception, imperfect-information, and sticky-price models—attribute deviations of output and employment from the natural rate to various market imperfections. All the theories imply that output rises above the natural rate when the price level exceeds the expected price level, and that output falls below the natural rate when the price level is less than the expected price level.

2. Economists often express aggregate supply in a relationship called the Phillips curve. The Phillips curve says that inflation depends on expected inflation, the deviation of unemployment from its natural rate, and supply shocks. It implies that policymakers who control aggregate demand face a short-run tradeoff between inflation and unemployment.

3. If expected inflation depends on recently observed inflation, then inflation has inertia, which implies that reducing inflation requires either a beneficial supply shock or a period of high unemployment and reduced output. If people have rational expectations, however, then a credible change in policy might be able to influence expectations directly and, therefore, reduce inflation without causing a recession.

4. Recent developments in the theory of aggregate supply have tried to explain why wages and prices are sticky in the short run. They have also challenged the natural-rate hypothesis by suggesting ways in which recessions can leave permanent scars on the economy.

KEY CONCEPTS

Sticky-wage model

Worker-misperception model

Imperfect-information model

Sticky-price model

Phillips curve

Demand-pull inflation

Cost-push inflation

Sacrifice ratio

Rational expectations

New classical economics

New Keynesian economics

Menu costs

Aggregate-demand externality

Coordination failure

Natural-rate hypothesis

Hysteresis

QUESTIONS FOR REVIEW

1. Explain the four theories of aggregate supply. On what market imperfection does each theory rely? What do the theories have in common?

2. How is the Phillips curve related to aggregate supply?

3. Why is inflation inertial?

4. Explain the differences between demand-pull inflation and cost-push inflation.

5. Under what circumstances might it be possible to reduce inflation without causing a recession?

6. Explain two ways in which a recession might raise the natural rate of unemployment.

PROBLEMS AND APPLICATIONS

1. Consider the following changes in the sticky-wage model.

   a. Suppose that labor contracts specify that the nominal wage be fully indexed for inflation. That is, the nominal wage is to be adjusted to fully compensate for changes in the consumer price index. How does full indexation alter the aggregate supply curve implied by the model?

   b. Suppose now that indexation is only partial. That is, for every increase in the CPI, the nominal wage rises, but by a smaller percentage. How does partial indexation alter the aggregate supply curve implied by the model?

2. In the sticky-price model, describe the aggregate supply curve in the following special cases. How do these cases compare to the short-run aggregate supply curve we discussed in Chapter 8?

   a. No firms have flexible prices ($s = 1$).

   b. The desired price does not depend on aggregate output ($a = 0$).

3. Suppose that an economy has the Phillips curve

$$\pi = \pi_{-1} - 0.5(u - 0.06).$$

   a. What is the natural rate of unemployment?

   b. Graph the short-run and long-run relationship between inflation and unemployment.

   c. How much cyclical unemployment is necessary to reduce inflation by 5 percentage points? Using Okun's law, compute the sacrifice ratio.

d. Inflation is running at 10 percent. The Fed wants to reduce it to 5 percent. Give two scenarios that will achieve that goal.

4. According to the rational-expectations approach, if everyone believes that policymakers are committed to reducing inflation, the cost of reducing inflation—the sacrifice ratio—will be lower than if the public is skeptical about the policymakers' intentions. Why might this be true? How might credibility be achieved?

5. Assume that people have rational expectations and that the economy is described by the sticky-wage or sticky-price model. Explain why each of the following propositions is true:

a. Only unanticipated changes in the money supply affect real GNP. Changes in the money supply that were anticipated when wages and prices were set do not have any real effects.

b. If the Fed chooses the money supply at the same time that people are setting wages and prices, so that everyone has the same information about the state of the economy, then monetary policy cannot be used systematically to stabilize output. Hence, a policy of keeping the money supply constant will have the same real effects as a policy of adjusting the money supply in response to the state of the economy. (This is called the *policy irrelevance proposition.*)

c. If the Fed sets the money supply substantially after people have set wages and prices, so the Fed has collected more information about the state of the economy, then monetary policy can be used systematically to stabilize output.

6. Suppose that an economy has the Phillips curve

$$\pi = \pi_{-1} - 0.5(u - u^n)$$

and that the natural rate of unemployment is given by an average of the past two years' unemployment:

$$u^n = 0.5(u_{-1} + u_{-2}).$$

a. Why might the natural rate of unemployment depend on recent unemployment (as is assumed in the above equation)?

b. Suppose that the Fed follows a policy to reduce permanently the inflation rate by one percentage point. What effect will that policy have on the unemployment rate over time?

c. What is the sacrifice ratio in this economy? Explain.

d. What do these equations imply about the short-run and long-run tradeoff between inflation and unemployment?

Chapter 12

The Macroeconomic
Policy Debate

The Federal Reserve's job is to take away the punch bowl just as the party gets going.

William McChesney Martin

What we need is not a skilled monetary driver of the economic vehicle continuously turning the steering wheel to adjust to the unexpected irregularities of the route, but some means of keeping the monetary passenger who is in the back seat as ballast from occasionally leaning over and giving the steering wheel a jerk that threatens to send the car off the road.

Milton Friedman

Disagreement among economists peaks during discussions of economic policy. The two quotations above—the first from a former chairman of the Federal Reserve, the second from a prominent critic of the Fed— exemplify the diversity of opinion over how macroeconomic policy should be conducted.

Some economists, such as William McChesney Martin, view the economy as inherently unstable. They argue that the economy experiences frequent shocks to aggregate demand and aggregate supply. Unless policymakers use monetary and fiscal policy to stabilize the economy, these shocks will lead to unnecessary and inefficient fluctuations in output, unemployment, and inflation. According to the popular saying, macroeconomic policy should "lean against the wind," stimulating the economy when it is depressed and slowing the economy when it is overheated.

Other economists, such as Milton Friedman, view the economy as naturally stable. They blame bad economic policies for the large and inefficient fluctuations we have sometimes experienced. They argue that economic policy should not try to "fine tune" the economy. Instead, economic policymakers should recognize their limitations and be satisfied if they do no harm.

Over the years, this debate has continued with numerous protagonists putting forth varied arguments for their positions. The fundamental issue is how economic policymakers should use the theory of economic fluctuations developed in the last four chapters. In this chapter we ask two questions that have arisen in this debate. First, should monetary and fiscal policy take an active role in trying to stabilize the economy, or should policy remain passive? Second, should policymakers be free to use their discretion in responding to changing economic conditions, or should they be committed to following a fixed policy rule?

12-1 Should Policy Be Active or Passive?

Policymakers in the federal government view economic stabilization as one of their primary responsibilities. The analysis of macroeconomic policy is a regular duty of the Council of Economic Advisers, the Congressional Budget Office, the Federal Reserve, and other government agencies. When Congress or the president is considering a major change in fiscal policy, or when the Federal Reserve is considering a major change in monetary policy, foremost in the discussion are whether the change will influence inflation and unemployment and whether aggregate demand needs to be stimulated or depressed.

Although the government has long conducted monetary and fiscal policy, the view that it has a responsibility to stabilize the economy is more recent. The Employment Act of 1946 was a key piece of legislation in which the government held itself accountable for macroeconomic performance. The act states that "it is the continuing policy and responsibility of the Federal Government to . . . promote full employment and production." This law was written while the memory of the Great Depression was still fresh. The lawmakers who wrote this act believed, as many economists do, that in the absence of an active government role in the economy, events like the Great Depression could occur regularly.

To many economists the case for active government policy is clear and simple. Recessions are periods of high unemployment, low incomes, and reduced economic well-being. The model of aggregate demand and aggregate supply shows how shocks to the economy cause recessions. It also shows how monetary and fiscal policy can prevent recessions by responding to these shocks. These economists consider it wasteful not to use these policy instruments to stabilize the economy.

Other economists are critical of the government's attempts to stabilize the economy. These critics argue that the government should take a "hands off" approach to macroeconomic policy. At first, this view might seem surprising. If our model shows how to prevent or reduce the severity of recessions, why do these critics want the government to refrain from using monetary and fiscal policy for economic stabilization? To find out, let's consider some of their arguments.

Lags in the Implementation and Effects of Policies

Monetary and fiscal policy influence the economy only after substantial lags, and the lags vary in length. These long and variable lags make attempts to stabilize the economy more difficult.

Economists distinguish between two lags in the conduct of stabilization policy: the inside lag and the outside lag. The **inside lag** is the time between a shock to the economy and the policy action responding to that shock. This lag arises because it takes time for policymakers both to recognize that a shock has occurred and to put appropriate policies into effect. The **outside lag** is the time between a policy action and its influence on the economy. This lag arises because policies do not immediately influence spending, income, and employment.

Fiscal policy has a long inside lag. Changes in spending or taxes normally require the approval of the president and both houses of Congress. The legislative process is often slow and cumbersome. For example, the 1964 tax cut, which was designed to stimulate the economy, was first proposed by President Kennedy in 1962. This delay makes fiscal policy an imprecise tool for stabilizing the economy.

Monetary policy has a long outside lag. Monetary policy works through interest rates, which in turn influence investment. But many firms make investment plans far in advance. Therefore, a change in monetary policy is thought to begin to alter real GNP only about six months after the change is made.

The long and variable lags associated with monetary and fiscal policy certainly make stabilizing the economy more difficult. Advocates of passive policy argue that, because of these lags, attempts to stabilize the economy are all too often destabilizing. Suppose that the economy's condition changes between the time when a policy action begins and the time when the policy affects the economy. In this case, active policy may end up stimulating the economy when it is overheated or depressing the economy when it is cooling off. Advocates of active policy admit that such lags do require policymakers to be cautious. But, they argue, these lags do not necessarily imply that policy should be completely passive, especially in the face of a severe and protracted economic downturn.

Some government stabilization policies, called **automatic stabilizers**, are designed to reduce these lags. Automatic stabilizers are policies that stimulate or depress the economy when necessary without any deliberate policy change. For example, the system of income taxes automatically reduces taxes when the economy goes into a recession, without any change in the tax laws, because individuals and corporations pay less tax when their income falls. Similarly, the system of unemployment insurance automatically raises transfer payments when the economy moves into a recession, because unemployment rises. These two automatic stabilizers are a type of fiscal policy without any inside lag.

CASE STUDY 12-1

Profit Sharing as an Automatic Stabilizer

Economists often propose economic policies to improve the automatic-stabilizing powers of the economy. The economist Martin Weitzman has made one of the most novel suggestions: profit sharing. Today, most labor contracts specify a fixed wage. For example, General Motors might pay assembly-line workers $20 an hour. Weitzman recommends that the workers' total pay should depend on their firm's profits. A profit-sharing contract for General Motors might pay workers $10 for each hour of work, but in addition the workers would divide among themselves a share of the firm's profit.

Weitzman argues that profit sharing would act as an automatic stabilizer. Under the current wage system, a fall in demand for a firm's product causes the firm to lay off workers: it is no longer profitable to employ them at the old wage. The firm will rehire these workers only if the wage falls or if demand recovers. Under a profit-sharing system, Weitzman argues, firms would be more likely to maintain employment after a fall in demand. Under our hypothetical profit-sharing contract for General Motors, for example, each additional hour of work would cost the firm only $10; the rest of the compensation for additional workers would come from the workers' share of profits. Because the marginal cost of labor would be so much lower under profit sharing, a fall in demand would not normally cause a firm to lay off workers.

To provide evidence for the advantages of profit sharing, Weitzman points to Japan. Most Japanese workers receive a high fraction of their compensation in the form of year-end bonuses. Weitzman argues that, because of these bonuses, Japanese workers "think of themselves more as permanently employed partners than as hired hands." And, as Weitzman's theory predicts, employment in Japan is much more stable than in countries without any form of profit sharing.

The *New York Times* dubbed Weitzman's proposal "the best idea since Keynes." Advocates of this proposal want the government to provide tax incentives to encourage firms to adopt profit-sharing plans. Others, however, have expressed skepticism, wondering why, if profit sharing is such a good idea, firms and workers don't sign such contracts without prodding from the government. Whether profit sharing would help stabilize the economy, as Weitzman suggests, remains an open question.[1]

---

[1] Martin L. Weitzman, *The Share Economy* (Cambridge, Mass.: Harvard University Press, 1984).

The Difficult Job of Economic Forecasting

Because economic policy influences the economy after a substantial lag, successful stabilization policy requires the ability to predict accurately future economic conditions. If we cannot predict whether the economy will be in a boom or a recession in six months or a year, we cannot evaluate whether monetary and fiscal policy should now be trying to expand or contract aggregate demand. Unfortunately, economic developments are often unpredictable, at least with our current understanding of the economy.

One way forecasters try to look ahead is with the **index of leading indicators**. This index is composed of eleven data series—such as stock prices, the number of building permits issued, the value of orders for new plants and equipment, and the money supply—that often fluctuate in advance of the economy. Hence, a fall in the leading indicators may signal a coming recession.

Another way forecasters look ahead is with models of the economy. Both government agencies and private forecasting firms maintain large-scale computer models. These models are made up of many equations, each representing a part of the economy. After making assumptions about the path of the exogenous variables, such as monetary policy, fiscal policy, and oil prices, these models yield predictions about unemployment, inflation, and other endogenous variables. One must always keep in mind, however, that the validity of these predictions is only as good as the model and the assumptions about the exogenous variables.

Drawing by Dana Fradon; © 1988 The New Yorker Magazine, Inc.

"It's true, Caesar. Rome is declining, but I expect it to pick up in the next quarter."

CASE STUDY 12-2

Two Episodes in Economic Forecasting

Economic forecasting is a crucial input to private and public decision-making. Business executives rely on forecasts when deciding how much to produce and how much to invest. Government policymakers also rely on them when developing economic policies.

How accurate is economic forecasting? We can answer this question by looking at how well forecasters have done in the past.

The most severe economic downturn in U.S. history, the Great Depression of the 1930s, caught economic forecasters by surprise. Even after the stock market crash of 1929, they remained confident that the economy would not suffer a substantial setback. In late 1931, when the economy was clearly in bad shape, the eminent economist Irving Fisher predicted that it would recover quickly. Subsequent events showed that these forecasts were much too optimistic.[2]

Figure 12-1 shows how economic forecasters did during the recession of 1982, the most severe economic downturn in the United States since the Great Depression. This figure shows the actual unemployment rate and six attempts to predict it for the following five quarters. You can see

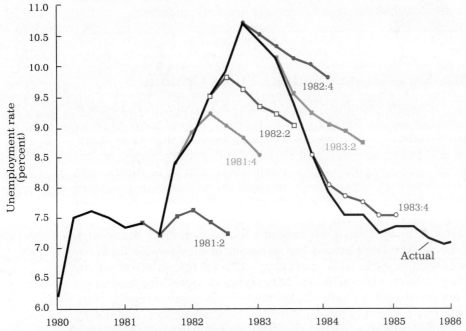

Source: The unemployment rate is from the U.S. Department of Labor. The predicted unemployment rate is the median forecast of about twenty forecasters surveyed by the American Statistical Association and the National Bureau of Economic Research.

Figure 12-1 **Forecasting the Recession of 1982.** The solid black line shows the actual unemployment rate from the first quarter of 1980 to the first quarter of 1986. The symbols show the unemployment rate predicted at six points in time: the second quarter of 1981, the fourth quarter of 1981, the second quarter of 1982, and so on. For each forecast, the symbols mark the current unemployment rate and the forecast for the subsequent five quarters. Notice that the forecasters missed both the rapid rise in the unemployment rate and the subsequent rapid decline.

---

[2] Kathryn M. Dominguez, Ray C. Fair, and Matthew D. Shapiro, "Forecasting the Depression: Harvard versus Yale," *American Economic Review* 78 (September 1988): 595–612. This article shows how badly economic forecasters did during the Great Depression, and it argues that one could not have done any better with the modern forecasting techniques available today.

that the forecasters did well predicting unemployment one quarter ahead. The more distant forecasts, however, were often inaccurate. For example, in the second quarter of 1981, forecasters were predicting little change in the unemployment rate over the next five quarters; yet only two quarters later unemployment began to rise sharply. The rise in unemployment to almost 11 percent in the fourth quarter of 1982 caught the forecasters by surprise. After the depth of the recession became apparent, the forecasters failed to predict how rapid the subsequent decline in unemployment would be.

These two episodes—the Great Depression and the recession of 1982—show that many of the most dramatic economic events are unpredictable. Although economic forecasts are an essential input to private and public decisionmaking, these forecasts are very uncertain.

Ignorance, Expectations, and the Lucas Critique

The prominent macroeconomist Robert Lucas once wrote, "As an advice-giving profession we are in way over our heads." Even many of those who frequently advise policymakers would agree with this assessment. Economics is a young science, and there is still much that we do not know. This ignorance suggests that economists should be cautious when advising policymakers. Economists cannot be completely confident when they make assessments about the effects of alternative economic policies.

Although there are many topics about which economists' knowledge is limited, Lucas has emphasized the question of how people form expectations of the future. Expectations play a crucial role in the economy because they influence the behavior of consumers, investors, and other economic actors. People's expectations depend on many things, including the economic policies being pursued by the government. Estimating the effect of a policy change on the economy therefore requires knowing how people's expectations will respond to the policy change. Lucas has argued that traditional methods of policy evaluation do not adequately take into account this impact of policy on expectations. This criticism of traditional policy evaluation is known as the **Lucas critique**.[3]

We saw one example of the Lucas critique in Chapter 11 when we discussed the cost of reducing inflation. Traditional estimates of the sacrifice ratio—the percentage points of GNP that must be forgone to reduce inflation by one percentage point—rely on the assumption that expected inflation depends on past inflation. Advocates of the rational-expectations approach claim that reducing inflation can be much less

---

[3] Robert E. Lucas, Jr. "Econometric Policy Evaluation: A Critique," *Carnegie Rochester Conference on Public Policy* 1 (Amsterdam: North-Holland Publishing Company, 1976), 19–46; reprinted in Robert E. Lucas, Jr., *Studies in Business Cycle Theory* (Cambridge, Mass.: MIT Press, 1981).

costly because expectations will respond to a credible change in policy. In other words, they claim that traditional estimates of the sacrifice ratio are unreliable because they are subject to the Lucas critique.

The Historical Record

Any judgment about whether government policy should play an active role in the economy must rely largely on how one evaluates the historical record. If the economy has experienced many large shocks to aggregate supply and aggregate demand, and if policy has successfully insulated the economy from these shocks, then the case for active policy would be clear. Conversely, if the economy has experienced few large shocks, and if the fluctuations we have observed can be traced to inept economic policy, then the case for passive policy would be clear. In other words, one's view of stabilization policy should be influenced by whether policy has historically been stabilizing or destabilizing. For this reason, the debate over macroeconomic policy frequently turns into a debate over macroeconomic history.

Yet history does not settle the debate over stabilization policy. Disagreements over history arise because it is not easy to identify the sources of economic fluctuations. The historical record therefore permits more than one interpretation.

The Great Depression is a case in point. Economists' views on macroeconomic policy are often related to their views on the cause of the Depression. Some economists believe that a large contractionary shock to private spending caused the Depression. They assert that policymakers should have responded by stimulating aggregate demand. Other economists believe that the large fall in the money supply caused the Depression. They assert that the Depression would have been avoided if the Fed had been pursuing a passive monetary policy of increasing the money supply at a steady rate. Hence, depending on one's beliefs about its cause, the Great Depression can be viewed as an example of why active monetary and fiscal policy is necessary, or why it is dangerous.

CASE STUDY 12-3

Is the Stabilization of the Economy a Figment of the Data?

Keynes wrote *The General Theory* in the 1930s, and in the wake of the Keynesian revolution, governments around the world began to view economic stabilization as one of their primary responsibilities. Some economists believe that the invention of Keynesian theory has had a profound influence on the behavior of the economy. Comparing data from before World War I and after World War II, they find that real GNP and unemployment have become much more stable. This, some Keynesians claim, is the best argument for active stabilization policy: it has worked.

In a series of provocative and influential papers, Christina Romer has challenged this assessment of the historical record. She argues that the measured reduction in volatility reflects not an improvement in economic policy and performance but rather an improvement in the economic data. The older data are much less accurate than the newer data. Romer claims that the higher volatility of unemployment and real GNP reported for the period before World War I is largely a figment of the data.

Romer uses various techniques to make her case. One way is to try to construct more accurate data for the earlier period. This task is difficult because data sources are not readily available. A second way is to try to construct less accurate data for the recent period—that is, data that are comparable to the older data and thus suffer from the same imperfections. After constructing new "bad" data, Romer finds that the recent period appears much more volatile—indeed, almost as volatile as the early period—suggesting that the volatility of the early period may be largely an artifact of data construction.

Romer's work is an important part of the continuing debate over whether macroeconomic policy has improved the performance of the economy. Although her work remains controversial, most economists now believe that the stabilization of the economy is much smaller than was once thought.[4]

12-2 Should Policy Be Conducted by Rule or by Discretion?

A second topic of frequent debate among economists is whether economic policy should be conducted by rule or by discretion. Policy is conducted by rule if policymakers announce in advance how policy will respond to various economic situations and are committed to following through on this announcement. Policy is conducted by discretion if policymakers are free to size up the economic situation case by case and choose whatever policy seems appropriate at the time.

The debate over rules versus discretion is distinct from the debate over passive versus active policy. Policy can be conducted by a rule and yet be either passive or active. For example, a passive policy rule might specify that the money supply will grow steadily at 3 percent per year. An active policy rule might specify that

$$\text{Money Growth} = 3\% + (\text{Unemployment Rate} - 6\%).$$

[4] Christina D. Romer, "Spurious Volatility in Historical Unemployment Data," *Journal of Political Economy* 94 (February 1986): 1–37; Christina D. Romer, "Is the Stabilization of the Postwar Economy a Figment of the Data?" *American Economic Review* 76 (June 1986): 314–334.

Under this rule, the money supply will grow at 3 percent if the unemployment rate is 6 percent, but for every percentage point the unemployment rate exceeds 6 percent, money growth will increase by an extra percentage point. This rule indicates that the Fed will try to stabilize the economy by increasing money growth when the economy is in a recession.

We begin this section by discussing the reasons that policy might be improved by a commitment to a fixed policy rule. We then examine several possible policy rules.

Distrust of Policymakers and the Political Process

Some economists believe that economic policy is too important to be left to the discretion of policymakers. Although this assessment is more political than economic, it is central to how one evaluates the role of economic policy. If politicians are incompetent or opportunistic, then one may not want to give them the discretion to use the powerful tools of monetary and fiscal policy.

Incompetence in economic policy arises for several reasons. Some economists view the political process as erratic, perhaps because it reflects the shifting power of special interest groups. In addition, macroeconomics is complicated, and politicians often do not have sufficient knowledge of it to make informed judgments. This ignorance allows charlatans to propose appealing but incorrect solutions to complex problems. The political process often cannot weed out the advice of charlatans from that of competent economists.

Opportunism in economic policy arises when the objectives of policymakers conflict with the well-being of the public. Some economists fear that politicians use macroeconomic policy to further their own electoral ends. If citizens vote on the basis of economic conditions prevailing at the time of the election, then politicians have an incentive to pursue policies that will look good during election years. A president might cause a recession soon after coming into office in order to lower inflation and then stimulate the economy as the next election approaches to lower unemployment; this would ensure that both inflation and unemployment are low on election day. This manipulation of the economy for electoral gain, called the **political business cycle**, has been the subject of extensive research by economists and political scientists.[5]

Distrust of the political process leads some economists to advocate placing economic policy outside the realm of politics. Some have proposed constitutional amendments, such as a balanced-budget amendment, that would tie the hands of legislators and insulate the economy from both incompetence and opportunism.

---

[5] William Nordhaus, "The Political Business Cycle," *Review of Economic Studies* 42 (1975): 169–190; Edward Tufte, *Political Control of the Economy* (Princeton, N. J.: Princeton University Press, 1978).

CASE STUDY 12-4

The Economy Under Republican and Democratic Presidents

How does the political party in power affect the economy? Researchers working at the boundary between economics and political science have been studying this question. One intriguing finding is that the two political parties in the United States appear to conduct systematically different macroeconomic policies.

Table 12-1 presents the growth in real GNP in each of the four years of the presidential terms since 1948. Notice that there is usually a recession in the second year of Republican administrations. Five of the seven years in which real GNP fell were second years of Republican administrations. By contrast, the economy is usually booming in the second year of Democratic administrations.

Table 12-1   Real GNP Growth During Democratic and Republican Administrations

Democratic Administrations

President	First	Second	Third	Fourth
Truman	0.0	8.5	10.3	3.9
Kennedy/Johnson	2.6	5.3	4.1	5.3
Johnson	5.8	5.8	2.9	4.1
Carter	4.7	5.3	2.5	−0.2
Average	3.3	6.2	5.0	3.3

Republican Administrations

President	First	Second	Third	Fourth
Eisenhower I	4.0	−1.3	5.6	2.1
Eisenhower II	1.7	−0.8	5.8	2.2
Nixon	2.4	−0.3	2.8	5.0
Nixon/Ford	5.2	−0.5	−1.3	4.9
Reagan I	1.9	−2.5	3.6	6.8
Reagan II	3.4	2.8	3.4	3.9
Average	3.1	−0.4	3.3	4.1

One interpretation of this finding is that the two parties have different preferences regarding inflation and unemployment. That is, rather than viewing politicians as opportunistic, perhaps one should view them as merely partisan. Republicans seem to dislike inflation more than Democrats. Therefore, Republicans pursue contractionary policies soon after coming into office and are willing to endure a recession in order to reduce inflation. Democrats pursue more expansionary policies to reduce unemployment and are willing to endure the higher inflation that results. Examining growth in the money supply shows that monetary policy is, in fact, less inflationary during Republican administrations. Thus, it seems that the two political parties pursue dramatically different policies, and that the political process is one source of economic fluctuations.

Even if one accepts this interpretation of the evidence, it is not clear whether it argues for or against fixed policy rules. On the one hand, a policy rule would insulate the economy from these political shocks. Under a fixed rule, the Fed would be unable to alter monetary policy in response to the changing political climate. The economy might be more stable, and long-run economic performance might be improved. On the other hand, a fixed policy rule would reduce the voice of the electorate in influencing macroeconomic policy.[6]

The Time Inconsistency of Discretionary Policy

If we suppose that policymakers are thoughtful and well-meaning, discretion at first glance appears obviously superior to a fixed policy rule. Discretionary policy is, by its nature, flexible. As long as policymakers are intelligent and benevolent, there might appear to be little reason to deny them flexibility in responding to changing economic conditions.

Yet a case for rules over discretion arises from the problem of **time inconsistency** of policy. In some situations policymakers may want to announce in advance the policy they will follow in order to influence the expectations of private decisionmakers. But later, after the private decisionmakers have acted on the basis of their expectations, these policymakers may be tempted to renege on their announcement. Understanding that policymakers may be inconsistent over time, private decisionmakers are led to distrust policy announcements. In this situation, policymakers may want to consider making a commitment to a fixed policy rule.

Time inconsistency is illustrated most simply in an example involving not economics but politics—specifically, public policy about negotiating with terrorists over the release of hostages. The announced policy of the United States and many other nations is that we will not negotiate over hostages. Such an announcement is intended to deter terrorists: if there is nothing to be gained from kidnapping hostages, rational terrorists won't kidnap any. In other words, the purpose of the announcement is to influence the expectations of terrorists and thereby their behavior.

---

[6] Alberto Alesina, "Macroeconomics and Politics," *NBER Macroeconomics Annual* 3 (1988): 13–52.

But, in fact, unless the policymakers are credibly committed to the policy, the announcement has little effect. Terrorists know that once hostages are taken, the temptation to make some concession to obtain the hostages' release can be overwhelming. The only way to deter rational terrorists is somehow to take away the discretion of policymakers and commit them to a rule of never negotiating. If policymakers were truly unable to make concessions, the incentive for terrorists to take hostages would be largely eliminated.

The same problem arises less dramatically in the conduct of monetary policy. Consider the dilemma of a Federal Reserve that cares about both inflation and unemployment. According to the Phillips curve, the tradeoff between inflation and unemployment depends on expected inflation. The Fed would prefer everyone to expect low inflation so that it will face a favorable tradeoff. To reduce expected inflation, the Fed often announces that low inflation is the paramount goal of monetary policy.

But an announcement of a policy of low inflation is by itself not credible. Once expectations are formed, the Fed has an incentive to renege on its announcement in order to reduce unemployment. Private economic actors understand the incentive to renege and therefore do not believe the announcement in the first place. Just as a president facing a hostage crisis is sorely tempted to negotiate their release, a Federal Reserve with discretion is sorely tempted to inflate in order to reduce unemployment. And just as terrorists discount announced policies of never negotiating, private economic actors discount announced policies of low inflation.

The surprising implication of this analysis is that policymakers can sometimes better achieve their goals by having their discretion taken away from them. In the case of rational terrorists, there will be fewer hostages taken and fewer hostages killed if policymakers are committed to following the seemingly harsh rule of refusing to negotiate for hostages' freedom. In the case of monetary policy, there will be lower inflation without higher unemployment if the Fed is committed to a policy of zero inflation.

The time inconsistency of policy arises in many other contexts. Here are some examples:

- The government may announce that it will not tax income from capital to encourage investment. But after the capital is in place, the government may be tempted to renege on its promise because the taxation of existing capital does not distort economic incentives.

- The government may announce that it will prosecute vigorously all tax evaders to induce compliance with the tax laws. But after the taxes have been evaded, the government may be tempted to call a "tax amnesty," under which tax evaders can avoid jail if they pay back taxes, in order to collect some extra revenue.

- The government may announce that it will give a temporary monopoly to inventors of new products to encourage innovation. But after a product has been invented, the government may be tempted to revoke the patent to make the product more widely available to consumers.

- Your professor may announce that this course will end with an exam to encourage you to work hard. But after you have studied and learned all the material, the professor may be tempted to cancel the exam so that he or she won't have to grade it.

In each of these cases, rational agents understand the incentive for the policymaker to renege, and this expectation affects their behavior. And in each case, the solution is to take away the policymaker's discretionary power with a commitment to a fixed policy rule.[7]

CASE STUDY 12-5

Alexander Hamilton versus Time Inconsistency

Time inconsistency has long been a problem associated with discretionary economic policy. In fact, it was one of the first problems to be addressed by Alexander Hamilton, whom President George Washington appointed the first Secretary of the Treasury in 1789.

The issue at hand was how to deal with the debts that the new nation had accumulated in the process of fighting for its independence. When the debts were incurred, the government promised to honor them when the war was over. But after the war, many Americans advocated defaulting on the debt because repaying the creditors would require taxation, which is always costly and unpopular.

Hamilton opposed this time inconsistency. He knew that the nation would likely need to borrow again sometime in the future. In his *First Report on the Public Credit*, which he presented to Congress in 1790, he wrote

> If the maintenance of public credit, then, be truly so important, the next inquiry which suggests itself is: By what means is it to be effected? The ready answer to which question is, by good faith; by a punctual performance of contracts. States, like individuals, who observe their engagements are respected and trusted, while the reverse is the fate of those who pursue an opposite conduct.

Thus, Hamilton proposed that the nation make a commitment to a policy rule of honoring its debts.

The policy rule that Hamilton originally proposed has continued for over two centuries. Today, when Congress debates spending priorities,

---

[7] The appendix to this chapter examines more analytically the time-inconsistency problem in monetary policy. For more on time inconsistency, see Finn E. Kydland and Edward C. Prescott, "Rules Rather Than Discretion: The Inconsistency of Optimal Plans," *Journal of Political Economy* 85 (June 1977): 473–492; and Robert J. Barro and David Gordon, "A Positive Theory of Monetary Policy in a Natural Rate Model," *Journal of Political Economy* 91 (August 1983): 589–610.

no one proposes defaulting on the public debt, as was common in Hamilton's day. In the case of government debt, everyone now agrees that there are substantial benefits to a fixed policy rule.

Rules for Monetary Policy

Even if one is convinced that policy rules are superior to discretion, the debate over macroeconomic policy is not over. If the Fed were to commit to a rule for monetary policy, what rule should it choose? Let's discuss briefly three policy rules that various economists advocate.

Some economists, called **monetarists**, advocate that the Fed keep the money supply growing at a steady rate. The quotation at the beginning of this chapter from Milton Friedman—the most famous monetarist—exemplifies this view of monetary policy. Monetarists believe that fluctuations in the money supply are responsible for most large fluctuations in the economy. They therefore believe that steady growth in the money supply would prevent most large fluctuations in output and employment.

Although a monetarist policy rule might have prevented many of the economic fluctuations we have experienced historically, most economists believe that it is not the best possible policy rule. Steady growth in the money supply stabilizes aggregate demand only if the velocity of money is stable. But the large fall in velocity in the early 1980s, which we discussed in Chapter 8, shows that velocity is sometimes unstable. Most economists therefore believe that a policy rule needs to allow the money supply to adjust to changes in the economy.

A second policy rule that economists widely advocate is a nominal GNP target. Under this rule, the Fed would announce a planned path for nominal GNP. If nominal GNP rose above the target, the Fed would reduce money growth to dampen aggregate demand. If it fell below the target, the Fed would raise money growth to stimulate aggregate demand. Since a nominal GNP target would allow monetary policy to adjust to changes in the velocity of money, most economists believe it would lead to greater stability in output and prices than a monetarist policy rule.

A third policy rule that is often advocated is a target for the price level. Under this rule, the Fed would announce a planned path for the price level and adjust the money supply when the actual price level deviated from the target. Proponents of this rule usually believe that price stability should be the primary goal of monetary policy.

Notice that all of these rules are expressed in terms of some nominal variable—the money supply, nominal GNP, or the price level. One can also imagine policy rules expressed in terms of real variables. For example, the Fed might try to target the unemployment rate at 5 percent.

The problem with such a policy rule is that no one knows exactly what the natural rate of unemployment is. If the Fed chose a target for the unemployment rate below the natural rate, the result would be accelerating inflation. Conversely, if the Fed chose a target for the unemployment rate above the natural rate, the result would be accelerating deflation. For this reason, economists rarely advocate rules for monetary policy expressed solely in terms of real variables, even though real variables such as unemployment and real GNP are the best measures of economic performance.

Rules for Fiscal Policy

Although most discussion of policy rules centers on monetary policy, economists and politicians also frequently propose rules for fiscal policy. The rule that has received the most attention is the balanced-budget rule. Under a balanced-budget rule, the government would not be allowed to spend more than it receives in tax revenue. Many state governments operate under such a fiscal policy rule, since a balanced budget is required in many state constitutions. A recurring topic of political debate is whether the federal constitution should similarly require a balanced budget for the federal government.

Most economists oppose a strict rule requiring the government to balance its budget. Three considerations lead them to believe that a budget deficit or surplus is sometimes appropriate.

First, a budget deficit or surplus can help stabilize the economy. In essence, a balanced-budget rule would revoke the automatic stabilizing powers of our system of taxes and transfers. When the economy goes into a recession, taxes automatically fall, and transfers automatically rise. While these automatic responses help stabilize the economy, they push the budget into deficit. A strict balanced-budget rule would require that the government raise taxes or reduce spending in a recession, which would further depress aggregate demand.

Second, a budget deficit or surplus can be used to minimize the distortion of incentives caused by the tax system. High tax rates impose a cost on society by discouraging economic activity. The higher the tax rates, the greater the social cost of taxes. The total social cost of taxes is minimized by keeping tax rates relatively stable, rather than making them high in some years and low in others. Economists call this policy *tax smoothing*. To keep tax rates smooth, a deficit is necessary in years of unusually low income (recessions) and unusually high expenditure (wars).

Third, a budget deficit can be used to shift a tax burden from current to future generations. For example, some economists argue that if the current generation fights a war to maintain freedom, future generations benefit. To make the future beneficiaries pay some of the costs, the current generation can finance the war with a budget deficit. The government can retire the debt issued during the war by levying taxes on the next generation.

These considerations lead many economists to reject a balanced-budget rule. At the very least, a rule for fiscal policy needs to take account of the recurring episodes, such as recessions and wars, during which a budget deficit is a reasonable policy response.

CASE STUDY 12-6

The Debt-GNP Ratio Over Two Hundred Years

If we look back over the course of U.S. history, we can see that the indebtedness of the federal government has varied substantially over time. Figure 12-2 shows the ratio of the federal debt to GNP since 1790. The government debt, relative to the size of the economy, varies from close to zero in the 1830s to a maximum of 129 percent of GNP in 1946.

Historically, the primary cause of increases in the government debt is war. The debt-GNP ratio rises sharply during major wars and falls slowly during peacetime. The notable exception is the 1980s, when the federal government ran substantial budget deficits in peacetime.

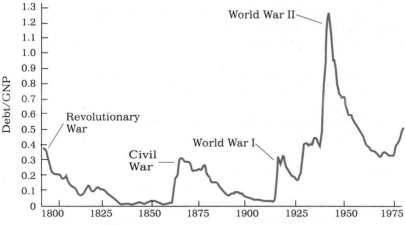

Source: U.S. Department of Treasury, U.S. Department of Commerce, and T.S. Berry, "Production and Population Since 1789," Bostwick Paper No. 6, Richmond, 1988.

Figure 12-2 **The Ratio of Government Debt to GNP Since 1790.** This figure shows that the U.S. government debt, relative to the size of the U.S. economy, rises sharply during wars and declines slowly during peacetime. The exception is the 1980s, during which the debt-GNP ratio rose without a major military conflict.

Many economists think that this historical pattern is the appropriate way to run fiscal policy. For reasons of both tax-smoothing and generational equity, deficit financing of wars appears optimal. The deficits of the 1980s were more controversial, however. Many economists have criticized these budget deficits as imposing an unjustifiable burden on future generations.[8]

12-3   Conclusion: Making Policy in an Uncertain World

In this chapter we have examined whether policy should take an active or passive role in responding to economic fluctuations and whether policy should be conducted by rule or by discretion. You have seen that there are many arguments on both sides of these questions. What is clear is that there is no simple and compelling case for any particular view of macroeconomic policy. In the end, you must weigh the various arguments, both economic and political, and decide for yourself what kind of role the government should play in trying to stabilize the economy.

For better or worse, economists play a key role in the formulation of economic policy. Because of the complexity of the economy, this role is often difficult. Yet it is also inevitable. Economists cannot sit back and wait until our knowledge of the economy has been perfected before giving advice. In the meantime, someone must advise economic policymakers. That job, difficult as it sometimes is, falls to economists.

The role of economists in the policymaking process goes beyond giving advice to policymakers. Even economists not directly involved in making economic policy influence policy indirectly through their research and writing. In the conclusion of *The General Theory*, John Maynard Keynes wrote that

> . . . the ideas of economists and political philosophers, both when they are right and when they are wrong, are more powerful than is commonly understood. Indeed, the world is ruled by little else. Practical men, who believe themselves to be quite exempt from intellectual influences, are usually the slaves of some defunct economist. Madmen in authority, who hear voices in the air, are distilling their frenzy from some academic scribbler of a few years back.

This is as true today as it was when Keynes wrote it in 1935—except now that academic scribbler is often Keynes himself.

---

[8] For a critique of the deficits of the 1980s, see Benjamin M. Friedman, *Day of Reckoning: The Consequences of American Economic Policy Under Reagan and After* (New York: Random House, 1988).

Summary

1. Advocates of active policy view the economy as subject to frequent shocks that will lead to inefficient fluctuations in output and employment unless monetary and fiscal policy respond. Many believe that economic policy has been successful in stabilizing the economy.

2. Advocates of passive policy argue that because monetary and fiscal policies work with long and variable lags, attempts to stabilize the economy are likely to end up being destabilizing. In addition, they believe that our present understanding of the economy is too limited to be useful in formulating successful stabilization policy and that inept policy is a frequent source of economic fluctuations.

3. Advocates of discretionary policy argue that discretion gives more flexibility to policymakers in responding to various unforeseen economic situations.

4. Advocates of policy rules argue that the political process cannot be trusted. They believe that politicians make frequent mistakes in conducting economic policy, and sometimes use economic policy for their own political ends. In addition, advocates of policy rules argue that a commitment to a fixed policy rule is necessary to solve the problem of time inconsistency.

KEY CONCEPTS

Inside and outside lags

Automatic stabilizers

Index of leading indicators

Lucas critique

Political business cycle

Time inconsistency

Monetarists

QUESTIONS FOR REVIEW

1. What are the inside lag and the outside lag? Which has the longer inside lag—monetary or fiscal policy? Which has the longer outside lag? Why?

2. Why would more accurate economic forecasting make it easier for policymakers to stabilize the economy? Describe two ways economists try to forecast developments in the economy.

3. Describe the Lucas critique.

4. Why is macroeconomic history important for macroeconomic policy?

5. What is meant by the "time inconsistency" of economic policy? Why might policymakers be tempted to renege on an announcement they made earlier? In this situation, what is the advantage of a policy rule?

6. List three policy rules that the Fed might follow. Which of these would you advocate? Why?

7. Give three reasons that requiring a balanced budget might be too restrictive a rule for fiscal policy.

PROBLEMS AND APPLICATIONS

1. Suppose that the tradeoff between unemployment and inflation is determined by the Phillips curve:

$$u = u^n - \alpha(\pi - \pi^e),$$

where u denotes the unemployment rate, u^n the natural rate, π the rate of inflation, and π^e the expected rate of inflation. In addition, suppose that the Democratic party always follows a policy of high money growth and the Republican party always follows a policy of low money growth. What "political business cycle" pattern of inflation and unemployment would you predict if

a. every four years one of the parties took control based on a random flip of a coin?

b. the two parties took turns?

2. When cities pass laws limiting the rent landlords can charge on apartments, the laws usually apply to existing buildings and exempt buildings not yet built. Advocates of rent control argue that this exemption ensures that rent control does not discourage the construction of new housing. Evaluate this argument in light of the time-inconsistency problem.

3. The *cyclically adjusted budget deficit* is the budget deficit corrected for the effects of the business cycle. In other words, it is the budget deficit that the government would be running if unemployment were at the natural rate. (It is also called the *full-employment budget deficit.*) Some economists have proposed the rule that the cyclically adjusted budget deficit always be balanced. Compare this proposal to a strict balanced-budget rule. Which is preferable? What problems do you see with the rule requiring a balanced cyclically adjusted budget?

Time Inconsistency and the Tradeoff Between Inflation and Unemployment

In this appendix, we examine more analytically the time inconsistency argument for rules rather than discretion. This material is relegated to an appendix because we will need to use some calculus.

Suppose that the Phillips curve describes the relationship between inflation and unemployment. Letting u denote the unemployment rate, u^n the natural rate of unemployment, π the rate of inflation, and π^e the expected rate of inflation, unemployment is determined by

$$u = u^n - \alpha(\pi - \pi^e).$$

Unemployment is low when inflation exceeds expected inflation and high when inflation falls below expected inflation.

For simplicity, suppose also that the Fed chooses the rate of inflation. Of course, more realistically, the Fed controls inflation only imperfectly through its control of the money supply. But for the purposes of illustration, it is useful to assume that the Fed can control inflation perfectly.

The Fed likes low unemployment and low inflation. Suppose that the Fed's perceived loss from unemployment and inflation can be represented as

$$L(u, \pi) = u + \gamma\pi^2,$$

where the parameter γ represents how much the Fed dislikes inflation relative to unemployment. $L(u, \pi)$ is called the *loss function*. The Fed's objective is to make the loss as small as possible.

Having specified how the economy works and the Fed's objective, let's compare monetary policy made under a fixed rule and under discretion.

First, consider policy under a fixed rule. A rule commits the Fed to a particular level of inflation. As long as private agents understand that the Fed is committed to this rule, the expected level of inflation will be the level the Fed is committed to produce. Since expected inflation equals actual inflation ($\pi^e = \pi$), unemployment will be at its natural rate ($u = u^n$).

What is the optimal rule? Since unemployment is at its natural rate regardless of the level of inflation legislated by the rule, there is no benefit to having any inflation at all. Therefore, the optimal fixed rule requires that the Fed produce zero inflation.

Second, consider discretionary monetary policy. Under discretion, the economy works as follows:

1. private agents form their expectations of inflation π^e;

2. the Fed chooses the actual level of inflation π;

3. based on expected and actual inflation, unemployment is determined.

Under this arrangement, the Fed minimizes its loss $L(u, \pi)$ subject to the constraint that the Phillips curve imposes. When making its decision about the rate of inflation, the Fed takes expected inflation as already determined.

To find what outcome we would obtain under discretionary policy, we must examine what level of inflation the Fed would choose. By substituting the Phillips curve into the Fed's loss function we obtain

$$L(u, \pi) = u^n - \alpha(\pi - \pi^e) + \gamma\pi^2.$$

Notice that the Fed's loss is negatively related to unexpected inflation (the second term) and positively related to actual inflation (the third term). To find the level of inflation that minimizes this loss, differentiate with respect to π to obtain

$$dL/d\pi = -\alpha + 2\gamma\pi.$$

The loss is minimized when this derivative equals zero. This implies that

$$\pi = \alpha/(2\gamma).$$

Whatever level of inflation private agents expected, this is the "optimal" level of inflation for the Fed to choose. Of course, rational private agents understand the objective of the Fed and the constraint that the Phillips curve imposes. They therefore expect that the Fed will choose this level of inflation. Expected inflation equals actual inflation [$\pi^e = \pi = \alpha/(2\gamma)$], and unemployment equals its natural rate ($u = u^n$).

Now compare the outcome under optimal discretion to the outcome under the optimal rule. In both cases, unemployment is at its natural rate. Yet discretionary policy produces more inflation than does policy under the rule. Thus, optimal discretion is worse than the optimal rule, even though the Fed under discretion was attempting to minimize its loss $L(u, \pi)$.

At first it seems bizarre that the Fed can achieve a better outcome by being committed to a fixed rule. Why can't the Fed with discretion mimic the Fed committed to a zero inflation rule? The answer is that the Fed is playing a game against private decisionmakers who have rational expectations. Without being committed to a fixed rule of zero inflation, the Fed is not able to get private agents to expect zero inflation.

Suppose, for example, that the Fed simply announces that it will follow a zero inflation policy. Such an announcement by itself cannot be credible. Once expectations of inflation are formed, the Fed has the incentive to renege on its announcement in order to decrease unemployment. Private agents understand the incentive to renege and therefore do not believe the announcement in the first place.

This theory of monetary policy has an important corollary. Under one circumstance, the Fed with discretion achieves the same outcome as the Fed committed to a fixed rule of zero inflation. If the Fed dislikes inflation much more than it dislikes unemployment (so that γ is very large), inflation under discretion is near zero, since the Fed has little incentive to inflate. This finding provides some guidance to those who have the job of appointing central bankers. An alternative to imposing a fixed rule is to appoint an individual with a fervent distaste for inflation. Perhaps this is why even liberal politicians who are more concerned about unemployment than inflation often appoint conservative central bankers who are more concerned about inflation.

Chapter 13

The Open Economy in the
Short Run

We now extend our analysis of economic fluctuations to include the effects of international trade and finance. As we first discussed in Chapter 7, world markets play a crucial role in most modern economies. In other words, most modern economies are open. Open economies export some of the goods and services they produce, and they import some of the goods and services they consume. Open economies also borrow and lend in world financial markets.

In this chapter we discuss how open economies behave in the short run. Our primary goal is to understand how monetary and fiscal policies influence the aggregate income of an open economy. The model we develop in this chapter, called the **Mundell-Fleming model**, is an open-economy version of the *IS-LM* model. Both models assume that the price level is fixed and then show what causes fluctuations in aggregate income. Both also stress the interaction between the goods market and the money market. The key difference is that the *IS-LM* model assumes a closed economy, whereas the Mundell-Fleming model assumes a small open economy. The Mundell-Fleming model introduces the international considerations we discussed in Chapter 7 into the short-run model of income determination we developed in Chapters 9 and 10.

One of the lessons of the Mundell-Fleming model is that the behavior of an economy depends on the exchange-rate system it has adopted. We begin by assuming a floating exchange rate. That is, we assume that the central bank allows the exchange rate to adjust to changing economic conditions. We then examine how the economy operates under a fixed exchange rate, and we discuss the debate over whether exchange rates should be floating or fixed.

13-1   The Mundell-Fleming Model

In this section we build the Mundell-Fleming model.[1] In the following sections we use the model to evaluate the impact of various policies under floating and fixed exchange rates.

Components of the Model

The Mundell-Fleming model is made up of components that should be familiar to you from previous chapters. We begin by simply stating the three equations that make up the model. They are

$$Y = C(Y - T) + I(r) + G + NX(e) \qquad IS$$
$$M/P = L(r, Y) \qquad LM$$
$$r = r^*.$$

Before putting these equations together to make a short-run model of a small open economy, let's review each of them in turn.

The first equation describes the goods market. It states that aggregate income Y is the sum of consumption C, investment I, government purchases G, and net exports NX. Consumption depends positively on disposable income $Y - T$. Investment depends negatively on the interest rate r. Net exports depend negatively on the exchange rate e.

Recall that we define the exchange rate e as the amount of foreign currency per unit of domestic currency—for example, e might be 100 yen per dollar. For the purposes of the Mundell-Fleming model, we do not need to distinguish between the real and nominal exchange rates. In Chapter 7 we related net exports to the real exchange rate ϵ, which equals eP/P^*, where P is the domestic price level and P^* is the foreign price level. Because the Mundell-Fleming model assumes that prices are fixed, changes in the real exchange rate are proportional to changes in the nominal exchange rate. That is, when the nominal exchange rate rises, foreign goods become less expensive compared to domestic goods, which depresses exports and stimulates imports.

The second equation describes the money market. It states that the supply of real money balances, M/P, equals the demand, $L(r, Y)$. The demand for real balances depends negatively on the interest rate and positively on income. The money supply M is an exogenous variable determined by the Federal Reserve. Like the *IS-LM* model, the Mundell-Fleming model also takes the price level P as an exogenous variable.

The third equation states that the world interest rate r^* determines the interest rate in this economy. That is, the economy is sufficiently

---

[1] The Mundell-Fleming model was developed in the early 1960s. Mundell's contributions are collected in Robert A. Mundell, *International Economics* (New York: Macmillan, 1968). For Fleming's contribution, see J. Marcus Fleming, "Domestic Financial Policies under Fixed and under Floating Exchange Rates," *IMF Staff Papers* 9 (November 1962): 369–379.

small that it can borrow or lend as much as it wants in world financial markets without affecting the world interest rate.

These three equations fully describe the Mundell-Fleming model. Our job is to examine the implications of these equations for short-run fluctuations in a small open economy. If you do not understand the equations, you should review Chapters 7 and 9 before continuing.

The Mundell-Fleming model is most easily analyzed graphically. Yet because it has three endogenous variables—Y, r, and e—there is not a unique way to present the model in a two-dimensional graph. We therefore offer two alternative graphical presentations. In each case, we hold one of the variables constant and examine the relationship between the other two. Keep in mind that both graphs express the same model; they do not present different theories, only alternative ways to view the same theory.

The Model on a $Y-r$ Graph

One way to depict the Mundell-Fleming model is to use a graph in which income Y is on the horizontal axis and the interest rate r is on the vertical axis. This presentation is comparable to our analysis of the closed economy in the *IS-LM* model. As Figure 13-1 shows, the *IS* curve slopes downward, and the *LM* curve slopes upward. New in this graph is the horizontal line representing the world interest rate.

Two features of this graph deserve special attention. First, because the exchange rate influences the demand for goods, the *IS* curve is drawn for a given value of the exchange rate (say, 100 yen per dollar). An increase in the exchange rate (say, to 200 yen per dollar) makes U.S. goods more expensive relative to foreign goods, which reduces net exports. Hence, an increase in the exchange rate shifts the *IS* curve to the left. To remind us that the position of the *IS* curve depends on the exchange rate, the *IS* curve is labeled *IS(e)*.

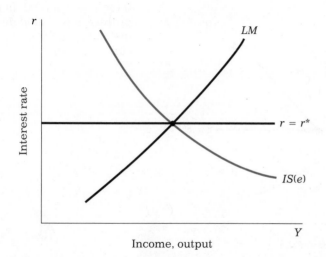

Figure 13-1 **The Mundell-Fleming Model on a $Y-r$ Graph.** This presentation of the Mundell-Fleming model is similar to that of the closed-economy *IS-LM* model. In the small open economy, however, the position of the *IS* curve depends on the exchange rate. The exchange rate adjusts to ensure that the *IS* curve crosses the point where the *LM* curve intersects the horizontal line that represents the world interest rate r^*.

Second, the three curves in Figure 13-1 all intersect at the same point. This might seem an unlikely coincidence. But, in fact, the exchange rate adjusts to ensure that all three curves pass through the same point.

To see why all three curves must intersect at a single point, let's imagine a hypothetical situation in which they did not, as in Figure 13-2A. Here the domestic interest rate—the point where the *IS* and *LM* curves intersect—would be higher than the world interest rate. Since the United States would be offering a higher rate of return than is available in world financial markets, investors from around the world would

A. The Exchange Rate Is Too Low

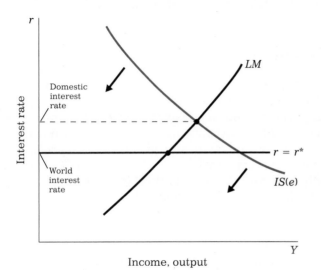

Income, output

B. The Exchange Rate Is Too High

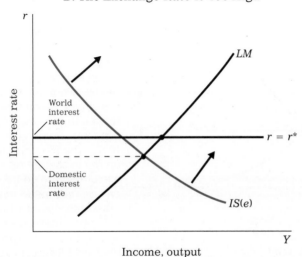

Income, output

Figure 13-2 **The Mundell-Fleming Model With the Exchange Rate at the Wrong Level.** This figure shows why the *IS* curve must intersect at the point at which the *LM* curve and the $r = r^*$ line cross. In panel A, because the three curves do not cross at the same point, the domestic interest rate would exceed the world interest rate. Foreign investors would try to invest their assets in the United States. In the process, they would bid up the dollar and shift the *IS* curve downward. In panel B, the domestic interest rate would be less than the world interest rate. U.S. investors would try to invest their assets abroad. In the process, they would depress the dollar and shift the *IS* curve upward.

want to buy U.S. assets. But first these foreign investors must convert their funds into dollars. In the process, they would bid up the value of the dollar. The rise in the exchange rate would shift the *IS* curve downward until the domestic interest rate equaled the world interest rate.

Alternatively, imagine that the *IS* and *LM* curves intersect at a point where the domestic interest rate is below the world interest rate, as in Figure 13-2B. Since the United States would be offering a lower rate of return, investors in the United States would want to invest in world financial markets. But, to be able to buy foreign assets, they must convert their dollars into foreign currency. In the process of doing so, they would depress the value of the dollar. The fall in the exchange rate would shift the *IS* curve upward until the domestic interest rate equaled the world interest rate.

To sum up, the equilibrium in this graph is found where the *LM* curve crosses the line representing the world interest rate. The exchange rate then adjusts and shifts the *IS* curve so that the *IS* curve crosses this point as well.

The Model on a $Y-e$ Graph

The second way to depict the Mundell-Fleming model is to use a graph in which income is on the horizontal axis and the exchange rate is on the vertical axis, as in Figure 13-3. In this case, the graph is drawn holding the interest rate constant at the world interest rate. Specifically, the two equations in this figure are

$$Y = C(Y - T) + I(r^*) + G + NX(e) \qquad\qquad IS^*$$
$$M/P = L(r^*, Y). \qquad\qquad LM^*$$

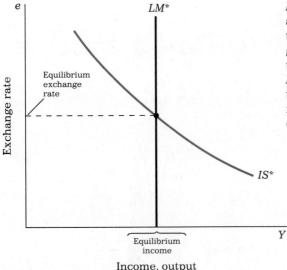

Figure 13-3 **The Mundell-Fleming Model on a $Y-e$ Graph.** This alternative presentation of the Mundell-Fleming model plots the goods-market equilibrium condition *IS** and the money-market equilibrium condition *LM** holding the interest rate constant at the world interest rate. It shows the equilibrium level of income and the equilibrium exchange rate.

We label these curves *IS** and *LM** to remind us that we are holding the interest rate constant at the world interest rate *r**. The equilibrium of the economy is found where the *IS** curve and the *LM** curve intersect. This intersection determines the exchange rate and level of income.

The *LM** curve is vertical because the exchange rate does not enter into the *LM** equation. Given the world interest rate, the *LM** equation determines aggregate income, regardless of the exchange rate. Figure 13-4 shows how the *LM** curve arises from the world interest rate and the *LM* curve, which relates the interest rate and income.

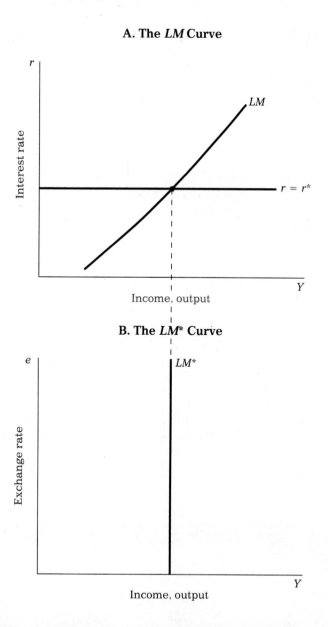

A. The *LM* Curve

r

Interest rate

LM

$r = r^*$

Y

Income, output

B. The *LM Curve**

e

*LM**

Exchange rate

Y

Income, output

Figure 13-4 **The *LM** Curve.** Panel A shows the standard *LM* curve together with a horizontal line representing the world interest rate *r**. These determine the level of income, regardless of the exchange rate. Therefore, as panel B shows, the *LM** curve is vertical.

A. The Net Exports Schedule

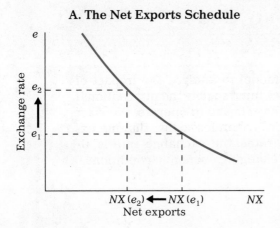

B. The Keynesian Cross

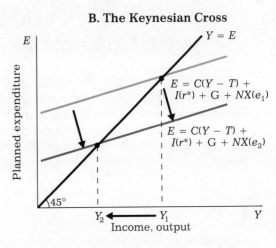

C. The *IS** Curve

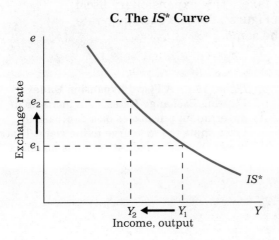

Figure 13-5   **The *IS** Curve.**   The *IS** curve is derived from the net exports schedule and the Keynesian cross. Panel A shows the net exports schedule: an increase in the exchange rate from e_1 to e_2 lowers net exports from $NX(e_1)$ to $NX(e_2)$. Panel B shows the Keynesian cross: a decrease in net exports from $NX(e_1)$ to $NX(e_2)$ reduces income from Y_1 to Y_2. Panel C shows the *IS** curve summarizing this relationship between the exchange rate and income: the higher the exchange rate, the lower the level of income.

The *IS** curve slopes downward because a higher exchange rate lowers net exports and thus lowers aggregate income. To show how this works, Figure 13-5 combines the net exports schedule and the Keynesian cross diagram to derive the *IS** curve. An increase in the exchange rate from e_1 to e_2 lowers net exports from $NX(e_1)$ to $NX(e_2)$. The reduction in net exports reduces planned expenditure and thus lowers income. Just as the standard *IS* curve combines the investment schedule and the Keynesian cross, the *IS** curve combines the net exports schedule and the Keynesian cross.

Throughout the rest of the chapter, we use the $Y - e$ diagram in our analysis, because it shows directly how the exchange rate responds to changes in policy. In all cases, however, we could use the $Y - r$ diagram and reach the same conclusions.

13-2   The Small Open Economy Under Floating Exchange Rates

Before using the Mundell-Fleming model to analyze the impact of economic policies in an open economy, we must specify the international monetary system in which the country has chosen to operate. We start with the system relevant for most major economies today: **floating exchange rates**. Under floating exchange rates, the exchange rate is allowed to fluctuate freely in response to changing economic conditions.

Fiscal Policy

Suppose that the government stimulates domestic spending by increasing government purchases or by cutting taxes. This expansionary fiscal policy shifts the IS^* curve outward, as in Figure 13-6. The exchange rate rises, and the level of income remains the same.

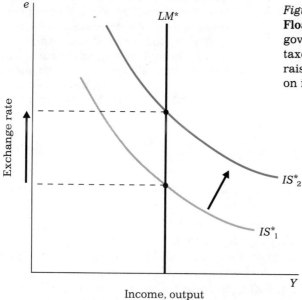

Figure 13-6   A Fiscal Expansion Under Floating Exchange Rates.   An increase in government purchases or a decrease in taxes shifts the IS^* curve to the right. This raises the exchange rate but has no effect on income.

This conclusion about fiscal policy stands in stark contrast to the conclusion implied by the closed-economy *IS-LM* model. In a closed economy, a fiscal expansion raises the interest rate and raises income. In a small open economy with a floating exchange rate, a fiscal expansion leaves income at the same level. The reason for the difference is that, in an open economy, the upward pressure on the domestic interest rate attracts foreign capital. The capital inflow from abroad raises the demand for dollars in the market for foreign exchange, which increases the exchange rate and reduces net exports. The fall in net exports offsets the expansion in the domestic demand for goods and services, so equilibrium income remains the same.

Monetary Policy

Suppose now that the central bank increases the money supply. Because the price level is assumed to be fixed, the increase in the money supply means an increase in real balances. The increase in real balances shifts the LM^* curve to the right, as in Figure 13-7. Hence, an increase in the money supply raises income and lowers the exchange rate.

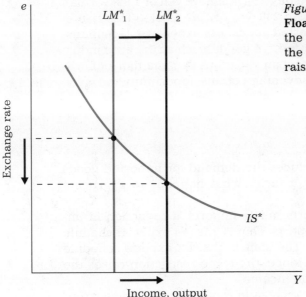

Figure 13-7 **A Monetary Expansion Under Floating Exchange Rates.** An increase in the money supply shifts the LM^* curve to the right, lowering the exchange rate and raising income.

Although monetary policy influences income in an open economy, as it does in a closed economy, the monetary transmission mechanism is different. Recall that in a closed economy, an increase in the money supply lowers the interest rate and thus raises the level of investment. In a small open economy, the interest rate is fixed by the world interest rate. When an increase in the money supply puts downward pressure on the domestic interest rate, it encourages domestic capital to flow to other countries, where it can earn a higher return. This capital outflow raises the supply of dollars in the market for foreign exchange, which lowers the exchange rate and raises net exports. Hence, in a small open economy, monetary policy influences income by altering the exchange rate rather than the interest rate.

CASE STUDY 13-1

The Rise in the Dollar, 1979–1982

In the early 1980s the United States experienced an unusual combination of tight monetary policy and loose fiscal policy. The chief goal of Fed Chairman Paul Volcker was to reduce the high rate of inflation inherited from the 1970s. At the same time, President Ronald Reagan wanted to fulfill his electoral promise to cut taxes and raise defense spending.

The Mundell-Fleming model predicts that both policies would raise the value of the dollar. And, indeed, the dollar rose relative to all major currencies. In 1979 the dollar could buy 218 Japanese yen or 1.83 German marks. In 1982 the dollar was worth 248 yen or 2.42 marks. This rise in the value of the dollar made imported goods less expensive. U.S. industries that compete against similar foreign goods, such as the auto industry, became less competitive. European vacations became more affordable, and many Americans took advantage of this opportunity to travel.

Trade Policy

Suppose that the government reduces the demand for imported goods by imposing an import quota or a tariff. What happens to aggregate income and the exchange rate?

Since net exports equal exports minus imports, a reduction in imports means an increase in net exports. That is, the net exports schedule shifts outward, as in Figure 13-8. The shift in the net exports schedule shifts the IS^* curve to the right. Hence, the trade restriction raises the exchange rate and has no effect on income.

A stated goal of policies to restrict trade is often to alter the current account NX. Yet, as we first saw in Chapter 7, such policies do not necessarily have that effect. The same conclusion holds in the Mundell-Fleming model under floating exchange rates. Recall that

$$NX(e) = Y - C(Y - T) - I(r) - G.$$

A trade restriction does not affect income, consumption, investment, or government purchases. It therefore does not affect the current account. Although the shift in the net exports schedule tends to raise NX, the increase in the exchange rate reduces NX by the same amount.

A. The Shift in the Net Exports Schedule

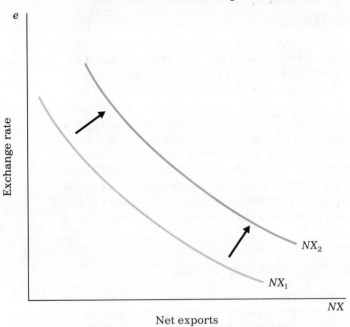

B. The Change in the Economy's Equilibrium

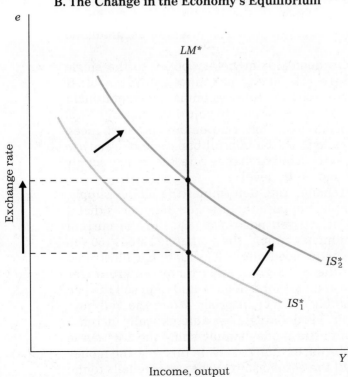

Figure 13-8   **A Trade Restriction Under Floating Exchange Rates.**   A tariff or an import quota shifts the net exports schedule outward. This causes the *IS** curve to shift outward, raising the exchange rate and leaving income the same.

13-3 The Small Open Economy Under Fixed Exchange Rates

We now turn to the second type of exchange-rate system: **fixed exchange rates**. In the 1950s and 1960s, most of the world's major economies, including the United States, operated within the Bretton Woods system—an international monetary system under which most governments agreed to fix exchange rates. The world abandoned this system in the early 1970s, beginning a period in which exchange rates were allowed to float freely. Recently, many European countries have reinstated a system of fixed exchange rates among themselves, and some economists have advocated a return to a worldwide system of fixed exchange rates. In this section we discuss how such a system works, and we examine the impact of economic policies on an economy with a fixed exchange rate.

How a Fixed-Exchange-Rate System Works

Under a system of fixed exchange rates, a central bank stands ready to buy or sell the domestic currency for foreign currencies at a predetermined price. Suppose, for example, that the Fed announced that it was going to fix the exchange rate at 100 yen per dollar. It would then stand ready to give $1.00 in exchange for 100 yen or to give 100 yen in exchange for $1.00. To carry out this policy, the Fed would need a reserve of dollars (which it can print) and a reserve of yen (which it must have accumulated in past transactions).

Fixing the exchange rate dedicates monetary policy to the single goal of keeping the exchange rate at the announced level. In other words, the essence of a fixed-exchange-rate system is the commitment of the central bank to allow the money supply to adjust to whatever level will ensure that the equilibrium exchange rate equals the announced exchange rate. Moreover, as long as the central bank stands ready to buy or sell foreign currency at the fixed exchange rate, the money supply adjusts automatically to the necessary level.

To see how fixing the exchange rate determines the money supply, consider the following example. Suppose that the Fed announces that it will fix the exchange rate at 100 yen per dollar. But, in the current equilibrium with the current money supply, the exchange rate is 150 yen per dollar, 50 yen above the announced rate. This situation is illustrated in Figure 13-9A. Notice that there is a profit opportunity: an arbitrager could buy 300 yen in the marketplace for 2 dollars, and then sell the yen to the Fed for 3 dollars, making 1 dollar in profit. When the Fed buys these yen from the arbitrager, the dollars it pays automatically increase the money supply. The rise in the money supply shifts the LM^* curve outward, lowering the equilibrium exchange rate. In this way, the money supply continues to rise until the equilibrium exchange rate falls to the announced level.

Conversely, suppose when the Fed announces that it will fix the exchange rate at 100 yen per dollar, the equilibrium is 50 yen per dollar. Figure 13-9B shows the situation. In this case, an arbitrager could make a profit by buying 100 yen from the Fed for 1 dollar and then selling the yen in the marketplace for 2 dollars. When the Fed sells these yen, the dollar it receives automatically reduces the money supply. The fall in the money supply shifts the *LM** curve inward, raising the equilibrium exchange rate. The money supply continues to fall until the equilibrium exchange rate rises to the announced level.

A. The Equilibrium Exchange Rate Is Greater Than the Fixed Exchange Rate

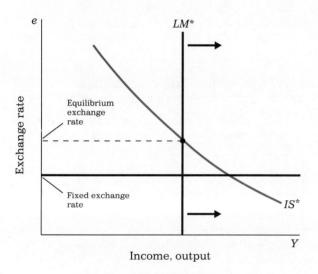

Income, output

B. The Equilibrium Exchange Rate Is Less Than the Fixed Exchange Rate

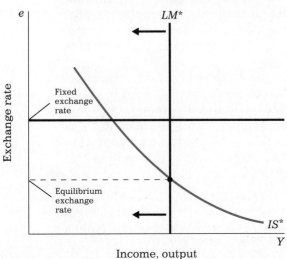

Income, output

Figure 13-9 **How a Fixed Exchange Rate Governs the Money Supply.** In panel A, the equilibrium exchange rate exceeds the fixed level. Arbitragers will buy foreign currency in foreign exchange markets and sell it to the Fed for a profit. This process automatically increases the money supply, shifting the *LM** curve and lowering the exchange rate. In panel B, the equilibrium exchange rate is below the fixed level. Arbitragers will buy dollars in foreign exchange markets and use them to buy foreign exchange from the Fed. This process automatically reduces the money supply, shifting the *LM** curve and raising the exchange rate.

It is important to understand that this exchange-rate system fixes the nominal exchange rate. Whether it also fixes the real exchange rate depends on the time horizon under consideration. If prices are flexible, as they are in the long run, then the real exchange rate can change even while the nominal exchange rate is fixed. Therefore, in the long run described in Chapter 7, a policy to fix the nominal exchange rate would not influence any real variable, including the real exchange rate. A fixed nominal exchange rate would influence only the money supply and the price level. Yet in the short run described by the Mundell-Fleming model, prices are fixed, so that a fixed nominal exchange rate implies a fixed real exchange rate as well.

CASE STUDY 13-2

The International Gold Standard

During most of the nineteenth century, the world's major economies operated under a gold standard. Each country maintained a reserve of gold and agreed to exchange one unit of its currency for a specified amount of gold. Through the gold standard, the world economies maintained a system of fixed exchange rates.

To see how an international gold standard fixes exchange rates, suppose that the U.S. Treasury stands ready to buy or sell an ounce of gold for $100, and the Bank of England stands ready to buy or sell an ounce of gold for 100 pounds. Together these policies fix the rate of exchange between dollars and pounds: one dollar must trade for one pound. Otherwise, the law of one price would be violated, and it would be profitable to buy gold in one country and sell it in the other.

Suppose, for example, that the exchange rate were two pounds per dollar. In this case, an arbitrager could buy 200 pounds for $100, use the pounds to buy 2 ounces of gold from the Bank of England, bring the gold to the United States, and sell it for $200 to the Treasury—making a $100 profit. Moreover, by bringing the gold to the United States from England, the arbitrager would increase the money supply in the United States and decrease the money supply in England.

Thus, during the era of the gold standard, the international transport of gold by arbitragers ensured that the money supply adjusted to maintain the system of fixed exchange rates. It did not completely fix exchange rates, however, because shipping gold across the Atlantic was costly. Yet the international gold standard did keep the exchange rate within a range dictated by transportation costs and thus prevented large and persistent movements in exchange rates.[2]

---

[2] For more on how the gold standard worked, see the essays in Barry Eichengreen, ed., *The Gold Standard in Theory and History* (New York: Methuen, 1985).

Fiscal Policy

Let's now examine how economic policies affect a small open economy with a fixed exchange rate. Suppose that the government stimulates domestic spending by increasing government purchases or by cutting taxes. This policy shifts the *IS** curve outward, as in Figure 13-10, putting upward pressure on the exchange rate. But since the money supply

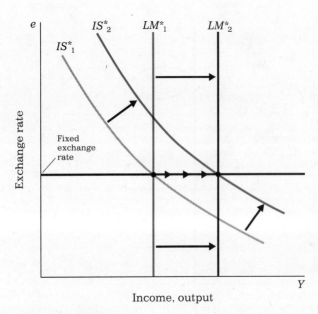

Figure 13-10 **A Fiscal Expansion Under Fixed Exchange Rates.** A fiscal expansion shifts the *IS** curve to the right. To maintain the fixed exchange rate, the Fed must increase the money supply and shift the *LM** curve to the right as well. Hence, in contrast to the case of floating exchange rates, under fixed exchange rates a fiscal expansion raises income.

adjusts to keep the exchange rate unchanged, the money supply must rise, shifting the *LM** curve outward. In contrast to the situation under floating exchange rates, a fiscal expansion under fixed exchange rates raises aggregate income. The rise in income occurs because a fiscal expansion under a fixed-exchange-rate system causes an automatic monetary expansion.

Monetary Policy

What happens if the Fed tries to increase the money supply—for example, by buying bonds from the public? The initial impact of this policy is to shift the *LM** curve outward, lowering the exchange rate, as in Figure 13-11. But, since the Fed is committed to buying and selling foreign currency at a fixed exchange rate, arbitragers quickly sell dollars to the Fed, causing the money supply and the *LM** curve to return to their initial positions. Hence, monetary policy as usually conducted is impossible under a fixed exchange rate. By agreeing to fix the exchange rate, the Fed gives up its control over the money supply.

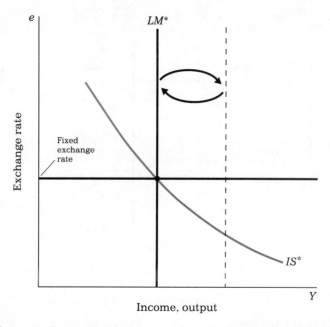

Figure 13-11   **A Monetary Expansion Under Fixed Exchange Rates.**   If the Fed tries to increase the money supply—for example, by buying bonds from the public—it will put downward pressure on the exchange rate.

To maintain the fixed exchange rate, the money supply and *LM** curve must return to their initial positions. Hence, under fixed exchange rates, normal monetary policy is impossible.

A country with a fixed exchange rate can, however, conduct a type of monetary policy: it can decide to change the level at which the exchange rate is fixed. A reduction in the value of the currency is called a **devaluation**, and an increase in its value is called a **revaluation**. In the Mundell-Fleming model, a devaluation shifts the *LM** curve outward; it acts like an increase in the money supply under a floating exchange rate. A devaluation thus expands net exports and raises aggregate income. Conversely, a revaluation shifts the *LM** curve inward, reduces net exports, and lowers aggregate income.

Trade Policy

Suppose that the government reduces imports by imposing an import quota or a tariff. This policy shifts the net exports schedule outward and thus shifts the *IS** curve outward, as in Figure 13-12. The shift in the *IS** curve tends to raise the exchange rate. To keep the exchange rate at the fixed level, the money supply must rise, shifting the *LM** curve outward.

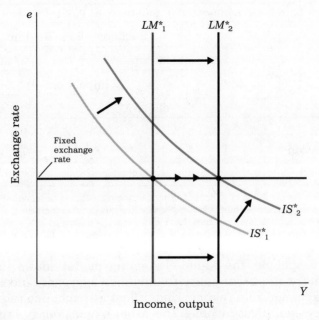

Figure 13-12 **A Trade Restriction Under Fixed Exchange Rates.**   A tariff or an import quota shifts the *IS** curve outward. This induces an increase in the money supply to maintain the fixed exchange rate. Hence, aggregate income increases.

The result of a trade restriction under a fixed exchange rate is very different from that under a floating exchange rate. Under a fixed exchange rate, a trade restriction raises aggregate income. Moreover, the trade restriction also raises the current account *NX*. Because the exchange rate is fixed, an outward shift in the net exports schedule implies an increase in net exports. To see this result another way, recall that

$$NX = S - I.$$

The expansion in income leads to an increase in saving, which implies an increase in net exports.

Summary of the Mundell-Fleming Model

The most important single lesson of the Mundell-Fleming model is that the effect of almost any economic policy on a small open economy depends on whether the exchange rate is floating or fixed. Table 13-1 summarizes our analysis of the effects of monetary, fiscal, and trade policies on income and the exchange rate. It also shows the effect of these policies on the current account. What is most striking is that all of the results are different under floating and fixed exchange rates.

Table 13-1   The Mundell-Fleming Model: Summary of Policy Effects

	Exchange-Rate Regime					
	Floating			Fixed		
	Impact on:					
Policy	Y	e	NX	Y	e	NX
Fiscal Expansion	0	↑	↓	↑	0	0
Monetary Expansion	↑	↓	↑	0	0	0
Import Restriction	0	↑	0	↑	0	↑

NOTE: This table shows the direction of impact of various economic policies on income Y, the exchange rate e, and the current account NX. A "↑" indicates the variable increases; a "↓" indicates it decreases; a "0" indicates no effect. Remember that the exchange rate is defined as the amount of foreign currency per unit of domestic currency (for example, 100 yen/dollar).

To be more specific, the Mundell-Fleming model shows that the power of monetary and fiscal policy to influence aggregate income depends on the exchange-rate regime. Under floating exchange rates, only monetary policy can affect income. The usual expansionary impact of fiscal policy is offset by a rise in the value of the currency. Under fixed exchange rates, only fiscal policy can affect income. The normal potency of monetary policy on income is lost because the money supply is dedicated to maintaining the exchange rate at the announced level.

13-4 Should Exchange Rates Be Floating or Fixed?

Having analyzed how an economy works under floating and fixed exchange rates, we turn to the question of which exchange-rate regime is preferable. The international monetary system is often a topic of heated debate among international economists and policymakers. Historically, most economists have favored a system of floating exchange rates. Yet, in recent years, some have advocated a return to fixed exchange rates.

The primary argument in favor of a floating exchange rate is that it allows monetary policy to be used for other purposes. Under fixed rates, monetary policy is subjugated to the single goal of maintaining the exchange rate at its announced level. Yet the exchange rate is only one macroeconomic variable among many that monetary policy can influence and about which policymakers are concerned. A system of floating exchange rates leaves monetary policymakers free to pursue other goals, such as stabilizing employment or prices.

Advocates of fixed exchange rates argue that exchange-rate uncertainty makes international trade more difficult. After the world abandoned the Bretton Woods system of fixed exchange rates in the early 1970s, both real and nominal exchange rates became more volatile than anyone had expected. Some economists attribute this volatility to irrational and destabilizing speculation by international investors. Business executives often claim that this volatility is harmful because it increases the uncertainty associated with international business transactions. Yet, despite this exchange-rate volatility, the amount of world trade has continued to increase under floating exchange rates.

Advocates of fixed exchange rates sometimes argue that a commitment to a fixed exchange rate is one way to discipline the monetary authority and prevent excessive growth in the money supply. Yet there are many other policy rules to which the central bank could be committed. A policy of fixing the exchange rate should be compared to the policy rules we discussed in Chapter 11, such as nominal GNP targeting. Fixing the exchange rate has the advantage of being simpler to implement than some other policy rules, since the money supply adjusts automatically, but this policy probably leads to greater instability in income and employment.

In the end, the choice between floating and fixed rates is not as stark as it may seem at first. During periods of fixed exchange rates, countries can change the value of their currency if maintaining the exchange rate conflicts too severely with other goals. During periods of floating exchange rates, countries often use formal or informal targets for the exchange rate when deciding whether to expand or contract the money supply. Hence, we rarely observe exchange rates that are completely fixed or completely floating. Instead, under both systems, stability of the exchange rate is usually one among many of the central bank's objectives.[3]

---

[3] For more on the debate over fixed versus flexible exchange rates, see Chapter 19 of Paul R. Krugman and Maurice Obstfeld, *International Economics: Theory and Policy* (Glenview, Ill.: Scott, Foresman and Company, 1988).

CASE STUDY 13-3

The European Monetary System

In March 1979, eight European countries—Belgium, Denmark, France, Germany, Ireland, Italy, Luxembourg, and the Netherlands—formed the *European Monetary System (EMS)*. The goal of the EMS is to limit fluctuations in the exchange rates among the currencies of the member countries. Relative to the currencies of countries not in the EMS, such as the U.S. dollar, these European currencies fluctuate together. An organization of countries like the EMS is called an **exchange-rate union**.

The EMS does not completely fix exchange rates. The central banks of the member countries can allow their exchange rates to fluctuate within narrow bands around specific targets. In addition, when maintaining the targets appears to be causing other economic problems, they can be changed. These changes in the targets typically occur every few years.

Proponents of the EMS argue that because the system reduces exchange-rate volatility, it is an important step toward making Europe more integrated economically. The EMS therefore complements the reduction in trade barriers scheduled for Europe in 1992. At the same time, the countries in the EMS lose some of their ability to conduct independent monetary policy. In fact, some policymakers view the EMS as the first step to the ultimate goal of a single currency for all of Europe.

13-5   A Concluding Reminder

In this chapter we have examined how a small open economy works in the short run when prices are sticky. We have seen how monetary and fiscal policy influence income and the exchange rate, and how the behavior of the economy depends on whether the exchange rate is floating or fixed. In closing, it is worth repeating a lesson from Chapter 7. The United States is neither a closed economy nor a small open economy: it is something in between.

A large open economy like the United States combines the behavior of a closed economy and the behavior of a small open economy. When analyzing policies in a large open economy, we need to consider both the closed-economy logic of Chapter 10 and the open-economy logic developed in this chapter. The appendix to this chapter presents a model for the intermediate case of a large open economy. The results of that model are, as one would guess, a mixture of the two polar cases we have already examined.

To see how we can draw on the logic of both the closed and small open economies and apply these insights to the United States, consider how a monetary contraction affects the economy in the short run. In a closed economy, a monetary contraction raises the interest rate, lowers investment, and thus lowers aggregate income. In a small open economy with a floating exchange rate, a monetary contraction raises the exchange rate, lowers net exports, and thus lowers aggregate income. The interest rate is unaffected, however, because it is determined by world financial markets.

The U.S. economy contains elements of both cases. Because the United States is large enough to affect the world interest rate and because capital is not perfectly mobile across countries, a monetary contraction does raise the interest rate and depress investment. At the same time, however, a monetary contraction also raises the value of the dollar, thereby depressing net exports. Hence, although the Mundell-Fleming model does not precisely describe an economy like that of the United States, it does predict correctly what happens to international variables such as the exchange rate, and it shows how international interactions alter the effects of monetary and fiscal policies.

Summary

1. The Mundell-Fleming model is the *IS-LM* model for a small open economy. It takes the price level as given and then shows what causes fluctuations in income and the exchange rate.

2. The Mundell-Fleming model shows that fiscal policy does not influence aggregate income under floating exchange rates. A fiscal expansion causes the currency to appreciate, which reduces net exports and offsets the usual expansionary impact on aggregate income. Fiscal policy does influence aggregate income under fixed exchange rates.

3. The Mundell-Fleming model shows that monetary policy does not influence aggregate income under fixed exchange rates. Any attempt to expand the money supply is futile, because the money supply must adjust to ensure that the exchange rate stays at its announced level. Monetary policy does influence aggregate income under floating exchange rates.

4. There are advantages to both floating and fixed exchange rates. Floating exchange rates leave monetary policymakers free to pursue objectives other than exchange rate stability. Fixed exchange rates reduce some of the uncertainty in international business transactions.

KEY CONCEPTS

Mundell-Fleming model

Floating exchange rates

Fixed exchange rates

Devaluation

Revaluation

Exchange-rate union

QUESTIONS FOR REVIEW

1. In the Mundell-Fleming model with floating exchange rates, explain what happens to aggregate income, the exchange rate, and the current account when taxes are raised. What would happen if exchange rates were fixed rather than floating?

2. In the Mundell-Fleming model with floating exchange rates, explain what happens to aggregate income, the exchange rate, and the current account when the money supply is reduced. What would

happen if exchange rates were fixed rather than floating?

3. In the Mundell-Fleming model with floating exchange rates, explain what happens to aggregate income, the exchange rate, and the current account when a quota on imported cars is removed. What would happen if exchange rates were fixed rather than floating?

4. What are the advantages of floating exchange rates and fixed exchange rates?

PROBLEMS AND APPLICATIONS

1. Use the Mundell-Fleming model to predict what would happen to aggregate income, the exchange rate, and the current account under both floating and fixed exchange rates in response to each of the following shocks:

  a. A fall in consumer confidence about the future induces consumers to spend less and save more.

  b. The introduction of a stylish line of Toyotas makes some consumers prefer foreign cars over domestic cars.

  c. The introduction of automatic teller machines reduces the demand for money.

2. The Mundell-Fleming model takes the world interest rate r^* as an exogenous variable. Let's consider what happens when this variable changes.

  a. What might cause the world interest rate to rise?

  b. In the Mundell-Fleming model with a floating exchange rate, what happens to aggregate income, the exchange rate, and the current account when the world interest rate rises?

  c. In the Mundell-Fleming model with a fixed exchange rate, what happens to aggregate income, the exchange rate, and the current account when the world interest rate rises?

3. Business executives and policymakers are often concerned about the "competitiveness" of American industry (the ability of U.S. industries to sell their goods profitably in world markets).

  a. How would a change in the exchange rate affect competitiveness?

b. Suppose you wanted to make American industries more competitive but did not want to alter aggregate income. What combination of monetary and fiscal policies would you pursue?

4. Suppose that higher income implies higher imports and thus lower net exports. That is, the net exports function is

$$NX = NX(e, Y).$$

Examine the effects of a fiscal expansion on output and the current account under

a. a floating exchange rate,

b. a fixed exchange rate.

How does your answer compare to those given in Table 13-1?

5. Suppose that money demand depends on consumption rather than on income, so that the equation for the money market becomes

$$M/P = L[r, C(Y - T)].$$

Analyze the impact of a tax cut on the exchange rate and income under both floating and fixed exchange rates.

6. Suppose that the price level relevant for money demand includes the price of imported goods and that the price of imported goods depends on the exchange rate. That is, the money market is described by

$$M/P = L(r, Y),$$

where

$$P = \lambda P_d + (1 - \lambda)P_f/e.$$

The parameter λ is the share of domestic goods in the price index P. Assume the price of domestic goods P_d and the price of foreign goods measured in foreign currency P_f are fixed.

a. Explain why in this model the LM^* curve is upward sloping rather than vertical.

b. What is the impact of expansionary fiscal policy under floating exchange rates in this model? Explain. Contrast with the standard Mundell-Fleming model.

c. The effect of the exchange rate on the price level is sometimes called an "endogenous supply shock." Why might it be called this?

A Short-Run Model of the Large Open Economy

In the appendix to Chapter 7 we presented a model of a large open economy. The model differed from the model of a small open economy because it did not assume that the country could borrow or lend at the world interest rate in unlimited amounts. Instead, the model assumed that the more the country borrowed, the higher the interest rate it had to pay. Here we sketch the analogous model for the short run when prices are fixed.

The three equations of the model are

$$Y = C(Y - T) + I(r) + G + NX(e)$$
$$M/P = L(r, Y)$$
$$NX(e) = -CF(r).$$

The first two equations are the same as those used in the Mundell-Fleming model of this chapter. The third equation, taken from the Chapter 7 appendix, states that the current account NX always balances the capital flow CF and that the capital flow depends on the domestic interest rate.

To see what this model implies, substitute the third equation into the first, so the model becomes

$$Y = C(Y - T) + I(r) + G - CF(r) \qquad IS$$
$$M/P = L(r, Y). \qquad LM$$

These two equations are much like the two equations of the closed-economy *IS-LM* model. The only difference is that expenditure now depends on the interest rate for two reasons. As before, a higher interest rate implies lower investment. But now, a higher interest rate also implies a larger capital flow and thus lower net exports.

To analyze this model, we can use the three graphs in Figure 13-13. Panel A shows the *IS-LM* diagram. As in the closed-economy model in Chapters 9 and 10, the interest rate r is on the vertical axis, and income Y is on the horizontal axis. The *IS* and *LM* curves together determine the equilibrium level of income and the equilibrium interest rate.

A. The *IS-LM* Model

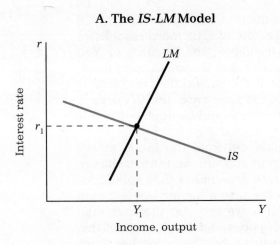

Income, output

Figure 13-13 A Short-Run Model of a Large Open Economy. Panel A shows that the *IS* and *LM* curves determine the interest rate r_1 and income Y_1. Panel B shows that r_1 determines the capital flow CF_1. Panel C shows that CF_1 and the net-exports schedule determine the exchange rate e_1.

B. The Capital Flow From Abroad

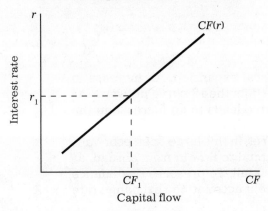

Capital flow

C. The Market for Foreign Exchange

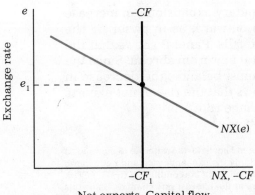

Net exports, Capital flow

The new capital-flow term in the *IS* equation, $-CF(r)$, makes this *IS* curve flatter than it would be in a closed economy. The more responsive the capital flow is to the interest rate, the flatter the *IS* curve is. You might recall from the appendix of Chapter 7 that the small open economy represents the extreme case in which the capital flow is infinitely elastic at the world interest rate. In this extreme case, the *IS* curve is completely flat. Hence, a small open economy would be depicted in this figure with a horizontal *IS* curve.[4]

Panels B and C show how the equilibrium from the *IS-LM* model determines the capital account, the current account, and the exchange rate. In panel B we see that the interest rate determines the capital flow from abroad. This curve slopes upward because a higher interest rate attracts more foreign investors. In panel C we see that the exchange rate adjusts to ensure that net exports of goods and services offset this capital flow. That is, the exchange rate ensures that the current account and the capital account balance.

Now let's use this model to examine the impact of policies under a floating exchange rate.

Fiscal Policy

Figure 13-14 examines the impact of a fiscal expansion. An increase in government purchases or a cut in taxes shifts the *IS* curve outward. As panel A illustrates, this shift in the *IS* curve leads to an increase in the level of income and an increase in the interest rate. These two effects are similar to those in a closed economy. Yet, in this large open economy, the higher interest rate induces more capital to flow in from abroad, as shown in panel B. Since *CF* rises, *NX* must fall. To preserve the balance between the capital account and the current account, the exchange rate appreciates, as in panel C.

Monetary Policy

Figure 13-15 examines the impact of a monetary expansion. An increase in the money supply shifts the *LM* curve outward, as in panel A. The level of income rises, and the interest rate falls. Panel B shows that the lower interest rate leads to a smaller capital flow from abroad. Since the capital account and the current account must balance, the decrease in *CF* implies an increase in *NX*. Panel C shows that the rise in net exports is produced by a depreciation of the exchange rate.

---

[4] A word of warning: Do not confuse the *IS* curve used here in Figure 13-13A with the *IS* curve used in Figure 13-1. In Figure 13-1, the *IS* curve is graphed holding the exchange rate and net exports *constant*. By contrast, in Figure 13-13A, the *IS* curve is graphed using the condition $NX(e) = -CF(r)$, which implies that net exports and the exchange rate vary as the interest rate changes. Since this *IS* curve is not drawn for a given exchange rate, changes in the exchange rate do not shift it.

A. The *IS-LM* Model

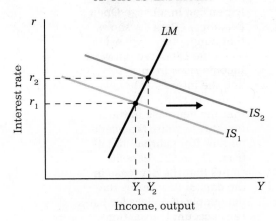

B. The Capital Flow From Abroad

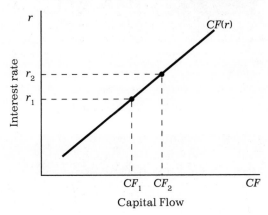

C. The Market for Foreign Exchange

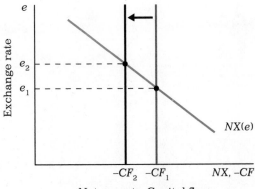

Figure 13-14 A Fiscal Expansion in a Large Open Economy. Panel A shows that a fiscal expansion shifts the *IS* curve outward. Income rises from Y_1 to Y_2, and the interest rate rises from r_1 to r_2. Panel B shows that the increase in the interest rate causes the capital flow from abroad to rise from CF_1 to CF_2. Panel C shows that the increase in the capital flow from abroad reduces the net supply of dollars for current-account transactions, which causes the exchange rate to appreciate from e_1 to e_2.

A. The *IS-LM* Model

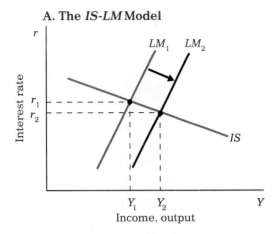

Figure 13-15 **A Monetary Expansion in a Large Open Economy.**   Panel A shows that a monetary expansion shifts the *LM* curve outward. Income rises from Y_1 to Y_2, and the interest rate falls from r_1 to r_2. Panel B shows that the decrease in the interest rate causes the capital flow from abroad to fall from CF_1 to CF_2. Panel C shows that the decrease in the capital flow raises the net supply of dollars for current-account transactions, which causes the exchange rate to depreciate from e_1 to e_2.

B. The Capital Flow From Abroad

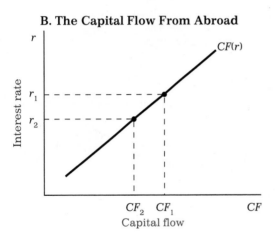

C. The Market for Foreign Exchange

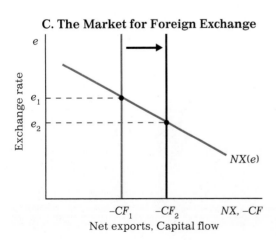

A Rule of Thumb

This model of the large open economy with a floating exchange rate does a good job of describing the U.S. economy today. Yet this model is more complicated and cumbersome than the model of the closed economy we studied in Chapters 9 and 10 and the model of the small open economy we developed in this chapter. Fortunately, there is a useful rule of thumb to help you determine how policies influence a large open economy without remembering all the details of the model: *The large open economy is an average of the closed economy and the small open economy. To find how any policy will affect any variable, find the answer in the two extreme cases and take an average.*

For example, how does a monetary contraction affect the interest rate and investment in the short run? In our closed-economy model, the interest rate rises, and investment falls. In our small-open-economy model, neither the interest rate nor investment changes. The effect in the large-open-economy model is an average of these two cases: a monetary contraction raises the interest rate and reduces investment, but only somewhat. Foreign capital flows into the economy and mitigates the rise in the interest rate and the fall in investment that would occur in a closed economy, but it does not flow in sufficient amounts to negate fully these effects.

This rule of thumb makes the simple models all the more valuable. Although they do not describe perfectly the world in which we live, they do provide a useful guide to the effects of economic policy.

Chapter 14

The Theory of Real Business Cycles

There are two schools of thought on the best way to explain short-run economic fluctuations. Most economists endorse the approach taken in the preceding chapters. They believe that the classical model cannot account for economic fluctuations and that, to explain the economy in the short run, we need a model in which prices are sticky.

Others question this judgment. A small but influential group, called the **new classical economists**, believes that one can explain short-run economic fluctuations while maintaining the assumptions of the classical model. They believe that it is best to assume that prices are fully flexible, even in the short run. Almost all microeconomic analysis is based on the premise that prices adjust to clear markets. New classical economists argue that macroeconomic analysis should be grounded on the same assumption.

The leading new classical explanation of economic fluctuations is called the theory of **real business cycles**. According to this theory, the assumptions that we have used to study the long run apply to the short run as well. Most important, real-business-cycle theory holds that the economy obeys the classical dichotomy: nominal variables, such as the money supply and the price level, are assumed not to influence real variables, such as employment and real GNP. To explain fluctuations in real variables, this theory emphasizes real changes in the economy, such as changes in fiscal policy and production technologies. Thus, the "real" in real-business-cycle theory refers to the theory's exclusion of nominal variables in explaining economic fluctuations.

In this chapter we examine the theory of real business cycles. Although a complete development of the theory would take many chapters, in this single chapter we can build a simplified model that exhibits the key elements of the approach. We can then discuss the pros and cons of this new classical view of economic fluctuations.

14-1 A Review of the Economy Under Flexible Prices

To see how real-business-cycle theory explains fluctuations, we use some of the economic relationships from previous chapters. These relationships appear in real-business-cycle theory, although often with different names attached to them. To build a real-business-cycle model, we begin with the *IS-LM* model, recalling how it behaves under flexible prices. We then modify it to develop a "real" model of short-run economic fluctuations.

The *IS-LM* model describes the economy using the following equations for the goods market and the money market:

$$Y = C(Y - T) + I(r) + G \qquad IS$$
$$M/P = L(r, Y). \qquad LM$$

The first equation states that output Y is the sum of consumption C, investment I, and government purchases G. Consumption depends on disposable income $Y - T$, and investment depends on the real interest rate r. The second equation states that the supply of real money balances M/P equals the demand, which is a function of the interest rate and the level of output. For simplicity, we are assuming that expected inflation equals zero, so that the nominal interest rate—which determines money demand—equals the real interest rate. These equations should be familiar from Chapters 9 and 10.

To analyze short-run fluctuations with the *IS-LM* model, we usually assume that the price level is fixed. If prices are flexible, however, then the price level adjusts so that output is at its natural rate:

$$Y = \overline{Y} = F(\overline{K}, \overline{L}).$$

These three equations determine three endogenous variables: the level of output Y, the real interest rate r, and the price level P.

Figure 14-1 shows the equilibrium of the economy under flexible prices. Output is at its natural rate $\overline{Y}$. The intersection of the *IS* curve and the vertical line at this level of output determines the interest rate. The price level adjusts to ensure that the *LM* curve crosses this point as well.

Note that the *LM* curve is not very important here. Because prices are flexible, the price level adjusts to produce an equilibrium in the money market. This adjustment of prices implies that the *LM* curve always crosses the intersection of the other two curves. For the purpose of understanding real variables, such as output and the real interest rate, we can ignore the money market.

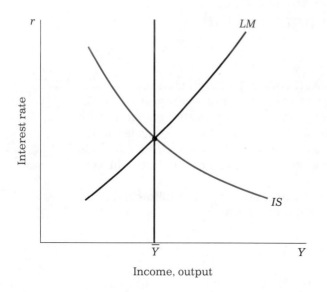

Figure 14-1 **The *IS-LM* Model With Flexible Prices.**   Under flexible prices, the level of output *Y* is determined by the supply of the factors of production and the production function. The interest rate is determined by the intersection of the *IS* curve and the vertical line at $\overline{Y}$, the natural rate of output. The price level adjusts so that the *LM* curve crosses the intersection of the other two curves.

We can therefore study the economy under flexible prices using the two relationships shown in Figure 14-2. First, the *IS* curve tells us how the demand for goods and services depends on the interest rate. For the remainder of this chapter, we call the *IS* curve the **real aggregate demand curve**. Second, the vertical line at the natural rate of output shows the supply of goods and services. We call this the **real aggregate supply curve**. The real interest rate adjusts to equilibrate the supply and demand for goods and services.

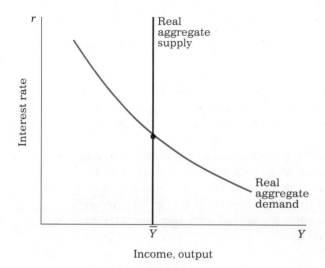

Figure 14-2 **The Two Key Relationships Under Flexible Prices.**   Under flexible prices, the two key relationships are real aggregate demand and real aggregate supply. Real aggregate demand shows the demand for goods and services as a function of the interest rate: it is another name for the *IS* curve. Real aggregate supply shows the supply of goods and services, which is determined by the supplies of capital and labor and by the available technology.

So far we have not said anything new. We have merely provided another way to express the model of national income that we first saw in Chapter 3. In the model discussed in Chapter 3, factor supplies and the production technology determine the supply of goods and services, and the real interest rate adjusts to ensure that the demand for goods and services equals the supply.

In interpreting Figure 14-2, do not confuse the real aggregate demand curve and the real aggregate supply curve with the aggregate demand curve and aggregate supply curve we analyzed in previous chapters. In previous chapters, the price level was on the vertical axis. In real-business-cycle theory, the price level is not of key importance, because it is a nominal variable and does not affect real variables. Here we are developing a completely different theory of economic fluctuations.

14-2 A Real-Business-Cycle Model

In this section we turn our model of the economy under flexible prices into a model of economic fluctuations. The new feature of this model is the behavior of labor supply. In the classical model discussed so far, the supply of labor is fixed, and this fixed supply determines the level of employment. Yet employment fluctuates substantially over the business cycle. Therefore, we must examine what causes fluctuations in labor supply.

After discussing the determinants of labor supply, we modify our classical model of aggregate income to include changes in labor supply. The supply of goods and services depends in part on the supply of labor. The greater the number of hours people are willing to work, the more output the economy can produce. We examine how, according to real-business-cycle theory, various events influence labor supply and aggregate income.

Intertemporal Substitution and Labor Supply

Real-business-cycle theory emphasizes that the quantity of labor supplied at any point in time depends on the economic incentives that workers face. When workers are well rewarded, they are willing to work more hours; when the rewards are less, they are willing to work fewer hours. Sometimes, if the reward for working is sufficiently small, workers will choose to forgo working altogether—at least temporarily. This willingness to reallocate working over time is called the **intertemporal substitution of labor**.

To see how intertemporal substitution affects labor supply, consider the following example. A college student finishing her sophomore year has two summer vacations left before graduation. She wishes to work for one of these summers, so she can buy a car after she graduates, and to relax during the other summer. How should she choose which summer to work?

Let W_1 be her real wage in the first summer, and W_2 the real wage she expects in the second summer. Choosing which summer to work involves comparing these two wages. Because the student can earn interest on money earned earlier, however, a dollar earned in the first summer is more valuable than a dollar earned in the second summer. Let r be the real interest rate. If the student works in the first summer and saves her earnings, she will have $(1 + r)W_1$ a year later. If she works in the second summer, she will have W_2. The intertemporal relative price—that is, the earnings from working the first summer relative to the earnings from working the second summer—is

$$\text{Intertemporal Relative Price} = \frac{(1 + r)W_1}{W_2}.$$

Hence, working the first summer is more attractive if the interest rate is high or if the wage is high relative to the wage expected to prevail in the future.

According to real-business-cycle theory, all workers perform this cost-benefit analysis to decide when to work and when to enjoy leisure. If the wage is temporarily high or if the interest rate is high, it is a good time to work. If the wage is temporarily low or if the interest rate is low, it is a good time to enjoy leisure.

Real-business-cycle theory uses the intertemporal substitution of labor to explain why employment and output fluctuate. Shocks to the economy that cause the interest rate to rise or the wage to be temporarily high cause people to want to work more. The increase in work effort raises the output of the economy.[1]

Real Aggregate Supply and Real Aggregate Demand

To build a real-business-cycle model, we must incorporate intertemporal substitution into our classical model of the economy. The key insight from our analysis of labor supply is that the interest rate influences the attractiveness of working today. The higher the interest rate, the greater the amount of labor supplied, and the greater the amount of output produced.

---

[1] The classic article emphasizing the role of intertemporal substitution in the labor market is Robert E. Lucas, Jr. and Leonard A. Rapping, "Real Wages, Employment, and Inflation," *Journal of Political Economy* 77 (September/October 1969): 721–754.

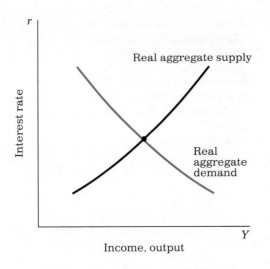

Figure 14-3 **Real Aggregate Demand and Real Aggregate Supply.** Because of intertemporal substitution, the real aggregate supply curve slopes upward: a higher interest rate makes working more attractive, which raises labor supply and thus output. The real interest rate adjusts to equilibrate real aggregate supply and real aggregate demand.

Figure 14-3 shows the real-business-cycle model of the economy. Because of intertemporal substitution, the real aggregate supply curve is now upward sloping rather than vertical—that is, a higher interest rate increases labor supply, which in turn increases the quantity of output supplied. Here, as before, the real interest rate adjusts to equilibrate the supply and demand for goods.

This model of the economy can explain fluctuations in output. Any shift in real aggregate demand or real aggregate supply changes equilibrium output. In addition, because of intertemporal substitution, the level of employment changes as well.

To explain shifts in real aggregate demand and real aggregate supply, real-business-cycle theorists have emphasized changes in fiscal policy and shocks to technology. We now examine these sources of short-run economic fluctuations.

Changes in Fiscal Policy

Suppose that government purchases increase, as they do, for example, during a war. Figure 14-4 shows how, according to real-business-cycle theory, this change affects the economy. For any given interest rate, the quantity of goods and services demanded is now higher. Therefore, the increase in government purchases shifts the real aggregate demand curve outward. Output and the interest rate both rise.

Note that there are similarities between this explanation of the effects of fiscal policy and the one we saw when we studied the *IS-LM* model in Chapter 10. An increase in government purchases shifts the real aggregate demand curve outward for the same reason that it shifts the *IS* curve outward in the *IS-LM* model: for any given interest rate, expenditure on goods and services is higher. In both cases, the result is

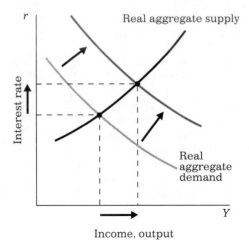

Figure 14-4 **An Increase in Government Purchases in the Real-Business-Cycle Model.** An increase in government purchases shifts the real aggregate demand curve outward. The result is higher output and a higher real interest rate.

higher output and a higher interest rate. Thus, the two models make similar predictions.

Yet there are important differences between the two explanations. In the *IS-LM* model, prices are sticky, and aggregate demand determines output and employment; labor supply and intertemporal substitution play no role in explaining how fiscal policy influences output. In the real-business-cycle model, prices are flexible, and workers intertemporally substitute. The expansion of output results from an increase in labor supply: people respond to the higher interest rate by choosing to defer leisure and to work longer hours.[2]

Shocks to Technology

Suppose that the technology available to the economy improves, perhaps because someone invents a new production process. According to real-business-cycle theory, this change affects the economy in two ways.

First, the improved technology increases the supply of goods and services. In other words, because the production function is now improved, more output is produced for any given interest rate. Therefore, the real aggregate supply curve shifts outward.

Second, the availability of the new technology raises the demand for goods. For example, suppose that the new technology is the invention of a faster computer. Firms wishing to buy these computers will raise their demand for investment goods. Therefore, the real aggregate demand curve shifts outward as well.

---

[2] To read more about the real-business-cycle interpretation of how changes in government purchases affect the economy, see Robert J. Barro, "Output Effects of Government Purchases," *Journal of Political Economy* 89 (December 1981): 1086–1121.

A. Real Aggregate Demand Shifts More Than Real Aggregate Supply

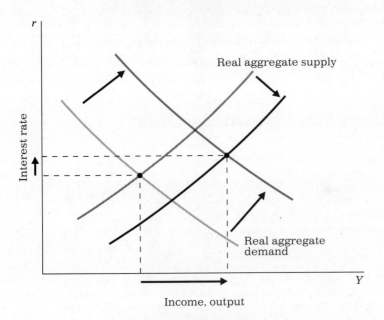

Income, output

Figure 14-5 **An Improvement in Technology in the Real-Business-Cycle Model.** A beneficial shock to the technology raises both real aggregate supply and real aggregate demand. In panel A, demand shifts more than supply. In panel B, demand shifts less than supply.

B. Real Aggregate Supply Shifts More Than Real Aggregate Demand

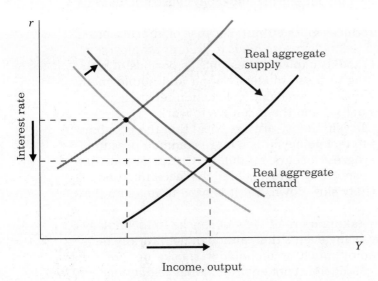

Income, output

Figure 14-5 shows these two effects. In panel A, the effect of the technology shock on demand is larger than the effect on supply, so output and the interest rate both rise. In panel B, the effect on demand is smaller than the effect on supply, so output rises and the interest rate falls. (Which case prevails depends on whether the shock is believed to be permanent or transitory. See Problem 1 at the end of the chapter.) The important lesson is that technology shocks change output and the interest rate. And, as we have seen, because of intertemporal substitution, shocks that change the interest rate influence employment as well.

14-3   The Debate Over Real-Business-Cycle Theory

Economists disagree on the validity of real-business-cycle theory. At the heart of the debate are four basic issues: the importance of technology shocks, the interpretation of unemployment, the neutrality of money, and the flexibility of wages and prices. We now examine each of these.

The Importance of Technology Shocks

Real-business-cycle theory assumes that the economy experiences fluctuations in its ability to turn inputs (capital and labor) into output (goods and services) and that these fluctuations in technology cause fluctuations in output and employment. When the available production technology improves, the economy produces more output. Because of intertemporal substitution, the improved technology also leads to greater employment. Many real-business-cycle models explain recessions as periods of technological regress. According to these models, output and employment fall during recessions because the available production technology deteriorates, which reduces output and the incentive to work.

Critics of real-business-cycle theory are skeptical that the economy experiences large shocks to technology. It is a more common presumption that technological progress occurs gradually. Critics argue that technological regress is especially implausible: the accumulation of technological knowledge may slow down, but it is hard to imagine that it would go in reverse.

Advocates respond by taking a broad view of shocks to technology. They argue that there are many events that, although not literally technological, affect the economy much as technology shocks do. For example, bad weather, the passage of strict environmental regulations, or increases in world oil prices are like adverse changes in technology: all of these events reduce our ability to turn capital and labor into goods and services. Whether these events are sufficiently common to explain the frequency and magnitude of business cycles is an open question.

CASE STUDY 14-1

The Solow Residual and the Business Cycle

To demonstrate the role of technology shocks in generating business cycles, the new classical economist Edward Prescott looked at data on the economy's inputs (capital and labor) and its output (GNP). For every year, he computed the **Solow residual**—the percentage change in output minus the percentage change in inputs, where the different inputs are weighted by their factor shares. The Solow residual measures the change in the economy's output of goods and services that cannot be explained by changes in the amounts of capital and labor. Prescott interprets it as a measure of the rate of technological progress.[3]

Figure 14-6 shows the Solow residual and the growth in output for the period 1948 to 1985. Notice that the Solow residual fluctuates substantially. It tells us, for example, that technology worsened by 3.5 percent in 1982 and improved by 3.4 percent in 1984. In addition, the Solow residual moves closely with output: in every year in which output fell, technology worsened. According to Prescott, these large fluctuations in the Solow residual show that technology shocks are an important source of economic fluctuations.

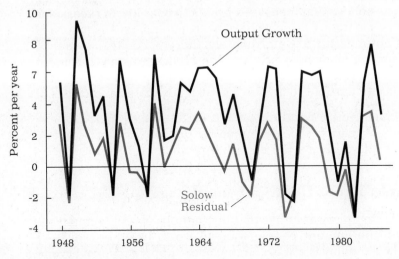

Figure 14-6 **Growth in Output and the Solow Residual.** The Solow residual, which some economists interpret as a measure of technology shocks, fluctuates together with the economy's output of goods and services.

---

[3] The appendix to Chapter 4 shows that the Solow residual is

$$\frac{\Delta A}{A} = \frac{\Delta Y}{Y} - \alpha\frac{\Delta K}{K} - (1 - \alpha)\frac{\Delta L}{L},$$

where A is total factor productivity, Y output, K capital, L labor, and α capital's share of income.

Prescott's interpretation of this figure is controversial, however. Many economists believe that the Solow residual does not accurately represent changes in technology over short periods of time. The standard explanation of the cyclical behavior of the Solow residual is that it reflects two problems of measurement.

First, during recessions, firms may continue to employ workers that they do not need, so that they will have these workers on hand when the economy recovers. This phenomenon is called **labor hoarding**. If firms do hoard labor, then labor input is overestimated in recessions, because the hoarded workers are probably not working as hard as usual. Labor hoarding makes the Solow residual more cyclical than the available production technology.

Second, when demand is low, firms may produce things that are not easily measured. In recessions, workers may clean the factory, organize the inventory, and do other useful tasks that standard measures of output fail to include. If so, then output is underestimated in recessions, which also makes the measured Solow residual more cyclical than technology.

Thus, economists can interpret the cyclical behavior of the Solow residual in different ways. Real-business-cycle theorists point to the low productivity in recessions as evidence for adverse technology shocks. Other economists believe that measured productivity is low in recessions because workers are not working as hard as usual and because more of their output is not measured. Unfortunately, there is no clear evidence on the importance of labor hoarding and the cyclical mismeasurement of output. Therefore, different interpretations of Figure 14-6 persist. This disagreement is one part of the debate between advocates and critics of real-business-cycle theory.[4]

The Interpretation of Unemployment

Real-business-cycle theory assumes that fluctuations in employment reflect changes in the amount people want to work. In other words, it assumes that the economy is always on the labor supply curve: everyone who wants a job at the prevailing wage can find one. To explain fluctuations in employment, advocates of this theory argue that changes in wages and interest rates cause intertemporal substitution in labor.

Critics of this theory believe that fluctuations in employment do not reflect changes in the amount people want to work. They believe that

---

[4] For the two sides of this debate, see Edward C. Prescott, "Theory Ahead of Business Cycle Measurement," and Lawrence H. Summers, "Some Skeptical Observations on Real Business Cycle Theory." Both are in *Quarterly Review*, Federal Reserve Bank of Minneapolis (Fall 1986).

desired employment is not very sensitive to the real wage and the real interest rate. They point out that the unemployment rate fluctuates substantially over the business cycle. The high unemployment in recessions suggests that the labor market does not clear: if people were voluntarily choosing not to work in recessions, they would not call themselves unemployed. These critics conclude that wages do not adjust to equilibrate labor supply and labor demand, as real-business-cycle models assume.

Advocates of real-business-cycle theory argue that unemployment statistics are difficult to interpret. The mere fact that the unemployment rate is high does not imply that intertemporal substitution is unimportant. Individuals who voluntarily choose not to work may call themselves unemployed to collect unemployment-insurance benefits. Or they may call themselves unemployed because, if they were offered the wage they receive in most years, they would be willing to work.

CASE STUDY 14-2

Looking for Intertemporal Substitution

Since intertemporal substitution of labor is a central element of real-business-cycle theory, much research has been aimed at examining whether it is an important determinant of labor supply. This research looks at data on wages and hours to see if people alter the amount they work in response to small changes in the real wage. If leisure were highly intertemporally substitutable, then individuals expecting increases in the real wage should work little today and much in the future. Those expecting decreases in their real wage should work hard today and enjoy leisure in the future.

Studies of labor supply find that expected changes in the real wage lead to only small changes in hours worked. Individuals appear not to respond to expected real-wage changes by substantially reallocating leisure over time. This evidence suggests that intertemporal substitution is not important, contrary to the claims of real-business-cycle theorists.

This evidence does not convince everyone, however. One reason is that the data are often far from perfect. For example, to study labor supply, we need data on wages; yet when a person is not working, we do not observe the wage he could have earned if he had taken a job. Thus, although these studies of labor supply find little evidence for intertemporal substitution, they do not end the debate over real-business-cycle theory.[5]

---

[5] Joseph G. Altonji, "Intertemporal Substitution in Labor Supply: Evidence from Micro Data," *Journal of Political Economy* 94 (June 1986, Part 2): S176–S215; Laurence Ball, "Intertemporal Substitution and Constraints on Labor Supply: Evidence from Panel Data," *Economic Inquiry* 28 (October 1990): 706–724.

The Neutrality of Money

Real-business-cycle theory assumes that money is neutral. That is, monetary policy is assumed not to affect real variables such as output and employment. The neutrality of money not only gives real-business-cycle theory its name, but it is also the most radical feature of the theory.

Critics argue that the evidence does not support the assumption of monetary neutrality. They point out that reductions in money growth and inflation are almost always associated with periods of high unemployment. Monetary policy appears to have a strong influence on the real economy.

Advocates of real-business-cycle theory argue that believers in monetary non-neutrality confuse the direction of causation between money and output. These advocates argue that the money supply is endogenous: fluctuations in output might cause fluctuations in the money supply, leading to the illusion of monetary non-neutrality. For example, when the output of the economy rises because of a beneficial technology shock, the quantity of money demanded rises; the Federal Reserve may raise the money supply to accommodate the greater demand. The direction of causation is hard to establish, because macroeconomists cannot conduct controlled experiments.[6]

The Flexibility of Wages and Prices

Real-business-cycle theory assumes that wages and prices adjust to clear markets. Advocates of this theory believe that the stickiness of wages and prices is not important for understanding economic fluctuations. They also believe that the assumption of flexible prices is superior methodologically to the assumption of sticky prices, because it ties macroeconomic theory more closely to microeconomic theory. Most of microeconomic analysis is based on the assumption that prices adjust to equilibrate supply and demand. Advocates of real-business-cycle theory believe that macroeconomists should base the analysis of economic fluctuations on the same assumption.

Critics point out that many wages and prices are not flexible. They believe that this inflexibility explains both the existence of unemployment and the non-neutrality of money. To explain why prices are sticky, they rely on the various new Keynesian theories that we discussed in Chapter 11.

---

[6] Robert G. King and Charles I. Plosser, "Money, Credit, and Prices in a Real Business Cycle," *American Economic Review* 74 (June 1984): 363–380.

F Y I **What Is New Classical Economics?**

Real-business-cycle theory is called *new classical* because it uses the assumptions of the classical model—especially flexible prices and monetary neutrality—to study short-run economic fluctuations. Yet real-business-cycle theory is not the only part of macroeconomics that bears the label "new classical." Most economists use the term broadly to describe the many challenges to the Keynesian orthodoxy that prevailed in the 1960s.

According to this broad definition, one can apply the label "new classical" to some of the ideas we discussed in earlier chapters, including rational expectations (Chapter 11), the Lucas critique (Chapter 12), and the problem of time inconsistency (Chapter 12). And, as we shall see, the Ricardian view of government debt (Chapter 16) can be called new classical. Some economists apply the label "new classical" to any model in which prices are fully flexible in the short run. By this definition, the worker-misperception and imperfect-information models of aggregate supply (Chapter 11) are new classical, even though they violate the classical dichotomy.

Although real-business-cycle theory is widely called new classical, in some ways the term is a misnomer, for the classical economists themselves never suggested that money was neutral in the short run. For example, David Hume, in his 1752 essay "Of Money," stressed that money was neutral only in the long run:

> In my opinion, it is only in the interval or intermediate situation, between the acquisition of money and the rise in prices, that the increasing quantity of gold or silver is favourable to industry. . . . The farmer or gardener, finding that their commodities are taken off, apply themselves with alacrity to the raising of more. . . . It is easy to trace the money in its progress through the whole commonwealth; where we shall find that it must first quicken the diligence of every individual, before it increases the price of labour.

In claiming that money is neutral in the short run, real-business-cycle theorists take the assumptions of classical economics more seriously than did the classical economists themselves.[7]

---

[7] For a textbook that emphasizes the new classical approach, see Robert J. Barro, *Macroeconomics*, 3d ed. (New York: Wiley, 1990). This book is recommended for advanced courses. The real-business-cycle model presented in this chapter is a highly simplified version of the one presented by Barro.

14-4   Conclusion

Real-business-cycle theory reminds us that we do not understand economic fluctuations as well as we would like. Fundamental questions about the economy remain open to dispute. Is the stickiness of wages and prices a key to understanding economic fluctuations? Does monetary policy have real effects?

How an economist answers these questions influences how he or she views the role of economic policy. Those economists who believe that wages and prices are sticky often believe that monetary and fiscal policy should be used to try to stabilize the economy. Price stickiness is a type of market imperfection. This imperfection leaves open the possibility that government policies can raise economic well-being.

By contrast, real-business-cycle theorists believe that government's ability to stabilize the economy is limited and that, even if the government could do so, it should not try. They view the business cycle as the natural and efficient response of the economy to changing technological possibilities. Most real-business-cycle models do not include any type of market imperfection. Therefore, in these models, the invisible hand of the marketplace guides the economy to an optimal allocation of resources.

These two views of economic fluctuations are a source of frequent and heated debate among economists. Much is at stake, both in economic science and in economic policy. It is this kind of debate that makes macroeconomics an exciting and attractive field of study.[8]

Summary

1. The theory of real business cycles is an alternative explanation of economic fluctuations. It applies the assumptions of the classical model, including the flexibility of wages and prices, to the short run.

2. Real-business-cycle models rely on the intertemporal substitution of labor. If the wage is temporarily high, or if the interest rate is high, working today is more attractive than working in the future. Individuals respond to these incentives by changing the amount of labor they supply.

3. Real-business-cycle models show how changes in fiscal policy or shocks to technology induce intertemporal substitution of labor and influence output and the real interest rate.

---

[8] To read more about real-business-cycle theory, see N. Gregory Mankiw, "Real Business Cycles: A New Keynesian Perspective," *Journal of Economic Perspectives* 3 (Summer 1989): 79–90; Bennett T. McCallum, "Real Business Cycle Models," in R. Barro, ed., *Modern Business Cycle Theory* (Cambridge, Mass.: Harvard University Press, 1989), 16–50; and Charles I. Plosser, "Understanding Real Business Cycles," *Journal of Economic Perspectives* 3 (Summer 1989): 51–77.

4. Advocates and critics of real-business-cycle theory disagree on whether technology shocks cause most economic fluctuations, whether high unemployment implies that the labor market does not clear, whether monetary policy affects real variables, and whether the short-run stickiness of wages and prices is important for understanding economic fluctuations.

KEY CONCEPTS

New classical economics

Real-business-cycle theory

Real aggregate demand curve

Real aggregate supply curve

Intertemporal substitution of labor

Solow residual

Labor hoarding

QUESTIONS FOR REVIEW

1. How does real-business-cycle theory explain fluctuations in employment?

2. According to real-business-cycle theory, how does an increase in government purchases affect the economy?

3. What are the four central disagreements in the debate over real-business-cycle theory?

PROBLEMS AND APPLICATIONS

1. According to real-business-cycle theory, permanent and transitory shocks should have very different effects on the economy. Let's therefore compare the effects of a transitory technology shock (such as good weather) and a permanent technology shock (such as the invention of a new production process).

　a. Which shock would have the larger impact on the demand for investment goods? Which shock would cause the larger shift in real aggregate demand?

　b. Which shock would raise the current real wage above the expected future real wage? Which shock would cause the larger shift in real aggregate supply?

　c. Compare the effects of the two shocks on output and the real interest rate.

2. Suppose that prices are fully flexible and that the output of the economy fluctuates because of shocks to technology, as real-business-cycle theory claims.

　a. If the Federal Reserve holds the money supply constant, what will happen to the price level as output fluctuates?

　b. If the Federal Reserve adjusts the money supply to stabilize the price level, what will happen to the money supply as output fluctuates?

　c. Many economists have observed that fluctuations in the money supply are positively correlated with fluctuations in output. Is this evidence against real-business-cycle theory?

Part Four

More on the Microeconomics Behind Macroeconomics

Chapter **15**

Consumption

How do households decide how much of their income to consume today and how much to save for the future? This is a microeconomic question, because it addresses the behavior of individual decisionmakers. Yet its answer is crucial for macroeconomics, because these consumption decisions affect how the economy as a whole behaves both in the long run and in the short run.

We saw that the consumption decision is crucial for long-run analysis when we studied economic growth. The Solow growth model of Chapter 4 shows that the saving rate is a key determinant of the steady-state capital stock and thus of the level of economic well-being. The saving rate measures how much of its income the present generation is putting aside for its own future and for future generations.

We saw that the consumption decision is crucial for short-run analysis when we studied aggregate demand. Since consumption is two-thirds of GNP, fluctuations in consumption are a key element of booms and recessions. The *IS-LM* model of Chapters 9 and 10 shows that changes in consumption can amplify shocks to the economy, and that the marginal propensity to consume is a key determinant of the fiscal policy multipliers.

In previous chapters we explained consumption with a function that relates consumption to disposable income: $C = C(Y - T)$. This approximation allowed us to develop simple models for long-run and short-run analysis. But this consumption function is too simple to provide a complete explanation of consumer behavior. We need a more sophisticated theory of the consumer to help refine our analysis. In this chapter we examine the consumption function in greater detail and develop a more thorough explanation of what determines aggregate consumption.

Since macroeconomics began as a field of study, many economists have written about the theory of consumer behavior and suggested alternative ways of interpreting the data on consumption and income. This chapter presents the views of four prominent economists, roughly in historical order. By examining the theories of consumer behavior developed by John Maynard Keynes, Irving Fisher, Franco Modigliani, and Milton Friedman, this chapter provides an overview of the diverse approaches to explaining consumption.

15-1 John Maynard Keynes and the Consumption Function

We begin our study of consumption with John Maynard Keynes's *General Theory*, which was published in 1936. Keynes made the consumption function central to his theory of economic fluctuations, and it has played a key role in macroeconomic analysis ever since. Alvin Hansen, one of Keynes's early followers, wrote that the "great contribution of Keynes' *General Theory* was the clear and specific formulation of the consumption function. This is an epoch-making contribution to the tools of economic analysis, analogous to, but even more important than, Marshall's discovery of the demand function."

Let's consider what Keynes thought about the consumption function, and then see what puzzles arose when his ideas were confronted with the data.

Keynes's Conjectures

Today, economists who study consumption rely on sophisticated techniques of data analysis. With the help of computers, they analyze aggregate data on the behavior of the overall economy from the national income accounts, and detailed data on the behavior of individual households from surveys. Because Keynes wrote in the 1930s, however, he had neither the advantage of these data nor the computers necessary to analyze such large data sets. Instead of relying on statistical analysis, Keynes made conjectures about the consumption function on the basis of introspection and personal experience.

First and most important, Keynes conjectured that the **marginal propensity to consume**—the amount consumed out of an additional dollar of income—is between zero and one. He wrote that the "fundamental psychological law, upon which we are entitled to depend with great confidence, . . . is that men are disposed, as a rule and on the average, to increase their consumption as their income increases, but not by as much as the increase in their income." The marginal propensity to consume was crucial to Keynes's policy recommendations for how to deal with widespread unemployment. The power of fiscal policy to influence the economy—as expressed by the fiscal policy multipliers—arises from the feedback between income and consumption.

Second, Keynes posited that the ratio of consumption to income, called the **average propensity to consume**, falls as income rises. He believed that saving was a luxury, so he expected the rich to save a higher proportion of their income than the poor. Although not essential for Keynes's own analysis, the postulate of a falling average propensity to consume became a central part of early Keynesian economics.

Third, Keynes thought that income is the primary determinant of consumption and believed that the interest rate does not have an important role. This conjecture stood in stark contrast to the beliefs of the classical economists who preceded him. The classical economists held that a higher interest rate encourages saving and discourages consumption. Keynes admitted that the interest rate could influence consumption as a matter of economic theory. Yet he wrote that "the main conclusion suggested by experience, I think, is that the short-period influence of the rate of interest on individual spending out of a given income is secondary and relatively unimportant."

On the basis of these three conjectures, the Keynesian consumption function is often written as

$$C = \overline{C} + cY \qquad\qquad \overline{C} > 0, 0 < c < 1,$$

where C is consumption, Y is disposable income, $\overline{C}$ is a constant sometimes called *autonomous consumption*, and c is the marginal propensity to consume. This consumption function, shown in Figure 15-1, is graphed as a straight line.

Notice that this consumption function exhibits the three properties that Keynes posited. It satisfies Keynes's first property because the marginal propensity to consume c is between zero and one, so that higher income leads to higher consumption and also to higher saving. This consumption function satisfies Keynes's second property because the average propensity to consume is

$$APC = C/Y = \overline{C}/Y + c.$$

As Y rises, $\overline{C}/Y$ falls, and so the average propensity to consume C/Y falls. (Note that, because the average propensity to consume is C/Y, it equals the slope of a line drawn from the origin to a point on the consumption function. Thus, in Figure 15-1, we can see that the APC falls as income rises.) And finally, this consumption function satisfies Keynes's third property because the interest rate is not included in this equation as a determinant of consumption.

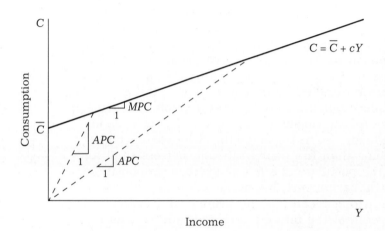

Figure 15-1 **The Keynesian Consumption Function.** This figure graphs a consumption function with the three properties that Keynes conjectured. First, the marginal propensity to consume c is between zero and one. Second, the average propensity to consume falls as income rises. Third, consumption is determined by current income.

The Early Empirical Successes

Soon after Keynes proposed the consumption function, economists started collecting and examining data to test his conjectures. The earliest studies indicated that the Keynesian consumption function is a good approximation of how consumers behave.

In some of these studies, researchers surveyed households and collected data on consumption and income. They found that households with higher income consumed more, which implies that the marginal propensity to consume is greater than zero. They also found that households with higher income saved more, which implies that the marginal propensity to consume is less than one. These data supported Keynes's prediction that the marginal propensity to consume is between zero and one. In addition, these researchers found that higher-income households saved a larger fraction of their income, which verified Keynes's conjecture that the average propensity to consume falls as income rises.

In other studies, researchers examined aggregate data on consumption and income for the period between the two world wars. These data also supported the Keynesian consumption function. In years when income was unusually low, such as during the depths of the Great Depression, both consumption and saving were low, indicating that the marginal propensity to consume is between zero and one. In addition, during those years of low income, the ratio of consumption to income was high, confirming Keynes's second conjecture. Finally, because the correlation between income and consumption was so strong, no other variable appeared to be important for explaining consumption. Thus, the data also confirmed Keynes's third conjecture that income is the primary determinant of how much people choose to consume.

Secular Stagnation, Simon Kuznets, and the Consumption Puzzle

Although the Keynesian consumption function met with early successes, two anomalies soon arose. Both concern Keynes's conjecture that the average propensity to consume falls as income rises.

The first anomaly came from a prediction some economists made during World War II. On the basis of the Keynesian consumption function, these economists reasoned that as incomes in the economy grew over time, households would consume a smaller and smaller fraction of their incomes. They feared that there might not be enough profitable investment projects to absorb all this saving. If so, the low consumption would lead to an inadequate demand for goods and services, resulting in a depression once the wartime demand from the government ceased. In other words, on the basis of the Keynesian consumption function, these economists hypothesized that the economy would experience what they called *secular stagnation*—a long depression of indefinite duration.

Fortunately for the economy, but unfortunately for the Keynesian consumption function, the end of World War II did not throw the country into another depression. Although incomes were much higher after the war than before, these higher incomes did not lead to large increases in the rate of saving. Keynes's conjecture that the average propensity to consume would fall as income rose appeared not to hold.

The second anomaly came from new data on consumption and income dating back to 1869. These data were constructed in the 1940s by the economist Simon Kuznets, who later received the Nobel Prize for this work. Kuznets discovered that the ratio of consumption to income was remarkably stable from decade to decade, despite large increases in income over the period he studied. Again, Keynes's conjecture that the average propensity to consume would fall as income rose appeared not to hold.

The finding that the average propensity to consume is constant over long periods of time presented a puzzle that motivated much of the subsequent work on consumption. Economists wanted to know why some studies confirmed Keynes's conjectures and others refuted them. That is, why did Keynes's conjectures hold up so well in the studies of household data and in the studies of short time-series, but fail so miserably when long time-series were examined?

Figure 15-2 illustrates this puzzle. The evidence suggested that there were two consumption functions. For the household data or for the short

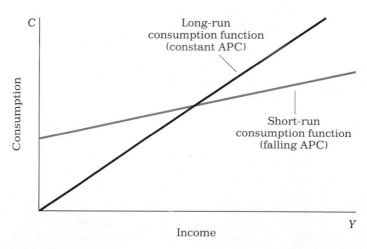

Figure 15-2 **The Consumption Puzzle.** Studies of household data and short time-series found a relationship between consumption and income similar to the one Keynes conjectured. In the figure, this relationship is called the short-run consumption function. But studies of long time-series found that the average propensity to consume did not vary systematically with income. This relationship is called the long-run consumption function. Notice that the short-run consumption function has a falling average propensity to consume, whereas the long-run consumption function has a constant average propensity to consume.

time-series, the Keynesian consumption function appeared to work well. Yet for the long time-series, the consumption function appeared to have a constant average propensity to consume. In Figure 15-2, these two relationships between consumption and income are called the short-run and long-run consumption functions. Economists needed to explain how these two consumption functions could be consistent with each other.

In the 1950s, Franco Modigliani and Milton Friedman proposed explanations of these seemingly contradictory findings. Both economists later won Nobel Prizes, in part because of their work on consumption. But before we see how Modigliani and Friedman tried to solve the consumption puzzle, we must discuss Irving Fisher's contribution to consumption theory. Both Modigliani's life-cycle hypothesis and Friedman's permanent-income hypothesis rely on the theory of consumer behavior proposed much earlier by Irving Fisher.

15-2   Irving Fisher and Intertemporal Choice

When people decide how much to consume and how much to save, they must balance the interests of the present against the interests of the future. The more consumption they enjoy today, the less they will be able to enjoy in the future. In making this tradeoff, households must look ahead to the income they expect to receive in the future and to the consumption of goods and services they hope to be able to afford.

The economist Irving Fisher developed the model with which economists analyze how rational, forward-looking consumers make intertemporal choices—that is, choices involving different periods of time. Fisher's model shows the constraints consumers face and how they choose consumption and saving.

The Intertemporal Budget Constraint

Almost everyone would prefer to increase the quantity or quality of the goods and services they consume—to wear nicer clothes, eat at better restaurants, or see more movies. The reason people consume less than they desire is that their consumption is constrained by their income. In other words, consumers face a limit on how much they can spend, called a *budget constraint*. When they are deciding how much to consume today versus how much to save for the future, they face an **intertemporal budget constraint**. To understand how people choose their level of consumption, we must examine this constraint.

To keep things simple, we examine the decision facing a consumer who lives for two periods. Period one represents the consumer's youth, and period two represents the consumer's old age. The consumer earns income Y_1 and consumes C_1 in period one, and earns income Y_2 and consumes C_2 in period two. (All variables are real—that is, adjusted for inflation.) Because the consumer has the opportunity to borrow and save, consumption in any single period can be either greater or less than income in that period.

We want to examine how the consumer's income in the two periods constrains consumption in the two periods. Note that, in the first period, saving equals income minus consumption. That is,

$$S = Y_1 - C_1,$$

where S is saving. In the second period, consumption equals the accumulated saving, including the interest earned on that saving, plus second-period income. That is,

$$C_2 = (1 + r)S + Y_2,$$

where r is the real interest rate. For example, if the interest rate is 5 percent, then for every dollar of saving in period one, the consumer enjoys an extra $1.05 of consumption in period two. Because there is no third period, the consumer does not save in the second period.

Note that these two equations still apply if the consumer is borrowing rather than saving in the first period. The variable S represents both saving and borrowing. If first-period consumption is less than first-period income, the consumer is saving, and S is greater than zero. If first-period consumption exceeds first-period income, the consumer is borrowing, and S is less than zero. For simplicity, we assume that the interest rate for borrowing is the same as the interest rate for saving.

To derive the consumer's budget constraint, combine the two equations above. Substitute the first equation for S into the second equation to obtain

$$C_2 = (1 + r)(Y_1 - C_1) + Y_2.$$

To make the equation easier to interpret, we must rearrange terms. To place all the consumption terms together, bring $(1 + r)C_1$ from the right-hand side to the left-hand side of the equation to obtain

$$(1 + r)C_1 + C_2 = (1 + r)Y_1 + Y_2.$$

Now divide both sides by $(1 + r)$ to obtain

$$C_1 + \frac{C_2}{1 + r} = Y_1 + \frac{Y_2}{1 + r}.$$

This equation relates consumption in the two periods to income in the two periods. It is the standard way of expressing the consumer's intertemporal budget constraint.

The consumer's budget constraint has a straightforward interpretation. If the interest rate is zero, the budget constraint says that total consumption in the two periods equals total income in the two periods.

In the usual case in which the interest rate is greater than zero, future consumption and future income are discounted by a factor $1 + r$. This **discounting** arises from the interest earned on savings. In essence, because the consumer earns interest on current income that is saved, future income is worth less than current income. Similarly, because future consumption is paid for out of savings that has earned interest, future consumption costs less than current consumption. The factor $1/(1 + r)$ is the price of second-period consumption measured in terms of first-period consumption: it is the amount of first-period consumption that the consumer must forgo to obtain one unit of second-period consumption.

Figure 15-3 graphs the consumer's budget constraint. Three points are marked on this figure. At point A, first-period consumption is Y_1 and second-period consumption is Y_2, so there is neither saving nor borrowing between the two periods. At point B, the consumer consumes nothing in the first period and saves all income, so second-period consumption is $[(1 + r)Y_1] + Y_2$. At point C, the consumer plans to consume nothing in the second period and borrows as much as possible against second-period income, so first-period consumption is $Y_1 + [Y_2/(1 + r)]$. Of course, these are only three of the many combinations of first- and second-period consumption that the consumer can choose: all the points on the line from B to C are possible.

The shaded area below the budget constraint shows other combinations of first-period and second-period consumption available to the consumer. The consumer can choose points below the budget constraint because he can discard some of his income. The important points are those on the budget constraint, however. As long as more consumption is preferred to less, the consumer will always choose a point on—rather than below—this budget line.

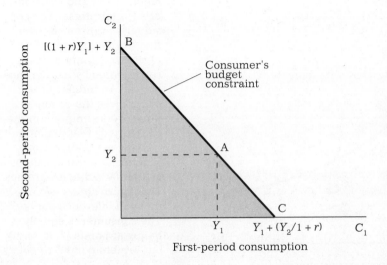

Figure 15-3 **The Consumer's Budget Constraint.** This figure shows the combinations of the first-period and second-period consumption that the consumer can choose. If he chooses points between A and B, he consumes less than his income in the first period and saves the rest for the second period. If he chooses points between A and C, he consumes more than his income in the first period and borrows to make up the difference.

Consumer Preferences

The consumer's preferences regarding consumption in the two periods can be represented by **indifference curves**. An indifference curve shows the combinations of first-period and second-period consumption that make the consumer equally happy.

Figure 15-4 shows two possible indifference curves. The consumer is indifferent among combinations W, X, and Y. Not surprisingly, if the consumer's first-period consumption is reduced, say from point W to point X, second-period consumption must increase for him to be kept equally happy. If first-period consumption is reduced again, from point X to point Y, the amount of extra second-period consumption he requires for compensation is greater.

The slope at any point on the indifference curve shows how much second-period consumption the consumer requires in order to be compensated for a one-unit reduction in first-period consumption. We call this slope the **marginal rate of substitution** between first-period consumption and second-period consumption. It tells us the rate at which the consumer is willing to substitute second-period consumption for first-period consumption.

We can see from Figure 15-4 that the marginal rate of substitution depends on the levels of consumption in the two periods. When first-period consumption is high and second-period consumption is low, such as at point W, the marginal rate of substitution is low: the consumer requires only a little extra second-period consumption to give up a unit of first-period consumption. When first-period consumption is low and second-period consumption is high, such as at point Y, the marginal rate of substitution is high: the consumer requires much additional second-period consumption to give up a unit of first-period consumption.

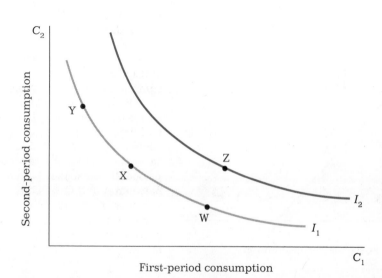

Figure 15-4 **The Consumer's Preferences.** The consumer's preferences over first-period and second-period consumption are represented by indifference curves. An indifference curve gives the combinations of consumption in the two periods that make the consumer equally happy. Higher indifference curves are preferred to lower ones. This figure shows two of many indifference curves. The consumer is equally happy at points W, X, and Y, but prefers point Z to points W, X, or Y.

The consumer is equally happy at all points on a given indifference curve, but he prefers some indifference curves to others. Because he prefers more consumption to less, higher indifference curves are preferred to lower ones. In Figure 15-4, the points on curve I_2 are preferred to the points on curve I_1.

The set of indifference curves gives a complete ranking of the consumer's preferences. They tell us that point Z is preferred to point W, but that may be obvious because point Z has more consumption in both periods. Yet compare point Z and point Y: point Z has more consumption in period one and less in period two. Which is preferred, Z or Y? Since Z is better than W, and W is equally preferred to Y, the indifference curves tell us that point Z is preferred to point Y. Hence, we can use the set of indifference curves to rank any combinations of first-period and second-period consumption.

Optimization

Having discussed the consumer's budget constraint and preferences, we can consider the decision about how much to consume. The consumer would like to end up with the best possible combination of consumption in the two periods—that is, on the highest possible indifference curve. But the budget constraint requires that the consumer also end up on or below the budget line, because the budget line measures the total resources available to him.

Figure 15-5 shows that many indifference curves cross the budget line. The highest indifference curve that the consumer can obtain without violating the budget constraint is the indifference curve that just barely touches the budget line, which is curve I_3 in the figure. The point at which the curve and line touch—point O for optimum—is the best combination of consumption available to the consumer in the two periods.

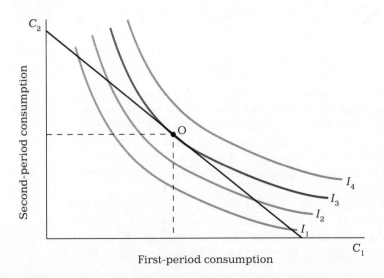

Figure 15-5 **The Consumer's Optimum.** The consumer achieves his highest level of satisfaction by choosing the point on the budget constraint that is on the highest indifference curve. At the optimum, the indifference curve is tangent to the budget constraint.

Notice that, at the optimum, the slope of the indifference curve equals the slope of the budget line. We say that the indifference curve is *tangent* to the budget line. The slope of the indifference curve is the marginal rate of substitution, and the slope of the budget line is one plus the real interest rate. We conclude that, at point O,

$$MRS = 1 + r.$$

The consumer chooses consumption in the two periods so that the marginal rate of substitution equals one plus the real interest rate.

How Changes in Income Affect Consumption

Now that we have seen how the consumer makes the consumption decision, let's examine how consumption responds to an increase in income. An increase in either Y_1 or Y_2 shifts the budget constraint outward, as in Figure 15-6. The higher budget constraint allows the consumer to choose a better combination of first- and second-period consumption—that is, the consumer can now reach a higher indifference curve.

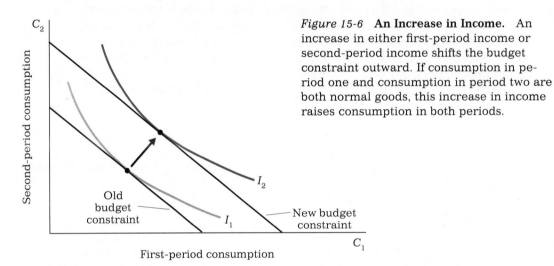

Figure 15-6 **An Increase in Income.** An increase in either first-period income or second-period income shifts the budget constraint outward. If consumption in period one and consumption in period two are both normal goods, this increase in income raises consumption in both periods.

Notice that, in Figure 15-6, the consumer chooses more consumption in both periods. Although not implied by the logic of the model alone, this situation is the most usual. If a consumer wants more of a good when his or her income rises, economists call it a **normal good**. The indifference curves in Figure 15-6 are drawn under the assumption that consumption in period one and consumption in period two are both normal goods.

The key implication of Figure 15-6 is that regardless of whether the increase in income occurs in the first period or the second period, the consumer spreads it over consumption in both periods. Because the consumer can borrow and lend between periods, the timing of the income is irrelevant to how much is consumed today (except, of course, that future income is discounted by the interest rate). The lesson of this analysis is that consumption depends on the present value of current and future income—that is, on

$$\text{Present Value of Income} = Y_1 + [Y_2/(1 + r)].$$

In contrast to Keynes's consumption function, Fisher's model says that consumption does not depend primarily on current income. Instead, consumption depends on the resources the consumer expects over his lifetime.

How Changes in the Real Interest Rate Affect Consumption

Let's now use Fisher's model to consider how a change in the real interest rate alters the consumer's choices. In general, there are two cases to consider: the case in which the consumer is initially saving and the case in which he is initially borrowing. Here we discuss the saving case, and Problem 1 at the end of the chapter asks you to analyze the borrowing case.

Figure 15-7 shows that an increase in the real interest rate rotates the consumer's budget line around the point (Y_1, Y_2). Therefore, this change alters the amount of consumption he chooses in both periods. You can see that, for the indifference curves drawn in this figure, first-period consumption falls and second-period consumption rises.

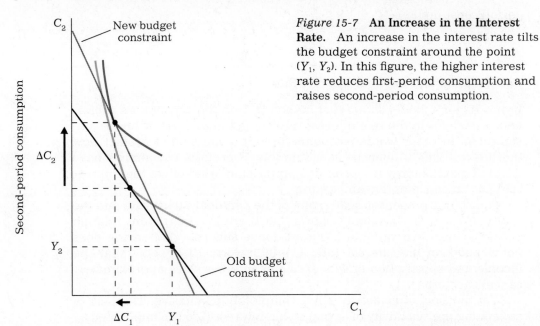

Figure 15-7 **An Increase in the Interest Rate.** An increase in the interest rate tilts the budget constraint around the point (Y_1, Y_2). In this figure, the higher interest rate reduces first-period consumption and raises second-period consumption.

First-period consumption

Economists decompose the impact of an increase in the real interest rate on consumption into two effects: an **income effect** and a **substitution effect**. Textbooks in microeconomics discuss these effects in detail. We summarize them briefly here.

The income effect is the change in consumption that results from the movement to a higher indifference curve. Because the consumer is a saver rather than a borrower, the increase in the interest rate makes him better off. If consumption in period one and consumption in period two are both normal goods, the consumer will want to spread this improvement in his welfare over both periods. This income effect tends to make the consumer choose more consumption in both periods.

The substitution effect is the change in consumption that results from the change in the relative price of consumption in the two periods. In particular, consumption in period two becomes less expensive relative to consumption in period one when the interest rate rises. That is, because the real interest rate earned on saving is higher, the consumer must now give up less first-period consumption to obtain an extra unit of second-period consumption. This substitution effect tends to make the consumer choose more consumption in period two and less consumption in period one.

The consumer's choice depends on both the income effect and the substitution effect. Both effects act to increase the amount of second-period consumption; hence, we can confidently conclude that an increase in the real interest rate increases second-period consumption. But the two effects have opposite impact on first-period consumption. Hence, the increase in the interest rate could either lower or raise first-period consumption.

CASE STUDY 15-1

Consumption and the Real Interest Rate

Irving Fisher's model shows that, depending on the consumer's preferences, changes in the real interest rate could either raise or lower consumption. In other words, economic theory alone cannot predict how the interest rate influences consumption. Therefore, economists have devoted much energy to examining empirically what effect the interest rate has on consumption and saving.

Figure 15-8 presents a scatterplot of the personal saving rate and the real interest rate. This figure shows that there is no apparent relation between these two variables. This evidence suggests that saving does not depend on the interest rate. In other words, it appears that the income and substitution effects of higher interest rates approximately cancel each other.

Yet this sort of evidence is not completely persuasive. The task of estimating the sensitivity of saving to the interest rate is complicated by

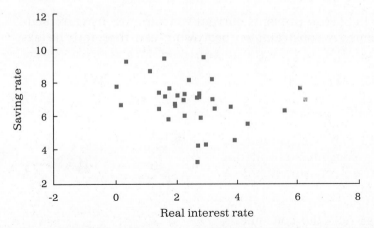

Figure 15-8 **A Scatterplot of Saving and the Interest Rate.** This figure uses annual data from 1954 to 1988 to examine whether there is any relationship between the personal saving rate and the real interest rate. No relationship is evident.

Source: The personal saving rate is personal disposable income minus consumer spending as a fraction of personal disposable income from the Department of Commerce. The real interest rate is the after-tax interest rate on one-year Treasury notes (the Department of Treasury) minus expected inflation; this was calculated assuming a tax rate of 30 percent. Expected inflation data are from the Livingston survey of expected inflation.

the identification problem discussed in Chapter 3. Nonetheless, more sophisticated examinations of the data usually find that the real interest rate has little effect on consumption and saving. Keynes's conjecture that consumption depends primarily on income and not on the interest rate has held up well in the face of much empirical testing.[1]

Constraints on Borrowing

Fisher's model assumes that the consumer can borrow as well as save. The ability to borrow allows current consumption to exceed current income. In essence, when the consumer borrows, he consumes some of his future income today. Yet for many people such borrowing is impossible. For example, a student wishing to enjoy spring break in Florida would probably be unable to finance this vacation with a bank loan. Let's examine how Fisher's analysis changes if the consumer cannot borrow.

---

[1] For some of the recent research on the relationship between consumption and the real interest rate, see Robert E. Hall, "Intertemporal Substitution and Consumption," *Journal of Political Economy* 96 (April 1988): 339–357; and John Y. Campbell and N. Gregory Mankiw, "Consumption, Income, and Interest Rates: Reinterpreting the Time-Series Evidence," *NBER Macroeconomics Annual* (1989): 185–216.

The inability to borrow prevents current consumption from exceeding current income. A constraint on borrowing can therefore be expressed as

$$C_1 \leq Y_1.$$

This inequality states that consumption in period one is less than or equal to income in period one. This additional constraint on the consumer is called a **borrowing constraint** or, sometimes, a *liquidity constraint*.

Figure 15-9 shows how this borrowing constraint restricts the consumer's set of choices. The consumer's choice must satisfy both the intertemporal budget constraint and the borrowing constraint. The shaded area represents the combinations of first-period consumption and second-period consumption that satisfy both constraints.

"What I'd like, basically, is a temporary line of credit just to tide me over the rest of my life."

Figure 15-10 shows how this borrowing constraint affects the consumption decision. There are two possibilities. In panel A, the consumer wishes to consume less in period one than he earns. The borrowing constraint is not binding in this case and, therefore, does not affect consumption. In panel B, the consumer would like to consume more than he earns in period one. In this case, the consumer consumes all of his first-period income, and the borrowing constraint prevents him from consuming more.

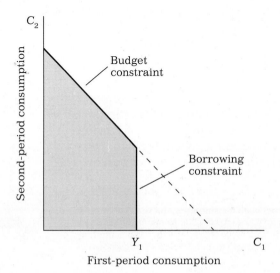

Figure 15-9   **A Borrowing Constraint.**   If the consumer cannot borrow, he faces the additional constraint that first-period consumption cannot exceed first-period income. The shaded area represents the combination of first-period and second-period consumption the consumer can choose.

A. The Borrowing Constraint Is Not Binding

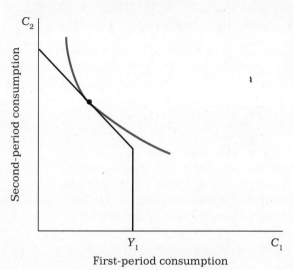

First-period consumption

Figure 15-10 **The Consumer's Optimum With a Borrowing Constraint.** When the consumer faces a borrowing constraint, there are two possible situations. In panel A, the consumer chooses first-period consumption to be less than first-period income, so the borrowing constraint is not binding and does not affect consumption.

B. The Borrowing Constraint Is Binding

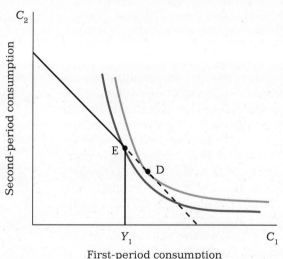

First-period consumption

In panel B, the borrowing constraint is binding. The consumer would like to borrow and choose point D. But because borrowing is not allowed, the best available choice is point E. When the borrowing constraint is binding, first-period consumption equals first-period income.

The analysis of borrowing constraints leads us to conclude that there are two consumption functions. For some consumers, the borrowing constraint is not binding, and consumption depends on the present value of lifetime income, $Y_1 + [Y_2/(1 + r)]$. For other consumers, the borrowing constraint binds, and the consumption function is $C_1 = Y_1$. *Hence, for those consumers who would like to borrow but cannot, consumption depends only on current income.*

The High Japanese Saving Rate

Japan has one of the world's highest saving rates, and many economists believe that this is a key to its economic success. Over the past 20 years, the net national saving rate in Japan has averaged about twice that in the United States. The Solow growth model in Chapter 4 shows that, in the long run, the saving rate is a primary determinant of a country's level of income. Because saving is so important for long-run economic performance, economists spend much time studying these international differences in saving.

Why do the Japanese consume a much smaller fraction of their income than Americans? One reason is that it is harder to borrow in Japan. Consider borrowing to buy a home, for example. In the United States, a person can usually buy a home with a down payment of 10 percent. A home-buyer in Japan can borrow much less: down payments of 40 percent are common. Moreover, housing prices are very high in Japan, primarily because land prices are high. Hence, high saving is necessary if a Japanese family is eventually to afford its own home.

Although constraints on borrowing are part of the explanation of high Japanese saving, there are many other differences between Japan and the United States that might contribute to the difference in the saving rates. The Japanese tax system encourages saving by taxing capital income very lightly. In addition, cultural differences may lead to differences in consumer preferences regarding present and future consumption. One prominent Japanese economist writes, "The Japanese are simply *different*. They are more risk averse and more patient. If this is true, the long-run implication is that Japan will absorb all the wealth in the world. I refuse to comment on this explanation."[2]

Many economists believe that the low U.S. saving rate is one of the biggest economic problems of the United States. As we discussed in Chapter 4, raising national saving is often a stated goal of economic policy. Keep in mind, however, that policies to increase saving have their costs. For example, home-buyers in the United States would not be happy if they faced the borrowing constraints that are so common in Japan.

---

[2] Fumio Hayashi, "Why Is Japan's Saving Rate So Apparently High?" *NBER Macroeconomics Annual* (1986): 147–210.

15-3 Franco Modigliani and the Life-Cycle Hypothesis

In a series of papers written in the 1950s, Franco Modigliani and his collaborators Albert Ando and Richard Brumberg used Irving Fisher's model of consumer behavior to study the consumption function. One of their goals was to solve the consumption puzzle—that is, to explain the apparently conflicting pieces of evidence that came to light when Keynes's consumption function was brought to the data. According to Fisher's model, consumption depends on a person's lifetime income. Modigliani emphasized that income varies over people's lives and that saving allows consumers to move income from those times in life when income is high to those times when it is low. This interpretation of consumer behavior formed the basis for his **life-cycle hypothesis**.[3]

The Hypothesis

Of the many reasons that income varies over a person's life, one of the most important is retirement. Most people plan to retire at about age 65 and expect a large drop in their income; yet they do not want a large drop in their consumption. Most people provide for their retirement by saving. Let's see what this motive for saving implies for the consumption function.

Consider a consumer who expects to live another T years, has wealth of W, and expects to earn income Y until she retires R years from now. What level of consumption will the consumer choose if she wishes to maintain a smooth level of consumption over her life?

The consumer's lifetime resources are composed of initial wealth W and lifetime earnings $R \times Y$. (For simplicity, we are assuming an interest rate of zero; if the interest rate were greater than zero, we would need to take account of interest earned on savings as well.) The consumer can divide up her lifetime resources among her T remaining years of life. We assume that she wishes to achieve the smoothest possible path of consumption over her lifetime. Therefore, she divides this total of $W + RY$ equally among the T years and each year consumes

$$C = (W + RY)/T.$$

We can write this person's consumption function as

$$C = (1/T)W + (R/T)Y.$$

---

[3] For references to the large body of work on the life-cycle hypothesis, a good place to start is the lecture Modigliani gave when he won the Nobel Prize. Franco Modigliani, "Life Cycle, Individual Thrift, and the Wealth of Nations," *American Economic Review* 76 (June 1986): 297–313.

For example, if the consumer expects to live for 50 more years and work for 30 more years, then $T = 50$ and $R = 30$, so her consumption function is

$$C = 0.02W + 0.6Y.$$

This equation says that consumption depends on both income and wealth. An extra dollar per year of income raises consumption by 60 cents per year, and an extra dollar of wealth raises consumption by 2 cents per year.

If every individual in the economy plans consumption like this, then the aggregate consumption function is much the same as the individual one. In particular, aggregate consumption depends on both wealth and income. That is, the economy's consumption function is

$$C = \alpha W + \beta Y,$$

where the parameter α is the marginal propensity to consume out of wealth, and the parameter β is the marginal propensity to consume out of income.

Implications

Figure 15-11 graphs the relationship between consumption and income predicted by the life-cycle model. For any given level of wealth, the model yields a conventional consumption function. Notice, however, that the intercept of the consumption function, αW, is not a fixed value but depends on the level of wealth.

This life-cycle model of consumer behavior can solve the consumption puzzle. The life-cycle consumption function implies that the average propensity to consume is

$$C/Y = \alpha(W/Y) + \beta.$$

Because wealth does not vary proportionately with income from person to person or from year to year, one should find that high income implies a low average propensity to consume when looking at data across individuals or over short periods of time. But, over long periods of time, wealth and income grow together, which implies a constant ratio W/Y and thus a constant average propensity to consume.

To make the same point somewhat differently, consider how the consumption function changes over time. As Figure 15-11 shows, for any given level of wealth, the life-cycle consumption function looks like the one Keynes suggested. But this function holds only in the short run when wealth is constant. In the long run, as wealth increases, the consumption function shifts upward, as in Figure 15-12. This upward shift prevents the average propensity to consume from falling as income increases. In this way, Modigliani reconciled the apparently conflicting studies of the consumption function.

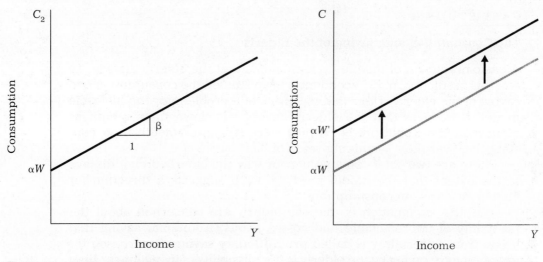

Figure 15-11 **The Life-Cycle Consumption Function.** The life-cycle model says that consumption depends on wealth as well as income. In other words, the intercept of the consumption function depends on wealth.

Figure 15-12 **How Changes in Wealth Shift the Consumption Function.** If consumption depends on wealth, then an increase in wealth shifts the consumption function upward.

The life-cycle model makes many other predictions as well. Most important, it implies that saving varies over a person's life in a predictable way. If a person begins adulthood with no wealth, she will accumulate wealth during her working years and then run down her wealth during her retirement years. Figure 15-13 illustrates the consumer's income, consumption, and wealth over her adult life. A key implication is that the young who are working save, while the old who are retired dissave.

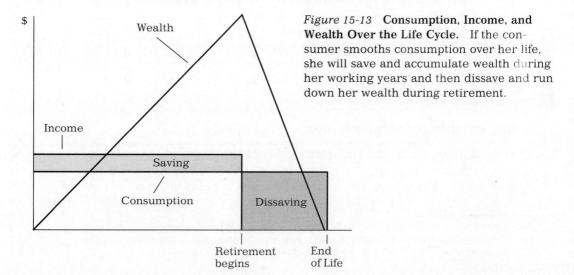

Figure 15-13 **Consumption, Income, and Wealth Over the Life Cycle.** If the consumer smooths consumption over her life, she will save and accumulate wealth during her working years and then dissave and run down her wealth during retirement.

CASE STUDY 15-3

The Consumption and Saving of the Elderly

A basic prediction of the life-cycle model is that the elderly dissave. To test this prediction, many economists have studied the consumption and saving of the elderly. Their findings present a problem for the life-cycle model. It appears that the elderly do not run down their wealth as quickly as one would predict if they were trying to smooth their consumption over their remaining years of life.[4]

There are two chief explanations for why the elderly do not dissave to the extent that the model predicts. Each suggests a direction for further research on consumption.

The first explanation is that the elderly are concerned about the possibility of unpredictable and costly events. Additional saving that arises from uncertainty is called **precautionary saving**. One reason for precautionary saving by the elderly is the possibility of living longer than expected and thus having to provide for a longer than average span of retirement. Another reason is the possibility of illness leading to large medical bills. If the elderly cannot buy insurance against these risks, they may respond by saving more in order to be better prepared for these contingencies.

The second explanation for the failure of the elderly to dissave is that they may want to leave bequests to their children, other relatives, or charities. Economists have studied bequests extensively and have proposed various theories of the bequest motive. We discuss some of this research in Chapter 16.

Overall, the research on the elderly suggests that the simplest life-cycle model cannot fully explain consumer behavior. There is no doubt that providing for retirement is an important motive for saving, but other motives, such as precautionary saving and bequests, appear important as well.

CASE STUDY 15-4

Saving and the Fear of Nuclear War

One of the more intriguing and controversial hypotheses about saving is that it fluctuates because of changes in the public's perception of the probability of nuclear war. Because people save to provide for consump-

---

[4] Albert Ando and Arthur Kennickell, "How Much (or Little) Life Cycle Saving Is There in Micro Data?" in Rudiger Dornbusch, Stanley Fischer, and John Bossons, eds., *Macroeconomics and Finance: Essays in Honor of Franco Modigliani* (Cambridge, Mass.: MIT Press, 1986).

tion in the future, an increase in the probability of nuclear war—and, hence, a decrease in the probability of surviving into the future—should reduce the amount people save.

Opinion polls indicate that the public has at times considered nuclear war to be a serious threat. In June 1981, for example, a Gallup poll asked, "How likely do you think we are to get into a nuclear war within the next ten years?" Nineteen percent of the respondents said that a nuclear war was "very likely," and another 28 percent said that it was "fairly likely."

Two pieces of evidence suggest that there is a link between the nuclear threat and saving. The first piece comes from time-series data.

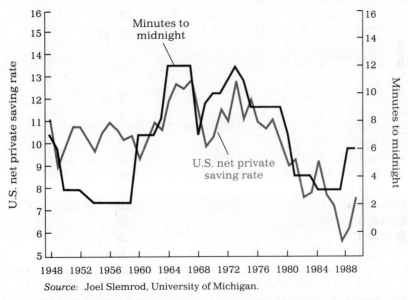

Source: Joel Slemrod, University of Michigan.

Figure 15-14 **Saving and the Threat of Nuclear War.** This figure shows that the net private saving rate fluctuates together with the threat of nuclear war. The threat of nuclear war is judged by the Bulletin of Atomic Scientists. The closer their clock is to midnight, the higher is the perceived threat of nuclear war.

Until recently, the Bulletin of Atomic Scientists regularly estimated the threat of nuclear war with their "minutes to midnight" clock; the higher the risk of nuclear war as estimated by the Bulletin, the closer it placed its clock to midnight. Figure 15-14 shows that the private saving rate fluctuates with the number of "minutes to midnight." When the threat of war is high, the saving rate is low.

The second piece of evidence comes from international data. Surveys conducted in various countries have asked people to judge the probability of nuclear war. Countries in which people perceive a high probability, such as the United States, tend to have low saving rates. Countries in which people perceive a low probability, such as Japan, tend to have high saving rates.

Economists differ about whether the perceived threat of nuclear war is an important—or even a plausible—determinant of national saving. Certainly, this hypothesized link between nuclear war and saving is one of the most unusual interactions between politics and economics.[5]

15-4 Milton Friedman and the Permanent-Income Hypothesis

In a book published in 1957, Milton Friedman proposed the **permanent-income hypothesis** to explain consumer behavior. Friedman's permanent-income hypothesis complements Modigliani's life-cycle hypothesis: both use Irving Fisher's theory of the consumer to argue that consumption should not depend on current income alone. But unlike the life-cycle hypothesis, which emphasizes that income follows a regular pattern over a person's lifetime, the permanent-income hypothesis emphasizes that people experience random and temporary changes in their incomes from year to year.[6]

The Hypothesis

Friedman suggested that we view current income Y as the sum of two components, **permanent income** Y^P and **transitory income** Y^T. That is,

$$Y = Y^P + Y^T.$$

Permanent income is the part of income that people expect to persist into the future. Transitory income is the part of income that people do not expect to persist. Put differently, permanent income is average income, and transitory income is the random deviation from that average.

---

[5] Joel Slemrod, "Saving and the Fear of Nuclear War," *Journal of Conflict Resolution* 30 (September 1986): 403–419; Joel Slemrod, "Fear of Nuclear War and Intercountry Differences in the Rate of Saving," *Economic Inquiry* 28 (October 1990): 647–657.

[6] Milton Friedman, *A Theory of the Consumption Function* (Princeton, N.J.: Princeton University Press, 1957).

To see how we might separate income into these two parts, consider these examples:

- Maria, who has a law degree, earned more this year than John, who is a high-school drop-out. Maria's higher income resulted from higher permanent income, because her education will continue to provide her a higher salary.

- Sue, a Florida orange grower, earned less than usual this year because a freeze destroyed her crop. Bill, a California orange grower, earned more than usual because the freeze in Florida drove up the price of oranges. Bill's higher income resulted from higher transitory income, because he is no more likely to have good weather next year than Sue.

These two examples show that different forms of income have different persistence. A good education provides a permanently higher income, whereas good weather provides only transitorily higher income. Although one can imagine intermediate cases, it is useful to keep things simple by supposing that there are only two kinds of income: permanent and transitory.

Friedman reasoned that consumption should depend primarily on permanent income, because consumers use saving and borrowing to smooth consumption in response to transitory changes in income. For example, if a person received a permanent raise of $10,000, his consumption would rise by about as much. Yet if a person won $10,000 in a lottery, he would not consume it all in one year. Instead, he would spread the extra consumption over the rest of his life. Assuming an interest rate of zero and a remaining lifespan of 50 years, consumption would rise by only $200 per year in response to the $10,000 prize. Thus, consumers spend their permanent income, but they save rather than spend most of their transitory income.

Friedman concluded that we should view the consumption function as approximately

$$C = \alpha Y^P,$$

where α is a constant. The permanent-income hypothesis, as expressed by this equation, states that consumption is proportional to permanent income.

Implications

The permanent-income hypothesis solves the consumption puzzle by suggesting that the standard Keynesian consumption function uses the wrong variable. According to the permanent-income hypothesis, consumption depends on permanent income; yet many studies of the consumption function try to relate consumption to current income.

Friedman argued that this *errors-in-variables problem* explains the seemingly contradictory findings.

Let's see what Friedman's hypothesis implies for the average propensity to consume. Divide both sides of his consumption function by Y to obtain

$$APC = C/Y = \alpha Y^P/Y.$$

According to the permanent-income hypothesis, the average propensity to consume depends on the ratio of permanent income to current income. When current income temporarily rises above permanent income, the average propensity to consume temporarily falls; when current income temporarily falls below permanent income, the average propensity to consume temporarily rises.

Now consider the studies of household data. Friedman reasoned that these data reflect a combination of permanent and transitory income. Households with high permanent income would have proportionately higher consumption. If all variation in current income came from the permanent component, one would not observe differences in the average propensity to consume across households. But some of the variation in income comes from the transitory component, and households with high transitory income would not have higher consumption. Therefore, researchers would find that high-income households had, on average, lower average propensities to consume.

Similarly, consider the studies of time-series data. Friedman reasoned that year-to-year fluctuations in income are dominated by transitory income. Therefore, years of high income should be years of low average propensities to consume. But over long periods of time—say, from decade to decade—the variation in income comes from the permanent component. Hence, in long time-series, one should observe a constant average propensity to consume.

CASE STUDY 15-5

The 1964 Tax Cut and the 1968 Tax Surcharge

The permanent-income hypothesis can help us to interpret how the economy responds to changes in fiscal policy. According to the *IS-LM* model of Chapters 9 and 10, tax cuts stimulate consumption and raise aggregate demand, and tax increases depress consumption and reduce aggregate demand. The permanent-income hypothesis states, however, that consumption responds only to changes in permanent income. Therefore, transitory changes in taxes will not have much impact on consumption and will have little effect on aggregate demand. If a change in taxes is to have a substantial effect on aggregate demand, it must be permanent.

Two changes in fiscal policy—the tax cut of 1964 and the tax surcharge of 1968—illustrate this principle. The tax cut of 1964 was a popular measure. It was announced to be a major and permanent reduction in tax rates. As we discussed in Chapter 9, this policy change had the intended effect of stimulating the economy.

The tax surcharge of 1968 arose in a very different political environment. It became law because the economic advisors of President Lyndon Johnson were concerned that the increase in government spending from the Vietnam War had excessively stimulated aggregate demand. To offset this effect, they recommended a tax increase. But Johnson, aware that the war was already unpopular, feared the political repercussions of a tax increase. He finally agreed to a temporary tax surcharge—in essence, a one-year increase in taxes. The tax surcharge did not have the desired effect of reducing aggregate demand. Unemployment continued to fall, and inflation continued to rise.

The lesson to be learned from these episodes is that a full analysis of tax policy must go beyond the simple Keynesian consumption function; it must take into account the distinction between permanent and transitory income. If consumers expect a tax change to be temporary, it will have a smaller impact on consumption and aggregate demand.

Rational Expectations and Consumption

The permanent-income hypothesis is founded on Fisher's model of intertemporal choice. It builds on the idea that forward-looking consumers base their consumption decisions not only on their current income but also on the income they expect to receive in the future. Thus, the permanent-income hypothesis highlights that consumption depends on people's expectations.

Recent research on consumption has combined this view of the consumer with the assumption of rational expectations. The rational-expectations assumption states that people optimally use all available information when forecasting the future. You might recall from Chapter 11 that this assumption has potentially profound implications for the costs of stopping inflation. It can also have profound implications for consumption.

The economist Robert Hall was the first to derive the implications of rational expectations for consumption. He showed that if the permanent-income hypothesis is correct, and if consumers have rational expectations, then changes in consumption over time should be unpredictable. Economists use the term **random walk** to describe the path of a variable whose changes are unpredictable. According to Hall, the combination of the permanent-income hypothesis and rational expectations implies that consumption follows a random walk.

Hall reasoned as follows. According to the permanent-income hypothesis, consumers face fluctuating income and try their best to smooth their consumption over time. At any moment, consumers choose consumption based on their current expectations of their lifetime incomes. Over time, they change their consumption because they receive news, which causes them to revise their expectations. For example, a person getting an unexpected raise increases consumption, whereas a person getting an unexpected demotion decreases consumption. If consumers are optimally using all available information, then the revisions in their expectations about their lifetime incomes should be unpredictable. Therefore, changes in their consumption should be unpredictable as well.

The evidence shows that the random-walk theorem does not describe the world exactly. That is, changes in aggregate consumption are somewhat predictable. Yet because the degree of predictability is small, some economists view the random-walk theorem—and therefore the rational expectations assumption—as a good approximation to reality.[7]

The rational-expectations approach to consumption has implications not only for forecasting but also for how economic policies affect the economy. *If consumers obey the permanent-income hypothesis and have rational expectations, then only unexpected policy changes influence consumption, and these changes have their effect when they change expectations.* For example, suppose that Congress today passes a tax increase to be effective next year. In this case, consumers receive the news about their lifetime incomes when Congress passes the law (or even earlier if the law's passage was predictable). The arrival of this news causes consumers to revise their expectations and reduce their consumption. The following year, when the tax hike goes into effect, consumption is unchanged because no news has arrived.

Hence, if the consumers have rational expectations, policymakers influence the economy not only through their actions but also through the public's expectation of their actions. Expectations, however, cannot be observed directly. Therefore, it is hard to know how and when changes in fiscal policy alter aggregate demand.

CASE STUDY 15-6

Do Consumers Anticipate Future Income?

The essence of Fisher's model of the consumer—and almost all subsequent work on consumption—is that consumption today depends not just on income today but also on income in the future. The more consumers expect to earn in the future, the more they should consume today.

---

[7] Robert E. Hall, "Stochastic Implications of the Life Cycle-Permanent Income Hypothesis: Theory and Evidence," *Journal of Political Economy* 86 (April 1978): 971–987.

The model therefore suggests that saving rates should help forecast future income growth. If consumers are saving a low fraction of current income, then they must be optimistic about future income. Conversely, if consumers are saving a high fraction of current income, then they must be pessimistic about future income. If this theory is correct, we should be able to examine data on the saving rate and find that periods of low saving are typically followed by periods of high income growth.[8]

Studies of time-series data on consumption and income provide support for this prediction. The saving rate does tend to rise when recessions are approaching, and booms are often preceded by low saving rates. Consumers do appear to look ahead to their future income when making their consumption decisions.

The evidence is not completely consistent with the theory, however. In particular, saving moves less than predicted. In other words, it appears that future income has a weaker influence on consumption, and current income has a stronger influence, than the permanent-income hypothesis predicts. One possible reason for this behavior is that some consumers may not have rational expectations: they may base their expectations of future income excessively on current income. Another possible reason is that some consumers are borrowing-constrained and therefore base their consumption on current income alone.[9]

15-5 Conclusion

In the work of Keynes, Fisher, Modigliani, and Friedman, we have seen a progression of views on consumer behavior. Keynes proposed that consumption depends largely on current income. Since then, economists have argued that consumers understand that they face an intertemporal decision. Consumers look ahead to their future resources and needs, implying a more complex consumption function than the one that Keynes proposed. Keynes suggested a consumption function of the form

$$\text{Consumption} = f(\text{Current Income}).$$

---

[8] *Mathematical Note:* To see how this works, consider our two-period example. Suppose that the interest rate is zero and that the consumer divides his total resources between the two periods, so that $C_1 = (Y_1 + Y_2)/2$. Then with simple algebraic rearrangement, you can show that $g = -2s$, where $g = (Y_2 - Y_1)/Y_1$ is the growth rate of income between the two periods and $s = (Y_1 - C_1)/Y_1$ is the first period saving rate. Hence, saving and subsequent growth are negatively related.

[9] John Y. Campbell, "Does Saving Anticipate Declining Labor Income?" *Econometrica* 55 (November 1982): 1249–1273; John Y. Campbell and N. Gregory Mankiw, "Consumption, Income, and Interest Rates: Reinterpreting the Time-Series Evidence," *NBER Macroeconomics Annual* (1989): 185–216.

The recent work suggests instead that

$$\text{Consumption} = f(\text{Current Income, Wealth, Expected Future Income, Interest Rates}).$$

In other words, current income is only one determinant of aggregate consumption.

Economists continue to debate the relative importance of these determinants of consumption. There remains disagreement, for example, on the effect of interest rates and the prevalence of borrowing constraints. One reason economists sometimes disagree about the effects of economic policy is that they are assuming different consumption functions. In the next chapter, we examine the debate about the impact of government debt, which is ultimately a debate about alternative views of consumer behavior.

Summary

1. Keynes conjectured that the marginal propensity to consume is between zero and one, that the average propensity to consume falls as income rises, and that current income is the primary determinant of consumption. Studies of household data and short time-series confirmed Keynes's conjectures. Yet studies of long time-series found no tendency for the average propensity to consume to fall as income rises over time.

2. Recent work on consumption builds on Irving Fisher's model of the consumer. In this model, the consumer faces an intertemporal budget constraint and chooses consumption for the present and the future to achieve the highest level of lifetime satisfaction. As long as the consumer can save and borrow, consumption depends on the consumer's lifetime resources.

3. The life-cycle hypothesis emphasizes that income varies somewhat predictably over a person's life and that consumers use saving and borrowing to smooth their consumption over their lifetimes. The hypothesis implies that consumption depends on both income and wealth.

4. The permanent-income hypothesis emphasizes that individuals experience both permanent and transitory fluctuations in their income. Because consumers can save and borrow, and because they want to smooth their consumption, consumption does not respond much to transitory income. Consumption depends primarily on permanent income.

KEY CONCEPTS

Marginal propensity to consume

Average propensity to consume

Intertemporal budget constraint

Discounting

Indifference curves

Marginal rate of substitution

Normal good

Income effect

Substitution effect

Borrowing constraint

Life-cycle hypothesis

Precautionary saving

Permanent-income hypothesis

Permanent income

Transitory income

Random walk

QUESTIONS FOR REVIEW

1. What were Keynes's three conjectures about the consumption function?

2. Describe the evidence that was consistent with Keynes's conjectures and the evidence that was inconsistent with them.

3. How do the life-cycle and permanent-income hypotheses resolve the seemingly contradictory pieces of evidence regarding consumption behavior?

4. Use Fisher's model of consumption to analyze an increase in second-period income. Compare the case in which the consumer faces a binding borrowing constraint and the case in which he does not.

PROBLEMS AND APPLICATIONS

1. The chapter uses the Fisher model to discuss a change in the interest rate for a consumer who saves some of his first-period income. Suppose, instead, that the consumer is a borrower. How does that alter the analysis? Discuss the income and substitution effects on consumption in both periods.

2. The chapter analyzes Fisher's model for the case in which the consumer can save or borrow at an interest rate of r and for the case in which the consumer can save at this rate but cannot borrow at all. Consider now the intermediate case in which the consumer can save at rate r_s and borrow at rate r_b, where $r_s < r_b$.

  a. What is the consumer's budget constraint in the case in which he consumes less than his income in period one?

  b. What is the consumer's budget constraint in the case in which he consumes more than his income in period one?

  c. Graph the two budget constraints and shade the area that represents the combination of first-period and second-period consumption the consumer can choose.

  d. Now add to your graph the consumer's indifference curves. Show three possible types of equilibria: one in which the consumer saves, one in which he borrows, and one in which he neither saves nor borrows.

  e. What determines first-period consumption in each of the three cases?

3. Explain whether borrowing constraints increase or decrease the potency of fiscal policy to influence aggregate demand in each of the following two cases:

    a. a temporary tax cut.

    b. an announced future tax cut.

4. In the discussion of the life-cycle hypothesis in the text, income is assumed to be constant during the period before retirement. For most people, however, income grows over their lifetimes. How does this growth in income influence the lifetime pattern of consumption and wealth accumulation shown in Figure 15-13 under the following conditions?

    a. Consumers can borrow, so that their wealth can be negative.

    b. Consumers face borrowing constraints, which prevents their wealth from falling below zero.

Do you consider case a or case b to be more realistic? Why?

5. Demographers predict that the fraction of the population that is elderly will increase over the next 20 years. What does the life-cycle model predict for the influence of this demographic change on the national saving rate?

6. One study found that the elderly who do not have children dissave at about the same rate as the elderly who do have children. What might this finding imply about the reason the elderly do not dissave as much as the life-cycle model predicts?

Chapter 16

Two Views of Government Debt

A billion here, a billion there, and pretty soon you're talking big money.

Senator Everett Dirksen

Throughout the 1980s, the federal government of the United States consistently ran large budget deficits. The government financed this excess of spending over revenue by borrowing in financial markets. Government debt rose by $1.97 trillion—from 33 percent of GNP in 1980 to 55 percent in 1989. Such a large peacetime increase in the government debt is unprecedented in the history of the United States.

The experience of the 1980s sparked a renewed interest among economists and policymakers in the economic effects of government debt. Some view the budget deficits of the 1980s as the worst mistake of economic policy since the Great Depression. Others think that the deficits matter very little.

This chapter presents the arguments on both sides of the debate. We begin by describing the traditional view of government debt, according to which government borrowing reduces national saving and crowds out capital accumulation. This view is held by most economists and has been implicit in the discussion of fiscal policy throughout this textbook. We then present an alternative view, called Ricardian equivalence, which is held by a small but influential minority of economists. According to the Ricardian view, government debt does not influence saving and capital accumulation.

We will see that the debate over government debt is largely a debate over the theory of consumption. In evaluating whether the traditional or the Ricardian view of government debt is correct, the key question is how fiscal policy influences consumer spending. To analyze the effects of government budget deficits on the economy, one must take a stand on whether consumers are short-sighted or forward-looking, on whether they face borrowing constraints or not, and on other aspects of consumer behavior.

16-1 The Traditional View of Government Debt

You are an economist working for the Congressional Budget Office (CBO). You receive a letter from the chair of the Senate Budget Committee:

Dear CBO Economist:

Congress is about to consider the president's request to cut all taxes by 20 percent. Before deciding whether to endorse the request, my committee would like your analysis. We see little hope of reducing government spending, so the tax cut would mean an increase in the budget deficit. How would the tax cut and budget deficit affect the economy and the economic well-being of the country?

Sincerely,
Committee Chair

Before responding to the senator, you open up your favorite economics textbook—this one, of course—to see what the models predict for such a change in fiscal policy.

To analyze the long-run effects of this policy change, you turn to the models in Chapters 3 and 4. The model in Chapter 3 shows that a tax cut stimulates consumer spending and reduces national saving. The reduction in saving raises the interest rate, which crowds out investment. The Solow growth model in Chapter 4 shows that lower investment eventually leads to a lower steady-state capital stock and a lower level of output. Because the economy starts with less capital than in the Golden Rule steady state, the reduction in steady-state capital implies lower consumption and reduced economic well-being.

To analyze the short-run effects of the policy change, you turn to the *IS-LM* model in Chapters 9 and 10. This model shows that a tax cut stimulates consumer spending, which implies an expansionary shift in the *IS* curve. The shift in the *IS* curve leads to an expansionary shift in the aggregate demand curve. In the short run, when prices are sticky, the expansion in aggregate demand leads to higher output and lower unemployment. Over time, as prices adjust, the economy returns to the natural rate of output, and the higher aggregate demand results in a higher price level.

To see how international trade affects your analysis, you turn to the open-economy models in Chapters 7 and 13. The model in Chapter 7 shows that reduced national saving causes a capital account surplus and a current account deficit. Although the inflow of capital from abroad lessens the effect of the fiscal policy change on capital accumulation, it implies that the United States becomes indebted to foreign countries. The fiscal policy change also causes the dollar to appreciate, which makes foreign goods cheaper in the United States and domestic goods more expensive abroad. The Mundell-Fleming model in Chapter 13 shows that this appreciation of the dollar and fall in net exports reduces the short-run expansionary impact of the fiscal change on output and employment.

With all these models in mind, you draft a response:

Dear Senator:

A tax cut financed by government borrowing would have many effects on the economy. The immediate impact of the tax cut would be to stimulate consumer spending. Higher consumer spending affects the economy both in the short run and in the long run.

In the short run, higher consumer spending would raise the demand for goods and services and thus raise output and employment. Interest rates would also rise, however, as investors competed for a smaller flow of saving. Higher interest rates would discourage investment and would encourage capital to flow in from abroad. The dollar would rise in value compared to foreign currencies, which would make American firms less competitive in world markets.

In the long run, the smaller national saving caused by the tax cut would mean a smaller capital stock and a greater foreign debt. Therefore, the output of the nation would be smaller, and a greater share of that output would be owed to foreigners.

The overall effect of the tax cut on economic well-being is hard to judge. Current generations may benefit from higher income and employment, although inflation would likely be higher as well. Future generations would bear much of the burden of today's budget deficits: they would be born into a nation with a smaller capital stock and a larger foreign debt.

Your faithful servant,
CBO Economist

The senator replies:

Dear CBO Economist:

Thank you for your letter. It made sense to me. But my committee yesterday heard testimony from a prominent economist who called herself a "Ricardian" and who reached quite a different conclusion. She said that a tax cut by itself would not stimulate consumer spending. She concluded that the budget deficit would therefore not have all the effects you listed. What's going on here?

Sincerely,
Committee Chair

After studying the next section, you write back to the senator, explaining in detail the debate over Ricardian equivalence.

16-2   The Ricardian View of Government Debt

Modern theories of consumer behavior emphasize that, because consumers are forward-looking, consumption does not depend on current income alone. The forward-looking consumer is at the heart of Franco Modigliani's life-cycle hypothesis and Milton Friedman's permanent-income hypothesis. The Ricardian view of government debt applies the logic of the forward-looking consumer to analyze the impact of fiscal policy.

The Basic Logic of Ricardian Equivalence

Consider the response of a forward-looking consumer to the tax cut that the Senate Budget Committee is considering. The consumer might reason as follows:

> The government is cutting taxes without any plans to reduce government spending. Does this policy alter my set of opportunities? Am I richer because of this tax cut? Should I consume more?
>
> Maybe not. The government is financing the tax cut by running a budget deficit. At some point in the future, the government will have to raise taxes to pay off the debt and accumulated interest. So the policy really represents a tax cut today coupled with a tax hike in the future. The tax cut merely gives me transitory income that eventually will be taken back. I am not any better off, so I will leave my consumption unchanged.

The forward-looking consumer understands that government borrowing today means higher taxes in the future. A tax cut financed by government debt does not reduce the tax burden; it merely reschedules it. It does not raise the consumer's permanent income and, therefore, does not increase consumption.

One can view this argument another way. Suppose that the government borrows $1,000 from the typical citizen to give that citizen a $1,000 tax cut. In essence, this policy is the same as giving the citizen a $1,000 government bond as a gift. One side of the bond says, "The government owes you, the bondholder, $1,000 plus interest." The other side says, "You, the taxpayer, owe the government $1,000 plus interest." Overall, the gift of a bond from the government to the typical citizen does not make the citizen richer or poorer, because the value of the bond is offset by the value of the future tax liability.

The general principle is that government debt is equivalent to future taxes, and if consumers are sufficiently forward-looking, future taxes are equivalent to current taxes. Hence, financing the government by debt is equivalent to financing it by taxes. This view, called **Ricardian equivalence**, is named after the famous nineteenth-century economist David Ricardo, because he first noted the theoretical argument.[1]

The implication of Ricardian equivalence is that a debt-financed tax cut leaves consumption unaffected. Households save the extra disposable income to pay for the future tax liability that the tax cut implies. This increase in private saving just offsets the decrease in public saving. National saving—the sum of private and public saving—remains the same. The tax cut therefore does not have all the effects that the traditional analysis predicts.

Take note that the logic of Ricardian equivalence does not imply that all changes in fiscal policy are irrelevant. Changes in fiscal policy do influence consumer spending if they influence present or future government purchases. For example, suppose that the government cuts taxes today because it plans to reduce government purchases in the future. If the consumer understands that this tax cut does not imply an increase in future taxes, he feels richer and raises his consumption. But note that it is the reduction in government purchases, rather than the reduction in taxes, that stimulates consumption: the announcement of a future reduction in government purchases would raise consumption today even if current taxes remained unchanged, because it would imply that taxes at some time in the future would be lower.

The Government Budget Constraint

To better understand the link between government debt and future taxes, it is useful to imagine that the economy lasts for only two periods. Period one represents the present, and period two the future. In period one, the government collects taxes T_1 and makes purchases G_1; in period two, it collects taxes T_2 and makes purchases G_2. Because the government can run a budget deficit or a budget surplus, taxes and purchases in any single period need not be closely related.

We want to see how the government's tax receipts in the two periods are related to its purchases in the two periods. Note that, in the first period, the budget deficit equals government purchases minus taxes. That is,

$$D = G_1 - T_1,$$

---

[1] Ironically, Ricardo was not a Ricardian. He was skeptical about the theory that now bears his name.

where D is the deficit. The government finances this deficit by selling an equal amount of government bonds. In the second period, the government must collect enough taxes to repay the debt, including the accumulated interest, and to pay for its second-period purchases. Thus,

$$T_2 = (1 + r)D + G_2,$$

where r is the interest rate.

To derive the equation linking taxes and purchases, combine the two equations above. Substitute the first equation for D into the second equation to obtain

$$T_2 = (1 + r)(G_1 - T_1) + G_2.$$

This equation relates purchases in the two periods to taxes in the two periods. To make the equation easier to interpret, we rearrange terms. After a little algebra, we obtain

$$T_1 + \frac{T_2}{1 + r} = G_1 + \frac{G_2}{1 + r}.$$

This equation is the **government budget constraint**. It states that the present value of government purchases equals the present value of taxes.

The government budget constraint shows how changes in fiscal policy today are linked to changes in fiscal policy in the future. If the government cuts first-period taxes without altering first-period purchases, then it enters the second period owing a debt to the holders of government bonds. This debt forces the government to choose between reducing purchases and raising taxes.

Figure 16-1 uses the Fisher diagram from Chapter 15 to show how a tax cut in period one affects the consumer under the assumption that the government does not alter its purchases in either period. In period one, the government cuts taxes by ΔT and finances this tax cut by borrowing. In period two, the government must raise taxes by $(1 + r)\Delta T$ to repay its debt and accumulated interest. Thus, the change in fiscal policy raises the consumer's income by ΔT in period one and reduces it by $(1 + r)\Delta T$ in period two. The consumer's set of opportunities is unchanged, however, because the present value of the consumer's lifetime income is the same as before the change in fiscal policy. Therefore, the consumer chooses the same level of consumption as he would have without the tax cut, which implies that private saving rises by the amount of the tax cut. Hence, by combining the government budget constraint and Fisher's model of intertemporal choice, we obtain the Ricardian result that a debt-financed tax cut does not affect consumption.

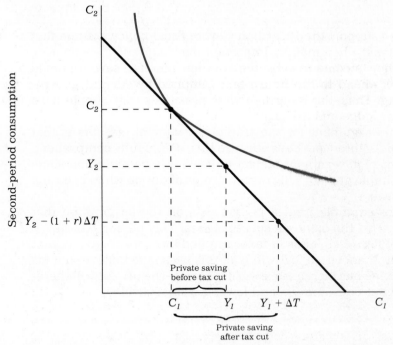

First-period consumption

Figure 16-1 **A Debt-Financed Tax Cut in the Fisher Diagram.** A debt-financed tax cut of ΔT raises first-period income. Yet if government purchases are unchanged, then the government budget constraint requires that second-period taxes be raised by $(1 + r)\Delta T$. Because the present value of income is unchanged, the budget constraint is unchanged, and the consumer chooses the same consumption as before the tax cut. Hence, Ricardian equivalence holds.

16-3 Consumers and Future Taxes

The essence of the Ricardian view is that when people choose their consumption, they rationally look ahead to the future taxes implied by government debt. But how forward-looking are consumers? Defenders of the traditional view of government debt believe that future taxes do not have as large an influence on current consumption as the Ricardian view assumes. Here are some of their arguments.[2]

---

[2] For a thorough survey of the debate over Ricardian equivalence, see Douglas Bernheim, "Ricardian Equivalence: An Evaluation of Theory and Evidence," *NBER Macroeconomics Annual (1987)*, 263–303.

Myopia

Economists who support the Ricardian view of fiscal policy assume that people are rational when making important decisions such as choosing how much of their income to consume and how much to save. Rational consumers look ahead to the future taxes implied by current government borrowing. Thus, the Ricardian view presumes that people have substantial knowledge and foresight.

One possible argument for the traditional view of tax cuts is that people are short-sighted, perhaps because they do not fully comprehend the implications of government budget deficits. It is possible that some people follow simple and not fully rational rules of thumb when choosing how much to save.

Suppose, for example, that a person acts on the assumption that future taxes will be the same as current taxes. This person will fail to take account of future changes in taxes implied by current government policies. A debt-financed tax cut will lead this person to believe that his permanent income has increased, even if it hasn't. The tax cut will therefore lead to higher consumption and lower national saving.

Borrowing Constraints

The Ricardian view of government debt is based on the permanent-income hypothesis. This view assumes that consumption does not depend on current income alone, but on permanent income, which includes both current and expected future income. According to the Ricardian view, a debt-financed tax cut increases current income, but it leaves permanent income and consumption unchanged.

Economists who hold the traditional view of government debt argue that the permanent-income hypothesis is not fully valid because some consumers face borrowing constraints. As we discussed in Chapter 15, a person facing a binding borrowing constraint can consume only his current income. For this person, current income rather than permanent income determines consumption; a debt-financed tax cut raises current income and raises consumption, even though future income is lower. In essence, when the government cuts current taxes and raises future taxes, it is giving taxpayers a loan. For individuals who wanted to obtain a loan but were unable to, the tax cut raises consumption.

Figure 16-2 uses the Fisher diagram to illustrate how a debt-financed tax cut raises consumption for a consumer facing a borrowing constraint. As we saw previously, this change in fiscal policy raises first-period income by ΔT and lowers second-period income by $(1 + r)\Delta T$. But the result is now different. Although the present value of income is the same, the consumer's set of opportunities is larger: the tax cut has loosened the borrowing constraint that prevents first-period consumption from exceeding first-period income. The consumer can now choose point B rather than point A.

You can see that the debate over government debt quickly evolves into a debate over consumer behavior. If many consumers would like to borrow to consume but cannot, then a debt-financed tax cut will stimulate consumption, as the traditional view assumes. Yet if borrowing constraints are unimportant for most consumers and if the permanent-income hypothesis is valid, then consumers are more likely to anticipate the future taxes implied by government debt.

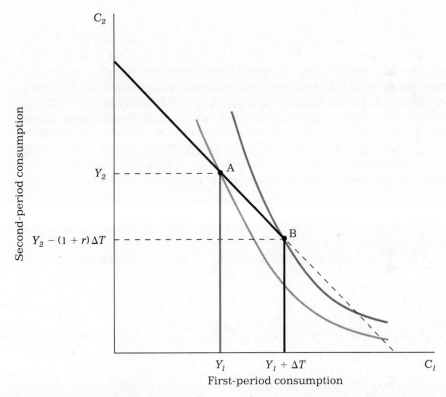

Figure 16-2 **How a Debt-Financed Tax Cut Relaxes a Borrowing Constraint.** The consumer here faces two constraints. The budget constraint says that the present value of consumption must not exceed the present value of income. The borrowing constraint says that first-period consumption must not exceed first-period income. A debt-financed tax cut of ΔT raises first- period income by ΔT and reduces second-period income by $(1 + r)\Delta T$. Because the present value of income is unchanged, the budget constraint is unchanged. Yet because first-period income is higher, the borrowing constraint allows a higher level of first-period consumption. The consumer now chooses point B rather than point A. Hence, Ricardian equivalence fails to hold.

Future Generations

A third argument for the traditional view of government debt is that
consumers expect the implied future taxes to fall not on them but on
future generations. Suppose, for example, that the government cuts
taxes today, issues 30-year bonds to finance the budget deficit, and then
raises taxes in 30 years to repay the loan. In this case, the government
debt represents a transfer of wealth from the next generation of taxpayers (which faces the tax hike) to the current generation of taxpayers
(which gets the tax cut). This transfer raises the lifetime resources of the
current generation, so it raises their consumption. In essence, a debt-
financed tax cut stimulates consumption because it gives the current
generation the opportunity to consume at the expense of the next generation.

The economist Robert Barro has provided a clever rejoinder to this
argument to support the Ricardian view. Barro argues that because
future generations are the children and grandchildren of the current
generation, we should not view them as independent economic actors.
Instead, he argues, the appropriate assumption is that current generations care about future generations. This altruism between generations
is evidenced by the gifts that many people give their children, often in
the form of bequests at the time of their death. The existence of bequests
suggests that many people are not eager to take advantage of the opportunity to consume at their children's expense.

According to Barro's analysis, the relevant decisionmaking unit is
not the individual who lives only a finite number of years, but the family
which continues indefinitely. In other words, an individual decides how
much to consume based not only on his own income but also on the
income of future members of his family. A debt-financed tax cut may
raise the income an individual receives in his lifetime, but it does not
raise his family's permanent income. Instead of consuming the extra
income from the tax cut, the individual saves it and leaves it as a bequest
to his children who will bear the future tax liability.

Again, we see that the debate over government debt is really a debate
over consumer behavior. The Ricardian view assumes that consumers
have a long time horizon. Barro's analysis of the family implies that the
consumer's time horizon, like the government's, is effectively infinite.
Yet it is possible that consumers do not look ahead to the tax liabilities
of future generations, perhaps because they do not care enough about
their children to leave them a bequest. In this case, a debt-financed tax
cut can alter consumption by redistributing wealth among generations.[3]

---

[3] Robert J. Barro, "Are Government Bonds Net Wealth?" *Journal of Political Economy* 81 (1974):
1095–1117.

C A S E   S T U D Y   16 - 1

Why Do Parents Leave Bequests?

The debate over Ricardian equivalence is partly a debate over how different generations are linked to each other. Robert Barro's defense of the Ricardian view is based on the assumption that parents leave their children bequests because they care about them. But is altruism really the reason that parents leave bequests?

One group of economists has suggested that parents use bequests to control their children. Parents often want their children to do certain things for them, such as phoning home regularly and visiting on holidays. Perhaps parents use the implicit threat of disinheritance to induce their children to be more attentive.

To test this "strategic bequest motive," these economists examined data on how often children visit their parents. They found that the more wealthy the parent, the more often the children visit. Moreover, only wealth that can be left as a bequest induces more frequent visits. Wealth that cannot be bequeathed, such as pension wealth which reverts back to the pension company in the event of an early death, does not encourage children to visit. These findings suggest that there may be more to the relationship between generations than mere altruism.[4]

16-4 Conclusion: Making a Choice

Having seen the alternative views of government debt, you should ask yourself two sets of questions.

First, which view do you agree with? If the government cuts taxes today, runs a budget deficit, and raises taxes in the future, how will the policy affect the economy? Will it stimulate consumption, as the traditional view holds? Or will consumers understand that their permanent income is unchanged and, therefore, offset the budget deficit with higher private saving?

Second, why do you hold the view that you do? If you agree with the traditional view of government debt, what is the reason? Do consumers fail to understand that higher government borrowing today means higher taxes tomorrow? Or do they ignore future taxes, either because

---

[4] B. Douglas Bernheim, Andrei Shleifer, and Lawrence H. Summers, "The Strategic Bequest Motive," *Journal of Political Economy* 93 (1985): 1045–1076.

they are borrowing-constrained or because future taxes fall on future generations with which they do not feel an economic link? If you hold the Ricardian view, do you believe that consumers have the foresight to see that government borrowing today implies future taxes to be levied on them or their descendants? Do you believe that consumers will save the extra income to offset that future tax liability?

One might have hoped that we could turn to the evidence to decide between these two views of government debt. Yet when economists examine historical episodes of large budget deficits, the evidence is inconclusive. History can be interpreted in different ways.

Consider, for example, the experience of the 1980s. The large budget deficits, caused mainly by the Reagan tax cut of 1981, seem to offer a natural experiment to test the two views of government debt. At first glance, this episode appears to support decisively the traditional view. The large budget deficits coincided with low national saving, high real interest rates, and a large current account deficit.

Yet those who hold the Ricardian view interpret the events of the 1980s differently. Perhaps saving was low in the 1980s because people were optimistic about future economic growth—an optimism that was also reflected in a booming stock market. Or perhaps saving was low because people expected that the tax cut would eventually lead not to higher taxes but, as Reagan promised, to lower government spending.

Because it is hard to rule out any of these interpretations, both views of government debt survive. Although one cannot be certain about which view is correct, one can be certain that the debate will continue as long as government debt remains a central issue in public policy.

Summary

1. According to the traditional view of government debt, a debt-financed tax cut stimulates consumer spending and lowers national saving. This increase in consumer spending raises aggregate demand and income in the short run, but leads to a lower capital stock and lower income in the long run.

2. According to the Ricardian view of government debt, a debt-financed tax cut does not stimulate consumer spending because it does not raise permanent income—it merely reschedules taxes from the present to the future.

3. The debate between the two views of government debt is ultimately a debate over how consumers behave. Are consumers rational or short-sighted? Do they face binding borrowing constraints? Are they economically linked to future generations through altruistic bequests? Economists' views of government debt hinge on their answers to these questions.

KEY CONCEPTS

Ricardian equivalence

Government budget constraint

QUESTIONS FOR REVIEW

1. According to the traditional view, how does a debt-financed tax cut affect public saving, private saving, and national saving?

2. According to the Ricardian view, how does a debt-financed tax cut affect public saving, private saving, and national saving?

3. Which view of government debt do you hold, and why?

PROBLEMS AND APPLICATIONS

1. Draft a letter to the senator of Section 16-1 explaining and evaluating the Ricardian view of government debt.

2. Chapter 15 discusses various views of the consumption function: Keynes's three conjectures, the life-cycle hypothesis, and the permanent-income hypothesis. What do these different views about consumption imply for the debate over government debt?

3. The Social Security system levies a tax on workers and pays benefits to the elderly. Suppose that Congress increases the tax and the benefits and, for simplicity, assume that the Congress announces that the increases will last for one year only.

   a. How would this change affect the economy?

   b. Does your answer depend on whether generations are altruistically linked?

Appendix

Is the Government Budget Deficit Correctly Measured?

This chapter discussed the traditional and Ricardian views of government budget deficits. The debate between these two competing views is central to the disagreements among economists over fiscal policy. Yet it is not the only source of controversy. Even economists who hold the traditional view that government borrowing has important effects on the economy argue among themselves about how best to evaluate fiscal policy.

Many arguments are over the question of how the budget deficit should be measured. Some economists believe that the deficit as currently measured is not a good indicator of the stance of fiscal policy. They believe that the budget deficit does not accurately gauge either the impact of fiscal policy on today's economy or the burden being placed on future generations of taxpayers. In this appendix, we discuss three problems with the usual measure of the budget deficit.

The general principle is that *the government budget deficit should accurately reflect the change in the government's overall indebtedness.* This principle seems simple enough. But its application is not as straightforward as one might expect.

Measurement Problem No. 1: Inflation

The least controversial of the measurement issues is the correction for inflation. Almost all economists agree that the government's indebtedness should be measured in real terms, not in nominal terms. The measured deficit should equal the change in the government's real debt, not the change in its nominal debt.

The budget deficit as commonly measured, however, does not correct for inflation. To see how large an error this induces, consider the following example. Suppose that the real government debt is not changing; in other words, in real terms, the budget is balanced. In this case, the nominal debt must be rising at the rate of inflation. That is, $\Delta D/D = \pi$, where π is the inflation rate and D is the stock of government debt. The government would look at the change in the nominal debt ΔD and would report a budget deficit of πD. Hence, most economists believe that the reported budget deficit is overstated by the amount πD.

One can make the same argument another way. The deficit is government expenditure minus government revenue. Part of expenditure is the interest paid on the government debt. Expenditure should include only the real interest paid on the debt rD, not the nominal interest paid iD. Because the difference between the nominal interest rate i and the real interest rate r is the inflation rate π, the budget deficit is overstated by πD.

This correction for inflation can be large, especially when inflation is high, and it can often change one's evaluation of fiscal policy. For example, in 1979, the federal government reported a budget deficit of $28 billion. Inflation was 8.6 percent, and the government debt held at the beginning of the year by the public (excluding the Federal Reserve) was $495 billion. The deficit was therefore overstated by

$$\pi D = 0.086 \times \$495 \text{ billion}$$
$$= \$43 \text{ billion}.$$

Thus, corrected for inflation, the reported budget deficit of $28 billion turns into a budget surplus of $15 billion! In other words, even though nominal government debt was rising, real government debt was falling.

Measurement Problem No. 2: Capital Assets

Many economists believe that an accurate assessment of the government's budget deficit requires accounting for the government's assets as well as its liabilities. In particular, when measuring the government's overall indebtedness, one should subtract government assets from government debt. Therefore, the budget deficit should be measured as the change in debt minus the change in assets.

Certainly, individuals and firms treat assets and liabilities symmetrically. When a person borrows to buy a house, we do not say that he is running a budget deficit. Instead, we offset the increase in assets (the house) against the increase in debt (the mortgage) and record no change in net wealth. Perhaps we should treat the government's finances the same way.

A budget procedure that accounts for assets as well as liabilities is sometimes called *capital budgeting*, because it takes into account changes in capital. For example, suppose that the government sells one of its office buildings or some of its land and uses the proceeds to reduce the government debt. Under current budget procedures, the reported deficit would be lower. Under capital budgeting, the revenue received from the sale would not lower the deficit, because the reduction in debt would be offset by a reduction in assets. Similarly, under capital budgeting, government borrowing to finance the purchase of a capital good would not raise the deficit.

The major difficulty with capital budgeting is that it is hard to decide which government expenditures should count as capital expenditures. For example, should the interstate highway system be counted as an asset of the government? If so, what is its value? What about the stockpile of nuclear weapons? Should spending on education be treated as expenditure on human capital? These difficult questions must be answered if the government is to adopt a capital budget.

Economists and policymakers disagree about whether the federal government should use capital budgeting. (Many state governments already use it.) Opponents of capital budgeting argue that, although the system is superior in principle to the current system, it is too difficult to implement in practice. Proponents of capital budgeting argue that even an imperfect treatment of capital assets would be better than ignoring them altogether.

Measurement Problem No. 3: Uncounted Liabilities

Some economists argue that the measured budget deficit is misleading because it excludes some important government liabilities. For example, consider the pensions of government workers. These workers provide labor services to the government today, but part of their compensation is deferred to the future. In essence, these workers are providing a loan to the government. Their future pension benefits represent a government liability not very different from government debt. Yet the accumulation of this liability is not included as part of the budget deficit.

Similarly, consider the Social Security System. In some ways, the system is similar to a pension plan. People pay some of their income into the system when young and expect to receive benefits when old. Perhaps accumulated future social security benefits should be included in the government's liabilities.

One might argue that Social Security liabilities are different from government debt, because the government can change the laws determining social security benefits. Yet, in principle, the government could always choose not to repay all of the government debt: the government honors its debt only because it chooses to do so. Promises to pay the holders of government debt may not be fundamentally different from promises to pay the future recipients of Social Security.

A particularly difficult form of government liability to measure is the *contingent liability*—the liability that is due only if a specified event occurs. For example, the government guarantees many forms of private credit, such as student loans, mortgages for low- and moderate-income families, and deposits in banks and savings and loan institutions. If the borrower repays the loan, the government pays nothing; if the borrower defaults, the government makes the repayment. When the government provides this guarantee, it undertakes a liability contingent on the borrower's default. Yet this contingent liability is not reflected in the budget deficit, in part because it is not clear what dollar value to attach to it.

Whither the Budget Deficit?

Economists differ in the importance they place on these measurement problems. Some believe that the problems are so severe that the measured budget deficit is almost meaningless. Most take these measurement problems seriously, but still view the measured budget deficit as a useful indicator of fiscal policy.

The undisputed lesson is that, to evaluate fully the course of fiscal policy, economists and policymakers must look at more than just the measured budget deficit. And, in fact, they do. The budget documents prepared annually by the Office of Management and Budget contain much detailed information on the government's finances, including data on capital expenditures and credit programs.

No economic statistic is perfect. Whenever one sees a number reported in the media, it is important to know what it is measuring and what it is leaving out. This is especially true for the government budget deficit.[5]

---

[5] To read more about the measurement problems of the government budget deficit, see Robert Eisner and Paul J. Pieper, "How to Make Sense of the Deficit," *The Public Interest* (Winter 1985): 101–118; and Laurence J. Kotlikoff, "Deficit Delusion," *The Public Interest* (Summer 1986): 53–65.

Chapter 17

Investment

Investment is the most volatile component of GNP. When expenditure on goods and services falls during a recession, much of the decline is usually due to a drop in investment spending. In the severe recession of 1982, for example, real GNP fell $105 billion from its peak in the third quarter of 1981 to its trough in the fourth quarter of 1982. Investment spending over the same period fell $152 billion, accounting for more than the entire fall in spending.

Economists study investment to better understand fluctuations in the economy's output of goods and services. In previous chapters our models of GNP used a simple investment function relating investment to the real interest rate: $I = I(r)$. That function states that an increase in the real interest rate reduces investment. In this chapter we look more closely at the theory behind this investment function.

There are three types of investment spending. **Business fixed investment** includes the equipment and structures that businesses buy to use in production. **Residential investment** includes the new housing that people buy to live in and that landlords buy to rent out. **Inventory investment** includes those goods that businesses put aside in storage, including materials and supplies, work in process, and finished goods. Figure 17-1 plots total investment and its three components in the United States during the past two decades. You can see that all types of investment fall substantially during recessions, which are shown as the shaded areas in the figure.

To account for these fluctuations, we build models in this chapter to explain each type of investment. As we develop these models, it is useful to keep in mind the following three questions:

• Why is investment negatively related to the interest rate?

• What causes the investment function to shift?

• Why does investment rise during booms and fall during recessions?

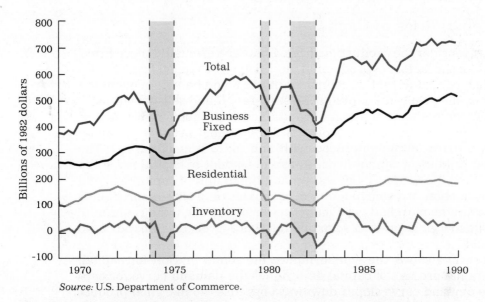

Source: U.S. Department of Commerce.

Figure 17-1 **The Three Components of Investment.** This figure shows total investment, business fixed investment, residential investment, and inventory investment in the United States from 1970 to 1990. Notice that all types of investment fall substantially during recessions, which are indicated here by the shaded areas.

At the end of the chapter, we return to these questions and summarize the lessons of the various models.

17-1 Business Fixed Investment

The standard model of business fixed investment is called the **neoclassical model of investment**. The neoclassical model examines the benefits and costs to firms of owning capital goods. The model shows how the level of investment—the addition to the stock of capital—is related to the marginal product of capital, the interest rate, and the tax rules affecting firms.

To develop the model, imagine that there are two kinds of firms in the economy. *Production firms* produce goods and services using capital that they rent. *Rental firms* make all of the investments in the economy; they buy capital and rent it out to the production firms. Of course, most firms in the real economy perform both functions: they produce goods and services, and they invest in capital for future production. For our analysis, however, it is instructive to separate these two activities by imagining that they take place in different kinds of firms.

The Rental Price of Capital

Let's first consider the production firms. Chapter 3 discussed these firms' demand for the factors of production. Recall how the typical firm decides how much capital to rent: it compares the cost and benefit of each unit of capital. The firm rents capital at a rental rate R and sells its output at a price P; the real cost of a unit of capital to the production firm is R/P. The real benefit of a unit of capital is the marginal product of capital MPK—the extra output produced with one more unit of capital. The marginal product of capital declines as the amount of capital rises: the more capital the firm has, the less an additional unit of capital will add to its production. We concluded that, to maximize profit, the firm rents capital until the marginal product of capital falls to equal the real rental price. The marginal-product schedule therefore gives the demand curve for capital.

Figure 17-2 shows the equilibrium in the rental market for capital. The marginal product of capital determines the demand curve for capital. The demand curve slopes downward because the marginal product of capital is low when the level of capital is high. At any point in time, the amount of capital in the economy is fixed, so the supply curve is vertical. The real rental price of capital adjusts to equilibrate supply and demand.

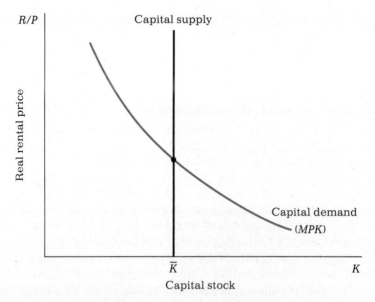

Figure 17-2 **The Rental Price of Capital.** The real rental price of capital adjusts to equilibrate the demand for capital (deter-mined by the marginal product of capital) and the fixed supply.

To see what variables influence the equilibrium rental price, consider the case of the Cobb-Douglas production function, which many economists consider a reasonable approximation of how the actual economy turns capital and labor into goods and services. Recall from Chapter 3 that the Cobb-Douglas production function is

$$Y = AK^{\alpha}L^{1-\alpha}.$$

The marginal product of capital of the Cobb-Douglas production function is

$$MPK = \alpha A(L/K)^{1-\alpha},$$

where K is capital, L labor, A a parameter measuring the level of technology, and α a parameter between zero and one that measures capital's share in output. Because the real rental price equals the marginal product of capital in equilibrium, we can write

$$R/P = \alpha A(L/K)^{1-\alpha}.$$

This expression identifies the variables that determine the real rental price. It shows that:

- The lower the stock of capital, the higher the real rental price of capital.

- The greater the amount of labor employed, the higher the real rental price of capital.

- The better the technology, the higher the real rental price of capital.

Events that reduce the capital stock (an earthquake), or raise employment (an expansion in aggregate demand), or improve the technology (a scientific discovery) raise the equilibrium real rental price of capital.

The Cost of Capital

Next consider the rental firms. Like car rental companies, their only activity is to buy capital goods and rent them out. We want to examine the incentive of these firms to increase or decrease their stock of capital, so we begin by considering the benefit and cost of owning capital.

The benefit of owning capital is the revenue from renting it to the production firms. The rental firm receives the real rental price of capital, R/P, for each unit of capital it owns and rents out.

The cost of owning capital is more complex. For each period of time that it rents out a unit of capital, the rental firm bears three costs:

1. When a rental firm buys a unit of capital and rents it out, it loses the interest it could have earned by depositing the purchase price of the capital in the bank. Or, equivalently, if the firm borrows to buy the capital, it must pay interest on the loan. If P_K is the purchase price of a unit of capital, and i is the nominal interest rate, then iP_K is the interest cost.

2. While the rental firm is renting out the capital, the price of the capital can change. If the price of capital falls, the firm loses, because the firm's asset has fallen in value. If the price of capital rises, the firm gains, because the firm's asset has risen in value. The cost of this loss or gain is $-\Delta P_K$.

3. While the capital is rented out, it suffers wear and tear, called **depreciation**. If δ is the rate of depreciation—the fraction of value lost per period because of wear and tear—then the dollar cost of depreciation is δP_K.

The total cost of renting out a unit of capital for one period is therefore

$$\text{Cost of Capital} = iP_K - \Delta P_K + \delta P_K$$
$$= P_K(i - \Delta P_K/P_K + \delta).$$

The cost of capital depends on the price of capital, the interest rate, the rate at which capital prices are changing, and the depreciation rate.

For example, consider the cost of capital to a car rental company. The company buys cars at \$10,000 each and rents them out to other businesses. The company faces an interest rate i of 10 percent per year, so the interest cost iP_K is \$1,000 per year for each car the company owns. Car prices are rising at 6 percent per year, so, excluding wear and tear, the firm gets a capital gain ΔP_K of \$600 per year. Cars depreciate at 20 percent per year, so the loss due to wear and tear δP_K is \$2,000 per year. Therefore, the company's cost of capital is

$$\text{Cost of Capital} = \$1,000 - \$600 + \$2,000$$
$$= \$2,400.$$

Hence, the cost to the car rental company of keeping a car in its capital stock is \$2,400 per year.

To make the expression for the cost of capital simpler and easier to interpret, we assume that the price of capital goods rises with the prices of other goods. In this case, $\Delta P_K/P_K$ equals the overall rate of inflation π. Because $i - \pi$ equals the real interest rate r, we can write the cost of capital as

$$\text{Cost of Capital} = P_K(r + \delta).$$

This equation states that the cost of capital depends on the price of capital, the real interest rate, and the depreciation rate.

Finally, we want to express the cost of capital relative to other goods in the economy. The **real cost of capital**—the cost of buying and renting out a unit of capital measured in units of the economy's output—is

$$\text{Real Cost of Capital} = (P_K/P)(r + \delta).$$

This equation states that the real cost of capital depends on the relative price of a capital good P_K/P, the real interest rate r, and the depreciation rate δ.

The Determinants of Investment

Now consider a rental firm's decision about whether to increase or decrease its capital stock. For each unit of capital, the firm earns real revenue R/P and bears the real cost $(P_K/P)(r + \delta)$. The real profit per unit of capital is

$$
\begin{aligned}
\text{Profit Rate} &= \text{Revenue} - \quad \text{Cost} \\
&= \quad R/P \quad - (P_K/P)(r + \delta).
\end{aligned}
$$

Since the real rental price in equilibrium equals the marginal product of capital, we can write the profit rate as

$$\text{Profit Rate} = MPK - (P_K/P)(r + \delta).$$

The rental firm makes a profit if the marginal product of capital is greater than the cost of capital. It incurs a loss if the marginal product is less than the cost of capital.

We can now see the economic incentives that lie behind the rental firm's investment decision. The firm's decision regarding its capital stock—that is, whether to add to it or to let it depreciate—depends on whether owning and renting out capital is profitable. The change in the capital stock, called **net investment**, depends on the difference between the marginal product of capital and the cost of capital. *If the marginal product of capital exceeds the cost of capital, firms find it profitable to add to their capital stock. If the marginal product of capital falls short of the cost of capital, they let their capital stock shrink.*

We can also now see that the separation of economic activity between production and rental firms—although useful to clarify our thinking—is not necessary for our conclusion regarding how firms determine their investment. For a firm that both uses and owns capital, the benefit of an extra unit of capital is the marginal product of capital, and the cost is the cost of capital. Like a firm that owns and rents out capital, this firm adds to its capital stock if the marginal product exceeds the cost of capital. Thus, we can write

$$\Delta K = I_n \, [MPK - (P_K/P)(r + \delta)],$$

where $I_n(\quad)$ is the function showing how much net investment responds to the incentive to invest.

We can now derive the investment function. Total spending on business fixed investment is the sum of net investment and the replacement of depreciated capital. The investment function is

$$I = I_n \, [MPK - (P_K/P)(r + \delta)] + \delta K.$$

Business fixed investment depends on the marginal product of capital, the cost of capital, and the amount of depreciation.

This model shows why investment depends on the interest rate. An increase in the real interest rate raises the cost of capital. It therefore reduces the amount of profit from owning capital and reduces the incentive to accumulate more capital. Similarly, a decrease in the real interest rate reduces the cost of capital and stimulates investment. For this reason, the investment schedule relating investment to the interest rate slopes downward, as in Figure 17-3.

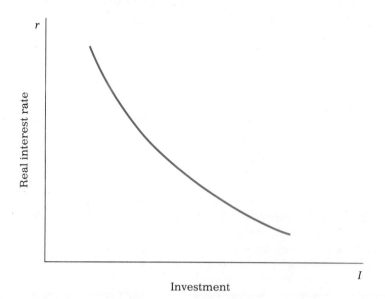

Figure 17-3 **The Investment Function.** Business fixed investment increases when the interest rate falls, because a lower in- terest rate reduces the cost of capital and therefore makes owning capital more profitable.

The model also shows what causes the investment schedule to shift. Any event that raises the marginal product of capital increases the profitability of investment and causes the investment schedule to shift outward, as in Figure 17-4. For example, a technological innovation that increases the production function parameter *A* raises the marginal product of capital and, for any given interest rate, raises the amount of capital goods that rental firms wish to buy.

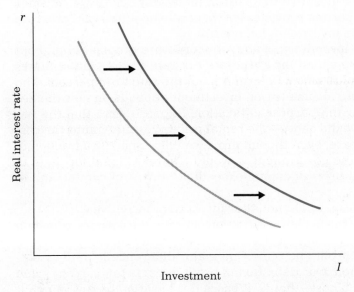

Figure 17-4 **Shifts in the Investment Function.** An increase in the mar- ginal product of capital shifts the investment function outward.

Finally, consider what happens as this adjustment of the capital stock continues over time. If the marginal product begins above the cost of capital, the capital stock will rise and the marginal product will fall. If the marginal product of capital begins below the cost of capital, the capital stock will fall and the marginal product will rise. Eventually, as the capital stock adjusts, the marginal product of capital approaches the cost of capital. When the capital stock reaches a steady-state level, we can write

$$MPK = (P_K/P)(r + \delta).$$

Thus, in the long run, the marginal product of capital equals the real cost of capital. The speed of adjustment toward the steady state depends on how quickly firms adjust their capital stock, which in turn depends on how costly it is to build, deliver, and install new capital.[1]

Taxes and Investment

Many provisions of the federal tax code influence firms' accumulation of capital. Sometimes policymakers change these provisions in order to shift the investment function and influence aggregate demand. Although taxes influence the incentive to invest in many ways, here we consider two of the most important provisions of corporate taxation: the corporate income tax and the investment tax credit.

The **corporate income tax** is a tax on corporate profits. Throughout most of the past 40 years, the corporate tax rate in the United States was 46 percent; the 1986 Tax Reform Act cut the rate to 34 percent. The effect of a corporate income tax on investment depends on how the law defines "profit" for the purpose of taxation. Suppose, first, that the law defined profit as we did above—the rental price of capital minus the cost of capital. In this case, even though firms would be sharing a fraction of their profits with the government, it would still be rational for them to invest if the rental price of capital exceeded the cost of capital, and to disinvest if the rental price fell short of the cost of capital. A tax on profit, measured in this way, would not alter investment incentives.

Yet, because of the tax law's definition of profit, the corporate income tax does influence investment. There are many differences between the law's definition of profit and ours. One major difference is in the treatment of depreciation. Our definition of profit deducts the current value of depreciation as a cost—that is, it bases depreciation on how much it would cost today to replace worn out capital. Under the corporate tax, however, firms deduct depreciation using historical cost—that is, a value based on the price of the capital when it was originally purchased. In periods of inflation, replacement cost is greater than historical cost, so the corporate tax tends to understate the value of depreciation and overstate profit. As a result, the tax law sees a profit and levies a tax even when economic profit is zero, which makes owning capital less attractive. For this and other reasons, many economists believe that the corporate income tax discourages investment.

The **investment tax credit** is a tax provision that encourages the accumulation of capital. The investment tax credit reduces a firm's taxes

---

[1] Economists often measure capital goods in units such that the price of one unit of capital equals the price of one unit of other goods and services ($P_K = P$). This was the approach taken implicitly in Chapter 4, for example. In this case, the steady-state condition says that the marginal product of capital net of depreciation, $MPK - \delta$, equals the real interest rate r.

by a certain amount for each dollar spent on capital goods. Because a firm recoups part of its expenditure on new capital in lower taxes, the credit reduces the effective purchase price of a unit of capital. That is, the investment tax credit reduces P_K. Thus, the investment tax credit reduces the cost of capital and raises investment.

Many economists believe that the investment tax credit is one of the most effective ways to stimulate investment. In 1985 the investment tax credit was 10 percent. Yet the Tax Reform Act of 1986, which reduced the corporate income tax rate, also eliminated the investment tax credit.[2]

CASE STUDY 17-1

The Swedish Investment Funds System

Tax incentives for investment are one tool policymakers can use to control aggregate demand. For example, an increase in the investment tax credit reduces the cost of capital, shifts the investment function outward, and raises aggregate demand. Similarly, a reduction in the tax credit reduces aggregate demand by making investment more costly.

From the mid-1950s to the mid-1970s, the government of Sweden attempted to control aggregate demand by encouraging or discouraging investment. A system called the *investment fund* subsidized investment, much like an investment tax credit, during periods of recession. When government officials decided that economic growth had slowed, they authorized a temporary investment subsidy. When the officials concluded that the economy had recovered sufficiently, they revoked the subsidy. Eventually, however, Sweden abandoned the use of temporary investment subsidies to control the business cycle, and the subsidy became a permanent feature of Swedish tax policy.

Should investment subsidies be used to combat economic fluctuations? Some economists believe that, for the two decades it was in effect, the Swedish policy reduced the magnitude of the business cycle. Others believe that this policy can have unintended and perverse effects: for example, if the economy begins to slow down, firms may anticipate a future subsidy and delay investment, making the slowdown worse. Thus, the implications of this policy are complex, which makes its effect on economic performance hard to evaluate.[3]

---

[2] To read more about how taxes influence investment, see Robert E. Hall and Dale W. Jorgenson, "Tax Policy and Investment Behavior," *American Economic Review* 57 (June 1967): 391–414.

[3] John B. Taylor, "The Swedish Investment Funds System as a Stabilization Rule," *Brookings Papers on Economic Activity*, no. 1 (1982): 57–106.

The Stock Market and Tobin's *q*

Many economists see a link between fluctuations in investment and fluctuations in the stock market. The term *stock* refers to the shares in the ownership of corporations, and the **stock market** is the market in which these shares are traded. Because firms are more valuable when they have many opportunities for profitable investment, stock prices reflect the incentives to invest.

The Nobel-Prize-winning economist James Tobin proposed that firms base their investment decisions on the following ratio, which is now called **Tobin's *q***:

$$q = \frac{\text{Market Value of Installed Capital}}{\text{Replacement Cost of Installed Capital}}.$$

The numerator of Tobin's *q* is the worth of the economy's capital as valued by the stock market. The denominator is the price of the capital if it were purchased today.

Tobin reasoned that net investment should depend on whether *q* is greater or less than one. If *q* is greater than one, then the stock market values installed capital at more than its replacement cost. In this case, managers can raise the market value of their firms' stock by buying more capital. Conversely, if *q* is less than one, the stock market values capital at less than its replacement cost. In this case, managers will not replace capital as it wears out.

Although at first the *q* theory of investment may appear quite different from the neoclassical model developed above, in fact the two theories are closely related. The connection comes from the observation that Tobin's *q* depends on current and future expected profits from installed capital. If the marginal product of capital exceeds the cost of capital, then installed capital earns profits. These profits make the rental firms desirable to own, which raises the market value of these firms' stock, implying a high value of *q*. Similarly, if the marginal product of capital falls short of the cost of capital, then installed capital is incurring losses, implying a low market value and a low value of *q*.

The advantage of Tobin's *q* as a measure of the incentive to invest is that it reflects the expected future profitability of capital as well as the current profitability. For example, suppose that Congress legislates a reduction in the corporate income tax beginning next year. This expected fall in the corporate tax implies greater profits for the owners of capital. These higher expected profits raise the value of the stock market today, raise Tobin's *q*, and therefore encourage investment today. Thus, Tobin's *q* theory of investment emphasizes that investment decisions depend not only on current economic policies, but also on policies expected to prevail in the future.

Tobin's *q* theory is useful also because it provides a simple way of interpreting the role of the stock market in the economy. Suppose, for example, that you observe a fall in stock prices. Because the replacement cost of capital is fairly stable, a fall in the stock market usually implies a fall in Tobin's q. A fall in q reflects investors' pessimism about the current or future profitability of capital. According to q theory, the fall in q will lead to a fall in investment, which could lower aggregate demand. In essence, q theory gives a reason to expect fluctuations in the stock market to be closely tied to fluctuations in output and employment. Thus, it is not surprising that the stock market is one of the most closely watched indicators of the course of economic activity.[4]

Financing Constraints

When a firm wants to invest in new capital, such as building a new factory, it often raises the necessary funds in financial markets. This financing may take several forms—obtaining loans from banks, selling bonds to the public, or selling shares in future profits on the stock market. The neoclassical model assumes that if a firm is willing to pay the cost of capital, the financial markets will make the funds available.

Yet sometimes firms face **financing constraints**—limits on the amount they can raise in financial markets. Financing constraints can prevent firms from undertaking profitable investments. When a firm is unable to raise funds in financial markets, the amount it can spend on new capital goods is limited to the amount it is currently earning. Financing constraints influence the investment behavior of firms just as borrowing constraints influence the consumption behavior of households. Borrowing constraints cause households to determine their consumption on the basis of current rather than permanent income; financing constraints cause firms to determine their investment on the basis of their current cash flow rather than expected profitability.

To see the impact of financing constraints, consider the effect of a short recession on investment spending. A recession reduces employment, the rental price of capital, and profits. If firms expect the recession to be short-lived, however, they will want to continue investing, knowing that their investments will be profitable in the future. That is, a short recession will have only a small effect on Tobin's q. For firms that can raise funds in financial markets, the recession should have only a small effect on investment.

Quite the opposite is true for firms that face financing constraints. The fall in current profits restricts the amount that these firms can spend on new capital goods and may prevent them from making profitable investments. Financing constraints make investment more sensitive to current economic conditions.

---

[4] To read more about the relationship between the neoclassical model of investment and q theory, see Fumio Hayashi, "Tobin's Marginal q and Average q: A Neoclassical Approach," *Econometrica* 50 (January 1982): 213–224; Lawrence H. Summers, "Taxation and Corporate Investment: A q-theory Approach," *Brookings Papers on Economic Activity* 1 (1981): 67–140.

17-2 Residential Investment

We now turn to another component of investment spending—residential investment. In this section we present a simple model to show what determines the amount of residential investment. Residential investment includes the purchase of new housing both by people who plan to live in it themselves and by landlords who plan to rent it to others. For simplicity, our model assumes that all housing is of the first type—that is, it is all owner-occupied.

The Stock Equilibrium and the Flow Supply

There are two parts to the model. First, the market for the existing stock of houses determines the equilibrium housing price. Second, the housing price determines the flow of residential investment.

Figure 17-5A shows how the relative price of housing P_H/P is determined by the supply and demand for the existing stock of houses. At any point in time, the supply of houses is fixed. We represent this stock with a vertical supply curve. The demand curve for houses slopes downward, because high prices cause people to live in smaller houses, to share residences, or sometimes even to become homeless. The price of housing adjusts to equilibrate supply and demand.

Figure 17-5B shows how the relative price of housing determines the supply of new houses. Construction firms buy materials and hire labor to build houses, and then sell the houses at the market price. Their costs depend on the overall price level P, and their revenue depends on the price of houses P_H. The higher the relative price of housing, the greater the incentive to build houses, and the more houses are built. The flow of new houses—residential investment—therefore depends on the equilibrium price as set in the market for existing houses.

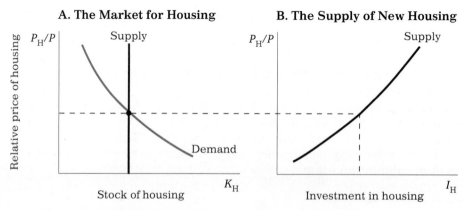

A. The Market for Housing   **B. The Supply of New Housing**

Figure 17-5 **The Determination of Residential Investment.**   The relative price of housing adjusts to equilibrate supply and demand for housing. The relative price then determines the flow of new housing that construction firms build.

This model of residential investment is closely related to the *q* theory of business fixed investment. According to *q* theory, business fixed investment depends on the market price of installed capital relative to its replacement cost; this relative price, in turn, depends on the expected profits from owning installed capital. According to this model of the housing market, residential investment depends on the relative price of housing. The relative price of housing, in turn, depends on the demand for housing, which depends on the imputed rent that individuals expect to receive from their housing. Hence, the relative price of housing plays much the same role for residential investment as Tobin's *q* does for business fixed investment.

Changes in Housing Demand

When the demand for housing shifts, the equilibrium housing price changes, which in turn affects residential investment. The demand curve for housing can shift for various reasons. An economic boom raises national income and therefore the demand for housing. A large increase in the population, perhaps due to immigration, also raises the demand for housing. Figure 17-6A shows that an expansionary shift in demand raises the equilibrium price. Figure 17-6B shows that the increase in the housing price increases residential investment.

One of the most important determinants of housing demand is the real interest rate. Many people take out loans—mortgages—to buy their homes; the interest rate is the cost of the loan. Even the few people who do not have to borrow to purchase a home will respond to the interest rate, because the interest rate is the opportunity cost of holding their wealth in housing rather than putting it in a bank. A reduction in the interest rate therefore raises housing demand, housing prices, and residential investment.

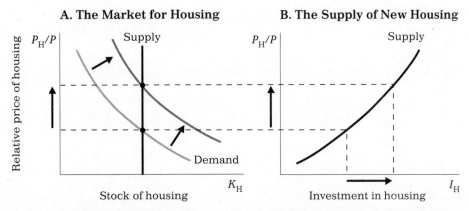

A. The Market for Housing **B. The Supply of New Housing**

Figure 17-6 **An Increase in Housing Demand.** An increase in housing demand, perhaps due to a fall in the interest rate, raises housing prices and residential investment.

//

F Y I **What Price House Can You Afford?**

When someone takes out a mortgage to buy a house, the bank often places a ceiling on the size of the loan. That ceiling depends on the person's income and the market interest rate. A typical bank requirement is that the monthly mortgage payment—including both interest and repayment of principal— not exceed 28 percent of the borrower's income.

Table 17-1 shows how the interest rate affects the loan ceiling. The home-buyer in the example has an income of $30,000 and is applying for a 30-year mortgage. The bank is assumed to use the standard 28 percent limit on the size of the loan.

As you can see, if the home-buyer is up against the borrowing limit, as many are, small changes in the interest rate can have a large influence on the amount he or she can spend on a house. An increase in the interest rate from 8 to 10 percent reduces the maximum loan from $95,398 to $79,766—a fall of 16 percent. An increase in the interest rate therefore reduces housing demand, which in turn depresses housing prices and residential investment.

It is noteworthy—and a bit puzzling—that banks make this calculation using the nominal rather than the real interest rate. The real interest rate measures the true cost of borrowing to buy a house, because the price of the house will normally rise at the overall rate of inflation. Yet bank rules use nominal interest rates when computing mortgage eligibility. Because of these bank rules, residential investment spending depends on nominal as well as real interest rates.

Table 17-1   How High Interest Rates Reduce Mortgage Eligibility and Housing Demand

Assumptions:
30-year mortgage, $30,000 annual income, 28 percent limit on mortgage payment

Interest Rate	Maximum Possible Loan
5%	$130,397
6	116,754
7	105,215
8	95,398
9	86,997
10	79,766
11	73,504
12	68,053
13	63,280
14	59,078
15	55,360

//

CASE STUDY 17-2

Taxes, Babies, and the Housing Boom of the 1970s

During the 1970s the United States experienced a nationwide boom in housing. The price of a new single-family home relative to the CPI rose 30 percent from 1970 to 1980. Economists do not know with certainty what caused the increase in housing prices during this period, but two hypotheses have been proposed.

One hypothesis is that the rise in inflation and the failure of federal tax law to index for inflation caused an increase in housing demand. The federal income tax subsidizes homeownership in two ways: it does not require homeowners to pay tax on the imputed rent on their homes, and it allows homeowners to deduct mortgage interest when computing their taxable income. Because the nominal interest rate on mortgages rises when inflation rises, the value of this subsidy is higher at higher rates of inflation. Inflation and nominal interest rates rose substantially in the 1970s, which increased the tax benefits of homeownership.

A second hypothesis is that the baby boom of the 1950s caused a rise in housing demand in the 1970s. Figure 17-7 shows the number of births each year from 1910 to 1989. Note that after World War II, births rose markedly—from 2.86 million in 1945 to a peak of 4.30 million in 1957. In the 1970s, the members of this large baby-boom generation began reaching adulthood and forming their own households. Therefore, the demand for housing grew rapidly, and housing prices rose.

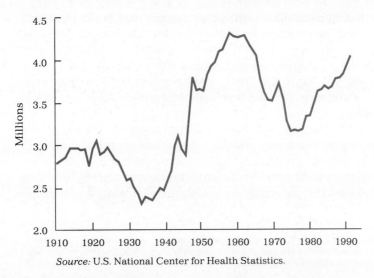

Source: U.S. National Center for Health Statistics.

Figure 17-7 **The Number of Births in the United States.** The number of births fluctuates substantially over time. These demographic fluctuations are one source of fluctuations in housing demand.

This baby-boom hypothesis suggests that the demand for new housing will fall during the 1990s. In the 1970s births fell substantially—reaching a low of 3.14 million in 1973. In the 1990s this small baby-bust generation will be reaching adulthood. Some economists predict that because of this slowdown in the growth of the adult population, real housing prices will fall during the 1990s.[5]

17-3   Inventory Investment

Inventory investment is one of the smallest components of spending, averaging about 1 percent of total GNP. Yet its remarkable volatility makes it important. In a typical recession, more than half of the fall in spending comes from a decline in inventory investment.

Reasons for Holding Inventories

Inventories serve many purposes. Before presenting a model to explain fluctuations in inventory investment, let's discuss some of the motives firms have for holding inventories.

One use of inventories is to smooth the level of production over time. Consider a firm that experiences temporary booms and busts in sales. Rather than adjusting production to match the fluctuations in sales, it may be cheaper to produce goods at a steady rate. When sales are low, the firm produces more than it sells and puts the extra goods into inventory. When sales are high, the firm produces less than it sells and takes goods out of inventory. This motive for holding inventories is called **production smoothing**.

A second reason for holding inventories is that inventories may allow a firm to operate more efficiently. Retail stores, for example, can sell merchandise more effectively if they have goods on hand to show to customers. Manufacturing firms keep inventories of spare parts in order to reduce the time that the assembly line is shut down when a machine

---

[5] James M. Poterba, "Tax Subsidies to Owner-Occupied Housing: An Asset Market Approach," *Quarterly Journal of Economics* 99 (1984): 729–752; N. Gregory Mankiw and David N. Weil, "The Baby Boom, the Baby Bust, and the Housing Market," *Regional Science and Urban Economics* 19 (May 1989): 235–258.

breaks. In some ways, we can view **inventories as a factor of production**: the more inventories a firm holds, the more output it can produce.

A third reason for holding inventories is to avoid running out of goods when sales are unexpectedly high. Firms often have to make production decisions before knowing how much customers will demand. For example, a publisher must decide on how many copies of a new book to print before knowing whether the book will be popular. If demand exceeds production and there are no inventories, the good will be out of stock for a period, and the firm will lose sales and profit. Inventories can prevent this from happening. This motive for holding inventories is called **stock-out avoidance**.

A fourth explanation of inventories is dictated by the production process. Many goods require a number of steps in production and, therefore, take time to produce. When a product is only partly completed, its components are counted as part of a firm's inventory. These inventories are called **work in process**.

CASE STUDY 17-3

Seasonal Fluctuations and Production Smoothing

Economists have spent much time studying data on production, sales, and inventories to test alternative theories of inventory holding. Much of this research examines whether the production-smoothing theory accurately describes the behavior of firms. Contrary to what many economists expected, most of the evidence suggests that firms do not use inventories to smooth production over time.

The clearest evidence against production smoothing comes from industries with seasonal fluctuations in demand. In many industries, sales fluctuate regularly over the course of a year. For example, the toy industry sells more of its output in December than in January. One might expect that firms would build up inventories in times of low sales and draw them down in times of high sales.

Yet, in most industries, firms do not use inventories to smooth production over the year. Instead, the seasonal pattern in production closely matches the seasonal pattern in sales. The evidence from seasonal fluctuations suggests that, in most industries, firms see little benefit to smoothing production.[6]

---

[6] Jeffrey A. Miron and Stephen P. Zeldes, "Seasonality, Cost Shocks, and the Production Smoothing Model of Inventories," *Econometrica* 56 (July 1988): 877–908.

The Accelerator Model of Inventories

Because there are many motives for holding inventories, there are many models of inventory investment. One simple model that explains the data well, without endorsing a particular motive, is the **accelerator model**. This model was developed about half a century ago, and it is sometimes applied to all types of investment. Here we apply it to the type for which it works best—inventory investment.

The accelerator model of inventories assumes that firms hold a stock of inventories that is proportional to the firms' level of output. That is, if N is the stock of inventories and Y is output, then

$$N = \beta Y,$$

where β is a parameter reflecting how much inventory firms wish to hold as a proportion of output. There are many reasons for setting the level of inventories in this way. When output is high, manufacturing firms have more materials and supplies on hand waiting to be used, and they have more goods in the process of being completed. When the economy is booming, retail firms want to have more merchandise on the shelves to show customers.

Inventory investment I is the change in the stock of inventories ΔN. Therefore,

$$I = \Delta N = \beta \Delta Y.$$

The accelerator model predicts that inventory investment will be proportional to the change in output. When output rises, firms want to hold more inventories, so they invest in them. When output falls, firms want to hold fewer inventories, so they disinvest—that is, they allow their inventories to run down.

We can now see how the model earned its name. Because the variable Y is the rate at which firms are producing goods, ΔY is the "acceleration" of production. Hence, the model says that inventory investment depends on whether the economy is speeding up or slowing down.

CASE STUDY 17-4

The Evidence for the Accelerator Model

To see how well the accelerator model fits the data, look at Figure 17-8. This figure is a scatterplot of annual data from the national income accounts for the United States. On the horizontal axis is the change in real GNP. On the vertical axis is real inventory investment.

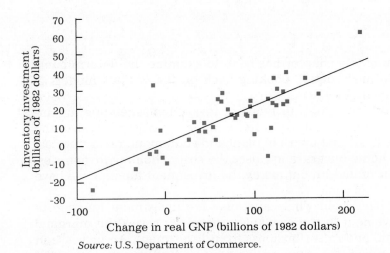

Source: U.S. Department of Commerce.

Figure 17-8 **The Evidence for the Accelerator Model.** This scatterplot
shows that inventory investment is
high in years when real GNP rises
and is low in years when real GNP
falls.

The positive association between the change in GNP and inventory
investment supports the prediction of the accelerator model. The line
drawn through these points shows the following relationship:

$$I = 0.2\Delta Y.$$

For every dollar that GNP rises, there is 20 cents of inventory investment.

Inventories and the Real Interest Rate

Like other components of investment, inventory investment depends on
the real interest rate. When a firm holds a good in inventory and sells it
tomorrow, rather than selling it today, it gives up the interest it could
have earned between today and tomorrow. Thus, the real interest rate
measures the opportunity cost of holding inventories.

When the real interest rate rises, holding inventories becomes more
costly, so rational firms try to reduce their stock. Therefore, an increase
in the real interest rate depresses inventory investment. For example,
in the 1980s many firms adopted "just in time" production plans, which
are designed to reduce the amount of inventory by producing goods just
before sale. The high real interest rates that prevailed during most of
this decade are one possible explanation for this change in business
strategy.

17-4 Conclusion

The purpose of this chapter has been to examine the determinants of investment in more detail. Looking back on the various models of investment, three themes arise.

First, we have seen that all types of investment spending are inversely related to the real interest rate. A higher interest rate raises the cost of capital to firms that invest in plant and equipment, raises the cost of borrowing to home-buyers, and raises the cost of holding inventories. Thus, the models of investment justify the investment function we have used throughout this book.

Second, we have seen what can cause the investment function to shift. An improvement in the available technology raises the marginal product of capital and raises business fixed investment. An increase in the population raises the demand for housing and raises residential investment. Most important, various economic policies, such as changes in the investment tax credit and the corporate income tax, alter the incentives to invest and therefore shift the investment function.

Third, we have learned why investment is so volatile over the business cycle: investment spending depends on the output of the economy as well as on the interest rate. In the neoclassical model of business fixed investment, higher employment raises the marginal product of capital and therefore the incentive to invest. Higher income also raises the demand for houses, which raises housing prices and residential investment. Higher output raises the stock of inventories firms wish to hold and therefore stimulates inventory investment. Our models predict that an economic boom should stimulate investment, and a recession should depress it. This is exactly what we observe.

Summary

1. The marginal product of capital determines the real rental price of capital. The real interest rate, the depreciation rate, and the relative price of capital goods determine the cost of capital. According to the neoclassical model, firms invest if the rental price is greater than the cost of capital, and disinvest if the rental price is less than the cost of capital.

2. Various parts of the federal tax code influence the incentive to invest. The corporate income tax discourages investment, and the investment tax credit—which has now been repealed in the United States—encourages it.

3. An alternative way of expressing the neoclassical model is to state that investment depends on Tobin's q, the ratio of the market value of installed capital to its replacement cost. This ratio reflects the current and expected future profitability of capital.

4. In contrast to the assumption of the neoclassical model, firms cannot always raise funds to finance investment. Financing constraints make investment sensitive to firms' current cash flow.

5. Residential investment depends on the relative price of housing. Housing prices in turn depend on the demand for housing and the fixed supply. An increase in housing demand, perhaps due to a reduction in the interest rate, raises housing prices and residential investment.

6. Firms have various motives for holding inventories of goods: smoothing production, using them as a factor of production, avoiding stockouts, and storing work in process. One model of inventory investment that works well without endorsing a particular motive is the accelerator model, according to which the stock of inventories is proportional to GNP. It implies that inventory investment depends on the change in GNP.

KEY CONCEPTS

Business fixed investment	Stock market
Residential investment	Tobin's q
Inventory investment	Financing constraints
Neoclassical model of investment	Production smoothing
Depreciation	Inventories as a factor of production
Real cost of capital	Stock-out avoidance
Net investment	Work in process
Corporate income tax	Accelerator model
Investment tax credit	

QUESTIONS FOR REVIEW

1. In the neoclassical model of business fixed investment, under what conditions will firms find it profitable to add to their capital stock?

2. What is Tobin's q, and what does it have to do with investment?

3. Explain why an increase in the interest rate reduces the amount of residential investment.

4. List four reasons firms might hold inventories.

PROBLEMS AND APPLICATIONS

1. Use the neoclassical model of investment to explain the impact of each of the following on the rental price of capital, the cost of capital, and investment:

   a. Anti-inflationary monetary policy raises the real interest rate.

   b. An earthquake destroys part of the capital stock.

   c. An immigration of foreign workers increases the size of the labor force.

2. Suppose that the government levies a tax on oil companies equal to a proportion of the value of the company's oil reserves. (The government assures the firms that the tax is for one time only.) According to the neoclassical model, what effect will the tax have on business fixed investment by these firms? What if these firms face financing constraints?

3. The *IS-LM* model developed in Chapters 9 and 10 assumes that investment depends only on the interest rate. Yet our theories of investment suggest that investment might also depend on national income: higher income might induce firms to invest more.

a. Explain why investment might depend on national income.

b. Suppose that investment is determined by

$$I = \bar{I} + aY,$$

where a is a constant between zero and one. With investment set this way, what are the fiscal-policy multipliers in the Keynesian cross model? Explain.

c. Suppose that investment depends on both income and the interest rate. That is, the investment function is

$$I = \bar{I} + aY - br,$$

where a is a constant between zero and one, and b is a constant greater than zero. Use the *IS-LM* model to consider the short-run impact of an increase in government purchases on national income Y, the interest rate r, consumption C, and investment I. How might this investment function alter the conclusions implied by the basic *IS-LM* model?

Chapter **18**

Money Supply and
Money Demand

Money supply and money demand are central to much of macroeconomic analysis. In Chapter 6 we discussed how economists use the term "money" and showed how the money supply influences prices and interest rates in the long run when prices are flexible. In Chapters 9 and 10 we saw that the supply and demand for money are key elements of the *IS-LM* model, which describes the short run when prices are sticky.

In this chapter we examine money supply and money demand more closely. We see that the banking system plays a key role in determining the money supply, and we discuss various policy instruments that the Federal Reserve can use to alter the money supply. We also discuss the motives behind money demand, and we analyze the individual's decision about how much money to hold.

18-1 Money Supply

Chapter 6 introduced the concept of "money supply" in a highly simplified manner. In that chapter we defined the quantity of money as the number of dollars held by the public, and we assumed that the Federal Reserve controls the supply of money by increasing or decreasing the number of dollars in circulation through open-market operations. Although acceptable as a first approximation, this explanation is not complete, because it omits the role of the banking system in determining the money supply. We now present a fuller explanation.

In this section we see that the money supply is determined not only by Fed policy, but also by the behavior of individuals who hold money and of banks in which money is held. We begin by recalling that the money supply includes both currency in the hands of the public and the deposits at banks that people can use on demand for transactions, such as checking accounts. That is, letting M denote the money supply, C currency, and D demand deposits, we can write

$$\text{Money Supply} = \text{Currency} + \text{Demand Deposits}$$
$$M \quad = \quad C \quad + \quad D.$$

To understand the money supply, one must understand the interaction between currency and demand deposits, and how Fed policy influences these two components of the money supply.

100-Percent-Reserve Banking

We begin by imagining a world without banks. In such a world, all money takes the form of currency, and the quantity of money is simply the number of dollars in the hands of the public. For this discussion, suppose that there is $1,000 of currency in this economy.

Now introduce banks. At first, suppose that banks accept deposits but do not make loans. The deposits that banks have received but have not lent out are called **reserves**. Some reserves are held in the vaults of local banks throughout the country, but most are held at a central bank, such as the Federal Reserve. In our hypothetical economy, all deposits are held as reserves: banks simply accept deposits, place the money in reserve, and leave the money there until the depositor makes a withdrawal or writes a check against the balance. This system is called **100-percent-reserve banking**.

Suppose that people deposit the economy's entire $1,000 in Firstbank. Figure 18-1 shows the **balance sheet**—the accounting statement of assets and liabilities—of Firstbank. The bank's assets are the $1,000 it holds as reserves; the bank's liabilities are the $1,000 it owes to depositors. Unlike banks in our economy, this bank is not making loans, so it will not earn profit from its assets. The bank presumably charges depositors a small fee to cover its costs. The advantage to being a depositor is that keeping money in the bank is safer than keeping it in one's wallet.

Firstbank's Balance Sheet	
Assets	Liabilities
Reserves $1,000	Deposits $1,000

Figure 18-1   **A Balance Sheet Under 100-Percent-Reserve Banking.**   A bank's balance sheet shows its assets and liabilities. Under 100-percent-reserve banking, banks hold all deposits as reserves.

What is the money supply in this economy? Before the creation of Firstbank, the money supply was the $1,000 of currency. After the creation of Firstbank, the money supply is the $1,000 of demand deposits. A dollar deposited in a bank reduces currency by one dollar and raises deposits by one dollar, so the money supply remains the same. *If banks hold 100 percent of deposits in reserve, the banking system has no influence on the supply of money.*

Fractional-Reserve Banking

Now imagine that banks start to use some of their deposits to make loans—for example, to families who are buying houses or to firms that are investing in new plants and equipment. The advantage to banks is that interest can be charged on the loans. The banks must keep some reserves on hand so that reserves are available whenever depositors want to make withdrawals. But as long as the amount of new deposits approximately equals the amount of withdrawals, a bank need not keep all of its deposits in reserve. Thus, bankers have an incentive to make loans. When they do so, we have **fractional-reserve banking**, a system under which banks keep only a fraction of their deposits in reserve.

Figure 18-2A shows the balance sheet of Firstbank after it makes a loan. This balance sheet assumes that the *reserve-deposit ratio*—the fraction of deposits kept in reserve—is 20 percent. Therefore, Firstbank keeps $200 of the $1,000 in deposits in reserve and lends out the remaining $800.

A. Firstbank's Balance Sheet

Assets		Liabilities	
Reserves	$200	Deposits	$1,000
Loans	$800		

B. Secondbank's Balance Sheet

Assets		Liabilities	
Reserves	$160	Deposits	$800
Loans	$640		

C. Thirdbank's Balance Sheet

Assets		Liabilities	
Reserves	$128	Deposits	$640
Loans	$512		

Figure 18-2 **Balance Sheets Under Fractional-Reserve Banking.** This figure shows how $1,000 in reserves leads to a much greater quantity of deposits. Thus, under a fractional-reserve system, banks create money.

Notice that Firstbank increases the supply of money by $800 when it makes this loan. Before the loan is made, the money supply is $1,000, equaling the deposits in Firstbank. After the loan is made, the money supply is $1,800: the depositor still has a demand deposit of $1,000, but now the borrower holds $800 in currency. *Thus, in a system of fractional-reserve banking, banks create money.*

The creation of money does not stop with Firstbank. If the borrower deposits the $800 in another bank (or if the borrower uses the $800 to pay someone who then deposits it), the process of money creation continues. Figure 18-2B shows the balance sheet of Secondbank. Secondbank receives the $800 in deposits, keeps 20 percent, or $160, in reserve, and then loans out $640. Secondbank thus creates $640 of money. If this $640 is eventually deposited in Thirdbank, this bank keeps 20 percent, or $128, in reserve and loans out $512, and so on. With each deposit and loan, more money is created.

Although this process of money creation can continue through an infinite number of banks, it does not create an infinite amount of money. Letting *rr* denote the reserve-deposit ratio—in our example, *rr* = 0.2— the amount of money that the original $1,000 creates is:

Original Deposit   = $1,000
Firstbank Lending   = $(1 - rr) \times \$1,000$
Secondbank Lending = $(1 - rr)^2 \times \$1,000$
Thirdbank Lending   = $(1 - rr)^3 \times \$1,000$

$\cdot$ $\cdot$
$\cdot$ $\cdot$
$\cdot$ $\cdot$

Total Money Supply = $[1 + (1 - rr) + (1 - rr)^2$
$\qquad\qquad\qquad + (1 - rr)^3 + \ldots] \times \$1,000$
$\qquad\qquad\quad = (1/rr) \times \$1,000$

Thus, each $1 of reserves generates $$(1/rr)$ of money. In our example, *rr* = 0.2, so the original $1,000 generates $5,000 of money.[1]

The banking system's ability to create money constitutes the primary difference between banks and other financial institutions. As we first discussed in Chapter 3, financial markets have the important function of transferring the economy's resources from those individuals who wish to save some of their income for the future to those individuals and firms who wish to borrow to buy investment goods to be used in future production. This process is called **financial intermediation**. Many different institutions in the economy act as financial intermediaries: the most prominent examples are the stock market, the bond market, and the banking system. Yet, of these financial institutions, only banks have the legal authority to create assets that are part of the money supply, such as checking accounts. Therefore, banks are the only financial institutions that directly influence the money supply.

Note that although the system of fractional-reserve banking creates money, it does not create wealth. When a bank loans out some of its reserves, it gives borrowers the ability to make transactions and therefore increases the supply of money. The borrowers are also undertaking a debt obligation to the bank, however, so the loan does not make them wealthier. In other words, the creation of money by the banking system increases the economy's liquidity, not its wealth.

---

[1] *Mathematical Note:* The last step in the derivation of the total money supply uses the algebraic result for the sum of an infinite geometric series (which we used previously in computing the multiplier in Chapter 9). This result states that if x is a number between -1 and 1, then

$$1 + x + x^2 + x^3 + \ldots = 1/(1 - x).$$

In this application, $x = (1 - rr)$.

A Model of the Money Supply

Now that we have seen how banks create money, let's examine in more detail what determines the money supply. Here we present a model of the money supply under fractional-reserve banking. The model has three exogenous variables:

- The **monetary base** B is the total number of dollars held by the public as currency C and by the banks as reserves R. It is directly controlled by the Federal Reserve.

- The **reserve-deposit ratio** rr is the fraction of deposits that banks hold in reserve. It is determined by the business policies of banks and the laws regulating banks.

- The **currency-deposit ratio** cr expresses the preferences of the public about how much money to hold in the form of currency C and how much to hold in the form of demand deposits D.

Our model shows how the money supply depends on the monetary base, the reserve-deposit ratio, and the currency-deposit ratio. It allows us to examine how Fed policy and the choices of banks and individuals influence the money supply.

We begin with the definition of the money supply:

$$M = C + D.$$

The currency-deposit ratio cr tells us how currency depends on deposits. That is,

$$C = cr \times D.$$

Substitute this into the first equation to obtain

$$M = (cr \times D) + D$$
$$= (cr + 1)D.$$

Rearranging terms, we get

$$D = M/(cr + 1).$$

This equation shows that the quantity of demand deposits is proportional to the money supply.

Next, note that by definition the monetary base is the sum of currency and bank reserves:

$$B = C + R.$$

The reserve-deposit ratio rr tells us what fraction of deposits banks hold in reserve. Thus,

$$R = rr \times D.$$

Substituting this expression and the equation for currency into the equation for the money base, we obtain

$$B = (cr \times D) + (rr \times D)$$
$$= (cr + rr)D.$$

Rearranging terms, we get

$$D = B/(cr + rr).$$

This equation shows that the quantity of demand deposits is proportional to the monetary base.

To solve for the money supply, put together the two equations for demand deposits. They state

$$M/(cr + 1) = D = B/(cr + rr).$$

This can be written as

$$M = \frac{cr + 1}{cr + rr} \times B.$$

This equation shows how the money supply depends on the three exogenous variables. Note that the money supply is proportional to the monetary base. The factor of proportionality, $(cr + 1)/(cr + rr)$, is denoted m and is called the **money multiplier**. We can write

$$M = m \times B.$$

Each dollar of the monetary base leads to m dollars of money supply. Because the monetary base has a multiplied effect on the money supply, the monetary base is sometimes called **high-powered money**.

Here's a numerical example approximately describing the U.S. situation in 1990. Suppose that the monetary base B is $300 billion, the reserve-deposit ratio rr is 0.1, and the currency-deposit ratio cr is 0.4. In this case, the money multiplier is

$$m = \frac{0.4 + 1}{0.4 + 0.1} = 2.8,$$

and the money supply is

$$M = 2.8 \times 300 = 840.$$

Thus, each dollar of the monetary base generates 2.8 dollars of money, so the total money supply is $840 billion.

We can now see how changes in the three exogenous variables—B, rr, and cr—cause the money supply to change:

1. The money supply is proportional to the monetary base. Therefore, an increase in the monetary base leads to the same percentage increase in the money supply.

2. The lower the reserve-deposit ratio, the more loans banks make, and the more money banks create from every dollar of reserves. Therefore, a decrease in the reserve-deposit ratio raises the money multiplier and the money supply.

3. The lower the currency-deposit ratio, the fewer dollars of the monetary base the public holds as currency, the more base dollars banks hold as reserves, and the more money banks can create. Therefore, a decrease in the currency-deposit ratio raises the money multiplier and the money supply.

With this model in mind, we can discuss the ways in which the Fed influences the money supply.

The Three Instruments of Monetary Policy

In previous chapters we made the simplifying assumption that the Federal Reserve controls the money supply directly. In fact, the Fed controls the money supply indirectly by altering either the monetary base or the reserve-deposit ratio. To do this, the Fed has at its disposal three instruments of monetary policy: open-market operations, reserve requirements, and the discount rate.

Open-market operations are the purchases and sales of government bonds by the Fed. When the Fed buys bonds from the public, the dollars it pays for the bonds increase the monetary base and thereby increase the money supply. When the Fed sells bonds to the public, the dollars it receives reduce the monetary base and thus decrease the money supply. Open-market operations are the policy instrument that the Fed uses most often. In fact, the Fed conducts open-market operations in New York bond markets every weekday.

Reserve requirements are Fed regulations that impose on banks a minimum reserve-deposit ratio. An increase in reserve requirements raises the reserve-deposit ratio and thus lowers the money multiplier and the money supply. Changes in reserve requirements are the least frequently used of the Fed's three policy instruments.

The **discount rate** is the interest rate that the Fed charges when it makes loans to banks. Banks borrow from the Fed when they find themselves with too few reserves to meet reserve requirements. The lower the discount rate, the cheaper are borrowed reserves, and the more banks borrow at the Fed's discount window. Hence, a reduction in the discount rate raises the monetary base and the money supply.

Although these three instruments—open-market operations, reserve requirements, and the discount rate—give the Fed substantial power to influence the money supply, the Fed does not have complete control over the money supply. Bank discretion in conducting business can cause the money supply to change in ways the Fed did not anticipate. For example, banks may choose to hold **excess reserves**—that is, reserves above the reserve requirement. The higher the amount of excess reserves, the higher the reserve-deposit ratio, and the lower the money supply. As another example, the Fed cannot precisely control the amount banks borrow from the discount window. The less banks borrow, the smaller the monetary base, and the smaller the money supply. Hence, the money supply sometimes moves in directions that the Fed did not intend.

CASE STUDY 18-1

Bank Failures and the Money Supply in the 1930s

Between August 1929 and March 1933, the money supply fell 28 percent. As we discussed in Chapter 10, some economists believe that this large decline in the money supply was the primary cause of the Great Depression. But, in that chapter, we did not discuss why the money supply fell so dramatically.

The three variables that determine the money supply—the monetary base, the reserve-deposit ratio, and the currency-deposit ratio—are shown in Table 18-1 for 1929 and 1933. You can see that the fall in the money supply cannot be attributed to a fall in the monetary base: in fact, the monetary base rose 18 percent over this period. Instead, the money supply fell because the money multiplier fell 38 percent. The money

Table 18-1 The Money Supply and Its Determinants: 1929 and 1933	August 1929	March 1933
Money Supply	**26.5**	**19.0**
Currency	3.9	5.5
Demand deposits	22.6	13.5
Monetary Base	**7.1**	**8.4**
Currency	3.9	5.5
Reserves	3.2	2.9
Money Multiplier	**3.7**	**2.3**
Reserve-deposit ratio	0.14	0.21
Currency-deposit ratio	0.17	0.41

Source: Adapted from Milton Friedman and Anna Schwartz, *A Monetary History of the United States, 1867–1960* (Princeton, N.J.: Princeton University Press, 1963), Appendix A.

multiplier fell because the currency-deposit and reserve-deposit ratios both rose substantially.

Most economists attribute the fall in the money multiplier to the large number of bank failures in the early 1930s. From 1930 to 1933, more than 9,000 banks suspended operations, often defaulting on their depositors. The bank failures caused the money supply to fall by altering the behavior of both depositors and bankers.

Bank failures raised the currency-deposit ratio by reducing public confidence in the banking system. People feared continuing bank failures, and they began to view currency as a more desirable form of money than demand deposits. When they began to withdraw their deposits, they drained the banks of reserves. The process of money creation reversed itself, as banks responded to lower reserves by reducing their outstanding balance of loans.

In addition, the bank failures raised the reserve-deposit ratio by making bankers more cautious. Having just observed many bank runs, bankers became apprehensive about operating with a small amount of reserves. They therefore increased their holdings of reserves to well above the legal minimum. Just as individuals responded to the banking crisis by holding more currency relative to deposits, bankers responded by holding more reserves relative to loans. These changes resulted in a large fall in the money multiplier.

Although it is easy to explain why the money supply fell, it is more difficult to decide whether to blame the Federal Reserve. One might argue that the monetary base did not fall, so the Fed should not be blamed. Critics of Fed policy during this period make two arguments. First, they claim that the Fed should have taken a more vigorous role in preventing bank failures by acting as a *lender of last resort* when banks needed cash during bank runs; this would have helped maintain confidence in the banking system and prevented the large fall in the money multiplier. Second, they point out that the Fed could have responded to the fall in the money multiplier by increasing the monetary base even more than it did. Either of these actions would likely have prevented such a large fall in the money supply, which in turn might have reduced the severity of the Great Depression.

Since the 1930s, many policies have been put into place that make such a large and sudden fall in the money multiplier less likely today. Most important, the system of federal deposit insurance maintains public confidence in the banking system and thus prevents large swings in the currency-deposit ratio. Deposit insurance, however, can be a costly policy: in the late 1980s and early 1990s, the federal government incurred the large expense of bailing out many insolvent savings and loan institutions. Yet deposit insurance does help stabilize the banking system and the money supply.

18-2 Money Demand

We now turn to the other side of the money market and examine what determines money demand. In previous chapters, we used simple money demand functions. We started with the quantity theory, which assumes that the demand for real balances is proportional to income. That is, the quantity theory assumes

$$(M/P)^d = kY,$$

where k is a constant. We then considered a more general and realistic money demand function that assumes the demand for real balances depends on both the interest rate and income:

$$(M/P)^d = L(i, Y).$$

We used this money demand function when we discussed how to stop a hyperinflation in Chapter 6 and when we developed the *IS-LM* model in Chapters 9 and 10.

The purpose of studying money demand in more detail is to gain insight about the money demand function. Just as studies of the consumption function rely on microeconomic models of the consumption decision, studies of the money demand function rely on microeconomic models of the money demand decision. In this section we first discuss in broad terms the different ways to model money demand. We then develop one prominent model.

When we first introduced the concept of "money" in Chapter 6, we noted that money serves three functions: it is a unit of account, a store of value, and a medium of exchange. The first function—money as a unit of account—does not by itself generate any demand for money, because one can quote prices in dollars without holding any. Money can serve its other two functions, however, only if people hold it. Theories of money demand, therefore, emphasize the role of money either as a store of value or as a medium of exchange.

Portfolio Theories of Money Demand

Theories of money demand that emphasize the role of money as a store of value are called **portfolio theories**. These theories stress that people hold money as part of their portfolio of assets. The key insight of these theories is that money offers a different combination of risk and return than other assets. In particular, money offers a safe (nominal) return, whereas the prices of stocks and bonds may fall. Thus, some economists have suggested that people choose to hold money as part of their optimal portfolio.[2]

---

[2] James Tobin, "Liquidity Preference as Behavior Toward Risk," *Review of Economic Studies* 25 (February 1958): 65–86.

Portfolio theories predict that the demand for money should depend on the risk and return offered by money and by the various assets individuals can hold instead of money. In addition, money demand should depend on total wealth, because wealth measures the size of the portfolio to be allocated among money and the alternative assets. For example, we might write the money demand function as

$$(M/P)^d = L(r_s, r_b, \pi^e, W),$$

where r_s is the expected real return on stock, r_b is the expected real return on bonds, π^e is the expected inflation rate, and W is real wealth. An increase in r_s or r_b lowers money demand, because other assets become more attractive. An increase in π^e also lowers money demand, because money becomes less attractive. (Recall that $-\pi^e$ is the expected real return to holding money.) An increase in W raises money demand, because higher wealth means that there is a larger portfolio to allocate among alternative assets.

From the standpoint of portfolio theories, we can view our money demand function, $L(i, Y)$, as a useful simplification. First, it uses real income Y as a proxy for real wealth W. Second, the only return variable it includes is the nominal interest rate, which is the sum of the real return on bonds and expected inflation (that is, $i = r_b + \pi^e$). According to portfolio theories, however, the money demand function should include the expected returns on other assets as well.

Economists disagree about whether portfolio theories are useful for studying money demand. The validity of portfolio theories probably depends on which measure of money one uses. The most narrow measures of money, such as $M1$, include only currency and checking accounts. These forms of money earn zero or very low rates of interest. There are other assets—such as savings accounts, Treasury bills, certificates of deposit, and money market mutual funds—that earn higher rates of interest and have the same risk characteristics as currency and checking accounts. Economists say that money ($M1$) is a **dominated asset**: as a store of value, there are other assets that are always better. Thus, it would not be optimal for people to hold money as part of their portfolio, implying that portfolio theories cannot explain the demand for these dominated forms of money.

Portfolio theories are more plausible as theories of money demand if one adopts a broad measure of money. The broad measures include many of those assets that dominate currency and checking accounts. $M2$, for example, includes savings accounts and money market mutual funds. When examining why people hold assets in the form of $M2$, rather than bonds or stock, the portfolio considerations of risk and return may be paramount. Hence, although the portfolio approach to money demand may not be plausible when applied to $M1$, it may be the right theory to explain the demand for $M2$ or $M3$.

Currency and the Underground Economy

How much currency are you holding right now in your wallet? How many $100 bills?

In the United States in 1990, currency outstanding per person equaled about $1,000. About half of this currency was in $100 bills. Most people find this amount of currency to be surprising, because they hold much smaller amounts and in smaller denominations.

Some of this currency is used by people in the underground economy—that is, by those engaged in illegal activity such as the drug trade and by those trying to hide income in order to evade taxes. People whose wealth was earned illegally may have fewer options for investing their portfolio, because by holding wealth in banks, bonds, or stock, they assume a greater risk of detection. Perhaps, for criminals, currency is not a dominated asset: it may be the best store of value available.

Transactions Theories of Money Demand

Theories of money demand that emphasize the role of money as a medium of exchange are called **transactions theories**. These theories acknowledge that money is a dominated asset and emphasize that money, unlike other assets, is held to make purchases. These theories best explain why people hold narrow measures of money, such as currency and checking accounts, as opposed to holding assets that dominate them, such as savings accounts or Treasury bills.

Transactions theories of money demand take many different forms, depending on how one models the process of obtaining money and making transactions. All of these theories assume that money has the cost of earning a low rate of return and the benefit of making transactions more convenient. Individuals decide how much money to hold by trading off these costs and benefits.

To see how transactions theories explain the money demand function, let's develop explicitly one prominent model of this type. The **Baumol-Tobin model** was developed in the 1950s by economists William Baumol and James Tobin and remains one of the leading theories of money demand.[3]

The Baumol-Tobin Model of Cash Management

The Baumol-Tobin model explicitly analyzes the costs and benefits of holding money. The benefit of holding money is convenience: people

---

[3] William Baumol, "The Transactions Demand for Cash: An Inventory Theoretic Approach," *Quarterly Journal of Economics* 66 (November 1952): 545–556; James Tobin, "The Interest Elasticity of the Transactions Demand for Cash," *Review of Economics and Statistics* (August 1956): 241–247.

hold money to avoid making a trip to the bank every time they wish to purchase something. The cost of this convenience is the forgone interest they would have received had they left the money deposited in a savings account that paid interest.

To see how people trade off these benefits and costs, consider an individual who plans to spend Y dollars gradually over the course of a year. (For simplicity, assume that the price level is constant, so real spending is constant over the year.) How much money should he hold in the process of spending this amount? That is, what is the optimal size of average cash balances?

Consider the possibilities. He could withdraw the Y dollars at the beginning of the year and gradually spend the money. Figure 18-3A shows his money holdings over the course of the year under this plan. His money holdings begin the year at Y and end the year at zero, averaging $Y/2$ over the year.

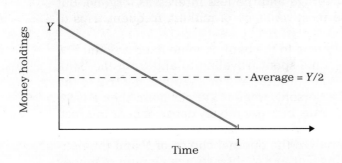

A. Money Holdings With One Trip to Bank

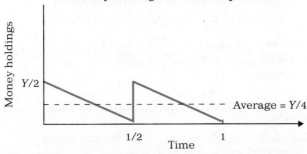

B. Money Holdings With Two Trips to Bank

Figure 18-3 **Money Holdings Over the Year.** This figure shows how average money holdings depend on the number of trips a person makes to the bank each year. (continued)

A second possible plan is to make two trips to the bank. In this case, he withdraws $Y/2$ dollars at the beginning of the year, gradually spends this amount over the first half of the year, and then makes another trip to withdraw $Y/2$ for the second half of the year. Figure 18-3B shows that money holdings over the year vary between $Y/2$ and zero, averaging $Y/4$. This plan has the advantage that less money is held on average, so less interest is forgone, but it has the disadvantage of requiring two trips to the bank rather than one.

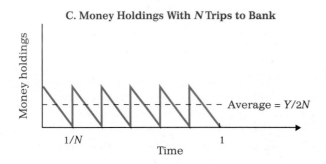

C. Money Holdings With *N* Trips to Bank

Figure 18-3 **Money Holdings Over the Year.** (continued.)

More generally, suppose the individual makes *N* trips to the bank over the course of the year. On each trip, he withdraws *Y/N* dollars; he then spends the money gradually over the following 1/*N*th of the year. Figure 18-3C shows that money holdings vary between *Y/N* and zero, averaging *Y*/(2*N*).

The question is, what is the optimal choice of *N*? The greater *N* is, the less money is held on average and the less interest is forgone. But as *N* increases, so does the inconvenience of making frequent trips to the bank.

Suppose that the cost of going to the bank is some fixed amount *F*. *F* represents the value of the time spent traveling to and from the bank and waiting in line to make the withdrawal. For example, if a trip to the bank takes 15 minutes and a person's wage is $12 per hour, then *F* is $3. Also, let *i* denote the interest rate; because money does not bear interest, *i* measures the opportunity cost of holding money.

Now we can explicitly analyze the optimal choice of *N* and the optimal amount of money holding. For any *N*, the average amount of money holding is *Y*/(2*N*), so the forgone interest is *iY*/(2*N*). Because *F* is the cost per trip to the bank, the total cost of making trips to the bank is *FN*. The total cost the individual bears is the sum of the forgone interest and the cost of trips to the bank:

$$\text{Total Cost} = \text{Forgone Interest} + \text{Trips to Bank}$$
$$= \quad iY/(2N) \quad + \quad FN.$$

The larger the number of trips *N*, the smaller the forgone interest, and the larger the cost of going to the bank.

Figure 18-4 shows how total cost depends on *N*. There is one value of *N* that minimizes total cost. This optimal value of *N* is[4]

$$N^* = \sqrt{\frac{iY}{2F}}.$$

---

[4] *Mathematical Note:* Deriving this expression for the optimal choice of *N* requires simple calculus. Differentiate total cost *C* with respect to *N* to obtain

$$dC/dN = -iYN^{-2}/2 + F.$$

At the optimum, *dC/dN* = 0, which yields the formula for *N**.

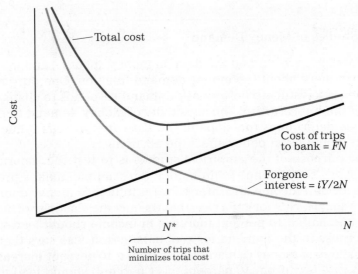

Figure 18-4 **The Cost of Money Holding.**
This figure shows how forgone interest, the cost of trips to the bank, and total cost de-pend on the number of trips N. There is one value of N, denoted N^*, that minimizes total cost.

At this value of N, average money holding is

$$\text{Average Money Holding} = Y/(2N^*)$$
$$= \sqrt{\frac{YF}{2i}}.$$

This expression shows that the individual holds more money if the fixed cost of going to the bank, F, is higher, if expenditure Y is higher, or if the interest rate i is lower.

So far, we have been interpreting the Baumol-Tobin model as a model of the demand for currency. That is, we have used it to explain the amount of money held outside of banks. Yet one can interpret the model more broadly. Imagine an individual who holds a portfolio of monetary assets (currency and checking accounts) and non-monetary assets (stocks and bonds). Monetary assets are used for transactions but offer a low rate of return. Let i be the difference in the return between monetary and non-monetary assets, and let F be the cost of transferring non-monetary assets into monetary assets, such as a brokerage fee. The decision about how often to pay the brokerage fee is analogous to the decision about how often to make a trip to the bank. Therefore, the Baumol-Tobin model describes this individual's demand for monetary assets. By showing that money demand depends positively on expendi-ture Y and negatively on the interest rate i, the model provides a mi-croeconomic justification for the money demand function, $L(i, Y)$, that we have used throughout this book.

CASE STUDY 18-3

Empirical Studies of Money Demand

Many economists have studied the data on money, income, and interest rates to learn more about the money demand function. One purpose of these studies is to estimate how money demand responds to changes in income and the interest rate. The sensitivity of money demand to these two variables determines the slope of the *LM* curve; it thus influences how monetary and fiscal policy affect the economy.

Another purpose of the empirical studies is to test the theories of money demand. The Baumol-Tobin model, for example, makes precise predictions for how income and interest rates influence money demand. The model's square-root formula says that the income elasticity of money demand is one-half: a 10 percent increase in income should lead to a 5 percent increase in the demand for real balances. It also says that the interest elasticity of money demand is one-half: a 10 percent increase in the interest rate (say, from 10 percent to 11 percent) should lead to a 5 percent decrease in the demand for real balances.

Most empirical studies of money demand do not confirm these predictions. They find that the income elasticity of money demand is larger than one-half and that the interest elasticity is smaller than one-half. Thus, although the Baumol-Tobin model may capture part of the story behind the money demand function, it is not completely correct.

One possible explanation for the failure of the Baumol-Tobin model is that some people may have less discretion over their money holdings than the model assumes. For example, consider a person who must go to the bank once a week to deposit her paycheck; while at the bank, she takes advantage of her visit to withdraw the currency needed for the coming week. For this person, the number of trips to the bank, N, does not respond to changes in expenditure or the interest rate. Because N is fixed, average money holdings ($Y/2N$) are proportional to expenditure and insensitive to the interest rate.

Now imagine that the world is populated with two sorts of people. Some obey the Baumol-Tobin model, so they have income and interest elasticities of one-half. The others have a fixed N, so they have an income elasticity of one and an interest elasticity of zero. In this case, the overall money demand function is a weighted average of the two groups. The income elasticity will be between one-half and one, and the interest elasticity will be between one-half and zero, as the empirical studies find.[5]

---

[5] To learn more about the empirical studies of money demand, see Stephen M. Goldfeld, "The Demand for Money Revisited," *Brookings Papers on Economic Activity*, no. 1 (1973): 577–638; and David Laidler, *The Demand for Money: Theories and Evidence*, 3rd ed. (New York: Harper and Row, 1985).

18-3 Conclusion: Microeconomic Models for Macroeconomics

Now that we have finished our study of money supply and money demand, let's step back and look at the overall theme of the past several chapters. We have examined a variety of microeconomic models, such as the permanent income theory of consumption, the neoclassical theory of investment, and the Baumol-Tobin model of cash management. The purpose of these models is to shed light on macroeconomic phenomena through an analysis of individual behavior.

These chapters should give you a taste of modern research in macroeconomics. Over the past two decades, much progress in macroeconomics has come from the development and testing of microeconomic models. Most often, these models do not seek to overturn macroeconomic theory; instead, they seek to refine it. Most macroeconomists believe that the continuing integration of microeconomics and macroeconomics holds out the greatest promise for further progress in understanding the economy.

Summary

1. The system of fractional-reserve banking creates money, because each dollar of reserves generates many dollars of demand deposits.

2. The supply of money depends on the monetary base, the reserve-deposit ratio, and the currency-deposit ratio. An increase in the monetary base leads to a proportionate increase in the money supply. A decrease in the reserve-deposit ratio or in the currency-deposit ratio increases the money multiplier and thus the money supply.

3. The Federal Reserve changes the money supply using three policy instruments. It can increase the monetary base by making an open-market purchase of bonds or by lowering the discount rate. It can reduce the reserve-deposit ratio by relaxing reserve requirements.

4. Portfolio theories of money demand stress that money is a store of value. They predict that the demand for money depends on the risk and return on money and alternative assets.

5. Transactions theories of money demand, such as the Baumol-Tobin model, stress that money is a medium of exchange. They predict that the demand for money depends positively on expenditure and negatively on the interest rate.

KEY CONCEPTS

Reserves

100-percent-reserve banking

Balance sheet

Fractional-reserve banking

Financial intermediation

Monetary base

Reserve-deposit ratio

Currency-deposit ratio

Money multiplier

High-powered money

Open-market operation

Reserve requirements

Discount rate

Excess reserves

Portfolio theories

Dominated asset

Transactions theories

Baumol-Tobin model

QUESTIONS FOR REVIEW

1. Explain how banks create money.

2. What are the three ways in which the Federal Reserve can influence the money supply?

3. Why might a banking crisis lead to a fall in the money supply?

4. Explain the difference between portfolio and transactions theories of money demand.

5. According to the Baumol-Tobin model, what determines how often people go to the bank? What does this decision have to do with money demand?

PROBLEMS AND APPLICATIONS

1. The money supply fell during the years 1929 to 1933 because both the currency-deposit ratio and the reserve-deposit ratio increased. Use the model of the money supply and the data in Table 18-1 to answer the following hypothetical questions about this episode.

   a. What would have happened to the money supply if the currency-deposit ratio had risen but the reserve-deposit ratio had remained the same?

   b. What would have happened to the money supply if the reserve-deposit ratio had risen but the currency-deposit ratio had remained the same?

   c. Which of the two changes was more responsible for the fall in the money supply?

2. Let's see what the Baumol-Tobin model says about how often you should go to the bank to withdraw cash.

   a. How much do you buy per year using currency (as opposed to checks or credit cards)? This is your value of Y.

   b. How long does it take you to go to the bank? What is your hourly wage? Use these two figures to compute your value of F.

   c. What interest rate do you earn on the money you leave in your bank account? This is your value of i. (Be sure to write i in decimal form—that is, 6 percent should be expressed 0.06.)

   d. According to the Baumol-Tobin model, how many times should you go to the bank each year, and how much should you withdraw each time?

e. In practice, how often do you go to the bank, and how much do you withdraw?

f. Compare the predictions of the Baumol-Tobin model to your behavior. Does the model describe how you actually behave? If not, why not? How would you change the model to make it a better description of your behavior?

3. In Chapter 6, we defined the velocity of money as the ratio of nominal expenditure to the quantity of money. Let's now use the Baumol-Tobin model to examine what determines velocity.

a. Recalling that average money holdings equal $Y/(2N)$, write velocity as a function of the number of trips to the bank N. Explain your result.

b. Use the formula for the optimal number of trips to express velocity as a function of expenditure Y, the interest rate i, and the cost of a trip to the bank F.

c. What happens to velocity when the interest rate rises? Explain.

d. What happens to velocity when the price level rises? Explain.

e. As the economy grows, what should happen to the velocity of money? (*Hint:* Think about how economic growth will influence Y and F.)

f. Suppose now that the number of trips to the bank is fixed rather than discretionary. What does this assumption imply about velocity?

What We Know, What We Don't

*If all economists were laid end to end, they would not
reach a conclusion.*

George Bernard Shaw

*The theory of economics does not furnish a body of
settled conclusions immediately applicable to policy. It
is a method rather than a doctrine, an apparatus of the
mind, which helps its possessor to draw correct
conclusions.*

John Maynard Keynes

The first chapter of this book states that the purpose of macroeconomics
is to understand economic events and to improve economic policy. Now
that we have developed and used many of the most important models
in the macroeconomist's toolbox, we can assess whether macroeconomists have achieved these goals.

Any fair assessment of macroeconomics today must admit that the
science is incomplete. There are some principles that almost all macroeconomists accept and on which we can rely when trying to analyze
events or formulate policies. Yet there are also many questions about
the economy that remain open to debate. In this last chapter we briefly
review the central lessons of macroeconomics, and we discuss the most
pressing unresolved questions.

The Four Most Important Lessons of
Macroeconomics

We begin with four lessons that have recurred throughout this book
and that most economists today would endorse. Each lesson tells us how
policy can influence a key economic variable—output, inflation, or unemployment—either in the long run or in the short run.

Lesson No. 1: In the long run, a country's capacity to produce goods and services determines the standard of living of its citizens.

Of all the measures of economic performance introduced in Chapter 2 and used throughout this book, the one that best measures economic well-being is GNP. Real GNP measures the economy's total output of goods and services and, therefore, a country's ability to satisfy the needs and desires of its citizens. Perhaps the most important question in macroeconomics is what determines the level and growth of GNP.

The models we developed in Chapters 3 and 4 identify the long-run determinants of GNP. In the long run, GNP depends on the factors of production—capital and labor—and on the technology for turning capital and labor into output. GNP grows when the factors of production increase or when the available technology improves.

This lesson has an obvious but important corollary: public policy can raise GNP in the long run only by improving the productive capability of the economy. There are many ways in which policymakers can attempt to do this. Policies that raise national saving—either through higher public saving or higher private saving—eventually lead to a larger capital stock. Policies that raise the efficiency of labor—such as those that improve education or increase technological progress—lead to a more productive use of capital and labor. All of these policies raise the economy's output of goods and services and, thereby, the standard of living. Economists disagree, however, about what is the best way to raise the economy's productive capability.

Lesson No. 2: In the short run, aggregate demand influences the amount of goods and services that a country produces.

Although the economy's ability to *supply* goods and services is the sole determinant of GNP in the long run, in the short run GNP depends also on the aggregate *demand* for goods and services. Aggregate demand is of key importance because prices are sticky in the short run. The *IS-LM* model developed in Chapters 9 and 10 shows what causes changes in aggregate demand and, therefore, short-run fluctuations in GNP.

Because aggregate demand influences output in the short run, all of the variables that affect aggregate demand can influence economic fluctuations. Monetary policy, fiscal policy, and shocks to the money and goods markets are often responsible for year-to-year changes in output and employment. Since aggregate demand is crucial to short-run fluctuations, policymakers monitor the economy closely. Before making any change in monetary or fiscal policy, they want to know whether the economy is in a boom or a recession.

Lesson No. 3: In the long run, the rate of money growth determines the rate of inflation, but it does not affect the rate of unemployment.

In addition to GNP, inflation and unemployment are among the most closely watched measures of economic performance. In Chapter 2 we discussed how these two variables are measured, and in subsequent chapters we developed models to explain how they are determined.

The long-run analysis of Chapter 6 stresses that growth in the money supply is the ultimate determinant of inflation. That is, in the long run, a currency loses real value over time if and only if the central bank prints more and more of it. This lesson can explain the decade-to-decade variation in the inflation rate that we have observed in the United States, as well as the far more dramatic hyperinflations that various countries have experienced from time to time.

We have also seen many of the long-run effects of high money growth and high inflation. In Chapter 6 we saw that, according to the Fisher effect, high inflation raises the nominal interest rate (so that the real interest rate remains unaffected). In Chapter 7 we saw that high inflation leads to a depreciation of the currency in the market for foreign exchange.

The long-run determinants of unemployment are very different. The classical dichotomy—the irrelevance of nominal variables in the determination of real variables—implies that growth in the money supply does not affect unemployment in the long run. As we discussed in Chapter 5, the natural rate of unemployment is determined by the rates of job separation and job finding, which in turn are determined by the process of job search and by the rigidity of the real wage.

These conclusions imply that persistent inflation and persistent unemployment are unrelated problems. To combat inflation in the long run, policymakers must reduce the growth in the money supply. To combat unemployment, they must alter the structure of labor markets. Hence, in the long run, there is no tradeoff between inflation and unemployment.

Lesson No. 4: In the short run, policymakers who control monetary and fiscal policy face a tradeoff between inflation and unemployment.

Although inflation and unemployment are not related in the long run, in the short run there is a tradeoff between these two variables, which is illustrated by the short-run Phillips curve. As we discussed in Chapter 11, policymakers can use monetary and fiscal policies to expand aggregate demand, which lowers unemployment and raises inflation. Or they can use these policies to contract aggregate demand, which raises unemployment and lowers inflation.

Policymakers face a fixed tradeoff between inflation and unemployment only in the short run. Over time, the short-run Phillips curve shifts for two reasons. First, supply shocks, such as changes in the price of oil, change the short-run tradeoff; an adverse supply shock offers policymakers the cruel choice between higher inflation or higher unemployment. Second, when people change their expectations of inflation, the short-run tradeoff between inflation and unemployment changes. The adjustment of expectations ensures that the tradeoff exists only in the short run. That is, only in the short run does unemployment deviate from its natural rate, and only in the short run does monetary policy have real effects. In the long run, the classical model of Chapters 3 through 7 describes the world.

The Four Most Important Unresolved Questions of Macroeconomics

So far, we have been discussing some of the broad lessons about which most economists would agree. We now turn to four questions about which there is continuing debate. Some of the disagreements are over the validity of alternative economic theories; others concern the ways in which economic theory should be applied to economic policy.

Question No. 1: How should policymakers try to raise the economy's natural rate of output?

The economy's natural rate of output depends on the amount of capital, the amount of labor, and the level of technology. Therefore, any policy designed to raise output in the long run must aim to increase the amount of capital, improve the use of labor, or enhance the available technology. None of these goals, however, can be achieved simply and costlessly.

The Solow growth model of Chapter 4 shows that increasing the amount of capital requires raising the economy's rate of saving and investment. Therefore, many economists advocate policies to raise national saving. Yet the Solow model also shows that raising the capital stock requires a period of reduced consumption for current generations. Some argue that policymakers should not encourage current generations to make this sacrifice, because technological progress will ensure that future generations are better off than current generations. Moreover, even those who advocate increased saving and investment disagree about how to encourage additional saving and whether the investment should be in privately-owned plants and equipment or in public infrastructure, such as roads and schools.

To improve the economy's use of its labor force, most policymakers would like to lower the natural rate of unemployment. Yet, as we discussed in Chapter 5, there is no easy way to achieve this goal. Although reducing unemployment insurance benefits would decrease the amount of frictional unemployment, and reducing the minimum wage would decrease the amount of wait unemployment, these policies would also hurt some of those members of society most in need. Many policies aimed at reducing unemployment achieve greater economic efficiency at the cost of greater economic inequality.

Raising the rate of technological progress is, according to some economists, the most important objective for public policy. The Solow growth model shows that persistent growth in living standards ultimately requires continuing technological progress. This conclusion suggests that the worldwide slowdown in productivity growth that began in the early 1970s may have been the worst economic development of the past half century. Economists have not been successful at explaining this slowdown, and policymakers have not been successful at finding ways to reverse it.

Question No. 2: Should policymakers try to stabilize the economy?

The model of aggregate supply and aggregate demand developed in Chapters 8 through 11 shows how various shocks to the economy cause economic fluctuations and how monetary and fiscal policy can influence these fluctuations. Some economists believe that policymakers should use this analysis in an attempt to stabilize the economy. They believe that monetary and fiscal policy should act to offset shocks in order to keep output and employment close to their natural rates.

Yet, as we discussed in Chapter 12, others are skeptical about our ability to stabilize the economy. These economists emphasize the long and variable lags inherent in economic policymaking, the poor record of economic forecasting, and our still-limited understanding of the economy. They conclude that the best policy is a passive one. In addition, many of these economists believe that policymakers are all too often opportunistic or suffer from the problem of time inconsistency. They conclude that policymakers should not be given discretion over monetary and fiscal policy but should be committed to following a fixed policy rule.

A related question is whether the benefits of economic stabilization—assuming stabilization could be achieved—would be large or small. According to the natural-rate hypothesis, stabilization policy cannot alter the average level of output and unemployment; it can only reduce the magnitude of fluctuations around the natural rate. Thus, successful stabilization policy would eliminate booms as well as recessions. Some economists have suggested that the average gain from stabilization would be small.

Finally, not all economists endorse the model of economic fluctuations developed in Chapters 8 through 11, which assumes sticky prices and monetary non-neutrality. According to real-business-cycle theory, which we discussed in Chapter 14, economic fluctuations are the optimal response of the economy to changing technology. Advocates of this approach believe that policymakers should not stabilize the economy, even if it were possible.

Question No. 3: How costly is inflation, and how costly is reducing inflation?

Whenever prices are rising, policymakers confront the question of whether to pursue policies to reduce the rate of inflation. To make this decision, they must compare the cost of allowing inflation to continue to the cost of reducing it. Yet economists cannot offer accurate estimates of either of these two costs.

The cost of inflation is a topic on which economists and laymen frequently disagree. When inflation reached 10 percent per year in the late 1970s, opinion polls showed that the public viewed inflation as a major economic problem. Yet, as we discussed in Chapter 6, when economists try to identify the social costs of inflation, they can point only to shoeleather costs, menu costs, the costs of a nonindexed tax system, and so on. These costs become large when countries experience hyperinflation, but they seem relatively minor at the moderate rates of inflation experienced in the United States. Some economists believe that the public confuses inflation with other economic problems that coincide with inflation. For example, growth in productivity and real wages slowed in the 1970s; some laymen might have viewed inflation as the cause of the slowdown in real wages. Yet it is also possible that economists are mistaken: perhaps inflation is in fact very costly, and we have yet to figure out why.

The cost of reducing inflation is a topic on which economists often disagree among themselves. As we discussed in Chapter 11, the standard view—as described by the short-run Phillips curve—is that reducing inflation requires a period of low output and high unemployment. According to this view, the cost of reducing inflation is measured by the sacrifice ratio, which gives the number of percentage points of one year's GNP that must be forgone to reduce inflation by one percentage point.

Some economists think that the cost of reducing inflation can be much smaller than standard estimates of the sacrifice ratio indicate. According to the rational-expectations approach discussed in Chapter 11, if a disinflationary policy is announced in advance and is credible, people will adjust their expectations quickly, so the disinflation need not cause a recession. According to the real-business-cycle models discussed in Chapter 14, prices are fully flexible, and money is neutral, so disinflationary monetary policy will not affect the economy's output of goods and services.

Other economists believe that the cost of reducing inflation is much larger than standard estimates of the sacrifice ratio indicate. The theories of hysteresis discussed in Chapter 11 suggest that a recession caused by disinflationary policy could raise the natural rate of unemployment. If so, then the cost of reducing inflation is not merely a temporary recession but a persistently higher level of unemployment.

Because the costs of inflation and disinflation remain open to debate, economists frequently offer conflicting advice to policymakers. Perhaps with further research, we can reach a consensus on the benefits of low inflation and the best way to achieve that goal.

Question No. 4: What are the consequences of government budget deficits?

Throughout the 1980s and early 1990s, the large budget deficits of the U.S. federal government have been a primary topic of debate among economic policymakers. As we discussed in Chapter 16, it is also a topic about which economists disagree.

Most of the models in this book, and most economists, take the traditional view of government debt. According to this view, a budget deficit leads to lower national saving, lower investment, and a current-account deficit. In the long run, it leads to a smaller steady-state capital stock and a larger foreign debt. Those who hold the traditional view conclude that budget deficits place a burden on future generations.

Yet advocates of the Ricardian view of government debt are skeptical of these conclusions. They stress that a budget deficit represents merely a substitution of future taxes for current taxes. As long as consumers are forward-looking, as the theories of consumption presented in Chapter 15 assume, they will save today to meet their or their children's future tax liability. Therefore, these economists believe that budget deficits have only a minor effect on the economy.

Conclusion

Economists and policymakers must deal with ambiguity. The current state of macroeconomics offers many insights, but it also leaves many questions open. The challenge for economists is to find answers to these questions and to expand our knowledge. The challenge for policymakers is to use the knowledge we now have to improve economic performance. Both challenges are formidable, but neither is insuperable.

Glossary

Accelerator model: The model according to which investment depends on the change in output. *(p. 458)*

Accommodating policy: A policy that yields to the effect of a shock and thereby prevents the shock from being disruptive; for example, a policy that raises aggregate demand in response to an adverse supply shock, sustaining the effect of the shock on prices and keeping output at the natural rate. *(p. 231)*

Accounting profit: The amount of revenue remaining for the owners of a firm after all the factors of production except capital have been compensated. (Cf. economic profit.) *(p. 52)*

Acyclical: Moving in no consistent direction over the business cycle. (Cf. countercyclical, procyclical.) *(p. 294)*

Adverse selection: An unfavorable sorting of individuals by their own choices; for example, in efficiency-wage theory, when a wage cut induces good workers to quit and bad workers to remain with the firm. *(p. 131)*

Aggregate: Total for the whole economy. *(p. 10)*

Aggregate demand curve: The negative relationship between the price level and the aggregate quantity of output demanded that arises from the interaction between the goods market and the money market. *(p. 217)*

Aggregate demand externality: The macroeconomic impact of one firm's price adjustment on the demand for all other firms' products. *(p. 313)*

Aggregate supply curve: The relationship between the price level and the aggregate quantity of output firms produce. *(p. 221)*

Animal spirits: Exogenous and perhaps self-fulfilling waves of optimism and pessimism about the state of the economy which, according to some economists, influence the level of investment. *(p. 269)*

Appreciation: A rise in the value of a currency relative to other currencies in the market for foreign exchange. (Cf. depreciation.) *(p. 191)*

Arbitrage: The act of buying an item in one market and selling it at a higher price in another market in order to profit from the price differential in the two markets. *(p. 201)*

Automatic stabilizer: A policy that reduces the amplitude of economic fluctuations without regular and deliberate changes in economic policy; for example, an income tax system which automatically reduces taxes when income falls. *(p. 324)*

Average propensity to consume (*APC*): The ratio of consumption to income (*C/Y*). *(p. 393)*

Balance sheet: An accounting statement that shows assets and liabilities. *(p. 464)*

Balanced budget: A budget in which receipts equal expenditures. *(p. 62)*

Baumol-Tobin model: A model of money demand positing that people choose optimal money holdings by comparing the opportunity cost of the forgone interest from holding money and the benefit of making less frequent trips to the bank. *(p. 474)*

Bond: A document representing an interest-bearing debt of the issuer, usually a corporation or the government. *(p. 158)*

Borrowing constraint: A restriction on the amount a person can borrow from financial institutions, limiting that person's ability to spend his or her future income today; also called a liquidity constraint. *(p. 406)*

Budget constraint: The limit that income places on expenditure. (Cf. intertemporal budget constraint.) *(p. 397)*

Budget deficit: A shortfall of receipts from expenditure. *(p. 62)*

Budget surplus: An excess of receipts over expenditure. *(p. 62)*

Business cycle: The economy-wide fluctuations in output, incomes, and employment. *(p. 214)*

Business fixed investment: Equipment and structures that businesses buy for use in future production. *(p. 440)*

Capital: 1. The stock of equipment and structures used in production. 2. The funds to finance the accumulation of equipment and structures. *(p. 44)*

Capital account: The amount of capital accumulation financed from abroad; domestic investment minus domestic saving. *(p. 181)*

Central bank: The institution responsible for the conduct of monetary policy, such as the Federal Reserve in the United States. *(p. 145)*

Classical dichotomy: The theoretical separation of real and nominal variables in the classical model, which implies that nominal variables do not influence real variables. (Cf. neutrality of money.) *(p. 170)*

Classical model: A model of the economy derived from the ideas of the classical, or pre-Keynesian, economists; a model based on the assumptions that wages and prices adjust to clear markets and that monetary policy does not influence real variables. (Cf. Keynesian model.) *(p. 12)*

Closed economy: An economy that does not engage in international trade. (Cf. open economy.) *(p. 56)*

Cobb-Douglas production function: A production function of the form $F(K, L) = AK^{\alpha}L^{1-\alpha}$, where K is capital, L is labor, and A and α are parameters. *(p. 54)*

Commodity money: Money that is intrinsically useful and would be valued even if it did not serve as money. (Cf. fiat money.) *(p. 142)*

Competition: A situation in which there are many individuals or firms so that the actions of any one of them do not influence market prices. *(p. 47)*

Constant returns to scale: A property of a production function whereby a proportionate increase in all factors of production leads to an increase in output of the same proportion. *(p. 45)*

Consumer price index (CPI): A measure of the overall level of prices that shows the cost of a fixed basket of consumer goods relative to the cost of the same basket in a base year. *(p. 15)*

Consumption: Goods and services purchased by consumers. *(p. 25)*

Consumption function: A relationship showing the determinants of consumption; for example, a relationship between consumption and disposable income, $C = C(Y - T)$. *(p. 57)*

Contractionary policy: Policy that reduces aggregate demand, real income, and employment. (Cf. expansionary policy.)

Coordination failure: A situation in which decisionmakers reach an outcome that is inferior for all of them because of their inability to jointly choose strategies that would result in a preferred outcome. *(p. 316)*

Corporate income tax: The tax levied on the accounting profit of corporations. *(p. 448)*

Cost of capital: The amount forgone by holding a unit of capital for one period, including interest, depreciation, and the gain or loss from the change in the price of capital. *(p. 443)*

Cost-push inflation: Inflation resulting from shocks to aggregate supply. (Cf. demand-pull inflation.) *(p. 306)*

Countercyclical: Moving in the opposite direction from output, incomes, and employment over the business cycle; rising during recessions and falling during recoveries. (Cf. acyclical, procyclical.) *(p. 294)*

CPI: *See* consumer price index.

Crowding out: The reduction in investment that results when expansionary fiscal policy raises the interest rate. *(p. 66)*

Currency: The sum of outstanding paper money and coins. *(p. 146)*

Current account: The receipts from exports minus the payments for imports, including the export and import of services from factors of production. *(p. 182)*

Cyclical unemployment: The unemployment associated with short-run economic fluctuations; the deviation of the unemployment rate from the natural rate. *(p. 303)*

Debt-deflation: A theory according to which an unexpected fall in the price level redistributes real wealth from debtors to creditors and, therefore, reduces total spending in the economy. *(p. 281)*

Deflation: A decrease in the overall level of prices. (Cf. disinflation, inflation.)

Deflator: *See* GNP deflator.

Demand deposits: Assets that are held in banks and can be used on demand to make transactions, such as checking accounts. *(p. 146)*

Demand-pull inflation: Inflation resulting from shocks to aggregate demand. (Cf. cost-push inflation.) *(p. 305)*

Depreciation: 1. The reduction in the capital stock that occurs over time because of aging and use. *(p. 27)* 2. A fall in the value of a currency relative to other currencies in the market for foreign exchange. (Cf. appreciation.) *(p. 191)*

Devaluation: An action by the central bank to decrease the value of a currency under a system of fixed exchange rates. (Cf. revaluation). *(p. 360)*

Diminishing marginal product: A characteristic of a production function whereby the marginal product of a factor falls as the amount of the factor increases while all other factors are held constant. *(p. 48)*

Discount rate: The interest rate that the Fed charges when it makes loans to banks. *(p. 469)*

Discounting: The reduction in value of future expenditure and receipts, compared to current expenditure and receipts, resulting from the presence of a positive interest rate. *(p. 399)*

Discouraged workers: Individuals who have left the labor force because they believe that there is little hope of finding a job. *(p. 137)*

Disinflation: A reduction in the rate at which prices are rising. (Cf. deflation, inflation.)

Disposable income: Income remaining after the payment of taxes. *(p. 57)*

Dominated asset: An asset that offers an inferior return compared to another asset in all possible realizations of future uncertainty. *(p. 473)*

Double coincidence of wants: A situation in which two individuals each have precisely the good that the other wants. *(p. 142)*

Economic profit: The amount of revenue remaining for the owners of a firm after all the factors of production have been compensated. (Cf. accounting profit.) *(p. 51)*

Efficiency of labor: A variable in the Solow growth model that measures the health, education, skill, and knowledge of the labor force. *(p. 100)*

Efficiency units of labor: A measure of the labor force that incorporates both the number of workers and the efficiency of each worker. *(p. 100)*

Efficiency-wage theories: Theories of real-wage rigidity and unemployment according to which firms raise labor productivity and profits by keeping real wages above the equilibrium level. *(p. 130)*

Elasticity: The percent change in a variable caused by a one-percent change in another variable.

Endogenous variable: A variable that is explained by a particular model; a variable whose value is determined by the model's solution. (Cf. exogenous variable.) *(p. 6)*

Equilibrium: A state of balance between opposing forces, such as the balance of supply and demand in a market. *(p. 7)*

Euler's theorem: The mathematical result economists use to show that economic profit must be zero if the production function has constant returns to scale and if factors are paid their marginal products. *(p. 52)*

***Ex ante* real interest rate:** The real interest rate anticipated when a loan is made; the nominal interest rate minus expected inflation. (Cf. *ex post* real interest rate.) *(p. 157)*

***Ex post* real interest rate:** The real interest rate actually realized; the nominal interest rate minus actual inflation. (Cf. *ex ante* real interest rate.) *(p. 157)*

Excess reserves: Reserves held by banks above the amount mandated by reserve requirements. *(p. 470)*

Exchange rate: The rate at which a country makes exchanges in world markets. (Cf. nominal exchange rate, real exchange rate.) *(p. 190)*

Exchange-rate union: A group of countries that agree to limit exchange-rate fluctuations among their currencies. *(p. 364)*

Exogenous variable: A variable that a particular model takes as given; a variable whose value is independent of the model's solution. (Cf. endogenous variable.) *(p. 6)*

Expansionary policy: Policy that raises aggregate demand, real income, and employment. (Cf. contractionary policy.)

Exports: Goods and services sold to other countries. *(p. 25)*

Factor of production: An input used to produce goods and services; for example, capital or labor. *(p. 44)*

Factor price: The amount paid for one unit of a factor of production. *(p. 46)*

Factor share: The proportion of total income being paid to a factor of production. *(p. 53)*

Federal Reserve (the Fed): The central bank of the United States. *(p. 145)*

Fiat money: Money that is not intrinsically useful and is valued only because it is used as money. (Cf. commodity money.) *(p. 142)*

Financial intermediation: The process by which resources are allocated from those individuals who wish to save some of their income for future consumption to those individuals and firms who wish to borrow to buy investment goods for future production. *(p. 466)*

Financing constraint: A limit on the quantity of funds a firm can raise—such as through borrowing—in order to buy capital. *(p. 451)*

Fiscal policy: The government's choice regarding levels of spending and taxation. *(p. 62)*

Fisher effect: The one-for-one influence of expected inflation on the nominal interest rate. *(p. 155)*

Fisher equation: The equation stating that the nominal interest rate is the sum of the real interest rate and expected inflation ($i = r + \pi^e$). *(p. 155)*

Fixed exchange rate: An exchange rate that is set by the central bank's willingness to buy and sell the domestic currency for foreign currencies at a predetermined price. (Cf. floating exchange rate.) *(p. 356)*

Flexible prices: Prices that adjust quickly to equilibrate supply and demand. (Cf. sticky prices.) *(p. 12)*

Floating exchange rate: An exchange rate that the central bank allows to change in response to changing economic conditions and economic policies. (Cf. fixed exchange rate.) *(p. 352)*

Flow: A variable measured as a quantity per unit of time. (Cf. stock.) *(p. 18)*

Fractional-reserve banking: A system in which banks keep only some of their deposits on reserve. (Cf. 100-percent reserve banking.) *(p. 465)*

Frictional unemployment: The unemployment that results because it takes time for workers to search for the jobs that best suit their skills and tastes. (Cf. wait unemployment.) *(p. 122)*

GDP: *See* gross domestic product.

General equilibrium: The simultaneous equilibrium of all the markets in the economy. *(p. 74)*

GNP: *See* gross national product.

Gold standard: A monetary system in which gold serves as money or in which all money is convertible into gold. *(p. 142)*

Golden rule: The saving rate in the Solow growth model that leads to the steady state in which consumption per worker (or consumption per efficiency unit of labor) is maximized. *(p. 89)*

Government purchases: Goods and services bought by the government. (Cf. transfer payments.) *(p. 25)*

Government-purchases multiplier: The change in aggregate income resulting from a one-dollar change in government purchases. *(p. 241)*

Gross domestic product (GDP): The total income earned domestically, including the income earned by foreign-owned factors of production; the total expenditure on domestically produced goods and services. *(p. 180)*

Gross national product (GNP): The total income of all citizens of a nation, including the income from factors of production used abroad; the total expenditure on the nation's output of goods and services. *(p. 15)*

GNP deflator: The ratio of nominal GNP to real GNP; a measure of the overall level of prices that shows the cost of the currently produced basket of goods relative to the price of that basket in a base year. *(p. 23)*

High-powered money: The sum of currency and bank reserves; also called the monetary base. *(p. 468)*

Hyperinflation: Extremely high inflation. *(p. 140)*

Hysteresis: The long-lasting influence of history, such as on the natural rate of unemployment. *(p. 317)*

Identification problem: The difficulty of isolating a particular relationship in data when two or more variables are related in more than one way. *(p. 72)*

Imperfect-information model: The model of

aggregate supply emphasizing that individuals do not always know the overall price level because they cannot observe the prices of all goods and services in the economy. *(p. 295)*

Import quota: A legal limit on the amount of a good that can be imported. *(p. 198)*

Imports: Goods and services bought from other countries. *(p. 25)*

Imputed value: An estimate of the value of a good or service that is not sold in the marketplace and therefore does not have a market price. *(p. 20)*

Income effect: The change in consumption of a good resulting from a movement to a higher or lower indifference curve, holding the relative price constant. (Cf. substitution effect.) *(p. 404)*

Index of leading indicators: *See* leading indicators.

Indifference curves: A graphical representation of preferences that shows different combinations of goods producing the same level of satisfaction. *(p. 400)*

Inflation: An increase in the overall level of prices. *(p. 29)*

Inflation tax: The revenue raised by the government through the creation of money; seigniorage. *(p. 141)*

Inside lag: The time between a shock hitting the economy and the policy action taken to respond to the shock. (Cf. outside lag.) *(p. 324)*

Insiders: Workers who are already employed and therefore have an influence on wage bargaining. (Cf. outsiders.) *(p. 129)*

Interest rate: The market price at which resources are transferred between the present and the future; the return to saving and the cost of borrowing. *(p. 60)*

Intermediation: *See* financial intermediation.

Intertemporal budget constraint: The budget constraint applying to expenditure and income in more than one period of time. *(p. 397)*

Intertemporal substitution of labor: The willingness of people to trade off working in one period for working in future periods. *(p. 377)*

Inventory investment: The change in the quantity of goods that firms hold in storage, including materials and supplies, work in process, and finished goods. *(p. 440)*

Investment: Goods purchased by individuals and firms to add to their stock of capital. *(p. 25)*

Investment tax credit: A provision of the corporate income tax that reduces a firm's tax when it buys new capital goods. *(p. 448)*

***IS* curve:** The negative relationship between the interest rate and the level of income that arises in the market for goods and services. (Cf. *IS-LM* model, *LM* curve.) *(p. 237)*

***IS-LM* model:** A model of aggregate demand that shows what determines aggregate income for a given price level by analyzing the interaction between the goods market and the money market. *(p. 236)*

Keynesian cross: A simple model of income determination, based on the ideas in Keynes's *General Theory*, which shows how changes in spending can have a multiplied effect on aggregate income. *(p. 237)*

Keynesian model: A model derived from the ideas of Keynes's *General Theory*; a model based on the assumptions that wages and prices do not adjust to clear markets and that aggregate demand determines the economy's output and employment. (Cf. classical model.) *(p. 235)*

Labor-augmenting technological progress: Advances in productive capability that raise the efficiency of labor. *(p. 100)*

Labor force: Those in the population who have a job or are looking for a job. *(p. 33)*

Labor-force participation rate: The percent of the adult population in the labor force. *(p. 34)*

Labor hoarding: The phenomenon of firms employing workers whom they do not need when the demand for their products is low, so that they will still have these workers when demand recovers. *(p. 384)*

Large open economy: An open economy that can influence its domestic interest rate; an economy that, by virtue of its size, can have a substantial impact on world markets and, in particular, on the world interest rate. (Cf. small open economy.) *(p. 208)*

Laspeyres price index: A measure of the level of prices based on a fixed basket of goods. (Cf. Paasche price index.) *(p. 31)*

Leading indicators: Economic variables that fluctuate in advance of the economy's output and thus signal the direction of economic fluctuations. *(p. 326)*

Life-cycle hypothesis: The theory of consumption that emphasizes the role of saving and borrowing as transferring resources from those times in life when income is high to those times in life when income is low, such as from working years to retirement. *(p. 409)*

Liquid: Readily convertible into the medium of exchange; easily used to make transactions. *(p. 159)*

Liquidity constraint: A restriction on the amount a person can borrow from a financial institution, which limits the person's ability to spend his future income today; also called a borrowing constraint. *(p. 406)*

Liquidity-preference theory: A simple model of the interest rate, based on the ideas in Keynes's *General Theory*, which says that the interest rate adjusts to equilibrate the supply and demand for real money balances. *(p. 250)*

LM curve: The positive relationship between the interest rate and the level of income (while holding the price level fixed) that arises in the market for real money balances. (Cf. *IS-LM* model, *IS* curve.) *(p. 237)*

Loanable funds: The flow of resources available to finance capital accumulation. *(p. 65)*

Lucas critique: The argument that traditional policy analysis does not adequately take into account the impact of policy changes on people's expectations. *(p. 328)*

M1, M2, M3: Various measures of the stock of money, where larger numbers signify a broader definition of money. *(p. 146)*

Macroeconometric model: A model that uses data and statistical techniques to describe the economy quantitatively, rather than just qualitatively. *(p. 268)*

Macroeconomics: The study of the economy as a whole. (Cf. microeconomics.) *(p. 3)*

Marginal product of labor (MPL): The amount of extra output produced when the labor input is increased by one unit. *(p. 48)*

Marginal product of capital (MPK): The amount of extra output produced when the capital input is increased by one unit. *(p. 51)*

Marginal propensity to consume (MPC): The increase in consumption resulting from a one-dollar increase in disposable income. *(p. 57)*

Marginal rate of substitution (MRS): The rate at which a consumer is willing to give up

some of one good in exchange for more of another; the slope of the indifference curve. *(p. 400)*

Market-clearing model: A model that assumes that prices freely adjust to equilibrate supply and demand. *(p. 11)*

Medium of exchange: The item widely accepted in transactions for goods and services; one of the functions of money. (Cf. store of value, unit of account.) *(p. 141)*

Menu cost: The cost of changing a price. *(p. 165)*

Microeconomics: The study of individual markets and decisionmakers. (Cf. macroeconomics.) *(p. 10)*

Model: A simplified representation of reality, often using diagrams or equations, that shows how variables interact. *(p. 6)*

Monetarism: The doctrine according to which changes in the money supply are the primary cause of economic fluctuations, implying that a stable money supply would lead to a stable economy. *(p. 336)*

Monetary base: The sum of currency and bank reserves; also called high-powered money. *(p. 467)*

Monetary neutrality: *See* neutrality of money.

Monetary policy: The central bank's choice regarding the supply of money. *(p. 145)*

Monetary transmission mechanism: The process by which changes in the money supply influence the amount that households and firms wish to spend on goods and services. *(p. 266)*

Money: The stock of assets used for transactions. (Cf. commodity money, fiat money.) *(p. 141)*

Money demand function: A function showing the determinants of the demand for real money balances; for example, $(M/P)^d = L(i, Y)$. *(p. 149)*

Money multiplier: The increase in the money supply resulting from a one-dollar increase in the monetary base. *(p. 468)*

Moral hazard: The possibility of dishonest behavior in situations in which behavior is imperfectly monitored; for example, in efficiency-wage theory, the possibility that low-wage workers may shirk their responsibilities and risk getting caught and fired. *(p. 131)*

Multiplier: *See* government-purchases multiplier, money multiplier, or tax multiplier.

Mundell-Fleming model: The *IS-LM* model for a small open economy. *(p. 345)*

Mundell-Tobin effect: The fall in the real interest rate that results when an increase in expected inflation raises the nominal interest rate, lowers real money balances and real wealth and, thereby, reduces consumption and raises saving. *(p. 172)*

National income accounting: The accounting system that measures GNP and many other related statistics. *(p. 16)*

National income accounts identity: The equation showing that GNP is the sum of consumption, investment, government purchases, and net exports. *(p. 25)*

National saving: A nation's income minus consumption and government purchases; the sum of private and public saving. *(p. 64)*

Natural rate of unemployment: The steady-state rate of unemployment; the rate of unemployment toward which the economy gravitates in the long run. *(p. 118)*

Natural-rate hypothesis: The premise that fluctuations in aggregate demand influence output, employment, and unemployment only in the short run, and that in the long run these variables return to the levels implied by the classical model. *(p. 317)*

Neoclassical model of investment: The theory according to which investment depends on the deviation of the marginal product of capital from the cost of capital. *(p. 441)*

Net exports: Exports minus imports. *(p. 25)*

Net investment: The amount of investment after the replacement of depreciated capital; the change in the capital stock. *(p. 445)*

Neutrality of money: The property that a change in the money supply does not influence real variables. (Cf. classical dichotomy.) *(p. 170)*

New classical economics: The school of thought according to which economic fluctuations can be explained while maintaining the assumptions of the classical model. (Cf. new Keynesian economics.) *(p. 312)*

New Keynesian economics: The school of thought according to which economic fluctuations can be explained only by admitting a role for some microeconomic imperfection, such as sticky wages or prices. (Cf. new classical economics.) *(p. 312)*

Nominal: Measured in current dollars; not adjusted for inflation. (Cf. real.) *(p. 170)*

Nominal exchange rate: The rate at which one country's currency trades for another country's currency. (Cf. real exchange rate.) *(p. 190)*

Nominal interest rate: The return to saving and the cost of borrowing without adjustment for inflation. (Cf. real interest rate.) *(p. 60)*

Normal good: A good that a consumer demands in greater quantity when his or her income rises. *(p. 402)*

Okun's law: The negative relationship between unemployment and real GNP, according to which a decrease in unemployment of one percentage point is associated with additional growth in real GNP of approximately two percent. *(p. 35)*

100-percent reserve banking: A system in which banks keep all deposits on reserve. (Cf. fractional reserve banking.) *(p. 464)*

Open economy: An economy in which people can freely engage in international trade in goods and capital. (Cf. closed economy.) *(p. 176)*

Open-market operations: The purchase or sale of government bonds by the central bank for the purpose of increasing or decreasing the money supply. *(p. 145)*

Outside lag: The time between a policy action and its influence on the economy. (Cf. inside lag.) *(p. 324)*

Outsiders: Workers who are not employed and therefore have no influence on wage bargaining. (Cf. insiders.) *(p. 129)*

Paasche price index: A measure of the level of prices based on a changing basket of goods. (Cf. Laspeyres price index.) *(p. 31)*

Permanent income: Income that people expect to persist into the future; normal income. (Cf. transitory income.) *(p. 414)*

Permanent-income hypothesis: The theory of consumption according to which people choose consumption based on their permanent income, and use saving and borrowing to smooth consumption in response to transitory variations in income. *(p. 414)*

Phillips curve: A negative relationship between inflation and unemployment; in its modern form, a relationship among inflation, cyclical unemployment, expected inflation, and supply shocks, derived from the short-run aggregate supply curve. *(p. 302)*

Pigou effect: The increase in consumer spending that results when a fall in the price level raises real money balances and, thereby, consumers' wealth. *(p. 281)*

Political business cycle: The fluctuations in output and employment resulting from the manipulation of the economy for electoral gain. *(p. 331)*

Portfolio theories of money demand: Theories that explain how much money people choose to hold and that stress the role of money as a store of value. (Cf. transactions theories of money demand.) *(p. 472)*

Precautionary saving: The extra saving that results from uncertainty regarding, for example, longevity or future income. *(p. 412)*

Present value: The amount today that is equivalent to an amount to be received in the future, taking into account the interest that could be earned over the interval of time. *(p. 403)*

Private saving: Disposable income minus consumption. *(p. 64)*

Procyclical: Moving in the same direction as output, incomes, and employment over the business cycle; falling during recessions and rising during recoveries. (Cf. acyclical, countercyclical.) *(p. 294)*

Production function: The mathematical relationship showing how the quantities of the factors of production determine the quantity of goods and services produced; for example, $Y = F(K, L)$. *(p. 45)*

Production smoothing: The motive for holding inventories according to which a firm can reduce its costs by keeping the amount of output it produces steady and allowing its stock of inventories to respond to fluctuating sales. *(p. 456)*

Profit: The income of firm owners; firm revenue minus firm costs. (Cf. accounting profit, economic profit.) *(p. 48)*

Public saving: Government receipts minus government spending; the budget surplus. *(p. 64)*

Purchasing-power parity: The doctrine according to which goods must sell for the same price in every country, implying that the nominal exchange rate reflects differences in price levels. *(p. 201)*

q-theory of investment: The theory according to which expenditure on capital goods depends on the ratio of the market value of installed capital to its replacement cost. *(p. 450)*

Quantity equation: The identity stating that the product of the money supply and the velocity of money equals nominal expenditure $(MV = PY)$; coupled with the assumption of stable velocity, an explanation of nominal expenditure called the quantity theory of money. *(p. 147)*

Quantity theory of money: The doctrine emphasizing that changes in the quantity of money lead to changes in nominal expenditure. *(p. 150)*

Quota: *See* import quota.

Random walk: The path of a variable whose changes over time are unpredictable. *(p. 417)*

Rational expectations: An approach that assumes that people optimally use all available information—including information about current and prospective policies—to forecast the future. *(p. 309)*

Real: Measured in constant dollars; adjusted for inflation. (Cf. nominal.) *(p. 170)*

Real aggregate demand curve: In real-business-cycle theory, the negative relationship arising from the goods market between the real interest rate and the aggregate quantity of output demanded. *(p. 376)*

Real aggregate supply curve: In real-business-cycle theory, the positive relationship arising from intertemporal substitution in the labor market between the real interest rate and the aggregate quantity of output supplied. *(p. 376)*

Real-business-cycle theory: The theory according to which economic fluctuations can be explained by real changes in the economy (such as changes in technology) and without any role for nominal variables (such as the money supply). *(p. 374)*

Real exchange rate: The rate at which one country's goods trade for another country's goods. (Cf. nominal exchange rate.) *(p. 192)*

Real interest rate: The return to saving and the cost of borrowing after adjustment for inflation. (Cf. nominal interest rate.) *(p. 60)*

Real money balances: The quantity of money expressed in terms of the quantity of goods and services it can buy; the quantity of money divided by the price level (M/P). *(p. 149)*

Recession: A sustained period of falling real income. *(p. 22)*

Rental price of capital: The amount paid to rent one unit of capital. *(p. 47)*

Reserve requirements: Regulations imposed on banks by the central bank that specify a minimum reserve-deposit ratio. *(p. 469)*

Reserves: The money that banks have received from depositors but have not used to make loans. *(p. 464)*

Residential investment: New housing bought by people to live in and by landlords to rent out. *(p. 440)*

Revaluation: An action undertaken by the central bank to raise the value of a currency under a system of fixed exchange rates. (Cf. devaluation.) *(p. 360)*

Ricardian equivalence: The theory according to which forward-looking consumers fully anticipate the future taxes implied by government debt, so that government borrowing today coupled with a tax increase in the future to repay the debt has the same effect on the economy as a tax increase today. *(p. 426)*

Sacrifice ratio: The number of percentage points of a year's real GNP that must be forgone to reduce inflation by one percentage point. *(p. 309)*

Saving: See national saving, private saving, and public saving.

Seasonal adjustment: The removal of the regular fluctuations in an economic variable that occur as a function of the time of year. *(p. 28)*

Sectoral shift: A change in the composition of demand among industries or regions. *(p. 122)*

Seigniorage: The revenue raised by the government through the creation of money; the inflation tax. *(p. 152)*

Shock: An exogenous change in an economic relationship, such as the aggregate demand or aggregate supply curve. *(p. 226)*

Shoeleather cost: The cost of inflation from reducing real money balances, such as the in-

convenience of needing to make more frequent trips to the bank. *(p. 164)*

Small open economy: An open economy that takes its interest rate as given by world financial markets; an economy that, by virtue of its size, has a negligible impact on world markets and, in particular, on the world interest rate. (Cf. large open economy.) *(p. 183)*

Solow growth model: A model showing how saving, population growth, and technological progress determine the level of and growth in the standard of living. *(p. 77)*

Solow residual: The growth in total factor productivity, measured as the percentage change in output minus the percentage change in inputs, where the inputs are weighted by their factor shares. *(p. 115)*

Stabilization policy: Public policy aimed at keeping output and employment at their natural-rate levels. *(p. 226)*

Stagflation: A situation of falling output and rising prices; combination of stagnation and inflation. *(p. 230)*

Steady state: A condition in which key variables are not changing. *(p. 83)*

Sticky prices: Prices that adjust sluggishly and, therefore, do not always equilibrate supply and demand. (Cf. flexible prices.) *(p. 12)*

Sticky-price model: The model of aggregate supply emphasizing the slow adjustment of the prices of goods and services. *(p. 296)*

Sticky-wage model: The model of aggregate supply emphasizing the slow adjustment of nominal wages. *(p. 289)*

Stock: 1. A variable measured as a quantity at a point in time. (Cf. flow.) *(p. 18)* 2. Shares of ownership in a corporation. *(p. 450)*

Stock market: A market in which shares of ownership in corporations are bought and sold. *(p. 450)*

Stock-out avoidance: The motive for holding inventories according to which firms keep extra goods on hand to prevent running out if sales are unexpectedly high. *(p. 457)*

Store of value: A way of transferring purchasing power from the present to the future; one of the functions of money. (Cf. medium of exchange, unit of account.) *(p. 141)*

Substitution effect: The change in consumption of a good resulting from a movement along an indifference curve because of a change in the relative price. (Cf. income effect.) *(p. 404)*

Tariff: A tax on imported goods. *(p. 198)*

Tax multiplier: The change in aggregate income resulting from a one-dollar change in taxes. *(p. 243)*

Time inconsistency: The tendency of policymakers to announce policies in advance in order to influence the expectations of private decisionmakers, and then to follow different policies after those expectations have been formed and acted upon. *(p. 333)*

Tobin's *q*: The ratio of the market value of installed capital to its replacement cost. *(p. 450)*

Total factor productivity: A measure of the level of technology; the amount of output per unit of input, where different inputs are combined on the basis of their factor shares. (Cf. Solow residual.) *(p. 115)*

Transactions theories of money demand: Theories that explain how much money people choose to hold and that stress the role of money as a medium of exchange. (Cf. portfolio theories of money demand.) *(p. 474)*

Transfer payments: Payments from the government to individuals that are not in exchange for goods and services, such as Social Security payments. (Cf. government purchases.) *(p. 61)*

Transitory income: Income that people do not expect to persist into the future; current income minus normal income. (Cf. permanent income.) *(p. 414)*

Underground economy: Economic transactions that are hidden in order to evade taxes or because the activity is illegal. *(p. 474)*

Unemployment insurance: A government program under which unemployed workers can collect benefits for a certain period of time after losing their jobs. *(p. 122)*

Unemployment rate: The percentage of the labor force that does not have a job. *(p. 15)*

Unit of account: The measure in which prices and other accounting records are recorded; one of the functions of money. (Cf. medium of exchange, store of value.) *(p. 141)*

Value-added: The value of a firm's output minus the value of the intermediate goods the firm purchased. *(p. 20)*

Velocity of money: The ratio of nominal expenditure to the money supply; the rate at which money changes hands. *(p. 148)*

Wage: The amount paid for one unit of labor. *(p. 47)*

Wage rigidity: The failure of wages to adjust to equilibrate labor supply and labor demand. *(p. 126)*

Wait unemployment: The unemployment resulting from wage rigidity and job rationing. (Cf. frictional unemployment.) *(p. 126)*

Worker-misperception model: The model of aggregate supply emphasizing that workers sometimes perceive incorrectly the overall level of prices. *(p. 291)*

Work in process: Goods in inventory that are in the process of being completed. *(p. 457)*

World interest rate: The interest rate prevailing in world financial markets. *(p. 183)*

Index

Accelerator model of inventories, 458–459, 461
Accommodating policy, 231
Accounting profit, 52
Adverse selection, 130–131
Aggregate demand
  defined, 217
  effect of shift in, 222–224
  exogenous shocks to, 226–228
  monetary and fiscal policy as determinants of, 274–275, 483
  role in determining short-run fluctuations, 483
Aggregate demand curve
  algebra of, 273–274
  definition and derivation of, 270–273
  differentiation from real-aggregate-demand curve of, 377
  IS-LM as a model of, 236
  in long- and short-run equilibria, 224–225, 233
Aggregate-demand externality, 313
Aggregate supply
  defined, 221
  expressed in Phillips curve, 319
  four models of, 288–301, 319
  shocks to, 229–232
  See also Phillips curve
Aggregate supply curve
  differentiation from real-aggregate-supply curve of, 377
  international differences in, 299–300
  long- and short-run, 221–222, 233
Aggregate supply and demand model, 216
  inflation inertia in, 305
Akerlof, George A., 314n
Alaska, gold discovery in, 169
Alesina, Alberto, 333n
Altonji, Joseph G., 385n
Altruism between generations, 432–433
Ando, Albert, 409, 412n

Angell, Norman, 145n
Animal spirits, 269
Appreciation (of currency), 200
Arbitrage, 201–203
Austen, Jane, 42
Australia, gold discovery in, 169
Automatic stabilizers, 324–325
Autonomous consumption, 394
Average propensity to consume, 393–397
  in life-cycle model, 410
  in permanent-income hypothesis, 416

Balanced budget, 62
Balance sheet
  under fractional-reserve banking, 465
  under 100-percent-reserve banking, 464
Ball, Laurence, 298n, 300n, 316n, 385n
Banking system
  effect on money supply of, 470
  failures in 1930s in, 470–471
  reserves in, 464
  role of, 463–466
  See also Excess reserves; Reserves
Barro, Robert J., 67n, 68n, 108n, 335n, 380n, 387n, 388n, 432–433
Barsky, Robert B., 28n, 158n
Barter economy, 142–143
Battalio, Raymond C., 317n
Baum, Frank, 168–169
Baumol, William, 474n
Baumol-Tobin model of cash management, 474–478
Becker, Gary S., 108n
Beil, Richard O., 317n
Benjamin, Daniel K., 68n, 123, 124n
Bequests, 412, 432–433
  See also Strategic bequest motive
Bernanke, Ben, 279n

Bernheim, B. Douglas, 429*n*, 433*n*

Berry, T. S., 338*f*

Bils, Mark J., 295*n*

Blanchard, Olivier Jean, 108*n*, 314*n*, 315*n*, 318*n*

Blinder, Alan, 164*n*, 217*n*

Bolivian hyperinflation, 166–167

Bond market, 466

Bonds, 472–473, 477

Bordo, Michael D., 68*n*

Borrowing constraint
    consumer, 405–408, 451
    government, 430–431
    in Japan, 408
    See also Liquidity constraint

Boskin, Michael J., 107*n*

Bossons, John, 412*n*

Bretton Woods System, 356

Britain, 123–124

Brown, Charles, 127*n*

Brown, E. Cary, 279*n*

Brumberg, Richard, 409

Brunner, Karl, 277*n*

Bruno, Michael, 129*n*

Bryan, William Jennings, 168

Budget constraint
    consumer, 397, 399
    government, 427–429

Budget deficit, 43, 62, 487–488
    cyclically adjusted or full-employment, 341
    measurement of, 436–439
    rules for, 337–339
    in the United States, 69, 186–187, 434
    See also Capital budgeting; Contingent
        liability; Debt, government

Budget surplus, 62

Bulow, Jeremy I., 132*n*

Bush, George, 77

Business cycle, 214
    See also Political business cycle; Real-
        business-cycle theory

Business fixed investment, 440
    decision for total spending for, 446
    model of, 441–451
    See also Neoclassical model of investment

Campbell, John Y., 405*n*, 419*n*

Canada
    investment and income in, 88–89
    importance of international trade for, 176
    imports and exports in, 177
    labor unions in, 129–30

Capital
    change in stock of (net investment), 445
    cost of, 443–446, 460
    depreciation of, 81–84, 86–87, 444–446
    effect of increase in, 112–114
    as factor of production, 44
    firm ownership of, 52
    international flow of, 181–182, 208–209
    rental price of, 442–445
    renting of, 47, 51
    See also Capital accumulation; Depreciation
        of capital; Interest rate; Rental price of
        capital

Capital account
    defined, 181–182, 206
    effect of protectionist trade policy on, 198
    effect of public policy on, 185–189
    in model of open economy, 183–185

Capital accumulation
    Golden Rule level of, 89–95
    nation's rate of, 103–104
    supply and demand of goods as determinants
        of, 79–89

Capital budgeting, 438

Capital demand, 51

Capital stock
    steady-state level of, 81–84, 87–91
    See also Depreciation, rate of; Investment;
        Saving rate

Cecchetti, Stephen G., 217*n*

Central bank, 145, 151, 160–161, 170
    role with fixed exchange rate, 356
    See also Federal Reserve (the Fed)

Chad, investment and income in, 88–89

Cipolla, Carlo M., 53*n*

Clark, John Bates, 214

Clark, Kim B., 132*n*

Classical dichotomy, 170, 171, 216
    in real business cycle theory, 374
    vertical aggregate supply curve satisfies, 222

Classical economic theory, 235–236

Classical economists, 394

Closed economy and open economy
    comparison of effect of fiscal policy on, 352–
        353
    comparison of effect of monetary policy on,
        353–354
    goods and services in, 56

Cobb, Charles, 53

Cobb-Douglas production function, 53–55, 92–
    93, 443

Commodity money, 142–144, 170

Competition, 47–52

Constant returns to scale, 45, 52, 53–55, 76

Constraints. *See* Borrowing constraint; Budget constraint; Liquidity constraint

Consumer
budget constraint of, 397–402
choices of, 401–402, 404
expectations of, 76
preferences of, 400–401, 404
in Ricardian view of government debt, 426–429
time horizon of, 432
See also Discounting; Indifference curves; Intertemporal budget constraint; Marginal rate of substitution

Consumer confidence, 76

Consumer price index (CPI), 29–30, 37
vs. GNP deflator, 30–33
effect of changes in, 168

Consumption
defined, 90
as expenditure component of GNP, 24–26, 56–59
factors affecting, 402–405
Fisher's theory of, 397–408
in Great Depression, 278
Keynes's theory of, 393–397, 419–420
random walk of, 417–418
rational expectations, implications for, 417–418
and real interest rate, 404–405
See also Average propensity to consume; Consumer; Consumption function; Intertemporal budget constraint; Marginal propensity to consume *(MPC)*; Marginal rate of substitution; Steady-state consumption

Consumption function
defined, 57
Fisher's theory of, 397–408
in Great Depression, 278
in Keynesian cross, 237–238
Keynes's theory of, 393–397, 419–420
in life-cycle hypothesis, 410
in permanent-income hypothesis, 415
recent work on, 420
short- and long-run, 396–397
in Solow model, 80–81
in U.S. data, 58–59
See also Autonomous consumption; Average propensity to consume; Consumption; Intertemporal budget constraint; Marginal rate of substitution

Contingent liability, 439

Cooper, Russell, 316*n*, 317*n*

Coordination failure, 315–317

Corporate income tax, 448, 460

Cost of capital, real, 445–448

Cost of living. *See* Consumer price index (CPI)

Cost-push inflation, 306, 307

Countercyclical real wage, 294–295

CPI. *See* Consumer price index (CPI)

Crowding out
of capital accumulation, 423
of investment, 68, 265, 274

Currency, 146
depreciation and appreciation of, 200
devaluation and revaluation of, 360
effect of inflation on value of, 200
as store of value, 474
See also Demand deposits

Currency-deposit ratio, 469–471

Current account
defined, 182
effect of protectionist trade policy on, 198
effect of public policy on, 185–189
in model of open economy, 183–185
relation of real exchange rate to, 194–195

Cyclical unemployment, 305

Debt, government
and fiscal policy, 337–339
relation to government deficit, 18
Ricardian view of, 387, 423, 426–429
traditional view of, 424–425

Debt-deflation theory, 281–283

Debt-GNP ratio, 338–339

Deflation
between 1880 and 1896, 168
in 1930s, 280–283

DeJong, Douglas V., 317*n*

Demand
origin of, 63
for real money balances, 149
relation to consumption function of, 80–81
See also Aggregate demand; Aggregate demand curve

Demand curve
for capital, 442
in economic models, 7–8
See also Aggregate demand curve

Demand deposits, 146

Demand-pull inflation, 305, 307

Deposit insurance, 283, 471

Depreciation
  of capital, 81–84, 86–87, 444–446
  of currency, 200
Devaluation (of currency), 360
Diminishing marginal product, 48–49
Dirksen, Everett, 423
Discounting, 398–399
Discount rate (of Federal Reserve), 469–470
Discouraged workers, 137
Disinflation, 308–312
Disposable income, 57–59
Dissaving, 411–412
Dominated asset, 473
Dominguez, Kathryn M., 327n
Dornbusch, Rudiger, 161n, 315n, 412n
Double coincidence of wants, 142
Douglas, Paul, 53
DRI model, 268–269

Eckstein, Otto, 269t
Economic disturbances. *See* Shocks
Economic fluctuations, 214–215
  causes of, 226
  differences in long- and short-run, 215–216
  seasonal changes in, 28–29
  theory of real business cycles for, 374
  See also Business cycle; Recession; Solow
    residual
Economic forecasting, 326–328
Economic growth, 77–109
  role of Solow model in study of, 107–108
  sources of, 112–116
  world slowdown in, 106–107, 109
  See also Solow growth model
Economic policy
  active or passive, 323–324, 330, 340
  by discretion, 330, 333–335, 340, 342–344
  effect of lag in, 324, 326
  goals of makers of, 302
  by rule, 330–339, 340, 342–344
  for stabilization, 323–324
  See also Fiscal policy; Monetary policy;
    Stabilization policy; Time inconsistency
Economic profit, 51–52
Economic statistics, 15
Economic theory, classical. *See* Classical
  economic theory
Efficiency of labor, 100

models to explain level and growth of, 108
  relation of total factor productivity to, 106,
    115
Efficiency units of labor, 100–102
Efficiency-wage theories, 130–131
Eichengreen, Barry, 358n
Einstein, Albert, 3
Eisner, Robert, 439n
Elasticity, 478
Employment
  natural-rate level of, 225, 228
  real-business-cycle theory interpretation of,
    384–385
Employment Act of 1946, 323
Endogenous variables
  in economic models, 6–9, 13
  in *IS-LM* model, 263, 284
  in Mundell-Fleming model, 346–347
  role in forecasting of, 326
Equilibrium of supply and demand, 7–8
Ethiopia, investment and income in, 88–89
Euler's theorem, 52n, 114
European Monetary System (EMS), 364
Ex ante real interest rate, 157
Excess reserves, 470
Exchange rate, nominal
  defined, 190, 206
  determinants of, 199–200
  with fixed exchange rate system, 358
  relation to real exchange rate of, 192
Exchange rate, real
  computation of, 192–193
  defined, 192, 206
  determinants of, 194–195
  effect of fixed exchange rate system on, 358
  effect of protectionist trade policy on, 198
  effect of public policy on, 196
  relation to net exports of, 193
  See also Terms of trade
Exchange rates
  comparing German mark and American dollar,
    200
  computation of percent changes in, 199
  in Mundell-Fleming model, 346–349
  See also Arbitrage; Purchasing-power parity
Exchange-rate system
  in open economy, 345–363
  See also Fixed exchange rate; Floating
    exchange rate
Exchange-rate union, 364

Exogenous variables
    in economic models, 6–9, 13
    effect on empirical relationships of, 72–73
    effect on price and quantity of, 216
    in *IS-LM* model, 263, 284
    in models of the economy, 326
    money supply dependence on, 468–469
    in Mundell-Fleming model, 346–347
    role in forecasting of, 326
    as shocks, 269–270
    technological progress as, 105–106
    turned into endogenous variable, 107–108
Expectations formation, 309–310, 328–329
Exports, 176, 199
Ex post real interest rate, 157
Externality, 108, 313

Factor demand, 48–51
    See also Capital demand; Factors of
        production; Labor demand
Factor prices
    defined, 46
    determination of real, 51
    effect of technological progress on, 102
Factors of production
    defined, 44
    demand for, 46–48
    as determinant of level of output, 44, 150
    effect of increase in, 112
    returns to, 51–55
    See also Accounting profit; Economic profit
Fair, Ray C., 5–6, 327n
Fair Labor Standards Act (1938), 127
Federal Reserve (the Fed), 145, 170
    accommodating policy of, 231
    influence over money supply of, 145, 469–471
    as lender of last resort, 471
    open-market operations of, 145, 469–470
    reserves of, 464
Feldstein, Martin S., 105n
Fiat money, 142, 144–145, 154, 170, 226
Financial intermediation, 466
Financial markets, 64–65, 451, 466
Financing constraints, 451
Firm, competitive
    demand for factors of production, 48–51
    economic profit of, 51–52
    profit-maximizing goal of, 47–48

Fiscal policy
    budget deficit rules in, 337–339
    as determinant of aggregate demand, 274–275
    effect in large open economy of, 370
    effect of lags in, 324
    effect on *IS* curve of, 246–247, 264, 284
    effect on national saving of, 62–69
    in ending hyperinflation, 161, 163
    with floating exchange rate, 352–353
    interdependence with monetary policy of,
        266–269
    interpretation using permanent-income
        hypothesis, 416–417
    in *IS-LM* model, 265
    in Keynesian consumption function theory,
        393
    in Keynesian cross, 238, 240
    in open economy, 352–353, 359, 370–371
    proposed alternative rules for, 337–338
    in real business cycle theory, 379–380
    U.S., in 1930s, 279, 283
    U.S., in 1980s, 69
    tax smoothing effect of, 337
    See also Automatic stabilizers; Contractionary
        policy; Expansionary policy; Government
        purchases; Government-purchases
        multiplier; Government spending; Tax
        laws
Fiscal-policy multipliers, 268–269
Fischer, Stanley, 107n, 108n, 154n, 161n, 291n,
    412n
Fisher, Irving, 155, 157–158, 327
    on consumption function, 397–408
    intertemporal choice, model of, 397–408, 417,
        418–419
Fisher effect, 155, 156n, 157, 171
Fisher equation, 155, 158
    See also Fisher effect
Fixed exchange rate, 4, 345, 356–358, 365
    arguments for, 362–363
    under gold standard, 358
Flexible vs. sticky prices, 11–12, 215, 224–225
Fleming, J. Marcus, 34n
Floating exchange rate, 345–355, 365
    arguments for, 362–363
    in large open economy, 368–373
    small open economy with, 352–355
Flows, 16–18
    balancing of, 62–65
    of dollars, 43
    of goods and services, 178

Flows *(continued)*
　international, 181–190
　stocks vs., 18
Fluctuations. *See* Economic fluctuations
Ford, Gerald, 140
Ford, Henry, 131
Ford Motor Company, 131–132
Forecasting. *See* Economic forecasting.
Forsythe, Robert, 317n
Fractional-reserve banking, 465–466
　See also Reserve-deposit ratio
Franklin, Benjamin, 176
France, imports and exports in, 177
Free Silver movement, 168–169
Frictional unemployment, 122–123, 130, 138,
　318
　See also Sectoral shift
Friedman, Benjamin M., 229n, 339n
Friedman, Milton, 152, 277n, 280, 287, 293n,
　304, 322, 336, 397, 470n
　permanent-income hypothesis of, 414–419,
　420, 426
Function, 9–10

Game theory. *See* Coordination failure
GDP. *See* Gross domestic product
Geary, Patrick T., 295n
General equilibrium model, 43, 74
Germany
　hyperinflation in interwar, 162–163
　imports and exports in, 177
　inflation rate in, 140
　postwar economic growth in, 86–87
GNP. *See* Gross national product (GNP)
GNP deflator, 23–24, 30–33
　vs. CPI, 30–33
Golden Rule level of capital accumulation
　defined, 102, 108–109
　effect of population growth on, 98
　in steady-state consumption, 89–93, 108–109,
　424
　transition to, 93–95
Goldfeld, Stephen M., 478n
Gold standard, 142, 158, 168–169, 226, 358
Goods market. *See* IS curve
Gordon, David, 335n
Gordon, Robert J., 309n
Government budget constraint, 427–429
Government budget deficit. *See* Budget deficit
Government debt. *See* Debt, government

Government purchases
　effect of increase in, 66–68
　as expenditure component of GNP, 24–25, 61–
　62, 65–68
　of goods and services, 61
Government-purchases multiplier, 241–243, 268,
　269
　See also Tax multiplier
Government spending
　financing of, 152–154
　transfer payments as, 61–62
　wartime purchases, 67–68
Gray, JoAnna, 291n
Great Depression, 235, 253, 277–283, 328, 329,
　470–471
Greece, seignorage in, 154
Griliches, Zvi, 107n
Gross domestic product (GDP), 180, 206
Gross national product (GNP)
　components of, 24–25, 56
　computation of, 19–21
　defined, 15, 180, 206
　determinants of real and nominal, 150
　expenditures in, 24–25
　growth of real, 77
　investment as component of, 440
　as measure of economy's performance, 16–17
　nominal, 22–24, 37
　real, 22–24, 28–29, 37, 77
　real vs. nominal, 21–23, 30
　seasonal cycles and, 29
　treatment of imputations in, 20–21
　treatment of intermediate goods and value-
　added in, 20
　treatment of inventories in, 19
　See also Debt-GNP ratio; GNP deflator;
　Imputed value; Okun's law; Sacrifice
　ratio; Value-added
Growth. *See* Economic growth
Grubel, Herbert G., 130n

Hall, Robert E., 119n, 161n, 162n, 163n, 310n,
　405n, 417–418, 449n
Hamilton, Alexander, 335–336
Hamilton, James D., 232n
Hansen, Alvin, 393
Hayashi, Fumio, 408n, 451n
Heller, Walter W., 244n
Heston Alan, 88n
Hicks, John R., 237n
High-powered money, 468

Holmes, Sherlock, 15
Human capital, 108
Hume, David, 387
Hyperinflation
    in Bolivia, 166–167
    defined, 140
    in interwar Germany, 162–163
    method to end, 160–161
    in Mexico, 200
Hysteresis theory, 317–319

Identification problem, 72–73
Imperfect-information model, 295–296, 299, 319
Import quota, 198, 354, 361
Imports, 4, 176, 199
Imputed value, 20–21
Income
    effect of falling prices on, 281–283
    effect on consumption of increase in (Fisher
        model), 402–403
    in Keynesian consumption function theory,
        393–395
    measures of, 26–28
    in permanent-income hypothesis, 414–416
    See also Disposable income; National
        income; Normal good; Permanent
        income; Transitory income
Income distribution, 46
Income effect, 404
Income velocity of money, 149
Indexation for inflation, 168
Index of leading indicators. See Leading
        indicators
Indifference curves, 400–402
Infinite geometric series, 242
Inflation
    commitment by rule or discretion to, 342–344
    determined by changing level of money
        supply, 151
    effect of, 141, 200
    effect of money growth on, 155
    effect on nominal interest rate, 155
    forces changing rate of, 305–307
    inertia of, 305, 310, 319
    measuring, 29–30
    real money balances with high, 164
    reduction of, 308–312
    relation of price level to, 151
    relation of real and nominal interest rates to,
        155

social costs of expected, 164–165, 171
social costs of unexpected, 166–168, 171
uncertainty in, 168
variation in, 140
    See also Cost-push inflation; Demand-pull
        inflation; Disinflation; Hyperinflation;
        Phillips curve; Shoeleather cost of
        inflation; Stagflation
Inflation, expected
    determinants of, 305
    in IS curve, 282
    in long- and short-run, 308
    in Phillips curve, 319
Inflation tax, 141, 153–154
Inside lags (in stabilization policy), 324
Insiders in labor force, 129
Interest rate
    dependence of investment on, 69–73
    relation to velocity of, 257
    role to equilibrate supply and demand, 62–65
    See also Discount rate (of Federal Reserve);
        Interest rate, nominal; Interest rate, real
Interest rate, nominal
    as cost of holding money, 171
    defined, 60, 155, 171
    effect of money growth on, 155
    See also Fisher equation
Interest rate, real, 60
    defined, 60, 155
    dependence of inventory investment on, 459
    as determinant of housing demand, 453–454
    effect on consumption of (Fisher model), 403–
        405
    ex ante and ex post forms of, 157
    link to investment of, 60
    See also Ex ante real interest rate; Ex post
        real interest rate; Fisher equation
Interest rate, world, 183–185, 346–351, 354
Intermediation. See Financial intermediation
International trade and finance
    exchange rates and, 190–203, 352–364
    flow of capital and goods in, 183–190
    international comparisons of, 176–177
    role of net exports in, 178–180
    significance of, 176–177
    See also Exchange rate, nominal; Exchange
        rate, real; Open economy, small; Open
        economy, large; Trade policy
Intertemporal budget constraint, 397–400,
    420
Intertemporal choice model, 417

Intertemporal substitution of labor, 377–378, 382, 385

Inventories
effect on economic equilibrium of, 239–240
as factor of production, 456–457, 461
in GNP accounting, 19
reasons for holding, 456–457, 461

Inventory investment, 440
effect of real interest rate on, 459
See also Accelerator model of inventories; Just-in-time production plan; Production smoothing; Stock-out avoidance; Work in process

Investment
components of, 440–441
defined, 25, 58–61
determinants of, 445–448
as expenditure component of GNP, 24–26, 58–61
factors changing demand for, 69–71
link to real interest rate of, 60, 72–73
planned, 244–245
See also IS curve; Net investment

Investment function, 60

Investment tax credit, 448–449

IS curve
algebra of, 248–250
defined, 237
derivation of, 244–245
expected inflation as variable in, 282
factors creating shift in, 246–248
fiscal policy and, 246–247
with fixed exchange rate, 361
during Great Depression, 278–279
loanable-funds interpretation of, 247
in Mundell-Fleming model, 347–351
as real aggregate demand curve, 376
shocks to, 269–270
See also Keynesian cross

IS-LM model
defined, 236–237
equations expressing, 259
equilibrium in, 284
intersection of curves in, 264
Mundell-Fleming model version of, 345–362, 365
real-business-cycle theory using, 375
role of, 260, 263, 269, 270, 284
showing influence of policy, 263–269, 424
See also Equilibrium, of the economy; Price level; Prices, flexible

Israel, hyperinflation in, 140

Italy
imports and exports in, 177
seigniorage in, 154

Japan
bonuses in, 325
borrowing constraints and saving rate in, 408
imports and exports in, 177
investment and income in, 88–89
postwar economic growth in, 86–87

Job rationing, 126–127

John, Andrew, 316n

Johnson, Lyndon, 417

Jorgenson, Dale W., 107n, 449n

Just-in-time production plan, 459

Katz, Lawrence F., 124n, 125n, 131n

Kennan, John, 295n

Kennedy, John F., 244, 324

Kennickell, Arthur, 412n

Keynes, John Maynard, 244, 250, 263, 269
on aggregate demand, 312–313
consumption function theory of, 393–397, 405
on employment increase, 294
influence of theory of, 329–330
on intellectual influence, 339
on Lenin's views of currency, 140
national income theory of, 235–236

Keynesian consumption function, 394

Keynesian cross, 237–240, 241, 244–247, 260

Keynesian model of national income, 275

King, Robert G., 386n

King, Stephen R., 309n

Kiyotaki, Nobuhiro, 314n

Kochin, Levis A., 68n, 123, 124n

Kotlikoff, Laurence J., 43n

Krugman, Paul R., 363n

Kuznets, Simon, 395–396

Kydland, Finn E., 335n

Labor
effect on output of increases in, 113–114
as factor of production, 44
See also Efficiency of labor

Labor-augmenting technological progress, 100

Labor demand, 49–50, 290

Labor force
defined, 33
discouraged workers in, 137

factors changing composition of, 135
insiders and outsiders in, 129, 318
Labor-force participation rate, 34
Labor hoarding, 384
Labor supply
  in real-business-cycle theory, 377, 385
  See also Intertemporal substitution of labor
Labor unions. *See* Unions, labor
Lags (in stabilization policy). *See* Inside lags;
  Outside lags
Laidler, David, 478*n*
Large open economy. *See* Open economy, large
Laspeyres price index, 31
Law of one price, 201
  See also Arbitrage; Purchasing-power parity
Leading indicators, 326
Leimer, Dean R., 105*n*
Lesnoy, Selig S., 105*n*
Life-cycle hypothesis, 409–411, 420
Lilien, David M., 135*n*
Liquid asset, 159, 251
Liquidity, banking system creation of, 466
Liquidity constraint, 406
Liquidity preference. *See* Theory of liquidity
  preference
Littlefield, Henry M., 169*n*
LM curve
  algebra of, 258–259
  defined, 237, 250, 260
  derivation of, 254–255
  factors creating shift in, 255–257
  with fixed exchange rate, 356–357
  in Mundell-Fleming model, 347–351
  quantity theory interpretation of, 257
  shocks to, 270
  See also Theory of liquidity preference
Loanable funds, theory of interest rate, 64–65
Long run vs. short run, 11–12, 215–216, 224–
  225, 275–276, 482–485
Lucas, Robert E., Jr., 108*n*, 296*n*, 299–300, 328,
  378*n*
Lucas critique, 328–329, 387

*M*1, 146–147, 473
*M*2, 146–147
*M*3, 146–147
McCallum, Bennett T., 388*n*
McKinley, William, 168–169
Macroeconomic models
  accelerator model of inventories, 458–459,
  461

aggregate demand model, 236
aggregate supply, four models of, 288–301,
  319
business fixed investment model, 441–451
general equilibrium model, 43, 74
imperfect-information model, 295–296, 299,
  319
intertemporal choice model, 417
IS-LM model, 259, 260, 263–270, 284, 345–
  362, 365, 375, 424
Keynesian model of national income, 275
life-cycle model, 410–411
model of aggregate supply and aggregate
  demand, 216–233
money supply model, 467, 469
Mundell-Fleming model, 345–362, 365, 425
neoclassical model of investment, 441, 451,
  460
model of large open economy, 208–210, 424–
  425
model of large open economy in the short
  run, 368–373
model of small open economy, 183–185
real-business-cycle model, 377–382, 388
residential investment model, 452–456
Solow growth model, 77, 79, 96–99, 100–109,
  408, 424
sticky-price model, 296–298, 299–300, 319
sticky-wage model, 288–291, 294–295, 319
worker-misperception model, 291–293, 294–
  295, 319
Macroeconometric models, 268
Macroeconomic policy. *See* Fiscal policy;
  Monetary policy; Trade policy
Macroeconomics
  defined and described, 3–5, 11, 13
  role of microeconomics in, 10–11
Maddison, Angus, 106*t*
Mankiw, N. Gregory, 108*n*, 298*n*, 300*n*, 314*n*,
  315*n*, 316*n*, 388*n*, 405*n*, 419*n*, 456*n*
Marginal product of capital (*MPK*), 51, 91–93,
  99, 102, 108, 112–113
  for Cobb-Douglas production function, 54–55
  determines real rental price of capital, 114,
  442, 460
  estimation of net, 103–104
  in investment function, 446–448
  relation to cost of capital of, 445
  See also Rental price of capital, real
Marginal product of labor (*MPL*), 48–50, 53, 54–
  55
Marginal product of land, 53

Marginal propensity to consume *(MPC)*, 57, 238, 393–395

Marginal rate of substitution, 400, 402

Market clearing, 11–12

Market prices, 47–48

Martin, William McChesney, 322

Marx, Karl
  consumption function of, 110—111
  incomes of capital and labor theory of, 46
  prediction for return to capital, 103

Menu costs, 165, 171, 313–314

Mexico
  hyperinflation in, 200
  investment and income in, 88

Meyer, Bruce D., 124*n*, 125*n*

Microeconomics, 10–11, 13

Minimum-wage laws, 127–128, 138

Miron, Jeffrey A., 28*n*, 457*n*

Models
  building economic, 42
  defined, 6–9
  use of, 11–12
  See also Macroeconomic models

Modigliani, Franco
  consumption-function explanation, 397
  life-cycle hypothesis of, 409–414, 420, 426

Monetarist theory, 336

Monetary base, 467–468, 469, 470
  See also High-powered money

Monetary neutrality, 170

Monetary policy
  as component of stabilization policy, 226–228
  defined, 145
  as determinant of aggregate demand, 274–275
  effect in large open economy of, 370, 372
  effect in long- and short-run of, 215–216
  effect of changes in, 265–266
  effect of lags in, 324
  effect on inflation rate of, 306–307
  effect on *LM* curve of, 284
  with fixed exchange rate, 356, 359–360
  with floating exchange rate, 353–354
  instruments used by Federal Reserve, 469
  interdependence with fiscal policy of, 266–269
  to lower inflation, 254
  in open economy, 353–354, 370–371
  proposed alternative rules for, 336–337

Monetary system, international, 362–364

Monetary transmission mechanism, 266, 353–354

Money
  creation of, 465–466
  functions of, 141–142
  measurement of quantity of, 146
  as medium of exchange, 142, 170
  neutrality of, 386
  as store of value, 141, 170
  types of, 142–145
  as unit of account, 142, 170
  See also Commodity money; Currency; Fiat money; Income velocity of money; Liquid asset; Money demand function; Money supply; Quantity theory of money; Real money balances; Transactions velocity of money; Velocity of money

Money demand function, 149–150, 158
  determinants of, 472–473
  effect on *LM* curve of, 270
  function of nominal interest rate in, 158–159
  portfolio theories of, 472–473
  studies of, 478
  transaction theories of, 474

Money hypothesis of the Great Depression, 280

Money market. *See LM* curve

Money multiplier, or tax multiplier, 470–471

Money stock. *See* Money supply

Money supply
  components of, 463–464
  control of, 145–146
  defined, 467
  dependence on exogenous variables, 468–469, 470
  determinants of, 463–464, 467–469
  determines nominal value of output, 150
  effect of change in, 150–151, 266, 483–484
  effect of fixed exchange rate on, 356
  effect of growth on inflation rate, 150–154
  effect on aggregate demand of, 218–220, 226
  effect on economy of, 147
  effect on *LM* curve of, 257
  during Great Depression, 277–283
  measures of, 146–147
  model of, 467–469
  See also Monetary transmission mechanism

Moral hazard, 131

MPC. See Marginal propensity to consume *(MPC)*

MPK. See Marginal product of capital *(MPK)*

MPL. See Marginal product of labor *(MPL)*

Multiplier. *See* Government-purchases multiplier; Money multiplier; Tax multiplier

Mundell, Robert A., 346n
Mundell-Fleming model
    components of, 346–347, 425
    for small open economy, 345–362, 365
    on $Y - e$ graph, 349–351
    on $Y - r$ graph, 347–349, 351
Mundell-Tobin effect, 172
Murphy, Kevin, 135n
Mussa, Michael, 162n

National income
    definition and data for, 27–28
    determinants of, 264, 269
    division of, 51
    See also Economic growth; Solow growth
        model
National income accounts, 16–19, 24–28
    in closed economy, 178
    in open economy, 178–180
National income accounts identity, 179–180, 247
    capital and current accounts in, 182
    in terms of total income, 180–181
    See also Net exports
National saving
    defined, 64
    effect of public policy on, 104
    effect of Social Security system on, 105
    evaluating, 103–104
    influences on, 78
    Ricardian equivalence view of, 427
National spending
    components in open economy of, 178–180
    in GNP, 24–25
    See also Spending hypothesis
Natural-rate hypothesis, 317–318, 319
Natural rate level of output. See Output, full-
        employment or natural rate level
Natural rate of employment. See Output, full-
        employment or natural rate level
Natural rate of unemployment, 222, 305, 312
    alteration by recession of, 317–318
    defined, 118, 137
    effect of unemployment insurance on, 123
    model of, 119, 136
    with monetary policy rules, 336–337
    See also Cyclical unemployment; Hysteresis
        theory
Neoclassical model of investment, 441–451, 460
Neoclassical theory of distribution, 46
Net exports, 179–182

in closed economy, 56
as expenditure component of GNP, 24–26
in national income accounting, 178–182
relation to real exchange rate of, 193
in small open economy, 205
with tariff, 198
Net investment, 445–446, 450
Net national product (NNP), 27
Nevins, Alan, 132
New classical economics, 312, 374, 383, 387
    See also Lucas critique; Rational
        expectations; Real-business-cycle theory;
        Time inconsistency
New Keynesian economics, 312–313, 386
NNP. See Net national product
Nominal interest rate. See Interest rate, nominal
Nordhaus, William, 331n
Normal good, 402

Obstfeld, Maurice, 363n
Okun, Arthur M., 35, 244n, 309n
Okun's law, 35–36, 234, 303–304, 309, 312
Olson, Mancur, 107n
100-percent-reserve banking, 464
OPEC (Organization of Petroleum Exporting
        Countries), 33, 135, 231–232, 304, 307
Open economy, large
    effect of economic policy on, 211
    model of, 208–210, 424–425
    rule of thumb for policy analysis of, 373
    short-run model of, 368–373
    United States as, 204–205
Open economy, small
    effect of fiscal policy on, 352–353
    effect of monetary policy on, 353–354
    with fixed exchange rates, 356–360
    with floating exchange rates, 352–355
    measures of total income in, 180–181
    model of, 183–185
    Mundell-Fleming model for, 345–362, 365
    national income accounting in, 178–180
Open-market operations (of Federal Reserve),
        145, 469–470
Optimization (of consumption), 401–402
Output
    factors influencing, 45–46
    long-run level of, 222
    relation of aggregate demand to quantity of,
        217–220
    supply and demand as determinants of, 63–65

Output, full-employment or natural-rate level, 222, 225, 228, 229
  deviations from, 291, 293, 296, 301, 319
  as real aggregate supply curve, 376
Outside lags (in stabilization policy), 324
Outsiders in labor force, 129

Paasche price index, 31
Permanent income, 414–417
Permanent-income hypothesis, 414–418, 420
Phelps, Edmund, 89n, 304
Phillips, A. W., 304
Phillips curve, 302–304
  to express and analyze aggregate supply, 319
  short-run, 307–308, 310
  shows inflation rise and fall, 305–309
Pieper, Paul J., 439n
Pigou, Arthur, 281
Pigou effect, 281
Plosser, Charles I., 386n, 388n
Policy. See Public policy
Policy irrelevance proposition, 321
Political business cycle, 331
Poole, William, 229n
Population growth, 96–99
  international comparisons of, 99
Portfolio theories of money demand, 472–473
Poterba, James M., 456n
PPI. See Producer price index
Precautionary saving, 412
Prescott, Edward C., 335n, 383–384
Price indices, 29–33, 37
Price level
  defined, 150–151
  determination of, 173–175
  effect of falling, 281
  effect of money on, 159–160
  effect of unexpected changes in, 289–291
  effect on aggregate demand of, 233
  in IS-LM model, 263
  from 1929–1933, 280
  in real-business-cycle theory, 377
  relation of aggregate demand to, 217–220
  relation to inflation rate of, 151
  See also Inflation; IS-LM model
Prices
  effect of changing, 165
  effect of demand shift on, 222

flexible and sticky, 11–13, 276
  relative, 170, 314, 453
  short-run stickiness of, 215–216, 313–314
  staggered adjustment of, 314–315
  See also Factor prices; Market prices; Menu
    costs; Rental price of capital
Prices, flexible, 11–13, 276
  economy with, 375–377
  in long-run equilibrium, 224
Price shocks. See Aggregate demand; Aggregate
    supply; OPEC (Organization of
    Petroleum Exporting Countries); Shocks
Price stickiness
  with expectation of, 316
  in short-run aggregate supply curve, 222
  in short-run equilibrium, 215–217
  in sticky-price model, 296–298
Private saving. See Saving
Procyclical real wage, 294, 298
Producer price index (PPI), 30
Production function, 44, 45
  in comparison of steady states, 91
  as determinant of level of output, 44, 150
  effect of technological progress on, 114–116
  with efficiency of labor variable, 100
  returns to scale in, 45, 76
  in Solow model, 79–80
  See also Constant returns to scale;
    Diminishing marginal product; Total
    factor productivity
Production smoothing, 456–457
Profit, 48, 52
  See also Accounting profit; Economic profit
Profit-sharing as automatic stabilizer, 325
Public policy
  consideration of duration of unemployment
    by, 133
  effect on saving of, 104–105
  to encourage capital accumulation, 109
  related to frictional unemployment, 122–123,
    138
  related to natural rate of unemployment, 121,
    122, 485–486
  related to technological progress, 106
  related to unemployed workers, 118, 137
  role in raising GNP, 483
  and role in stabilizing the economy, 486
  and tradeoff between inflation and
    unemployment, 483–484
  See also Economic policy; Fiscal policy;
    Monetary policy; Stabilization policy;
    Trade policy

Public saving. *See* Saving
Purchasing-power parity, 201–204

q theory of investment. *See* Tobin's *q*
Quantity equation, 147–149, 150, 158
Quantity theory of money, 141, 147–152
   effect of money growth, 155
   equation for, 218, 257
   statement of, 151, 170–171
   See also LM curve; Money demand function;
     Money supply; Quantity equation; Real
     money balances
Quota. *See* Import quota

Radford, R. A., 143*n*
Raff, Daniel M. G., 132*n*
Random walk theorem for consumption, 417–
   418
Rapping, Leonard A., 378*n*
Rational expectations
   effect of, 328–329
   implications for consumption function, 417–
     418
   as new classical economics, 387
   theory of, 309–311, 319
Reagan, Ronald, 69, 140, 354, 434
Real aggregate demand curve, 376–377
Real aggregate supply curve, 376–377, 379
Real-business-cycle theory, 312, 377–382, 388
   arguments for and against, 382–386. 389
   neutrality of money in, 386, 387
   as part of new classical economics, 387
   See also Classical dichotomy; Intertemporal
     substitution of labor
Real cost of capital. *See* Cost of capital, real
Real interest rate. *See* Interest rate, real
Real money balances, 149
   between 1929–1931, 280
   demand for liquidity of, 159
   effect of increase in, 265
   in quantity equation, 218
   supply and demand of, 250, 257
Real rental price of capital. *See* Rental price of
   capital, real
Real wage. *See* Wages, real
Recession, 214, 226, 228–229
   effect of, 451
   effect on inventory investment of, 456
   indication of, 36
   possible effect of, 317–319

as result of coordination failure, 315–316
of 1982 (U.S.), 328
Rental price of capital, 47–51
   equals marginal product of capital *(MPK)*, 114
   in investment, 442–451
   real, 51, 102–103, 114, 442–443, 445, 460
Reserve-deposit ratio, 465, 469, 470–471
Reserve requirements (of Federal Reserve),
   469–470
Reserves, 464, 470
Residential investment, 440
Residential investment model, 452–456
Returns to scale. *See* Constant returns to scale
Revaluation (of currency), 360
Revenue, 48
Ricardian equivalence, 425, 427
Ricardian view of government debt, 387, 423,
   430–432, 434
Ricardo, David, 427
Risk aversion, 168
Rockoff, Hugh, 169*n*
Romer, Christina, 330
Romer, David, 108*n*, 298*n*, 300*n*, 314*n*, 315*n*,
   316*n*
Romer, Paul, 108*n*
Ross, Thomas W., 317*n*
Rotemberg, Julio, 298*n*

Sachs, Jeffrey, 129*n*
Sacrifice ratio, 308–309, 310, 312
   effect of hysteresis on, 318
   estimates of, 328–329
Samuelson, Paul, 263
Sargent, Thomas J., 161*n*, 162*n*, 163*n*, 310
Saving
   effect of public policy on, 104–105
   effect of Social Security system on, 105
   in Fisher intertemporal choice model, 398–
     399
   in Keynesian consumption function theory,
     393
   in national income accounting, 64
   prediction of life-cycle model for, 411–412
   role in economic growth, 104
   See also Borrowing constraint; Dissaving;
     National saving
Saving rate, 408
   effect of different, 108
   of the elderly, 412
   and fear of nuclear war, 412–413
   steady states resulting from, 87–89, 92

Schwartz, Anna J., 68n, 152, 277n, 280, 470n
Sectoral shift
    causes and effect of, 135–136
    defined, 122
Secular stagnation, 395
Seigniorage, 152–154, 161, 171
Shapiro, Matthew D., 327n
Shleifer, Andrei, 433n
Shocks
    accommodating policy for, 231
    to aggregate demand and supply, 226–232,
        233–234
    effect on inflation rate of, 306
    exogenous variables as, 269–270
    to technological progress, 380–382
Shoeleather cost of inflation, 164, 171
Short run vs. long run, 11–12, 215–216, 224–
        225, 275–276, 482–485
Silver. See Free Silver movement
Silver, Stephen, 295n
Simonsen, Mario Henrique, 315n
Slemrod, Joel, 414n
Small open economy. See Open economy, small
Social Security system
    adjustment to benefits in, 168
    defined, 105
    effect on saving, 105
Solow, Robert M., 78n, 115n, 305
Solow growth model, 77, 424
    development of, 79
    prediction about factor prices, 103
    predictions with technological progress of,
        100–102, 105–106
    prediction with population growth of, 96–99
    role in study of economic growth of, 107–109
Solow residual, 115, 383–384
South Africa, gold discovery in, 169
Spending hypothesis of the Great Depression,
        278–279
Spiegelman, Robert G., 125n
Stabilization policy, 226–232
    argument against use of, 323–324
    inside and outside lags in, 324
    prediction important for, 326
    See also Automatic stabilizers
Stagflation, 230–232
Staggering of wages and prices. See Prices;
        Wages
Standards of living, international comparisons
        of, 78
Steady state
    of capital stock, 81–84, 87–91

choice of, 89–91
and consumption, 89–92
defined, 84
effect of population growth on, 96–99
with technological progress, 100–102
    See also Golden Rule
Sticky vs. flexible prices, 11–12, 215, 224–225
Sticky-price model, 296–298, 299–300, 319
Sticky-wage model, 288–291, 294–95, 319
Stock market, 450–451, 466
Stock-out avoidance, 457
Stocks, 472–473, 477
Stocks vs. flows, 18
Strategic bequest motive, 433
Substitution effect, 404
Summers, Lawrence H., 123n, 128n, 318n,
        384n, 433n, 451n
Summers, Robert, 88n, 99n
Sumner, Scott, 295n
Supply
    of real money balances, 149
    relation to production function of, 79–80
    See also Aggregate supply; Aggregate supply
        curve
Supply curve
    for capital, 442
    in economic models, 7–8
    See also Aggregate supply curve
Sweden
    collective bargaining in, 129
    investment incentive program in, 449

Tariffs, 198, 354
Tax laws, 68–70
Tax multiplier, 243
Tax reduction, 68–69
Tax smoothing, 337
Taylor, John B., 315n, 449n
Technological progress
    effect on efficiency of labor, 100
    effect on production function of, 114, 151
    efforts to understand, 105–106
    in real-business-cycle theory, 380–382
    role in investment demand change of, 69
    Solow residual as measure of, 115
    See also Labor-augmenting technological
        progress
Temin, Peter, 277n
Terms of trade, 192
Theory of liquidity preference, 250–255, 260,
        265

Time inconsistency, 333–334, 342–344
  and new classical economics, 387
Tobin, James, 450, 472*n*, 474*n*
  See also Baumol-Tobin model of cash
    management; Mundell-Tobin effect
Tobin's *q*, 450–451, 461
  See also Residential investment model
Topel, Robert H., 135*n*
Total factor productivity
  effect on output of, 115
  factors influencing, 115–116
  measurement of, 115
  slow growth of, 106–107, 116
  See also Solow residual
Trade deficit. *See* Current account
Trade, international, 142, 176
Trade policy
  with fixed exchange rate, 361
  with floating exchange rate, 354–355
  function of, 198
  protectionist, 178, 198–199
Transaction theories of money demand, 474
Transactions velocity of money, 148
Transfer payments
  as government spending, 61–62
  of Social Security system, 105
Transitory income, 414–417
Tufte, Edward, 331*n*

Uncertainty. *See* Precautionary saving
Uncertainty in inflation, 168, 169
Underground economy, 474
Unemployment, 118–138
  cyclical, 305
  determinants of, 120–132
  duration of, 132–133, 138
  effect of wage rigidity on, 126–127
  effect on inflation rate of, 305
  with fixed rule for inflation, 342–344
  natural rate of, 118–121, 222, 305
  public policy related to, 118, 137
  real-business-cycle theory interpretation of,
    384–385
  relation to real GNP of, 35–36
  See also Unemployment insurance;
    Unemployment rate
Unemployment insurance
  in Canada, 130
  effect on frictional unemployment of, 122–
    123, 138
  effect on job finding rate of, 124–125

  experience rating system in, 123
  interwar experience in Britain with, 123–124
Unemployment rate
  defined, 15, 33–34, 37
  differences in, 133–134, 138
  model of natural, 119–121
  in Sweden, 129
  upward trend in, 134–136, 138
  See also Cyclical unemployment;
    Discouraged workers; Frictional
    unemployment; Natural rate of
    unemployment; Okun's law; Phillips
    curve; Wait unemployment
Unions, labor
  in Canada, 129–130
  effect on wage rigidity of, 128–129
  in Sweden, 129
United Kingdom
  effect of 1980s recession in, 318
  importance of trade for, 176
  imports and exports in, 177
  interest rates in, 1730–1920, 67–68
  unemployment in 1980s in, 318
  See also Britain
United States
  birthrate in, 455
  consumption function in, 58–59
  importance of trade for, 176
  imports and exports in, 177
  inflation and unemployment in, 306–307
  inflation of 1978–1981, 32–33
  inflation rate in, 140
  inflation rate and nominal interest rate in,
    156
  inflation reduction in, 354
  investment and income in, 88–89
  as large open economy, 204–205, 364–365
  macroeconomic data in, 4
  money growth and inflation in, 152–153
  money supply during Great Depression, 470
  oil prices in, 231–232
  Okun's law and, 35–36
  presidential elections and economic
    performance in, 5–6
  ratio of labor income to capital income in,
    55
  real GNP in, 112, 215, 332
  recession of 1982 in, 228–229
  saving rate in, 408
  sources of economic growth in, 116
  stagflation in, 231–232

United States *(continued)*
    unemployment rate in, 35–36, 118–119, 133–
        136
    velocity of money in, 228–229

Value-added, 20
Van Huyck, John B., 317*n*
Variables
    nominal, 170
    real, 169–170, 171
    See also Endogenous variables; Exogenous
        variables
Velocity of money
    assumption of constant, 150, 257
    effect of change in, 151
    income and transactions velocity of, 148–149
    monetary policy response to, 227–229
Volcker, Paul, 254, 307, 311–312, 354

Wage rigidity
    causes of, 127–131
    effect of minimum-wage laws on, 127
    effect of union actions on, 128–130, 138
    effect on unemployment of, 126–127
    efficiency-wage theories as cause of, 130–131,
        138
    See also Minimum-wage laws
Wages
    staggered adjustment of, 314–315
    sticky, 315

    See also Sticky-wage model; Worker-
        misperception model
Wages, nominal
    effect of stickiness of, 288–289
    setting of, 288–289
    in worker-misperception model, 291–293
Wages, real, 126
    with actual price level, 289
    in Canada, 129–130
    cyclical behavior of, 294–295
    defined, 50
    in worker-misperception model, 291–293
Wait unemployment, 126–127, 131, 132, 138
Wealth redistribution
    among generations, 432
    caused by unexpected price-level changes,
        281
Weil, David N., 108*n*, 456*n*
Weitzman, Martin L., 325
The Wizard of Oz, 168–169
Woodbury, Stephen A., 125*n*
Worker-misperception model, 291–293, 294–
        295, 319
Work in process, 457
World interest rate. *See* Interest rate, world

Yellen, Janet, 131*n*, 314*n*

Zaire, saving rate in, 88–89
Zambia, investment and income in, 88
Zeldes, Stephen P., 457*n*

U.S. Federal Government
Budget Deficit
(Adjusted for Inflation)

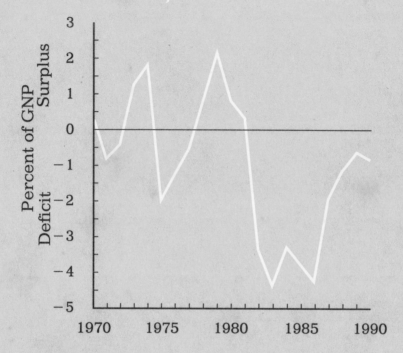

Money Growth (*M*2)

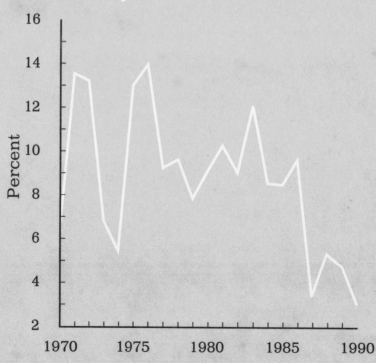